AMAZING GRACE

366 Inspiring Hymn Stories for Daily Devotions

Kenneth W. Osbeck

KREGEL PUBLICATIONS
Grand Rapids, Michigan 49501

Amazing Grace: 366 Hymn Stories for Personal Devotions,
by Kenneth W. Osbeck. © 1990 by Kregel Publications,
a division of Kregel, Inc., P.O. Box 2607, Grand Rapids,
MI 49501. All rights reserved.

Unless otherwise indicated, Scripture quotations are from
the *Holy Bible*, New International Version, copyright ©
1973, 1978, 1984 by the International Bible Society. Used
by permission of Zondervan Bible Publishers.

Cover Design: Brian Fowler

Library of Congress Cataloging-in-Publication Data

Osbeck, Kenneth W., 1924–
   Amazing grace: 366 hymn stories for personal
devotions / Kenneth W. Osbeck.
     p.   cm.
   Includes index.

   1. Hymns—Devotional use. 2. Devotional calendars.
3. Hymns, English—History and criticism. 4. Hymns,
English—United States—History and criticism. I. Title.

| BV340.072 | 1990 | 245'.21—dc20 | 90-37888 |
| | | | CIP |

ISBN 0-8254-3425-4 (pbk.)

3 4 5 Printing/Year 94 93 92 91

Printed in the United States of America

Contents

Preface

Even a casual visit to a bookstore will impress a viewer with the many "how-to" or self-improvement books that are available today. *How to be happy, be healthy, be successful, be a good parent . . .* and the list goes on.

But what are the "how-to's" for an effective spiritual life? Are there daily practices that Christians should pursue?

First and foremost, *there needs to be an appreciative awareness of God's amazing grace in our lives*: grace that adopted us as sinners and made us members of the heavenly kingdom; grace that sustains and directs our daily steps; and the grace that will ultimately usher us to our eternal home.

Secondly, let me suggest these key words that also need to be a vital part of every believer's daily experience:

Praise—Prayer—Love

A daily life of *praise*, thanksgiving, and the adoration of God.

A daily life of *prayer*, fellowship, and a communion with God.

A daily life of *love*, a delight in the personal assurance of God's love and a desire to share His love with others.

Two basic resource books are available to help us in this spiritual well-being: the Bible, and the church hymnal. Regular study of the Bible, God's infallible rule of faith and practice, is an absolute essential for Christian living. Nothing ever replaces our daily need for His trustworthy Word. Through the ages, however, devout believers from every Christian community have responded to God and His inspired revelation with their own expressions. The church hymnal, a most important heritage of the Christian church, is one of the finest collections of man's thoughts and feelings about God. When these choice responses are further enhanced with appropriate melodies, harmonies, and rhythms, there exists a reservoir of unusual spiritual strength and encouragement.

Spend time each day with the two resource books now blended together into these daily devotionals. Allow God to speak directly to you through the Scriptures. Also, consider thoughtfully how other sincere believers have related to God with their "psalms, hymns, and spiritual songs." Then respond to Him with your own expressions of *praise, prayer,* and *love*. Carry a musical truth with you throughout each day. Let the non-Christian world observe a living demonstration of a joyful faith. And as you do, you will become increasingly aware of God's amazing grace and His power that enables you to live an effective and victorious Christian life. Perhaps these words, written more than two centuries ago, will begin to have new meaning for you:

Amazing grace—how sweet the sound—that saved a wretch like me!

I once was lost but now am found, was blind but now I see.

'Twas grace that taught my heart to fear, and grace my fears relieved;

How precious did that grace appear the hour I first believed.

The Lord has promised good to me, His word my hope secures;

He will my shield and portion be as long as life endures.

Thru many dangers, toils and snares, I have already come;

'Tis grace hath brought me safe thus far, and grace will lead me home.

—*John Newton, 1725-1807*
(See page 170)

"I am in myself, incapable of standing a single hour without continual fresh supplies of strength and grace from the fountain-head."

—*John Newton*

Hymns breathe the praise of the saints,
The vision of the prophets,
The prayers of the penitent and the spirit of the martyrs.

They bring solace to the sad, assurance to the perplexed,
Faith to the doubter and comfort to the oppressed.

They span the centuries of history and bridge the barriers of
    denominations.

Study them to be pure in heart;
Sing them to be joyful in spirit,

Store them in the mind to possess a treasury of worship.

—*Unknown*

January

• Guidance • Aspiration • Prayer • Worldwide Evangelism

ANOTHER YEAR IS DAWNING
Frances Ridley Havergal, 1836-1879

Teach us to number our days aright, that we may gain a heart of wisdom.
(Psalm 90:12)

It is always challenging to approach a new year and to realize anew that our days upon this earth are so rapidly passing. How important it is that we pause with the psalmist and pray for a "heart of wisdom" that will enable us this year to live each new day in a way that brings all glory to our God.

> I with Thee would begin, O my Savior so dear, on the way that I still must pursue; I with Thee would begin every day granted here, as my earnest resolve I renew—To be and remain Thine forever. —*From the Swedish*

In January of 1874, the many friends of Frances Ridley Havergal received a New Year's greeting with the heading, "A Happy New Year! Ever Such May it Be!" Following this greeting appeared her text, still considered to be one of the finest New Year's prayers of consecration ever written:

> Another year is dawning, Dear Father, let it be, in working or in waiting another year with Thee; another year of progress, another year of praise, another year of proving Thy presence all the days.

> Another year of mercies, of faithfulness and grace; another year of gladness in the shining of Thy face; another year of leaning upon Thy loving breast; another year of trusting, of quiet, happy rest.

> Another year of service, of witness for Thy love; another year of training for holier work above. Another year of dawning, Dear Father, let it be, on earth, or else in heaven, another year for Thee. Amen.

One can well imagine that those who received this greeting card from Miss Havergal that year read her words thoughtfully. They were written by one who had already become widely known throughout England as "the consecration poet." It was said of her that she always lived her words before she wrote them. Her life was one of constant and complete commitment to God. Her many talents—an accomplished pianist and vocalist, proficiency in seven languages, a keen mind (memorization of the entire New Testament, Psalms, Isaiah, and the Minor Prophets)—were all dedicated to serving God and others during the new year. May that be our challenge for this new year as well!

🍎 *For Today:* Deuteronomy 1:30, 31; Joshua 3:4; Psalm 39:4; Isaiah 58:11

Begin this new year with a fervent prayer such as the one written by Frances Havergal that God will give your life a renewed purpose and power as you earnestly seek to represent Him in a worthy manner.

Aurelia tune   Samuel S. Wesley, 1810-1876

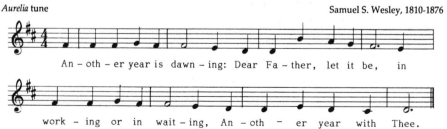

An - oth - er year is dawn - ing: Dear Fa - ther, let it be, in

work - ing or in wait - ing, An - oth - er year with Thee.

O JESUS, I HAVE PROMISED

John E. Bode, 1816–1874

God is not unjust; He will not forget your work and the love you have shown Him as you have helped His people and continue to help them . . . show this same diligence to the very end, in order to make your hope sure. (Hebrews 6:10, 11)

> I asked the New Year for some motto sweet,
> Some rule of life by which to guide my feet.
> I asked and paused; it answered soft and low,
> "God's will to know."   —*Unknown*

The beginning of the new year is usually a time for reflecting on and evaluating the past as well as for setting serious goals for the future. Because it is so easy to get caught up in a blur of daily sameness, special days and events are important in life. We need these highlights for our growth and development.

"O Jesus, I Have Promised" was written by an English clergyman on such a special day. It was penned especially for a confirmation service in which John Bode's own daughter and two sons were making their life's vows of commitment to God and His service. He told his three children: "I have written a hymn containing all the important truths I want you to remember when you are fully confirmed."

Without doubt, the three children of John Bode never forgot that confirmation service and their father's concern for them as they sang these words throughout their lives:

> O Jesus, I have promised to serve Thee to the end; be Thou forever near me, my Master and my Friend: I shall not fear the battle if Thou art by my side, nor wander from the pathway if Thou wilt be my guide.

> O let me feel Thee near me—the world is ever near; I see the sights that dazzle, the tempting sounds I hear: My foes are ever near me, around me and within; but Jesus, draw Thou nearer, and shield my soul from sin.

> O Jesus, Thou hast promised to all who follow Thee, that where Thou art in glory, there shall Thy servant be; and, Jesus, I have promised to serve Thee to the end; O give me grace to follow, my Master and my Friend.

Do you need to stop today and do some reflecting and evaluating?

❦ *For Today:* Ecclesiastes 5:5; John 12:26; Romans 12:11; Colossians 3:24; Revelation 14:13

Think seriously about ways in which your spiritual life can be deepened and developed during this coming year. Why not begin even now?

Angel's Story tune   Arthur H. Mann, 1850–1929

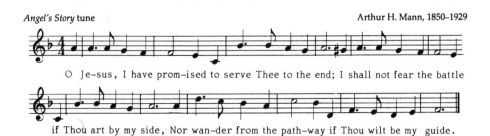

O Je-sus, I have prom–ised to serve Thee to the end; I shall not fear the battle

if Thou art by my side, Nor wan–der from the path–way if Thou wilt be my guide.

O GOD, OUR HELP IN AGES PAST

Isaac Watts, 1674–1748

Lord, You have been our dwelling place throughout all generations. Before the mountains were born or You brought forth the earth and the world, from everlasting to everlasting You are God. (Psalm 90:1, 2)

It has been wisely said that no thinking person ever regarded the beginning of a new year with indifference. Each of us faces many concerns and questions as we stand on the threshold of the unknown future.

The mystery of time is the subject of this hymn text, a paraphrase of Psalm 90. The hymn is considered by many to be one of the finest ever written and perhaps the best known of the 600 hymns by Isaac Watts, often called the "father of English hymnody."

At an early age Isaac displayed unusual talent in writing poetic verse. As a young man he became increasingly concerned with the congregational singing in the English speaking churches. Only ponderous metrical psalms were used until this time. To use any words other than the actual words of Scripture would have been considered an insult to God.

Challenged by his father to "write something better for us to sing, " young Watts began to create new versions of the psalms with inspiring and expressive style. Eventually, at the early age of 25, he published an important hymnal titled *The Psalms of David in the Language of the New Testament.* In addition to "O God, Our Help in Ages Past," several of Watts' other paraphrases based on psalm settings are hymn texts still widely sung today. They include such favorites as "Joy to the World," Psalm 98; and "Jesus Shall Reign," Psalm 72.

After more than 250 years, Isaac Watts' hymn is still a timely reminder of God's faithfulness throughout the past and His sure promises for our future.

> O God, our help in ages past, our hope for years to come, our shelter from the stormy blast, and our eternal home.
>
> Under the shadow of Thy throne still may we dwell secure; sufficient is Thine arm alone, and our defense is sure.
>
> Before the hills in order stood or earth received her frame, from everlasting Thou art God, to endless years the same.
>
> Time, like an ever rolling stream, bears all its sons away; they fly, forgotten, as a dream dies at the opening day.
>
> O God, our help in ages past, our hope for years to come, be Thou our guide while life shall last, and our eternal home.

❧ *For Today:* Psalm 33:20; 48:14; 90; Isaiah 26:4

Live confidently in the assurance that the One who has directed your steps to this moment of time is worthy of your complete trust for the days ahead.

St. Anne tune   Atributed to William Croft, 1678–1727

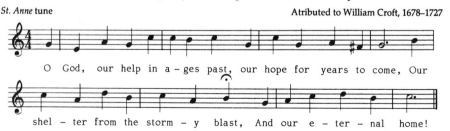

O God, our help in a-ges past, our hope for years to come, Our shel-ter from the storm-y blast, And our e-ter-nal home!

GUIDE ME, O THOU GREAT JEHOVAH

William Williams, 1717–1791

Since You are my rock and my fortress, for the sake of Your name lead and guide me. (Psalm 31:3)

The need for daily guidance is one of the believer's greatest concerns. How easily our lives can go astray without the assurance of divine leadership. Today's featured text is one of the great hymns of the church on this subject. It is a product of the revival movement that swept through Wales during the 18th century. This revival was led by a 24-year-old Welsh preacher, Howell Harris, who stirred the land with his fervent evangelistic preaching and his use of congregational singing.

One of the lives touched by Harris' ministry was 20-year-old William Williams. Young Williams, the son of a wealthy Welsh farmer, was preparing to become a medical doctor. But, upon hearing the stirring challenge by evangelist Howell Harris, Williams dedicated his life to God and the Christian ministry. William Williams, like Harris, decided to take all of Wales as his parish and for the next 43 years travelled 100,000 miles on horseback, preaching and singing the gospel in his native tongue. He became known as the "sweet singer of Wales."

The vivid, symbolic imagery of this text is drawn wholly from the Bible. The general setting is the march of the Israelites from Egypt to Canaan. Although the Israelites' sin and unbelief kept them from their destination for 40 years, God provided for their physical needs with a new supply of manna each day.

Twice during the Hebrews' years of wandering, they became faint because of lack of water. At the command of God, Moses struck a large rock with his wooden staff. Out of it flowed a pure, crystalline stream that preserved their lives. God also continued to guide them with a pillar of cloud by day and the pillar of fire by night.

> Guide me, O Thou great Jehovah, pilgrim thru this barren land;
> I am weak, but Thou art mighty—Hold me with Thy pow'rful hand:
> Bread of Heaven, Bread of Heaven, feed me till I want no more.
>
> Open now the crystal fountain, whence the healing stream doth flow;
> Let the fire and cloudy pillar lead me all my journey through;
> Strong Deliverer, strong Deliverer, be Thou still my strength and shield.
>
> When I tread the verge of Jordan, bid my anxious fears subside;
> Bear me thru the swelling current; land me safe on Canaan's side:
> Songs of praises, songs of praises, I will ever give to Thee.

❧ *For Today:* Psalm 16:11; 32:8; Isaiah 58:11; Romans 8:14

Claim God's promises for your life in even the small decisions you will be called upon to make this day. Begin to praise Him—

Cwm Rhondda tune   John Hughes, 1873–1932

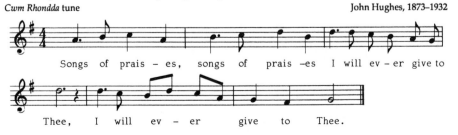

Songs of prais-es, songs of prais-es I will ev-er give to Thee, I will ev-er give to Thee.

HOW FIRM A FOUNDATION

1787 "K"—in Rippon's *Selection of Hymns*

So we say with confidence, "The Lord is my helper; I will not be afraid. What can man do to me?" (Hebrews 13:6)

A believer's stability in this life, as well as his confidence for eternity, rests solely on the written promises of God's Word. The direction of the living God for our lives is very definite. It is found in a firm foundation—the written revelation: "Thus saith the Lord."

In the first stanza the sure foundation of the Christian faith is established as being the Word of God. This challenging question is posed: What more can God do than provide His very Word as a completed revelation of Himself to man? The succeeding verses personalize precious promises from His Word:

Verse Two—Isaiah 41:10—"Fear thou not, for I am with thee, be not dismayed, for I am thy God . . ."
Verse Three—Isaiah 43:2—"When thou passest through the waters, I will be with thee . . ."
Verse Four—2 Corinthians 12:9—"My grace is sufficient for thee; for my strength is made perfect in weakness . . ."
Verse Five—Hebrews 13:5—"I will never leave thee, nor forsake thee . . ."

The authorship of the text has always been a mystery to hymnologists. Its first appearance was in 1787 in *Selection of Hymns,* published by Dr. John Rippon, pastor of the Carter's Lane Baptist Church in London. He was one of the most popular and influential dissenting ministers of his time.

How firm a foundation, ye saints of the Lord, is laid for your faith in His excellent Word! What more can He say than to you He hath said—To you, who for refuge to Jesus have fled?

Fear not, I am with thee—O be not dismayed, for I am thy God, I will still give thee aid; I'll strengthen thee, help thee, and cause thee to stand, upheld by my gracious, omnipotent hand.

When thru the deep waters I call thee to go, the rivers of woe shall not thee overflow; for I will be with thee thy troubles to bless, and sanctify to thee thy deepest distress.

When thru fiery trials thy pathway shall lie, My grace, all-sufficient, shall be thy supply; the flame shall not hurt thee—I only design thy dross to consume and thy gold to refine.

The soul that on Jesus hath leaned for repose, I will not, I will not desert to his foes; that soul, tho all hell should endeavor to shake, I'll never—no, never—no, never forsake.

❦ *For Today:* Psalm 36:1; 118:6, 7; Hebrews 13:5, 6

Plant your feet firmly on the "thus saith the Lord" and live life confidently in that strength. Carry this musical message with you knowing that—

Foundation tune   American melody

What more can He say than to you He hath said— To you, who for ref - uge to Je - sus have fled.

AS WITH GLADNESS MEN OF OLD

William C. Dix, 1837–1898

After Jesus was born in Bethlehem in Judea, during the time of King Herod, Magi (Wise Men) from the east came to Jerusalem and asked, "Where is the One who has been born king of the Jews? We saw His star in the east and have come to worship Him." (Matthew 2:1, 2)

The period in the church year that begins with January 6 and extends to Ash Wednesday is known as Epiphany.

Epiphany marks the time that the Christ Child was revealed to the wise men in His first manifestation to the Gentiles as the Light of the whole world. It is generally believed by Bible scholars that these wise men from the East arrived approximately 2 years after the birth of Christ. The earnestness of their search, their worship and gifts, and their desire to return home to share their spiritual experience with others have much to teach us. In many churches, Epiphany is ushered in with a special week of prayer, a renewed commitment to evangelism, and a worldwide concern for missions.

Epiphany should be a strong reminder to all Christians that God wants not only our worship but also our willingness to share His message with others both at home and abroad. The gospel of good news must be heard beyond the walls of our church buildings. May we be challenged to share God's love both by word and deed with those He brings into our lives each day.

As with gladness men of old did the guiding star behold—as with joy they hailed its light, leading onward, beaming bright—so, most gracious Lord, may we evermore be led to Thee.

As with joyful steps they sped to that lowly manger bed, there to bend the knee before Him whom heav'n and earth adore. So may we with willing feet ever seek Thy mercy seat.

As they offered gifts most rare at that manger rude and bare, so may we with holy joy, pure and free from sin's alloy, all our costliest treasures bring, Christ, to Thee, our heav'nly King.

Holy Jesus, every day keep us in the narrow way; and, when earthly things are past, bring our ransomed souls at last where they need no star to guide, where no clouds Thy glory hide.

❦ *For Today:* Ezekiel 3:18; Matthew 2:1–12; John 4:35; Ephesians 1:3–8; James 5:19, 20.

Reflect once again on the importance of the wise men—their difficult journey to Bethlehem, their worship and gifts, and the return to their homelands to share what they had learned. Then begin this Epiphany season with the prayer—

Dix tune   Conrad Kocher, 1786–1872

So, most gra - cious Lord, may we Ev - er - more be led to Thee.

TEACH ME TO PRAY

Words and Music by Albert S. Reitz, 1879–1966

Let us then approach the throne of grace with confidence, so that we may receive mercy and find grace to help us in our time of need. (Hebrews 4:16)

One of the most important emphases during this season of Epiphany is that of prayer, both for our own daily guidance and as the undergirding power needed for the spiritual journey of our local church.

What is prayer? To many, prayer is regarded as a foolish repetition of words, a refuge for weaklings, or a childish petition for material needs. How sadly this reservoir of spiritual power is undervalued when perceived in these terms, just as we would underestimate electricity if we talked of it only in terms of a 40-watt bulb.

For the child of God, prayer is far more than the mere gratification of our human whims. It is the practice of the presence of Almighty God in every activity of our daily lives.

> Prayer is so simple. It is like quietly opening a door and slipping into the very presence of God. —*Unknown*

Rev. Albert S. Reitz left this account:

> When I was pastor of the Rosehill Baptist Church, we had a heart-warming Day of Prayer under the leadership of the Evangelical Prayer Union of Los Angeles. The next morning in my study the Lord gave the words and the music then followed.

As you read these words, may they challenge you to recognize the importance of an earnest prayer life.

> Teach me to pray, Lord, teach me to pray; this is my heart cry day unto day; I long to know Thy will and Thy way; teach me to pray, Lord, teach me to pray.

> Power in prayer, Lord, power in prayer, here 'mid earth's sin and sorrow and care; men lost and dying, souls in despair—O give me power, power in prayer!

> My weakened will, Lord, Thou canst renew; my sinful nature Thou canst subdue; fill me just now with power anew, power to pray and power to do!

> Teach me to pray, Lord, teach me to pray; Thou art my Pattern day unto day; Thou art my surety now and for aye; teach me to pray, Lord, teach me to pray.

> **Chorus:** Living in Thee, Lord, and Thou in me; constant abiding, this is my plea; grant me Thy power boundless and free: Power with men and power with Thee.

❦ *For Today:* Matthew 5:44; 21:22; Mark 11:25; Luke 18:1.

Practice God's presence even amidst the noise and clamor of your busy day. Don't forget to pray for the ongoing ministry of your church. Carry this tuneful message to help—

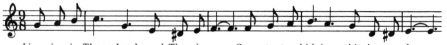

Liv – ing in Thee, Lord, and Thou in me; Con–stant a–bid–ing, this is my plea;

Grant me Thy pow–er, bound–less and free: Pow–er with men and pow–er with Thee.

SWEET HOUR OF PRAYER

William W. Walford, 1772-1850

And pray in the Spirit on all occasions with all kinds of prayers and requests. With this in mind, be alert and always keep on praying for all the saints. (Ephesians 6:18)

No one is poor who can by prayer open the storehouse of God. —*Louis Paul Lehman*

Through the ages, devout believers in Christ have recognized the necessity of maintaining an intimate relationship with God through His ordained channel of prayer. It has often been said that prayer is as basic to spiritual life as breathing is to our natural lives. It is not merely an occasional impulse to which we respond when we are in trouble; prayer is a way of life.

Nevertheless, we need to set aside a special time for prayer. We need that daily "Sweet Hour of Prayer." This song is thought to have been written in 1842 by William Walford, an obscure and blind lay preacher who was the owner of a small trinket shop in the little village of Coleshill, England.

The first two stanzas of today's hymn remind us of the blessings of prayer—relief for our troubled lives and the assurance of a God who is concerned about our every need. The final stanza anticipates the day when we will no longer need to pray, for we'll be at home in heaven with our Lord.

There is also an interesting reference in this verse to a Mount Pisgah—the place where God instructed Moses in Deuteronomy 3:27 to go and merely view the promised land since, because of disobedience, he would never be permitted to enter it.

Sweet hour of prayer, sweet hour of prayer, that calls me from a world of care and bids me at my Father's throne make all my wants and wishes known! In seasons of distress and grief my soul has often found relief, and oft escaped the tempter's snare by thy return, sweet hour of prayer.

Sweet hour of prayer, sweet hour of prayer, thy wings shall my petition bear to Him whose truth and faithfulness engage the waiting soul to bless; and since He bids me seek His face, believe His Word and trust His grace, I'll cast on Him my ev'ry care, and wait for thee, sweet hour of prayer.

Sweet hour of prayer, sweet hour of prayer, may I thy consolation share, till from Mount Pisgah's lofty height I view my home and take my flight: This robe of flesh I'll drop, and rise to seize the everlasting prize, and shout, while passing thru the air, "Farewell, farewell, sweet hour of prayer."

❦ *For Today:* Matthew 6:5, 6; 7:11; 18:19; 21:22; Luke 18:1-8

Earnestly purpose to spend additional time throughout this new year in prayer and communion with God. Allow this musical message to help you in the—

Sweet Hour tune   William B. Bradbury, 1816-1868

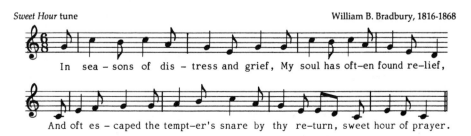

In sea-sons of dis-tress and grief, My soul has oft-en found re-lief,

And oft es-caped the tempt-er's snare by thy re-turn, sweet hour of prayer.

PRAYER IS THE SOUL'S SINCERE DESIRE

James Montgomery, 1771-1854

Men ought always to pray, and not to faint. (Luke 18:1 KJV)

Living a life without prayer is like building a house without nails.   —*Unknown*

Prayer is releasing the energies of God. For prayer is asking God to do what we cannot do ourselves.   —*Selected*

Except for Charles Wesley or Isaac Watts, no writer has made a greater contribution to English hymnody than the author of this text, James Montgomery. He wrote more than 400 hymns, many of which are still in popular use: "Stand Up and Bless the Lord," "Angel From the Realms of Glory," "In the Hour of Trial," and "According to Thy Gracious Word."

Though trained for the ministry, Montgomery spent his lifetime as a journalist and newspaper editor. He became widely known for his writings and poetry, yet when once asked, "Which of your poems will live?" he replied, "None, sir, except a few of my hymns." His words were prophetic. It is by his hymns that Montgomery is remembered, rather than by his more classic poetry.

Many have acclaimed this hymn as one of the finest definitions and descriptions of prayer to be found in short form. Such colorful metaphors as "hidden fire," "a sign," "a falling tear," "an upward glance," "vital breath," and "native air" describe in poetic language the mystic meaning of prayer—understood by experience, yet often difficult to express in words. Perhaps those terms will lead you to a new appreciation for the "soul's sincere desire."

> Prayer is the soul's sincere desire, uttered or unexpressed, the motion of a hidden fire that trembles in the breast.
>
> Prayer is the burden of a sigh, the falling of a tear, the upward glancing of an eye when none but God is near.
>
> Prayer is the simplest form of speech that infant lips can try; prayer, the sublimest strains that reach the Majesty on high.
>
> Prayer is the Christian's vital breath, the Christian's native air; his watchword at the gates of death: He enters heav'n with prayer.
>
> O Thou by whom we come to God, the Life, the Truth, the Way! The path of prayer Thyself hast trod: Lord, teach us how to pray!

🐦 *For Today:* Matthew 6:5-8; Luke 11:1-4; Colossians 4:2, 12; 1 Thessalonians 5:17

Reflect on the importance of prayer in your daily life. Determine to make an even greater use of this spiritual power throughout the day. Use this musical reminder—

St. Agnes tune   John B. Dykes, 1823-1876

Prayer is the soul's sin-cere de-sire, Ut-tered or un-ex-pressed,

The mo-tion of a hid-den fire That trem-bles in the breast.

WHAT A FRIEND WE HAVE IN JESUS

Joseph Scriven, 1819-1886

A man that hath friends must show himself friendly: And there is a friend that sticketh closer than a brother. (Proverbs 18:24 KJV)

A true friend loves and accepts us just as we are, stays close to us in good or in bad, and is always ready to help in time of need. Because the author of this hymn text found just such a friend in his Lord, he decided to spend his entire life showing real friendship to others.

Joseph Scriven had wealth, education, a devoted family, and a pleasant life in his native Ireland. Then unexpected tragedy entered. On the night before Scriven's scheduled wedding, his fiancée drowned. In his deep sorrow, Joseph realized that he could find the solace and support he needed only in his dearest friend, Jesus.

Soon after this tragedy, Scriven dramatically changed his lifestyle. He left Ireland for Port Hope, Canada, determined to devote all of his extra time in being a friend and helper to others. He often gave away his clothing and possessions to those in need, and he worked—without pay—for anyone who needed him. Scriven became known as "the Good Samaritan of Port Hope."

When Scriven's mother became ill in Ireland, he wrote a comforting letter to her, enclosing the words of his newly written poem with the prayer that these brief lines would remind her of a never-failing heavenly Friend. Sometime later, when Joseph Scriven himself was ill, a friend who came to call on him happened to see a copy of these words scribbled on scratch paper near his bed. The friend read the lines with interest and asked, "Who wrote those beautiful words?"

"The Lord and I did it between us," was Scriven's reply.

What a Friend we have in Jesus, all our sins and griefs to bear! What a privilege to carry everything to God in prayer! O what peace we often forfeit, O what needless pain we bear, all because we do not carry everything to God in prayer.

Have we trials and temptations? Is there trouble anywhere? We should never be discouraged—Take it to the Lord in prayer. Can we find a friend so faithful who will all our sorrows share? Jesus knows our every weakness—Take it to the Lord in prayer.

Are we weak and heavy laden, cumbered with a load of care? Precious Savior, still our refuge—Take it to the Lord in prayer. Do thy friends despise, forsake thee? Take it to the Lord in prayer; in His arms He'll take and shield thee—Thou wilt find a solace there.

❦ ***For Today:*** Psalm 6:9; Mark 11:24; John 15:13-16; 1 John 5:14, 15

Like Joseph Scriven, we too can find relief from our burdens when we turn to our Lord as a friend. Allow this musical truth to help you realize—

Converse tune   Charles C. Converse, 1832-1918

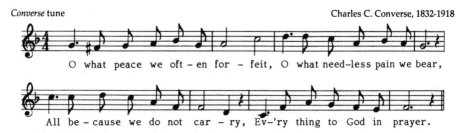

O what peace we oft-en for-feit, O what need-less pain we bear,

All be-cause we do not car-ry, Ev-'ry thing to God in prayer.

DAY BY DAY

Lina Sandell Berg, 1832-1903
Translated by Andrew L. Skoog, 1856-1934

Have I not commanded you? Be strong and courageous. Do not be terrified; do not be discouraged, for the Lord your God will be with you wherever you go. (Joshua 1:9)

It is a common tendency for people to look ahead. They wonder—what will happen next? That's why the pseudo science of astrology is booming today as never before. Because we are apprehensive of the future, wondering when some health problem or perhaps a financial difficulty will surprise us, we long for a reassuring word of comfort.

"Day by Day" was written by a young Swedish woman who learned early in life the all-important lesson of living each day with the conscious presence and strength of her Lord. Lina Sandell has often been called the "Fanny Crosby of Sweden" for her many contributions to gospel hymnody. From her pen flowed approximately 650 hymns which strongly influenced the waves of revival that swept the Scandinavian countries during the latter half of the 19th century.

At the age of 26 Lina had an experience that greatly influenced her life. She was accompanying her father aboard ship to the city of Gothenburg, Sweden, across Lake Vattern. The ship gave a sudden lurch and Lina's father, a devout Lutheran minister, fell overboard and drowned before the eyes of his devoted daughter. Although Lina had written many hymn texts prior to this tragic experience, now more than ever poetic thoughts that expressed a tender, child-like trust in her Lord began to flow freely from her broken heart.

> Day by day and with each passing moment, strength I find to meet my trials here; trusting in my Father's wise bestowment, I've no cause for worry or for fear. He whose heart is kind beyond all measure gives unto each day what He deems best—lovingly, its part of pain and pleasure, mingling toil with peace and rest.

> Ev'ry day the Lord Himself is near me with a special mercy for each hour; all my cares He fain would bear, and cheer me, He whose name is Counsellor and Pow'r. The protection of His child and treasure is a charge that on Himself He laid: "As thy days, thy strength shall be in measure," this the pledge to me He made.

❦ *For Today:* Deuteronomy 33:25; Psalm 55:22; Isaiah 14:3; 2 Corinthians 12:9; Hebrews 4:16

Practice the kind of deep and peaceful trust that Lina Sandell has expressed in this hymn. Focus only on the challenges and difficulties of today and trust the Lord for tomorrow. Sing this message as you go—

Oscar Ahnfelt, 1813-1882

The pro-tec-tion of His child and treasure is a charge that on Himself He laid.

"As thy days, thy strength shall be in mea-sure," This the pledge to me He made.

JESUS, SAVIOR, PILOT ME

Edward Hopper, 1818–1888

Thou wilt show me the path of life. In Thy presence is fulness of joy; at Thy right hand there are pleasures for evermore. (Psalm 16:11 KJV)

"Lord, save us; we perish," the disciples cried, and instantly Christ arose to rebuke the winds of the storm and calm the sea. Today's hymn expresses in 19th century sailor's language the universal human need for divine help.

Edward Hopper, a gentle, humble man, was a Presbyterian minister with an honorary Doctor of Divinity degree. His most fruitful ministry, however, was with the sailors at the small Church of the Sea and Land in the New York harbor area, where he ministered until his death. Hopper wrote today's text especially for the spiritual needs of these sailors from around the world; it became their favorite hymn.

"Jesus, Savior, Pilot Me" uses only three of the original six verses written by Dr. Hopper. One of the omitted stanzas is an interesting reminder of our constant need for Christ even when there are no disturbing storms and life seems calm.

> Though the sea be smooth and bright, sparkling with the stars of night, and my ship's path be ablaze with the light of halcyon [peaceful] days, still I know my need of Thee; Jesus, Savior, pilot me.

Edward Hopper died at the age of 70 as he was sitting peacefully in his study, pencil in hand, working on a new poem about heaven. At his funeral this tribute was given: "Suddenly the gentle, affectionate spirit of Edward Hopper entered the heavenly port, as he had requested—safely piloted by that never-failing friend, Jesus, whose divine voice was still tenderly whispering to him, 'Fear not, I will pilot thee.'"

> Jesus, Savior, pilot me over life's tempestuous sea; unknown waves before me roll, hiding rocks and treach'rous shoal; chart and compass come from Thee— Jesus, Savior, pilot me!

> As a mother stills her child, Thou canst hush the ocean wild; boist'rous waves obey Thy will when Thou say'st to them, "Be still." Wondrous Sov'reign of the sea, Jesus, Savior, pilot me!

> When at last I near the shore, and the fearful breakers roar 'twixt me and the peaceful rest—then, while leaning on Thy breast, may I hear Thee say to me, "Fear not—I will pilot thee."

❧ ***For Today:*** Psalm 89:9; 107:28–30; Matthew 8:23–27; James 1:6

Join the sailors' chorus in a sincere plea to our faithful pilot for His constant guidance in our lives during this new year. Sing this prayer as you go—

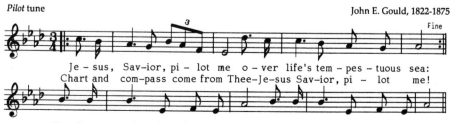

Pilot tune

John E. Gould, 1822-1875

Je - sus, Sav-ior, pi - lot me o - ver life's tem - pes - tuous sea:
Chart and com-pass come from Thee—Je-sus Sav-ior, pi - lot me!

Un - known waves be - fore me roll, Hiding rocks and treach'rous shoal;

HE LEADETH ME

Joseph H. Gilmore, 1834–1918

He makes me lie down in green pastures, He leads me beside quiet waters, He restores my soul. (Psalm 23:2)

The blessedness and awe of being led by Almighty God Himself so impressed the author of this text that he wrote these beloved words spontaneously—and these exact words have been sung by believers around the world for more than a century. Although Joseph Gilmore became a distinguished university and seminary professor, an author of several textbooks in Hebrew and English literature, and a respected Baptist minister, he is best remembered today for this one hymn, hurriedly written when he was just 28.

Gilmore scribbled down these lines while visiting with friends after preaching about the truths of the 23rd Psalm at the Wednesday evening service of the First Baptist Church in Philadelphia. He left this account:

> At the close of the service we adjourned to Deacon Watson's pleasant home, where we were being entertained. During our conversation the blessedness of God's leading so grew upon me that I took out my pencil, wrote the text just as it stands today, handed it to my wife, and thought no more of it.

Without telling her husband, Mrs. Gilmore sent the verses to the *Watchman and Reflector Magazine,* where it first appeared the following year. Three years later Joseph Gilmore went to Rochester, New York, as a candidate to become the pastor of Second Baptist Church. He recalls:

> Upon entering the chapel I took up a hymnal, thinking—I wonder what they sing here. To my amazement the book opened up at "He Leadeth Me," and that was the first time I knew that my hurriedly written lines had found a place among the songs of the church.

William Bradbury, an important American contributor to early gospel hymnody, added two additional lines to the chorus: "His faithful foll'wer I would be, for by His hand He leadeth me." Does that describe you?

> He leadeth me! O blessed thought! O words with heav'nly comfort fraught! Whate'er I do, where'er I be, still 'tis God's hand that leadeth me.

> Lord, I would clasp Thy hand in mine, nor ever murmur nor repine; content, whatever lot I see, since 'tis my God that leadeth me!

> And when my task on earth is done, when by Thy grace the vict'ry's won, e'en death's cold wave I will not flee, since God thru Jordan leadeth me.

> **Chorus:** He leadeth me, He leadeth me, by His own hand He leadeth me; His faithful foll'wer I would be, for by His hand He leadeth me.

❦ *For Today:* Psalm 23; 139:10, 24; Isaiah 41:13, 14; John 16:13

Visualize a loving shepherd tenderly leading his sheep. Then be especially responsive to God's guidance. Reflect on this tuneful thought—

William B. Bradbury, 1816–1868

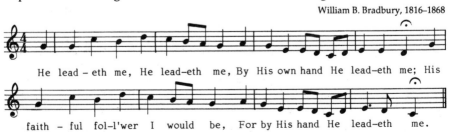

He lead - eth me, He lead-eth me, By His own hand He lead-eth me; His

faith - ful fol-l'wer I would be, For by His hand He lead-eth me.

TRUSTING JESUS

Edgar Page Stites, 1836–1921

Trust in the Lord, and do good; so shalt thou dwell in the land, and verily thou shalt be fed. Delight thyself also in the Lord; and He shall give thee the desires of thine heart. Commit thy way unto the Lord; trust also in Him, and He shall bring it to pass. (Psalm 37:3-5 KJV)

"Simply trusting every day" along a "stormy way," "in danger" when "the path is drear" "if the way is clear"—what a valuable lesson for each of us to learn. We are so prone to look ahead in life to see how our problems will be solved or where our path will lead. We waste much time and energy in worrying instead of simply trusting, delighting, and committing our ways to the Lord. That's how to find His strength and wisdom to face our problems and responsibilities for tomorrow and all the days ahead. Edgar Stites, an obscure but active lay worker, had learned that spiritual lesson. He discovered that "while He leads I cannot fall." God's way in our lives is always far superior to the path we might have chosen.

The writer of "Trusting Jesus" was a faithful member of the Methodist church in Cape May, New Jersey. After serving in the Civil War, he worked as a riverboat pilot and later as a home missionary in the Dakotas. He wrote several other hymns, including the very popular "Beulah Land."

Mr. Stites' poem first appeared in a newspaper in 1876. It was then given to evangelist D. L. Moody, who in turn asked his associate, Ira Sankey, to compose a suitable tune for the words. The hymn was widely used in the Moody-Sankey evangelistic services, and through the years Christians have responded to the implicit, child-like faith expressed so well in this simple but inspiring hymn.

> Simply trusting ev'ry day, trusting thru a stormy way; even when my faith is small, trusting Jesus—that is all.

> Brightly does His Spirit shine into this poor heart of mine; while He leads I cannot fall, trusting Jesus—that is all.

> Singing if my way is clear, praying if the path be drear; if in danger, for Him call, trusting Jesus—that is all.

> **Chorus:** Trusting as the moments fly, trusting as the days go by; trusting Him whate'er befall, trusting Jesus—that is all.

❧ *For Today:* Deuteronomy 33:25; Psalm 84:11; Proverbs 3:5; Ephesians 6:16; 1 John 5:4, 5

Consciously commit every problem or concern to Jesus, trusting Him fully to guide you in the right way and deliver you from all useless worry. Sing this truth as you go—

Ira D. Sankey, 1840-1908

Trust – ing as the mo – ments fly, Trust–ing as the days go by; Trust–ing Him what–e'er be–fall, Trust – ing Je – sus, that is all.

GOD LEADS US ALONG

Words and Music by George A. Young, 19th century

You guide me with Your counsel, and afterward You will take me into glory. Whom have I in heaven but You? And being with You, I desire nothing on earth. (Psalm 73:24, 25)

The more clearly we see the sovereignty of God and depend on His providential care, the less perplexed we will be by life's calamities.

> He does not lead me year by year, nor even day by day;
> But step by step my path unfolds; my Lord directs the way. —*Unknown*

The author and composer of "God Leads Us Along" was an obscure preacher and carpenter who spent a lifetime humbly serving God in small rural areas. Often the salary was meager and life was difficult for his family. Through it all, however, George Young and his wife never wavered in their loyalty to God and His service.

The story is told that after much struggle and effort, the George Young family was finally able to move into their own small home, which they had built themselves. Their joy seemed complete. But then, while Young was away holding meetings in another area, hoodlums who disliked the preacher's gospel message set fire to the house, leaving nothing but a heap of ashes. It is thought that out of that tragic experience, George Young completed this hymn, which reaffirms so well the words of Job 35:10: "God my Maker, who gives songs in the night." The words of this hymn have since been a source of great comfort and encouragement to countless numbers of God's people as they experienced the "night" times of their lives:

> In shady, green pastures, so rich and so sweet, God leads His dear children along; where the water's cool flow bathes the weary one's feet, God leads His dear children along.
> Sometimes on the mount where the sun shines so bright, God leads His dear children along; sometimes in the valley, in the darkest of night, God leads His dear children along.
> Tho sorrows befall us and Satan oppose, God leads His dear children along; thru grace we can conquer, defeat all our foes, God leads His dear children along.
> **Chorus:** Some thru the waters, some thru the flood, some thru the fire, but all thru the blood; some thru great sorrow, but God gives a song, in the night season and all the day long.

❦ *For Today:* Deuteronomy 1:30, 33; Joshua 3:4; Isaiah 58:11; Matthew 6:34

Determine for this day and for this new year to trust God more fully—regardless of the circumstances that may come your way. Sing this musical truth as a helpful reminder—

Some thru great sor - row, but God gives a song, In the night sea-son

and all the day long.

GOD MOVES IN A MYSTERIOUS WAY

William Cowper, 1731–1800

Oh, the depth of the riches of the wisdom and knowledge of God! How unsearchable His judgments. . . . (Romans 11:33)

> Good when He gives, supremely good, nor less when He denies.
> Even crosses from His sovereign hand are blessings in disguise.   —*Unknown*

The hymn "God Moves in a Mysterious Way" has been acclaimed as one of the finest songs ever written on the theme of God's providence. This label is made all the more amazing by the fact that the hymn text was written by an English poet who lived a lifetime of mental distress. William Cowper's emotional upsets included an 18-month stay in an insane asylum and later several attempted suicides. During his time in the asylum, Cowper began reading the Bible. At the age of 33 he had a genuine conversion experience. Yet he was periodically haunted by deep depressions, voices, and visions, and the overwhelming thought that God had forsaken him and would doom him to hell.

But between these times of mental melancholia, William Cowper was a gifted writer. Several of his secular works achieved great literary fame. For nearly two decades he worked closely with John Newton in Olney, England, and eventually their combined talents produced the famous *Olney Hymns* hymnal. In this ambitious collection of 349 hymns, 67 were written by Cowper, including such favorites as "O For a Closer Walk With God" and "There Is a Fountain."

"God Moves in a Mysterious Way" was originally titled "Conflict: Light Shining Out Of Darkness." It is thought to be Cowper's final hymn text and a reflection of God's leading throughout his own lifetime. There is even speculation that it was written following a failed attempt at suicidal drowning. Regardless of the original motivation for their writing, these words have since been used to bring much comfort to God's people for nearly two centuries:

> God moves in a mysterious way His wonders to perform; He plants His footsteps in the sea and rides upon the storm.
>
> You fearful saints, fresh courage take: The clouds you so much dread are big with mercy, and shall break in blessings on your head.
>
> Judge not the Lord by feeble sense, but trust Him for His grace; behind a frowning providence faith sees a smiling face.
>
> Blind unbelief is sure to err and scan His work in vain; God is His own interpreter, and He will make it plain.

❦ ***For Today:*** Proverbs 23:30; Matthew 11:25, 26; 2 Corinthians 1:9

Pause to thank God for the various and perhaps unusual ways He has directed your life to this very moment. Resolve to trust Him more fully in the days ahead. Sing this hymn as you remember that—

Dundee tune   Scottish Psalter, 1621

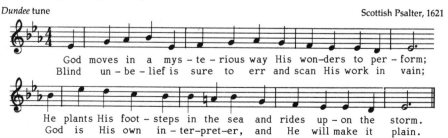

God moves in a mys-te-rious way His won-ders to per-form;
Blind un-be-lief is sure to err and scan His work in vain;

He plants His foot-steps in the sea and rides up-on the storm.
God is His own in-ter-pret-er, and He will make it plain.

THE KING OF LOVE MY SHEPHERD IS

Henry W. Baker, 1821–1877

For He is our God and we are the people of His pasture, the flock under His care. (Psalm 95:7)

The beloved words of Psalm 23 have undoubtedly provided greater comfort and encouragement to God's people through the years than any other portion of Scripture. In times of deep need, how eloquently these tender words from the psalmist David minister to our wounded spirits. This psalm has also formed the textual basis for more sacred music than any other scriptural setting. But to many devout Christians the best-loved hymn based on Psalm 23 is this paraphrase by an English musician, Sir Henry Baker. In this text Baker skillfully combines thoughts of King David with lessons from the New Testament. For example, the words from the third stanza are based on the parable of the lost sheep in Luke 15:5. The fourth stanza includes the phrase "Thy cross before to guide me." Here the shepherd is identified as Christ by the inclusion of the cross symbolism.

Sir Henry William Baker is highly regarded by students of hymnody for his work as the editor-in-chief of one of the most monumental hymnals ever published, *Hymns, Ancient and Modern,* a book which sold more than 60 million copies after it was published in 1861. See how these words can direct you again to the love of the Good Shepherd.

> The King of Love my Shepherd is, whose goodness faileth never;
> I nothing lack if I am His and He is mine forever.
>
> Where streams of living water flow my ransomed soul He leadeth,
> and where the verdant pastures grow, with food celestial feedeth.
>
> Perverse and foolish oft I strayed, but yet in love He sought me,
> and on His shoulder gently laid, and home rejoicing brought me.
>
> In death's dark vale I fear no ill with Thee, dear Lord, beside me;
> Thy rod and staff my comfort still, Thy cross before to guide me.
>
> Thou spread'st a table in my sight; Thine unction grace bestoweth;
> and O what transport of delight from Thy pure chalice floweth!
>
> And so through all the length of days Thy goodness faileth never:
> Good Shepherd, may I sing Thy praise within Thy house for ever!

🍂 *For Today:* Psalm 23; John 10:9; Hebrews 2:14, 15; 1 Peter 2:25

Take time to read and meditate again on the 23rd Psalm. Reflect on the tender love and care that an earthly shepherd has for his sheep. Relate this to your heavenly Shepherd's guidance and care for your life. Let this musical message help you—

Dominius Regit Me tune

John B. Dykes, 1823–1876

The King of Love my Shep-herd is, Whose good-ness fail-eth nev - er;

I noth - ing lack if I am His And He is mine for ev - er.

SURELY GOODNESS AND MERCY

John W. Peterson, 1921–
Alfred B. Smith, 1916–

Answer me, O Lord, out of the goodness of Your love; in Your great mercy turn to me. (Psalm 69:16)

Charles Haddon Spurgeon, known as the "Prince of Preachers" of the 19th century, labored for more than 20 years on his unrivaled commentary of the Psalms, a seven-volume work entitled *The Treasury of David.* "Only those who have meditated profoundly upon the Psalms," wrote Spurgeon, "can have any adequate conception of the wealth they contain." Meditate on this comment that Mr. Spurgeon made about the 23rd Psalm, the basis of this hymn:

> The sweetest word of the whole is that monosyllable, "my." He does not say, "The Lord is the shepherd of the world at large, and leadeth forth the multitude as his flock." If He is a shepherd to no one else, He is a shepherd to me. He cares for me, watches over me, and preserves me. The words are in the present tense. Whatever be the believer's position, he is even now under the pastoral care of Jehovah.

Two well-known names in the field of gospel music, John W. Peterson and Alfred B. Smith, collaborated in 1958 to write this popular paraphrase of Psalm 23. Mr. Smith recalls the humorous touch that provided the initial inspiration for this song:

> It was written after receiving a letter from one of the descendants of P. P. Bliss, telling of Bliss's first country school teacher, Miss Murphy, whom he dearly loved. It told of her teaching the class (before they could read or write) to memorize the 23rd Psalm. When the part "surely goodness and mercy" was reached, little Philip thought it said, "surely good Miss Murphy shall follow me all the days of my life." This little incident focused our thoughts on the phrase which became the heart and title of the song.

> A pilgrim was I, and a wan-d'ring, in the cold night of sin I did roam, when Jesus the kind Shepherd found me, and now I am on my way home.

> He restoreth my soul when I'm weary, He giveth me strength day by day; He leads me beside the still waters; He guards me each step of the way.

> When I walk thru the dark lonesome valley, my Savior will walk with me there; and safely His great hand will lead me to the mansions He's gone to prepare.

> **Chorus:** Surely goodness and mercy shall follow me all the days of my life; and I shall dwell in the house of the Lord forever, and I shall feast at the table spread for me. Surely goodness and mercy shall follow me all the days, all the days of my life.

❦ *For Today:* Exodus 15:13; Psalm 16:11; 23; Revelation 19:9

Carry the truth of this musical message with you as you live in the joy and confidence of your heavenly Father's love and care for you—

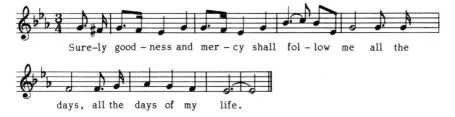

Sure–ly good – ness and mer – cy shall fol – low me all the

days, all the days of my life.

BE STILL, MY SOUL

Katharina von Schlegel, 1697–?
English Translation-Jane L. Borthwick, 1813–1897

Be still, and know that I am God; I will be exalted among the nations, I will be exalted in the earth.   (Psalm 46:10)

Spiritual revivals throughout history have always been accompanied by an outburst of new song. This was especially true of the 16th century reformation movement when, following centuries of dormancy during the Middle Ages, congregational singing was rediscovered. However, by the 17th century the church was once more cold and non-evangelistic. Again God lit the fires of revival in the latter half of that century with a movement known as the Pietistic Revival in Germany, which was similar to the Puritan and Wesleyan movements in England. The Pietistic movement also gave birth to many rich German hymns, one of which incorporates the contributions of three persons.

Katharina von Schlegel was the outstanding woman of this revival movement. Little is known of her other than that she was a Lutheran and may have been the canoness of an evangelical women's seminary in Germany. However, we do know that she contributed a number of lyrics to a collection of spiritual songs published in 1752.

Approximately 100 years after it was written, this hymn text was translated into English by Jane Borthwick, a scholar noted for her fine work in translating German texts. This hymn tune is an arrangement of one movement from Jean Sibelius' "Finlandia." Sibelius was Finland's best-known composer, and his music is generally characterized by a strong nationalistic fervor.

God has used the talents of these three individuals from different lands to provide His people with a hymn that teaches so well the biblical truth that we all need to relearn daily: "They that wait upon the Lord shall renew their strength . . ." (Isaiah 40:31).

> Be still, my soul—the Lord is on thy side! Bear patiently the cross of grief or pain; leave to thy God to order and provide—In ev'ry change He faithful will remain. Be still, my soul—thy best, thy heav'nly Friend thru thorny ways leads to a joyful end.
>
> Be still, my soul—thy God doth undertake to guide the future as He has the past; thy hope, thy confidence let nothing shake—All now mysterious shall be bright at last. Be still, my soul—the waves and winds still know His voice who ruled them while He dwelt below.

❦ *For Today:* Proverbs 3:5; Isaiah 30:15; 40:31; Hebrews 10:35

Determine to live by the truth that "the Lord is on thy side!" Remember that "All now mysterious shall be bright at last—"

Finlandia tune   Jean Sibelius, 1865–1957

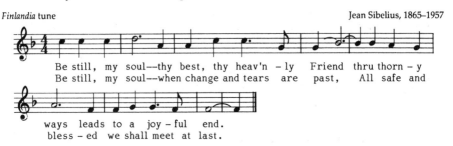

Be still, my soul—thy best, thy heav'n – ly Friend thru thorn – y
Be still, my soul—when change and tears are past, All safe and

ways leads to a joy – ful end.
bless – ed we shall meet at last.

DEAR LORD AND FATHER OF MANKIND

John Greenleaf Whittier, 1807–1892

In repentance and rest is your salvation, in quietness and trust is your strength. (Isaiah 30:15)

So often in our modern lives we attack our problems with frantic and hurried activity, creating unnecessary stress for ourselves. We easily forget that our heavenly Father can assist us in meeting our daily challenges with serenity and calm assurance. We need the quiet confidence in God and a peaceful resting in His eternal love that is reflected in this beautiful text by John Greenleaf Whittier, "America's beloved Quaker poet." Whittier's poetic lines remind us of this so clearly, admonishing us to listen carefully for God's "still small voice of calm" in the midst of all of life's turbulency.

Whittier was a good example of quiet godly life in his speech, dress, and writings. It has been said that he "left upon our literature the stamp of genius and upon our religion the touch of sanity."

"A good hymn is the best use to which poetry can be devoted, though I do not claim to have succeeded in writing one," wrote Whittier. Hymnal editors, however, have collected and edited enough of his poems to make seventy-five hymns.

John Greenleaf Whittier's life expressed the steadfast rest in his heavenly Father's love that these words suggest. As you read, why not decide now to let Him guide you and give you peace in this hectic world.

> Dear Lord and Father of mankind, forgive our fev'rish ways! Reclothe us in our rightful mind; in purer lives Thy service find, in deeper rev'rence, praise.

> In simple trust like theirs who heard, beside the Syrian sea, the gracious calling of the Lord, let us, like them, without a word rise up and follow Thee.

> Drop Thy still dews of quietness till all our strivings cease; take from our souls the strain and stress, and let our ordered lives confess the beauty of Thy peace.

> Breathe thru the heats of our desire Thy coolness and Thy balm; let sense be dumb, let flesh retire; speak thru the earthquake, wind and fire, O still small voice of calm.

❦ *For Today:* Mark 1:16–20; Ephesians 4:6; 2 Timothy 1:9; 1 Peter 2:9; 1 John 1:9

Breathe this prayer as you begin your activities today—"Lord, grant to me a quiet mind, that trusting Thee . . . for Thou art kind . . . I may go on without a fear, for Thou, my Lord, art always near." Use this musical message to remember—

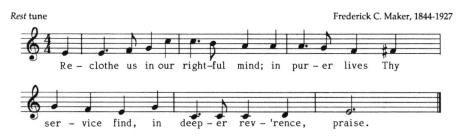

Rest tune   Frederick C. Maker, 1844-1927

Re – clothe us in our right–ful mind; in pur – er lives Thy

ser – vice find, in deep – er rev – 'rence, praise.

STILL, STILL WITH THEE

Harriet B. Stowe, 1812–1896

Morning by morning, O Lord, You hear my voice; morning by morning I lay my requests before You and wait in expectation. (Psalm 5:3)

"How precious to me are Your thoughts, O God! . . . When I awake, I am still with Thee". This was the phrase that inspired Harriet Beecher Stowe as she meditated one morning on Psalm 139:17, 18. In the midst of a busy and productive life—as a writer, an avid crusader against world-wide slavery, and a mother of six—it was Harriet Stowe's practice to rise at 4:30 each morning to "see the coming of the dawn, hear the singing of the birds, and to enjoy the over-shadowing presence of her God."

As a devoted mother and the wife of a seminary professor, Harriet still found time to write numerous hymns, a volume of religious verse, and approximately 40 books dealing with the various social problems of her time. Her best known novel was *Uncle Tom's Cabin,* which had a strong influence against slavery just before the Civil War.

In later life, as she looked back over many of the difficulties she had experienced in her busy years of raising a family while engaging in many pursuits, Harriet wrote, "I thank God there is one thing running through all of them—from the time I was 13 years old [the age of her conversion]—and that is the intense unwavering sense of Christ's educating, guiding presence and care."

It is commonly agreed by hymnists that for sheer poetic beauty, there are few hymn texts that excel these lines:

Still, still with Thee—when purple morning breaketh, when the bird waketh and the shadows flee; fairer than morning, lovelier than daylight, dawns the sweet consciousness—I am with Thee!

Alone with Thee amid the mystic shadows—the solemn hush of nature newly born; alone with Thee in breathless adoration, in the calm dew and freshness of the morn.

Still, still with Thee—as to each new-born morning a fresh and solemn splendor still is giv'n; so doth this blessed consciousness, awaking, breathe each day nearness unto Thee and heav'n!

So shall it be at last in that bright morning, when the soul waketh and life's shadows flee; O in that hour, fairer than daylight dawning, shall rise the glorious tho't—I am with Thee!

❦ *For Today:* Job 19:25–27; Psalm 139:17, 18; Colossians 3:4; 1 John 4:13

Live this day with a fresh awareness of God's beauty in nature and of His companionship in your life. Let this musical message remind you—

Consolation tune   Felix Mendelssohn, 1809-1847

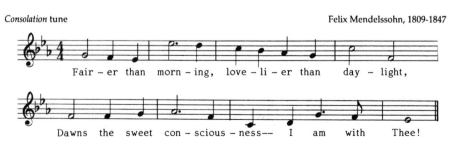

Fair – er than morn – ing, love – li – er than day – light,

Dawns the sweet con – scious – ness–– I am with Thee!

JESUS SAVES!

Priscilla J. Owens, 1829-1907

Sing to the Lord, praise His name; proclaim His salvation day after day. Declare His glory among the nations, His marvelous deeds among all peoples. (Psalm 96:2, 3)

The heart of the Christian gospel is a person, not a church or a system of doctrinal interpretation. To evangelize is to proclaim the good news of Jesus Christ—that He came to this world, died for our sins, and was raised from the grave according to the Scriptures. And, as the reigning Lord, He now meets every human need with His forgiveness of sins and the indwelling gift of His Holy Spirit to all who repent and believe.

Today, however, many false teachers claim that God speaks equally through all religions and ideologies. Those who believe this do not consider a personal faith in the person and work of Christ to be essential. We must reject as derogatory to our Lord and His gospel every teaching that makes this boast. The Bible is dogmatic: "For there is one God and one mediator between God and man, the man Christ Jesus" (1 Timothy 2:5).

Priscilla J. Owens, a Baltimore public school teacher for 49 years, wrote these stirring soul-winning words for a missionary service in the Sunday school of the Union Square Methodist Church. Fourteen years later, William Kirkpatrick wedded his vibrant music to her words. Through the years they have challenged God's people with the urgency of soul winning.

> We have heard the joyful sound: Jesus saves! Jesus saves! Spread the tidings all around: Jesus saves! Jesus saves! Bear the news to every land; climb the steeps and cross the waves; onward!—'tis our Lord's command; Jesus saves! Jesus saves!

> Waft it on the rolling tide; Jesus saves! Jesus saves! Tell to sinners far and wide: Jesus saves! Jesus saves! Sing, ye islands of the sea; echo back, ye ocean caves; earth shall keep her jubilee: Jesus saves! Jesus saves!

> Sing above the battle strife, Jesus saves! Jesus saves! By His death and endless life, Jesus saves! Jesus saves! Sing it softly through the gloom, when the heart for mercy craves; sing in triumph o'er the tomb;—Jesus saves! Jesus saves!

> Give the winds a mighty voice, Jesus saves! Jesus saves! Let the nations now rejoice,—Jesus saves! Jesus saves! Shout salvation full and free; highest hills and deepest caves; this our song of victory,—Jesus saves! Jesus saves!

❦ *For Today:* Psalm 67:2; Isaiah 52:7; Mark 16:15; Acts 1:8; Romans 1:16

Try to speak to someone about trusting Jesus and Him alone for salvation from sin and the satisfaction of every need. Carry this musical message that—

William Kirkpartick, 1838-1921

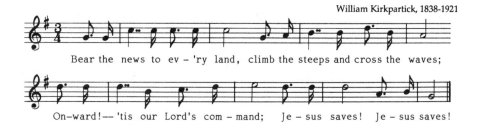

Bear the news to ev - 'ry land, climb the steeps and cross the waves;

On—ward!-- 'tis our Lord's com - mand; Je - sus saves! Je - sus saves!

GO YE INTO ALL THE WORLD

Words and Music by James McGranahan, 1840-1907

Go into all the world and preach the good news to all creation. (Mark 16:15)

Give us a watchword for the hour, a thrilling word, a word of power;
A battlecry, a flaming breath that calls to conquer even death.
A word to rouse the Church from rest, to heed the Master's last request;
The call is given: Christians arise, our watchword is EVANGELIZE!

—Author unknown

As members of the church of Jesus Christ, how we need to be reminded continually of our Lord's final request! We settle down so easily in our individual comforts and in the security of our church routines. Worldwide evangelization will become a realistic possibility only when the Spirit of God renews His people personally with a vision and passion for the spiritual needs of a lost world . . . when in His power we are willing to go . . . to evangelize!

James McGranahan, author and composer of this hymn, is a well-known name in the field of early gospel music. After the sudden death of Philip Bliss in 1876, McGranahan became the songleader in the evangelistic campaigns conducted by Major D. W. Whittle in England and throughout America. Known for his fine tenor voice and a commanding personality, he pioneered in using male choirs in his services. McGranahan collaborated with Ira Sankey and other gospel musicians in many publications. "Go Ye Into All the World" was widely used as a missionary challenge in their great crusade meetings. These words still speak pointedly to us today.

Far, far away, in heathen darkness dwelling, millions of souls forever may be lost; who, who will go, salvation's story telling, looking to Jesus, minding not the cost.

See o'er the world wide open doors inviting—Soldiers of Christ, arise and enter in! Christians, awake! your forces all uniting, send forth the gospel; break the chains of sin.

God speed the day, when those of ev'ry nation "Glory to God!" triumphantly shall sing; Ransomed, redeemed, rejoicing in salvation, shout "Hallelujah, for the Lord is King!"

Chorus: "All pow'r is given unto Me; all pow'r is given unto Me; go ye into all the world and preach the gospel, and lo, I am with you alway."

❦ *For Today:* Matthew 9:37, 38; 28:18-20; 1 Corinthians 15:3, 4

Seek to read some pertinent article on the status of world missions. Ask God to show you a more significant role in this great endeavor. Meditate on the truth of Christ's command in this hymn's chorus—

"All pow'r is giv—en un—to Me, All pow'r is giv—en un—to Me, Go ye

in—to all the world and preach the gos—pel, And lo, I am with you al—way."

FROM GREENLAND'S ICY MOUNTAINS

Reginald Heber, 1783-1826

Then He said to His disciples, "The harvest is plentiful but the workers are few. Ask the Lord of the harvest, therefore, to send out workers into His harvest field." (Matthew 9:37, 38)

We hear many missionary sermons in our churches, but not often do we sing such a beautifully worded and challenging missionary hymn as this one, which was quickly and spontaneously written by Reginald Heber. These well-chosen words and ideas inspire us to spread the blessings of salvation to all people and nations until our Lord "in bliss returns to reign."

Heber was a minister in the Anglican church in England. With his keen interest in world missions, he did much through his writings and influence to promote the missionary activity that greatly increased during his lifetime.

In the summer of 1819, Heber was asked by his father-in-law if he knew a worthy hymn that could be used at a missionary service the next Sunday. Reginald went at once to his study for a few minutes of quiet meditation and soon returned with the first stanzas of this text. His family was very pleased with it. Heber, however, feeling the hymn was still incomplete, returned to his study and completed the triumphant final verse.

Five years later the tune was composed specifically for Heber's text by the noted American educator and church musician, Lowell Mason. It is said that Mason composed this tune with a great sense of inspiration.

Today, Reginald Heber is ranked as one of the foremost 19th century English hymnists, having written 57 well-known hymns, including "Holy, Holy, Holy." As a result of his zeal for missions, he became an Anglican bishop to Calcutta, India, but died there at the age of 43. Notice how large is the Lord's harvest field.

> From Greenland's icy mountains, from India's coral strand, where Afric's sunny fountains roll down their golden sand, from many an ancient river, from many a palmy plain, they call us to deliver their land from error's chain.

> Shall we, whose souls are lighted with wisdom from on high, shall we to men benighted the lamp of life deny? Salvation! O salvation! The joyful sound proclaim till earth's remotest nation has learned Messiah's name.

> Waft, waft, ye winds, His story, and you, ye waters, roll, till like a sea of glory it spreads from pole to pole; till o'er our ransomed nature the Lamb for sinners slain, Redeemer, King, Creator, in bliss returns to reign.

❦ ***For Today:*** Matthew 28:19, 20; Mark 16:15; John 4:35; Acts 1:8

Pray especially for some foreign missionary in your church, that the truth of this musical message might become a greater reality in today's world—

Missionary Hymn tune   Lowell Mason, 1792-1872

Sal - va - tion! O sal - va - tion! The joy-ful sound pro-claim,   till
Till o'er our ran-somed na - ture the Lamb for sin - ners slain,   Re-

earth's re - mot - est na - tion has learned Mes - si - ah's name.
deem - er, King, Cre - a - tor, in bliss re - turns to reign.

IN CHRIST THERE IS NO EAST OR WEST

John Oxenham, 1852-1941

There is neither Jew nor Greek, slave nor free, male nor female, for you are all one in Christ Jesus. (Galatians 3:28)

One of the clear teachings of the Bible is that the gospel does not presuppose the superiority of any race or culture. In the past, missionary endeavor has too frequently imposed "our" culture on others while spreading the gospel, often putting native believers in bondage to another culture rather than to Christ and the Scriptures alone.

Written in 1908 by the noted English writer, John Oxenham, this missionary hymn text was part of a script for a pageant at a giant missionary event sponsored by the London Missionary Society's exhibition, The Orient in London. It is estimated that over a quarter of a million people viewed this presentation. It was continued from 1908-1914 both in England and in the United States.

An interesting account of the impact of this hymn relates an incident during the closing days of World War II when two ships were anchored together, one containing Japanese aliens, and the other American soldiers, all waiting to be repatriated. For an entire day they lined the rails, glaring at one another. Suddenly someone began to sing "In Christ There Is No East Or West." Then another on the opposite ship joined in. Soon there was an extraordinary chorus of former enemies unitedly praising God with these words:

> In Christ there is no East or West, in him no South or North, but one great fellowship of love thru out the whole wide earth.

> In Him shall true hearts ev'rywhere their high communion find; His service is the golden cord close-binding all mankind.

> Join hands then, brothers of the faith, whate'er your race may be; who serves my Father as a son is surely kin to me.

> In Christ now meet both East and West, in Him meet South and North; all Christly souls are one in Him throughout the whole wide earth.

Words from "Bees in Amber" by John Oxenham

🐝 *For Today:* Acts 10:34, 35; Romans 9:1-3; Ephesians 4:3; Philippians 1:27; 1 Peter 3:8

Purpose to pray each day of the week for the work of the gospel in a different area of the world: Africa, Asia, Europe, Latin America, the Middle East, the Pacific, the Caribbean . . . . Perhaps this musical message will be a helpful reminder—

St. Peter tune   Alexander R. Reinagle, 1799-1877

In Christ there is no East or West, in Him no South or North, but one great fel-low-ship of love thru - out the whole wide earth.

CHRIST FOR THE WORLD WE SING

Samuel Wolcott, 1813-1886

Therefore go and make disciples of all nations, baptizing them in the name of the Father and of the Son and of the Holy Spirit, and teaching them to obey everything I have commanded you. And surely I will be with you always, to the very end of the age. (Matthew 28:19, 20)

The task of worldwide evangelization is a staggering challenge. It is estimated that the world's population is presently about 5 billion people, with two-thirds of mankind still unreached with the gospel. Also one-third of the human race is nearly destitute, lacking the basic necessities for survival. Yet we are told that by the year 2,000 the population will add another billion, and that in the next 100 years the population will double to more than 10 billion people. All this time, other world religions are also pressing their claims with increasing vigor. Islam is growing at a rate of 16 percent annually, Hinduism at 12 percent. Christianity's growth is estimated at less then 10 percent.

Samuel Wolcott, author of this missionary text, had a burning zeal for the spread of the gospel and the spiritual needs of the world. In his earlier years he had been a missionary to Syria before poor health forced his return to America. Later he served as pastor in numerous Congregational churches, as well as acting as secretary of the Ohio Home Missionary Society. It was while pastoring the Plymouth Congregational Church in Cleveland, Ohio, that he wrote this text. He stated:

> The Young Men's Christian Association of Ohio met in one of our churches with their motto in evergreen letters over the pulpit, "Christ for the World, and the World for Christ."

Pastor Wolcott was so moved by this motto that he promptly wrote these words, which have since been widely used to challenge Christians to have a vision for the needs of our entire world.

> Christ for the world we sing! The world to Christ we bring with loving zeal: The poor and them that mourn, the faint and overborne, sinsick and sorrow worn, whom Christ doth heal.

> Christ for the world we sing! The world to Christ we bring with fervent prayer: The wayward and the lost, by restless passions tossed, redeemed at countless cost from dark despair.

> Christ for the world we sing! The world to Christ we bring with joyful song: The newborn souls, whose days, reclaimed from error's ways, inspired with hope and praise, to Christ belong.

❦ ***For Today:*** Psalm 22:27; Mark 13:10; 16:15; Romans 10:12-15

Ask God to give you a worldwide vision for the furtherance of the gospel. Determine to take a greater interest in your church's mission program. Allow this hymn to help—

Italian Hymn tune   Felice de Giardini, 1716-1796

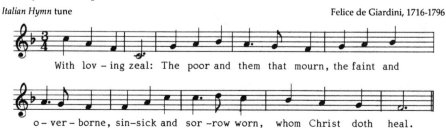

With lov-ing zeal: The poor and them that mourn, the faint and

o-ver-borne, sin–sick and sor –row worn, whom Christ doth heal.

WE'VE A STORY TO TELL

Words and Music by H. Ernest Nichol, 1862-1928

All nations will come and worship before You, for Your righteous acts have been revealed. (Revelation 15:4)

"A story to tell. A song to be sung. A message to give. A Savior to show." Here is a concise summary of the task of worldwide evangelization—a gospel that must be demonstrated as well as proclaimed.

Evangelism began well. The early Christians, though often fiercely persecuted by the Romans, were successful. By A.D. 380, Christianity was recognized as the official religion throughout the empire. Yet for the next 1,000 years and more, the flame of evangelism burned low. The 16th century Protestant Reformation movement saw a brief revival of evangelical fervor, but not until the 18th century did Protestants make their first serious attempt to organize missionary work. The expansion of missions in the 18th and 19th centuries was clearly connected with the waves of revival that were sweeping across Europe and North America.

Since the close of World War II, the cause of world missions has grown markedly. It is estimated that presently more than 250,000 missionaries are sent out every year, with many of these workers coming from Third World countries.

But the task is far from finished. More than two-thirds of the world's population is yet unreached with the good news of Christ. The Wycliffe Bible translators report that there are still 723 tribes without a Bible translation. Nearly every mission board desperately needs more workers.

"We've a Story to Tell" was written and composed by an English musician, H. Ernest Nichol, in 1896. These words are still widely sung by young and old alike and represent the missionary zeal that should always burn in our hearts:

> We've a story to tell to the nations that shall turn their hearts to the right, a story of truth and mercy, a story of peace and light, a story of peace and light.

> We've a song to be sung to the nations that shall lift their hearts to the Lord; a song that shall conquer evil and shatter the spear and sword, and shatter the spear and sword.

> We've a message to give to the nations—that the Lord who reigneth above hath sent us His Son to save us and show us that God is love, and show us that God is love.

> We've a Savior to show to the nations who the path of sorrow hath trod, that all of the world's great peoples might come to the truth of God, might come to the truth of God.

> **Chorus:** For the darkness shall turn to dawning, and the dawning to noon-day bright, and Christ's great kingdom shall come to earth, the kingdom of love and light.

❦ *For Today:* Psalm 67:2; Matthew 22:14; Mark 16:15; Luke 24:47; John 12:46

Take time to write a letter of appreciation to a missionary from your church. Let this musical message be an encouragement, both to you and to them—

And Christ's great king-dom shall come to earth, The king-dom of love and light.

O ZION, HASTE

Mary Ann Thomson, 1834-1923

May Your ways be known on earth, Your salvation among all nations. (Psalm 67:2)

The Christian church is God's appointed means of spreading the gospel around the world. A church that is not a missionary church will quench the Spirit of God and miss His blessing. God's agenda for history is "that all nations might believe and obey Him" (Romans 16:26). All too often, however, the church has allowed itself to become self-centered, merely maintaining the status quo and failing to respond actively to this biblical directive.

That's why we need missionary hymns like this one. Its author, Mary Ann Thomson, was born in London, England, but spent most of her life in Philadelphia, Pennsylvania, where she was active in the Church of the Annunciation. She wrote a number of hymns and poems, this being the only one to survive, however. She wrote "O Zion, Haste" out of a stressful experience in 1868. One night, as she was watching her child who was ill with typhoid fever, the desire to write a missionary hymn pressed upon her. Some have felt that perhaps Mrs. Thomson had made a covenant with God that if he would spare her child, she would consecrate him to His service. The opening line of the final stanza, "give of thy sons to bear the message glorious," could indicate this. May these words move us from lethargy to evangelism.

> O Zion, haste, thy mission high fulfilling, to tell to all the world that God is Light, that He who made all nations is not willing one soul should perish, lost in shades of night.
>
> Behold, how many thousands still are lying, bound in the darksome prison-house of sin, with none to tell them of the Savior's dying, or of the life He died for them to win.
>
> Proclaim to every people, tongue and nation that God in whom they live and move is love: Tell how He stooped to save His lost creation, and died on earth that man might live above.
>
> Give of thy sons to bear the message glorious; give of thy wealth to speed them on their way; pour out thy soul for them in prayer victorious; and all thou spendest Jesus will repay.
>
> **Refrain:** Publish glad tidings, tidings of peace; tidings of Jesus, redemption, and release.

❦ *For Today:* Isaiah 52:7; Luke 24:47; Acts 1:8; Romans 10:15; 16:26

Prayerfully consider how your church could have a greater impact on worldwide missions. At the right time, share your thoughts with the pastor and other leaders. Carry the urgency for missions with you with this hymn's refrain—

Tidings tune   James Welch, 1837-1901

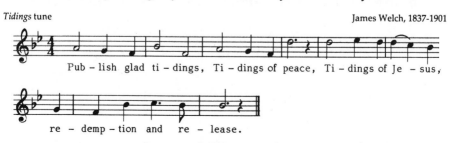

Pub - lish glad ti - dings, Ti - dings of peace, Ti - dings of Je - sus,
re - demp - tion and re - lease.

SO SEND I YOU

E. Margaret Clarkson, 1915-

Then I heard the voice of the Lord saying, "Whom shall I send? And who will go for us?" And I said, "Here am I. Send me!" (Isaiah 6:8)

Isolated from Christian fellowship and feeling very lonely, Margaret Clarkson was a 23-year-old school teacher in a gold-mining camp town in northern Ontario, Canada. Her friends and family were many miles away. As she meditated on John 20:21 one evening, God spoke to her through the phrase "So send I you." She realized that this lonely area was the place to which God had sent her. This was her mission field. As she quickly set down her thoughts in verse, one of the finest and most popular missionary hymns of the 20th century was born.

Miss Clarkson has authored many articles and poems for Christian and educational periodicals. For more than 30 years she was involved in the Toronto, Canada, public school system in various educational capacities.

Because of a physical disability, Miss Clarkson has been unable to fulfill her early desire of going to a foreign mission field. Yet her distinguished career in education, her many inspiring writings, and this challenging missionary hymn have accomplished much for the kingdom of God, even though she has remained in Canada.

These words have been greatly used by God to challenge many to respond to God's call for service with the words of the prophet Isaiah, "Here am I . . . send me!"

So send I you to labor unrewarded, to serve unpaid, unloved, unsought, unknown, to bear rebuke, to suffer scorn and scoffing—So send I you to toil for me alone.

So send I you to bind the bruised and broken, o'er wand'ring souls to work, to weep, to wake, to bear the burdens of a world a-weary—So send I you to suffer for My sake.

So send I you to loneliness and longing, with heart a-hung-'ring for the loved and known, forsaking home and kindred, friend and dear one—So send I you to know my love alone.

So send I you to leave your life's ambition, to die to dear desire, self-will resign, to labor long and love where men revile you—So send I you to lose your life in Mine.

So send I you to hearts made hard by hatred, to eyes made blind because they will not see, to spend—tho it be blood—to spend and spare not—So send I you to taste of Calvary. "As the Father hath sent Me, so send I you."

❦ *For Today:* Matthew 9:37, 38; John 4:35; 20:21; Acts 1:8

Enter your "mission field" today with the confidence you have been placed there by your heavenly Father. Carry this musical message with you—

John W. Peterson, 1921-

"As the Fa-ther hath sent Me, So send I you."

TAKE THE NAME OF JESUS WITH YOU

Lydia Baxter, 1809-1874

And whatever you do, whether in word or deed, do it all in the name of the Lord Jesus, giving thanks to God the Father through Him. (Colossians 3:17)

"What's in a name?" This was the probing question asked by Romeo in Shakespeare's play *Romeo and Juliet.* Christians have long realized that the whispered name "Jesus" can bring comfort and cheer to someone suffering or bereaved, and it can bring joyful hope to the fearful or depressed heart.

The writer of this hymn text knew well the meaning of that special name "Jesus". Although Lydia Baxter was a bed-ridden invalid much of her life, she remained continually cheerful and patient. "I have a very special armor," she would tell her friends. "I have the name of Jesus. When the tempter tries to make me blue or despondent, I mention the name of Jesus, and he can't get through to me anymore."

"Take the Name of Jesus With You" was written by Mrs. Baxter on her sick bed just four years before her death in 1874 at the age of 65. Throughout her lifetime she was known as an avid student of the Bible who loved to discuss the significance of scriptural names with her friends. She would inform them that Samuel means "asked of God," Hannah—"grace," Sarah—"princess," and Naomi—"pleasantness." But the name that meant everything to Lydia Baxter was the name "Jesus."

This hymn was used often during the Moody-Sankey evangelistic campaigns in the latter part of the 19th century. These words are still a comforting reminder of the peace and joy that result as we carry His precious Name throughout this life, and of the "joy of heav'n" that awaits us.

> Take the name of Jesus with you, child of sorrow and of woe; it will joy and comfort give you—Take it, then, where'er you go.
>
> Take the name of Jesus ever, as a shield from ev'ry snare; if temptations round you gather, breathe that holy name in prayer.
>
> O the precious name of Jesus! How it thrills our souls with joy, when His loving arms receive us and His songs our tongues employ!
>
> At the name of Jesus bowing, falling prostrate at His feet, King of kings in heav'n we'll crown Him when our journey is complete.
>
> **Chorus:** Precious name, O how sweet! Hope of earth and joy of heaven.

❦ *For Today:* Proverbs 18:10; John 1:12; Acts 4:12; Philippians 2:9, 10

Breathe the name of Jesus often as you go about your daily tasks, letting Him share each concern or blessing that comes your way. Carry this musical reminder with you for today and the days ahead—

William H. Doane, 1832-1915

Pre – cious name, O how sweet! Hope of earth and joy of heav'n

Pre – cious name, O how sweet! Hope of earth and joy of heav'n.

TURN YOUR EYES UPON JESUS

Words and Music by Helen H. Lemmel, 1864-1961

Let us fix our eyes on Jesus, the author and perfector of our faith, who for the joy set before Him endured the cross, scorning its shame, and sat down at the right hand of the throne of God. (Hebrews 12:2)

> I've seen the face of Jesus . . .It was a wondrous sight!
> Oh, glorious face of beauty, Oh gentle touch of care;
> If here it is so blessed, what will it be up there?   —*W. Spencer Walton*

In our fast-paced daily life, how easy it is to get caught up in the "things of earth" so that eternal values become blurred and almost forgotten. As we conclude the first month's journey through this new year, we need today's hymn to remind us that we must continue to make Christ the central core of our lives—to pursue the Kingdom of God and His righteousness—if we are to be victorious believers.

In 1918, Helen Howarth Lemmel, the author and composer of this hymn, was given a tract by a missionary friend. As she read it, Helen's attention was focused on this line: "So then, turn your eyes upon Him, look full into His face, and you will find that the things of earth will acquire a strange new dimness." She related:

> Suddenly, as if commanded to stop and listen, I stood still, and singing in my soul and spirit was the chorus of the hymn with not one conscious moment of putting word to word to make rhyme, or note to note to make melody. The verses were written the same week, after the usual manner of composition, but none the less dictated by the Holy Spirit.

Since that day, Helen Lemmel's hymn has been translated into many languages and used by God to challenge believers around the world with the necessity of living devoted lives for His glory.

> O soul, are you weary and troubled? No light in the darkness you see? There's light for a look at the Savior, and life more abundant and free!

> Thru death into life everlasting He passed, and we follow Him there; over us sin no more hath dominion—For more than conq'rors we are!

> His word shall not fail you—He promised; believe Him, and all will be well: Then go to a world that is dying, His perfect salvation to tell!

> **Chorus:** Turn your eyes upon Jesus; look full in His wonderful face, and the things of earth will grow strangely dim in the light of His glory and grace.

❧ *For Today:* Isaiah 45:22; Matthew 6:33; Colossians 3:1-4

Purpose to enjoy more fully the fellowship of Christ now and throughout the remainder of this new year. Let these words remind you to face each situation with confidence—

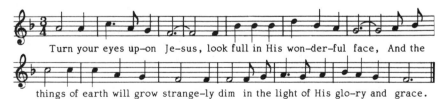

Turn your eyes up-on Je-sus, look full in His won-der-ful face, And the things of earth will grow strange-ly dim in the light of His glo-ry and grace.

February

• *God's Love to Us* • *Our Love for God*
• *Love for Our Fellow-man*

WALK IN THE LIGHT

Bernard Barton, 1784-1849

But if we walk in the light, as He is in the light, we have fellowship with one another, and the blood of Jesus, His Son, purifies us from every sin. (1 John 1:7)

> How beautiful to walk in the steps of the Savior
> Led in paths of light.
> —*E. Hewitt*

Walking in the light means walking as Christ walked while here on earth—seeking to imitate His life style in all that we do. When we walk in the light, our paths become illuminated and purposeful, and there is a glow of warmth and love in our lives that makes us want to care for the needs of others. This life of love is not merely a soft sentimental feeling—but rather a life of action.

Sometimes we as Christians seem to minimize this basic quality in our lives. We spend our time seeking the unusual and "deep" truths of the Scriptures or arguing with those with whom we may differ. A life devoid of Christ's tender love for others, both fellow-believers and non-believers, can negate much of our Christian witness. The Bible teaches that a life without love, counts for nothing (1 Corinthians 13:1-3).

Walking in the light is in the present tense. It is a new experience with God each day. It is always helpful to recall God's faithfulness and leading in the past. But our past blessings must always be blended into the present wonder of walking this day with the Lord.

The author of "Walk in the Light," Bernard Barton, was known as England's "Quaker Poet." Although he never rose above the position of a bank clerk, his reputation as a man of letters was recognized by many literary leaders of his day. In all, Barton had 10 books of verse published, from which about 20 hymns came into usage.

"Walk in the Light" first appeared in Barton's *Devotional Verses*, published in 1926. Make walking in the light your experience today.

> Walk in the light! So shalt thou know that fellowship of love His Spirit only can bestow, who reigns in light above.

> Walk in the light! And thou shalt find thy heart made truly His, who dwells in cloudless light enshrined, in Whom no darkness is.

> Walk in the light! And thou shalt own thy darkness passed away, because that light hath on thee shone in which is perfect day.

> Walk in the light! And thine shall be a path, though thorny, bright: For God, by grace, shall dwell in thee, and God Himself is light.

❦ **For Today:** Psalm 36:9; John 8:12; Romans 12:10; 2 Corinthians 4:6

Consciously leave time in your schedule to be responsive to the needs of another. Share Christ and His love with them.

Manoah tune

From Henry W. Greatorex's *Collections*, 1851

Walk in the light! So shalt thou know that fel-low-ship of love His Spir-it on-ly can be-stow, Who reigns in light a-bove.

JESUS, THOU JOY OF LOVING HEARTS

Attributed to Bernard of Clairvaux, 1091-1153
Translated by Ray Palmer, 1808-1887

I have told you this so that My joy may be in you and that your joy may be complete. (John 15:11)

This song is another of the fine hymn texts that originated during the Middle Ages. It is thought to have been written by a monk—one of the most prominent religious leaders of his day. An important part of the medieval church was the role of the monks and their monasteries. Since these churchmen were among the few who could read and write, their institutions became powerful influences in shaping the religious and cultural development of Western civilization.

As a young man, Bernard became abbot of the monastery of Clairvaux, France. His influence was soon felt throughout Europe. It is said that he commanded kings, emperors, and prelates—and they obeyed him. In 1146 he was commissioned by the pope to lead a second preaching crusade against the Moslems. Because of his eloquence and strong preaching, great crowds followed him. One of the conditions for those joining the Crusade was a personal conversion experience. It is recorded that multitudes of vicious men were dramatically changed through Bernard's preaching. They carried a cross unashamedly as a symbol of their commitment to Christ and this crusade.

Bernard wrote a number of books, chiefly on such subjects as church government, monasticism and other church-related topics. It is generally agreed that he wrote a long 192-line poem titled "Dulcis Jesus Memorial" ("Joyful Rhythm on the Name of Jesus"). In 1858 Ray Palmer, an American Congregational preacher, translated from the Latin a portion of this medieval poem attributed to Bernard for the hymn "Jesus, Thou Joy of Loving Hearts." This hymn text aptly describes the preciousness of Christ in each believer's life.

> Jesus, Thou joy of loving hearts, Thou fount of life, Thou light of men, from the best bliss that earth imparts, we turn unfilled to Thee again.

> Thy truth unchanged hath ever stood; Thou savest those that on Thee call; to them that seek Thee, Thou art good; to them that find Thee, all in all.

> Our restless spirits yearn for Thee, where'er our changeful lot is cast; glad when Thy gracious smile we see, blest when our faith can hold Thee fast.

> O Jesus, ever with us stay; make all our moments calm and bright; chase the dark night of sin away; shed o'er the world Thy holy light.

❦ ***For Today:*** John 6:35; Ephesians 2:14-18; Colossians 1:13, 14; 1 Peter 1:8

Live with the awareness that even with the "best bliss that earth imparts," without an intimate awareness of Christ, life will be empty. Make His presence the goal of your activities.

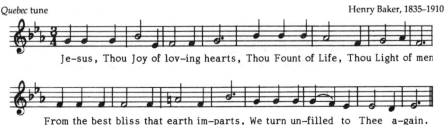

Quebec tune   Henry Baker, 1835–1910

Je-sus, Thou Joy of lov-ing hearts, Thou Fount of Life, Thou Light of men

From the best bliss that earth im-parts, We turn un-filled to Thee a-gain.

O THE DEEP, DEEP LOVE OF JESUS

S. Trevor Francis, 1834-1925

I pray that you, being rooted and established in love, may have power, with all the saints, to grasp how wide and long and high and deep is the love of Christ. (Ephesians 3:17, 18)

Who can fully grasp the dimensions of God's great love for us? Yet the Scriptures teach that we are to have a growing awareness of divine love. Love is the very heart and essence of God, not only for the lovely but for the vilest of sinners. Christ did not die merely to display God's love—He died because God is love (1 John 4:8). If the New Testament teaches us anything, it teaches us about God's love in searching for lost men. Becoming a Christian in a very real sense is simply putting ourselves in the way of being found by God—to stop running from His loving pursuit.

As we mature in the Christian faith, we begin to realize that every situation that comes our way is an opportunity for God's love to be made more evident in our lives. Once we realize this, our attitude changes dramatically toward suffering people as well as toward ourselves when we are called to suffer. Then even during those times when our spiritual fervor declines and our devotion to God subsides, despite these shortcomings, God's love remains unfailing—continually working for our eternal good.

The author of this text, S. Trevor Francis, was a prominent lay leader with the Plymouth Brethren in England and was known as an effective devotional speaker throughout Great Britain and around the world.

> O the deep, deep love of Jesus—vast, unmeasured, boundless free! Rolling as a mighty ocean in its fullness over me, underneath me, all around me, is the current of Thy love—leading onward, leading homeward, to my glorious rest above.

> O the deep, deep love of Jesus—spread His praise from shore to shore! How He loveth, ever loveth, changeth never, nevermore. How He watches o'er His loved ones, died to call them all His own; how for them He intercedeth, watcheth o'er them from the throne.

> O the deep, deep love of Jesus, love of ev'ry love the best! 'Tis an ocean vast of blessing; 'tis a haven sweet of rest. O the deep, deep love of Jesus—'tis a heav'n of heav'ns to me; and it lifts me up to glory, for it lifts me up to Thee.

🐦 *For Today:* Romans 5:8; 8:35-39; Ephesians 3:14-20; 1 John 4:8; Revelation 1:5, 6

Ask God to enlarge your understanding of His great love and the ability to share it with others. Reflect on this musical truth—

Ebenezer tune — Thomas I. Williams, 1869-1944

O the deep, deep love of Je - sus-- Vast, un - meas - ured, bound - less free.

LOVE DIVINE, ALL LOVES EXCELLING

Charles Wesley, 1707-1788

This is how God showed His love among us: He sent His one and only Son into the world that we might live through Him. (1 John 4:9)

We must never underestimate the power of love in our human relationships—whether marriages, family, business associations, or friendships. The divine love of God for man far excels all other forms of love.

"Love Divine . . ." is another of the more than 6500 hymns by Charles Wesley, the "sweet bard of Methodism." This fine text —written in 1747—touches various elements of Christian doctrine. It extols the love of God as expressed in the incarnation of Christ. Then it refers to the Wesleyan concept of entire sanctification—that any believer might live without consciously sinning and thereby find the promised "rest" mentioned in Hebrews 4:9. The "Alpha and Omega" of verse two (first and last letters of the Greek alphabet) also reflect this Wesleyan teaching, that the experiences of conversion and sanctification are thought of as the "beginning of faith" and the "end or object of faith." The third stanza emphasizes the truth that the Spirit of God indwells the temple or body of each believer, while the fourth stanza anticipates the glorious culmination of our faith when "we cast our crowns before Thee, lost in wonder, love and praise."

Although Christians may have differences of interpretation regarding the doctrine of sanctification, we can agree on this basic truth: It ought to be a normal desire for each believer to grow in the grace of our Lord.

Love divine, all loves excelling, joy of heav'n, to earth come down; fix in us Thy humble dwelling; all Thy faithful mercies crown. Jesus, Thou art all compassion; pure, unbounded love Thou art; visit us with Thy salvation; enter ev'ry trembling heart.

Breathe, O breathe Thy loving Spirit into ev'ry troubled breast! Let us all in Thee inherit; let us find that second rest. Take away our bent to sinning, Alpha and Omega be; end of faith, as its beginning, set our hearts at liberty.

Come, almighty to deliver, let us all Thy life receive; suddenly return, and never, nevermore Thy temples leave. Thee we would be always blessing, serve Thee as Thy hosts above, pray and praise Thee without ceasing, glory in Thy perfect love.

Finish then Thy new creation; pure and spotless let us be; let us see Thy great salvation perfectly restored in Thee. Changed from glory into glory, till in heav'n we take our place, till we cast our crowns before Thee, lost in wonder, love and praise.

❦   *For Today:* John 3:14-21; Philippians 1:6; Colossians 1:28; 1 John 3:11-24

God's love must dominate our hearts, minds, and wills. Pray that this will become increasingly true in your life. Carry this portion of the hymn with you—

Beecher tune   John Zundel, 1815-1882

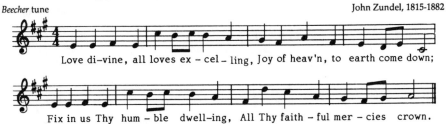

Love di-vine, all loves ex – cel – ling, Joy of heav'n, to earth come down;

Fix in us Thy hum – ble dwell–ing, All Thy faith – ful mer – cies crown.

IMMORTAL LOVE—FOREVER FULL

John Greenleaf Whittier, 1807-1892

To know this love that surpasses knowledge—that you may be filled to the measure of all the fullness of God. (Ephesians 3:19)

> Love is Silence—when your words would hurt.
> Love is Patience—when your neighbor's curt.
> Love is Deafness—when a scandal flows.
> Love is Thoughtfulness—for others' woes.
> Love is Promptness—when stern duty calls.
> Love is Courage—when misfortune falls.
>
> —*Unknown*

The Bible teaches that the three cardinal virtues of the Christian life are *faith, hope, love,* with love as the greatest (1 Corinthians 13:13). These virtues in a person's life are the most convincing evidences of a personal relationship with Christ. True faith must always lead to a life of love for God and others. It also gives purpose for this life and the glorious hope of spending eternity with our King of Love. Our love relationship with others should be characterized as sacrificial, sensitive, and sharing. We should relate to people even as Jesus did. He loved individuals simply for themselves and met and accepted them at the place of their personal need.

In 1867 John Greenleaf Whittier, a Quaker and recognized as one of America's finest poets, wrote a 38 stanza poem titled "Our Master." This hymn text with its emphasis upon the constancy of God's immortal love was taken from that poem. It was Whittier who once stated "a good hymn is the best use to which poetry can be directed." The musical setting by William V. Wallace, a Scottish violinist and composer, was adapted from a longer love song, "Waft, Ye Winds," written by Wallace in 1856.

> Immortal Love—forever full, forever flowing free, forever shared, forever whole, a never ebbing sea!
>
> We may not climb the heav'nly steeps to bring the Lord Christ down; in vain we search the lowest deeps, for Him no depths can drown.
>
> But warm, sweet, tender, even yet a present help is He; and faith has still its Olivet, and love its Galilee.
>
> The healing of His seamless dress is by our beads of pain; we touch Him in life's throng and press, and we are whole again.
>
> Thru Him the first fond prayers are said our lips of childhood frame; the last low whispers of our dead are burdened with His name.
>
> O Lord and Master of us all, whate'er our name or sign, we own Thy sway, we hear Thy call, we test our lives by Thine!

❦ ***For Today:*** Psalm 139; Jeremiah 31:3; Romans 8:38, 39; 1 John 4:19

Reflect on the constancy of our Lord's immortal love as you meditate on this thoughtful hymn text.

Serenity tune

William V. Wallace, 1812-1865

Im- mor - tal Love--for-ev-er full, For - ev - er flow-ing free, For-
O Lord and Mas-ter of us all, What-e'er our name or sign, We

ev - er shared, for - ev - er whole, A nev - er ebb - ing sea!
own Thy sway, we hear Thy call, We test our lives by Thine!

THE LOVE OF GOD

Words and Music by Frederick M. Lehman, 1868-1953

The Lord your God is with you, He is mighty to save. He will take great delight in you, He will quiet you with His love, He will rejoice over you with singing. (Zephaniah 3:17)

Never has God's eternal love been described more vividly than in the words of this greatly loved hymn: "measureless," "strong," "evermore endure . . . "

The unusual third stanza of the hymn was a small part of an ancient lengthy poem composed in 1096 by a Jewish songwriter, Rabbi Mayer, in Worms, Germany. The poem, entitled "Hadamut," was written in the Arabic language. The lines were found one day in revised form on the walls of a patient's room in an insane asylum after the patient's death. The opinion has since been that the unknown patient, during times of sanity, adapted from the Jewish poem what is now the third verse of "The Love of God."

The words of this third stanza were quoted one day at a Nazarene campmeeting. In the meeting was Frederick M. Lehman, a Nazarene pastor, who described his reaction:

> The profound depths of the lines moved us to preserve the words for future generations. Not until we had come to California did this urge find fulfillment, and that at a time when circumstances forced us to hard manual labor. One day, during short intervals of inattention to our work, we picked up a scrap of paper and added the first two stanzas and chorus to the existing third verse lines.

Pastor Lehman completed the hymn in 1917. His daughter Claudia (Mrs. W. W. Mays) assisted him with the music.

> The love of God is greater far than tongue or pen can ever tell,
> It goes beyond the highest star and reaches to the lowest hell,
> The guilty pair, bowed down with care, God gave His Son to win:
> His erring child He reconciled and pardoned from His sin.
>
> When years of time shall pass away and earthly thrones and kingdoms fall,
> When men, who here refuse to pray, on rocks and hills and mountains call,
> God's love so sure shall still endure, all measureless and strong:
> Redeeming grace to Adam's race—the saints' and angels' song.
>
> Could we with ink the ocean fill and were the skies of parchment made,
> Were ev'ry stalk on earth a quill and ev'ry man a scribe by trade
> To write the love of God above would drain the ocean dry,
> Nor could the scroll contain the whole tho stretched from sky to sky.
>
> **Chorus:** O love of God, how rich and pure! How measureless and strong! It shall forevermore endure—the saints' and angels' song.

❦ **For Today:** John 15:9; Ephesians 3:1, 19; 1 John 3:1; Revelation 1:5, 6

Consciously try to personalize and experience the truth of this hymn in every situation that comes your way. Carry this musical message with you realizing that—

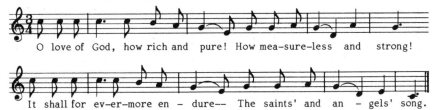

O love of God, how rich and pure! How mea–sure–less and strong!

It shall for ev–er–more en – dure-- The saints' and an – gels' song.

JESUS, LOVER OF MY SOUL

Charles Wesley, 1707-1788

The Lord is good, a refuge in times of trouble. He cares for those who trust in Him. (Nahum 1:7)

The universal recognition of a personal dependence upon the infinite God has no doubt made this appealing hymn the best loved of the more than 6500 texts of Charles Wesley. Written shortly after Charles' "heart-warming" experience at the Adlersgate Hall in London in 1738, this text has since brought comfort and inspiration to countless numbers during "the storms of life."

The simple yet vivid language of this hymn gives it a special quality. Some have called it the "finest heart-hymn in the English language." Also the exaltation of Christ is truly noteworthy in such picturesque terms as "lover," "healer," "fountain," "wing," and "pilot." But possibly the greatest appeal of these lines is the assurance they give of Christ's consolation and protection through all of life and then for eternity.

There is no authenticated information as to what particular situation caused Wesley to write this text. A frightening storm at sea that he experienced while returning home from America may account for the nautical references. A story also has been mentioned of a bird flying into Charles' cabin for safety, while another incident is given of his hiding under a hedge after an attack by an angry mob opposing his ministry. Still others see this text as a picture of Wesley's own life as a young man as he struggled to find his peace with God before his dramatic Aldersgate conversion experience.

How important it is that we learn the truth taught in these words!

Jesus, lover of my soul, let me to Thy bosom fly. While the nearer waters roll, while the tempest still is high! Hide me, O my Savior, hide—till the storm of life is past; safe into the haven guide, O receive my soul at last!

Other refuge have I none—hangs my helpless soul on Thee. Leave, ah, leave me not alone; still support and comfort me! All my trust on Thee is stayed—All my help from Thee I bring. Cover my defenseless head with the shadow of Thy wing.

Thou, O Christ, art all I want, more than all in Thee I find. Raise the fallen, cheer the faint, heal the sick and lead the blind. Just and holy is Thy name—I am all unrighteousness; false and full of sin I am; Thou art full of truth and grace.

Plenteous grace with Thee is found, grace to cover all my sin; let the healing streams abound; make and keep me pure within. Thou of life the fountain art— Freely let me take of Thee; spring Thou up within my heart; rise to all eternity.

❦ *For Today:* Psalm 37:39, 40; 2 Corinthians 1:3-7; Revelation 7:17

Remember to fly to Christ for refuge whenever the "storm of life" becomes overwhelming. He alone is our refuge and the one true foundation of life.

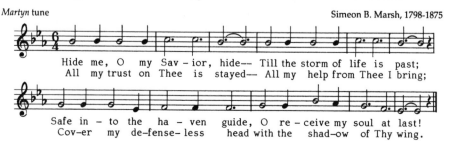

Martyn tune   Simeon B. Marsh, 1798-1875

Hide me, O my Sav-ior, hide— Till the storm of life is past;
All my trust on Thee is stayed— All my help from Thee I bring;

Safe in - to the ha - ven guide, O re-ceive my soul at last!
Cov-er my de-fense-less head with the shad-ow of Thy wing.

O LOVE THAT WILT NOT LET ME GO

George Matheson, 1842-1902

I have loved you with an everlasting love; I have drawn you with lovingkindness. (Jeremiah 31:3)

The writing of this thoughtful and artistically constructed text is most remarkable! It was authored by an esteemed Scottish minister who was totally blind and who described the writing as the "fruit of much mental suffering." Many conjectures have been made regarding the cause of the "mental suffering." Fortunately, Dr. George Matheson did leave this account:

> My hymn was composed in the manse of Innelan on the evening of the 6th of June, 1882, when I was 40 years of age. I was alone in the manse at that time. It was the night of my sister's marriage, and the rest of the family were staying overnight in Glasgow. Something happened to me, which was known only to myself, and which caused me the most severe mental suffering. The hymn was the fruit of that suffering. It was the quickest bit of work I ever did in my life. I had the impression of having it dictated to me by some inward voice rather than of working it out myself. I am quite sure that the whole work was completed in five minutes, and equally sure that it never received at my hands any retouching or correction. I have no natural gift of rhythm. All the other verses I have ever written are manufactured articles; this came like a dayspring from on high.

A very popular account for the writing of this hymn, though never fully substantiated, claims that it was the result of the reminder at his sister's wedding of the great disappointment that Matheson had experienced just before he was to have been married to his college financee. When told of his impending total blindness, she is said to have informed him, "I do not wish to be the wife of a blind preacher."

It is very possible that the lingering memory of this rejection from an earthly lover prompted George Matheson to write this beautiful expression of an eternal love that will never be broken:

> O Love that wilt not let me go, I rest my weary soul on Thee; I give Thee back the life I owe, that in Thine ocean depths its flow may richer, fuller be.

> O Light that follow'st all my way, I yield my flick'ring torch to Thee; my heart restores its borrowed ray, that in Thy sunshine's blaze its day may brighter, fairer be.

> O Joy that seekest me thru pain, I cannot close my heart to Thee; I trace the rainbow thru the rain, and feel the promise is not vain that morn shall tearless be.

> O Cross that liftest up my head, I dare not ask to fly from Thee; I lay in dust life's glory dead, and from the ground there blossoms red life that shall endless be.

❦ **For Today:** Romans 8:35-39; 1 John 3:1; Revelation 1:5, 6

Rest securely in God's eternal love, regardless of the human difficulty or suffering you may be experiencing. Allow this musical message to help you—

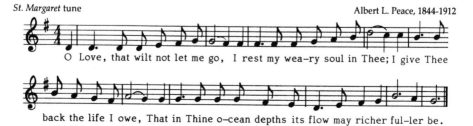

St. Margaret tune

Albert L. Peace, 1844-1912

O Love, that wilt not let me go, I rest my wea-ry soul in Thee; I give Thee

back the life I owe, That in Thine o–cean depths its flow may richer ful–ler be.

I AM HIS AND HE IS MINE

George Wade Robinson, 1838-1877

Your life is now hidden with Christ in God. (Colossians 3:3)

Spiritual maturity is a growing appreciation of God simply for who He is. Only then can we begin to revel in our eternal union with Him. This realization gives all of life a different perspective. Life takes on a new dignity, worth, and meaning. Even nature is viewed differently—"earth around is sweeter green . . . " Learning to abide in Christ means that we live with a calmer, more relaxed attitude because we rely on God rather than ourselves—"things that once were wild alarms cannot now disturb my rest." John Wesley often spoke of this kind of life as "living with a loose rein." Our union with Christ also makes us victors when we realize that "while God and I shall be," nothing in life can ever separate us from this eternal love relationship (Romans 8:35).

The author of this text, George Wade Robinson, was a pastor of Congregational churches in England. The composer, James Mountain, was an Anglican minister who became greatly influenced by the Moody-Sankey campaigns in England in the early 1870's. Mountain later devoted his life to the work of evangelism both in Great Britain and world-wide. "I Am His and He Is Mine" first appeared in James Mountain's collection, *Hymns of Consecration and Faith*, published in 1876. The truths this hymn presents so well become more meaningful each time we sing it.

Loved with everlasting love, led by grace that love to know—Spirit, breathing from above, Thou hast taught me it is so! O this full and perfect peace, O this transport all divine— In a love which cannot cease, I am His and He is mine.

Heav'n above is softer blue; earth around is sweeter green; something lives in ev'ry hue Christless eyes have never seen! Birds with gladder songs o'erflow, flow'rs with deeper beauties shine, since I know, as now I know, I am His and He is mine.

Things that once were wild alarms cannot now disturb my rest; closed in everlasting arms, pillowed on the loving breast! O to lie forever here, doubt and care and self resign, while He whispers in my ear—I am His and He is mine.

His forever, only His—Who the Lord and me shall part? Ah, with what a rest of bliss Christ can fill the loving heart! Heav'n and earth may fade and flee, first-born light in gloom decline, but while God and I shall be, I am His and He is mine.

❦ *For Today:* Song of Solomon 6:3; John 14:1-8; 15:9-11; Galatians 2:20

Take time to truly meditate upon God and all that He is. Then revel and rejoice in the glorious truth that you are inseparably united with Him.

Everlasting Love tune   James Mountain, 1844-1933

O this full and per-fect peace, O this trans-port all di-vine—
Heav'n and earth may fade and flee, First-born light in gloom de-cline,

In a love which can-not cease, I am His and He is mine.
But while God and I shall be, I am His and He is mine.

AND CAN IT BE THAT I SHOULD GAIN?

Charles Wesley, 1707-1788

To Him who loves us and has freed us from our sins by His blood. . . . (Revelation 1:5)

Can any believer contemplate the "amazing love" of Calvary without sharing the awe and wonder of Charles Wesley's questions in today's hymn? Written a short time after his "heart-warming" Aldersgate experience on May 20, 1738, this song of grateful adoration for God's great plan of redemption has been one of the most deeply moving and treasured hymns for more than 200 years.

Even though he had a strict religious training in his youth, education at Oxford University, and missionary service in the new colony of Georgia, Charles Wesley had no peace or joy in his heart and life. Returning to London after a discouraging time in America, he met with a group of Moravians in the Aldersgate Hall and came to realize that "salvation is by faith alone." In his journal of May 20th he wrote:

> At midnight I gave myself to Christ, assured that I was safe, whether sleeping or waking. I had the continual experience of His power to overcome all temptation, and I confessed with joy and surprise that He was able to do exceeding abundantly for me above what I can ask or think.

In this spirit of joyous enthusiasm, Charles began to write new hymns with increased fervor. He travelled throughout Great Britain with his older brother John a quarter of a million miles, mostly on horseback, leading great crowds in singing his hymns in mass outdoor services of 40,000 people.

With every new spiritual experience or thought that crossed Charles' mind, a new hymn was born. Even on his deathbed it is said that he dictated to his wife a final hymn of praises to the Lord he had loved so intimately and served so effectively.

> And can it be that I should gain an int'rest in the Savior's blood? Died He for me, who caused His pain? For me, who Him to death pursued?

> He left His Father's throne above, so free, so infinite His grace! Emptied Himself of all but love, and bled for Adam's helpless race.

> No condemnation now I dread; I am my Lord's and He is mine: Alive in Him, my living Head, and clothed in righteousness divine.

> **Refrain:** Amazing love! how can it be that Thou, my God, shouldst die for me?

❧ *For Today:* Romans 5:8; Colossians 1:12-14; Hebrews 9:11, 12; 1 Peter 1:18, 19; Revelation 5:9

Live in the joy and freedom of being "alive in Him" and free of all condemnation. Carry this musical truth with you—

Sagina tune   Thomas Campbell, 1777-1844

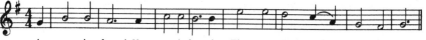

A – maz – ing love! How can it be that Thou, my God, shouldst die for me?

THE WONDER OF IT ALL

Words and Music by George Beverly Shea, 1909-

What is man that You are mindful of him, the Son of Man that You care for Him?
(Hebrews 2:6)

What many Christians need today is a rebirth of wonder and awe. We know the gospel intellectually, but it seldom reaches our emotions and will. We take the incarnation, resurrection, ascension, the indwelling Holy Spirit, and the eternal reign of Christ merely as theological concepts without letting them grip our inmost being. And the wonder that this great God knows, loves and cares for us doesn't often thrill us as it should. We even become very blase when we witness a life that has been dramatically transformed by the love of God. Our spiritual condition can be likened to those Christians at the church in Laodicea mentioned in Revelation 3:14-22: "neither cold nor hot"—just lukewarm. We need to recapture the wonder of it all.

George Beverly Shea, one of the all-time favorite gospel singers, gives this account of the writing of this hymn in his book *Songs That Lift the Heart:*

> England figures in the story behind this hymn written in 1955. I was on my way to Scotland for meetings there aboard the *S.S. United States* bound for Southampton when inspiration came from conversation with another passenger. He wanted to know what went on at our meetings and after detailing the sequence of things at a typical Billy Graham Crusade meeting, I found myself at a loss for words when I tried to describe the response that usually accompanied Mr. Graham's invitation to become a Christian. "What happens then never becomes commonplace . . . watching people by the hundreds come forward . . . oh, if you could just see the wonder of it all."
>
> "I think I should," he answered. Then he wrote these words on a card and handed it back to me: THE WONDER OF IT ALL.
>
> "That sounds like a song to me." Later that night, I wrote words on that theme and roughed out a melody to go with them.

* * * *

> There's the wonder of sunset at evening, the wonder as sunrise I see; but the wonder of wonders that thrills my soul is the wonder that God loves me.
>
> There's the wonder of springtime and harvest, the sky, the stars, the sun; but the wonder of wonders that thrills my soul is a wonder that's only begun.
>
> **Refrain:** O, the wonder of it all! The wonder of it all! Just to think that God loves me. O, the wonder of it all! The wonder of it all! Just to think that God loves me.

❦ *For Today:* Psalm 8; 2 Corinthians 5:19; Ephesians 2:10; 3:19.

Take time to reflect with awe on the wonder of your personal relationship with the God of the universe. Determine to live throughout the day with this attitude as you think of "the wonder of it all."

O, the won-der of it all! The won-der of it all! Just to think that God loves me.

WHAT WONDROUS LOVE IS THIS

Anyone who is hung on a tree is under God's curse. (Deuteronomy 21:23)

Greater love has no one than this, that he lay down his life for his friends. (John 15:13)

> Not father or mother has loved you as God has, for it was that you might be happy He gave His only Son. When He bowed His head in the death hour, love solemnized its triumph; the sacrifice there was complete. —*Henry Wadsworth Longfellow*

This beloved hymn, with its plaintive modal sound, is one of the best known of our authentic American folk hymns. Like all true folk music, the origins of this text and music remain unknown. It is simply the product of devout people who, when reflecting seriously on the sacrificial gift of God's Son, respond spontaneously with amazed adoration for this "wondrous love."

One typical folk hymn characteristic found in these words is the repetition of key phrases such as "O my soul" and "I'll sing on." Since folk music is generally learned aurally without the assistance of the printed page or musical notation, such repetition is necessary. Note also how effectively the curving melodic lines enhance the thought and personal application of the words.

The hymn first appeared in 1835 in a collection titled *William Walker's Southern Harmony.* These simply stated words with their appealing music have since ministered to people everywhere, extolling the profound truth of Christ's love for each of us. Allow the hymn to move you to awe even now.

> What wondrous love is this, O my soul, O my soul! What wondrous love is this, O my soul! What wondrous love is this that caused the Lord of bliss to bear the dreadful curse for my soul, for my soul, to bear the dreadful curse for my soul.
>
> When I was sinking down, sinking down, when I was sinking down, sinking down; when I was sinking down beneath God's righteous frown, Christ laid aside His crown for my soul; Christ laid aside His crown for my soul.
>
> To God and to the Lamb I will sing, I will sing; to God and to the Lamb I will sing; to God and to the Lamb who is the great "I Am," while millions join the theme, I will sing, I will sing; while millions join the theme, I will sing.
>
> And when from death I'm free, I'll sing on, I'll sing on, and when from death I'm free, I'll sing on; and when from death I'm free, I'll sing and joyful be, and through eternity I'll sing on, I'll sing on, and through eternity I'll sing on.

❧ *For Today:* Numbers 21:8; Jeremiah 31:3; John 3:14-18; 1 John 3:1; Revelation 1:5, 6

Reflect once again on the wondrous love of Christ in your behalf. Determine to share your Lord and His wondrous love with another.

Wondrous Love tune   *William Walker's Southern Harmony, 1835*

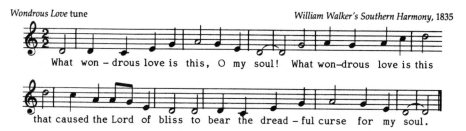

What won-drous love is this, O my soul! What won-drous love is this that caused the Lord of bliss to bear the dread-ful curse for my soul.

MY SAVIOR'S LOVE

Words and Music by Charles H. Gabriel, 1856-1932

Live a life of love, just as Christ loved us and gave Himself for us as a fragrant offering and sacrifice to God. (Ephesians 5:2)

> Love saw a guilt of sin, and sought a basis of pardon.
> Love saw the defilement of sin, and sought a way of cleansing.
> Love saw the depravity of sin, and sought a means of restoration.
> Love saw the condemnation of sin, and sought a method of justification.
> Love saw the death of sin, and sought a way of life.
> Love sought—Love found!   —*Unknown*

Historians have noted that the ancient Greeks expressed three levels of love: *Eros* Love—a "give me" kind of love; *Philia* Love—a "give and take" kind of love. "You love me and I'll love you;" and *Agape* Love—an "unconditional" kind of love. "I love you simply for who you are."

Our Savior's love was *agape* love in its highest form. He loved us enough to leave heaven's best, to suffer humiliation and death for a world of rebellious sinners. Only when we are gathered in glory with the ransomed of the ages and see His face will we fully know the meaning of this divine love. In the meantime, however, the scriptural command is that we are to live a life of love that ministers to the needs of others as a "fragrant offering and sacrifice to God."

"My Savior's Love" was written by Charles H. Gabriel, the most popular and prolific gospel song writer of the 1910-20 decade, which was the height of the Billy Sunday/Homer Rodeheaver evangelistic crusades. This song first appeared in the hymnal titled *Praises*, published in 1905.

> I stand amazed in the presence of Jesus the Nazarene, and wonder how He could love me, a sinner condemned, unclean.

> For me it was in the garden He prayed, "Not My will, but Thine;" He had no tears for His own griefs but sweat drops of blood for mine.

> In pity angels beheld Him, and came from the world of light to comfort Him in the sorrows He bore for my soul that night.

> He took my sins and my sorrows; He made them His very own; He bore the burden to Calv'ry and suffered and died alone.

> When with the ransomed in glory His face I at last shall see, 'twill be my joy thru the ages to sing of His love for me.

> **Chorus:** How marvelous! how wonderful! and my song shall ever be: How marvelous! how wonderful is my Savior's love for me!

❦ *For Today:* John 3:16; 15:12, 13; Ephesians 2:4-7; 1 John 3:16; 4:9, 10

Try to approach each event of the day with this question: "How would Jesus have shown His love in this situation?"

William B. Bradbury, 1816–1868

How mar-vel-ous! How won-der-ful! Is my Sav-ior's love for me!

I LOVE THEE

An American Folk Hymn taken from *Ingall's Christian Harmony*, 1805

O love the Lord, all ye saints. (Psalm 31:23)

> Blest be Thy love, dear Lord, that taught us this sweet way,
> Only to love Thee for Thyself, and for that love obey.
> —J. Austin

Secular songs of romantic expressions abound on this day. For the Christian, a hymn about love is also appropriate for Valentine's Day, and no sweeter expression of one's love for Christ can be found than these anonymous lines from an early American folk hymn.

For the early Christians, February 14 was a special day. Tradition tells us that a man by the name of Valentine was a Christian doctor who went about doing good deeds wherever he could, in imitation of his Master. Valentine became a good friend and helper to the Christians, who were being persecuted by the cruel powers of the Roman Empire. It is believed that the good doctor was eventually imprisoned because of his loyalty to his fellow "followers of the Way." After he was beheaded on February 14, that day was observed each year in Valentine's honor by the early Christians.

As time went on, however, Valentine and his deeds of kindness were forgotten. Because February was near the beginning of spring, with its feelings of romance, the day became a secular holiday celebrating romantic love. Tokens of love and affection were given to sweethearts and friends, starting the custom that we still practice today.

Dr. Valentine gave his life for his fellow Christians because of his deep love for Christ. We too can express our love for the Savior with these simply stated yet profound words . . . "but how much I love Thee my actions will show."

> I love Thee, my Savior, I love Thee, my Lord; I love Thee, my Savior, I love Thee, my God: I love Thee, I love Thee, and that Thou dost know; but how much I love Thee my actions will show.

> O Jesus my Savior, with Thee I am blest, my life and salvation, my joy and my rest: Thy name be my theme and Thy love be my song; Thy grace shall inspire both my heart and my tongue.

> Oh who's like my Savior? He's heaven's bright king; He smiles and He loves me and helps me to sing: I'll praise Him, I'll praise Him with notes loud and clear; while rivers of pleasure my spirit shall cheer.

❦ ***For Today:*** Deuteronomy 6:5; 30:20; Luke 10:27; 1 John 4:19

On this special day dedicated to expressions of love, we can make it truly a "holy day" with our love for Christ and by sharing His love and concern for others. Sing this musical testimony—

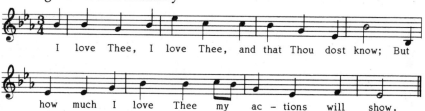

MY JESUS, I LOVE THEE

William R. Featherston, 1846-1873

We love Him because He first loved us. (1 John 4:19)

And shall I use these ransomed powers of mine
For things that only minister to me?
Lord, take my tongue, my hands, my heart, my all,
And let me live and love for Thee!   —*Unknown*

The spiritual depth of "My Jesus, I Love Thee" is made all the more remarkable by the knowledge that it was written by a teenager. William Ralph Featherston of Montreal, Canada, is thought to have written these lines of heartfelt gratitude to Christ at the time of his conversion experience when only 16. It is believed he then sent a copy of his poem to an aunt in Los Angeles, and somehow the text appeared anonymously in print in an English hymnal, *The London Book,* in 1864.

Several years later, a well-known American Baptist pastor, Dr. A. J. Gordon, discovered the anonymous hymn in the English hymnbook and decided to compose a better melody for it. With its new tune the hymn has since been included in nearly every evangelical hymnal and has been sung frequently by believers everywhere during hushed moments of rededication to God.

How marvelous are the workings of God in bringing together expressions such as these, providing a hymn that has been used in a remarkable way for more than a century to direct Christians to a deeper relationship with their Lord. May these words cause each of us even now to renew our devotion to God so that this love for Christ may be reflected in all of the activities of this day.

My Jesus, I love Thee, I know Thou art mine—For Thee all the follies of sin I resign; my gracious Redeemer, my Savior art Thou: If ever I loved Thee, my Jesus, 'tis now.

I love Thee because Thou hast first loved me and purchased my pardon on Calvary's tree; I love Thee for wearing the thorns on Thy brow: If ever I loved Thee, my Jesus, 'tis now.

I'll love Thee in life, I will love Thee in death, and praise Thee as long as Thou lendest me breath; and say when the death-dew lies cold on my brow, "If ever I loved Thee, my Jesus, 'tis now."

In mansions of glory and endless delight, I'll ever adore Thee in heaven so bright; I'll sing with the glittering crown on my brow, "If ever I loved Thee, my Jesus, 'tis now."

❦ ***For Today:*** John 14:23; Ephesians 2:4, 5; 1 Peter 1:8; 2:9; 1 John 4:7-21

Express your own love for the Savior in fresh and fervent words; reflect on what He has done for you, what He is presently doing, and the future glory that still awaits. Determine to demonstrate your loving devotion for Christ with an encouraging word or deed for some needy individual.

Gordon tune   Adoniram J. Gordon, 1836-1895

My gra - cious Re - deem - er, my Sav - ior art Thou:

If ev - er I loved Thee, my Je - sus, 'tis now.

MORE LOVE TO THEE

Elizabeth Prentiss, 1818-1878

And this is my prayer: That your love may abound more and more in knowledge and depth of insight, so that you may be able to discern what is best and may be pure and blameless until the day of Christ, filled with the fruit of righteousness that comes through Jesus Christ—to the glory and praise of God. (Philippians 1:9–11)

To love Christ more is the deepest need, the constant cry of my soul . . . out in the woods, and on my bed, and out driving, when I am happy and busy, and when I am sad and idle, the whisper keeps going up for more love, more love, more love!

These were the words of Elizabeth Prentiss, wife of a Presbyterian minister and author of this hymn text. She was often described by her many friends as "a very bright-eyed little woman with a keen sense of humor, who cared more to shine in her own happy household than in a wide circle of society." Although Elizabeth was strong in spirit, she was frail in body. Throughout her life she was almost an invalid, scarcely knowing a moment free of pain.

"More Love to Thee" was written by Mrs. Prentiss during a time of great personal sorrow, following the loss of two children in a short period of time. For weeks Elizabeth was inconsolable. In her diary she wrote, "empty hands, a worn-out, exhausted body, and unutterable longings to flee from a world that has so many sharp experiences."

During this period of grief, Mrs. Prentiss began meditating upon the story of Jacob in the Old Testament. She noted how God met him in a very special way during his moments of sorrow and need. Elizabeth prayed earnestly that she too might have a similar experience. While she was meditating and praying one evening, these four stanzas were born—words that have since become a universal prayer for devout believers everywhere:

More love to Thee, O Christ, more love to Thee! Hear Thou the prayer I make on bended knee; this is my earnest plea: More love, O Christ, to Thee. . . .

Once earthly joy I craved, sought peace and rest; now Thee alone I seek—give what is best; this all my prayer shall be: More love, O Christ, to Thee. . . .

Let sorrow do its work, send grief and pain; sweet are Thy messengers, sweet their refrain, when they can sing with me, more love, O Christ, to Thee. . . .

Then shall my latest breath whisper Thy praise; this be the parting cry my heart shall raise; this still its prayer shall be: More love, O Christ, to Thee.

❦ **For Today:** 2 Thessalonians 3:5; James 1:12; 1 Peter 1:8; 1 John 4:19; Jude 21

Try to look beyond your problems. Resolve that regardless of life's circumstances, your love for Christ will continue to grow and be strong. Carry this musical prayer with you—

William H. Doane, 1832-1915

This is my ear-nest plea: More love, O Christ, to Thee,
More love to Thee, More love to Thee!

JESUS LOVES EVEN ME

Words and Music by Philip P. Bliss, 1838-1876

As the Father has loved Me, so have I loved you. Now remain in my love. (John 15:9)

The wonder of Jesus' deep love for each of us has been expressed in this text in beautiful but childlike language by the noted musician of early gospel music, Philip P. Bliss. After attending a service where the hymn "O How I Love Jesus" was sung repeatedly, Bliss thought, "Have I not been singing enough about my poor love for Jesus and shall I not rather sing of His great love for me?" Soon he completed both the words and music of one of the all-time favorite children's hymn, which is widely sung and enjoyed by adults as well.

Philip Bliss was the dynamic and very talented song writer and associate of evangelists D. L. Moody and Major Daniel W. Whittle. Bliss' commanding height and impressive personality made his singing and song leading outstanding features in any evangelistic service. His gift for writing gospel hymns was also exceptional. Still widely used today are such other Bliss favorites as: "Wonderful Words of Life," "It Is Well With My Soul," "Hold the Fort," "Hallelujah, What a Savior," and "Almost Persuaded." One of his music colleagues, George C. Stebbins, stated:

> There has been no writer of verse since his time who has shown such a grasp of the fundamental truths of the gospel, or such a gift for putting them into a poetic and singable form.

The third stanza of this simple but very appealing hymn is especially meaningful when we realize that Philip Bliss died suddenly at the age of 38 in a tragic train accident. His many stirring hymns, however, have lived on. They all focus clearly on important biblical truths, but none is more moving than the reminder in this text that Jesus loves even me.

> I am go glad that our Father in heav'n tells of His love in the Book He has giv'n; wonderful things in the Bible I see—this is the dearest that Jesus loves me.

> Tho I forget Him and wander away, still He doth love me wherever I stray; back to His dear loving arms would I flee when I remember that Jesus loves me.

> O if there's only one song I can sing when in His beauty I see the great King, this shall my song in eternity be: "O what a wonder that Jesus loves me!"

> **Chorus:** I am so glad that Jesus loves me, Jesus loves me, Jesus loves me; I am so glad that Jesus loves me, Jesus loves even me.

❧ *For Today:* Romans 5:8; 2 Corinthians 5:21; 1 John 4:9-12

Take time to thank your Lord once more for His great love for you personally, a love that cannot be comprehended but can only be gratefully accepted by faith. Sing as you go—

I am so glad that Je - sus loves me, Je - sus loves me, Je - sus loves me;

I am so glad that Je - sus loves me, Je - sus loves e - ven me.

HE LIFTED ME

Words and Music by Charles H. Gabriel, 1856-1932

He lifted me out of the slimy pit, out of the mud and mire; He set my feet on a rock and gave me a firm place to stand. He put a new song in my mouth, a hymn of praise to our God. (Psalm 40:2, 3)

O the love that sought me! O the blood that bought me!
O the grace that brought me to the fold!
Wondrous grace that brought me to the fold!   —*W. Spencer Walton*

Occasionally it is good for each of us as Christians to reflect seriously on a question such as this: "Where would I be today if God had not transformed my life, established my ways, and given me a life of joy and praise?" With all of the allurements of sin so rampant in today's society, we must readily confess that except for the love and grace of God, we too could find ourselves with broken and shameful lives. But we have been accepted into the beloved and made children of the heavenly kingdom. Through the redemptive work of Christ, we have been given a new and higher "plane" on which to live. With the author and composer Charles Gabriel we can only exclaim, "O praise His name, He lifted me!" Such divine love on our behalf calls forth a response of thankful gratitude and a sincere desire to see other needy individuals share this redemptive experience.

Charles H. Gabriel was one of the best known and most prolific gospel songwriters of the late 19th and early 20th century eras. His fame as a successful composer became widely known, especially with the use of his songs by Homer Rodeheaver in the large Billy Sunday evangelistic campaigns. "He Lifted Me" first appeared in the collection *Revival Hymns,* published in 1905.

In loving kindness Jesus came my soul in mercy to reclaim, and from the depths of sin and shame thru grace He lifted me.

He called me long before I heard, before my sinful heart was stirred, but when I took him at His word, forgiv'n He lifted me.

His brow was pierced with many a thorn; His hands by cruel nails were torn when from my guilt and grief, forlorn, in love He lifted me.

Now on a higher plain I dwell, and with my soul I know 'tis well; yet how or why, I cannot tell, He should have lifted me.

Chorus: From sinking sand He lifted me; with tender hand He lifted me; from shades of night to plains of light, O praise His name, He lifted me!

❦ **For Today:** Psalm 40; Isaiah 61:10; Philippians 3:8; Revelation 1:5

Express gratitude and praise to God for His transforming power and love in your life. Determine to share your testimony with another. Use this musical testimony as a reminder—

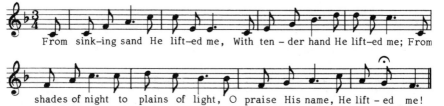

From sink-ing sand He lift-ed me, With ten-der hand He lift-ed me; From shades of night to plains of light, O praise His name, He lift-ed me!

WHY SHOULD HE LOVE ME SO?

Words and Music by Robert Harkness, 1880-1961

For God so loved the world that He gave His one and only Son, that whoever believes in Him shall not perish but have eternal life. (John 3:16)

In the deepest sense, love is a prerequisite of the whole Christian faith. It begins with God since His basic attribute is love (1 John 4:8). The Father then supplied a model of sacrificial love by providing salvation for man through the atoning work of Christ. Also He gave us the indwelling Holy Spirit so we could respond to Him and seek to imitate His love in service to others. How our society languishes for a living demonstration of God's love by Christians in every relationship of life!

Reflecting seriously on God's redemptive love in sending His only Son to suffer and die for each of us personally should create within us a deep sense of unworthiness and devotion. Why should the Creator of the universe do all this for me? I was rebellious, a sinner, an enemy of God . . . yet He pursued and loved me. The amazing thrill of the gospel is that we do not have to become good first in order to be loved by God. We are already loved just as we are. It is impossible to define and describe divine love and the transformation it produces in the life that receives it by faith. But this love can be experienced by anyone who desires it.

Author and composer Robert Harkness was an Australian gospel musician who traveled extensively in round-the-world tours as a pianist with some of the leading evangelists of his day. Harkness wrote several hundred gospel songs, which were first featured in these campaigns. He also prepared a correspondence course, "Evangelistic Piano Playing," that has been widely used through the years.

> Love sent my Savior to die in my stead; why should He love me so? Meekly to Calvary's cross He was led; why should He love me so?

> Nails pierced His hands and His feet for my sin; why should He love me so? He suffered sore my salvation to win; why should He love me so?

> O how He agonized there in my place; why should He love me so? Nothing withholding my sin to efface; why should He love me so?

> **Chorus:** Why should He love me so? Why should He love me so? Why should my Savior to Calvary go? Why should He love me so?

❦ ***For Today:*** Romans 5:8; 8:35-39; Galatians 5:6; 1 Peter 1:22; 1 John 3:1

Reflect seriously on all that Christ did to provide us with personal salvation and a restored fellowship with Almighty God. In the light of this, consider your own unworthiness. With a grateful response, carry this musical question with you as you go thinking of "why should He love me so?"

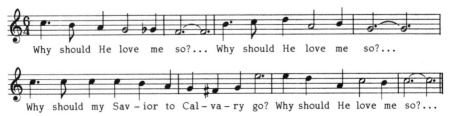

Why should He love me so?... Why should He love me so?...

Why should my Sav – ior to Cal – va – ry go? Why should He love me so?...

HOW CAN I HELP BUT LOVE HIM?

Words and Music by Elton M. Roth, 1891-1951

For Christ's love compels us, because we are convinced that one died for all, and therefore all died. And He died for all, that those who live should no longer live for themselves but for Him who died for them and was raised again. (2 Corinthians 5:14, 15)

> When I stand before the throne, dressed in beauty not my own;
> When I see Thee as Thou art, love Thee with unceasing heart;
> Then, Lord, shall I fully know—not till then—how much I owe.   *—Unknown*

We all need a strong compelling force to move us through life. Without this force we become stagnant. We can be driven by many different motives—wealth, power, prestige. The apostle Paul's compulsion was an intense awareness of Christ's atoning love for man and the responsibility he felt to share this truth with others. The apostle was so gripped by Christ that he counted his own life as nothing in the light of that love (Acts 20:24). Paul abandoned all ambitions as he sought to be a worthy follower and proclaimer of divine love.

Who can do anything other than love Christ after personally experiencing His divine love? Our love relationship with Christ will be demonstrated by our obedience to Him and the doing of His will for our lives (John 15:10). This obedience is not motivated by a desire for reward or a fear of punishment. It is simply a response of love for all that our Lord has done for us and for what He means in our daily lives.

The author and composer of this gospel hymn, Elton M. Roth, was a traveling music evangelist for a period of time. Later he taught music in various Bible schools, including Biola College in Los Angeles. Mr. Roth published many anthems and over 100 hymns, including the popular "In My Heart There Rings a Melody."

> Down from His splendor in glory He came into a world of woe, took on Himself all my guilt and my shame—why should He love me so?
>
> I am unworthy to take of His grace, wonderful grace so free; yet Jesus suffered and died in my place, e'en for a soul like me.
>
> He is the fairest of thousands to me; His love is sweet and true; wonderful beauty in Him I now see, more than I ever knew.
>
> **Refrain:** How can I help but love Him when He loved me so? How can I help but love Him when He loved me so?

❧ **For Today:**   Jeremiah 31:2, 3; 2 Corinthians 5:14; 1 Peter 1:8; 1 John 4:19; Jude 21

Pray that God will let your life overflow with His love and joy. Begin with your family and go on from there.

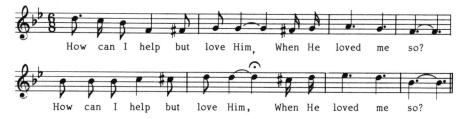

WHEN LOVE SHINES IN

Carrie E. Breck, 1855-1934

Let your light shine before men, that they may see your good deeds and praise your Father in heaven. (Matthew 5:16)

Our emotional soundness and even our physical health depend on the quality of our love for God. And as a result, we gain an attitude of love and concern for our fellowmen. Negative feelings of hate, anger, and selfishness can destroy the well-being of any individual. How important it is to allow God's love to shine into our lives, not only for the good it brings to others but also for the health it brings to our own lives.

True Christian love always seeks to lighten the burden of others and to bring happiness into their lives. We love others not only for what they are but also for what they can become once they too experience the warmth of divine love. Our lives can never remain the same once we learn to share God's love in word and deed each day. The closer we get to Christ, the closer we get to one another.

But believers are not known simply because they do good deeds. They do good works because they have experienced the supernatural love of Christ. The praise for this transformed life is then directed to the heavenly Father—never to themselves.

Carrie Breck, the author of "When Love Shines In," was known as a deeply devoted Christian and life-long Presbyterian. She wrote more than 2,000 poems while a mother of five children.

> Jesus comes with pow'r to gladden, when love shines in; ev'ry life that woe can sadden, when love shines in. Love will teach us how to pray; love will drive the gloom away, turn our darkness into day—when love shines in.

> How the world will grow with beauty, when love shines in, and the heart rejoice in duty, when love shines in. Trials may be sanctified, and the soul in peace abide; life will all be glorified—when love shines in.

> Darkest sorrow will grow brighter, when love shines in, and the heaviest burden lighter, when love shines in. 'Tis the glory that will throw light to show us where to go; O the heart shall blessing know—when love shines in.

> We may have unfading splendor, when love shines in, and a friendship true and tender, when love shines in. When earth's vict'ries shall be won, and our life in heav'n begun, there will be no need of sun—when love shines in.

> **Chorus:** When love shines in, how the heart is tuned to singing, when love shines in; in joy and peace to others bringing—when love shines in!

❧ *For Today:* Song of Solomon 8:7; Proverbs 4:18; Colossians 1:12

Seek by the Holy Spirit's enablement to radiate Christ's love in word and deed. Carry this musical truth with you—

William J. Kirkpatrick, 1838-1921

THEY'LL KNOW WE ARE CHRISTIANS BY OUR LOVE

Words and Music by Peter Scholtes, 1938-

A new commandment I give you: Love one another. As I have loved you, so you must love one another. All men will know that you are My disciples if you love one another. (John 13:34, 35)

It's easy to talk sentimentally about love. It's much more difficult to apply it to needy people and situations. The Scriptures clearly teach, however, that the proof of God's presence within our lives is our willingness to share His love with humanity. The earthly badge of our heavenly citizenship is our love relationship with others.

A life of love is a deliberate choice on our part. We must choose this lifestyle against our natural bent for self-centeredness. Soon, with the Holy Spirit's enablement, our new life of love becomes a natural behavior. Then the emotional feelings of inner fulfillment follow. Responding to the needs of others will never be a duty; rather it should be a privilege of normal Christian living. Our love in action will bring joy to a brother or sister in Christ and even show nonbelievers that we are Christians not only in name but in deed as well.

> We are one in the Spirit, we are one in the Lord, we are one in the Spirit, we are one in the Lord, and we pray that all unity may one day be restored: And they'll know we are Christians by our love, by our love; Yes, they'll know we are Christians by our love.

> We will walk with each other, we will walk hand in hand, we will walk with each other, we will walk hand in hand, and together we'll spread the news that God is in our land: And they'll know we are Christians by our love, by our love; Yes, they'll know we are Christians by our love.

> We will work with each other, we will work side by side, we will work with each other, we will work side by side, and we'll guard each man's dignity and save each man's pride: And they'll know we are Christians by our love, by our love; Yes, they'll know we are Christians by our love.

> All praise to the Father, from whom all things come, and all praise to Christ Jesus, His only Son, and all praise to the Spirit, who makes us one: And they'll know we are Christians by our love; Yes, they'll know we are Christians by our love.

❦ *For Today:* Matthew 22:39; John 17:22; 1 Corinthians 16:14; 1 Peter 1:22; 1 John 3:23

Look around in your local church. Is there someone needing a helping hand? Does a new mother need a meal taken in or the washing done? Can you help an elderly person with some home repairs? Consider this—

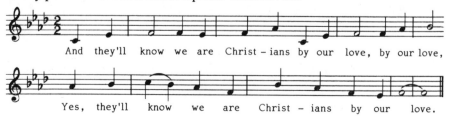

And they'll know we are Christ-ians by our love, by our love,

Yes, they'll know we are Christ - ians by our love.

LET US BREAK BREAD TOGETHER

Traditional Spiritual

They devoted themselves to the apostles' teaching and to the fellowship, to the breaking of bread and to prayer . . . All the believers were together and had everything in common. (Acts 2:42, 44)

The local church has been described as a laboratory where believers learn to love one another regardless of color, nationality, or financial status. Our common heavenly citizenship is the one dominant tie that binds our hearts together. One of the basic results of our weekly corporate worship should be the growing bond of love and unity that develops between believers. This bond of fellowship should result in God's family members learning to care, honor, and serve one another in love. We should treat others with the same tenderness and understanding that we have experienced from God Himself. This determination to live in a love relationship with fellow believers is infinitely more important than the issues or differences that may separate us.

Christian unity does not mean that we must eliminate all diversities. We should be able to differ with each other while maintaining love, respect, and a warm, unified spirit. When our differences get out of hand and hard feelings develop, however, the communion service should always be a reminder that we must reconcile our differences and once more restore a spirit of unity within the body of Christ. The bread and cup of the Lord's Supper should remind us of this truth each time we participate together (1 Corinthians 11:17-34).

> Let us break bread together on our knees; let us break bread together on our knees; when I fall on my knees, with my face to the rising sun, O Lord, have mercy on me.

> Let us drink the cup together on our knees; let us drink the cup together on our knees; when I fall on my knees, with my face to the rising sun, O Lord, have mercy on me.

> Let us praise God together on our knees; let us praise God together on our knees; when I fall on my knees, with my face to the rising sun, O Lord, have mercy on me.

❧ **For Today:** Psalm 133:1; Matthew 26:26-30; Luke 24:30; Romans 15:5, 6; Hebrews 10:25

Reflect on this statement: I should value not only those for whom Christ died, but above all those in whom Christ now lives. Consider how a more loving and caring relationship could be promoted among the members of your local church. Ponder this important matter—

SAVIOR, TEACH ME, DAY BY DAY

Jane E. Leeson, 1807-1882

If anyone loves Me, he will obey my teaching. My Father will love him, and we will come to him and make our home with him. (John 14:23)

It is wonderful to have experienced God's gift of love in days past, but the real challenge of victorious Christian living is knowing God in a new and fresh way each day. This is what gives our lives zest and enables us to face any new challenge. But this daily learning about our Savior is more than merely pursuing theological knowledge. Biblical knowledge must always be joined with a loving relationship with Christ, since knowledge in itself can easily develop into a false spiritual pride. For many of us, our greatest need is simply to be reminded of what we already know and to translate our knowledge into loving action. Our love for God is not really genuine until we have learned to share it with others.

There are numerous laws on the statute books of our land that attempt to teach us to be better people. The Christian, however, is also governed by two other basic commands: "Thou shalt love the Lord, thy God, with all thy soul, and with all thy mind . . . thou shalt love thy neighbor as thyself" (Matthew 22:37, 39). And even beyond this, we are to treat one another with the same tender spirit that we have experienced from our Lord (Philippians 2:5).

"Savior, Teach Me, Day by Day," which was originally written for children, spurs us on to the kind of service our Lord was talking about. Its basic theme—learning to love Christ who first loved us—involves a response of action: obedience (stanza 1); "prompt to serve" (stanza 2); "strong to follow" (stanza 3); and living joyously (stanza 4). The hymn was first published in 1842.

The author, Jane Eliza Leeson, was a rather unknown English writer of religious verse. She was a member of a strange and spurious sect known as the Holy Catholic Apostolic Church. In later life Miss Leeson became a member of the Roman Catholic Church. Yet her one enduring hymn still speaks to each of us of every age:

> Savior, teach me, day by day, love's sweet lesson to obey; sweeter lesson cannot be, loving Him who first loved me.

> With a child's glad heart of love, at Thy bidding may I move, prompt to serve and follow Thee, loving Him who first loved me.

> Teach me thus Thy steps to trace, strong to follow in Thy grace, learning how to love from Thee, loving Him who first loved me.

> Love in loving finds employ, in obedience all her joy; ever new that joy will be, loving Him who first loved me.

❦ ***For Today:*** Psalm 18:1; 2 Corinthians 10:17; Philippians 1:9; 1 John 3:18

Ask the question, "What have I learned about God during the past few days?" Also, "What new insights do I wish to learn this day?"

Posen tune   George C. Strattner, 1650-1705

Sav - ior, teach me, day by day, Love's sweet les - son to o - bey;

Sweet - er les - son can - not be, Lov - ing Him who first loved me.

BLEST BE THE TIE THAT BINDS

John Fawcett, 1740-1817

Whoever loves his brother lives in the light, and there is nothing in him to make him stumble. (1 John 2:10)

"We just cannot break the ties of affection that bind us to you dear friends." As Mary Fawcett assured the little congregation at Wainsgate, England, of the bond of love that she and her husband felt for their poor peasant parishioners, Pastor John decided to express his feelings in a poem about the value of Christian fellowship.

The following Sunday, John Fawcett preached from Luke 12:15: "A man's life consists not in the abundance of the things he possesses." He closed his sermon by reading his new poem, "Brotherly Love."

At the age of 26, John Fawcett and his new bride, Mary, began their ministry at an impoverished Baptist church in Wainsgate. After seven years of devoted service in meager circumstances, they received a call to the large and influential Carter's Lane Baptist Church in London. After the wagons were loaded for the move, the Fawcetts met their tearful parishioners for a final farewell. "John, I cannot bear to leave. I know not how to go!" "Nor can I either," said the saddened pastor. "We shall remain here with our people." The order was then given to unload the wagons.

John and Mary Fawcett carried on their faithful ministry in the little village of Wainsgate for a total of 54 years. Their salary was estimated to be never more than the equivalent of $200.00 a year, despite Fawcett's growing reputation as an outstanding evangelical preacher, scholar, and writer. Among his noted writings was an essay, "Anger," which became a particular favorite of King George III. It is reported that the monarch promised Pastor Fawcett any benefit that could be conferred. But the offer was declined with this statement: "I have lived among my own people, enjoying their love; God has blessed my labors among them, and I need nothing which even a king could supply." Such was the man who gave us these loving words:

> Blest be the tie that binds our hearts in Christian love! The fellowship of kindred minds is like to that above.

> Before our Father's throne we pour our ardent prayers; our fears, our hopes, our aims are one, our comforts and our cares.

> We share our mutual woes, our mutual burdens bear; and often for each other flows the sympathizing tear.

> When we asunder part it gives us inward pain; but we shall still be joined in heart, and hope to meet again.

🍎 ***For Today:*** Psalm 133; Matthew 18:20; John 13:34, 35; Hebrews 13:1

Appreciate anew your Christian friends and fellow church members. Seek to show, as John Fawcett did, a loving concern for the needs of others.

Dennis tune   Hans G. Naegeli, 1773-1836

GOD BE WITH YOU

Jeremiah E. Rankin, 1828-1904

The grace of our Lord Jesus be with you. (Romans 16:20)

> It is my joy in life to find at every turning of the road,
> The strong arms of a comrade kind to help me onward with my load.
> And since I have no gold to give, and love alone can make amends—
> My daily prayer is, while I live, "God, make me worthy of my friends."   —*Unknown*

Often we hear someone tell us glibly to "have a good day!" Would not a far better farewell for Christians be the loving wish of today's hymn text—"God be with you"? The added thought of "till we meet again" suggests a sincere desire for continued friendship.

The writer of this hymn text, Dr. Jeremiah Rankin, pastored several prominent Congregational churches throughout the East until 1889, when be became president of Howard University, the noted school for the education of black students. A powerful preacher and an excellent leader and promoter of congregational singing, Rankin wrote much poetry, including the still popular hymn "Tell It to Jesus." He also edited a number of well-known gospel songbooks.

No other hymn except perhaps "Blest Be the Tie That Binds" has been as widely used as this one as a closing benediction in church services. "God Be With You" was a favorite in the Moody and Sankey meetings throughout North America and England. It became the official closing song for the Christian Endeavor Conventions around the world. And still today, no finer farewell can be expressed by Christians to one another as they leave a place of worship than the sincere wish, "God be with you till we meet again."

> God be with you till we meet again, by His counsels guide, uphold you, with His sheep securely fold you—God be with you till we meet again.
>
> God be with you till we meet again, 'neath His wings protecting hide you, daily manna still provide you—God be with you till we meet again.
>
> God be with you till we meet again, when life's perils thick confound you, put His arms unfailing round you—God be with you till we meet again.
>
> God be with you till we meet again, keep love's banner floating o'er you, smite death's threat'ning wave before you—God be with you till we meet again.
>
> **Chorus:** Till we meet, till we meet, till we meet at Jesus' feet, till we meet, till we meet—God be with you till we meet again.

❦ *For Today:* Exodus 33:14; Acts 20:32; 1 Peter 5:7-10

Avoid trite and casual greetings and farewells. Instead, practice a genuine concern for others. Try saying goodbye to friends or family with some of the lovely wishes expressed in this text: God be with you . . . guide, uphold you, hide you, put His arms around you.

William G. Tomer, 1833-1896

Till we meet..... till we meet.... God be with you till we meet a-gain.

IT'S JUST LIKE HIS GREAT LOVE

Edna R. Worrell, 19th century

How great is the love the Father has lavished on us, that we should be called children of God! And that is what we are! (1 John 3:1)

The greatest demonstration of love is God's gift of Jesus Christ to a lost world. It is impossible to comprehend fully this divine love; it can only be learned experientially. As we grow in our love relationship with the Lord, we begin to realize in part the magnitude of His love. This love is unconditional—He loves us regardless of our failures or successes. This love is impartial—it includes everyone. This love is infinite and eternal—simply because God Himself is love! And this love is personal—He loves each of us as if we were the only one in His world to love.

Discouragement is common to each of us, especially in our moments of self-pity or as we are made aware of our shortcomings. In times like these, introspection—continually looking within—only makes us more miserable. Rather, we need to look up. We need to focus on Christ and His great love for us, to remember that we are "children of God," and to rely on His promise that our eternal destiny is heaven. Such a reflection will assuredly change any gloom to song and restore once more a walk of sweet fellowship with our Lord. Then we will have the joy of knowing that Jesus will keep us from day to day because of His great love.

A Friend I have, called Jesus, whose love is strong and true, and never fails how e'er 'tis tried, no matter what I do; I've sinned against this love of His, but when I knelt to pray, confessing all my guilt to Him, the sin-clouds rolled away.

Sometimes the clouds of trouble bedim the sky above. I cannot see my Savior's face; I doubt His wondrous love; but He, from heaven's mercy seat, beholding my despair, in pity bursts the clouds between and shows me He is there.

When sorrow's clouds o'ertake me and break upon my head, when life seems worse than useless and I were better dead, I take my grief to Jesus then, nor do I go in vain, in pity bursts the clouds between and shows me He is there.

Oh, I could sing forever of Jesus' love divine, of all His care and tenderness for this poor life of mine; His love is in and over all, and wind and waves obey when Jesus whispers "Peace, be still!" and rolls the clouds away.

Chorus: It's just like Jesus to roll the clouds away; it's just like Jesus to keep me day by day. It's just like Jesus all along the way; it's just like His great love.

❦ *For Today:* Luke 19:10; Ephesians 3:18, 19; 1 John 3:16; 4:9, 10

Determine to live joyfully as one who knows what it means to be loved and forgiven by God's great love. Carry this musical truth with you—

It's just like Je-sus to roll the clouds a-way, It's just like Je-sus to keep me

day by day, It's just like Je-sus all a-long the way, It's just like His great love.

SWEETER AS THE YEARS GO BY

Words and Music by Lelia N. Morris, 1862-1929

The righteous will flourish like a palm tree, they will grow like a cedar of Lebanon; planted in the house of the Lord, they will flourish in the courts of our God. They will still bear fruit in old age, they stay fresh and green, proclaiming, "The Lord is upright; He is my Rock, and there is not wickedness in Him." (Psalm 92:12-15)

For the believer, growing older should mean a greater awareness of God's love and fellowship as well as a time of greater usefulness in Christian service. The golden years can and should be the most fruitful time of life. A lifetime of companionship with God should result in a mellow and gracious Christ-like spirit. Because there are fewer demands and pressures for life's necessities, the older Christian should have opportunities for effective ministry that he never before attempted.

There is nothing more tragic, however, than to see a professing Christian become disgruntled and self-centered in later years. It is true that we simply bring into full bloom the traits that were begun in our early years. If we wish to have positive and productive attitudes in our senior years, we must begin to develop these traits while we are still young.

Author and composer Mrs. Lelia Morris was an active worker in the Methodist church. She continued to write gospel songs during the last 15 years of her life, even after going blind in her early fifties. "Sweeter as the Years Go By" was written during the early years of her blindness. It is said that during this difficult time in her life, Mrs. Morris used a 28-foot long blackboard with music lines on it to help her hymn writing. In all, Lelia Morris wrote more than 1,000 hymn texts, as well as many of the tunes. Her handicap never deterred her from being effective and productive for God. Even in blindness she found her Lord sweeter as the years went by.

Of Jesus' love that sought me, when I was lost in sin; of wondrous grace that brought me back to His fold again; of heights and depths of mercy, far deeper than the sea, and higher than the heavens, my theme shall ever be.

He trod in old Judea life's pathway long ago; the people thronged about Him His saving grace to know; He healed the broken hearted, and caused the blind to see; and still His great heart yearneth in love for even me.

'Twas wondrous love which led Him for us to suffer loss—to bear without a murmur the anguish of the cross; with saints redeemed in glory let us our voices raise, till heaven and earth re-echo with our Redeemer's praise.

Refrain: Sweeter as the years go by, sweeter as the years go by; richer, fuller, deeper, Jesus' love is sweeter, sweeter as the years go by.

❦ *For Today:* Psalm 92:12, 14; Proverbs 16:31; John 15:10, 11

Seek out a respected elderly person. Learn his secret for a contented and useful life with God. Keep this musical message upon your lips—

Sweet–er as the years go by, Sweet–er as the years go by; Rich–er,full–er,

deep–er, Je – sus' love is sweet – er, Sweet – er as the years go by.

IN HEAVENLY LOVE ABIDING

Anna L. Warning, 1823-1910

But because of His great love for us, God, who is rich in mercy, made us alive with Christ even when we were dead in transgressions—it is by grace you have been saved. And seated us with Him in the heavenly realms in Christ Jesus. (Ephesians 2:4-6)

Those who were born on this day are special people—they celebrate only one fourth as many birthdays as the rest of us. But the Bible tells us of something else that makes someone special—spiritual rebirth:

But you are a chosen people, a royal priesthood, a holy nation, a people belonging to God, that you may declare the praises of Him who called you out of darkness into His wonderful light. (1 Peter 2:9)

The Scriptures also teach that as believers we enjoy many special privileges. We are heavenly people—our citizenship is in the heavenlies with Christ. Even now we are seated positionally with Him in glory. In Christ we have access to His storehouse of riches; we are the possessors of all heavenly blessings. We have been given a heaven-born nature that responds to spiritual nourishment— the Living and Written Word. While we seek to be worthy representatives for God in this life, our affections are already centered on things above. This occupation with heavenly values enables us to rise above the mundane circumstances and storms that often cross our earthly paths and provides the enablement we need to live a life of daily victory. And while we await the day of our final victory, we live in the enjoyment of our future inheritance. In a sense, then, we are "in heavenly love abiding" already.

The author of this hymn text, Anna Laetitia Warning, was raised as a Quaker in South Wales but later joined the Anglican church. In later life she took on a busy ministry of visiting prisoners in jail. She was known and loved for her gentle but cheerful spirit.

In heavenly love abiding, no change my heart shall fear; and safe is such confiding, for nothing changes here. The storm may roar without me; my heart may low be laid, but God is round about me, and can I be dismayed?

Wherever He may guide me, no fear shall turn me back; my Shepherd is beside me, and nothing shall I lack. His wisdom ever waketh; His sight is never dim; He knows the way He taketh, and I will walk with Him.

Green pastures are before me, which yet I have not seen; bright skies will soon be o'er me, where darkest clouds have been. My hope I cannot measure; my path to life is free; my Savior is my treasure, and He will walk with me.

❧ *For Today:* Ephesians 1:3-14; Philippians 3:20; Colossians 3:1, 2

Live this day as an heir of the heavenly kingdom. Face each situation that may arise with the absolute confidence that God is round about you.

Seasons tune   Felix Mendelssohn, 1809-1847

The storm may roar with-out me, My heart may low be laid, But God is round a-bout me, And can I be dis-mayed?

March

- *Sunday School Favorites*
- *Songs For and About Children/Youth*

BRING THEM IN

Alexcenah Thomas, 19th century

I have other sheep that are not of this sheep pen. I must bring them also. They too will listen to my voice, and there shall be one flock and one shepherd. (John 10:16)

During this month our attention is often focused on the ministry of our Sunday schools. The Sunday school has been the church's chief agency for reaching and teaching children for the past two centuries. It would be impossible to measure the extent of its spiritual influence during that time.

The Sunday school movement began in England during the lifetime of Robert Raikes (1736-1811), who was often called the "founder of the modern Sunday school." Raikes became intensely concerned with the spiritual and social conditions of the great masses of poor illiterate children. Since education was reserved for the wealthy, four out of five poor children had no schooling. Child labor was shamefully exploited. In the midst of these conditions Raikes began taking children off the streets and teaching them biblical truths as well as the ability to read and write.

Later the followers of John and Charles Wesley, the Methodists, began establishing Sunday schools, first in England and then in America following the Revolutionary War. Still later the Sunday school movement was encouraged further by the founding of the American Sunday School Union in 1824. As this concern for children developed, it became apparent to Christian leaders that music is a natural means for working with children, since most children respond readily to musical activities. This desire to reach and teach children for Christ through appropriate songs was one of the important factors that led to the rise of the gospel song movement during the latter half of the 19th century.

"Bring Them In" has been widely used since being published in 1885 by its composer William Ogden, who was known for his work with children's music.

> Hark! 'tis the Shepherd's voice I hear, out in the desert dark and drear, calling the sheep who've gone astray far from the Shepherd's fold away.

> Who'll go and help this Shepherd king, help Him the wand'ring one to find? Who'll bring the lost ones to the fold where they'll be sheltered from the cold?

> Out in the desert hear their cry, out on the mountains wild and high. Hark! 'tis the Master speaks to thee, "Go find my sheep where'er they be."

> **Chorus:** Bring them in, bring them in, bring them in from the fields of sin; bring them in, bring them in, bring the wand'ring ones to Jesus.

❦ *For Today:* Psalm 96:2, 3; Proverbs 11:30; Matthew 13:39; Matthew 18:12

Spend time in prayer for your church Sunday school—the leaders and teachers who have assumed the important responsibility of ministering the Christian faith to children and youth. At your first opportunity let them know of your prayerful concern and appreciation for their work.

William Odgen, 1841-1897

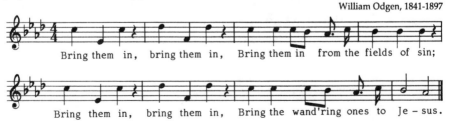

Bring them in, bring them in, Bring them in from the fields of sin;

Bring them in, bring them in, Bring the wand'ring ones to Je - sus.

JESUS LOVES ME

Anna B. Warner, 1820-1915

I tell you the truth, anyone who will not receive the kingdom of God like a little child will never enter it. (Luke 18:17)

The story is told of a brilliant professor at Princeton Seminary who always left his graduation class with these words: "Gentlemen, there is still much in this world and in the Bible that I do not understand, but of one thing I am certain—'Jesus loves me, this I know, for the Bible tells me so'—and gentlemen, that is sufficient!"

Without doubt the song that has been sung more by children than any other hymn is this simply stated one by Anna Warner. Written in 1860, it is still one of the first hymns taught to new converts in other lands.

Miss Warner wrote this text in collaboration with her sister Susan. It was part of their novel *Say and Seal,* one of the best selling books of that day. Today few individuals would know or remember the plot of that story, which once stirred the hearts of many readers. But the simple poem spoken by one of the characters, Mr. Linden, as he comforts Johnny Fax, a dying child, still remains the favorite hymn of countless children around the world.

> Jesus loves me! this I know, for the Bible tells me so. Little ones to Him belong; they are weak but He is strong.

> Jesus loves me! loves me still, tho I'm very weak and ill, that I might from sin be free, bled and died upon the tree.

> Jesus loves me! He who died heaven's gate to open wide; He will wash away my sin, let His little child come in.

> Jesus loves me! He will stay close beside me all the way. Thou hast bled and died for me; I will henceforth live for Thee.

> **Chorus:** Yes, Jesus loves me! The Bible tells me so.

William Bradbury, the composer of the music, was one of the leading contributors to the development of early gospel music in America. He became recognized as one of the pioneers in children's music both for the church and in the public schools. In 1861 Bradbury composed the music for Anna Warner's text and personally added the chorus to her four stanzas. The hymn appeared the following year in Bradbury's hymnal collection, *The Golden Sower.* It had an immediate response.

❦ *For Today:* Genesis 33:5; Psalm 127:3; Matthew 11:25; Mark 10:16

"If there is anything that will endure the eye of God, because it still is pure, it is the spirit of a little child, fresh from His hand, and therefore undefiled." Ask God to give you this kind of spirit.

William B. Bradbury, 1816-1868

Yes, Je – sus loves me! Yes, Je – sus loves me! Yes, Je – sus loves me! The Bi – ble tells me so.

O HOW I LOVE JESUS

Frederick Whitfield, 1829-1904

We love because He first loved us. (1 John 4:19)

This simply stated, lilting musical testimony has been another of the Sunday school favorites since it was first published in leaflet form in 1855. It has since been translated into various languages and has been included in numerous evangelical hymnals.

The words express so well the response of believers of any age as we reflect on all that Christ has done and continues to do for us daily. Indirectly, the hymn also exalts the written Word, for it is only through the study of the revealed written Word that we gain a true knowledge of the Living Word.

The text originally included eight stanzas. Several interesting verses not found in present hymnals include these words:

> It tells me of a Father's smile that beams upon His child.
> It cheers me through this little while, through deserts waste and wild.
>
> It bids my trembling soul rejoice, and dries each rising tear.
> It tells me in a still small voice, to trust and not to fear.

The author, Frederick Whitfield, was an Anglican church clergyman. He is credited with more than 30 books of religious verse. The anonymous tune is a typical 19th century American folk song used in the campground meetings of that time.

Even a century after they were written, these ageless words are still appropriate for expressing our love and devotion for Christ:

> There is a name I love to hear; I love to sing its worth; it sounds like music in mine ear, the sweetest name on earth.
>
> It tells me of a Savior's love, who died to set me free; it tells me of His precious blood, the sinner's perfect plea.
>
> It tells me what my Father hath in store for ev'ry day, and, tho I tread a darksome path, yields sunshine all the way.
>
> It tells of One whose loving heart can feel my deepest woe, who in each sorrow bears a part that none can bear below.
>
> **Chorus:** O how I love Jesus, O how I love Jesus, O how I love Jesus—because He first loved me!

❧ *For Today:* John 14:23; Philippians 2:9-11; 1 Peter 1:8; 1 John 4:7-21; Jude 21

Breathe a prayer expressing your love to Christ for all that He means to you. Thank Him for initiating His love on your behalf. Thank Him also for the daily sunshine He gives. Carry this little musical nugget with you throughout the day—

American Melody

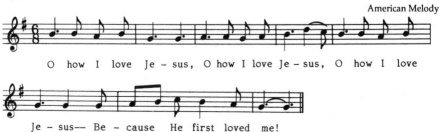

O how I love Je - sus, O how I love Je - sus, O how I love

Je - sus— Be - cause He first loved me!

WONDERFUL WORDS OF LIFE

Words and Music by Philip P. Bliss, 1838-1876

The words I have spoken to you are spirit and they are life. (John 6:63)

One of the basic precepts of the Sunday school movement has always been that God's Word must be carefully and systematically studied by believers of all ages.

> Study it carefully, think of it prayerfully,
> Till in your heart its precepts dwell;
> Slight not its history, ponder its mystery,
> None can e'er prize it too fondly or well.
>
> *—Unknown*

One of the earnest concerns of many present leaders is the biblical ignorance of so many church people. Often precious Sunday school time is spent in teaching everything but the Bible itself. Yet the churches that do teach the Scriptures diligently and apply their teachings to modern living are the churches that are experiencing the greatest growth. We never outgrow our need for the Bible; it becomes more helpful to us with the years.

We must also realize that God's truth revealed to us is never contrary or apart from the Bible. Often there have been those who have claimed to have extra revelations through visions which supercede the Scriptures. God's Word clearly warns against this false assertion (Jeremiah 23:16).

Philip P. Bliss was one of the most important names in the development of early gospel music. Before his tragic death at age 38, he wrote many favorites still enjoyed by congregations. "Wonderful Words of Life" was written by Bliss in 1874, for the first issue of a Sunday school paper, *Words of Life*. These words still speak to both young and old of the importance of God's Word in our daily lives:

> Sing them over again to me—wonderful words of life; let me more of their beauty see—wonderful words of life. Words of life and beauty, teach me faith and duty:

> Christ, the blessed one, gives to all wonderful words of life; sinner, list to the loving call—wonderful words of life. All so freely given, wooing us to heaven:

> Sweetly echo the gospel call—wonderful words of life; offer pardon and peace to all—wonderful words of life. Jesus, only Savior, sanctify forever:

> **Refrain:** Beautiful words, wonderful words of life.

❦ **For Today:** Psalm 119:103, 172; Jeremiah 15:16; Matthew 4:4

Reflect on whether God's Word has the place of importance in your life that it should have. Consider ways that this could be improved. Sing this musical reminder—

Beau – ti – ful words, won – der – ful words, Won – der – ful words of Life; Beau-ti – ful words, won – der- ful words, Won–der–ful words of Life.

THY WORD IS LIKE A GARDEN, LORD

Edwin Hodder, 1837-1904

How sweet are Your words to my taste, sweeter than honey to my mouth! I gain understanding from Your precepts; therefore I hate every wrong path. (Psalm 119:103, 104)

For the child of God, the daily reading of the Scriptures is the nourishment of the soul. The Bible's value has been described in many ways as the traveller's map, the pilgrim's staff, the pilot's compass, the soldier's sword, and the Christian's charter. Someone has offered this sage advice regarding the use of the Bible: "Read it to be wise, believe it to be safe, and practice it to be holy. Read it slowly, frequently, and prayerfully. It is a mine of wealth, a paradise of glory, and a river of pleasure."

> Read this book for whatever you can accept and take the rest on faith. You will live
> and die a better man.   —*Abraham Lincoln*

Although just a lay amateur writer in England, Edwin Hodder was also impressed with the miraculous quality of the Bible. So in this hymn, first published in 1863, Hodder paints comparative pictures that both young and old can understand easily. Verse one begins with the thought that even casual seekers can find something from God's written landscape that will beautify their lives merely by "plucking a lovely cluster." Stanza one continues to say, however, that it is not enough to be casual in this garden of beauty. Rather, we must earnestly search and dig into its mighty depths for "jewels rich and rare."

Verse two extends the thought further that God's Word, like the starry host, is fathomless in giving guidance for life's journey. Finally, the hymn reminds us that there is an earnestness confronting each believer in the form of a warfare against sin and unrighteousness. For this battle we require the aid of God's Holy Word.

> Thy Word is like a garden, Lord, with flowers bright and fair; and ev'ryone who seeks may pluck a lovely cluster there. Thy Word is like a deep, deep, mine, and jewels rich and rare are hidden in its mighty depths for ev'ry searcher there.

> Thy Word is like a starry host—A thousand rays of light are seen to guide the traveler and make his pathway bright. Thy Word is like an armory where soldiers may repair and find, for life's long battle-day, all needful weapons there.

> O may I love Thy precious Word, may I explore the mine; may I its fragrant flowers glean, may light upon me shine. O may I find my armor there, Thy Word my trusty sword! I'll learn to fight with ev'ry foe the battle of the Lord!

❦ *For Today:* Psalm 119:105; 130; John 5:39; 6:63; 2 Timothy 3:16

Allow the Bible's relevance, beauty, and simplicity to thrill your soul. Reflect on this musical reminder to help—

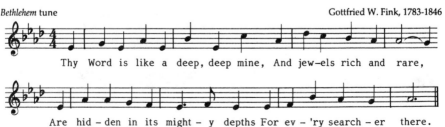

Bethlehem tune   Gottfried W. Fink, 1783-1846

NO, NOT ONE!

Johnson Oatman, Jr., 1856-1922

I no longer call you servants, because a servant does not know his master's business. Instead, I have called you friends. . . . (John 15:15)

> He became poor that we might become rich (James 2:5).
> He was born that we might be born again (John 1:14).
> He became a servant that we might become sons (Galatians 4:6, 7).
> He had no home that we might have a home in heaven (Matthew 8:20).
> He was made sin that we might be made righteous (2 Corinthians 5:21).
> He died that we might live (John 5:24, 25).

This is another of our favorite Sunday school songs that extols, in child-like language, our living Lord. It has a typical gospel song character in that it employs a repetitive phrase—"No, not one"—which allows people of all ages and backgrounds to join heartily together in the praise of Christ. Gospel songs such as this can teach even the youngest child the truth of the pre-eminence of our Lord and His nearness in every situation of our lives.

The author, Johnson Oatman, Jr., was an ordained Methodist minister, but he worked most of his life in the insurance business. He wrote numerous gospel hymn texts including "Higher Ground" and "Count Your Blessings."

The composer, George C. Hugg, was an active lay musician-choir director in various churches in the Philadelphia area. He too was active in writing and publishing Sunday school songs during this time.

In times of stress and loneliness, these simple words with their easily sung tune, that many of us first sang in our earliest Sunday school classes, still minister to us today:

> There's not a friend like the lowly Jesus, no, not one! no, not one! None else could heal all your soul's diseases, no, not one! no, not one!

> No friend like Him is so high and holy, no, not one! no, not one! And yet no friend is so meek and lowly, no, not one! no, not one!

> There's not an hour that He is not near us, no, not one! no, not one! No night so dark but His love can cheer us, no, not one! no, not one!

> Did ever saint find this Friend forsake him? no, not one! no, not one! Or sinner find that He would not take him? no, not one! no, not one!

> Was e'er a gift like the Savior given? no, not one! no, not one! Will He refuse us a home in heaven? no, not one! no, not one!

> **Refrain:** Jesus knows all about our struggles; He will guide till the day is done. There's not a friend like the lowly Jesus, no, not one! no, not one!

❦ *For Today:* Proverbs 18:24; Matthew 11:29; John 8:12; 2 Corinthians 5:1; Revelation 3:20

When a difficult situation arises, let the simple, child-like truth of this music minister to your need.

George C. Hugg, 1848-1907

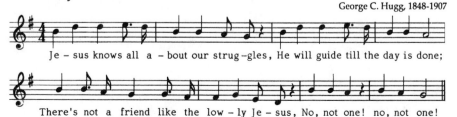

Je - sus knows all a - bout our strug –gles, He will guide till the day is done;

There's not a friend like the low – ly Je – sus, No, not one! no, not one!

BRIGHTEN THE CORNER

Ina Duley Ogdon, 1877-?

Christ gave Himself for us to redeem us from all wickedness and to purify for Himself a people that are His very own, eager to do what is good. (Titus 2:14)

"Do not wait until some deed of greatness you may do . . . but brighten the corner where you are!" These words were born out of frustration when the talented speaker, Mrs. Ina Odgon, was selected to be on the Chautauqua Circuit. This would give her the opportunity to reach thousands around the country with her brilliant oratory. Just before she was to leave on the tour, her father was injured seriously in an automobile accident. Ina felt it necessary to cancel her plans so she could take care of her father.

At first Mrs. Ogdon felt much anger and resentment against God for allowing this tragedy to happen. Gradually, however, she determined that she would be happy and remain "true to the many duties near" her. She would do her best to "brighten the corner" where God had placed her. Ina completed this poem in 1913. Later it was set to its lilting music by the well-known musician, Charles Gabriel, and it became the popular theme song of the Billy Sunday-Homer Rodeheaver campaigns. Interestingly, Mrs. Ogdon no doubt ministered effectively to more people with these challenging words, born out of despair, than she would have done with her speaking tours on the Chautauqua Circuit.

> Do not wait until some deed of greatness you may do. Do not wait to shed your light afar. To the many duties ever near you now be true; brighten the corner where you are.

> Just above are clouded skies that you may help to clear; let not narrow self your way debar. Tho into one heart alone may fall your song of cheer, brighten the corner where you are.

> Here for all your talent you may surely find a need, here reflect the Bright and Morning Star. Ever from your humble hand the bread of life may feed; brighten the corner where you are.

> **Chorus:** Brighten the corner where you are! Brighten the corner where you are! Someone far from harbor you may guide across the bar; brighten the corner where you are!

❦ *For Today:* Matthew 5:16; Acts 26:20; 1 Timothy 6:16; Titus 2:7; Titus 2:14; James 2:20

Resolve that regardless of the frustrating and mundane duties you may face, you will, with God's help, do them cheerfully as unto the Lord, seeking to bring some spark of joy and kindness into the life of another. Carry this little musical reminder with you throughout the day—

Charles H. Gabriel, 1856-1932

SAVIOR, LIKE A SHEPHERD LEAD US

Dorothy A. Thrupp, 1799-1847

I will instruct you and teach you in the way you should go; I will counsel you and watch over you. (Psalm 32:8)

Divine guidance is the very essence of Christianity. The Bible equates being guided by the Spirit of God with being a child of God (Romans 8:14). But even as our natural children can sometimes rebel against parental authority, so we too can forsake God's leading in our lives and seek to go our own ways. God's leading, then, doesn't just happen. There must be the sincere desire and willingness to be guided. With implicit faith we must recognize that God has a planned path for each of His children, and we must deeply desire to follow that path wherever it leads. Scriptural promises such as Jeremiah 29:11 become our source of daily encouragement:

For I know the plans I have for you, declares the Lord, plans to prosper you and not to harm you, plans to give you hope and a future.

The author of this popular hymn, Dorothy Thrupp, was born and lived in London, England. She was a rather prolific writer of children's hymns and devotional materials although she seldom signed her name to any of her works. When she did, she would use a pseudonym. For this reason it has never been fully proven that she was the actual author of "Savior, Like a Shepherd Lead Us." The hymn first appeared unsigned in her collection *Hymns for the Young*, in 1836.

Savior, like a shepherd lead us; much we need Thy tender care; in Thy pleasant pastures feed us; for our use Thy folds prepare: Blessed Jesus, blessed Jesus, Thou has bought us, Thine we are; blessed Jesus, blessed Jesus, Thou hast bought us, Thine we are.

We are Thine—do Thou befriend us; be the Guardian of our way; keep Thy flock, from sin defend us; seek us when we go astray: Blessed Jesus, blessed Jesus, hear, O hear us when we pray; blessed Jesus, blessed Jesus, hear, O hear us when we pray.

Thou has promised to receive us, poor and sinful tho we be; Thou hast mercy to relieve us, grace to cleanse and pow'r to free: Blessed Jesus, blessed Jesus, early let us turn to Thee; blessed Jesus, blessed Jesus, early let us turn to Thee.

Early let us seek Thy favor; early let us do Thy will; blessed Lord and only Savior, with Thy love our bosoms fill: Blessed Jesus, blessed Jesus, Thou hast loved us; love us still; blessed Jesus, blessed Jesus, Thou hast loved us, love us still.

❦ ***For Today:*** Psalm 23; Proverbs 16:1, 3, 6, 9; Isaiah 40:11; John 10:14-16, 27

Walk the path one step at a time in the confidence of God's leading and presence. Do not become burdened by the distant future. Sing this musical truth as you go—

Bradbury tune   William B. Bradbury, 1816-1868

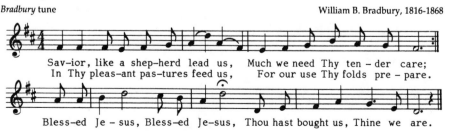

Sav-ior, like a shep-herd lead us, Much we need Thy ten-der care;
In Thy pleas-ant pas-tures feed us, For our use Thy folds pre-pare.
Bless-ed Je-sus, Bless-ed Je-sus, Thou hast bought us, Thine we are.

THE LORD'S MY SHEPHERD

Scottish Psalter, 1650

My sheep listen to my voice; I know them, and they follow Me. (John 10:27)

I will commit my way, O Lord, to Thee, nor doubt Thy love, though dark the way
may be; Nor murmur, for the sorrow is from God, and there is comfort even in Thy rod.
—*Unknown*

One of the characteristics of the relationship that exists between a shepherd and his flock is that sheep can always distinguish the voice of their particular shepherd. The sheep's responsibility is simply to listen and follow.

As Christians, we worship and acknowledge God as our Creator and Redeemer. But how comforting it is to realize that this same great God is also "my Shepherd." In time of stress, I can rest securely in His strong arms. With the Good Shepherd leading, even death's dark vale need not be feared since death to the believer is simply a release to God's eternal home.

As members of Christ's flock, we too must recognize our heavenly Shepherd's voice. To do so, we must always remain close enough to hear it.

Whether you turn to the right or to the left, your ears will hear a voice behind you saying, "This is the way; walk in it." (Isaiah 30:21)

This lovely setting of the 23rd Psalm was originally put in stanza form for the Scottish Psalter of 1650, a collection that contained only the 150 psalms arranged in metrical form for congregational singing. The charming and child-like tune has only recently begun to appear in American hymnals. "The Lord's My Shepherd". . . for many children the first Bible verse learned and often the last repeated before entering "death's dark vale." A psalm of priceless heritage!

The Lord's my Shepherd—I'll not want; He makes me down to lie in pastures green. He leadeth me the quiet waters by.

My soul He doth restore again, and me to walk doth make within the paths of righteousness, e'en for His own name's sake.

Yea, tho I walk thru death's dark vale, yet will I fear no ill, for Thou art with me, and Thy rod and staff me comfort still.

My table Thou hast furnished in presence of my foes; my head Thou dost with oil anoint, and my cup overflows.

Goodness and mercy all my life shall surely follow me, and in God's house forevermore my dwelling place shall be.

🌿 ***For Today:*** Psalm 23; 78:52; Jeremiah 29:11; John 10:1-6; Hebrews 13:20, 21; 1 Peter 5:7

Be sensitive to God's inner voice with directions for your life. Determine to follow wherever He indicates. Abandon yourself to His divine guidance. Sing as you go—

Crimond tune

Jessie Seymour Irvine, 1836-1887

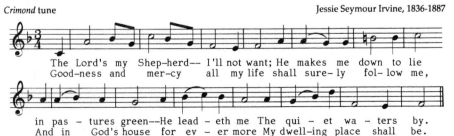

The Lord's my Shep-herd— I'll not want; He makes me down to lie
Good-ness and mer-cy all my life shall sure-ly fol-low me,

in pas - tures green--He lead - eth me The qui - et wa - ters by.
And in God's house for ev - er more My dwell-ing place shall be.

SHEPHERD OF EAGER YOUTH

Clement of Alexandria, c. 170-c. 220
Translated by Henry Martyn Dexter, 1821-1890

Remember your Creator in the days of your youth, before the days of trouble come and the years approach when you will say, "I find no pleasure in them!" (Ecclesiastes 12:1)

> Someone cried, "Where must the seed be sown to bring the most fruit when it is grown?"
> The Master heard as He said and smiled, "Go plant it for Me in the heart of a child."
> —*Unknown*

It is vitally important that our children be led to a personal relationship with Christ and instructed in His Word when they are young. What truth there is in these familiar statements: "To save a child is to save a life," or "Give me a child till he/she is seven and I care not who gets him after that." D. L. Moody, the noted evangelist, once said: "If I could relive my life, I would devote my entire ministry to reaching children for God."

Christian nurturing of our children requires consistent discipline. Webster defines discipline as "training which corrects, strengthens, and perfects." Discipline goes far beyond merely being punitive. Discipline and training have done their job only when they result in a changed character and the desire to live with self-control. Although there may be times when our youth may rebel and react against their early Christian training, they can never get completely away from it (Proverbs 22:6).

"Shepherd of Eager Youth" is the oldest Christian hymn of which the authorship is known. Clement of Alexandria wrote this text in the Greek language sometime between A.D. 202 and the time of his death in A.D. 220. The title in the original Greek could literally be translated "Tamer of Steeds Unbridled." It was evidently used as a hymn of Christian instruction for new young converts from heathenism.

> Shepherd of eager youth, guiding in love and truth thru devious ways—Christ, our triumphant King, we come Thy name to sing; hither Thy children bring tributes of praise.

> Thou art our Holy Lord, the all-subduing Word, healer of strife; Thou didst Thyself abase that from sin's deep disgrace Thou mightest save our race and give us life.

> Ever be near our side, our shepherd and our guide, our staff and song; Jesus, Thou Christ of God, by Thy enduring word lead us where Thou hast trod, make our faith strong.

❦ ***For Today:*** Deuteronomy 32:46; 1 Timothy 4:12; 1 Peter 2:25

Reflect on this truth: The prized possession of any church is its youth. Seek to speak a word of encouragement to some young person.

Italian Hymn tune   Felice De Giardini, 1716-1796

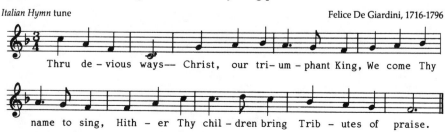

Thru de - vious ways— Christ, our tri - um - phant King, We come Thy name to sing, Hith - er Thy chil - dren bring Trib - utes of praise.

DARE TO BE A DANIEL

Words and Music by Philip P. Bliss, 1838-1876

But Daniel resolved not to defile himself. . . . (Daniel 1:8)

> Doubt sees the obstacles—Faith sees the way.
> Doubt sees the darkest night—Faith sees the day.
> Doubt dreads to take a step—Faith soars on high.
> Doubt questions, "Who believes?"—Faith answers, "I."   —*Unknown*

The book of Daniel is really a textbook of instruction and an example of how God's people can live in difficult conditions and come through victoriously. Even as the Jewish people were living in Babylonian captivity, so Christians today are pilgrims and sojourners in a foreign culture. We, like Daniel and his friends, must exercise our implicit faith in God's purposes and leading for our lives. We too must resolve in advance that we will not be defiled by the world. And whether our God delivers us or not from the fiery furnace, we will remain faithful to Him (Daniel 3:17, 18).

Daniel and his friends also personify for us Christian courage at its best—not merely a desperate type of courage for some emergency situation, but a quiet steadfast courage that enables us to live in a Christ-like manner each day. It takes courage to be an unpopular minority when truth and right are involved. It takes courage to defend God's name when everyone else is using it in blasphemy. It takes courage to be another Daniel in a godless society.

This is another of the fine Sunday school songs by Philip P. Bliss, one of the truly important contributors to both early gospel hymnody and the rise of the Sunday school movement. Bliss, like many other Christian leaders, realized the unusual potential of teaching our youth spiritual truths through appropriate songs.

> Standing by a purpose true, heeding God's command, honor them, the faithful few! All hail to Daniel's Band!

> Many mighty men are lost, daring not to stand, who for God had been a host, by joining Daniel's Band!

> Many giants, great and tall, stalking thro' the land, headlong to the earth would fall, if met by Daniel's Band!

> Hold the gospel banner high! On to vict'ry grand! Satan and His host defy, and shout for Daniel's Band!

> **Refrain:** Dare to be a Daniel; dare to stand alone! Dare to have a purpose firm! Dare to make it known.

❦ *For Today:* Daniel 6:7, 10, 16, 22, 23; Psalm 27:14; Ephesians 6:11

God is still seeking people who by faith will dare to prove His greatness and will represent Him courageously—regardless of the circumstances. Let this musical line be the desire of your life—

I WOULD BE TRUE

Howard A. Walter, 1883-1918

I have chosen the way of truth; I have set my heart on Your laws. (Psalm 119:30)

The yearning to achieve a trustworthy, strong, brave yet humble character is an unusual goal for a young person, especially in today's self-seeking and materialistic society. The text for "I Would Be True," however, was written by a young man in his early twenties in a poem that he titled "My Creed."

After graduating with honors from Princeton University in 1905, Howard Arnold Walter spent a year teaching the English language in Japan. While there he sent a copy of his "creed" to his mother back home in Connecticut. Mrs. Walter sent the poem to *Harper's Magazine,* where it appeared in the May, 1907 issue.

Returning to the United States, Howard Walter entered Hartford Seminary and upon graduation served as an assistant minister at the Asylum Hill Congregational Church in Hartford, Connecticut. One day he showed his poem to an itinerant Methodist lay preacher, Joseph Peek. Although Peek had no technical knowledge of music, he immediately whistled a tune suited to Walter's words.

Several years later Howard Walter left for India to teach and minister to Mohammedan students. In 1918, a severe influenza epidemic there caused the death of this devoted young man. His credo lives on, however, in the numerous lives of those who have since sung this hymn and realized anew that God is more interested in what we are as a person than even what we may do for Him. In an environment today that can easily corrupt even the purest of minds, how important it is that we seek God's daily help to live a life that is true.

> I would be true, for there are those who trust me; I would be pure, for there are those who care. I would be strong, for there is much to suffer; I would be brave, for there is much to dare.
>
> I would be friend of all—the foe, the friendless; I would be giving, and forget the gift. I would be humble, for I know my weakness; I would look up, and laugh, and love, and lift.
>
> I would be prayerful thru each busy moment; I would be constantly in touch with God, I would be tuned to hear His slightest whisper; I would have faith to keep the path Christ trod.

❧ **For Today:** Psalm 51:2, 10; 2 Corinthians 7:1; Philippians 4:8

Make this credo your personal goal. Above all, be "in touch with God" and "tuned to his slightest whisper." Be a Christian who is known for his integrity. Carry this portion of the hymn with you as you go—

Joseph Yates Peek, 1843-1911

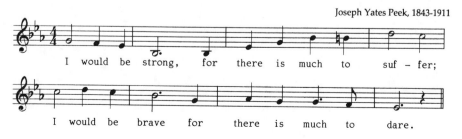

I would be strong, for there is much to suf - fer;

I would be brave for there is much to dare.

YIELD NOT TO TEMPTATION

Words and Music by Horatio R. Palmer, 1834-1907

Watch and pray so that you will not fall into temptation. (Matthew 26:41)

Temptations are common to everyone, even mature Christians. The noblest souls are often the ones most tempted. It seems that Satan assaults Christians in positions of leadership with his strongest weapons. Therefore, we must all be on our constant spiritual guard.

Jesus' 40 day temptation in the wilderness dramatically instructs us how to overcome Satan's attacks. In each temptation, Jesus answered the devil with Scripture. All of the scriptural quotations Jesus used were from the book of Deuteronomy, an indication of the importance of being well-acquainted with the Old Testament (Deuteronomy 8:3; Matthew 4:4).

It is impossible to isolate ourselves from all of life's temptations. The allurements of modern living are ever near. But we are not alone in this struggle. "We have One who has been tempted in every way, just as we are—yet without sin" (Hebrews 4:15). And "because He Himself suffered when He was tempted, He is able to help those who are being tempted" (Hebrews 2:18). Regardless of the temptation, our Lord understands what we are facing and stands ready to provide the strength to resist and to emerge victorious.

Horatio R. Palmer, author and composer, was an American musician. One day while he was working on a music theory exercise, the idea for this hymn suddenly came to him. He wrote it down as quickly as possible and with few exceptions the hymn has remained as it was written. The hymn has been an excellent teaching song for both young and old in learning how to face the daily temptations of life.

> Yield not to temptations for yielding is sin; each vict'ry will help you some other to win; fight manfully onward, dark passions subdue; look ever to Jesus—He'll carry you through.

> Shun evil companions, bad language disdain; God's name hold in rev'rence, nor take it in vain; be thoughtful and earnest, kind-hearted and true; look ever to Jesus—He'll carry you through.

> To him that o'er-cometh God giveth a crown; thru faith we will conquer tho often cast down; He who is our Savior our strength will renew; look ever to Jesus—He'll carry you through.

> **Chorus:** Ask the Savior to help you, comfort, strengthen and keep you; He is willing to aid you—He will carry you through.

🎵 *For Today:* Psalm 97:10; Matthew 6:13; 1 Corinthians 10:13; James 1:14, 15, 2 Peter 2:9; Revelation 3:10

Ask God to make you a victor over all temptations that may come your way. Carry this musical reminder to help you—

STANDING ON THE PROMISES

Words and Music by R. Kelso Carter, 1849-1928

For all the promises of God in Him are yea, and in Him Amen, unto the glory of God by us. (2 Corinthians 1:20 KJV)

All of us have times in life when a crisis or problem seems larger than we can possibly bear, and we become very fearful. Often, however, the Lord has to get our attention through such an adversity to cause us once more to rely solely on His promises.

Bible scholars have pointed our that the phrase "fear not" appears in the Bible 365 times—a reassuring promise for each day of the year. A daily dependence upon the divine promises is the only real remedy for our human fears. Often even well-intentioned parents make hasty promises to their children, promises they are unable to fulfill. How different are the promises of God! They are "yea and amen," the only assurances on which we can securely stand.

The author and composer, Russell Kelso Carter, was an unusually talented and versatile person. At various times in his 79 year lifetime he was an athlete, an active Methodist minister, a sheep rancher, a professor and publisher of various textbooks, and in his later years a practicing physician in Baltimore. In addition to "Standing on the Promises," Carter wrote a number of other hymn texts and tunes as well as assisting in compiling the 1891 hymnal *Hymns for the Christian Life* for the Christian Missionary Alliance denomination. Mr. Carter's fruitful life reflects the truth of this hymn—that only as we stand on God's promises are we enabled to live with purpose for God's glory.

> Standing on the promises of Christ my King, thru eternal ages let His praises ring; glory in the highest I will shout and sing, standing on the promises of God.
>
> Standing on the promises that cannot fail, when the howling storms of doubt and fear assail, by the living Word of God I shall prevail, standing on the promises of God.
>
> Standing on the promises of Christ the Lord, bound to Him eternally by love's strong cord, overcoming daily with the Spirit's sword, standing on the promises of God.
>
> Standing on the promises I now can see perfect, present cleansing in the blood for me; standing in the liberty where Christ makes free, standing on the promises of God,
>
> Standing on the promises I cannot fall, list'ning ev'ry moment to the Spirit's call, resting in my Savior as my all in all, standing on the promises of God.
>
> **Chorus:** Standing, standing, standing on the promises of God my Savior. Standing, standing, I'm standing on the promises of God.

❧ *For Today:* Psalm 34:18; Psalm 55:22; 2 Peter 1:4

Claim a scriptural promise as especially for you this day. Live confidently in its truth. Carry this tune as a reminder—

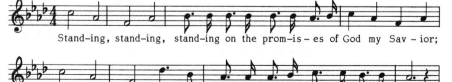

Stand–ing, stand–ing, stand–ing on the prom–is–es of God my Sav–ior;

Stand – ing, stand – ing, I'm stand – ing on the prom – is – es of God.

MORE SECURE IS NO ONE EVER

Lina Sandell Berg, 1832-1903

My salvation and my honor depend on God; He is my mighty rock, my refuge. (Psalm 62:7)

A sincere love for God and a heart filled with gratitude following a miraculous healing experience prompted the tender lines of this hymn, set to a child-like Swedish folk melody.

Lina Sandell was the daughter of a Lutheran pastor in Smöland, Sweden. Since early childhood she had been confined to bed with a paralysis that doctors considered hopeless. One Sunday morning, while her parents were at church, Lina began reading her Bible and praying. She was suddenly healed. With a thankful heart, Lina began writing verses that expressed her feelings for God. As a result, at the age of 16 she published her first book of meditations and poems. One of her earliest hymn texts during this time was "Tryggare Kan Ingen Vara" or "More Secure Is No One Ever."

In the following years Lina had experiences that must have tested her faith, as expressed in a stanza of this hymn—"What He takes or what He gives us . . ." When she was 26, Lina accompanied her father on a trip across Lake Vattern. When the ship lurched suddenly, Pastor Sandell was thrown overboard and drowned as his devoted daughter stood helplessly by. Then after her marriage to C. O. Berg, Lina met tragedy once more with the death of their first son at birth.

Lina's sweet trusting faith in her Lord did not seem shaken by the sorrows in her life. Instead, more songs than ever began to flow from her broken heart. In all, she wrote more than 650 hymns before her death in 1903. These heart-warming gospel songs had much influence on the powerful revival surge that swept the Scandinavian countries during the mid-19th century. And still today these words minister to our lives:

> More secure is no one ever than the loved ones of the Savior—not yon star on high abiding, nor the bird in home-nest hiding.

> Neither life nor death can ever from the Lord His children sever, for His love and deep compassion comforts them in tribulation.

> Little flock to joy then yield thee! Jacob's God will ever shield thee; rest secure with this Defender—At His will all foes surrender.

> What He takes or what He gives us shows the Father's love so precious; we may trust His purpose wholly—'Tis His children's welfare solely.

❧ *For Today:* Matthew 18:14; 2 Thessalonians 3:3; 1 Peter 5:10, 11

Rest securely in the love and protection of your heavenly Father—much like a child in the arms of a parent. Allow this hymn to help you realize that—

Tryggare Kan Ingen Vara tune   Swedish melody

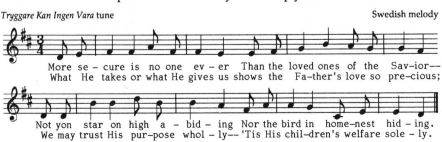

More se - cure is no one ev - er Than the loved ones of the Sav-ior—
What He takes or what He gives us shows the Fa-ther's love so pre-cious;

Not yon star on high a - bid - ing Nor the bird in home-nest hid - ing.
We may trust His pur-pose whol - ly— 'Tis His chil-dren's welfare sole - ly.

LEANING ON THE EVERLASTING ARMS

Elisha A. Hoffman, 1839-1929

The eternal God is your refuge, and underneath are the everlasting arms.
(Deuteronomy 33:27)

When close friends or family members turn to us for comfort in their grief following the loss of a loved one, often we find it difficult to express just the right words of consolation. One day successful author, business man, and devout Presbyterian layman Anthony J. Showalter received sorrowful letters from two different friends, telling him of their recent bereavements. In sending messages of comfort to them, Mr. Showalter included Deuteronomy 33:27—

"The eternal God is your refuge, and underneath are the everlasting arms . . . "

As he concluded his letters the thought occurred to him that this verse would be a fine theme for a hymn. Almost spontaneously he jotted down the words and music for the refrain of this soon-to-be favorite.

Feeling that he should have some assistance in completing a text based on this comforting verse from Deuteronomy, Mr. Showalter asked his friend Elisha A. Hoffman, a pastor and author of more than 2,000 gospel songs, to furnish the stanzas. The hymn then was published in 1887 in the *Glad Evangel for Revival, Camp and Evangelistic Meetings Hymnal.*

It is not surprising that "Leaning on the Everlasting Arms," with its assurance of God's steadfast care and guidance and the peace that is ours as we enjoy the intimacy of His fellowship, has been another of the gospel song favorites enjoyed by all ages. Each day we need to relearn the truths of these words:

> What a fellowship, what a joy divine, leaning on the everlasting arms; what a blessedness, what a peace is mine, leaning on the everlasting arms.

> O how sweet to walk in this pilgrim way, leaning on the everlasting arms; O how bright the path grows from day to day, leaning on the everlasting arms.

> What have I to dread, what have I to fear, leaning on the everlasting arms? I have blessed peace with my Lord so near, leaning on the everlasting arms.

> **Chorus:** Leaning, leaning, safe and secure from all alarms; leaning, leaning, leaning on the everlasting arms.

❦ *For Today:* Psalm 17:8; Psalm 57:1; Psalm 91:2; Proverbs 14:26; 1 John 1:7

When the events of today seem difficult, or even overwhelming, apply the lesson of leaning on "those everlasting arms," as you learn to rest and relax in His loving care. Share the truth of Deuteronomy 33:27 with another needing encouragement. Use this little musical message as your theme song for today—

A. J. Showalter, 1858-1924

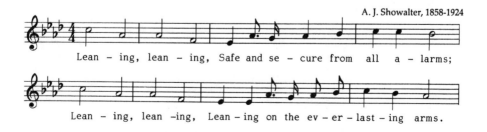

Lean - ing, lean - ing, Safe and se - cure from all a - larms;

Lean - ing, lean - ing, Lean - ing on the ev - er - last - ing arms.

TRUST AND OBEY

John H. Sammis, 1846-1919

But Samuel replied, "Does the Lord delight in burnt offerings and sacrifices as much as in obeying the voice of the Lord? To obey is better than sacrifice, and to heed is better than the fat of rams." (1 Samuel 15:22)

Life can often be a restless, disrupted existence until we give ourselves wholeheartedly to something beyond ourselves and follow and obey it supremely. Such implicit trust in God's great love and wisdom with a sincere desire to follow His leading should be every Christian's goal. Our willingness to trust and obey is always the first step toward God's blessing in our lives.

In 1886 Daniel B. Towner, director of the music department at Moody Bible Institute, was leading the music for evangelist D. L. Moody's series of meetings in Brockton, Massachusetts. A young man rose to give a testimony, saying, "I am not quite sure—but I am going to trust, and I am going to obey." Mr. Towner jotted down this statement and sent it to the Rev. J. H. Sammis, a Presbyterian minister and later a teacher at Moody, who wrote the present five stanzas.

Salvation is God's responsibility. Our responsibility is to trust in that salvation and then to obey its truths. "Trust and Obey" presents a balanced view of a believer's trust in Christ's redemptive work, and it speaks of the resulting desire to obey Him and do His will in our daily lives. Then, and only then, do we experience real peace and joy.

> When we walk with the Lord in the light of His Word, what a glory He sheds on our way! While we do His good will He abides with us still, and with all who will trust and obey.

> Not a shadow can rise, not a cloud in the skies, but His smile quickly drives it away; not a doubt nor a fear, not a sigh nor a tear, can abide while we trust and obey.

> Not a burden we bear, not a sorrow we share, but our toil He doth richly repay; not a grief nor a loss, not a frown nor a cross, but is blest if we trust and obey.

> But we never can prove the delights of His love until all on the altar we lay, for the favor He shows and the joy He bestows are for them who will trust and obey.

> Then in fellowship sweet we will sit at His feet, or we'll walk by His side in the way; what He says we will do, where He sends we will go—Never fear, only trust and obey.

> **Chorus:** Trust and obey—for there's no other way to be happy in Jesus—but to trust and obey.

🐦 ***For Today:*** Psalm 37:3-5; John 8:31; John 14:23; James 2:14-26; 1 John 2:6

Experience the glory and abiding presence of Christ as you determine to trust Him more completely and obey His leading more fully in all that you do. Carry this musical reminder with you remembering—

Daniel B. Towner, 1850-1919

Trust and o - bey— For there's no oth - er way To be hap - py in Je - sus— But to trust and o - bey.

I MUST TELL JESUS

Words and Music by Elisha A. Hoffman 1839-1929

The Lord stood at my side and gave me strength. . . . (2 Timothy 4:17)

Oh, help me, Lord, to take the time
To set all else aside,
That in the secret place of prayer
I may with you abide.   —*Unknown*

One of the loneliest feelings we can have comes when we face a time of need without having a loving friend to talk to about it. Everyone needs at least one trusted friend in whom to confide.

Pastor Elisha A. Hoffman, author and composer of more than 2,000 gospel songs, gives the following account of the writing of this well-loved hymn:

> During a pastorate in Lebanon, Pennsylvania, there was a woman to whom God permitted many visitations of sorrow and affliction. Coming to her home one day, I found her much discouraged. She unburdened her heart, concluding with the question, "Brother Hoffman, what shall I do? What shall I do?" I quoted from the Word, then added, "You cannot do better than to take all of your sorrows to Jesus. You must tell Jesus."
>
> For a moment she seemed lost in mediation. Then her eyes lighted as she exclaimed, "Yes, I must tell Jesus."
>
> As I left her home I had a vision of that joy-illuminated face . . . and I heard all along my pathway the echo, "I must tell Jesus . . . I must tell Jesus."

Pastor Hoffman quickly wrote the words and soon completed the music as well. Since its publication in 1894 in *Pentecostal Hymns,* this hymn text has reminded many believers that they have a heavenly Friend who is always available to hear and help:

> I must tell Jesus all of my trials; I cannot bear these burdens alone: In my distress He kindly will help me; He ever loves and cares for His own.
>
> I must tell Jesus all of my troubles; He is a kind, compassionate friend; if I but ask Him, He will deliver, make of my troubles quickly an end.
>
> O how the world to evil allures me! O how my heart is tempted to sin! I must tell Jesus, and He will help me over the world the vict'ry to win.
>
> **Chorus:** I must tell Jesus! I must tell Jesus! I cannot bear my burdens alone; I must tell Jesus! I must tell Jesus! Jesus can help me, Jesus alone.

❦ *For Today:* Psalm 6:9; Proverbs 14:26; John 14:14; Hebrews 2:18; Hebrews 10:22

Determine to go to Jesus with all of the concerns, temptations or trials that may arise. Share this truth with another who may also be hurting. Carry this tune with you knowing that—

I must tell Je-sus! I must tell Je-sus! I can-not bear my bur-dens a - lone;

I must tell Je-sus! I must tell Je-sus! Je-sus can help me, Je-sus a - lone.

BE THOU MY VISION

Text—Irish hymn, c. 8th century • Music—Irish Melody
Translated by Mary E. Byrne, 1880-1931
Versified by Eleanor H. Hull, 1860-1935

Where there is no vision, the people perish: but he that keepeth the law, happy is he. (Proverbs 29:18)

Truly our visionary attitude throughout life is often the difference between success and mediocrity. One is reminded of the classic story of the two shoe salesmen who were sent to a primitive island to determine business potential. The first salesman wired back, "Coming home immediately. No one here wears shoes." The second man responded, "Send a boatload of shoes immediately. The possibilities for selling shoes here are unlimited."

For the Christian, vision is a true awareness of Christ in all of His fullness and enabling power. This ancient 8th century hymn text from Ireland is still meaningful for us today with its expression of a yearning for the presence and leading of God in our lives. The earnest prayer is enhanced by such quaint but tender phrases as "Lord of my heart," "Thy presence my light," "bright heav'n's Sun," and "heart of my heart." The text states that when we allow God to have first place in our lives, He becomes our treasure; we care no more for the pursuit of riches or "man's empty praise."

The entire Irish poem was first translated into English in 1905 by Mary Bryne, a research worker and writer for the Board of Intermediate Education in Dublin, Ireland. Several years later Eleanor Hull, a writer of English history and literature, put the prose into verse form and included it in her book of poems, *The Poem Book of the Gael.* The melody for this hymn is a traditional Irish tune.

Be Thou my Vision, O Lord of my heart—Nought be all else to me save that Thou art: Thou my best thought, by day or by night—waking or sleeping, Thy presence my light.

Be Thou my Wisdom, and Thou my true Word—I ever with Thee and Thou with me, Lord; Thou my great Father, I Thy true Son—Thou in me dwelling, and I with Thee one.

Riches I heed not, nor man's empty praise—Thou mine inheritance, now and always; Thou and Thou only, first in my heart—High King of heaven, my Treasure Thou art.

High King of heaven, my victory won, may I reach heaven's joys, O bright heav'n's Sun! Heart of my own heart, whatever befall, still be my Vision, O Ruler of all.

❦ *For Today:* Matthew 13:44-52; Ephesians 2:13-22; Philippians 3:12

Ask God to give you a vision of some task that you can do for Him that will require your complete reliance upon His enabling power to accomplish it well. Carry this hymn with you—

Published by Chatto and Windus, Limited, London, England.

HIGHER GROUND

Johnson Oatman Jr., 1856-1922

I press on toward the goal to win the prize for which God has called me heavenward in Christ Jesus. (Philippians 3:14)

How sad it is to observe someone who has never lived up to his real potential. It is tragic to watch an individual who has great ability that is never used simply because he or she lacks the incentive to pursue a worthy goal. Similarly, it is disappointing to see a Christian fail to evidence spiritual growth of any kind. Scripture teaches that Christian maturity or Christlikeness is a process in which we advance from one level to the next, step by step. But the secret of such development is to have an intense desire to fulfill the purpose God has for our lives.

"Higher Ground" has been a favorite with many Christians since it was first published in 1898. It expresses so well this universal desire for a deeper spiritual life, continuing on a higher plane of fellowship with God than we have ever before experienced.

The author of this stirring text was Johnson Oatman, Jr., a businessman who wrote 3,000 gospel songs in his leisure time. Oatman was ordained by the Methodist Episcopal denomination but never pastored a church. His hymns were always well received, even though he was paid no more than $1.00 for any of his texts.

The music for "Higher Ground" was composed by Charles H. Gabriel, music editor of the Rodeheaver Publishing Company. He wrote the music and sometimes the texts for more than 8,000 gospel songs, many of which were especially popular in the Billy Sunday-Homer Rodeheaver campaigns from 1910-1920. This song was used often in the great camp meetings of this era and the singing of it would often bring forth shouts of "Glory, hallelujah!"

> I'm pressing on the upward way; new heights I'm gaining every day— Still praying as I'm onward bound, "Lord, plant my feet on higher ground."

> My heart has no desire to stay where doubts arise and fears dismay; tho some may dwell where these abound, my prayer, my aim is higher ground.

> I want to live above the world, tho Satan's darts at me are hurled; for faith has caught the joyful sound, the song of saints on higher ground.

> I want to scale the utmost height and catch a gleam of glory bright; but still I'll pray till heav'n I've found, "Lord, lead me on to higher ground."

> **Chorus:** Lord, lift me up and let me stand by faith on heaven's table-land; A higher plane than I have found—Lord, plant my feet on higher ground.

❦ *For Today:* Matthew 6:33; 1 Corinthians 9:24-27; Philippians 3:12-16

Reflect on some particular area of life that with God's enablement could be lived on a higher level. Use this musical prayer to help—

Charles H. Gabriel, 1856-1932

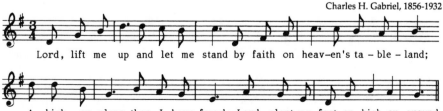

Lord, lift me up and let me stand by faith on heav–en's ta – ble – land;

A high – er plane than I have found––Lord, plant my feet on high–er ground.

REDEEMED

Fanny J. Crosby, 1820-1915

Give thanks to the Lord, for he is good; His love endures forever. Let the redeemed of the Lord say this— (Psalm 107:1, 2)

All my theology is reduced to this narrow compass—Christ Jesus came into this world to save sinners. —*Archibald Alexander*

The word *redeemed* implies the idea of a slave standing on the trader's auction block being offered to the highest bidder. At last the price is paid by a compassionate new owner, who then gives the slave his unconditional freedom. But the freed slave, out of gratitude to his new owner, offers himself as a loving bond servant for life to his redeemer.

Man has been separated from God by sin and has become a slave of Satan. But man has been redeemed. Because Christ paid the ransom we owed to divine justice, we have been freed from the shackles of sin's bondage and God's eternal wrath. Out of gratitude for this deliverance, we cling to our new master and lovingly determine to serve Him forever. A realization of redemption causes the ransomed to sing repeatedly, "Redeemed—how I love to proclaim it, redeemed by the blood of the Lamb. . . ."

This popular gospel song by Fanny Crosby first appeared with William Kirkpatrick's jubilant tune in the hymnal *Songs of Redeeming Love*, published in 1882. It is another of the more than 8,000 hymns by the blind American poetess, Fanny Jane Crosby, the most important writer of gospel hymn texts in American history.

Redeemed—how I love to proclaim it! Redeemed by the blood of the Lamb; redeemed thru His infinite mercy —His child, and forever, I am.

Redeemed and so happy in Jesus; no language my rapture can tell; I know that the light of His presence with me doth continually dwell.

I think of my blessed Redeemer. I think of Him all the day long; I sing, for I cannot be silent; His love is the theme of my song.

I know I shall see in His beauty the King in whose law I delight, who lovingly guardeth my footsteps and giveth me songs in the night.

Chorus: Redeemed, redeemed, redeemed by the blood of the Lamb; redeemed, redeemed, His child, and forever, I am.

❧ *For Today:* Romans 3:24-26; Ephesians 1:7; Colossians 1:12-14; 1 Peter 1:18, 19

One of the strongest evidences for the validity of the gospel is a redeemed, vibrant life. Determine with the Holy Spirit's help to be such a demonstration. Carry this musical testimony with you as you go—

William J. Kirkpatrick, 1838-1921

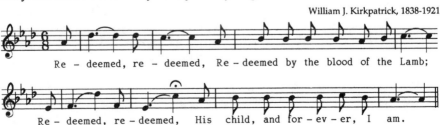

Re - deemed, re - deemed, Re - deemed by the blood of the Lamb;

Re - deemed, re - deemed, His child, and for - ev - er, I am.

NOTHING BUT THE BLOOD

Words and Music by Robert Lowry, 1826-1899

". . . without the shedding of blood there is no forgiveness." (Hebrews 9:22)

The teaching of the Bible, in both the Old and New Testaments, is very clear regarding God's forgiveness of man's sin. Only a perfect blood sacrifice would satisfy the Father's requirement of holiness. Throughout the Old Testament much is told about the blood atonements that the priests had to make on behalf of their people (Exodus 30:10; Leviticus 17:11). But the blood of bulls and goats could never satisfy God's justice for man's past, present and future sin. Only the shedding of divine blood would do. The Father's gift of salvation to man required His Son's live blood. Now when God looks at us, He sees Christ's shed blood and declares us righteous for Jesus' sake. Our acceptance with God the Father rests completely upon the merits of the blood of Jesus Christ.

> Not all the blood of beasts on Jewish altars slain
> Could give the guilty conscience peace, or wash away the stain.
> But Christ, the heav'nly Lamb, takes all our sins away;
> A sacrifice of nobler name and richer blood than they.   —*Isaac Watts*

Robert Lowry was a popular Baptist pastor in various churches throughout the East. In later life he became interested in writing and publishing gospel songs. Today he is best remembered for his many contributions to our hymnal with songs such as "Nothing But the Blood," published in 1876. Though simply stated both textually and musically (a five note melodic range and just two chords), this gospel song has had an important place in the church's ministry in teaching both young and old the absolute necessity of trusting implicitly in the precious blood of Christ for this life and for eternity.

> What can wash away my sin? Nothing but the blood of Jesus; what can make me whole again? Nothing but the blood of Jesus.
>
> For my pardon this I see—nothing but the blood of Jesus; for my cleansing, this my plea—nothing but the blood of Jesus.
>
> Nothing can for sin atone—nothing but the blood of Jesus; naught of good that I have done—nothing but the blood of Jesus.
>
> This is all my hope and peace—nothing but the blood of Jesus; this is all my righteousness—nothing but the blood of Jesus.
>
> **Refrain:** Oh! precious is the flow that makes me white as snow; no other fount I know, nothing but the blood of Jesus.

❦ *For Today:* Isaiah 1:18; Zechariah 13:1; Romans 3:24, 25; Revelation 12:11

Recognize anew your total dependence on Christ's shed blood. Thank Him with these musical lines—

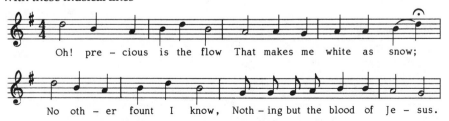

THERE SHALL BE SHOWERS OF BLESSING
Daniel W. Whittle, 1840-1901

I will send down showers in season; there will be showers of blessing. (Ezekiel 34:26)

How disheartening it is to see a once fertile field that has been rendered hardened and useless by a drought. Land that was intended to produce a rich harvest for its owner lies barren and lifeless. As Christians, God desires that our lives bear much fruit for Him. But the soil of our hearts must be right if we want the seeds of righteousness to grow. The parable of the sower in Matthew 13 teaches that it is possible to have four different kinds of soil in our lives: An unconcerned soil, a shallow soil, a polluted soil, and a good soil—one that responds and produces a bountiful harvest.

At times many Christians feel as though they are in a spiritual drought. God seems removed. Spiritual activities are just routine business. Prayer and Bible reading become monotonous. Christian friends seem critical and irritating. We feel that life is really a valley of dry bones (Ezekiel 37:1-4). Then we cry out to God for a fresh outpouring of His grace, not just drops of mercy but showers of blessing. And soon the answer comes—perhaps in the form of a Scripture passage, a sermon, a song, an encouraging remark, a new insight. Our souls revive and we are once again able to "raise a harvest of righteousness" (James 3:18).

"There Will Be Showers of Blessing" was the product of one of the outstanding gospel duos of the past century, Major Daniel Whittle, the evangelist, and musician James McGranahan. Together these two travelled extensively for a number of years in a very successful evangelism ministry. They also collaborated on a number of popular gospel songs still widely used today. This hymn first appeared in *Gospel Hymns No. 4,* 1883.

"There shall be showers of blessing"—this is the promise of love; there shall be seasons refreshing, sent from the Savior above.

"There shall be showers of blessing"—precious reviving again; over the hills and the valleys sound of abundance of rain.

"There shall be showers of blessing"—send them upon us, O Lord; grant to us now a refreshing; come and now honor Thy Word.

"There shall be showers of blessing"—O that today they might fall, now as to God we're confessing, now as on Jesus we call!

Chorus: Showers of blessing, showers of blessing we need; mercy drops round us are falling, but for the showers we plead.

❦ *For Today:* Genesis 12:3; Deuteronomy 7:13; Psalm 72:6; 1 Peter 1:3

If perhaps you should feel "spiritually dry," first reflect on the condition of the soil of your heart. Then claim God's promise for "showers of blessing." Sing as you go—

James McGranahan, 1840-1907

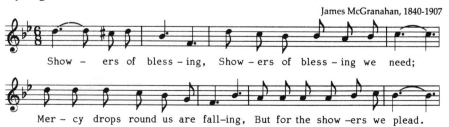

Show - ers of bless - ing, Show - ers of bless - ing we need;

Mer - cy drops round us are fall-ing, But for the show -ers we plead.

LET THE LOWER LIGHTS BE BURNING

Words and Music by Philip P. Bliss, 1838-1876

Let your light shine before men, that they may see your good deeds and praise your Father in heaven. (Matthew 5:16)

> I do not ask for mighty words to leave the crowd impressed,
> But grant my life may ring so true my neighbors shall be blessed.
> I do not ask for influence to sway the multitude;
> Give me a "word in season" for the soul in solitude.   —*Unknown*

The lower lights surrounding a lighthouse guide the boats in the harbor away from the treacherous rocks and into the channel. The interesting analogy in this hymn was suggested to author and composer Philip P. Bliss as he listened to D. L. Moody tell a sermon anecdote about a pilot during a storm.

"Brethren," concluded Mr. Moody, "the Master will take care of the great lighthouse. Let us keep the lower lights burning." Bliss, as he often did, immediately put this challenging thought into a hymn. He usually worked rapidly, completing both the text and the music in one sitting.

Bliss first met Dwight L. Moody in Chicago in 1869 and soon joined him and his music associate, Ira Sankey, in their evangelistic campaigns. A prolific composer of gospel hymns, Bliss continued to write and publish until his death at the age of 38 in a tragic train accident at Ashtabula, Ohio, during the Christmas season of 1876. Yet his many songs, including "Jesus Loves Even Me," "Hold the Fort," "Hallelujah, What a Savior," "Wonderful Words of Life," and many more, still live on today to bless and inspire our lives.

We may not all be powerful lighthouses, such as Mr. Moody, Ira Sankey, or Philip Bliss, but God calls us each to be "lower lights" wherever we are to guide some fainting, struggling person to the eternal haven with deeds that direct all the praise to our heavenly Father.

> Brightly beams our Father's mercy from His lighthouse evermore, but to us He gives the keeping of the lights along the shore.
>
> Dark the night of sin has settled. Loud the angry billows roar; eager eyes are watching, longing for the lights along the shore.
>
> Trim your feeble lamp, my brother! Some poor sailor tempest tossed, trying now to make the harbor, in the darkness may be lost.
>
> **Chorus:** Let the lower lights be burning! Send a gleam across the wave! Some poor fainting, struggling seaman you may rescue, you may save.

❦   *For Today:*   Daniel 12:3; Matthew 5:1-16; James 5:19, 20

Resolve to keep a gleam burning for Christ by words and actions so that some seeking individual may be directed into a calm and secure relationship with the Lord. Use this musical message as a reminder—

Let the low - er lights be burn–ing! Send a gleam a –cross the wave!

Some poor faint - ing, strug–gling sea–man You may res–cue, you may save.

WHEN HE COMETH

William O. Cushing, 1823-1902

When Christ, who is your life, appears, then you also will appear with Him in glory. (Colossians 3:4)

The scriptural promise of Christ's second coming is always a thrilling truth for believers to ponder. Beyond that, the thought of the Savior creating a jeweled crown from little children who love Him is a fascinating pictorial concept. William Orcutt Cushing conceived the idea for his "Jewel Song" text from the promise in Malachi 3:17: "And they shall be mine, saith the Lord of Hosts, in that day when I make up my jewels." Pastor Cushing wrote the text for the children in his own Sunday school in 1856.

Several years later, William Cushing suffered a period of deep despair in his life. After the death of his wife, he developed a creeping paralysis and the loss of his speech at the age of 47. He was forced to retire from the ministry after 27 years as an active and successful pastor in Disciples of Christ churches. When he pleaded, "Lord, give me something to do for Thee," God answered, giving him the gift of writing appealing hymn texts. He worked with such talented musicians as Ira Sankey and George Root to produce more than 300 gospel hymns during his remaining years. Such hymns as "Hiding in Thee," "Under His Wings," and "There'll Be No Dark Valley" are just a few of his texts that have since contributed much to the lives of Christians everywhere.

William Cushing's picturesque words in today's hymn, "They shall shine in their beauty—bright gems for His crown," could also be used to describe his own qualities of character. He was known by his many friends to be a noble, sweet, deeply spiritual Christian. Loved by all, Cushing continued to inspire and encourage others despite his handicap until the end of his life at the age of 79.

> When He cometh, when he cometh to make up His jewels, all His jewels, precious jewels, His loved and His own.
>
> He will gather, He will gather the gems for His kingdom, all the pure ones, all the bright ones, His loved and His own.
>
> Little children, little children who love their Redeemer, are the jewels, precious jewels, His loved and His own.
>
> **Chorus:** Like the stars of the morning, His bright crown adorning, they shall shine in their beauty—bright gems for His crown.

❦ ***For Today:*** Zechariah 9:16; Matthew 16:27; Matthew 24:27, 29, 30, 31, 36, 42, 44; Acts 1:11; Titus 2:12, 13

Strive to live in the expectancy that Christ could return today. Carry this little children's hymn with you. Share the truth of this song with your family as you have opportunity.

George F. Root, 1820-1895

WE ARE CLIMBING JACOB'S LADDER

Negro Spiritual

He had a dream in which he saw a stairway resting on earth, with its top reaching to heaven, and the angels of God were ascending and descending on it. (Genesis 28:12)

This delightful children's song was inspired by the account of Jacob's dream at Bethel as recorded in Genesis 28:10-22. In this dream, Jacob saw a stairway or ladder resting on earth with its top reaching to heaven, with God's angels or messengers ascending and descending on it.

From Jacob's dream we learn that the gap between earth and heaven can be bridged. Although God revealed Himself in times past to various individuals as He did to Jacob, His full self-revelation required a God-Man—the Son of God in all of His deity and the Son of Man in full humanity to span the mighty gulf. Jesus Christ became the "ladder" for man to reach heaven and to enjoy even now a restored fellowship with the heavenly Father.

In times past, God used dreams to speak to people, as He did to Job (Job 33:15), Joseph (Genesis 37:5-9), Solomon (1 Kings 3:5, 15), Daniel (Daniel 7) and the wise men (Matthew 2:11-12). But with the completion of the Bible, our divine guidance is much more reliably known through the Holy Spirit's illumination of the Scriptures than through dreams and visions that we may experience. In fact, God's Word clearly warns against this kind of instruction (Jeremiah 23:16). It is this claim to extra revelation that forms the basis of all false cults.

As is true of all real spirituals and folk songs, there is no known author or composer of "Jacob's Ladder." It was first heard about 1825, and it has been a favorite with young and old since.

> We are climbing Jacob's ladder; we are climbing Jacob's ladder; we are climbing Jacob's ladder, soldiers of the cross.
>
> Sinner, do you love my Jesus? Sinner, do you love my Jesus? Sinner, do you love my Jesus? soldiers of the cross.
>
> If you love Him, why not serve Him? If you love Him, why not serve Him? If you love Him why not serve Him? soldiers of the cross.
>
> We are climbing higher, higher; we are climbing higher, higher; we are climbing higher, higher, soldiers of the cross.

❦ *For Today:* Genesis 27, 28, 29; John 1:51; Ephesians 4:13; 2 Peter 3:18

Keep this perspective in all you do: As Christians we are merely travelers in this life, moving forward and upward to our heavenly home. Even now, however, we have God's messengers to help us live victoriously. Give Christ your thanks for making all of this possible. Use this little spiritual to help you as you reflect on these truths—

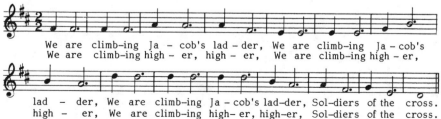

WE'RE MARCHING TO ZION

Isaac Watts, 1674-1748

You have come to Mount Zion, to the heavenly Jerusalem, the city of the living God. (Hebrews 12:22)

Should we sing psalms or hymns in our church services? This was the controversy stirring many congregations during the 17th and 18th centuries. Isaac Watts was the life-long champion of the "humanly composed" hymn while the majority of the English-speaking churches insisted on the traditional psalm settings. Tempers frequently flared, and some churches actually split in the heat of this decidedly unharmonious musical conflict. In some churches a compromise was reached. The psalm setting would be sung in the early part of the service with a hymn used at the close, during which time the parishioners could leave or simple refuse to sing.

Isaac Watts' "Come, We That Love the Lord" was no doubt written in part to refute his critics, who termed his hymns "Watts' Whims," as well as to provide some subtle barbs for those who refused to sing his hymns: "Let those refuse to sing who never knew our God; but children of the heavenly King may speak their joys abroad." The hymn first appeared in Watts' *Hymns and Spiritual Songs of 1707* and was titled "Heavenly Joy on Earth."

Still today there exists a controversy within some evangelical congregations regarding the use of traditional versus contemporary sacred music. Although we may each have our own preference, cultural differences such as this should never be a cause for disrupting the unity of any group of believers. This epigram by Augustine, the early church theologian, is still worthy of our earnest consideration: "Let there be in the essentials, unity. In all non-essentials, liberty. In all things, charity."

Come, we that love the Lord, and let our joys be known; join in a song with sweet accord, and thus surround the throne.

Let those refuse to sing who never knew our God; but children of the heav'nly King may speak their joys abroad.

The hill of Zion yields a thousand sacred sweets before we reach the heav'nly fields, or walk the golden streets.

Then let our songs abound and ev'ry tear be dry; we're marching thru Immanuel's ground to fairer worlds on high.

Chorus: We're marching to Zion, beautiful, beautiful Zion; we're marching upward to Zion, the beautiful city of God.

❦ *For Today:* Psalm 149:1; Isaiah 35:10; Habakkuk 3:17, 18; 1 Peter 4:13

Determine to follow the suggestion of this hymn: "Let our joys [not our minor differences] be known and thus surround the throne." Rejoice in the truth that the best is yet to come—"fairer worlds on high."

Robert Lowry, 1826-1899

We're march-ing to Zi - on, Beau-ti - ful, beau - ti- ful Zi - on;

We're march - ing up - ward to Zi - on the beau - ti - ful cit - y of God.

WHEN THE ROLL IS CALLED UP YONDER

Words and Music by James M. Black, 1856-1938

For the Lord Himself will come down from heaven, with a loud command, with the voice of the archangel and with the trumpet call of God, and the dead in Christ will rise first. (1 Thessalonians 4:15)

The calm assurance of a future heavenly home is one of the greatest blessings for every Christian. It has been said that only those with an absolute confidence in their hereafter truly know to live victoriously in this life. Having a personal relationship with Christ means that we need have no fear that we will not hear "the trumpet call of God," whether we are still alive or asleep in Jesus.

James M. Black was an active Methodist layman, a music teacher, and a composer and publisher of numerous gospel songs. He related this experience:

> While a teacher in the Sunday school and president of a young people's society , I one day met a girl, 14 years old, poorly clad and a child of a drunkard. She accepted my invitation to attend the Sunday school and join the young people's society. One evening at a consecration meeting, when members answered the roll call by repeating Scripture texts, she failed to respond. I spoke of what a sad thing it would be when our names are called from the Lamb's Book of Life, if one of us should be absent. When I reached my home, my wife saw that I was deeply troubled. Then the words in the first stanza came to me in full. In fifteen minutes more, I had composed the other two verses. Going to the piano, I played the music just as it is found today in the hymnbooks.

The subsequent death of the missing girl from pneumonia, after an illness of just 10 days, furnished the dramatic finale to this account and gives a poignancy to the "roll call" song. Since its publication in 1894, this simply worded gospel song with its rather ordinary music has captured the hearts of innumerable believers. These sincere expressions have provided Christians with a singable vehicle of praise for the glorious future that still awaits them.

> When the trumpet of the Lord shall sound and time shall be no more, and the morning breaks eternal bright and fair— When the saved of earth shall gather over on the other shore, and the roll is called up yonder I'll be there.

> On that bright and cloudless morning when the dead in Christ shall rise and the glory of His resurrection share— When the chosen ones shall gather to their home beyond the skies, and the roll is called up yonder I'll be there.

> Let us labor for the Master from the dawn till setting sun. Let us talk of all His wondrous love and care; then when all of life is over and our work on earth is done, and the roll is called up yonder I'll be there.

> **Chorus:** When the roll is called up yonder, when the roll is called up yonder, when the roll is called up yonder—when the roll is call up yonder I'll be there.

❧ *For Today:* John 6:40; 1 Corinthians 15:40-42; 1 Thessalonians 4:13-18

Give God praise for the certainty about your eternal destiny that you as a child of God enjoy. Live this day in that confidence.

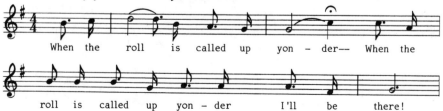

WHEN WE ALL GET TO HEAVEN

Eliza E. Hewitt, 1851-1920

After that, we who are still alive and are left will be caught up with them in the clouds to meet the Lord in the air. And so we will be with the Lord forever. Therefore encourage each other with these words. (1 Thessalonians 4:17, 18)

For the child of God, the end of this earthly pilgrimage is just the beginning of a glorious new life.

> This glorious hope revives our courage for the way,
> When each in expectation lives and longs to see the day
> When from sorrow, toil, pain and sin, we shall be free,
> And perfect love and joy shall reign throughout all eternity. *—John Fawcett*

Our services of worship even now should be a foretaste of that day of rejoicing when those from every tribe, language, people, and nation see our Lord and together "we'll sing and shout the victory."

The author of this hymn text, Eliza Hewitt, a school teacher in Philadelphia, was another Christian lay worker deeply devoted to the Sunday school movement during the latter half of the 19th century. Like many of the other gospel song writers of this time, Eliza wrote her songs with the goal of reaching and teaching children with the truths of the gospel. She often attended the Methodist camp meetings at Ocean Grove, New Jersey. It was here that she collaborated with Emily Wilson, wife of a Methodist District Superintendent in Philadelphia, in the writing of this popular gospel hymn, a favorite of both young and old alike. It was first published in 1898.

The anticipation of heaven has often been described as the oxygen of the human soul. "Everyone who has this hope in him purifies himself, just as He is pure" (1 John 3:3).

> Sing the wondrous love of Jesus, sing His mercy and His grace; in the mansions bright and blessed He'll prepare for us a place.

> While we walk the pilgrim pathway clouds will over-spread the sky; but when trav'ling days are over not a shadow, not a sigh.

> Let us then be true and faithful, trusting, serving ev'ry day; just one glimpse of Him in glory will the toils of life repay.

> Onward to the prize before us! Soon His beauty we'll behold; soon the pearly gates will open—We shall tread the streets of gold.

> **Chorus:** When we all get to heaven, what a day of rejoicing that will be! When we all see Jesus, we'll sing and shout the victory.

❦ *For Today:* Psalm 16:11; Isaiah 35:10; John 14:2, 3; 1 Corinthians 15:54-57

Allow your imagination to anticipate that day in heaven when the entire family of God is gathered for an endless celebration of praise. Allow this glorious hope to brighten your day and to keep you "true, faithful, trusting, serving . . ." Sing this musical truth as you go—

Emily D. Wilson, 1865-1942

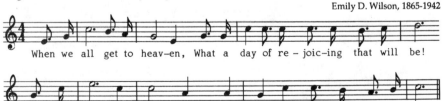

When we all get to heav-en, What a day of re - joic-ing that will be!

When we all see Je - sus, We'll sing and shout the vic - to - ry.

NOW THE DAY IS OVER

Sabine Baring-Gould, 1834-1924

I will lie down and sleep in peace, for You alone, O Lord, make me dwell in safety. (Psalm 4:8)

Upon God's care I lay me down, as a child upon its mother's breast;
No silken couch, nor softest bed could ever give me such deep rest. —*Unknown*

Trusting God throughout the day allows us to rest peacefully at night. Fear and anxiety are the chief causes of the tension that leads to disturbed rest. And sound rest is an absolute necessity for the renewing of our bodies, minds, and emotions. Only a peaceful relationship with God and with others allows us this total renewal at the close of each day. We must learn to relax and release our cares and burdens to the Lord and then claim His promised rest.

'Tis sweet to keep my hand in His, while all is dim—
To close my weary, aching eyes, and trust in Him! —*Unknown*

Whenever there are those occasional times when sleep eludes us, it is important to center our thoughts on God, the Scriptures, and the loving concern of the Lord rather than upon the solving of life's many problems.

"Now the Day is Over" was written by Sabine Baring-Gould (composer of "Onward, Christian Soldiers"). The author, a minister in the Anglican church, was recognized as one of England's most prolific writers of his time. Baring-Gould wrote this charming text for the children of his parish at Horbury Bridge, near Wakefield, England. It was based on Proverbs 3:24—"When thou liest down, thou shalt not be afraid; yea, thou shalt lie down, and thy sleep shall be sweet." The hymn first appeared in the *Church Times* on March 16, 1865. It is still a favorite hymn with children everywhere.

Now the day is over, night is drawing nigh; shadows of the evening steal across the sky.

Jesus, give the weary calm and sweet repose; with Thy tend'rest blessing may mine eyelids close.

Thru the long night-watches may Thine angels spread their white wings above me, watching round my bed.

When the morning wakens, then may I arise pure and fresh and sinless in Thy holy eyes.

❧ *For Today:* Psalm 3:5; Psalm 37:7; Psalm 63:1-8; Psalm 139:11, 12

Determine to begin and end each day with your mind centered on God. Thank Him for providing the renewal of your body, mind, and emotions. Sing and share this lovely children's hymn before retiring—

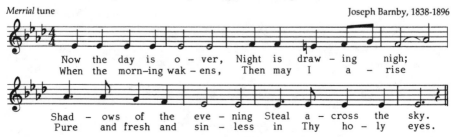

Merrial tune   Joseph Barnby, 1838-1896

Now the day is o - ver, Night is draw - ing nigh;
When the morn-ing wak - ens, Then may I a - rise

Shad - ows of the eve - ning Steal a - cross the sky.
Pure and fresh and sin - less in Thy ho - ly eyes.

TELL ME THE STORIES OF JESUS

William H. Parker, 1845-1929

He explained to them what was said in all of the Scriptures concerning Himself. (Luke 24:27)

Children love to hear stories. It is critically important that we build upon this natural response and fill their minds with truths about Christ that will give them a solid foundation upon which to build their lives. Although Sunday schools are important, parental influence and instruction in the home are foundations of Christian education. The stories of Jesus—His birth, His life, His death, His resurrection, His ascension, and His promised return to take us to heaven—for the child of God of any age are always fresh, exciting, and spiritually refreshing. They never grow old.

Telling the stories of Jesus must also be the mission of our Sunday schools. Portrayals of the person and work of Christ must always be the core of every Christian education curriculum along with appropriate songs that enhance the teaching of the Scriptures. Although such emphases as character school, arts and crafts, and game times have their place in the church program, nothing ever equals the importance of providing our youth with sound, relevant biblical instruction.

William H. Parker was an English Baptist layman greatly interested in the work of Sunday schools. He wrote this text in 1885 after returning from teaching his Sunday school class and reflecting upon the oft-repeated request of the children, "Teacher, tell us another story." This text pictures so vividly the important events of our Lord's life from Galilee to Calvary.

Tell me the stories of Jesus I love to hear; things I would ask Him to tell me if He were here: Scenes by the wayside, tales of the sea, stories of Jesus, tell them to me.

First let me hear how the children stood round His knee; and I shall fancy His blessing resting on me: Words full of kindness, deeds full of grace, all in the lovelight of Jesus' face.

Into the city I'd follow the children's band, waving a branch of the palm tree high in my hand; one of His heralds, yes, I would sing loudest hosannas! Jesus is King.

Show me that scene in the garden, of bitter pain. Show me the cross where my Savior for me was slain. Sad ones or bright ones, so that they be stories of Jesus, tell them to me.

❦ *For Today:* Deuteronomy 6:7; Isaiah 40:30, 31; Matthew 20:28; Mark 8:31

Consider creative ways that biblical truths can be communicated to children— visual aids, dramatizations, musical records—both at home and in Sunday school. Seriously reflect as a parent (or a grandparent) whether you are doing everything possible to further your children's spiritual training.

Frederic A. Challinor, 1866-1952

Tell me the sto - ries of Je - sus I love to hear;

Sto - ries of Je - sus— Tell them to me.

April

• Christ's Suffering and Death • Palm Sunday
• Resurrection • Lord's Supper

LEAD ME TO CALVARY

Jennie Evelyn Hussey, 1874-1958

Consider Him who endured such opposition from sinful men, so that you will not grow weary and lose heart. (Hebrews 12:3)

This is the season of the year when we give special attention to Christ's suffering, death, and victorious resurrection. In the church calendar, an awareness of these events begins with the Christian observance of Lent, a 40-day period (excluding Sundays) that is set aside each year prior to Easter to concentrate on the circumstances that led to the death of God's Son on a Roman cross. (Easter is always the first Sunday after the full moon that occurs on or after March 21—the spring equinox. This date was first set in A.D. 325 by the ancient church). The Lenten period should result in a spiritual self-examination and in rededicated living for each devout believer, preparing us for the celebration of our risen Lord.

The cross of Christ is either a blessing or a curse, depending on our response to it. Either it leads to our eternal redemption, or it condemns us to eternal damnation. This is demonstrated by the two thieves who hung on either side of the Savior. One responded and received divine mercy; the other rebelled his way into hell. God never violates man's free will and forces His love on anyone. But He has never rejected anyone who cries out to Him in believing faith. It is man who rejects God and the salvation that He provided at Calvary.

Jennie Hussey was a life-long Quaker. Much of her life was a time of hardship and suffering, especially in her care of an invalid sister. Yet Jennie was known for her cheerful and courageous attitude. In all she wrote approximately 150 hymn texts. "Lead Me to Calvary" first appeared in *New Songs of Praise and Power* in 1921. These thoughtful words can deepen our spiritual lives as we move further through this important Lenten season.

King of my life I crown Thee now—Thine shall the glory be; lest I forget Thy thorn-crowned brow, lead me to Calvary.

Show me the tomb where Thou wast laid, tenderly mourned and wept; angels in robes of light arrayed guarded Thee whilst Thou slept.

Let me like Mary, thru the gloom, come with a gift to Thee; show to me now the empty tomb—lead me to Calvary.

May I be willing, Lord, to bear daily my cross for Thee; even Thy cup of grief to share—Thou hast borne all for me.

Chorus: Lest I forget Gethsemane, lest I forget Thine agony, lest I forget Thy love to me, lead me to Calvary.

🍃 *For Today:* Isaiah 53:5; John 19:17; 1 Corinthians 15:3; Galatians 2:20

Ask God to use this Lenten season to awaken your appreciation of His suffering and death at Calvary and to be more desirous of sharing His love with others. Carry this musical reminder with you—

William J. Kirkpatrick, 1838-1921

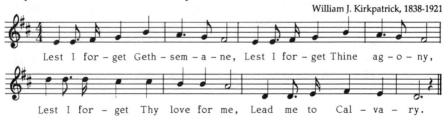

Lest I for - get Geth - sem - a - ne, Lest I for - get Thine ag - o - ny,

Lest I for - get Thy love for me, Lead me to Cal - va - ry.

IN THE HOUR OF TRIAL

James Montgomery, 1771-1854

No temptation has seized you except what is common to man. And God is faithful; He will not let you be tempted beyond what you can bear. But when you are tempted, He will also provide a way out so that you can stand up to it. (1 Corinthians 10:13)

Crisis situations are often the important pivotal points in our lives. Our response to these traumatic times—the loss of a loved one, a change in employment, a mistreatment by a trusted friend—will be the foundation stones upon which our lives are built. Maintaining the glow of our first love for God despite all the stresses of life is a major concern. The third stanza of this hymn teaches so well what our attitude should be when difficulties come our way: A desire to know what God is saying through the experience and a willingness to cast our cares on Him.

This beloved hymn was written by one of England's foremost hymn writers, James Montgomery. It was first published in 1853 with the title "Prayers on a Pilgrimage." The text is based on the incident of Peter's denial of his Lord in the courtyard of the high priest (Mark 14:54, 66-72).

"In the Hour of Trial" also teaches that believers, like Peter, are capable of rebelling and straying from the fellowship of their Lord. The Bible gives this warning: "If you think you are standing firm, be careful that you don't fall!" (1 Corinthians 10:12). The antidote to sin's allurements is the ability to keep our minds centered on Christ and His redemptive work for us. And like Peter, we can have our fellowship with God restored when we return to Him in brokenness and true humility. Peter's remorse was the start of his spiritual greatness. Like Peter, we must let our pride and self-sufficiency become our Christ confidence if our lives are to count for the Lord.

In the hour of trial, Jesus, plead for me; lest by base denial I depart from Thee: When Thou seest me waver, with a look recall, nor for fear or favor suffer me to fall.

With forbidden pleasures would this vain world charm, or its sordid treasures spread to work me harm; bring to my remembrance sad Gethsemane, or, in darker semblance, cross-crown'd Calvary.

Should Thy mercy send me sorrow, toil, and woe, or should pain attend me on my path below, grant that I may never fail Thy hand to see; grant that I may ever cast my care on Thee.

❦ *For Today:* Mark 14:54, 66-72; John 16:33; 17:15; Galatians 6:14

Be sensitive to the possibility of denying your Lord even in some small word or deed. Share with another believer who has strayed from God the truth of a new beginning with Christ.

Penitence tune   Spencer Lane, 1843-1903

When Thou seest me wa - ver, With a look re - call,

Nor for fear or fa - vor-- Suf - fer me to fall.

WHEN I SURVEY THE WONDROUS CROSS

Isaac Watts, 1674-1748

Carrying His own cross, He went out to the place of the Skull (which in Aramaic is called Golgotha). Here they crucified Him. (John 19:17, 18)

While preparing for a communion service in 1707, Isaac Watts wrote this deeply moving and very personal expression of gratitude for the amazing love that the death of Christ on the cross revealed. It first appeared in print that same year in Watts' outstanding collection, *Hymns and Spiritual Songs.* The hymn was originally titled "Crucifixion to the World by the Cross of Christ." Noted theologian Matthew Arnold called this the greatest hymn in the English language. In Watts' day, texts such as this, which were based only on personal feelings, were termed "hymns of human composure" and were very controversial, since almost all congregational singing at this time consisted of ponderous repetitions of the Psalms. The unique thoughts presented by Watts in these lines certainly must have pointed the 18th century Christians to a view of the dying Savior in a vivid and memorable way that led them to a deeper worship experience, even as it does for us today.

Young Watts showed unusual talent at an early age, learning Latin when he was 5, Greek at 9, French at 11 and Hebrew at 12. As he grew up, he became increasingly disturbed by the uninspiring psalm singing in the English churches. He commented, "The singing of God's praise is the part of worship most closely related to heaven; but its performance among us is the worst on earth." Throughout his life, Isaac Watts wrote over 600 hymns and is known today as the "father of English hymnody." His hymns were strong and triumphant statements of the Christian faith, yet none ever equalled the colorful imagery and genuine devotion of this emotionally stirring and magnificent hymn text.

> When I survey the wondrous cross on which the Prince of glory died, my richest gain I count but loss, and pour contempt on all my pride.
>
> Forbid it, Lord, that I should boast, save in the death of Christ, my God; all the vain things that charm me most—I sacrifice them to His blood.
>
> See, from His head, His hands, His feet, sorrow and love flow mingled down; did e'er such love and sorrow meet, or thorns compose so rich a crown?
>
> Were the whole realm of nature mine, that were a present far too small: Love so amazing, so divine, demands my soul, my life, my all.

❧ *For Today:* Matthew 26:28; Luke 7:47; Romans 5:6-11; Galatians 6:14

Can you say with Isaac Watts: "my soul, my life, my all"? Sing as you go—

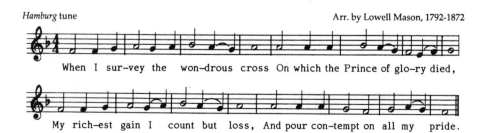

Hamburg tune   Arr. by Lowell Mason, 1792-1872

When I sur-vey the won-drous cross On which the Prince of glo-ry died,

My rich-est gain I count but loss, And pour con-tempt on all my pride.

WOUNDED FOR ME

W. G. Ovens, 1870-1945 (verse 1)
Gladys W. Roberts, 1888-? (verses 2-5)

To this you were called, because Christ suffered for you, leaving you an example, that you should follow in His steps. (1 Peter 2:21)

Death by crucifixion was one of the worst forms of dying. No Roman citizen was ever crucified; this horrible death was reserved only for Rome's enemies. The Roman scourge was a most dreadful instrument of torture and suffering. It was made of sinews of oxen, and sharp bones were inter-twisted among the sinews so that every time the lash came down upon a body, these pieces of bone inflicted fearful lacerations and literally tore off chunks of flesh from the person's bones. This is what Christ endured in accomplishing our redemption. But the physical suffering was not the worst. Rather, the weight of human sin and the separation from God the Father because of His wrath against sin were the real causes of the Savior's death.

But simply knowing about Christ's suffering and death is not enough. We must personally appropriate this to our own lives. We must say, "It was for me!" We must allow the Holy Spirit to do in us subjectively all that Christ has done for us objectively. Then, after we have experienced this redemptive work in our own lives, we must humbly, lovingly, and thoughtfully "follow in His steps" and seek to restore others.

The five stanzas of this thoughtful hymn cover the whole story of redemption, from the Savior's suffering to His second coming. When this hymn is sung, then, all of the verses must be used; none can be deleted. Start softly and slowly and gradually build to a thrilling climax—"O how I praise Him—He's coming for me!"

Wounded for me, wounded for me, there on the cross He was wounded for me; gone my transgressions, and now I am free, all because Jesus was wounded for me.

Dying for me, dying for me, there on the cross He was dying for me; now in His death my redemption I see, all because Jesus was dying for me.

Risen for me, risen for me, up from the grave He has risen for me; now evermore from death's sting I am free, all because Jesus has risen for me.

Living for me, living for me, up in the skies He is living for me; daily He's pleading and praying for me, all because Jesus is living for me.

Coming for me, coming for me, one day to earth He is coming for me; then with what joy His dear face I shall see; O how I praise Him—He's coming for me!

❦ **For Today:** Psalm 65:3; 103:12; Isaiah 53; Ephesians 2:5

Let your soul rejoice as you review the complete redemption Christ has provided for you. Sing this hymn as you go realizing that He was—

W.G. Ovens, 1870-1945

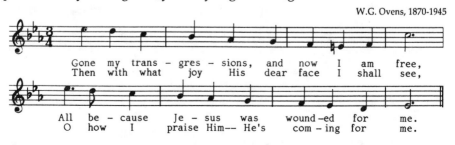

I GAVE MY LIFE FOR THEE

Frances R. Havergal, 1836-1879

And He died for all, that those who live should no longer live for themselves but for Him who died for them and was raised again. (2 Corinthians 5:15)

A vivid painting of Christ, wearing His crown of thorns as He stands before Pilate and the mob, is displayed in the art museum of Dusseldorf, Germany. Under the painting by Sternberg are the words, "This have I done for thee; what hast thou done for Me?" When Frances Havergal viewed the painting during a visit to Germany, she was deeply moved. As she gazed at it in tears, she scribbled down the lines of this hymn text on a scrap of paper. After returning to her home in England, she felt the poetry was so poor that she tossed the lines into a stove. The scorched scrap of paper amazingly floated out of the flames and landed on the floor, where it was found by Frances' father, Rev. William Havergal, an Anglican minister, a noted poet, and a church musician. He encouraged her to preserve the poem by composing the first melody for it. The present tune was composed for this text by the noted American gospel songwriter, Philip P. Bliss, and was first published in 1873.

When Christ cried out on the cross, "It is finished," victory over sin was won. All that is required of each of us is to personally appropriate that finished work. To show our gratefulness, however, our response should be, "Thank you, Lord, for giving your life for me. Now I want to live for You and serve You till the end of my days." This was the reaction of Miss Havergal, known as the "consecration poet," whose entire life was characterized by simple faith and spiritual saintliness. In spite of frail health, she lived an active life until her death at the age of 43. She wrote many beautifully phrased hymn texts, including "Take My Life and Let It Be" and "Like a River Glorious."

> I gave My life for thee; My precious blood I shed that thou might'st ransomed be and quickened form the dead; I gave, I gave My life for thee—what hast thou giv'n for Me?

> I suffered much for thee, more than thy tongue can tell, of bitt'rest agony to rescue thee from hell; I 've borne, I've borne it all for thee—what hast thou borne for Me?

> And I have brought to thee, down from My home above, salvation full and free, my pardon and My love; I bring, I bring rich gifts to thee—what hast thou brought to Me?

❧ *For Today:* Psalm 116:12-14; John 19:30; Romans 12:1, 2; Galatians 2:20

Allow your soul to respond in a new and fresh dedication to God as you reflect on all that Christ has done for you. Allow these musical questions to motivate your thinking—

Kenosis tune   Philip P. Bliss, 1838-1876

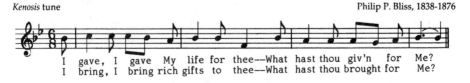

I gave, I gave My life for thee—What hast thou giv'n for Me?
I bring, I bring rich gifts to thee—What hast thou brought for Me?

NEAR THE CROSS

Fanny J. Crosby, 1820-1915

For God was pleased to have all His fullness dwell in Him, and through Him to reconcile to Himself all things, whether things on earth or things in heaven, by making peace through His blood, shed on the cross. (Colossians 1:19, 20)

The cross was a superb triumph over Satan, death, and hell. Never was Christ more a king than when He shouted from the cross—"It is finished." Out of the hideous suffering of Calvary He has carved His victory and His kingdom. The victory of the cross assures us that we no longer need to be kept separate from God—either in this life or for eternity. Even now we can enter into His presence "with confidence, so that we may receive mercy and find grace to help us in our time of need" (Hebrews 4:16). And the best is yet to come—"the golden strand just beyond the river."

As God's people, we should live daily with a sensitive awareness of Christ's cross. We should review its scenes of suffering as well as revel in its triumph. "Near the Cross," this simply stated hymn by Fanny Crosby, has been widely used by God to teach people this truth since its first publication in 1869.

As she did with many of her 8,000 hymn texts, Fanny Crosby wrote this poem to fit an existing tune that had been composed by William H. Doane. Although she worked with a number of other gospel musicians, William Doane was Fanny Crosby's principal collaborator. Doane was a very successful business man in Cincinnati, as well as a composer and publisher of numerous gospel songs. He was a very wealthy man when he died and he left much of his fortune to philanthropic causes, including the construction of the Doane Memorial Music Building at Moody Bible Institute in Chicago.

> Jesus, keep me near the cross—there a precious fountain, free to all, a healing stream, flows from Calv'ry's mountain.

> Near the cross, a trembling soul, love and mercy found me; there the Bright and Morning Star sheds its beams around me.

> Near the cross! O Lamb of God, bring its scenes before me; help me walk from day to day with its shadows o'er me.

> Near the cross I"ll watch and wait, hoping, trusting ever, till I reach the golden strand just beyond the river.

> **Chorus:** In the cross, in the cross be my glory ever, till my raptured soul shall find rest, beyond the river.

❦ ***For Today:*** John 6:47-51; 19:17, 18; Galatians 6:14; Ephesians 2:13

Determine that especially during this Lenten season you are going to review and revel more often in the cross of Christ and all that it means. Sing this musical prayer to help you remember—

William H. Doane, 1832-1915

BLESSED REDEEMER

Avis B. Christiansen, 1895-1985

When they came to the place called the Skull, there they crucified Him, along with the criminals—one on His right, the other on His left. (Luke 23:33)

A Hill with Three Crosses—
One cross where a thief died IN SIN
One cross where a thief died TO SIN
A center cross where a Redeemer died FOR SIN   —*Unknown*

It is thought that the day we call "Good Friday" originated from the term "God's Friday"—the day that Christ was led to the hill of Golgotha and crucified, assuring an eternal reconciliation for lost man. The Roman cross, intended to be an instrument of cruel death, instead became an instrument of new life and hope for the human race. God loved and valued each of us so highly that He was willing to pay the greatest price imaginable for our salvation.

The composer of this hymn, Harry Dixon Loes, was a popular music teacher at the Moody Bible Institute from 1939 until his death in 1965. One day while listening to a sermon on the subject of Christ's atonement entitled "Blessed Redeemer," Mr. Loes was inspired to compose this tune. He then sent the melody with the suggested title to Mrs. Christiansen, a friend for many years, asking her to write the text. The completed hymn first appeared in the hymnal *Songs of Redemption* in 1920.

Mrs. Avis Christiansen is to be ranked as one of the important gospel hymn writers of the 20th century. She has written hundreds of gospel hymn texts as well as several volumes of published poems. Throughout her long lifetime of 90 years, Mrs. Christiansen collaborated with many well-known gospel musicians to contribute several other choice hymns to our hymnals, including "Blessed Calvary" and "I Know I'll See Jesus Some Day."

Up Calv'ry's mountain, one dreadful morn, walked Christ my Savior, weary and worn; facing for sinners death on the cross, that He might save them from endless loss.

"Father, forgive them!" thus did He pray, e'en while His life-blood flowed fast away; praying for sinners while in such woe—no one but Jesus ever loved so.

O how I love Him, Savior and Friend! How can my praises ever find end! Thru years unnumbered on heaven's shore, my tongue shall praise Him forevermore.

Chorus: Blessed Redeemer, precious Redeemer! Seems now I see Him on Calvary's tree, wounded and bleeding, for sinners pleading—blind and unheeding—dying for me!

🎵 **For Today:** Matthew 27:39-43; John 19:17, 18, 33, 34; Colossians 2:13-20

Since Christ has paid the price of our redemption in full, all we have to do is believe, receive, rejoice and represent Him. Reflect on this musical truth—

Harry Dixon Loes, 1892-1965

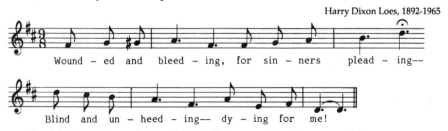

Wound - ed and bleed - ing, for sin - ners plead - ing--

Blind and un - heed - ing-- dy - ing for me!

AT CALVARY

William R. Newell, 1868-1956

In Him we have redemption through His blood, the forgiveness of sins, in accordance with the riches of God's grace that He lavished on us with all wisdom and understanding. (Ephesians 1:7, 8)

Calvary, meaning "the place of the skull," is a place that everyone has heard about and that thousands of Holy Land tourists visit every year. But the significance of the events that took place on this hill nearly two thousand years ago are often not truly realized by many of those who merely view its location. "At Calvary" focuses our attention on the wondrous mercy and grace that Christ demonstrated through His death on the cross. The hymn exalts our Lord for conquering sin and death and bringing salvation to all who will accept Him as Redeemer and Lord. The "mighty gulf" between God and man was bridged with Christ's sacrificial atonement at Calvary.

William R. Newell was a noted evangelist, Bible teacher, and later assistant superintendent at the Moody Bible Institute. One day on his way to teach a class, he was meditating about Christ's suffering at Calvary and all that it meant to him as a lost sinner. These thoughts so impressed themselves on his mind that he stepped into an empty classroom and quickly scribbled down the lines of this hymn on the back of an envelope. A few minutes later he met his friend and colleague, Daniel B. Towner, music director at the institute, and showed him the text he had just written, suggesting that Towner try composing music for it. An hour later as Newell returned from class, Dr. Towner presented him with the melody and they sang their completed hymn together.

Following its publication in 1895, Christians everywhere have used this hymn enthusiastically to rejoice in the "riches of God's grace" made available "At Calvary."

> Years I spent in vanity and pride, caring not my Lord was crucified, knowing not it was for me He died on Calvary.
>
> By God's Word at last my sin I learned—then I trembled at the law I'd spurned, till my guilty soul imploring turned to Calvary.
>
> Now I've giv'n to Jesus ev'rything; now I gladly own Him as my King; now my raptured soul can only sing of Calvary.
>
> O the love that drew salvation's plan! O the grace that bro't it down to man! O the mighty gulf that God did span at Calvary!
>
> **Chorus:** Mercy there was great, and grace was free; pardon there was multiplied to me. There my burdened soul found liberty—at Calvary.

❦ *For Today:* Romans 5:6-11; 1 Corinthians 1:18; Colossians 1:19-23

Give joyful praise from a grateful heart for what the cross means—an instrument of human indignity became the means of our salvation.

Daniel B. Towner, 1850-1919

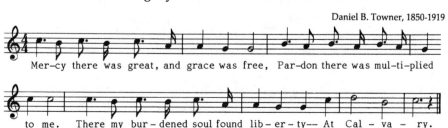

Mer-cy there was great, and grace was free, Par-don there was mul-ti-plied to me. There my bur-dened soul found lib-er-ty-- At Cal - va - ry.

THE OLD RUGGED CROSS

Words and Music by George Bennard, 1873-1958

He Himself bore our sins in His body on the tree, so that we might die to sins and live for righteousness; by His wounds you have been healed. (1 Peter 2:24)

The author and composer of this beloved hymn, George Bennard, began his Christian ministry in the ranks of the Salvation Army. Eight years later he was ordained by the Methodist Episcopal church, where his devoted ministry as an evangelist was highly esteemed for many years.

One time, after returning to his home in Albion, Michigan, Bennard passed through a particularly trying experience, one that caused him to reflect seriously about the significance of the cross and what the apostle Paul meant when he spoke of entering into the fellowship of Christ's sufferings (Philippians 3:10). George Bennard began to spend long hours in study, prayer, and meditation until one day he could say:

> I saw the Christ of the cross as if I were seeing John 3:16 leave the printed page, take form and act out the meaning of redemption. The more I contemplated these truths the more convinced I became that the cross was far more than just a religious symbol but rather the very heart of the gospel.

During these days of spiritual struggle, the theme for "The Old Rugged Cross" began to formulate itself in Bennard's mind. But an inner voice seemed to keep telling him to "wait." Finally, however, after returning to Michigan, he began to concentrate anew on his project. This time the words and melody began to flow easily from his heart. Shortly thereafter, Bennard sent a manuscript copy to Charles Gabriel, one of the leading gospel hymn writers of that time. Gabriel's prophetic words, "You will certainly hear from this song, Mr. Bennard," were soon realized as the hymn became one of the most widely published songs, either sacred or secular, throughout America.

> On a hill far away stood an old rugged cross, the emblem of suff'ring and shame; and I love that old cross where the dearest and best for a world of lost sinners was slain.

> O that old rugged cross, so despised by the world, has a wondrous attraction for me; for the dear Lamb of God left His glory above to bear it to dark Calvary.

> To the old rugged cross I will ever be true, its shame and reproach gladly bear; then He'll call me some day to my home far away, where His glory forever I'll share.

> **Chorus:** So I'll cherish the old rugged cross, till my trophies at last I lay down; I will cling to the old rugged cross, and exchange it some day for a crown.

❦ *For Today:* Isaiah 53:3-12; John 19:17-25; Romans 5:6-11; Hebrews 9:27, 28

Ponder the significance of Christ's cross in your salvation. Sing this musical testimony—

So I'll cher-ish the old rug-ged cross, Till my tro-phies at last I lay down;

I will cling to the old rug-ged cross, And ex-change it some day for a crown.

O SACRED HEAD, NOW WOUNDED

Attributed to Bernard of Clairvaux, 1091-1153
Translated into German by Paul Gerhardt, 1607-1676
Translated into English by James W. Alexander, 1804-1859

And when they had plaited a crown of thorns, they put it upon His head, and a reed in His right hand; and they bowed the knee before Him, and mocked Him, saying, "Hail, King of the Jews!" And they spit upon Him, and took the reed, and smote Him on the head. (Matthew 27:29, 30 KJV)

It is difficult to join our fellow believers each Lenten season in the singing of this passion hymn without being moved almost to tears. For more than 800 years these worshipful lines from the heart of a devoted medieval monk have portrayed for parishioners a memorable view of the suffering Savior.

This remarkable text has been generally attributed to Bernard of Clairvaux, the very admirable abbot of a monastery in France. Forsaking the wealth and ease of a noble family for a life of simplicity, holiness, prayer, and ministering to the physical and spiritual needs of others, Bernard was one of the most influential church leaders of his day. Martin Luther wrote of him, "He was the best monk that ever lived, whom I admire beyond all the rest put together."

"O Sacred Head, Now Wounded" was part of the final portion of a lengthy poem that addressed the various parts of Christ's body as He suffered on the cross. The seven sections of the poem considered His feet, knees, hands, side, breast, heart, and face. The stanzas of the hymn were translated into German in the 17th century and from German into English in the 19th century. God has preserved this exceptional hymn, which has led Christians through the centuries to more ardent worship of His Son.

O sacred Head, now wounded, with grief and shame weighed down, now scornfully surrounded with thorns Thy only crown; how art Thou pale with anguish, with sore abuse and scorn! How does that visage languish which once was bright as morn!

What Thou, my Lord, hast suffered was all for sinners' gain: Mine, mine was the transgression, but Thine the deadly pain. Lo, here I fall, my Savior! 'Tis I deserve Thy place; look on me with Thy favor; vouch-safe to me Thy grace.

What language shall I borrow to thank Thee, dearest Friend, for this Thy dying sorrow, Thy pity without end? O make me Thine forever! And, should I fainting be, Lord, let me never, never outlive my love to Thee!

❦ *For Today:* Isaiah 53; Matthew 27:39-43; Philippians 2:8; 1 Peter 3:18

Ponder anew your suffering Savior; then commit your life more fully to Him. Allow these musical truths to help you in your meditation—

Passion Chorale tune — Hans Leo Hassler, 1564-1612

O make me Thine for – ev – er! And, should I faint – ing be,

Lord, let me nev – er, nev – er Out – live my love to Thee!

ROCK OF AGES

Augustus M. Toplady, 1740-1778

For I do not want you to be ignorant of the fact, brothers, that our forefathers were all under the cloud and that they all passed through the sea . . . they all ate the same spiritual food and drank the same spiritual drink; for they drank from the spiritual rock that accompanied them and that rock was Christ. (1 Corinthians 10:1, 3, 4)

This fervent plea for Christ our eternal rock to grant salvation through His sacrifice and to be a place of refuge for the believer is one of the most popular hymns ever written. With strong emotional impact, it proclaims Christ's atonement on the cross to be the only means of salvation, making man's tears and efforts to justify himself of no avail. Also it urges us to find consolation and security in Christ our rock—even at the time of death.

Augustus Toplady's strong and passionate lines were actually written to refute some of the teachings of John and Charles Wesley during a bitter controversy with them concerning Arminianism (which stresses man's free will) versus John Calvin's doctrine of election. "Rock of Ages" was the climax to an article that Toplady wrote in *The Gospel Magazine* in 1776, in which he supported the doctrine of election by arguing that just as England could never pay her national debt, so man through his own efforts could never satisfy the eternal justice of a holy God. Despite the belligerent intent of this text, God has preserved this hymn for more than 200 years to bring blessing to both Arminian and Calvinistic believers around the world.

At the age of 16, as he sat in a barn and listened to the preaching of an uneducated man, Toplady was dramatically converted. Later, he became a powerful and respected minister of the Anglican church. While he was the busy pastor of several churches in England, Augustus Toplady wrote many hymn texts, but few have survived. "Rock of Ages" is the one for which he is known today.

> Rock of ages, cleft for me, let me hide myself in Thee; let the water and the blood, from Thy wounded side which flowed, be of sin the double cure, save from wrath and make me pure.

> Could my tears forever flow, could my zeal no languor know, these for sin could not atone—Thou must save and Thou alone: In my hand no price I bring; simply to Thy cross I cling.

> While I draw this fleeting breath, when my eyes shall close in death, when I rise to worlds unknown and behold Thee on Thy throne, Rock of Ages, cleft for me, let me hide myself in Thee.

❦ **For Today:** Exodus 17:1-6; 33:17-23; Psalm 78:35; Acts 4:12

Give sincere praise to Christ our "Rock of Ages" for His great gift of salvation and for His provision of a place of refuge for us, even unto death.

Toplady tune   Thomas Hastings, 1784-1872

THERE IS A FOUNTAIN

William Cowper, 1731-1800

But now in Christ Jesus you who once were far away have been brought near through the blood of Christ. (Ephesians 2:13)

William Cowper is viewed by some as one of the finest of all English writers. But Cowper's emotional life was one of great turmoil. At an early age he was directed by his father to study law. Upon completion of his studies, however, the prospect of appearing for his final examination before the bar so frightened him that it caused a mental breakdown and even an attempted suicide. Later he was placed in an insane asylum for 18 months. During this detention, he one day read from the Scriptures the passage in Romans 3:25 that Jesus Christ is "set forth to be a propitiation through faith in His blood, to declare His righteousness for the remission of sins that are past, through the forbearance of God." Through his reading of the Bible, Cowper soon developed a personal relationship with Christ and a sense of forgiveness of sin. This was in 1764, when he was 33 years old.

Three years later, Cowper was invited to move to Olney, England, where John Newton pastored the parish Anglican Church. It was here for nearly two decades that Newton and Cowper had a close personal friendship. In 1799 their combined talents produced the famous *Olney Hymns* hymnal, one of the most important single contributions made to the field of evangelical hymnody. In this ambitious collection of 349 hymns, sixty-seven were written by Cowper with the remainder by Newton.

"There Is a Fountain" was originally titled "Peace for the Fountain Opened." The hymn, with its vivid imagery, is based on the Old Testament text, Zechariah 13:1—"In that day there shall be a fountain opened to the house of David and to the inhabitants of Jerusalem for sin and uncleanness."

Only eternity will reveal the hosts who, through the singing of this hymn, have been made aware of the efficacy of Christ's complete atonement.

There is a fountain filled with blood drawn from Immanuel's veins, and sinners plunged beneath that flood lose all their guilty stains.

The dying thief rejoiced to see that fountain in his day, and there may I, though vile as he, wash all my sins away.

Dear dying Lamb, Thy precious blood shall never lose its pow'r, till all the ransomed Church of God be saved to sin no more.

E'er since by faith I saw the stream Thy flowing wounds supply, redeeming love has been my theme and shall be till I die.

When this poor lisping, stamm'ring tongue lies silent in the grave, then in a nobler, sweeter song, I'll sing Thy pow'r to save.

❦ **For Today:** John 19:34; Ephesians 1:7; Colossians 1:20; Hebrews 9:12-14

Carry the joy of "redeeming love" as your day's theme.

Cleansing Fountain tune   American melody

And   sin-ners plunged be - neath that flood Lose all their guilt -y stains.
Then in a   no - bler, sweet-er song, I 'll sing Thy pow'r to save.

IN THE GARDEN

C. Austin Miles, 1868-1945

Mary Magdalene went to the disciples with the news: "I have seen the Lord!" And she told them that He had said these things to her. (John 20:18)

It was in 1912 that music publisher Dr. Adam Geibel asked author and composer C. Austin Miles to write a hymn text that would be "sympathetic in tone, breathing tenderness in every line; one that would bring hope to the hopeless, rest for the weary, and downy pillows to dying beds." Mr. Miles has left the following account of the writing of this hymn:

> One day in April, 1912, I was seated in the dark room, where I kept my photographic equipment and organ. I drew my Bible toward me; it opened at my favorite chapter, John 20—whether by chance or inspiration let each reader decide. That meeting of Jesus and Mary had lost none of its power and charm.
> As I read it that day, I seemed to be part of the scene. I became a silent witness to that dramatic moment in Mary's life, when she knelt before her Lord, and cried, "Rabboni!"
> My hands were resting on the Bible while I stared at the light blue wall. As the light faded, I seemed to be standing at the entrance of a garden, looking down a gently winding path, shaded by olive branches. A woman in white, with head bowed, hand clasping her throat, as if to choke back her sobs, walked slowly into the shadows. It was Mary. As she came to the tomb, upon which she placed her hand, she bent over to look in, and hurried away.
> John, in flowing robe, appeared, looking at the tomb; then came Peter, who entered the tomb, followed slowly by John.
> As they departed, Mary reappeared; leaning her head upon her arm at the tomb, she wept. Turning herself, she saw Jesus standing, so did I. I knew it was He. She knelt before Him, with arms outstretched and looking into His face cried, "Rabboni!" I awakened in sun light, gripping the Bible, with muscles tense and nerves vibrating. Under the inspiration of this vision I wrote as quickly as the words could be formed the poem exactly as it has since appeared. That same evening I wrote the music.

* * * *

I come to the garden alone, while the dew is still on the roses; and the voice I hear, falling on my ear, the Son of God discloses.

He speaks, and the sound of His voice is so sweet the birds hush their singing; and the melody that He gave to me within my heart is ringing.

I'd stay in the garden with Him tho the night around me be falling; but He bids me go—thru the voice of woe, His voice to me is calling.

Refrain: And He walks with me, and He talks with me, and He tells me I am His own, and the joy we share as we tarry there, none other has ever known.

❦ *For Today:* Matthew 20:28; Matthew 28:5-9; John 20; Romans 5:6, 10, 11

Let your mind join Mary and the disciples in the garden when Christ first appeared to them following His resurrection. Respond as did Mary—"Rabboni!" (my Master). Carry this musical truth throughout the day—

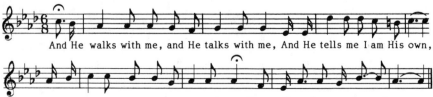

And He walks with me, and He talks with me, And He tells me I am His own,

And the joy we share as we tar-ry there, None oth-er has ev – er known.

THERE IS A GREEN HILL FAR AWAY

Mrs. Cecil Frances Alexander, 1823-1895

Finally Pilate handed Him over to them to be crucified. (John 19:16)

The full understanding of the depth of suffering that our Savior endured at Calvary for our redemption is difficult to grasp. When Mrs. Cecil Alexander, one of England's finest hymn writers, was attempting to explain to her Sunday school class the meaning of the phrase from the Apostles' Creed, "suffered under Pontius Pilate, was crucified, dead and buried," she felt inadequate. She had always believed that one of the most effective ways to teach sound spiritual truths to children is through the use of appropriate hymns. She decided, therefore, to put the details of Christ's suffering and death on the cross into a simply worded but appealing song that could be easily understood by the children in her class. Although the hymn with its direct style of wording and clearly expressed thoughts was originally intended for youth, it had an immediate appeal to adults as well. After the lilting melody was composed for the text in 1878 by George C. Stebbins, the hymn became widely used in the Moody-Sankey evangelistic campaigns, as it has been in church services since then.

Friends of Mrs. Alexander said that her life was even more beautiful than her writing. After her marriage to William Alexander, archbishop and primate of the Anglican church for all of Ireland, she engaged herself in parish duties and charity work. Her husband said of her, "From one poor home to another she went. Christ was ever with her, and all felt her influence." Mrs. Alexander had been active before her marriage in the Sunday school movement, and her love of children and interest in their spiritual instruction never diminished. Almost all of the 400 poems and hymns that she wrote were prompted by this concern.

Adults as well as children have loved this particular hymn, written by a devoted woman who had a sincere desire to help others to truly appreciate the extent of Christ's agony on the cross and the magnitude of His love.

There is a green hill far away, outside a city wall, where the dear Lord was crucified, who died to save us all.

We may not know, we cannot tell, what pains He had to bear; but we believe it was for us He hung and suffered there.

He died that we might be forgiv'n. He died to make us good, that we might go at last to heav'n, saved by His precious blood.

There was no other good enough to pay the price of sin; He only could unlock the gate of heav'n and let us in.

Chorus: O dearly, dearly has He loved! And we must love Him too, and trust in His redeeming blood, and try His works to do.

❦ *For Today:* John 19; Romans 5:6-11; Ephesians 1:7, 8; Titus 2:13, 14

Express your gratitude for Christ's "redeeming blood." Let the truth of His great love motivate you to "try His works to do."

Green Hill tune
George C. Stebbins, 1846-1945

O dear - ly, dear - ly has He loved! And we must love Him too,

And trust in His re deem - ing blood, And try His works to do.

IN THE CROSS OF CHRIST I GLORY

John Bowring, 1792-1872

May I never boast except in the cross of our Lord Jesus Christ, through which the world has been crucified to me, and I to the world. (Galatians 6:14)

The cross has been the most significant symbol of the Christian faith throughout church history. It is said that as many as 400 different forms or designs of it have been used—among them the usual Latin Cross, the Greek Cross, the Budded Cross. Regardless of design, the symbol of the cross should always remind us of the price that was paid by the eternal God for man's redemption. "In the Cross of Christ I Glory" is generally considered one of the finest hymns on this subject. It was written by John Bowring, one of the most remarkable men of his day as well as one of the greatest linguists who ever lived. It is said that he could converse in over 100 different languages before his death.

Some writers claim that John Bowring had visited Macao, on the South Chinese Coast, and was much impressed by the sight of a bronze cross towering on the summit of the massive wall of what had formerly been a great cathedral. This cathedral, originally built by the early Portuguese colonists, overlooked the harbor and had been destroyed by a typhoon. Only one wall, which was topped by the huge metal cross, remained. This scene is said to have so impressed Bowring that it eventually served as the inspiration for this hymn text.

The writing of the tune for this hymn is also most interesting. It was composed 24 years after Bowring's text by an American organist and choir leader of the Central Baptist Church of Norwich, Connecticut. The composer, Ithamar Conkey, was sorely disappointed at one Sunday morning service when only one choir member appeared, a faithful soprano by the name of Mrs.Beriah Rathbun. Before the evening service Conkey composed a new tune for this text and named it after his one faithful choir member.

The preaching of the cross may be a foolish message to many "but unto us who are saved it is the power of God" (1 Corinthians 1:18 KJV).

> In the cross of Christ I glory, tow'ring o'er the wrecks of time; all the light of sacred story gathers round its head sublime.

> When the woes of life o'er take me, hopes deceive and fears annoy, never shall the cross forsake me: Lo! it glows with peace and joy.

> When the sun of bliss is beaming light and love upon my way, from the cross the radiance streaming adds more luster to the day.

> Bane and blessing, pain and pleasure, by the cross are sanctified; peace is there that knows no measure, joys that thru all time abide.

❦ *For Today:* John 19; Romans 5:6-11; 1 Corinthians 1:17-19; Ephesians 2:16

Determine to allow the glory of Christ's cross to be evident in all that you do. Sing this musical testimony as you go realizing that—

Rathbun tune   Ithamar Conkey,1815-1867

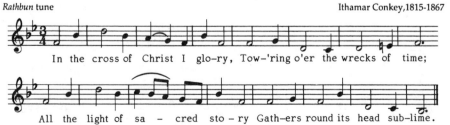

In the cross of Christ I glo-ry, Tow-'ring o'er the wrecks of time;

All the light of sa – cred sto – ry Gath-ers round its head sub-lime.

BENEATH THE CROSS OF JESUS

Elizabeth C. Clephane, 1830-1869

For the preaching of the cross is to them that perish foolishness; but unto us which are saved it is the power of God. (1 Corinthians 1:18 KJV)

There is no neutral ground when we face the cross: Either we accept its atoning work and become a new person, or we reject it and remain in our sinful self-centered state. When we take our stand with Christ and His redemption accomplished at Calvary, we are compelled to make two profound confessions: "The wonders of His glorious love and my own worthlessness."

This hymn of commitment was written by a frail Scottish Presbyterian woman of the past century, Elizabeth Clephane, who, despite her physical limitations, was known throughout her charming community of Melrose, Scotland, for her helpful, cheery nature. Among the sick and dying in her area she won the name of "Sunbeam." "Beneath the Cross of Jesus" was written by Miss Clephane in 1868, one year before her early death at the age of 39. She wrote eight hymns, all published posthumously. Besides this hymn, only one other has endured—"The Ninety and Nine," made popular by the tune composed for it by Ira D. Sankey.

It is obvious that Elizabeth, like most Scottish Presbyterians of her day, was an ardent Bible student, for her hymn is replete with biblical symbolism and imagery. For example:

"the mighty Rock" is a reference from Isaiah 32:2
"the weary land" is a reference from Psalm 63:1
"home within the wilderness" is a reference from Jeremiah 9:2
"rest upon the way" is a reference from Isaiah 28:12
"noontide heat" is a reference from Isaiah 4:6
"burden of the day" is a reference from Matthew 11:30

Beneath the cross of Jesus I fain would take my stand, the shadow of a mighty rock within a weary land; a home within the wilderness, a rest upon the way from the burning of the noon day heat and the burden of the day.

Upon that cross of Jesus mine eye at times can see the very dying form of One who suffered there for me; and from my smitten heart with tears two wonders I confess—the wonders of His glorious love and my own worthlessness.

I take, O cross, thy shadow for my abiding place—I ask no other sunshine than the sunshine of His face; content to let the world go by, to know no gain nor loss, my sinful self my only shame, my glory all the cross.

❦ *For Today:* Psalm 22:7; Matthew 27:33, 37; Luke 9:23; Galatians 6:14

"My glory all the cross." Determine to live the truth of this phrase. Reflect on these musical expressions—

St. Christopher tune   Frederick C. Maker, 1844-1927

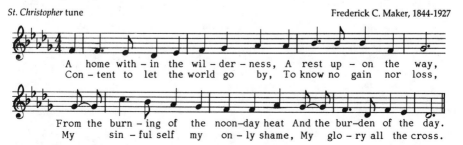

A home with-in the wil-der-ness, A rest up-on the way,
Con-tent to let the world go by, To know no gain nor loss,

From the burn-ing of the noon-day heat And the bur-den of the day.
My sin-ful self my on-ly shame, My glo-ry all the cross.

BURDENS ARE LIFTED AT CALVARY

Words and Music by John M. Moore, 1925-

Come to Me, all you who are weary and burdened, and I will give you rest. (Matthew 11:28)

Today's featured hymn was written in 1952 by one of our contemporary song writers, John M. Moore, currently a Baptist pastor and evangelist in Toronto, Canada. The hymn was prompted by an experience that Dr. Moore had while serving as the assistant superintendent of the Seaman's Chapel in Glasgow, Scotland, one of that area's outstanding evangelistic centers. He recalls:

I wrote "Burdens Are Lifted at Calvary" after a most interesting experience. The company secretary of a large shipping firm telephoned the Seaman's Chapel and requested that I visit a young merchant seaman who was lying critically ill in a Glasgow hospital. After getting permission fron the nursing sister, I went in to visit the young sailor. I talked for a few moments and then put my hand in my case for a tract, not knowing which one I would pull out. It happened to be a tract based on *Pilgrim's Progress,* with a color reproduction of Pilgrim coming to the cross with a great burden on his back. I showed the young seaman this picture and told him the story in brief, adding that Pilgrim's experience had been my experience too. I explained that when I came to the cross of Christ, my burden rolled away and my sense of sin and guilt before God was removed. He nodded his head when I asked him, "Do you feel this burden on your back today?" We prayed together and never shall I forget the smile of peace and assurance that lit up his face when he said that his burden was lifted!

Later that night, sitting by the fireside with paper and pen, I could not get the thought out of my mind—his burden is lifted! I started writing, but never for a moment did I imagine that this little hymn would become a favorite throughout the world. Since that time, I hear of people all over the world who are being blessed and saved through the singing of this hymn.

* * * *

Days are filled with sorrow and care; hearts are heavy and drear; burdens are lifted at Calvary—Jesus is very near.

Cast your care on Jesus today; leave your worry and fear; burdens are lifted at Calvary—Jesus is very near.

Troubled soul, the Savior can see ev'ry heartache and tear; burdens are lifted at Calvary—Jesus is very near.

Refrain: Burdens are lifted at Calvary, Calvary, Calvary. Burdens are lifted at Calvary; Jesus is very near.

❦ *For Today:* Psalm 147:3; John 6:35; John 20:31; Colossians 1:20

Reach out to someone who is deeply burdened by sin and earthly cares and share your testimony of faith in Christ and the truth of this song.

Bur-dens are lift-ed at Cal-va-ry, Cal-va-ry;
Bur-dens are lift-ed at Cal-va-ry— Je-sus is ver-y near.

JESUS PAID IT ALL

Elvina M. Hall, 1820-1889

"Come now, let us reason together," says the Lord, "Though your sins are like scarlet, they shall be as white as snow; though they are red as crimson, they shall be like wool." (Isaiah 1:18)

It has been stated that all religious systems can be spelled with just two letters—D O. The gospel of Christ, however, is spelled with four letters—D O N E! This hymn text, written by a lay woman named Elvina Hall, speaks pointedly to this basic truth, which is the very basis of our Christian faith.

Mrs. Hall wrote these words one Sunday morning while seated in the choir loft of the Monument Street Methodist Church in Baltimore, Maryland, supposedly listening to the sermon by her pastor, the Rev. George Schrick. One can imagine a conversation something like this following the service:

> Pastor Schrick, I must confess that I wasn't listening too closely to your message this morning. Because, you see, once you started preaching about how we can really know God's love and forgiveness, I began thinking about all that Christ has already done to provide our salvation. Then these words came to me, and I just had to get them down on paper. And the only paper I could find at the time was the flyleaf of this hymnal. So I scribbled the words on that.

The pastor recalled that the church organist, John Grape, had just previously given him a copy of a new tune that he had composed,which he had titled "All to Christ I Owe." To the amazement of all, they soon discovered that John Grape's tune fit perfectly with Elvina Hall's words scribbled on the flyleaf page of the hymnal. Since its first published appearance in 1874, this hymn has been widely used in churches, especially for the communion services.

> I hear the Savior say, "Thy strength indeed is small! Child of weakness, watch and pray; find in Me thine all in all."
>
> Lord, now indeed I find Thy pow'r, and Thine alone, can change the leper's spots and melt the heart of stone.
>
> For nothing good have I whereby Thy grace to claim—I'll wash my garments white in the blood of Calv'ry's Lamb.
>
> And when before the throne I stand in Him complete, "Jesus died my soul to save," my lips shall still repeat.
>
> **Chorus:** Jesus paid it all, all to Him I owe. Sin had left a crimson stain—He washed it white as snow.

❦ *For Today:* Romans 3:24-26; 1 Corinthians 6:11; Ephesians 1:7-9

Breathe a prayer of thanksgiving even now that our eternal standing with God is dependent only on the redemptive work of Christ. Seek to share this good news with someone who may be confused about this.

John T. Grape, 1835-1915

Je - sus paid it all, All to Him I owe; Sin had left a crim - son

stain-- He washed it white as snow.

HOSANNA, LOUD HOSANNA

Jennette Threlfall, 1821-1880

Hosanna to the Son of David! Blessed is He who comes in the name of the Lord!
Hosanna in the highest. (Matthew 21:9)

The week preceding Easter Sunday is known as Holy or Passion Week. These seven days have been described as the most intense and important week of history. The dramatic events that occurred during Christ's final days on earth are recorded in all four gospels (Matthew 21; Mark 11; Luke 19; John 12).

Palm Sunday: John 12:12-15— The only day of triumph known by Christ in His earthly ministry. A fulfilment of Old Testament prophecy (Zechariah 9:9).

The Lord's Holy Anger: 1. At a fig tree that bore no fruit (Matthew 21:18-19). 2. At the moneychangers who were misusing the temple (Matthew 21:12, 13).

The Last Supper: Matthew 26:26-28— Observed on Maundy Thursday.

The Foot Washing: John 13:1-10— An object lesson taught by Christ regarding the basic qualities of true discipleship: humility, purity, and servanthood.

The Song of Victory: Matthew 26:30— This last song was likely one of the imminent Hallel Psalms, Nos. 115-118.

Gethsemane: Matthew 26:36-46— Three times Jesus prayed, while His disciples slept, "O Father, if it be possible, let this cup pass from Me; nevertheless not as I will, but as Thou wilt!"

The Kiss of Betrayal: Mark 14:44; Luke 22:48— "Judas, are you betraying the Son of Man with a kiss?"

The Perverted Trial: Matthew 27:11-26— Christ charged with blasphemy and sentenced to die as a criminal against Rome.

The Crucifixion: Matthew 27:33-38— Most Christians believe He was crucified on what is now known as Good Friday. The church color for this day is black.

"Hosanna, Loud Hosanna" was written by Jennette Threlfall, an invalid English woman who was known for her cheery disposition as well as her many published poems. This text first appeared in the author's volume *Sunshine and Shadow,* in 1873.

Hosanna, loud hosanna, the little children sang; thru pillared court and temple the lovely anthem rang; to Jesus, who had blessed them close folded to His breast, the children sang their praises, the simplest and the best.

From Olivet they followed 'mid an exultant crowd, the victor palm branch waving, and chanting clear and loud; the Lord of men and angels rode on in lowly state, nor scorned that little children should on His bidding wait.

"Hosanna in the highest!" That ancient song we sing, for Christ is our Redeemer, the Lord of heav'n our King; O may we ever praise Him with heart and life and voice, and in His blissful presence eternally rejoice!

❦ *For Today:* Matthew 21:1-11; Mark 11:9, 10; John 12,13

Sing this Palm Sunday hymn with your family—

Ellacombe tune   From *Gesangbuch der Herzogl,* 1784

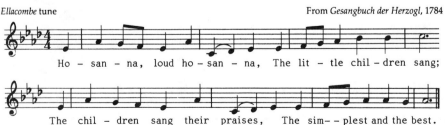

Ho - san - na, loud ho - san - na, The lit - tle chil - dren sang;

The chil - dren sang their praises, The sim- - plest and the best.

ALL GLORY, LAUD AND HONOR

Theodolph of Orleans, 760-821
Translated by John M. Neale, 1818-1866

The next day the great crowd that had come for the Feast heard that Jesus was on His way to Jerusalem. They took palm branches and went out to meet Him, shouting "Hosanna! Blessed is He who comes in the name of the Lord." (John 12:12, 13)

The triumphant procession began after the disciples obtained the colt (Luke 19:30). They were implicitly obedient in following their Lord's command, even though it no doubt seemed to be a trivial request. And still today—obedience is the key to our effective service for God.

The Palm Sunday procession also teaches us that our Lord is still leading His people—"bringing many sons to glory" (Hebrews 2:10), our heavenly Jerusalem, "whose architect builder is God" (Hebrews 11:10). Our responsibility is to be His faithful follower and to extol His name with our daily praises.

This Palm Sunday hymn was written approximately A.D. 820 by Bishop Theodolph of Orleans, France, while he was imprisoned at the monastery of Angers. Theodolph was well known in his day as a poet, pastor, and beloved bishop of Orleans. When Emperor Charlemagne died in 814, the bishop was put into a monastic prison by Charlemagne's son and successor, Louis I the Pious, for allegedly plotting against him. A well-known legend has long been associated with this hymn. It is believed by many that a short time before the bishop's death in 821, Louis was visiting in the area where the bishop was imprisoned and by chance passed under his cell. The bishop is said to have been singing and worshiping by himself. When the emperor heard this particular text being sung, he was so moved by the incident that he immediately ordered the bishop's release.

All glory, laud and honor to Thee, Redeemer, King, to whom the lips of children make sweet hosannas ring: Thou art the King of Israel, Thou David's royal Son, who in the Lord's name comest, the King and blessed One!

The company of angels are praising Thee on high, and mortal men and all things created make reply: The people of the Hebrews with palms before Thee went; our praise and prayer and anthems before Thee we present.

To Thee, before Thy passion, they sang their hymns of praise; to Thee, now high exalted, our melody we raise: thou didst accept their praises—accept the praise we bring, who in all good delightest, Thou good and gracious King!

❦ *For Today:* Matthew 21:1-17; Mark 11:10; Luke 28:37, 38; John 12:1-16

During this special week, let us consider seriously whether we truly love and serve Christ for any other reason other than for who He is. Let us exalt Him with this hymn—

St. Theodolph tune

Melchior Teschner, 1584-1635

Thou art the King of Is - rael, Thou Da - vid's roy - al Son,

Who in the Lord's name com - est, The King and bless - ed One!

THE DAY OF RESURRECTION

John of Damascus, early 8th century
English translation by John M. Neale, 1818-1866

Now thanks be unto God, which always causeth us to triumph in Christ. (2 Corinthians 2:14 KJV)

This hymn from the early eighth century is one of the oldest expressions found in most hymnals. Its origin is rooted in the liturgy of the Greek Orthodox Church. It was written by one of the famous monks of that church, John of Damascus, c. 676-c. 780.

The celebration of Easter has always been a spectacle of ecclesiastical pomp in the Greek Orthodox Church. Even today, as a vital part of the ceremony, the worshipers bury a cross under the high altar on Good Friday and dramatically resurrect it with shouts of "Christos egerthe" ("Christ is risen") on Easter Sunday. With this announcement begins a time of joyous celebration. Torches are lit, bells and trumpets peel, and salvos of cannons fill the air. The following account describes such a scene:

> Everywhere men clasped each other's hands, congratulated one another, and embraced with countenances beaming with delight, as though to each one separately some wonderful happiness had been proclaimed—and so in truth it was; and all the while rising above the mingling of many sounds, each one of which was a sound of gladness, the aged priests were distinctly heard chanting forth a glorious hymn of victory in tones so loud and clear, that they seemed to have regained the youth and strength to tell the world how "Christ is risen from the dead, having trampled death beneath His feet, and henceforth they that are in the tombs have everlasting life."

John M. Neale is generally regarded as one of the leading translators of ancient hymns. He was recognized as one of the most learned hymnologists of his day and had a knowledge of twenty languages.

The day of resurrection! Earth, tell it out abroad—the Passover of gladness, the Passover of God! From death to life eternal, from this world to the sky, our Christ hath brought us over with hymns of victory!

Our hearts be pure from evil, that we may see aright the Lord in rays eternal of resurrection light; and, list'ning to His accents, may hear, so calm and plain, His own "All hail!" and, hearing, may raise the victor strain.

Now let the heav'ns be joyful, let earth her song begin, let the round world keep triumph and all that is therein; let all things seen and unseen their notes in gladness blend, for Christ the Lord hath risen, our joy that hath no end!

❦ *For Today:* Matthew 28:1-9; Acts 2:24; 13:29, 20; 1 Corinthians 15:54-58.

Determine to make this Easter a spiritual highpoint celebration in your life and in the lives of your family members. Reflect on this portion of the hymn—

Greenland tune   Arranged from J. Michael Haydn, 1737-1806

The day of res – ur –rec – tion! Earth, tell it out a – broad––
Now let the heav'ns be joy – ful, Let earth her song be – gin,

Our Christ hath brought us o – ver with hymns of vic – to – ry!
For Christ the Lord hath ris – en, Our joy that hath no end!

THE STRIFE IS O'ER

Anonymous Latin hymn from approximately 1605
English translation by Francis Pott, 1832-1909

Where, O death, is your victory? Where, O death, is your sting? The sting of death is sin, and the power of sin is the law. But thanks be to God! He gives us the victory through our Lord Jesus Christ. (1 Corinthians 15:55, 56, 57)

The thrilling news from the empty tomb is that life has triumphed over death! This is a message that dispels our fears and gives us the sure hope that because Christ lives, we shall live also (John 14:19). Alleluia!

This inspiring Easter hymn first appeared anonymously in a Jesuit collection, *Symphonia Sirenum*, published in Cologne, Germany, in 1695. It was more than 150 years after its writing, however, before this hymn was used by English-speaking churches. In 1859 the translation was made by Francis Pott, an Anglican minister. The music is an adaptation from the "Gloria Patri," published in 1591 by Palestrina, the great 16th century Catholic composer and director of the performing choir at St. Peter's church in the Vatican. This musical arrangement was made by Dr. William H. Monk for inclusion in the well-known Anglican hymnal *Hymns Ancient and Modern*, 1861 edition. In making this musical adaptation from Palestrina's work, Dr. Monk used the first two phrases, repeated the first phrase and added original alleluias for the beginning and the end. (*Alleluia* is a Latin form of the Hebrew *Hallelujah*, which means "praise the Lord!"). It is interesting to note the interplay between the statements of fact related to Christ's resurrection that are contained in the first half of each stanza and the personal response to these factual truths as expressed in the last half of each verse, concluding with the jubilant "Alleluia!"

> The strife is o'er—the battle done, the victory of life is won; the song of triumph has begun: Alleluia!
>
> The pow'rs of death have done their worst, but Christ their legions hath dispersed; let shouts of holy joy outburst: Alleluia!
>
> The three sad days have quickly sped; He rises glorious from the dead; all glory to our risen Head! Alleluia!
>
> He closed the yawning gates of hell; the bars from heav'n's high portals fell; let hymns of praise His triumphs tell: Alleluia!
>
> Lord, by the stripes which wounded Thee, from death's dread sting Thy servants free, that we may live and sing to Thee: Alleluia!
>
> Alleluia! Alleluia! Alleluia!

❦ *For Today:* Isaiah 25:7-9; Romans 1:4; 6:9-10; Revelation 19:1, 2

Allow your soul to vibrate with the resounding "Alleluias" for all that the empty tomb means to you. Use this fine hymn to help realize—

Victory tune

Giovanni P. da Palestrina, c. 1525-1594
Adapted by William H. Monk, 1823-1889

The strife is o'er—the bat - tle done, The vic-to-ry of life is won; The song

of tri-umph has be-gun: Al-le-lu-ia! Al-le-lu-ia! Al-le-lu-ia! Al-le-lu-ia!

CHRIST THE LORD IS RISEN TODAY

Charles Wesley, 1707-1788

I am the First and the Last, I am the Living One; I was dead, and behold I am alive for ever and ever! (Revelation 1:17, 18)

What a glorious truth to ponder—Jesus is not the "Great I WAS" but rather the "Great I AM!" He is not only a historical fact but a present-day, living reality. The whole system of Christianity rests upon the truth that Jesus Christ rose from the grave and is now seated at the Father's right hand as our personal advocate.

"Christ the Lord is Risen Today" has been one of the church's most popular Easter hymns since it was first written by Charles Wesley just one year after his "heart-warming" experience at the Aldersgate Hall in London, England, in 1738. The first Wesleyan Chapel in London was a deserted iron foundry. It became known as the Foundry Meeting House. This hymn was written by Charles for the first service in that chapel.

Following his Aldersgate encounter with Christ, Charles began writing numerous hymns on every phase of the Christian experience, some 6,500 in all. It has been said that the hymns of Charles Wesley clothed Christ in flesh and blood and gave converts a belief they could easily grasp, embrace with personal faith, and if necessary, even die for.

If all of our eternity is to be realized on this side of the grave, we are hopeless and to be pitied (1 Corinthians 15:19). But for the Christian, the resurrection assures us of God's tomorrow. This anticipation makes it possible to live joyfully today, regardless of life's circumstances.

> Christ the Lord is ris'n today, Alleluia! Sons of men and angels say: Alleluia! Raise your joys and triumphs high, Alleluia! Sing, ye heav'ns, and earth reply: Alleluia!

> Lives again our glorious King, Alleluia! Where, O death, is now thy sting? Alleluia! Dying once He all doth save, Alleluia! Where thy victory, O grave? Alleluia!

> Love's redeeming work is done, Alleluia! Fought the fight, the battle won, Alleluia! Death in vain forbids Him rise, Alleluia! Christ has opened Paradise, Alleluia!

> Soar we now where Christ has led, Alleluia! Foll'wing our exalted Head, Alleluia! Made like Him, like Him we rise, Alleluia! Ours the cross, the grave, the skies, Alleluia!

❦ *For Today:* Matthew 28:1-9; Acts 2:24-28; 1 Corinthians 15:4, 20; 55-57

The message of the resurrection is to "come and see"—to personally experience the transforming power of the living Christ. Then—"to go and tell." Carry this hymn of triumph with you—

Easter Hymn tune   From *Lyra Davidica*, 1708

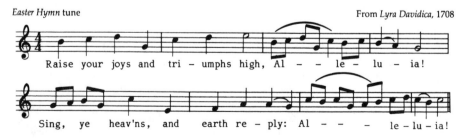

Raise your joys and tri - umphs high, Al – – le - lu – ia!

Sing, ye heav'ns, and earth re - ply: Al – – – le – lu – ia!

CHRIST AROSE

Robert Lowry, 1826-1899

Now if we died with Christ, we believe that we will also live with Him. For we know that since Christ was raised from the dead, He cannot die again; death no longer has master over Him. (Romans 6:8, 9)

"Alleluia, He is Risen!" "Alleluia, He is Risen Indeed!" If you and I had been living during the early Christian era, this undoubtedly would have been our greeting to one another as believers on an Easter Sunday. For the past century, however, many evangelical churches have been inspired anew in celebrating this triumphant day by singing "Christ Arose", written and composed by Robert Lowry in 1874.

Robert Lowry is a highly respected name among early gospel hymn writers. He served for a time as a professor of literature at Bucknell University, pastored several important Baptist churches in the East, and then became the music editor of the Biglow Publishing Company. It has often been said that the quality of Lowry's numerous publications did much to improve the cause of sacred music in this country.

During the Easter season of 1874, while having his devotions one evening, Robert Lowry was impressed with the events associated with Christ's resurrection, especially with these words recorded in Luke 24:6, 7:

He is not here, but is risen; remember how He spoke unto you when He was in Galilee, saying, the Son of Man must be delivered into the hands of sinful men and be crucified, and the third day rise again.

Soon Robert Lowry found himself seated at the little pump organ in the parlor of his home, and in a very spontaneous fashion, the words and music of "Christ Arose" gave expression to the thoughts that had been uppermost in his mind. The hymn was published the following year and has been an inspirational favorite with God's people ever since.

Low in the grave He lay—Jesus, my Savior! Waiting the coming day—Jesus, my Lord!

Vainly they watch His bed—Jesus, my Savior! Vainly they seal the dead—Jesus, my Lord.

Death cannot keep his prey—Jesus, my Savior! He tore the bars away—Jesus, my Lord!

Chorus: Up from the grave He arose, with a mighty triumph o'er His foes; He arose a Victor from the dark domain, and He lives forever with His saints to reign: He arose! He arose! Hallelujah! Christ arose!

❦ *For Today:* Matthew 27:5-66; John 19:41, 42; 1 Corinthians 15:4

Allow the truth of Christ's resurrection to thrill your life anew. Sing with triumph as you go—

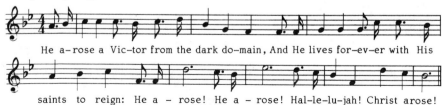

He a-rose a Vic-tor from the dark do-main, And He lives for-ev-er with His
saints to reign: He a - rose! He a - rose! Hal-le-lu-jah! Christ arose!

HE LIVES

Alfred H. Ackley, 1887-1960

He is not here; He has risen, just as He said. Come and see the place where He lay. (Matthew 28:6)

"Why should I worship a dead Jew?"

This challenging question was posed by a sincere young Jewish student who had been attending evangelistic meetings conducted by the author and composer of this hymn, Alfred H. Ackley. In his book, *Forty Gospel Hymn Stories,* George W. Sanville records Mr. Ackley's answer to this searching question, which ultimately prompted the writing of this popular gospel hymn:

> He lives! I tell you, He is not dead, but lives here and now! Jesus Christ is more alive today than ever before. I can prove it by my own experience, as well as the testimony of countless thousands.

Mr. Sanville continues:

> Mr. Ackley's forthright, emphatic answer, together with his subsequent triumphant effort to win the man for Christ, flowered forth into song and crystallized into a convincing sermon on "He Lives!" In his re-reading of the resurrections of the Gospels, the words "He is risen" struck him with new meaning. From the thrill within his own soul came the convincing song— "He Lives!" The scriptural evidence, his own heart, and the testimony of history matched the glorious experience of an innumerable cloud of witnesses that "He Lives," so he sat down at the piano and voiced that conclusion in song. He says, "The thought of His ever-living presence brought the music promptly and easily."

The hymn first appeared in *Triumphant Service Songs,* a hymnal published by the Rodeheaver Company in 1933. It has been a favorite with evangelical congregations since that time.

> I serve a risen Savior; He's in the world today; I know that He is living, whatever men may say; I see His hand of mercy, I hear His voice of cheer, and just the time I need Him He's always near.
>
> In all the world around me I see His loving care, and tho my heart grows weary I never will despair; I know that He is leading thru all the stormy blast; the day of His appearing will come at last.
>
> Rejoice, rejoice, O Christian, lift up your voice and sing eternal hallelujahs to Jesus Christ the King! The hope of all who seek Him, the help of all who find, none other is so loving, so good and kind.
>
> **Chorus:** He lives, He lives, Christ Jesus lives today! He walks with me and talks with me along life's narrow way. He lives, He lives, salvation to impart ! You ask me how I know He lives? He lives within my heart.

❦ **For Today:** Job 19:25; Romans 6:9, 10; Philippians 3:10, 11; Revelation 1:18

Determine to greet everyone in such a way that they will know unmistakably that Jesus is alive and living in your life. Sing as you go—

He lives, He lives, sal - va - tion to im - part! You ask me how I know He lives? He lives with - in my heart.

BECAUSE HE LIVES

Gloria Gaither, 1942-
William J. Gaither, 1936-

Because I live, you also will live. (John 14:19)

Christ's resurrection is our guarantee of at least two basic truths: First, He has the power to give His life to us and to bring us ultimately to glory to reign with Him forever. And second, His resurrection makes it possible for Him to live in our hearts and to be an integral part of our daily living.

For the past two decades the music of Gloria and Bill Gaither has greatly enriched evangelical hymnody. But the song that has especially highlighted the Gaither's ministry is one that reflects their own philosophy—the resurrection principle in the daily routines of life—"Because He Lives." Bill Gaither recalls the circumstances that prompted the writing of this favorite:

> We wrote "Because He Lives" after a period of time when we had had a kind of dry spell and hadn't written any songs for a while . . . Also at the end of the 1960's, our country was going through some great turmoil with the height of the drug culture, and the whole "God is Dead" theory was running wild in our country. Also it was the peak of the Vietnam war. During that time our little son was born— at least Gloria was expecting him. I can remember at the time we thought, "Brother, this is really a poor time to bring a child into the world." At times we were even quite discouraged by the whole thing. And then Benjy did come. We had two little girls whom we love very much, but this was our first son, and so that lyric came to us, "How sweet to hold our new-born baby and feel the pride and joy he gives, but better still the calm assurance that this child can face uncertain days because Christ lives." And it gave us the courage to say, "Because Christ lives we can face tomorrow" and keep our heads high.

* * * *

God sent His son—they called Him Jesus; He came to love, heal and forgive; He lived and died to buy my pardon; an empty grave is there to prove my Savior lives.

How sweet to hold a new-born baby and feel the pride and joy he gives; but greater still the calm assurance: This child can face uncertain days because Christ lives.

And then one day I'll cross the river; I'll fight life's final war with pain; and then, as death gives way to victory, I'll see the lights of glory—and I'll know He lives.

Chorus: Because He lives I can face tomorrow, because He lives all fear is gone; because I know He holds the future and life is worth the living—just because He lives.

❦ *For Today:* John 6:40; Colossians 3:3, 4; 2 Timothy 1:10; 1 John 5:11

Live in the joyous confidence that the living, victorious Christ is guiding your life. Carry this musical truth with you as you go—

William J. Gaither

Be – cause I know....... He holds the fu – ture,

And life is worth the liv – ing— just be – cause He lives.

ABIDE WITH ME

Henry F. Lyte, 1793-1847

But they constrained Him, saying, "Abide with us: for it is toward evening, and the day is far spent." And He went in to tarry with them. (Luke 24:29 KJV)

> Yes, life is like the Emmaus road, and we tread it not alone
> For beside us walks the Son of God, to uphold and keep His own.
> And our hearts within us thrill with joy at His words of love and grace,
> And the glorious hope that when day is done we shall see His blessed face.
> —*Avis Christiansen*

The author of this text, Henry F. Lyte, was an Anglican pastor. Though he battled tuberculosis all of his life, Lyte was known as a man strong in spirit and faith. It was he who coined the phrase "it is better to wear out than to rust out."

During his later years, Lyte's health progressively worsened so that he was forced to seek a warmer climate in Italy. For the last sermon with his parishioners at Lower Brixham, England, on September 4, 1847, it is recorded that he nearly had to crawl to the pulpit. His final words made a deep impact upon his people when he proclaimed, "It is my desire to induce you to prepare for the solemn hour which must come to all, by a timely appreciation and dependence on the death of Christ."

Henry Lyte's inspiration for writing "Abide with Me" came shortly before his final sermon, while reading from the account in Luke 24 of our Lord's appearance with the two disciples on their seven mile walk from Jerusalem to the village of Emmaus on that first Easter evening. How the hearts of those discouraged disciples suddenly burned within them when they realized that they were in the company of the risen, the eternal Son of God!

> Abide with me—fast falls the eventide. The darkness deepens—Lord, with me abide; when other helpers fail and comforts flee, help of the helpless, O abide with me!
>
> Swift to its close ebbs out life's little day; earth's joys grow dim; its glories pass away; change and decay in all around I see—O Thou who changest not, abide with me!
>
> I need Thy presence ev'ry passing hour—What but Thy grace can foil the tempter's pow'r? Who like Thyself my guide and stay can be? Thru cloud and sunshine, O abide with me.
>
> Hold Thou Thy word before my closing eyes. Shine thru the gloom and point me to the skies; heav'n's morning breaks and earth's vain shadows flee—In life, in death, O Lord, abide with me.

🌿 *For Today:* Psalm 139:7-12; Luke 24:13-35; 1 John 3:24

Relive the thrill expressed by the two Emmaus disciples when their spiritual eyes were opened and they first realized that they were in the presence of their risen Lord. Use this hymn to help—

Eventide tune   William H. Monk, 1823-1889

WERE YOU THERE?

Spiritual

It was the third hour when they crucified Him. (Mark 15:25)

Folk songs are generally described as songs of which the origins have been lost but which express the heartfelt traditions and experiences of a particular culture or people. Therefore, they become greatly cherished by each succeeding generation.

The Negro spirituals represent some of the finest of American folk music. These songs are usually a blending of an African heritage, harsh remembrances from former slavery experiences, and a very personal interpretation of biblical stories and truths. They especially employ biblical accounts that give hope for a better life—such as the prospects of heaven. They symbolize so well the attitudes, hopes and religious feeling of the black race in America.

To better understand a Negro spiritual, one must feel even as a black singer does that he or she is actually present and very much involved in the event itself. The event being sung—in this case the story of Christ's suffering, death, and ultimate resurrection—becomes a very intensely emotional experience. It is told with much feeling and freedom of spirit, generally without any instrumental accompaniment.

The lesson for each of us to learn from a Negro spiritual like this is that truths such as the redemptive work of Christ must have much more than just our mental assent. The biblical account must become a very personal conviction in our lives, and our very souls should be gripped by its emotional power.

> Were you there when they crucified my Lord?
>
> Were you there when they nailed Him to the tree?
>
> Were you there when they pierced Him in the side?
>
> Were you there when they laid Him in the tomb?
>
> Were you there when God raised Him from the dead?
>
> Sometimes I feel like shouting glory, glory, glory! When I think how God raised Him from the dead!

❦ *For Today:* Isaiah 53:4-12; Matthew 20:28; 1 Peter 2:24; Revelation 1:5, 6

Imagine yourself standing at the foot of the cross when Christ was tortured and crucified. Then place yourself outside the empty tomb when the angelic announcement "He is not here . . ." was given. Try to relive the emotional feelings that would have been yours. Allow this song to minister to you as you go through the day—

WORTHY IS THE LAMB

Words and Music by Don Wyrtzen, 1942-

You are worthy, our Lord and God, to receive glory and honor and power, for You created all things, and by Your will they were created and have their being. (Revelation 4:11)

> Come, let us join our cheerful songs with angels round the throne;
> Ten thousand thousand are their tongues, but all their joys are one.
> "Worthy the Lamb that died," they cry, "to be exalted thus."
> "Worthy is the Lamb," our lips reply "for He was slain for us."
> The whole creation joins as one to bless the sacred Name
> Of Him that sits upon the throne, and to adore the Lamb.
> —*Isaac Watts*

Heaven will be a place of great singing as we join voices with the angels and saints of the ages in praising the One who made it all possible.

This popular contemporary hymn is based directly on a text of Scripture that could well be the believers' theme throughout eternity:

Worthy is the Lamb that was slain to receive power, and riches, and wisdom, and strength, and honor, and glory, and blessing. (Revelation 5:12)

Don Wyrtzen, author and composer of this hymn and one of the outstanding gospel song writers of our day, recalls:

> In 1970, I was in Mexico City assisting evangelist Luis Palau conduct a series of crusades. Because the messages were in Spanish, I spent the time during the sermons writing new songs. One day I became particularly impressed with the great truth of Revelation 5:12, and I thought how effective this verse could be, if only the proper music was used to enhance it. I thought about the music used in the secular song "The Impossible Dream" and decided that a similar musical style would work well with these words. God has used this song to bless and inspire His people during these past years perhaps more than any other work I have been privileged to write, for which I will be eternally grateful to Him.

* * * *

Worthy is the Lamb that was slain, worthy is the Lamb that was slain, worthy is the Lamb that was slain, to receive: Power and riches and wisdom and strength, honor and glory and blessing! Worthy is the Lamb, worthy is the Lamb, worthy is the Lamb that was slain, worthy is the Lamb!

❦ **For Today:** John 1:29; 1 Peter 1:18, 19; Revelation 5:6-13; 13:8; 17:14

What is your response to the resurrected and now reigning Christ? Are you living daily in the awareness of His life-giving power? Are you joyfully anticipating the day when you will join the heavenly chorus extolling the One who alone is worthy of all praise? Why not begin even now?

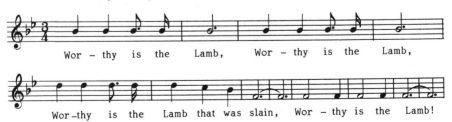

Wor - thy is the Lamb, Wor - thy is the Lamb,

Wor -thy is the Lamb that was slain, Wor - thy is the Lamb!

ACCORDING TO THY GRACIOUS WORD

James Montgomery, 1771-1854

For whenever you eat this bread and drink this cup, you proclaim the Lord's death until He comes. (1 Corinthians 11:26)

> Here, O my Lord, I see Thee face to face; here would I touch and handle things unseen, here grasp with firmer hand eternal grace, and all my weariness upon Thee lean. Here would I feed upon the bread of God, here drink with Thee the royal wine of heav'n. Here would I lay aside each earthly load, here taste afresh the calm of sin forgiv'n. —*Horatius Bonar*

In His sovereign wisdom our Lord knew that His followers through the centuries would need a continual reminder of the essential truths of their faith—the sacrificial death, the triumphant resurrection, and the victorious return of Christ. For His disciples, Christ shared the Last Supper and introduced the signs of the new covenant—His broken body and shed blood—symbolized by the bread and the cup. With this supper as the model, He then gave instructions that this feast of remembrance should occur regularly in our worship of Him until He comes. After that, it will culminate in heaven with the saints of the ages in the Wedding Supper of the Lamb (Revelation 19:7, 9). Not only should the communion service serve as a backward and forward reminder of what Christ has and will do for us, but it should also cause us to look within ourselves —"A man ought to examine himself before he eats of the bread and drinks of the cup" (1 Corinthians 11:28).

"According to Thy Gracious Word" by James Montgomery recounts vividly the sacrificial atonement of Christ and the believer's response to Christ's command in Luke 22:19—"This do in remembrance of Me."

> According to Thy gracious word, in meek humility, this will I do, my dying Lord: I will remember Thee.

> Thy body, broken for my sake, my bread from heav'n shall be; Thy testamental cup I take, and thus remember Thee.

> When to the cross I turn mine eyes and rest on Calvary, O Lamb of God, my sacrifice, I must remember Thee—

> Remember Thee and all Thy pains and all Thy love to me; yea, while a breath, a pulse remains will I remember Thee.

> And when these failing lips grow dumb and mind and mem' ry flee, when you shalt in Thy kingdom come, Jesus, remember me!

❦ *For Today:* Matthew 26:26-29; 1 Corinthians 10:16-21; 11:23-28

Reflect on this: Am I truly willing to take the backward, forward, and inward looks as I anticipate the next Communion Service? Use this musical reminder to help—

Manoah tune · From the "Greatorex collection," 1851

Ac - cord–ing to Thy gra - cious word, In meek hu – mil - i - ty,

This will I do, my dy - ing Lord: I will re - mem - ber Thee.

THE SPACIOUS FIRMAMENT

Joseph Addison, 1672-1719

The heavens declare the glory of God; the skies proclaim the work of His hands. (Psalm 19:1)

The month of May is generally regarded as the most beautiful month of the year. March winds and April showers have done their work, and now the earth is attired in all of its God-given beauty. Of all people, Christians should be the most appreciative of God's created world. Although we may never be able to understand fully and explain adequately all of the scientific details about creation, we can say with certainty, "I believe in God the Father Almighty, maker of heaven and earth" (Apostles' Creed); and with the writer of Hebrews, "By faith we understand that the universe was formed at God's command" (Hebrews 11:3). The wonder of God's spacious firmament should cause a flow of endless praise to our great Creator.

The Bible teaches that man is without excuse for not knowing God. The Creator has revealed Himself at least partially in nature (Romans 1:19-21) as well as internally in the human conscience (Romans 1:32; 2:14, 15). The full revelation of God, however, is only realized in the person and work of Jesus Christ—"the radiance of God's glory" (Hebrews 1:3).

"The Spacious Firmament" was written by Joseph Addison—one of England's outstanding writers. These verses were part of a larger essay titled "An Essay on the Proper Means of Strengthening and Confirming Faith in the Mind of Man." Addison prefaced his work with the words: "The Supreme Being has made the best arguments for His own existence in the formation of the heavens and earth." Addison's poem first appeared in *The Spectator* newspaper in 1712.

> The spacious firmament on high, with all the blue, ethereal sky, and spangled heavens, a shining frame, their great Original proclaim: Th' unwearied sun , from day to day, does his Creator's pow'r display; and publishes to ev'ry land the work of an almighty hand.
>
> What though in solemn silence, all move round this dark terrestrial ball? What though no real voice nor sound amid their radiant orbs be found? In reason's ear they all rejoice, and utter forth a glorious voice, forever singing as they shine, "The hand that made us is divine."

❦ *For Today:* Genesis 1:1-19; Psalm 19:1-6; Isaiah 40:26; Romans 1:20; Hebrews 11:1-4

Reflect again on the Genesis account of creation. Reaffirm your faith and confidence in God as the creator of this vast firmament. Determine to be more aware and appreciative of the many splendors of nature that we often take for granted. Consider this musical truth as you go—

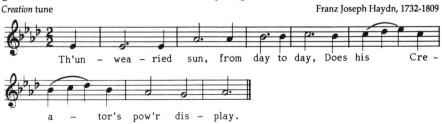

Creation tune — Franz Joseph Haydn, 1732-1809

Th'un - wea - ried sun, from day to day, Does his Cre - a - tor's pow'r dis - play.

May

• Creation and Nature • Christ's Ascension and Exaltation
• Pentecost and the Holy Spirit • Trinity Sunday
• Christian Home • National Holiday/Memorial Day

THIS IS MY FATHER'S WORLD

Maltbie D. Babcock, 1858-1901

The Lord loves righteousness and justice; the earth is full of His unfailing love. (Psalm 33:5)

Even though we are constantly reminded of the violence, tragedy, and ugliness in today's world, we can still rejoice that the beauty of nature all around is ours to enjoy. Who can deny the pleasure that comes from the sight of a glowing sunset or a majestic mountain, the sound of chirping birds or the roar of the surf, and the smell of new mown hay or roses or lilies.

Maltbie D. Babcock revealed his great admiration for nature in this lovely hymn text. Although he was recognized as one of the outstanding Presbyterian ministers of his generation, Dr. Babcock was also a skilled athlete who enjoyed all outdoor activity, especially his early morning walks. He would always comment, "I'm going out to see my Father's world." Since Dr. Babcock was an accomplished performer on the organ, the piano and the violin, we can see why nature seemed to him to be "the music of the spheres." In addition to being a tribute to nature, however, the hymn is a triumphant assertion of the unfailing power of God and the assurance of Christ's eventual reign—"and earth and heav'n be one."

As we follow Dr. Babcock's example and give praise to God for all the beauty of His world, we cannot help being concerned that much of the loveliness is being destroyed by human carelessness and greed. The real answer to our ecological problems must be a renewed appreciation of earth as "our Father's world" and a greater responsibility for taking proper care of it. Christians should be models of this concern.

> This is my Father's world, and to my list'ning ears all nature sings, and round me rings the music of the spheres. This is my Father's world! I rest me in the thought of rocks and trees, of skies and seas—His hand the wonders wrought.

> This is my Father's world—the birds their carols raise; the morning light, the lily white, declare their Maker's praise. This is my Father's world! He shines in all that's fair; in the rustling grass I hear Him pass—He speaks to me ev'rywhere.

> This is my Father's world—O let me ne'er forget that tho the wrong seems oft so strong God is the Ruler yet. This is my Father's world! The battle is not done; Jesus who died shall be satisfied, and earth and heav'n be one.

❦ **For Today:** Psalm 8; 24:1, 2; 145:1-13; Isaiah 45:18; 1 Corinthians 15:25, 26

Determine to cultivate a renewed awareness and appreciation of the marvels of God's creation all around you. Endeavor to be even more responsible as a caretaker of your Father's world. Sing this musical praise as you go—

Terra Betta tune   Franklin L. Sheppard, 1852-1930

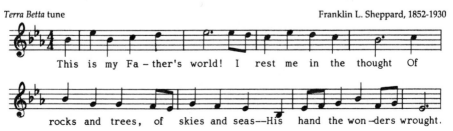

ALL CREATURES OF OUR GOD AND KING

Francis of Assisi, 1182-1226
English Translation by William Draper, 1855-1933

All Thy works shall praise Thee, O Lord; and Thy saints shall bless Thee. They shall speak of the glory of Thy kingdom, and talk of Thy power. (Psalm 145:10, 11)

All the magnificent wonders of nature reveal the majesty of God and glorify Him. From the grateful heart of a devoted Italian monk in the year of 1225 came this beautiful message. As a great lover of nature, Saint Francis saw the hand of God in all creation, and he urged men to respond with expressions of praise and alleluia.

Giovanni Bernardone, the real name of Saint Francis, demonstrated through his own life all the tender, humble, forgiving spirit and absolute trust in God that his hymn urges others to have. At the age of 25 Bernardone left an indulgent life as a soldier, renounced his inherited wealth, and determined to live meagerly and to imitate the selfless life of Christ.

Throughout his life Saint Francis appreciated the importance of church music and encouraged singing in his monastery. He wrote more than 60 hymns for this purpose. The beautiful expressions of praise in "All Creatures of Our God and King" have endured throughout the centuries. A prayer written by Saint Francis has also become familiar and well-loved:

> Lord, make me an instrument of Thy peace. Where there is hatred, let me sow love.
> Where there is injury, pardon, Where there is discord, unity.
> Where there is doubt, faith. Where there is error, truth.
> Where there is despair, hope. Where there is sadness, joy.
> Where there is darkness, light.
> For it is in giving, that we receive. It is in pardoning, that we are pardoned.
> It is in dying, that we are born to eternal life.

* * * *

All creatures of our God and King, lift up your voice and with us sing Alleluia, Alleluia! Thou burning sun with golden beam, thou silver moon with softer gleam: O praise Him, O praise Him! Alleluia, Alleluia! Alleluia!

Thou rushing wind that art so strong, ye clouds that sail in heav'n along, O praise Him! Thou rising morn, in praise rejoice; ye lights of evening, find a voice: O praise Him, O praise Him! Alleluia, Alleluia! Alleluia!

Dear mother earth, who day by day unfoldest blessings on our way, O praise Him! Alleluia! The flow'rs and fruits that in thee grow, let them His glory also show; O praise Him, O praise Him! Alleluia, Alleluia! Alleluia!

Let all things their Creator bless, and worship Him in humbleness—O praise Him! Alleluia! Praise, praise the Father, praise the Son, and praise the Spirit, Three in One: O praise Him, O praise Him! Alleluia, Alleluia! Alleluia!

❦ *For Today:* Psalm 145; Jeremiah 32:17-20; Romans 11:36; Revelation 14:7

Praise God continually for His many blessings and for the wonders of His creation. Sing as you go—

Lasst Uns Erfreuen tune   From the *Geistliche Kirchengesäng* of 1623

O praise Him, O praise Him! Al – le – lu – ia, Al – le –

lu – ia! Al – le – lu – ia!

JOYFUL, JOYFUL, WE ADORE THEE

Henry van Dyke, 1852-1933

But the fruit of the Spirit is love, joy . . . against such things there is no law. (Galatians 5:22)

While gazing at the magnificent Berkshire mountains of Massachusetts, Henry van Dyke described in "Joyful, Joyful," the many aspects of life that should bring us joy. He insisted that his text, written in 1911, be sung to the music of "Hymn of Joy" from Beethoven's *Ninth Symphony.* This combination of words and great music, makes "Joyful, Joyful, We Adore Thee" one of the most joyous expressions of any hymn in the English language.

One of the forceful ideas expressed by van Dyke is that God's gracious love for us should create a greater "brother love" for our fellow man. With God's help we can become victorious over strife and be "lifted to the joy divine" as we daily show more love to others.

Henry van Dyke was a distinguished Presbyterian minister who served as a moderator of his denomination for a time and as a Navy Chaplain in World War I. Later he was the ambassador to Holland and Luxembourg under President Wilson. He also served a number of years as a professor of literature at Princeton University. High honors came to him for his many devotional writings. Yet this one inspiring hymn is the reason Henry van Dyke is best remembered today:

> Joyful, joyful, we adore Thee, God of glory, Lord of love; hearts unfold like flow'rs before Thee, hail Thee as the sun above. Melt the clouds of sin and sadness, drive the dark of doubt away; giver of immortal gladness, fill us with the light of day!

> All Thy works with joy surround Thee, earth and heav'n reflect Thy ways; stars and angels sing around Thee, center of unbroken praise; field and forest, vale and mountain, bloss'ming meadow, flashing sea, chanting bird and flowing fountain call us to rejoice in Thee.

> Thou art giving and forgiving, ever blessing, ever blest, well-spring of the joy of living, ocean-depth of happy rest! Thou the Father, Christ our Brother—All who live in love are Thine: Teach us how to love each other; lift us to the joy divine.

> Mortals, join the mighty chorus which the morning stars began; father-love is reigning o'er us; brother-love binds man to man. Ever singing, march we onward, victors in the midst of strife; joyful music lifts us sunward in the triumph song of life.

❦ **For Today:** Job 38:7; Psalm 98; Habakkuk 3:17-19; 1 Peter 3:8, 9

Would it be possible for you to offer your praise to God for His matchless love in some creative way—original poetry, music, painting . . .?

Hymn to Joy tune   Ludwig van Beethoven, 1770-1827

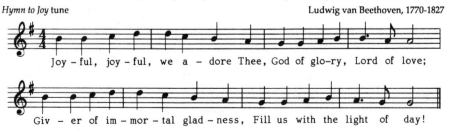

Joy - ful, joy - ful, we a - dore Thee, God of glo—ry, Lord of love;

Giv — er of im — mor — tal glad — ness, Fill us with the light of day!

FAIREST LORD JESUS!

Text from *Münster Gesangbuch*, 1677
4th verse translated by Joseph A. Seiss, 1823-1904

For by Him all things were created: things in heaven and on earth, visible and invisible, whether thrones or powers or rulers or authorities; all things were created by Him and for Him. (Colossians 1:16)

This lovely hymn extolling the beauty and virtues of Christ leads us to the praise and worship or our "beautiful Savior." The vivid comparisons of all the enjoyable sights of nature with Jesus, who is the very source and essence of all beauty, fill us with awe. Then we are reminded that our Savior outshines all creations of God, including the hosts of angels. How worthy He is of the deepest "glory and honor, praise, adoration now and forevermore!"

Little is known of the origin of this inspiring hymn. It is thought by some to have been sung in the 12th century by the German crusaders as they made their wearisome and dangerous trip to the Holy Land. Another source claims that this was one of the hymns used by the followers of John Hus. These were Moravian believers who were driven out of Bohemia in the bloody anti-Reformation purge of 1620. They settled in Silesia, now a part of Poland. "Fairest Lord Jesus" is thought to be a folk hymn that came from these devout Silesian peasants. The fourth verse, a fine translation by Joseph A. Seiss, emphasizes the dual nature of the Savior—"Son of God and Son of Man"—as well as the praise that will be eternally His.

Whatever the actual origin of the hymn may be, Christians for centuries have been blessed with this worshipful and joyful text, which focuses our view on the fair Son of God who reveals to us the glory of the Father.

Fairest Lord Jesus! Ruler of all nature! O Thou of God and man the Son! Thee will I cherish, Thee will I honor, Thou my soul's glory, joy and crown!

Fair are the meadows, fairer still the woodlands, robed in the blooming garb of spring; Jesus is fairer, Jesus is purer, who makes the woeful heart to sing.

Fair is the sunshine, fairer still the moonlight, and all the twinkling starry host: Jesus shines brighter, Jesus shines purer than all the angels heav'n can boast.

Beautiful Savior! Lord of the nations! Son of God and Son of Man! Glory and honor, praise, adoration now and forevermore be Thine!

❦ ***For Today:*** John 1:1, 3, 14; 5:23; 20:31; Philippians 2:9-11; Colossians 1:13, 15; 2:9; Hebrews 1:2, 3

Take time to reflect once again on the virtues of our lovely Lord Jesus. Offer thanks to God for the matchless gift of His Son. Worship Him with this musical expression—

Crusaders' Hymn tune

From *Schlesische Volkslieder*, 1842
Adapted by Richard S. Willis, 1819-1900

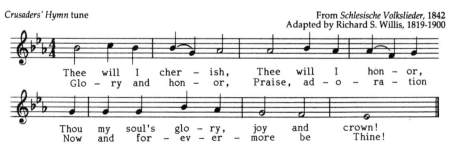

Thee will I cher - ish, Thee will I hon - or,
Glo - ry and hon - or, Praise, ad - o - ra - tion

Thou my soul's glo - ry, joy and crown!
Now and for - ev - er - more be Thine!

HOW GREAT THOU ART!

English Words by Stuart K. Hine, 1899-

Every day I will praise You and extol Your name for ever and ever. Great is the Lord and most worthy of praise; His greatness no one can fathom. (Psalm 145:2, 3)

Today's inspiring hymn of praise and adoration reminds us of God's unlimited power and love in creation and redemption. Although written in the past century, the hymn has become familiar to congregations just since the close of World War II. It especially became an international favorite after the Billy Graham Evangelistic Team used it in their crusades during the late 1940's and early 1950's.

The original text was written by a Swedish pastor, Carl Boberg, in 1886. While visiting a beautiful country estate, Boberg was caught in a sudden thunderstorm. The awesome and violent lightning and thunder quickly ended, leaving clear brilliant sunshine and the calm, sweet singing of the birds in the trees. Falling on his knees in awe and adoration of Almighty God, the pastor wrote nine stanzas of praise. Swedish congregations began to sing his lines to one of their old folk tunes. The text was later translated into German and Russian and ultimately into English by the Reverend S. K. Hine and his wife, English missionaries to the people of the Ukraine. When war broke out in 1939, it was necessary for the Hines to return to Britain, where Mr. Hine added the fourth stanza to this hymn. These four stanzas by Stuart Hine have since ministered and inspired God's people worldwide:

> O Lord my God, when I in awesome wonder consider all the worlds Thy hands have made, I see the stars, I hear the rolling thunder, Thy pow'r thruout the universe displayed!

> When thru the woods and forest glades I wander and hear the birds sing sweetly in the trees, when I look down from lofty mountain grandeur and hear the brook and feel the gentle breeze.

> And when I think that God, His Son not sparing, sent Him to die, I scarce can take it in—That on the cross, my burden gladly bearing, He bled and died to take away my sin!

> When Christ shall come with shout of acclamation and take me home, what joy shall fill my heart! Then I shall bow in humble adoration and there proclaim, my God, how great Thou art!

> **Refrain:** Then sings my soul, my Savior God, to Thee; how great Thou art, how great Thou art! Then sings my soul, my Savior God, to Thee; how great Thou art, how great Thou art!

❦ *For Today:* Deuteronomy 3:24; Psalm 48:1; Isaiah 40:26, 28; Romans 1:20

Take time to think once again about the unfathomable greatness of God and His wonderful redeeming love for each of us.

O Store Gud tune — Swedish melody

Then sings my soul, my Sav - ior God, to Thee; How great Thou art, how great Thou art!

UNTO THE HILLS AROUND DO I LIFT UP

John D. S. Campbell, 1845-1914

I will lift up my eyes to the hills—where does my help come from? My help comes from the Lord, the Maker of heaven and earth. (Psalm 121:1, 2)

The more we pursue God's majesty and greatness, the greater becomes our strength to live victoriously. Each day we need to take time to look away from ourselves and our petty complaints and focus our attention on our Creator God. Someone has observed that it is usually not so much the greatness of our troubles as the littleness of our spirit that makes us disgruntled complainers. A worthy starting point is to find inspiration from some part of God's creation. For the psalmist, it was looking at the hills all around him, reminders of God's power and authority. In another portion the psalmist reminds us that in time of need we should flee like a bird to our mountain and there find rest and security (Psalm 11:1). Yet the instruction is clear that though we receive inspiration from observing the majesty of creation, our real source of help must ultimately come from a personal relationship with God Himself, "the Lord, who heav'n and earth hath made."

The author of this text, John Douglas S. Campbell, was a well-known English personality of his day. He was a member of Parliament and the Governor General of Canada. Campbell was also a noted writer and a devoted Christian. The hymn first appeared in 1877. These inspiring words can still be a source of much comfort for any believer today:

> Unto the hills around do I lift up my longing eyes; O whence for me shall my salvation come, from whence arise? From God, the Lord, doth come my certain aid, from God, the Lord, who heav'n and earth hath made.

> He will not suffer that thy foot be moved: Safe shalt thou be. No careless slumber shall His eyelids close, who keepeth thee. Behold, our God, the Lord, He slumbereth ne'er, who keepeth Israel in His holy care.

> Jehovah is Himself thy keeper true, thy changeless shade; Jehovah thy defense on thy right hand Himself hath made. And thee no sun by day shall ever smite; no moon shall harm thee in the silent night.

> From ev'ry evil shall He keep thy soul, from ev'ry sin; Jehovah shall preserve thy going out, thy coming in. Above thee watching, He whom we adore shall keep thee henceforth, yea, forevermore.

❦ *For Today:* Psalm 11; 24; 121; Isaiah 40:9, 26; 41:10

Enjoy the majesty of some particular part of God's creation—a mountain, sunrise, sunset. Breathe a prayer of gratitude to the One who has made this possible. Determine to rely on Him more fully throughout this day. Carry this musical truth with you—

Sandon tune — Charles H. Purday, 1799-1885

From God, the Lord, doth come my cer-tain aid,

From God, the Lord, who heav'n and earth hath made.

HIS EYE IS ON THE SPARROW

Civilla D. Martin, 1869-1948

Are not two sparrows sold for a penny? Yet not one of them will fall to the ground apart from the will of your Father in heaven. And even the very hairs of your head are all numbered. So don't be afraid; you are worth more than sparrows. (Matthew 10:29-31)

Mrs. Civilla Martin, author of this gospel hymn text, tells of a visit in 1904 to a bedridden Christian friend. Mrs. Martin asked the woman if she ever got discouraged because of her physical condition. Her friend responded quickly: "Mrs. Martin, how can I be discouraged when my heavenly Father watches over each little sparrow and I know He loves and cares for me." Within just a few minutes Mrs. Martin completed the writing of her new text, which has since been a source of much encouragement to many of God's people.

It is interesting that our Lord chose the most common of all birds, sparrows of little value, to teach a profound truth: In God's eyes, no one is insignificant! He is vitally concerned with even the details of our lives. Notice also that the Bible uses another bird to teach this inspiring truth: "Those who hope in the Lord will soar on wings like eagles . . ." (Isaiah 40:31). With an awareness of God's concern for our lives and the promise of His enabling power to live victoriously, why should we be afraid?

Though the fig tree does not bud and there are no grapes on the vines, yet I will rejoice in the Lord, I will be joyful in God my Savior. (Habakkuk 3:17, 18)

Why should I feel discouraged, why should the shadows come, why should my heart be lonely and long for Heav'n and home, when Jesus is my portion? My constant Friend is He: His eye is on the sparrow, and I know He watches me; His eye is on the sparrow, and I know He watches me.

"Let not your heart be troubled," His tender word I hear, and resting on His goodness, I lose my doubts and fears; tho' by the path He leadeth but one step I may see: His eye is on the sparrow, and I know He watches me; His eye is on the sparrow, and I know we watches me.

Whenever I am tempted, whenever clouds arise, when songs give place to sighing, when hope within me dies, I draw the closer to Him; from care He sets me free; His eye is on the sparrow, and I know He watches me; His eye is on the sparrow, and I know He watches me.

Refrain: I sing because I'm happy, I sing because I'm free, for His eye is on the sparrow, and I know He watches me.

❦ *For Today:* Psalm 40:17; Matthew 6:28; Luke 12:6, 7, 22-31; James 1:1-11.

Rest and rejoice in the assurance of God's love. Seek to bring a word of cheerful encouragement to some sick or invalid individual. Remind him or her of God's concern and the truth of this song.

Charles H. Gabriel, 1856-1932

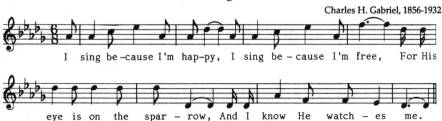

I sing be—cause I'm hap-py, I sing be-cause I'm free, For His eye is on the spar-row, And I know He watch-es me.

DAY IS DYING IN THE WEST

Mary A. Lathbury, 1841-1913

Ye shall have a song, as in the night when a holy solemnity is kept; and gladness of heart, as when one goeth with a pipe to come into the mountain of the Lord, to the mighty One of Israel. (Isaiah 30:29 KJV)

> Those evening clouds, that setting ray, and beauteous tints, sure to display their great Creator's praise;
> Then let the short-lived thing called man, whose life's comprised within a span, to Him his homage raise. —*Sir Walter Scott*

It is so easy to lose oneself in the majestic spectacles of the setting sun as it slowly fades over the horizon—yet forget to praise God, the source of all beauty. Mary Lathbury reminds us to "wait and worship" the "Lord most high" as we stand in awe at the passing of each day.

With a desire to encourage religious and cultural activities, Miss Lathbury worked with others to establish the Chautauqua Movement on the shores of beautiful Lake Chautauqua near Jamestown, New York. She became affectionately known as the "Poet Laureate and Saint of Chautauqua." In 1877, Mary was asked to write a hymn that would be suitable for the evening vesper services of Chautauqua. As she stood on the shore of the lake watching the magnificent setting sun one evening, Mary received the inspiration for the first two stanzas of her hymn. The final two stanzas were added 2 years later. After the music director of Chautauqua, Professor William Fisk Sherwin, composed a suitable melody for the text, "Day Is Dying in the West" was used that same summer. It has been used as the vesper hymn for all evening services of Chautauqua at its lovely New York site ever since.

> Day is dying in the west, heav'n is touching earth with rest; wait and worship while the night sets her evening lamps alight thru all the sky.

> Lord of life, beneath the dome of the universe, Thy home, gather us who seek Thy face to the fold of Thy embrace, for Thou art nigh.

> While the deep'ning shadows fall, heart of Love, enfolding all, thru the glory and the grace of the stars that veil Thy face, our hearts ascend.

> When forever from our sight pass the stars, the day, the night, Lord of angels, on our eyes let eternal morning rise, and shadows end.

> **Chorus:** Holy, holy, holy, Lord God of Hosts! Heav'n and earth are full of Thee! Heav'n and earth are praising Thee, O Lord most high!

🍒 *For Today:* Psalm 4:7, 8; 19:1, 2; 69:34; Isaiah 6:3

As you observe the setting sun or any of the wonders of God's creation, offer worship and praise to Him for the beauties He has provided for us.

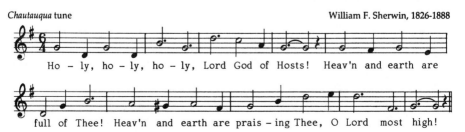

Chautauqua tune — William F. Sherwin, 1826-1888

Ho - ly, ho - ly, ho - ly, Lord God of Hosts! Heav'n and earth are
full of Thee! Heav'n and earth are prais - ing Thee, O Lord most high!

LOOK, YE SAINTS! THE SIGHT IS GLORIOUS

Thomas Kelly, 1769-1854

. . . Great and marvelous are Your deeds, Lord God Almighty. Just and true are Your ways, King of the ages. All nations will come and worship before You, for Your righteous acts have been revealed. (Revelation 15:3, 4)

Ascension Day, when we commemorate the translation of our Lord to heaven, is often a neglected observance in the lives of many Christians. It occurs 40 days after Easter, and though it never falls on a Sunday, the Lord's Day following Ascension Day is designated as Ascension Sunday. It is certainly one of the important events in the life of Christ, and it should be celebrated along with His birth, death, resurrection, sending of the Holy Spirit, and the promised second coming.

It is always thrilling to relive with our imagination the ascension scene on Mount Olivet described in Acts 1. There was the parting blessing from the Lord to His disciples and His final instructions regarding their mission to be worldwide witnesses after being empowered by the Holy Spirit. Then the One who had been nailed to a Roman cross just a short time before was dramatically taken up before their very eyes. And the two men dressed in white who suddenly appeared reminded the disciples that Christ's ascension must always be related to His return—"this same Jesus . . . will come back in the same way you have seen Him go into heaven" (Acts 1:10).

"Look, Ye Saints! The Sight Is Glorious" is generally regarded as one of the finest ascension hymns in the English language, one that is worthy of much greater use than it normally receives. Its author, Thomas Kelly, is recognized as one of Ireland's finest evangelical preachers, as well as one of its most distinguished spiritual poets of the 19th century.

Look, ye saints! the sight is glorious: See the Man of Sorrows now; from the fight returned victorious, ev'ry knee to Him shall bow: Crown Him! crown Him! Crowns become the Victor's brow.

Crown the Savior! angels, crown Him! rich the trophies Jesus brings; in the seat of pow'r enthrone Him, while the vault of heaven rings: Crown Him! crown Him! Crown the Savior King of kings.

Hark! those bursts of acclamation! Hark! those loud triumphant chords! Jesus takes the highest station—O what joy the sight affords! Crown Him! crown Him! King of kings and Lord of lords!

❦ **For Today:** Luke 24:50, 51; Acts 1:1-10; Philippians 2:6-11; Hebrews 2:9

Rejoice in the truth that your Lord not only rose triumphantly but ascended into heaven victoriously to be your personal representative before the Father. Learn and sing this hymn—

Coronae tune   William H. Monk, 1823-1889

Look, ye saints! the sight is glo–rious: See the Man of Sor – rows now;

From the fight re – turned vic – to – rious, Ev–'ry knee to Him shall bow.

CROWN HIM WITH MANY CROWNS

Matthew Bridges, 1800-1894 and Godfrey Thring, 1823-1903

His eyes are like blazing fire, and on His head are many crowns . . . He is dressed in a robe dipped in blood, and His name is the Word of God. (Revelation 19:12, 13)

Jesus Christ, the condescension of divinity and the exaltation of humanity.
—*Phillips Brooks*

The One who bore the crown of thorns while on the cross is now crowned with "many crowns" as the reigning monarch of heaven. Each crown in this hymn text exalts Christ for some specific aspect of His person or ministry: Stanza one for His eternal Kingship; stanza two for His love demonstrated in redemptive suffering; stanza three for His victorious resurrection and ascension; stanza four as a member of the Triune Godhead ever worthy of worship and praise.

This worshipful text is the combined effort of two distinguished Anglican clergymen, each of whom desired to write a hymn of exaltation to our suffering but now victorious Lord. Matthew Bridges' version first appeared in 1851 with six stanzas. Twenty-three years later Godfrey Thring wrote six additional stanzas, which appeared in his collection *Hymns and Sacred Lyrics.* The hymn's present form includes stanzas one, two, and four by Bridges and the third verse by Thring. The tune, "Diademata" (the Greek word for *crowns*), was composed especially for this text by George Elvey, a noted organist at St. George's Chapel in Windsor, England, where British royalty often attend.

Crown Him with many crowns, the Lamb upon His throne: Hark! how the heav'nly anthem drowns all music but its own! Awake, my soul, and sing of Him who died for thee, and hail Him as thy matchless King thru all eternity.

Crown Him the Lord of love: Behold His hands and side—rich wounds, yet visible above, in beauty glorified; no angel in the sky can fully bear that sight, but downward bends his wond'ring eye at mysteries so bright.

Crown Him the Lord of life: Who triumphed o'er the grave, who rose victorious to the strife for those He came to save; His glories now we sing, who died and rose on high, who died eternal life to bring and lives that death may die.

Crown Him the Lord of heav'n: One with the Father known; One with the Spirit thru Him giv'n from yonder glorious throne. To Thee be endless praise, for Thou for us hast died; be Thou, O Lord, thru endless days adored and magnified.

❦ *For Today:* Romans 14:9; Hebrews 2:7-10; Revelation 1:5, 6; 5:11-14; 19:1

Let your soul rejoice in the truth that you are related to the One "who died eternal life to bring and lives that death may die." Worship and praise Him even now with these musical lines—

Diademata tune   George J. Elvey, 1816-1893

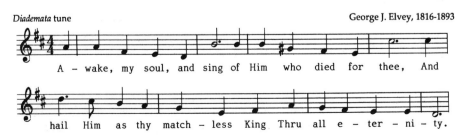

A - wake, my soul, and sing of Him who died for thee, And hail Him as thy match - less King Thru all e - ter - ni - ty.

GOLDEN HARPS ARE SOUNDING

Words and Music by Frances R. Havergal, 1836-1879

But you will receive power when the Holy Spirit comes on you; and you will be my witnesses in Jerusalem, and in all Judea and Samaria, and to the ends of the earth. After He said this, He was taken up before their very eyes, and a cloud hid Him from their sight. (Acts 1:8, 9)

Christ's resurrection is one of the most authenticated facts in history. During the 40-day interlude between Easter and the ascension, He was seen by such trusted witnesses as Peter, the entire group of disciples and apostles, a crowd of 500 of His followers, and finally by the apostle Paul (1 Corinthians 15:5-8). And many of these same individuals who saw His resurrected body also witnessed His ascent into heaven. The resurrection and the ascension, cornerstones of the Christian faith, have been historically documented. Christ's ascension assures us that Jesus is alive and ruling His kingdom while seated at the right hand of His Father. The ascension is also the guarantee that our Lord will personally return for His followers and escort us to the heavenly home He has prepared.

"Golden Harps Are Sounding" is one of our fine but unfamiliar hymns from the neglected "Ascension and Reign" section of many church hymnals. These are hymns that should be used not only during this Ascension Day season but also throughout the year to teach believers the importance of this event.

The author, Frances Havergal, wrote this Ascension Day hymn especially for a group of children while visiting their school. It is said to have been written within the space of ten minutes. "Golden Harps Are Sounding" is one of the few hymns for which Miss Havergal also composed her own tune, "Hermas."

Golden harps are sounding, angel voices ring, pearly gates are opened, opened for the King: Christ, the King of glory, Jesus, King of love, is gone up in triumph to His throne above.

He who came to save us, He who bled and died, now is crowned with glory at His Father's side: Never more to suffer, never more to die, Jesus, King of glory, is gone up on high.

Praying for His children in that blessed place, calling them to glory, sending them His grace: His bright home preparing, faithful ones, for you; Jesus ever liveth, ever loveth too.

Refrain: All His work is ended, joyfully we sing; Jesus hath ascended—Glory to our King!

❦ ***For Today:*** Psalm 24:7, 10; Luke 24:50; Acts 1:7-10; Romans 8:34; Hebrews 9:24

Share the thrilling account of Christ's ascension with your family members. Sing this musical truth together—

Hermas tune

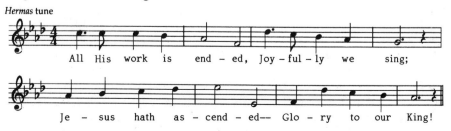

All His work is end - ed, Joy - ful - ly we sing;

Je - sus hath as - cend - ed-- Glo - ry to our King!

HAIL, THOU ONCE DESPISED JESUS!

John Bakewell, 1721-1819

He [God] raised Him from the dead and seated Him at His right hand in the heavenly realms, far above all rule and authority, power and dominion, and every title that can be given, not only in the present age but also in the one to come. (Ephesians 1:20, 21)

The author of this worshipful and strongly doctrinal hymn text presents a vivid contrast between the shame and suffering of Christ's earthly life and the greatness of His eternal glorification. We must never forget that the infant Jesus has moved on to take His place as the reigning Lord. Often at Christmas we become very sentimental about His lowly birth, or at Easter saddened as we recall His suffering and death. Sometimes our emphasis upon Christ's earthly ministry causes us to lose sight of His eternal deity. The Bible reminds us that "because Jesus lives forever, He has a permanent priesthood. Therefore He is able to save completely those who come to God through Him, because He always lives to intercede for them" (Hebrews 7:24, 25).

John Bakewell was a zealous lay evangelist who was associated with the Wesleyan movement during the mid 1700's. Something of the character of this man is indicated by the tribute on his tombstone in a grave site located in the same area where John Wesley is buried in London, England:

> Sacred to the memory of John Bakewell, who departed this life March 18, 1819, age 98. He adorned the doctrine of God, our Savior, and preached His glorious gospel about 70 years. "The memory of the just is blessed."

* * * *

Hail, Thou once despised Jesus! Hail, Thou Galilean King! Thou didst suffer to release us; Thou didst free salvation bring. Hail, Thou agonizing Savior, bearer of our sin and shame! By Thy merits we find favor; life is given through Thy name.

Jesus, hail! enthroned in glory, there forever to abide; all the heavenly hosts adore Thee, seated at Thy Father's side: There for sinners Thou art pleading; there Thou dost our place prepare, ever for us interceding till in glory we appear.

Worship, honor pow'r and blessing Thou art worthy to receive; loudest praises, without ceasing, meet it is for us to give. Help, ye bright angelic spirits, bring your sweetest, noblest lays; help to sing our Savior's merits; help to chant Immanuel's praise!

❦ ***For Today:*** Isaiah 53:3-6; Luke 24:26; Ephesians 1:18-22; Revelation 5:6-14

Lift your heart to the One who was slain but now liveth again—our Savior evermore. And because of His unchanging priesthood, He is ever accessible to us through prayer. Worship Him with these musical lines—

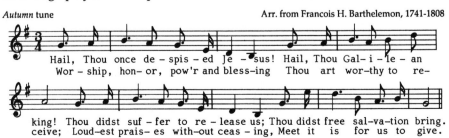

Autumn tune   Arr. from Francois H. Barthelemon, 1741-1808

HARK! TEN THOUSAND HARPS AND VOICES

Thomas Kelly, 1769-1854

Then I looked and heard the voice of many angels, numbering thousands upon thousands, and ten thousand times ten thousand. In a loud voice they sang: "Worthy is the Lamb, who was slain, to receive power and wealth and wisdom and strength and honor and glory and praise." (Revelation 5:11, 12)

As Christians we often reflect about anticipated sights of heaven—golden streets, jasper walls, crystal seas, jeweled crowns . . . but what about the sounds of heaven? From what we can learn from the Bible, heaven is a place of loud, inspiring sounds and much music.

The author of this hymn text, Thomas Kelly, saw with the eye of imagination the thrilling scene in heaven when the thousands upon thousands of angels give praise to Christ for His victorious mission to earth to accomplish man's redemption. And the thrilling truth is that someday we redeemed mortals will join that heavenly chorus. Throughout the ages our main occupation will be singing and playing our "glories to the King!" Alleluia!

This is another triumphant ascension hymn from the pen of Thomas Kelly, one of Ireland's finest evangelical preachers and spiritual poets of the 19th century. The hymn first appeared in one of Kelly's collections of hymns published in 1806. It was originally titled "Let All the Angels of God Worship Him."

Hark! ten thousand harps and voices sound the note of praise above; Jesus reigns and heav'n rejoices; Jesus reigns, the God of love. See, He sits on yonder throne: Jesus rules the world alone.

Sing how Jesus came from heaven, how He bore the cross below, how all pow'r to Him is given, how He reigns in glory now. 'Tis a great and endless theme—O, 'tis sweet to sing of Him.

King of glory, reign forever! Thine an everlasting crown. Nothing from Thy love shall sever those whom Thou hast made Thine own: Happy objects of Thy grace, destined to behold Thy face.

Savior, hasten Thine appearing; bring, O bring the glorious day, when, the awful summons hearing, heav'n and earth shall pass away. Then with golden harps we'll sing, "Glory, glory to our King!"

Refrain: Alleluia! Alleluia! Alleluia! A-men.

❦ *For Today:* Isaiah 60:19; Romans 8:35-39; Hebrews 1:6; 1 Peter 3:22; Revelation 22:3-5

Ponder anew the sights and sounds of heaven. Let your heart rejoice that you will be a part of that great eternal scene. Begin preparing now with these notes of praise—

Harwell tune   Lowell Mason, 1792-1872

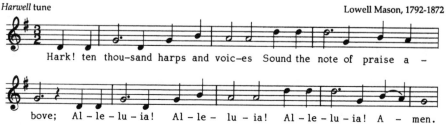

Hark! ten thou-sand harps and voic-es Sound the note of praise a - bove; Al - le - lu - ia! Al - le - lu - ia! Al - le - lu - ia! A - men.

THINE IS THE GLORY

Edmond L. Budry, 1854-1932
Translated by Richard B. Hoyle, 1875-1939

But thanks be to God! He gives the victory through our Lord Jesus Christ. (1 Corinthians 15:57)

In the ancient world, no celebration was considered more glorious than the march of triumphant returning warriors through their capital city. Many visual depictions have been made of the victorious Roman soldiers in the early centuries marching proudly through the streets and arches of Rome, leading captive slaves and hearing the boisterous approval of cheering admirers.

Christ our Savior fought the greatest battle of all time against the prince of this world and all of his legions. Our Lord returned triumphant to His Father, having conquered not only sin, death, and the grave, but Satan and hell also. Now He sits on the Father's right hand as the ruler of His kingdom and our personal advocate before God.

But the day of our celebration is just ahead. One can picture with imagination the procession that will occur in heaven when the Captain of Our Faith, Christ Himself, leads His Bride, the Church, through the heavenly portals amidst the shouts and songs of praise and glory to the "risen, conqu'ring Son."

"Thine Is the Glory" was originally written in 1884 in French—"A Toi la Gloire," by Edmond Budry, a pastor in Vevey, Switzerland. Nearly 40 years later, it was translated into English by Richard Hoyle and appeared in the *Cantate Domino Hymnal* used by the Student Christian Federation.

> Thine is the glory, risen, conqu'ring Son; endless is the vict'ry Thou o'er death hast won. Angels in bright raiment rolled the stone away, kept the folded grave clothes where Thy body lay.

> Lo! Jesus meets us, risen, from the tomb; lovingly He greets us, scatters fear and gloom; let His church with gladness hymns of triumph sing, for her Lord now liveth; death hath lost its sting.

> No more we doubt Thee, glorious Prince of Life! Life is naught without Thee; aid us in our strife; make us more than conqu'rors, through Thy deathless love; bring us safe through Jordan to Thy home above.

> **Refrain:** Thine is the glory, risen, conqu'ring Son; endless is the vict'ry Thou o'er death hast won.

❧ *For Today:* Romans 5:6, 10, 11; 1 Corinthians 15:50-58; Revelation 1:5, 6

Live in the triumphant promise of the joy that you will one day experience with all fullness when you share in the heavenly celebration with the saints of the ages. But for now, raise your voice in praise to our victorious Lord.

Maccabeus tune   George Frederick Handel, 1685-1759

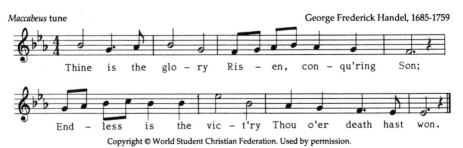

Thine is the glo - ry Ris - en, con - qu'ring Son;
End - less is the vic - t'ry Thou o'er death hast won.

REJOICE—THE LORD IS KING!

Charles Wesley, 1707-1788

After He had provided purification for sins, He sat down at the right hand of the Majesty in heaven. (Hebrews 1:3)

This text by Charles Wesley is another of the more than 6,500 hymns written by the "Sweet Bard of Methodism." Wesley wrote on hundreds of scriptural passages as well as on every conceivable phase of Christian experience and doctrine. This text was developed by Wesley to encourage his followers to have a more spontaneous joy in their lives as they became aware that Christ reigns victorious in heaven. It was based on the apostle Paul's instruction to the Christians at Philippi:

Rejoice in the Lord always. I will say it again: Rejoice! (Philippians 4:4)

It is important to remember that this instruction was written while Paul was a prisoner of Emperor Nero in Rome. The teaching of the entire Philippian letter is that it is possible to be a victor in life—regardless of the circumstances—when our faith is in an ascended, reigning Lord. There are twelve references to rejoicing in this one short book.

"Rejoice—the Lord is King!" first appeared in John Wesley's *Moral and Sacred Poems* in 1744, and two years later in Charles Wesley's collection, *Hymns for our Lord's Resurrection.*

Rejoice—the Lord is King! Your Lord and King adore! Rejoice, give thanks, and sing and triumph evermore! Lift up your heart, lift up your voice! Rejoice, again I say, rejoice!

Jesus the Savior reigns, the God of truth and love; when He had purged our stains He took His seat above: Lift up your heart, lift up your voice! Rejoice, again I say, rejoice!

His kingdom cannot fail—He rules o'er earth and heav'n; the keys of death and hell are to our Jesus giv'n: Lift up your heart, lift up your voice! Rejoice, again I say, rejoice!

He all His foes shall quell, shall all our sins destroy; and every bosom swell with pure seraphic joy: Lift up your heart, lift up your voice! Rejoice, again I say, rejoice!

Rejoice in glorious hope! Our Lord the Judge shall come and take His servants up to their eternal home: Lift up your heart, lift up your voice! Rejoice, again I say, rejoice!

❧ *For Today:* Philippians 4:4-9; Colossians 3:1; Hebrews 2:9

"Rejoice in the Lord always" is easy to quote but difficult to practice. Yet we must remember that this attitude of joy is not an option for the Christian but a scriptural command—the result of an intimate relationship with our reigning Lord. Carry this musical reminder as a help—

Darwall tune   John Darwall, 1731-1789

THE COMFORTER HAS COME

Frank Bottome, 1823-1894

And I will ask the Father. and He will give you another counselor to be with you forever—the Spirit of truth. (John 14:16)

One of the important days worthy of every Christian's recognition is Pentecost Sunday—an observance of the advent of the Holy Spirit. Pentecost Sunday occurs 50 days after Easter. The church color for this season is red, and the symbol is generally that of the dove. Other symbols for the Holy Spirit include:

Oil—It is the Holy Spirit that anoints and sets a believer apart for service.
Water—It is the Holy Spirit that cleanses us from the power of sin.
Light—It is the Holy Spirit that guides us in steps of truth and righteousness.
Fire— It is the Holy Spirit that purges and sets our devotion for God ablaze.
Wind—It is the Holy Spirit that refreshes our often parched hearts.

Jesus also referred to the Holy Spirit as the counselor—the Comforter—the "paraclete"—the one who would reside in each believer and always be ready to help and guide in times of need.

Following Christ's resurrection, the disciples' awareness of the Holy Spirit in their lives changed them from fearful, discouraged disciples into powerful proclaimers of the good news. This same awareness and appropriation of the Holy Spirit's enabling power is still a most necessary ingredient for effective representation of our Lord.

The text for this hymn, written by Frank Bottome, an American Methodist pastor, first appeared in the hymnal *Precious Times of Refreshing and Revival* in 1890.

O spread the tidings 'round, wherever man is found, wherever human hearts and human woes abound; let ev'ry Christian tongue proclaim the joyful sound: The Comforter has come!

The long, long night is past; the morning breaks at last, and hushed the dreadful wail and fury of the blast, as o'er the golden hills the day advances fast! The Comforter has come!

O boundless love divine! How shall this tongue of mine to wond'ring mortals tell the matchless grace divine—that I, a child of hell, should in His image shine! The Comforter has come!

Chorus: The Comforter has come, the Comforter has come! The Holy Ghost from heav'n—the Father's promise giv'n; O spread the tidings round, wherever man is found—The Comforter has come!

❦ **For Today:** John 7:39; John 15:26; Acts 2:1, 4, 38; 1 Thessalonians 4:8

Live in the conscious awareness of the Holy Spirit's presence and power. Ask Him to lead you as you witness to someone about Christ. Remember this truth as you go—

William J. Kirkpatrick, 1838-1921

O spread the ti - dings 'round, wher - ev - er man is found—

The Com - fort - er has come!

SPIRIT OF GOD, DESCEND UPON MY HEART

George Croly, 1780-1860

Not by might nor by power, but by My Spirit, says the Lord Almighty. (Zechariah 4:6)

Although it is always thrilling at Christmas to recall the events of our Savior's birth, or at Easter to celebrate His triumph over death, we must not forget Ascension or Pentecost. If Christ had never ascended to make intercession for us or had never sent the Holy Spirit to indwell and guide us, our relationship with the heavenly Father would be most incomplete.

One of the finest of all hymns for the Pentecost season is "Spirit of God, Descend Upon My Heart." It was written by Anglican minister George Croly, who was known among his associates as a "fundamentalist in theology, a fierce conservative in politics, and intensely opposed to all forms of liberalism." The hymn first appeared in 1854 in Croly's own hymnal, *Psalms and Hymns for Public Worship*. It was originally titled "Holiness Desired."

Each stanza contributes an important truth for our spiritual benefit:

Stanza One— A desire to change the focus of one's life from things temporal to things spiritual.

Spirit of God, descend upon my heart: Wean it from earth, through all its pulses move. Stoop to my weakness, mighty as Thou art, and make me love Thee as I ought to love.

Stanza Two— The total dedication of one's self to God.

Hast Thou not bid us love Thee, God and King? All, all Thine own—soul, heart and strength and mind. I see Thy cross—there teach my heart to cling: O let me seek Thee, and O let me find.

Stanza Three— A prayerful concern for knowing fully the Spirit's abiding presence.

Teach me to feel that Thou art always nigh; teach me the struggles of the soul to bear—to check the rising doubt, the rebel sigh; teach me the patience of unanswered prayer.

Stanza Four— A most beautiful metaphor of a Spirit-filled life: "my heart an altar, and Thy love the flame."

Teach me to love Thee as Thine angels love, one holy passion filling all my frame: The baptism of the heav'n descended Dove—my heart an altar and Thy love the flame.

❦ ***For Today:*** Psalm 51:10, 11; John 15:26; Romans 5:5; 8:1-4; Ephesians 4:29, 30

Pray even now that the Holy Spirit will give you a greater love and devotion for Christ and will teach and personalize more fully the truths of this hymn. Carry this musical prayer as you go—

Morecambe tune

Frederick C. Atkinson, 1841-1897

Spir - it of God, de - scend up - on my heart:

And make me love Thee as I ought to love.

GRACIOUS SPIRIT, DWELL WITH ME

Thomas T. Lynch, 1818-1871

I will give you a new heart and put a new spirit in you . . . and I will put My Spirit in you and move you to follow My decrees. (Ezekiel 36:26, 27)

An awareness and knowledge of the Holy Spirit's ministries is most important for every believer. Note briefly these ten specific ministries:

- Teaches truths about God and reveals Christ (John 16:12-15).
- Convicts us of wrong doing (John 16:8-11).
- Regenerates and renews us (Titus 3:5).
- Baptizes or places us into the body of Christ (1 Corinthians 12:13).
- Gives assurance of our salvation (Romans 8:16).
- Indwells and guides our lives (Romans 8:14; 1 Corinthians 6:19, 20).
- Prays for us (Romans 8:26).
- Fills our lives with joy and power (Ephesians 5:18).
- Seals and guarantees our eternal promise (Ephesians 4:30).
- Distributes gifts to the church (1 Corinthians 12:1-11).

In spite of a renewed awareness and appreciation of the Holy Spirit's ministries within recent years, these is also much theological difference between various groups of believers regarding terminologies and specifics. May we not become so engrossed with our theological differences about the Holy Spirit that we forfeit the practical benefits of living and walking in the Spirit and demonstrating the fruit of a Spirit-filled life to a lost world—"love, joy, peace, patience, kindness, goodness, faithfulness, gentleness and self-control" (Galatians 5:22). "Gracious Spirit, Dwell Within Me" also reminds us that the indwelling presence of the Holy Spirit should make us "gracious," "truthful," "mighty," and "holy."

> Gracious Spirit, dwell with me: I myself would gracious be; and with words that help and heal would Thy life in mine reveal; and with actions bold and meek would for Christ my Savior speak.

> Truthful Spirit, dwell with me: I myself would truthful be; and with wisdom kind and clear let Thy life in mine appear; and with actions brotherly speak my Lord's sincerity.

> Mighty Spirit, dwell with me: I myself would mighty be; mighty so as to prevail where unaided man must fail: ever by a mighty hope pressing on and bearing up.

> Holy Spirit, dwell with me: I myself would holy be; separate from sin, I would choose and cherish all things good, and whatever I can be, give to Him who gave me Thee!

❦ **For Today:** Romans 8:9; 1 Corinthians 6:19; Galatians 5:25; 1 Peter 1:22

Since the Holy Spirit is the most neglected and least understood Person of the Godhead, what can you do to help your church bring more attention to the importance of the Holy Spirit and His specific ministries?

Redhead tune   Richard Redhead, 1820-1901

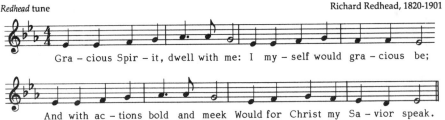

Gra – cious Spir – it, dwell with me: I my – self would gra – cious be;

And with ac – tions bold and meek Would for Christ my Sa – vior speak.

HOLY GHOST, WITH LIGHT DIVINE

Andrew Reed, 1787-1862

That the righteous requirements of the law might be fully met in us, who do not live according to the sinful nature but according to the Spirit. (Romans 8:4)

> As the earth can produce nothing unless it is fertilized by the sun, so we can do nothing worthwhile for God without the energizing Holy Spirit's power operating in our lives. —*Unknown*

> I used to ask God to help me. Then I asked if I might help Him. I ended up by asking Him to do His work through me. —*Hudson Taylor*

One of the marks of spiritual maturity in any believer's life is the growing conviction of the necessity of the Holy Spirit's presence and power for daily living. How natural it often seems to attempt to live our lives and even minister for God in our own wisdom and strength. How tragic it is when churches and religious organizations institutionalize themselves with dogma or legalistic rules and practices and gradually replace the invigorating ministry of the Holy Spirit in the lives of their people. It is said that religious movements often follow a predictable course: A Spirit-filled leader, an efficient machine, a dead monument.

"Holy Ghost, With Light Divine" has been for many years one of the church's important teaching hymns regarding the Holy Spirit's ministry. The first stanza tells us that we need a sensitivity to the Holy Spirit's presence in order to have clear directions for our lives. Then we are reminded that we need the Holy Spirit's ministry in order to live lives of purity and power (verse two). We also need the work of the Holy Spirit to balance the emotional sorrows of life with "joy divine" (verse three). Finally, we need the all-prevailing control by the Holy Spirit if our lives are to be totally committed and conformed to God (verse four).

This fine text, written by Anglican minister Andrew Reed, first appeared in a publication by its author in 1817.

> Holy Ghost, with light divine, shine upon this heart of mine; chase the shades of night away; turn my darkness into day.

> Holy Ghost, with pow'r divine, cleanse this guilty heart of mine; long hath sin without control held dominion o'er my soul.

> Holy Ghost, with joy divine, cheer this saddened heart of mine; bid my many woes depart; heal my wounded, bleeding heart.

> Holy Spirit, all divine, dwell within this heart of mine; cast down ev'ry idol-throne; reign supreme and reign alone.

❦ *For Today:* John 14:16-21; Acts 1:8; Romans 8:9-11; Ephesians 5:8, 9, 18

Try to engage in a conversation some respected Christian friend whose life clearly reflects Spirit control. Seek to learn more about this truth in a personal, first-hand manner. Sing this prayer as you go—

Mercy tune   Louis M. Gottschalk, 1829-1869

Ho-ly Ghost, with light di-vine, Shine up-on this heart of mine;
Ho-ly Spir-it, all di-vine, Dwell with-in this heart of mine;

Chase the shades of night a-way, Turn my dark-ness in-to day.
Cast down ev-'ry i-dol throne, Reign su-preme and reign a-lone.

BREATHE ON ME, BREATH OF GOD

Edwin Hatch, 1835-1889

As the Father has sent Me, I am sending you. And with that He breathed on them and said, "Receive the Holy Spirit." (John 20:21, 22)

The good news of the gospel relates not only to what Christ once did—His death, resurrection, ascension—but to what He presently offers: Forgiveness of sin, the reuniting of our eternal fellowship with the Creator, an advocate with the heavenly Father, and the energizing indwelling gift of the Holy Spirit.

When a person becomes a Christian, he or she receives the Holy Spirit within. Often, however, the Holy Spirit does not have control of that life even though He resides there. The Scriptures teach that we are to be filled with the Holy Spirit if we are to live overcoming lives. This is not some emotional, mystical event. To be "filled with the Spirit of God" means in a very practical way that a believer has surrendered completely to the Lordship of Christ and sincerely desires to be directed by the Holy Spirit in order to worthily exalt Christ and be an effective representative for God. One of the most compelling evidences of a Spirit-filled life is our consistent, Christ-like daily living.

The author of this choice text, Edwin Hatch, was an Anglican minister. He also served for a time as a professor of the classics at Trinity College in Canada. Dr. Hatch was widely known for his scholarship and lectures in early church history. Despite his scholarly attainments, Hatch was said to have possessed a faith as "simple and unaffected as a child's."

This prayer to the Holy Spirit desiring a unity between our earthly will and God's divine will first appeared in 1878 in a pamphlet titled "Between Doubt and Prayer." The hymn in its present form appeared later in the *Psalmist Hymnal,* published in 1886.

> Breathe on me, Breath of God; fill me with life anew, that I may love what Thou dost love and do what Thou wouldst do.
>
> Breathe on me, Breath of God, until my heart is pure, until with Thee I will one will—to do and to endure.
>
> Breathe on me, Breath of God, till I am wholly Thine, till all this earthly part of me glows with Thy fire divine.
>
> Breathe on me, Breath of God, so shall I never die, but live with Thee the perfect life of Thine eternity.

❦ ***For Today:*** John 3:5-7; 2 Corinthians 3:18; Galatians 5:5; 1 John 4:13

Invite the Holy Spirit to have a greater control of your life—to empower you to be an even more effective representative for God. Sing this prayer as you go—

Trentham tune — Robert Jackson, 1842-1914

Breathe on me, Breath of God, Fill me with life a-new,

That I may love what Thou dost love And do what Thou wouldst do.

BLESSED QUIETNESS

Manie P. Ferguson, 19th century

Do not let any unwholesome talk come out of your mouths, but only that which is helpful for building others up according to their needs, that it may benefit those who listen. And do not grieve the Holy Spirit of God, with whom you were sealed for the day of redemption. (Ephesians 4:29, 30)

The Holy Spirit performs many important ministries in the life of a Christian. One of these is to give us a calm and tranquil spirit, despite the stormy circumstances of life that may come our way.

One of the great tragedies of the Christian life, however, occurs when, through apathy or neglect or overt attitudes and actions, we allow the Holy Spirit's ministry to become grieved and even quenched, leaving us powerless and restless. Perhaps it might be due to: self-centeredness and lack of concern for the needs of others; negative and critical attitudes toward others; practicing known sin; or lack of times of worship and communion with God. Whatever the cause, this time of spiritual draught must be dealt with even as the psalmist prayed in Psalm 51: "Create in me a clean heart, O God, and renew a right spirit within me . . ."

The text for "Blessed Quietness" was written about 1900 by Manie Payne Ferguson after she had come into the Wesleyan experience of "holiness" or "entire sanctification" or—as some call it— "the filling of the Holy Spirit." Regardless of our theological terminology for the Holy Spirit's energizing ministry, the truth of these words is an essential in every believers' life—

Joys are flowing like a river since the comforter has come; He abides with us forever, makes the trusting heart His home.

Bringing life and health and gladness all around, this heav'nly guest banished unbelief and sadness, chang'd our weariness to rest.

Like the rain that falls from heaven, like the sunlight form the sky, so the Holy Ghost is given, coming on us from on high.

See, a fruitful field is growing, blessed fruit of righteousness; and the streams of life are flowing in the lonely wilderness.

What a wonderful salvation, where we always see His face! What a perfect habitation, what a quiet resting place!

Chorus: Blessed quietness, holy quietness—what assurance in my soul! On the stormy sea He speaks peace to me—how the billows cease to roll!

❦ *For Today:* Luke 11:13; John 14:18; Acts 5:32; Romans 8:16; Galatians 5:22

Be especially aware of attitudes, words, or actions that could grieve and quench the Holy Spirit's ministry in your life. Enjoy a life of "blessed quietness" as you walk with God. Carry this musical reminder with you—

W. S. Marchall, 19th century
Adapted by James M. Kirk, 1854-1945

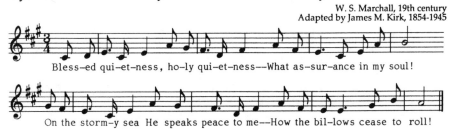

Bless—ed qui—et—ness, ho—ly qui—et—ness——What as—sur—ance in my soul!

On the storm—y sea He speaks peace to me——How the bil—lows cease to roll!

HOLY SPIRIT, FAITHFUL GUIDE

Words and Music by Marcus M. Wells, 1815-1895

I will not leave you comfortless; I will come to you. (John 14:18 KJV)

One of the Holy Spirit's ministries is to lead us each day wherever our heavenly Father desires us to best represent Him. When vital decisions must be made, the Holy Spirit can open the Scriptures to us and illuminate our minds. By this faithful guidance of the Holy Spirit, we come to love and follow the will of God for our daily living.

Many of our troubles occur because we fail to take counsel from the Holy Spirit and the Bible. Instead of first praying and seeking guidance, we act and then ask God to bless our actions. We must learn the lesson continually that effective Christian living is totally dependent upon an awareness and appreciation of the Holy Spirit's intimate presence in our lives; we must have a willingness to be directed and controlled by Him.

"Holy Spirit, Faithful Guide" was written and composed by an American farmer, Marcus M. Wells. He gave the following account for its writing:

> On a Saturday afternoon in October, 1858, while at work in my cornfield near Hardwick, New York, the sentiment of this hymn came to me. The next day, I finished the hymn and wrote a tune for it and sent it to Professor I. G. Woodbury.

The hymn appeared in the next month's issue of Woodbury's periodical, *The New York Musical Pioneer.* These tender words still minister to us today:

> Holy Spirit, faithful Guide, ever near the Christian's side, gently lead us by the hand, pilgrims in a desert land; weary souls fore'er rejoice, while they hear that sweetest voice whisp'ring softly, "Wand'rer come! Follow Me, I'll guide thee home."

> Ever-present, truest Friend, ever near Thine aid to lend, leave us not to doubt and fear, groping on in darkness drear; when the storms are raging sore, hearts grow faint, and hopes give o'er, whisper soflty, "Wand'rer come! Follow Me, I'll guide thee home."

> When our days of toil shall cease, waiting still for sweet release, nothing left but heav'n and prayer, knowing that our names are there, wading deep the dismal flood, pleading naught but Jesus' blood, whisper softly, "Wand'rer come! Follow Me, I'll guide thee home."

❦ ***For Today:*** John 14:16, 26; 15:26; 16:13; Romans 8:4, 26, 27; 1 John 3:24

Determine to be especially aware of and sensitive to the Holy Spirit's guidance, even in the minute decisions and actions of the day. Thank Him for His promised presence, even into eternity. Use this portion of the hymn to aid you in this exciting walk of faith.

Faithful Guide tune

Ho - ly Spir-it, faith-ful Guide, Ev - er near the Chris-tian's side,
Gent - ly lead us by the hand, Pil-grims in a des - ert land;

Whis - p'ring soft - ly, "Wan - d'rer come! Fol-low Me, I'll guide you home."

EVEN ME

Elizabeth Codner, 1824-1919

He will be like rain falling on a mown field, like showers watering the earth.
(Psalm 72:6)

The spiritual blessings of a Spirit-filled life are intended for every believer, not just for a favored few.

The author of this hymn text was Elizabeth Codner, the wife of an Anglican clergyman. She was having her personal devotions one day when she became deeply impressed with a verse of Scripture, Ezekiel 34:26:

I will cause the shower to come down in the season, there shall be showers of blessing.

Mrs. Codner thought about the importance of water in the dry country of Palestine and related this to the necessity of the daily refreshment of the Holy Spirit and the Scriptures in a believer's life. When she was still contemplating this truth, a group of young people from the parish called on her and told the news of their recent trip to Ireland. They related that certain cities and areas of the Emerald Isle had experienced a spiritual awakening during the time of their visit. The young people were thrilled to have been witnesses of this event. As they were describing their experience, Mrs. Codner began to pray that these young men would not be content merely to have been spectators of the Holy Spirit's ministry but would also desire a genuine outpouring of His power in their individual lives. With the words of Ezekiel 34:26 in mind, she challenged them with the remark, "While the Lord is pouring out such showers of blessing upon others, pray that some drops will fall on you."

The following Sunday morning, Mrs. Codner stayed home from church because of illness, and with the impact of the young people's experience still fresh in her mind, she penned these challenging words.

Lord, I hear of show'rs of blessing Thou art scatt'ring full and free; show'rs the thirsty land refreshing—let some drops now fall on me.

Love of God so pure and changeless, blood of Christ so rich and free, grace of God so strong and boundless: magnify them all in me.

Pass me not! Thy lost one bringing, bind my heart, O Lord, to Thee; while the streams of life are springing, blessing others, O bless me.

Refrain: Even me, even me, let Thy blessing fall on me.

❦ ***For Today:*** Psalm 72; Ezekiel 34:26-31; Luke 11:13; Romans 8:4

Recall and reflect on individuals whose lives have strongly evidenced the Holy Spirit's presence and power. Ask God in faith to make this your portion as well. Pray as you go—

William B. Bradbury, 1816-1868

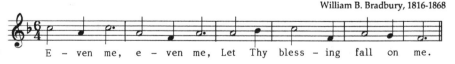

E - ven me, e - ven me, Let Thy bless - ing fall on me.

PRAISE YE THE TRIUNE GOD!

Elizabeth R. Charles, 1828-1896

I will praise Your name for Your love and Your faithfulness, for You have exalted above all things Your name and Your word. (Psalm 138:2)

Saints and angels join in praising Thee, the Father, Spirit, Son—
Evermore their voices raising to the Eternal Three in One. —*J. Montgomery*

The Sunday after Pentecost Sunday is the time when the Christian church has especially recognized the doctrine of the Trinity, the existence of the triune Godhead. This doctrine has been called one of the mystic truths of Scripture because of the difficulty in fathoming and explaining it. Yet it cannot be denied that the Bible does teach that while God is one, He exists in three co-equal Persons—Father, Son, and Holy Spirit. Scripture ascribes each member with such attributes as eternal, omnipotent, omniscient, and creator of the universe. Although the word *trinity* is not used, there are several passages in which all three Persons are expressly mentioned together: The great commission (Matthew 28:19), and the apostolic blessing (2 Corinthians 13:13).

The best of human analogies for explaining the trinity, such as ice, water, and steam being three distinct forms of the same element, always falls short. In the final analysis, we must accept this truth by faith and offer our worship and praise to each member of the Godhead.

This hymn text by Elizabeth Charles, one of England's gifted women of her day—author, poet, translator of German texts, musician and painter—is one of our finest Godhead hymns. The hymn does not present any complicated arguments. It simply directs a child-like praise to each member of the trinity for His loving care and concern for us. This we can understand.

Praise ye the Father for His loving kindness; tenderly cares He for His erring children; praise Him, ye angels, praise Him in the heavens, praise ye Jehovah!

Praise ye the Savior—great is His compassion; graciously cares He for His chosen people; young men and maidens, ye old men and children, praise ye the Savior!

Praise ye the Spirit, Comforter of Israel, sent of the Father and the Son to bless us; praise ye the Father, Son and Holy Spirit—Praise ye the Triune God!

❦ *For Today:* Psalm 139:7; Romans 8:9; 16:26; 1 John 5:7, 8; Jude 20; Revelation 1:4, 5

Though it is difficult to do, try explaining the meaning of the Trinity to some close Christian friend or member of your family. Offer this expression of praise throughout the day—

Flemming tune   Fredrich F. Flemming, 1778-1813

COME, THOU ALMIGHTY KING

Source unknown, c. 1757

Lift up your heads, O you gates; lift them up, you ancient doors, that the King of glory may come in. Who is He, this King of glory? The Lord Almighty—He is the King of glory. (Psalm 24:9, 10)

In his book *The Knowledge of the Holy*, A. W. Tozer left these choice words regarding the Trinity:

> The doctrine of the Trinity . . . is truth for the heart. The fact that it cannot be satisfactorily explained, instead of being against it, is in its favor. Such a truth had to be revealed; no one could have imagined it.

The doctrine of the Trinity has been controversial since the earliest days of Christianity. In A.D. 325, the Council of Nicaea affirmed its belief in the Triune Godhead. During the 16th century Reformation period, it was again denied by the Socinians. And still today many liberal theologians and groups are blatant in their denial. They often speak of God, the Father of all, Jesus, the mere man, and the divine influence of the Spirit of God. This form of blasphemy relegates each member of the Godhead to a role far less than that ascribed in the Bible.

This familiar Trinity hymn is also one of our most popular "opening hymns" for a Sunday morning worship service. It appeared anonymously in England in about 1757 to commemorate Trinity Sunday. It has been attributed by some to Charles Wesley since it first appeared in a pamphlet published by John Wesley.

This is a hymn that must always be sung with all four stanzas. To omit any of the first three would be to slight one of the members of the Godhead. The fourth stanza is a grand affirmation of the mysterious doctrine of the Trinity, that God is One yet Three and ever worthy of our love and adoration.

Come, Thou Almighty King, help us Thy name to sing; help us to praise: Father, all glorious, o'er all victorious, come and reign over us, Ancient of Days.

Come, Thou Incarnate Word, gird on Thy mighty sword, our prayer attend: Come and Thy people bless, and give Thy word success—Spirit of holiness, in us descend.

Come, Holy Comforter, Thy sacred witness bear in this glad hour: Thou who almighty art, now rule in ev'ry heart, and ne'er from us depart, Spirit of pow'r.

To the great One in Three eternal praises be, hence evermore: His sov'reign majesty, may we in glory see, and to eternity love and adore.

❦ *For Today:* Psalm 47; 103:19; John 8:54; 10:31-33; Acts 5:3, 4

Reflect again on the importance of having a proper perspective regarding the Godhead. What are the dangers of giving less than full and equal recognition of deity to each member of the Trinity? Carry this musical truth with you—

Italian Hymn tune — Felice de Giardini, 1716-1796

HAPPY THE HOME WHEN GOD IS THERE

Henry Ware Jr., 1794-1843

. . . But as for me and my household, we will serve the Lord. (Joshua 24:15)

The beauty of the home is order; the blessing of the home is contentment;
The glory of the home is hospitality; the crown of the home is godliness.

—Unknown

This is the season when our attention is especially directed to the basic social institution in society, the home, with special days for recognizing mothers, fathers, and children. The strength of any nation is the quality of its homes. "In love of home, the love of country has its rise" said Charles Dickens.

Home should be the holy of holies in a person's life, a place where ultimate love and acceptance are found between parents and with the children. The real test of a parent's spirituality is his home life—the daily demonstration of a Christ-like character. As parents, our responsibility is not only to feed and clothe our children's bodies, but to nurture their spirits, their minds, and their moral values. By word and by personal example we must carefully guide our children and fervently seek to show them what it means to be a Christian. Good parenting also involves maintaining strong lines of communication between all members of the family. This demands quality time spent together in discussions, social times, daily spiritual retreats, and weekly periods of instruction and worship in the local church.

This fine text was written by an ordained Unitarian minister, Henry Ware, who later became pastor of the Second Unitarian Church in Boston, Massachusetts. The well-known American poet, Ralph Waldo Emerson, served for a time as Ware's assistant. The hymn first appeared in *Selection of Hymns and Poetry for Use of Infant and Juvenile Schools and Families,* published in 1846.

Happy the home when God is there and love fills ev'ry breast, when one their wish and one their prayer and one their heav'nly rest.

Happy the home where Jesus' name is sweet to ev'ry ear, where children early lisp His fame and parents hold Him dear.

Happy the home where prayer is heard and praise is wont to rise, where parents love the sacred Word and all its wisdom prize.

Lord, let us in our homes agree this blessed peace to gain; unite our hearts in love to Thee, and love to all will reign.

❦ *For Today:* Deuteronomy 6:7 Proverbs 22:6; Ephesians 5:21-23; 6:4

Reflect on ways that you could improve the quality of your home. Does God really have His rightful place as the foundation of the home? Carry this musical message with you as you seriously consider these matters—

Beatitudo tune

John B. Dykes, 1825-1876

O PERFECT LOVE

Dorothy B. Gurney, 1858-1932

For this reason a man will leave his father and mother and be united to his wife, and the two will become one flesh. (Ephesians 5:31)

A perfect union of selfless and totally committed love, not an indulgent form of physical gratification, is God's plan for the human race. Kindness, patience, forgiveness, and demonstrated affection for each other are the ingredients of a happy marriage. The desire to put the needs and interests of one's mate first before your own is the basis of matrimonial harmony. Marriage has been instituted by God to be a picture of the sacrificial and unending love of Christ for His bride, the church, and the bride's loving and devoted responses to her Lord. Yet today we see an epidemic of broken marriages, lack of genuine faithfulness, self-centered conflicts between husbands and wives—even among professing Christians.

A beautiful portrayal of ideal married love is given in this wedding hymn as it describes the harmony that exists when God is the foundation of the marriage relationship. Dorothy Gurney, an English woman, was asked by her sister, who was soon to be married, if she would try writing some suitable words for a favorite hymn tune that could be used at the wedding. Dorothy went off by herself for only 15 minutes and returned with the text of "O Perfect Love." Her sister was delighted with it and insisted that it be sung at the wedding.

Mrs. Gurney stated that the writing of the hymn "was no effort whatever after the initial idea had come to me of the two-fold aspect of perfect union— love and life—and I have always felt that God helped me write it." Although this was the only hymn she wrote, it has been recognized as one of the finest wedding texts in the English language.

> O perfect love, all human thought transcending, lowly we kneel in prayer before Thy throne, that theirs may be the love which knows no ending, whom thou forevermore dost join in one.
>
> O perfect life, be Thou their full assurance of tender charity and steadfast faith, of patient hope, and quiet, brave endurance, with child-like trust that fears nor pain nor death.
>
> Grant them the joy which brightens earthly sorrow; grant them the peace which calms all earthly strife, and to life's day the glorious unknown morrow that dawns upon eternal love and life!

❦ *For Today:* Genesis 2:18-25; Mark 10:7-9; Ephesians 5:21-33; 1 Peter 3:7

Reflect on this statement: "A successful marriage requires falling in love many times, always with the same person." Determine to let your marriage more fully imitate Christ's love for His bride, the Church.

Sandringham tune   Joseph Barnby, 1839-1896

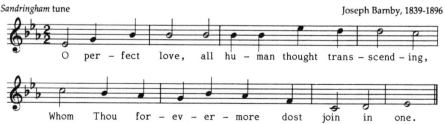

AMERICA THE BEAUTIFUL

Katharine Lee Bates, 1859-1929

Righteousness exalts a nation, but sin is a disgrace to any people. (Proverbs 14:34)

> After what I owe to God, nothing should be more dear or more sacred to me than the love and respect I owe to my country. —*Jacques Auguste de Thou*

Each time we join together in singing the vividly descriptive lines of "America the Beautiful," we are moved emotionally as we contemplate the wonders of our great nation. The scenic beauties, the courage of the early settlers, and the sacrifices of heroes in battle all stir us to avid appreciation of our country's heritage. But this national hymn does more than inspire us to praise our great nation. It also encourages us to pray for it. Each stanza is completed with an earnest plea for God's grace, God's healing, and His refining until we as a people achieve true brotherhood, law-abiding control, and nobility.

The author felt deeply about the message of her patriotic hymn:

> We must match the greatness of our country with the goodness of personal godly living. If only we could couple the daring of the Pilgrims with the moral teachings of Moses, we would have something in this country that no one could ever take from us.

As we consider this hymn, we are reminded that America owes its birth to the living, vital and dynamic faith in God that our founding fathers demonstrated. There is a real need today for a return to such a national dependence upon God as well as a renewed pride in our wonderful land.

Katherine Bates, who was a teacher and head of the English department at Wellesley College in Massachusetts, wrote the original lines of this text in 1893, while teaching summer school in Colorado Springs, Colorado, where the Rocky Mountains and Pike's Peak had especially impressed her.

> O beautiful for spacious skies, for amber waves of grain, for purple mountain majesties above the fruited plain! America, America! God shed His grace on thee, and crown thy good with brotherhood from sea to shining sea.

> O beautiful for pilgrim feet, whose stern, impassioned stress a thoroughfare for freedom beat across the wilderness! America! America! God mend thine ev'ry flaw, confirm thy soul in self-control, thy liberty in law.

> O beautiful for heroes proved in liberating strife, who more than self their country loved and mercy more than life! America! America! May God thy gold refine, till all success be nobleness, and ev'ry gain divine.

> O beautiful for patriot dream that sees, beyond the years, thine alabaster cities gleam—undimmed by human tears! America! America! God shed His grace on thee, and crown thy good with brotherhood from sea to shining sea.

❦ *For Today:* Isaiah 32:17; Romans 13:1-7; 1 Peter 2:13-17

Give thanks to God for the noble heritage and the many beauties of our great country He has entrusted to us. Raise your voice in praise to God and country—

Materna tune   Samuel A. Ward, 1847-1903

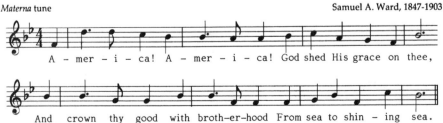

A - mer - i - ca! A - mer - i - ca! God shed His grace on thee,

And crown thy good with broth-er-hood From sea to shin - ing sea.

BATTLE HYMN OF THE REPUBLIC

Julia Ward Howe, 1819-1910

Some trust in chariots and some in horses, but we trust in the name of the Lord our God. (Psalm 20:7)

To have implicit trust in God's faithful care and protection is never easy in times of danger or strife. Yet even in the midst of the terrible Civil War between the Northern and Southern states, a remarkable woman named Julia Ward Howe proclaimed her confidence in God's triumphant power in this inspiring text.

Deeply anguished at the growing conflict between the two sections of the country, Mrs. Howe watched troops marching off to war singing "John Brown's Body," a song about a man who had been hanged in his efforts to free the slaves. Julia felt that the catchy camp meeting tune should have better words. In a desire to phrase her own feelings about the dreadful events of the time, she "scrawled the verses almost without looking at the paper." The national hymn first appeared in the *Atlantic Monthly Magazine* in 1862, as a battle song for the republic. Before long the entire nation became inspired by her text and united in singing the new words with the old tune.

Mrs. Howe's hymn has been acclaimed through the years as one of our finest patriotic songs. At one time it was sung as a solo at a large rally attended by President Abraham Lincoln. After the audience had responded with loud applause, the President, with tears in his eyes, cried out, "Sing it again!" It was sung again. And after more than a hundred years, Americans still join often in proclaiming, "Glory! Hallelujah! His truth is marching on!"

> Mine eyes have seen the glory of the coming of the Lord; He is trampling out the vintage where the grapes of wrath are stored; He hath loosed the fateful lightning of His terrible swift sword; His truth is marching on.
>
> I have seen Him in the watch-fires of a hundred circling camps; they have builded Him an altar in the evening dews and damps; I can read His righteous sentence by the dim and flaring lamps; His day is marching on.
>
> He has sounded forth the trumpet that shall never call retreat; He is sifting out the hearts of men before His judgment seat; O be swift, my soul, to answer Him; be jubilant, my feet! Our God is marching on.
>
> In the beauty of the lilies Christ was born across the sea, with a glory in His bosom that transfigures you and me; as He died to make men holy, let us die to make men free! While God is marching on.
>
> **Refrain:** Glory! Glory! Hallelujah! His truth is marching on.

❦ *For Today:* 2 Chronicles 7:14; Psalm 33:12; 144:15; 1 Peter 2:16

How can we best express our gratitude for those who have died defending their country? Try to honor them by continuing to support the truths for which they fought. Sing as you go—

American melody, c. 1852

Glo – ry! glo – ry! Hal – le – lu – jah! Glo – ry! glo–ry! Hal – le – lu- jah!

Glo – ry! glo – ry! Hal – le – lu – jah! His truth is march – ing on.

MY COUNTRY, 'TIS OF THEE

Samuel Francis Smith, 1808-1895

Blessed is the nation whose God is the Lord, the people He chose for His inheritance. (Psalm 33:12)

Men must be governed by God or they will be ruled by tyrants.   —*William Penn*

Moved deeply by the desire to create a national hymn that would allow the American people to offer praise to God for our wonderful land, a 24 year-old theological student penned these lines on a scrap of paper in less than 30 minutes in 1843. Yet even today many consider "My Country, 'Tis of Thee" their favorite patriotic hymn and call it our "unofficial national anthem."

The easily singable words of the song are matched with a popular international melody used by many nations, including England, where it accompanies "God Save the King/Queen." The emotionally powerful ideas that Smith expressed had an immediate response. The hymn soon became a national favorite. The stirring tributes to our fatherland in the first three stanzas lead to a worshipful climax of gratefulness to God and a prayer for His continued guidance.

Following his graduation from Harvard and the Andover Theological Seminary, Samuel Smith became an outstanding minister in several Baptist churches in the East. He composed 150 hymns during his 87 years and helped compile the leading Baptist hymnal of his day. He was also editor of a missionary magazine through which he exerted a strong influence in promoting the cause of missions. Later he became the secretary of the Baptist Missionary Union and spent considerable time visiting various foreign fields. Samuel Smith was truly a distinctive representative of both his country and his God.

> My country, 'tis of thee, sweet land of liberty, of thee I sing: Land where my fathers died, land of the pilgrims' pride, from ev'ry mountain side let freedom ring!
>
> My native country, thee, land of the noble free, thy name I love: I love thy rocks and rills, thy woods and templed hills; my heart with rapture thrills like that above.
>
> Let music swell the breeze, and ring from all the trees sweet freedom's song: Let mortal tongues awake; let all that breathe partake; let rocks their silence break, the sound prolong.
>
> Our father's God, to Thee, author of liberty, to Thee we sing: Long may our land be bright with freedom's holy light; protect us by Thy might, great God, our King!

❦ *For Today:* Psalm 33; Matthew 22:21; Acts 10:35; Romans 13:1-7

Spend time thinking of the many wonderful positive aspects of our great land and give praise to God for all of His past blessings. Pray for His continued guidance and protection in future days. Carry this musical message as you go—

America tune

From *Thesaurus Musicus*, 1744
Source unknown

Land where my fa – ther's died, Land of the pil – grims' pride,
Long may our land be bright with free–dom's ho– ly light;

From ev – 'ry moun – tain side let free – dom ring.
Pro–tect us by Thy might, Great God our King.

June

• Gospel • Salvation • Repentance • Forgiveness
• Invitation • Testimony

CHRIST RECEIVETH SINFUL MEN

Erdmann Neumeister, 1671-1756
Translated by Emma F. Bevan, 1827-1909

This man welcomes sinners and eats with them. (Luke 15:2)

> Did Christ o'er sinners weep, and shall our cheeks be dry?
> Let floods of penitential grief burst forth from every eye. —*John Newton*

The thrilling news of the gospel is that Jesus welcomes the nobodies of life and transforms them into somebodies. The pages of church history are filled with examples of people whose lives have been dramatically changed from vile sinners to spiritual saints.

Divine love is never forced on anyone. God created man with a free will, free even to reject Christ's provision for salvation. Our heavenly Father does not want to send to hell people who reject His Son—it is a place that was originally intended for the devil and his angels (Matthew 25:41). It cost God the cross and death of Jesus before He could forgive our sin and still remain a holy God. Although costly to God, salvation is a free gift to all who will receive it.

"Christ Receiveth Sinful Men" was originally written in 1718 by a Lutheran minister, Erdmann Neumeister, pastor of a church in Hamburg, Germany, for 41 years. He became widely known as an eloquent, forceful preacher as well as the author of approximately 650 hymns. More than a century later, an English lady hymnist, Emma Frances Bevan, translated this and a number of other German texts into the English language. Still today, this hymn reminds us clearly that Christ welcomes any repentant sinner who responds to His gracious invitation for forgiveness and a new life.

> Sinners Jesus will receive! Sound this word of grace to all who the heav'nly pathway leave, all who linger, all who fall.
>
> Come, and He will give you rest; trust Him for His word is plain; He will take the sinfulest; Christ receiveth sinful men.
>
> Now my heart condemns me not; pure before the law I stand; He who cleansed me from all spot satisfied its last demand.
>
> Christ receiveth sinful men, even me with all my sin; purged from ev'ry spot and stain, heav'n with Him I enter in.
>
> **Chorus:** Sing it o'er and o'er again: Christ receiveth sinful men; make the message clear and plain: Christ receiveth sinful men.

❦ ***For Today:*** Isaiah 55:7; Matthew 11:28, 29; Luke 15:1-7; Ephesians 1:6-8

Thank God again for His free gift of salvation that is extended to everyone. There are many today who believe that they must somehow make themselves better before they can be accepted by God. Determine to share this truth with such a one.

James McGranahan, 1840-1907

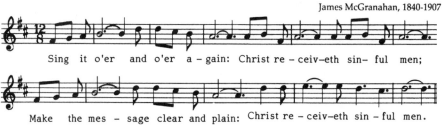

YE MUST BE BORN AGAIN

William T. Sleeper, 1819-1904

In reply Jesus declared, "I tell you the truth, unless a man is born again, [born from above] he cannot see the kingdom of God." (John 3:3)

Jesus made it clear that to be a member of His heavenly Kingdom, people must be twice-born—recipients of God's Spirit and possessors of eternal life. Such a person then begins to live by a new dimension and a new direction. He has a new disposition, a new nature, a new commitment, and a new purpose for living. A so-called Christianity that does not involve a personal conversion and change is not an authentic Christianity in the New Testament sense. Eternal life is a quality of life that begins with the new birth experience and continues in daily fellowship with God and His people both now and forever. But the new birth experience can never be adequately explained. It is more than knowledge and mental assent. To be understood, it must ultimately be experienced.

The composer of this hymn, George C. Stebbins, tells in his *Memoirs and Reminiscences* about the time he was assisting Dr. George F. Pentecost in an evangelistic crusade in Worcester, Massachusetts, when Dr. Pentecost one night preached on Christ's statement to Nicodemus in John 3:3 about the need of being born again. With the strong impression of this sermon still in his mind, Stebbins contacted one of the pastors in the city, William Sleeper, and asked his assistance in writing verses for the musical ideas he had for this text. "He acted at once upon my suggestion," said Stebbins, "and soon after came to me with the hymn that bears his name.

And another hymn was born that has since been used to confront individuals with the necessity of a new birth if they are ever to "see the kingdom of God."

A ruler once came to Jesus by night to ask Him the way of salvation and light; the Master made answer in words true and plain, "Ye must be born again."

Ye children of men, attend to the word so solemnly uttered by Jesus the Lord; and let not this message to you be in vain, "Ye must be born again"

O ye who would enter that glorious rest and sing with the ransomed the song of the blest, the life everlasting if ye would obtain, "Ye must be born again."

A dear one in heaven thy heart yearns to see, at the beautiful gate may be watching for thee; then list to the note of this solemn refrain, "Ye must be born again."

Chorus: Ye must be born again; I verily, verily say unto thee, "Ye must be born again."

❦ **For Today:** John 3:1-21; 17:3; Romans 8:16; 1 Peter 1:23

Share this truth with another who needs to hear and respond to the urgency of this message—

George C. Stebbins, 1846-1945

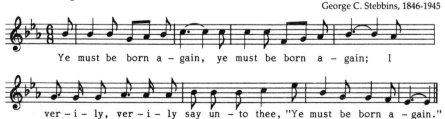

AMAZING GRACE

John Newton, 1725-1807 (verses 1-4), John P. Rees, 1828-1900 (verse 5)

And God is able to make all grace abound to you, so that in all things at all times . . . you will abound in every good work. (2 Corinthians 9:8)

Calling himself a "wretch" who was lost and blind, John Newton recalled leaving school at the age of 11 to begin life as a rough, debauched seaman. Eventually he engaged in the despicable practice of capturing natives from West Africa to be sold as slaves to markets around the world. But one day the grace of God put fear into the heart of this wicked slave trader through a fierce storm. Greatly alarmed and fearful of a shipwreck, Newton began to read *The Imitation of Christ* by Thomas à Kempis. God used this book to lead him to a genuine conversion and a dramatic change in his way of life.

Feeling a definite call to study for the ministry, Newton was encouraged and greatly influenced by John and Charles Wesley and George Whitefield. At the age of 39, John Newton became an ordained minster of the Anglican church at the little village of Olney, near Cambridge, England. To add further impact to his powerful preaching, Newton introduced simple heart-felt hymns rather than the usual psalms in his services. When enough hymns could not be found, Newton began to write his own, often assisted by his close friend William Cowper. In 1779 their combined efforts produced the famous *Olney Hymns* hymnal. "Amazing Grace" was from that collection.

Until the time of his death at the age of 82, John Newton never ceased to marvel at the grace of God that transformed him so completely. Shortly before his death he is quoted as proclaiming with a loud voice during a message, "My memory is nearly gone, but I remember two things: That I am a great sinner and that Christ is a great Savior!" What amazing grace!

Amazing grace—how sweet the sound—that saved a wretch like me! I once was lost but now am found, was blind but now I see.

'Twas grace that taught my heart to fear, and grace my fears relieved; how precious did that grace appear the hour I first believed!

Thru many dangers, toils and snares I have already come; 'tis grace hath brought me safe thus far, and grace will lead me home.

The Lord has promised good to me; His word my hope secures; He will my shield and portion be as long as life endures.

When we've been there ten thousand years, bright shining as the sun, we've no less days to sing God's praise than when we'd first begun.

❦ *For Today:* 1 Chronicles 17:16, 17; John 1:16, 17; Romans 5:20, 21

Ponder anew the magnitude of God's grace. Sing this musical truth—

Amazing Grace tune

American melody
From *Carrell & Clayton's Virginia Harmony*, 1831

A - maz - ing grace--how sweet the sound--That saved a wretch like me! I once was lost but now am found, Was blind but now I see.

GRACE! 'TIS A CHARMING SOUND

Philip Doddridge, 1702-1751 (verses 1, 3)
Augustus Toplady, 1740-1778 (verses 2, 4, 5)

For it is by grace you have been saved, through faith—and this is not from yourselves, it is the gift of God—not by works, so that no one can boast. (Ephesians 2:8, 9)

"Jesus died for all mankind"—every race and nation—and yet, He "died for me." And now the benefits of that death, a personal salvation and restored fellowship with Almighty God, are available to all who respond in faith and appropriate that truth. With the author of this hymn we cry out with heartfelt gratitude, "Saved by grace alone! This is all my plea."

Grace is the gift of God freely given to those who never deserved it. No merit or goodness precedes the forgiving love of God. Not only does God's grace relate to our eternal redemption, but it is a divine provision for our every daily need—spiritual, material, emotional, and physical.

"Grace ! 'Tis a Charming Sound" is the work of two well-known 18th century English ministers, Philip Doddridge and Augustus Toplady. Doddridge was known as a man of great ability and learning, authoring almost 400 hymns. Toplady was known for his strong Calvinistic convictions. Although he was converted as a young man through the influence of John Wesley and his Methodist followers, Augustus Toplady in later life became an ardent critic of the Wesleys and their Arminian or "free will" theology. Yet today Toplady is best remembered for his hymns such as this and "Rock of Ages," which transcend such theological barriers.

Grace! tis a charming sound, harmonious to the ear; Heav'n with the echo shall resound and all the earth shall hear.

'Twas grace that wrote my name in life's eternal book; 'twas grace that gave me to the Lamb, who all my sorrows took.

Grace taught my wand'ring feet to tread the heav'nly road; and new supplies each hour I meet, while pressing on to God.

Grace taught my soul to pray, and made mine eyes o'er-flow; 'twas grace which kept me to this day, and will not let me go.

O let Thy grace inspire my soul with strength divine; may all my pow'rs to Thee aspire, and all my days be Thine.

Chorus: Saved by grace alone! This is all my plea; Jesus died for all mankind, and Jesus died for me.

❦ *For Today:* Acts 15:11; 2 Corinthians 5:21; Titus 3:7; Hebrews 4:16; 1 Peter 5:10

Go forth joyfully with this musical testimony—

Ira D. Sankey, 1840-1908

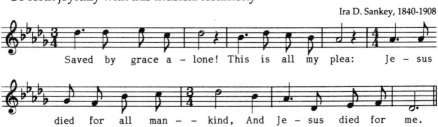

Saved by grace a - lone! This is all my plea: Je - sus
died for all man - - kind, And Je - sus died for me.

GRACE GREATER THAN OUR SIN

Julia H. Johnston, 1849-1919

But where sin increased, grace increased all the more, so that, just as sin reigned in death, so also grace might reign through righteousness to bring eternal life through Jesus Christ our Lord. (Romans 5:20, 21)

God's grace is not merely a sufficient grace; it is an abounding grace—"that you will abound in every good work" (2 Corinthians 9:8). His grace provides our eternal salvation as well as the enablement to know life more abundantly. It is available for our every problem and need.

Sometimes the argument is advanced that since God's grace covers all our sins, then we are free to live as we please. God's grace does provide for our freedom, but it is meant to free us from a slavery to our selfish, sinful nature in order that we might pursue "every good work"—to become all that God intends us to be.

Julia Johnston was for many years involved in the work of Sunday schools at the First Presbyterian Church of Peoria, Illinois, and as a writer of lesson materials for primary age children for the David C. Cook Publishing Company. She also wrote approximately 500 hymn texts. The composer of this hymn, Daniel B. Towner, was for many years the director of the music department at Moody Bible Institute. "Grace Greater Than Our Sin" first appeared in Towner's compilation, *Hymns Tried and True*, 1911.

Marvelous grace of our loving Lord, grace that exceeds our sin and our guilt! Yonder on Calvary's mount outpoured—there where the blood of the Lamb was spilt.

Sin and despair, like the seawaves cold, threaten the soul with infinite loss; grace that is greater—yes, grace untold—points to the Refuge, the mighty Cross.

Dark is the stain that we cannot hide; what can avail to wash it away? Look! there is flowing a crimson tide—whiter than snow you may be today.

Marvelous, infinite, matchless grace, freely bestowed on all who believe! You that are longing to see His face, will you this moment His grace receive?

Chorus: Grace, grace, God's grace, grace that will pardon and cleanse within; grace, grace, God's grace, grace that is greater than all our sin!

❦ *For Today:* Romans 3:24-26; 1 Corinthians 15:10; 2 Corinthians 8:9; Ephesians 1:6-8; Titus 2:11

What does the term "grace" mean to your life? Try to define it in your own words. Discuss your insights with another. Carry this musical truth as you go—

Daniel B. Towner, 1850-1919

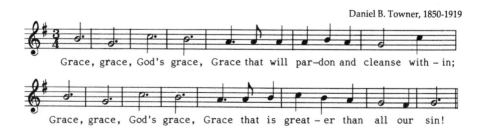

Grace, grace, God's grace, Grace that will par–don and cleanse with – in;

Grace, grace, God's grace, Grace that is great – er than all our sin!

SAVED BY GRACE

Fanny J. Crosby, 1820-1915

And I—in righteousness I will see Your face; when I awake, I will be satisfied with seeing Your likeness. (Psalm 17:15)

> I am living for the moment when my Savior's face I see—
> Oh, the thrill of that first meeting, when His glory shines on me!
> When His voice like sweetest music falls upon my waiting ear,
> And my name, amid the millions, from His precious lips I hear.
>
> —*Avis B. Christiansen*

The anticipation of seeing her Savior's face and praising Him for redeeming grace was a thrilling thought for blind Fanny Crosby to ponder, for the face of Christ as He opened the gate to heaven would be the first sight her eyes would ever behold. Written in 1891 when she was 71 years of age, "Some Day," as Fanny titled the text, was prompted by the final words of a dying pastor friend: "If each of us is faithful to the grace, which is given us by Christ, that same grace which teaches us how to live will also teach us how to die." Deeply moved by this thought, Fanny completed the lines in a matter of minutes under a sense of "divine inspiration." Of all her many hymn texts, this one always seemed to be her favorite. She called it her "heart-song." "Saved by Grace" was one of the favorite hymns of both D. L. Moody and his music associate, Ira Sankey. In their later campaigns, they used it at nearly every service.

As Ira Sankey lay dying, it is reported that he drifted into a final coma as he softly sang:

> Some day the silver chord will break, and I no more as now shall sing; but O the joy when I shall wake within the palace of the King!

> Some day my earthly house will fall—I cannot tell how soon 'twill be; but this I know—my All in All has now a place in heav'n for me.

> Some day, when fades the golden sun beneath the rosy-tinted west, my blessed Lord will say, "Well done!" and I shall enter into rest.

> Some day—till then I'll watch and wait, my lamp all trimmed and burning bright, that when my Savior opens the gate, my soul to Him may take its flight.

> **Chorus:** And I shall see Him face to face, and tell the story—Saved by grace; and I shall see Him face to face, and tell the story—Saved by grace.

❦ *For Today:* Acts 15:11; Ephesians 1:6, 7; 2:8; 1 Peter 1:3, 4

Take time to anticipate the moment when you, like Fanny Crosby, will see the face of Christ. Praise Him even now because you have been saved by His redeeming grace. Allow this musical truth to encourage your way and perhaps even share it with another.

George C. Stebbins, 1846-1945

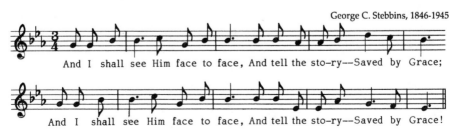

And I shall see Him face to face, And tell the sto-ry—Saved by Grace;

And I shall see Him face to face, And tell the sto-ry—Saved by Grace!

WONDERFUL GRACE OF JESUS

Words and Music by Haldor Lillenas, 1885-1959

For you know the grace of our Lord Jesus Christ, that though He was rich, yet for your sakes He became poor, so that you through His poverty might become rich. (2 Corinthians 8:9)

The wonderful grace of Jesus will be the theme that will echo throughout the corridors of heaven during all eternity. It should also be the joyful exclamation of every Christian now whenever he thinks of Calvary and the deep love of our Savior.

"Wonderful Grace of Jesus" is one of the most inspiring hymns in our hymnals, and it has been used extensively by both choirs and congregations since it was written and composed by Haldor Lillenas in 1918. Born in Norway, Mr. Lillenas came to the United States as a child. He married Bertha Mae Wilson, a songwriter also, and together they traveled extensively, furnishing songs and choirs for many of the leading song leaders in the country, including the noted Charles Alexander. Mr. Alexander found this hymn, among the approximately 4,000 that Lillenas wrote, to be particularly useful as a mass choir selection in the great crusades in the early years of this century. And the song has remained popular ever since. The reminder of Christ's "all sufficient grace" that is truly "deeper than the mighty rolling sea" and "higher than the mountain" still moves us to stand in awe each time we sing it in a church service.

Wonderful grace of Jesus, greater than all my sin; how shall my tongue describe it, where shall its praise begin? Taking away my burden, setting my spirit free, for the wonderful grace of Jesus reaches me.

Wonderful grace of Jesus, reaching to all the lost, by it I have been pardoned, saved to the uttermost; chains have been torn asunder, giving me liberty, for the wonderful grace of Jesus reaches me.

Wonderful grace of Jesus, reaching the most defiled, by its transforming power making him God's dear child, purchasing peace and heaven for all eternity—and the wonderful grace of Jesus reaches me.

Chorus: Wonderful the matchless grace of Jesus, deeper than the mighty rolling sea; higher than the mountain, sparkling like a fountain, all sufficient grace for even me; broader than the scope of my transgressions, greater far than all my sin and shame; O magnify the precious name of Jesus, praise His name!

🐝 *For Today:* Acts 15:11; Titus 3:7; Hebrews 4:16; 1 Peter 5:10

Contemplate again the "scope of your transgressions" and the forgiveness and love of Christ as He stretches out His hand to you. Praise His precious name as you go singing—

O mag-ni-fy the pre-cious name of Je-sus, PRAISE HIS NAME!

DEPTH OF MERCY

Charles Wesley, 1707-1788

You are kind and forgiving, O Lord, abounding in love to all who call on You. (Psalm 86:5)

Although Charles Wesley had been trained for the Anglican church ministry and had been active in religious activities, there came a time when he realized that he had never personally experienced God's love and mercy. His crisis experience occurred on May 20, 1738, as he met with a small group of Moravian believers in the Aldersgate Hall in London, England. That evening he wrote in his journal:

> At midnight I gave myself to Christ, assured that I was safe, whether sleeping or waking. I had the continual experience of His power to overcome all temptation, and confessed, with joy and surprise, that He was able to do exceedingly abundantly for me above what I can ask or think.

Following his "heart-warming" experience at Aldersgate, Charles with his brother John developed an intense desire to bring others to a personal conversion experience and to teach the great truths of the Scripture. To aid in these endeavors, Charles Wesley wrote more than 6,500 hymn texts on every aspect of the Christian life, fitting them to any popular tune that suited the meter and message of the lines.

The Wesleys spread their message of God's mercy and His power to transform lives to all social classes. They spent much time ministering to the cruelly treated prisoners of Newgate Prison in London and visited the dreadful Bedlam, a dungeon for the insane.

"Depth of Mercy" first appeared in the Wesley hymnal, *Hymns and Sacred Poems*, in 1741. It has 13 stanzas and was titled "After a Relapse Into Sin." These words suggest the personal experience of Charles before and after his "heart-warming" spiritual experience at Aldersgate.

> Depth of mercy! can there be mercy still reserved for me? Can my God His wrath forbear—me, the chief of sinners spare?

> I have long withstood His grace, long provoked Him to His face, would not harken to His calls, grieved Him by a thousand falls.

> Now incline me to repent; let me now my sins lament; now my foul revolt deplore, weep, believe, and sin no more.

> There for me my Savior stands, holding forth His wounded hands; God is love! I know, I feel, Jesus weeps and loves me still.

❧ *For Today:* Psalm 136:1; Isaiah 55:6, 7; Micah 7:18-20; Romans 2:4

The Hebrew word for "mercy" literally means "to get inside another's skin," to be completely identified with that person. This is what Christ has done for us. Now He asks that we demonstrate this same quality to others.

Aletta tune   William B. Bradbury, 1816-1868

Depth of mer–cy! can there be   Mer – cy still re – served for   me?
There for   me my Sav – ior stands, Hold–ing forth His   wound–ed hands;

Can my God His wrath for – bear––Me,   the chief of sin – ners spare?
God is love!   I   know, I   feel,   Je – sus weeps and loves me   still.

THERE'S A WIDENESS IN GOD'S MERCY

Frederick W. Faber, 1814-1863

But Thou, O Lord, art a God full of compassion, and gracious longsuffering, and plenteous in mercy and truth. (Psalm 86:15 KJV)

A wealth of truth about the depth of God's love and mercy is expressed simply but eloquently in this choice two-line hymn text written by Frederick William Faber in the middle of the 19th century. In addition to being known as a man with unusual personal charm, persuasive preaching ability, and excellent writing skills, Faber made his most lasting contribution with the 150 hymn texts he composed during his brief life of 49 years.

Frederick Faber had an unusual spiritual journey. Raised as a strict Calvinist, he strongly opposed the Roman Catholic Church. After education at Oxford, he became an ordained Anglican minister. Gradually, however, he was influenced by the Oxford Movement, which stressed that Anglican churches had become too evangelical—with too little emphasis on formal and liturgical worship. Eventually Faber renounced the Anglican State Church, became a Catholic priest, and spent his remaining years as Superior of the Catholic Brompton Oratory in London.

Faber had always realized the great influence that hymn singing had in Protestant evangelical churches. Determined to provide material for Catholics to use in the same way, he worked tirelessly in writing hymns and publishing numerous collections of them. In 1854 the Pope honored Frederick Faber with an honorary Doctor of Divinity degree in recognition of his many accomplishments. Today we are still grateful for this memorable declaration of the boundless love and mercy of our God to all mankind:

> There's a wideness in God's mercy, like the wideness of the sea; there's a kindness in His justice, which is more than liberty.
>
> There is welcome for the sinner, and more graces for the good; there is mercy with the Savior; there is healing in His blood.
>
> For the love of God is broader than the measure of man's mind; and the heart of the Eternal is most wonderfully kind.
>
> If our love were but more simple, we should take Him at His word; and our lives would be all sunshine in the sweetness of our Lord.

🐦 *For Today:* Psalm 36:5; 103:8-13; Ephesians 1:6-8; 1 John 1:7

Let yourself become immersed in the joy of realizing and accepting in a simple, trusting manner the great mercy of God. Praise and thank Him by singing as you go knowing that—

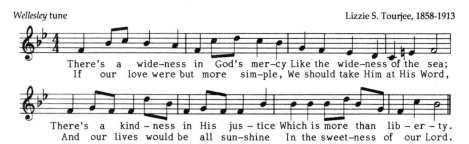

Wellesley tune   Lizzie S. Tourjee, 1858-1913

There's a wide–ness in God's mer–cy Like the wide–ness of the sea;
If our love were but more sim–ple, We should take Him at His Word,

There's a kind – ness in His jus – tice Which is more than lib – er – ty.
And our lives would be all sun–shine In the sweet–ness of our Lord.

ART THOU WEARY?

John M. Neale, 1818-1866
Adapted from the Greek of Stephen the Sabaite, 725-815

The Spirit and the bride say, "Come." And let him who hears say, "Come!" Whoever is thirsty, let him come; and whoever wishes, let him take the free gift of the water of life. (Revelation 22:17)

I have read in Plato and Cicero sayings that are very wise and very beautiful; but I have never read in either of them, "Come unto Me all ye that labor and are heavy burdened."
—*St. Augustine*

Inspired by Christ's loving offer of pardon and rest for the weary and distressed soul, an 8th century Greek monk named Stephen wrote these plaintive lines. From the age of 10 Stephen lived in the monastery of Mar Sabas in the wilderness of Judea. He eventually became the abbot of this monastery until his death at the age of 90. The mystic quality of the hymn's text reflects the introspective solitude of Stephen's life. He joins with "saints, apostles, prophets, and martyrs" to assert God's blessing upon all who respond to Him in simple faith.

This text in its present form is actually a paraphrase of Stephen's writing. It was done by John M. Neale, an English clergyman who discovered and translated many ancient Greek and Latin hymns. Neale published "Art thou Weary?" in his 1862 edition of *Hymns of the Eastern Church*.

"Art Thou Weary?" has been the favorite hymn of many notable people, including President Franklin D. Roosevelt. Its simple and direct arrangement of a question in the first line of each verse followed by the positive answer in each second line has given assurance of God's constant faithfulness to countless despairing persons.

Art thou weary, art thou languid, art thou sore distrest? "Come to Me," saith One, "and, coming, be at rest."

Hath He marks to lead me to Him, if He be my guide? "In His feet and hands are wound-prints, and His side."

If I still hold closely to Him, what hath He at last? "Sorrow vanquished, labor ended, Jordan passed."

If I ask Him to receive me, will He say me nay? "Not till earth and not till heaven pass away."

Finding, foll'wing, keeping, struggling, is He sure to bless? Saints, apostles, prophets, martyrs answer, "Yes."

❦ ***For Today:*** Psalm 23:2; 55:22; Matthew 11:28, 29; John 10:10

Come to Christ with any burden or sorrow in your life and be assured that He will hasten to meet you with open arms just as the father of the prodigal son did. Rest in the truth of these musical lines—

Stephanos tune

Henry W. Baker, 1821-1877

Art thou wea - ry, art thou lan - guid, Art thou sore dis - trest?

"Come to Me," saith One, "and, com - ing, Be at rest."

I HEARD THE VOICE OF JESUS SAY

Horatius Bonar, 1808-1889

Come, all you who are thirsty, come to the water; and you who have no money, come, buy and eat! Come, buy wine and milk without money and without cost. (Isaiah 55:1)

Thy grace first made me feel my sin; it taught me to believe. Then in believing, I found—and now I live, I live!   —*Horatius Bonar*

The heart of the Christian gospel is the gentle word "come." From the moment of a person's conversion until he or she is ushered into eternal glory, the Savior beckons with the gracious invitation "come." This word appears more than 500 times throughout the Scriptures.

The beautiful lines of this hymn by Horatius Bonar fill us with peace and buoyant joy. They calm us as we contemplate walking in the divine light of life that is shed on our ways as we respond in personal faith to the voice of Jesus.

Horatius Bonar was one of Scotland's most gifted and influential ministers and writers of the 19th century. He wrote more than 600 hymn texts throughout his life. "I Heard the Voice of Jesus Say" is generally considered to be his finest. Bonar wrote the lines while pastoring the Presbyterian church at Kelso, Scotland. He actually intended the hymn to be used by the children since he was always concerned that they learn the truths of the person and work of Christ. The text with its theme of revived life and joyous rest in Jesus has had universal appeal since its first publication in 1846.

I heard the voice of Jesus say, "Come unto Me and rest; lay down, thou weary one, lay down thy head upon My breast." I came to Jesus as I was, weary and worn and sad; I found in Him a resting place, and He has made me glad.

I heard the voice of Jesus say, "Behold, I freely give the living water—thirsty one, stoop down and drink, and live." I came to Jesus, and I drank of that life-giving stream; my thirst was quenched, my soul revived, and now I live in Him.

I heard the voice of Jesus say, "I am this dark world's Light; look unto Me—thy morn shall rise, and all thy day be bright." I looked to Jesus, and I found in Him my Star, my Sun; and in that Light of life I'll walk, till trav'ling days are done.

❧ *For Today:* Isaiah 55:1-3; Matthew 11:28; John 4:14; 8:12; Revelation 3:20; 22:17

Truly rest and be glad in the love of Jesus no matter what your concerns may be. Thank Him for the "Light of Life" that He has promised to shine on your path. Rejoice in the truth of this musical testimony—

Vox Dilecti tune   John B. Dykes, 1823-1876

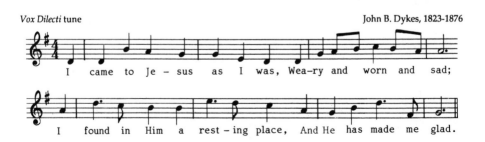

I came to Je - sus as I was, Wea-ry and worn and sad;

I found in Him a rest - ing place, And He has made me glad.

THE NINETY AND NINE

Elizabeth C. Clephane, 1830-1869

There will be more rejoicing in heaven over one sinner who repents than over ninety-nine righteous persons who do not need to repent. (Luke 15:7)

The Bible teaches that man does not seek after God, but that God initiates the search for lost man. "The Ninety and Nine," based on the parable in Luke 15:3-7, presents a vivid picture of this scriptural truth.

Written for children by an invalid woman named Elizabeth Clephane in Melrose, Scotland, the text appeared in a newspaper and caught the attention of Ira Sankey, the well-known music associate of evangelist D. L. Moody. Since he was on the way to their next evangelistic meetings in Edinburgh, Scotland, Mr. Sankey simply tucked the poem in his vest pocket and thought no more of it. During the service that afternoon, Mr. Moody concluded his stirring message on the Good Shepherd and abruptly asked Ira to close with an appropriate solo. Startled, Sankey suddenly remembered the poem in his pocket. He related that he breathed a quick prayer for divine help, struck the chord of A flat on his little pump organ, and began to sing, composing the melody as he went. When Sankey reached the end of the song, both he and Mr. Moody were in tears. During the invitation, many "lost sheep" responded to the call of Christ.

During their series of evangelistic meetings in Great Britain, Moody and Sankey held a service in Melrose, Scotland. The two sisters of Elizabeth Clephane were in the audience. To their surprise and delight, they heard their departed sister's poem set to a melody and delivered by the noted Ira Sankey with great spiritual impact.

> There were ninety and nine that safely lay in the shelter of the fold, but one was out on the hills away, far off from the gates of gold—Away on the mountains wild and bare, away from the tender Shepherd's care, away from the tender Shepherd's care.
>
> "Lord, Thou hast here Thy ninety and nine; are thy not enough for Thee?" but the Shepherd made answer: "This of Mine has wandered away from Me. And altho' the road be rough and steep, I go to the desert to find my sheep; I go to the desert to find My sheep."
>
> But all thro' the mountains, thunder-riv'n, and up from the rocky steep, there arose a glad cry to the gate of heav'n, "Rejoice! I have found My sheep!" And the angels echoed around the throne, "Rejoice, for the Lord brings back His own! Rejoice, for the Lord brings back His own."

❦   *For Today:*   Isaiah 55:7; Mark 2:17; Luke 15:3-7; 2 Peter 3:9

Lift your heart and voice in praise to God for sending His son to seek and find you when you were lost and indifferent to Him. Sing this portion of the hymn as you go—

Ira D. Sankey, 1840-1908

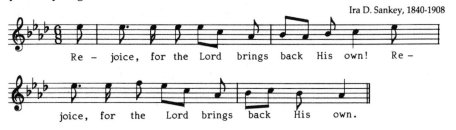

Re - joice, for the Lord brings back His own! Re - joice, for the Lord brings back His own.

LET JESUS COME INTO YOUR HEART

Words and Music by Lelia N. Morris, 1862-1929

I tell you, now is the time of God's favor, now is the day of salvation. (2 Corinthians 6:2)

Gospel songs that urgently ask people to respond to Christ's invitation for salvation have had a powerful influence in evangelism since they were first written shortly after the close of the American Civil War. Many believers can remember which song was used when they made their decision for Christ. Ira D. Sankey, often called the "father of the gospel song," once stated: "These songs were calculated to awaken the careless, to melt the hardened, and to guide inquiring souls to Jesus Christ."

"Let Jesus Come Into Your Heart," written and composed by Mrs. Lelia Morris, has been one of the these invitation hymns widely used by God to direct seeking sinners to a personal salvation experience. Its origin in 1898 was at a camp meeting in Mountain Lake Park, Maryland. A woman of culture and refinement responded to the altar call invitation. Mrs. Morris joined her there and with an arm around her shoulder whispered, "Just now your doubtings give o'er." The song leader of the camp meeting joined the duo and added another phrase, "Just now reject Him no more." Then the evangelist earnestly importuned, "Just now throw open the door." Mrs. Morris made the last appeal, "Let Jesus come into your heart." Shortly thereafter Mrs. Morris completed the thought and added the music before the camp meetings closed. Another song was born to guide countless numbers of inquiring souls to Jesus Christ.

If you are tired of the load of your sin, let Jesus come into your heart; if you desire a new life to begin, let Jesus come into your heart.

If 'tis for purity now that you sigh, let Jesus come into your heart: fountains for cleansing are flowing near by; let Jesus come into your heart.

If there's a tempest your voice cannot still, let Jesus come into your heart; if there's a void this world never can fill, let Jesus come into your heart.

If you would join the glad songs of the blest, let Jesus come into your heart; if you would enter the mansions of rest, let Jesus come into your heart.

Refrain: Just now, your doubtings give o'er; just now, reject Him no more; just now, throw open the door; let Jesus come into your heart.

❧ *For Today:* John 6:37; Acts 16:31; Hebrews 3:15; 1 John 1:9; Revelation 22:17

Be sensitive to the spiritual needs of those about you. Often you will be able to detect signs of a struggling soul searching for God. With gracious boldness share with such a one the message of this song—

ROOM AT THE CROSS FOR YOU

Words and Music by Ira R. Stanphill, 1914-

But God demonstrates His own love for us in this: While we were still sinners, Christ died for us. (Romans 5:8)

Out of the varied experiences of a fruitful life have come the many moving hymns of Ira F. Stanphill. As a child he traveled by covered wagon from Arkansas to New Mexico, then later moved to Oklahoma and Kansas. Converted at age 12, Stanphill began preaching at 22 in revival meetings and later served pastorates in Florida, Pennsylvania, and Texas. At 17 he wrote his first gospel song and traveled for several years with evangelists, playing the piano, organ, ukulele and accordian.

Mr. Stanphill began to write his own gospel hymns, and he employed the unusual practice of creating a text from titles suggested from the congregation during a service. He would explain:

"The basic reason I have written songs is that I love God and Christ has loved me. Most of my songs are the outgrowth of real experiences with Christ. I think they appeal to people because I have had trials, heartaches, and sorrow in my own life, and I know what I write about."

"Room at the Cross" was a title suggested to Ira in 1946 at one of his meetings. He wrote it on a scrap of paper, which he found in his pocket after returning home. Impressed with the title, he quickly wrote both words and music as they appear today. Since then the song has been recorded by numerous Christian artists, translated into Spanish, German, and Italian, and was used as the closing theme of the national broadcast *Revival Time* for many years. Only eternity will reveal the number who have been directed to Christ through this one gospel hymn that reminds us that there is always room at the cross for one more sinner.

The cross upon which Jesus died is a shelter in which we can hide; and its grace so free is sufficient for me, and deep is its fountain—as wide as the sea.

Tho millions have found Him a friend and have turned from the sins they have sinned, the Savior still waits to open the gates and welcome a sinner before it's too late.

The hand of my Savior is strong, and the love of my Savior is long; through sunshine or rain, through loss or in gain, the blood flows from Calv'ry to cleanse every stain.

Chorus: There's room at the cross for you; tho millions have come, there's still room for one—Yes, there's room at the cross for you.

❦ *For Today:* Acts 16:31; Romans 10:9, 10, 13; 1 Timothy 1:15; Hebrews 2:3

No one can hear the message of God's great love as displayed at Calvary and remain unmoved. Resolve to invite some needy sinner to come to the cross. Share this musical truth with that person—

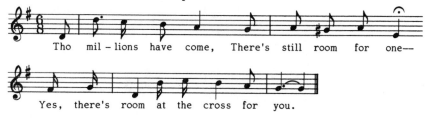

IN TIMES LIKE THESE

Words and Music by Ruth Caye Jones, 1902-1972

Simon Peter answered Him, "Lord, to whom shall we go? You have the words of eternal life." (John 6:68)

Wars, earthquakes, famines, violence, drugs, child abuse, humanism, the occult, New Age. . . .

When world events and ideologies like these seem ominous and unsettling to us or when personal sorrows or tragedies confront us, where can we go but to the Lord? How comforting it is to know that we can always flee to Him and rest securely on our "Solid Rock." During the fearful days at the height of World War II, when the stress and strain of daily living seemed almost overwhelming, the comforting hymn "In Times Like These" was written. In the midst of a busy day as a housewife, Ruth Caye Jones felt a direct inspiration from the Holy Spirit. She stopped her work to quickly put down both words and music just as they were given to her by God.

Since that day the hymn has been a blessing to countless Christians at special times of need. It has brought comfort during illness, has been used widely at funerals, has encouraged and challenged Christian workers, and has drawn many to salvation. Mrs. Jones experienced for herself the consolation the words of the song could bring as she spent time recovering form serious surgery a few years after it was written.

The Scriptures warn that world conditions will continue to get worse as we approach the end of this age and the return of Christ. In addition, we must prepare ourselves for the difficult times that come to everyone as life progresses. We can only remain firm when we know with conviction that our God is in control and that all things are working out for our ultimate good. In the meantime, we simply grip the "Solid Rock!"

> In times likes these you need a Savior; in times like these you need an anchor; be very sure, be very sure your anchor holds and grips the Solid Rock!
>
> In times like these you need the Bible; in times like these O be not idle; be very sure, be very sure your anchor holds and grips the Solid Rock!
>
> In times like these I have a Savior; in times like these I have an anchor; I'm very sure, I'm very sure my anchor hold and grips the Solid Rock!
>
> **Refrain:** This Rock is Jesus, yes, He's the One; this Rock is Jesus, the only One! Be very sure, be very sure your anchor holds and grips the Solid Rock!

❧ **For Today:** Job 13:13, 15; 19:25, 27; Psalm 56:11; Isaiah 26:3, 4

Whatever difficulties might surround you just now, be certain that you can sing with conviction this musical testimony—

JUST AS I AM

Charlotte Elliott, 1789-1871

Then Jesus declared, "I am the bread of life. He who comes to Me will never go hungry, and he who believes in Me will never be thirsty. All that the Father gives Me will come to Me, and whoever comes to Me I will never drive away." (John 6:35, 37)

Often we feel that if only we were in different circumstances or had some special talent, we could be a better witness for God and serve Him more effectively. Today's hymn was written by a bed-ridden invalid who felt useless to do anything except express her feelings of devotion to God. Yet Charlotte Elliott's simply worded text has influenced more people for Christ than any hymn ever written or perhaps any sermon ever preached.

As a young person in Brighton, England, Miss Elliott was known as "carefree Charlotte." She was a popular portrait artist and a writer of humorous verse. At the age of 30, however, a serious ailment made her an invalid for life. She became listless and depressed until a well-known Swiss evangelist, Dr. Caesar Malan, visited her. Sensing her spiritual distress, he exclaimed, "Charlotte, you must come just as you are—a sinner—to the Lamb of God who takes away the sin of the world!" Immediately placing her complete trust in Christ's redemptive sacrifice for her, Charlotte experienced inner peace and joy in spite of her physical affliction until her death at the age of 82.

Charlotte Elliott wrote approximately 150 hymns throughout her lifetime; today she is considered to be one of the finest of all English hymnwriters. "God sees, God guards, God guides me," she said. "His grace surrounds me and His voice continually bids me to be happy and holy in His service—just where I am!"

> Just as I am, without one plea but that Thy blood was shed for me, and that Thou bidd'st me come to Thee, O Lamb of God, I come! I come!

> Just as I am, tho tossed about with many a conflict, many a doubt, fightings and fears within, without, O Lamb of God, I come! I come!

> Just as I am, poor, wretched, blind—Sight, riches, healing of the mind, yea, all I need in Thee to find—O Lamb of God, I come! I come!

> Just as I am, Thou wilt receive, wilt welcome, pardon, cleanse, relieve; because Thy promise I believe, O Lamb of God, I come! I come!

❦ **For Today:** Psalm 51:1, 2; John 1:29; John 3:16; Ephesians 2:13

Give God thanks for His acceptance of us just as we are. As we respond in simple faith to Him, we will find "all that we need," not only for our personal salvation but also for the particular place of service that He has for us.

Woodworth tune   William B. Bradbury, 1816-1868

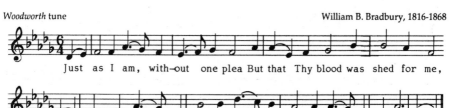

Just as I am, with-out one plea But that Thy blood was shed for me,

And that Thou bidd'st me come to Thee, O Lamb of God, I come! I come!

JESUS IS ALL THE WORLD TO ME

Words and Music by Will L. Thompson, 1847-1909

I consider everything a loss compared to the surpassing greatness of knowing Christ Jesus my Lord, for whose sake I have lost all things. I consider them rubbish, that I may gain Christ and be found in Him. (Philippians 3:8, 9)

The author and composer of this hymn, Will L. Thompson, was known as the "Bard of Ohio" for his respected musical talents. He wrote many successful secular and sacred songs and he edited and published numerous collections. But it is said of him that his greatest joy was writing and performing simple gospel songs about his Lord. He has provided Christian hymnody with two such enduring songs that have been mightily used by God: A testimony song for Christians, "Jesus Is All the World to Me," and an invitation song that has been influential in directing non-Christians to the Savior, "Softy and Tenderly."

The story is told of a visit that Will Thompson made to D. L. Moody's bedside as the famed evangelist lay dying. All visitation had been stopped, but when Moody heard that Will Thompson had called, he insisted upon seeing him. "Will," said Moody, "I would rather have written 'Softly and Tenderly Jesus Is Calling' than anything I have been able to do in my whole life!" Soon the well-known evangelist entered His eternal rest with these words of invitation that had been used so many times in his evangelistic campaigns once again upon his lips: "Come home, come home, ye who are weary, come home; earnestly, tenderly, Jesus is calling—calling, 'O sinner, come home.'"

And the words of this hymn by Will Thompson, published in his hymnal collection of 1904, have since been widely used by believers to express devotion to Christ and dependency upon Him for all of life's needs:

Jesus is all the world to me, my life, my joy, my all; He is my strength from day to day, without Him I would fall. When I am sad to Him I go; no other one can cheer me so; when I am sad He makes me glad—He's my friend.

Jesus is all the world to me, my friend in trials sore; I go to Him for blessings, and He gives them o'er and o'er. He sends the sunshine and the rain; He sends the harvest's golden grain; sunshine and rain, harvest of grain—He's my friend.

Jesus is all the world to me; I want no better friend; I trust Him now, I'll trust Him when life's fleeting days shall end. Beautiful life with such a friend, beautiful life that has no end; eternal life, eternal joy—He's my friend.

❧ *For Today:* John 15:14, 15; Philippians 1:21; 4:12; 1 Peter 2:21; 1 John 2:25

Reflect on this statement—There are three essentials for a happy life: (1) A faith to live by, (2) a self to live with, and (3) a purpose to live for. Carry this musical truth with you—

SAVED, SAVED!

Words and Music by Jack P. Scholfield, 1882-1972

Everyone who calls on the name of the Lord will be saved. (Romans 10:13)

> Indulgence says, "Drink your way out."
> Philosophy says, "Think your way out."
> Science says, "Invent your way out."
> Industry says, "Work your way out."
> Communism says, "Strike your way out."
> Militarism says, "Fight your way out."
> Christ says, "I AM THE WAY OUT!"
>
> —*Unknown*

We commonly use many terms to describe a Christian—"saved," "born again," "justified." Although these words are important to us who understand and appreciate them, they can sometimes be confusing and misunderstood by anyone who is unfamiliar with a biblical vocabulary. To people who are seeking, we must always be ready to explain these terms in language that is relevant to them. A personal encounter with Christ is much more important than the terminology we use to describe this salvation experience.

We must emphasize that it is Christ and Christ alone who saves—not the methods, procedures, or manipulations often used for those seeking salvation. No two experiences of salvation are necessarily alike. Coming to Jesus to experience His love and forgiveness is a very personal matter—not a prescribed procedure. Although simple enough for a child to understand and respond to, calling on the name of the Lord to be saved is much more than lips that merely speak glibly about Jesus. There must also be the evidence of a changed, committed life.

The author and composer of this hymn, Jack Scholfield, was a singing evangelist. He wrote "Saved, Saved!" in 1911 while assisting in evangelistic meetings. He explained, "The melody just came to me, almost as a gift. Then I simply tried to make the words fit the tune. It was popular from the start."

> I've found a Friend who is all to me; his love is ever true; I love to tell how He lifted me and what His grace can do for you.

> He saves me from ev'ry sin and harm, secures my soul each day; I'm leaning strong on His mighty arm—I know He'll guide me all the way.

> When poor and needy and all alone, in love He said to me, "Come unto Me and I'll lead you home to live with me eternally."

> **Chorus:** Saved by His pow'r divine, saved to new life sublime! Life now is sweet and my joy is complete, for I'm saved, saved, saved!

❦ **For Today:** John 14:6; Acts 4:12; Titus 3:3-7; Hebrews 9:12; 1 John 4:10

Seek to explain the simple plan of salvation to someone. Sing as you go—

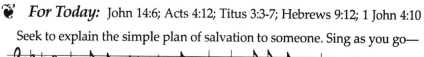

Saved by His pow'r di - vine, Saved to new life sub - lime!

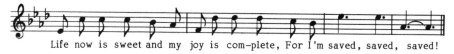

Life now is sweet and my joy is com-plete, For I'm saved, saved, saved!

NOW I BELONG TO JESUS

Words and Music by Norman J. Clayton, 1903-

If we live, we live to the Lord; and if we die, we die to the Lord. So, whether we live or die, we belong to the Lord. (Romans 14:8)

God is FOR us—that is good.
God is WITH us—that is better.
God is IN us—that is best!

—Unknown

We hear much these days about the problem of homeless people—people of the street with no place to go and no one who cares. Can we really appreciate the terrible state of despair and loneliness experienced by these masses? Man was created by God to enjoy His fellowship and the fellowship of family and friends. All of us have a need to belong to someone and something.

The greatest "belonging" in life is described by the Heidelberg Catechism, which begins its instruction in this way:

Question—"What is your only comfort in life and death?"

Answer—"That I, with body and soul, am not my own, but belong body and soul, in life and in death, to my faithful Savior, Jesus Christ . . . "

This popular gospel song by Norman Clayton speaks so well about this truth of the mystical union that exists between Christ and the believer—Christ in the believer and the believer in Christ. Who can fathom the mystery of a mortal believer's spirit being united with the divine Christ—a glorious relationship that begins for the believer at the moment of genuine response to the call of Christ and one that will last for eternity?

Norman Clayton has authored and composed numerous other fine gospel hymns, but "Now I Belong to Jesus" is still his most widely used song. This inspiring gospel song first appeared in *Word of Life Melodies No. 1* in 1943. Mr. Clayton writes that one of his greatest thrills in life was hearing a 10-year-old deaf girl sing his song at a camp for handicapped children.

Jesus my Lord will love me forever, from Him no pow'r of evil can sever; He gave His life to ransom my soul—Now I belong to Him!

Once I was lost in sin's degradation; Jesus came down to bring me salvation, lifted me up from sorrow and shame—Now I belong to Him!

Joy floods my soul, for Jesus has saved me, freed me from sin that long had enslaved me; His precious blood He gave to redeem—Now I belong to Him!

Chorus: Now I belong to Jesus; Jesus belongs to me—Not for the years of time alone, but for eternity.

❦ *For Today:* Song of Solomon 2:16; John 10:28; Colossians 1:27

Rise above the circumstances of this day and rejoice in the glorious truth that you and Christ are united for eternity. Carry this musical testimony with you—

Now I be - long to Je - sus, Je - sus be - longs to me—

Not for the years of time a - lone, But for e - ter - ni - ty.

THE SOLID ROCK

Edward Mote, 1797-1874

For no one can lay any foundation other than the one already laid, which is Jesus Christ. (1 Corinthians 3:11)

Life with Christ is an endless hope; without Him a hopeless end.   —*Unknown*

The Bible likens our life to a house. Some homes are built to last while others crumble easily in strong wind or rain. The difference is not in the severity of the storm but in the quality of the foundation upon which the structure is built. The author of this hymn text wisely chose "the solid rock" on which to build his own life, and he rested on Christ's "unchanging grace" until his homegoing at age 77.

Edward Mote knew nothing about God or the Bible as he grew up in London, England, the child of poor innkeepers. At the age of 16 he was genuinely converted to Christ. Mote later settled in a suburb of London where he became known as a successful cabinet maker and a devoted church layman.

After a time, a Baptist chapel was built in Horsham, Sussex, England, largely because of Edward's efforts. The grateful church members offered him the deed to the property. He refused it, saying, "I only want the pulpit, and when I cease to preach Christ, then turn me out of that." Here Mote ministered faithfully until forced to resign because of poor health one year before his death. He commented, "The truths I have been preaching, I am now living upon and they'll do very well to die upon."

During his busy life as a minister, Edward Mote wrote more than 150 hymn texts. In 1836 he published a collection titled *Hymns of Praise* and included "The Solid Rock" in it.

My hope is built on nothing less than Jesus' blood and righteousness; I dare not trust the sweetest frame, but wholly lean on Jesus' name.

When darkness veils His lovely face, I rest on His unchanging grace; in ev'ry high and stormy gale my anchor holds within the veil.

His oath, His covenant, His blood support me in the whelming flood; when all around my soul gives way, He then is all my hope and stay.

When He shall come with trumpet sound, O may I then in Him be found, dressed in His righteousness alone, faultless to stand before the throne.

Refrain: On Christ, the solid Rock, I stand—all other ground is sinking sand; all other ground is sinking sand.

❦ *For Today:* Matthew 7:24-27; John 14:6; Acts 4:12; Romans 5:1-5; Hebrews 6:17-20

Reflect on some of the shaky foundations upon which many of your friends seem to be building their lives. Determine to share Christ with them as you have opportunity. Carry this musical testimony with you as you go—

Solid Rock tune   William B. Bradbury, 1816-1868

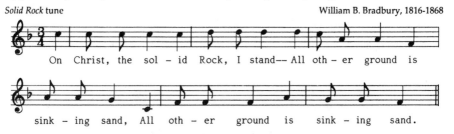

On Christ, the sol - id Rock, I stand–– All oth - er ground is sink - ing sand, All oth - er ground is sink - ing sand.

MY FAITH HAS FOUND A RESTING PLACE

Lidie H. Edmunds, 19th century

I know whom I have believed, and am convinced that He is able to guard what I have entrusted to Him for that day. (2 Timothy 1:12)

Saving faith is much more than a commitment to a creed, church, or a doctrinal system. It must be a commitment to a person—Jesus Christ. Doctrinal statements and creeds are important in defining and delineating truth, but they must never replace a personal relationship with "The Truth." We can get so caught up in our creedal statements, interpretations and arguments, or church traditions that we lose the sense of simple, child-like trust in Christ and his written Word. This was the concern of the apostle Paul—"I am afraid that just as Eve was deceived by the serpent's cunning, your minds may somehow be led astray from your sincere and pure devotion to Christ" (2 Corinthians 11:3). Again and again we must take inventory of ourselves and determine what is the real foundation of our spiritual lives and the source of our resting place—Christ or merely a creed?

Little is known about the author of this hymn text or the source of the tune other than that it is an old Norwegian melody. The hymn in its present form first appeared in the hymnal *Songs of Joy and Gladness,* published in 1891. It has become increasingly popular in recent years as a testimonial hymn in church services. May it testify of your faith in God.

My faith has found a resting place—not in device nor creed; I trust the ever living One—His wounds for me shall plead.

Enough for me that Jesus saves—this ends my fear and doubt; a sinful soul I come to Him—He'll never cast me out.

My heart is leaning on the Word—the written Word of God; salvation by my Savior's name—salvation thru His blood.

My great Physician heals the sick; the lost He came to save; for me His precious blood He shed; for me His life He gave.

Chorus: I need no other argument, I need no other plea; it is enough that Jesus died, and that He died for me.

🍂 *For Today:* Job 19:25, 27; Psalm 31:19; Isaiah 32:17; John 14:6; 1 John 5:13

Express your love and commitment to Christ anew in simple, child-like terms. Pray that all religious veneer may be stripped away and that others may simply see His pure reflection in all of your daily activities. Sing this musical testimony as you go—

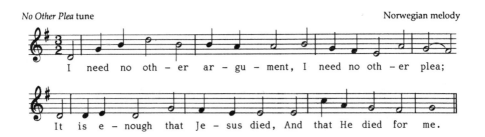

No Other Plea tune   Norwegian melody

I need no oth – er ar – gu – ment, I need no oth – er plea;

It is e – nough that Je – sus died, And that He died for me.

IN JESUS

James Procter, dates unknown

The fool says in his heart, "There is no God." (Psalm 14:1)

This song is the testimonial hymn of an avowed atheist who led others in a vain search for the true meaning of life before finding his answer in Jesus. James Proctor grew up in a Christian home and attended church and Sunday school regularly in Manchester, England. In his teens, however, he began to read extensively the writing of infidels and a group called The Free Thinkers. Gradually his faith in God began to be shaken. Eventually James renounced all interest in Christianity. He joined the Free Thinkers' Society and soon became its president.

Some time later, James Procter became seriously ill and feared that he would not live. Finally in desperation, he called for a minister of the gospel, who came to Procter's bedside and led him to a definite conversion. Soon after this, as Procter's sister sat beside his bed, he asked her to locate in his dresser two verses he had written earlier. Then he dictated to her with great excitement the closing two verses of "In Jesus." James wanted these lines to be particularly meaningful to his many friends in the Free Thinkers' Society as they would read his personal testimony.

Procter's faithful sister took her brother's poem to the well-known musician and composer, Robert Harkness, while he was assisting R. A. Torrey in an evangelistic campaign at the time in Manchester. Mr. Harkness soon completed the music while travelling to another meeting in London.

Every man has a god—even the atheist—a "no-god." The tragedy is that man becomes like his god—he grows into the image of what he worships and serves. That's why we must be "In Jesus."

> I've tried in vain a thousand ways my fears to quell, my hopes to raise; but what I need, the Bible says, is ever, only Jesus.

> My soul is night, my heart is steel—I cannot see, I cannot feel; for light, for life I must appeal in simple faith to Jesus.

> He died, He lives, He reigns, He pleads; there's love in all His words and deeds; there's all a guilty sinner needs forever more in Jesus.

> Tho' some should sneer, and some should blame, I'll go with all my guilt and shame; I'll go to Him because His name, above all names is Jesus.

❦ *For Today:* Deuteronomy 4:29; Psalm 10; 34:6; 94:3; John 17:3

Be prepared to enter into a conversation with someone who is struggling with doubts about the existence of God and a personal faith in Him. In a non-judgmental way, seek to answer these questions from your own experience. Learn and sing this little testimonial song written by a former atheist—

Robert Harkness, 1880-1961

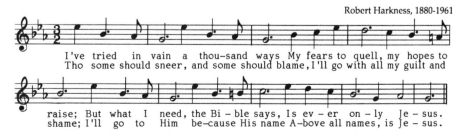

I've tried in vain a thou-sand ways My fears to quell, my hopes to
Tho some should sneer, and some should blame, I'll go with all my guilt and

raise; But what I need, the Bi – ble says, Is ev – er on – ly Je – sus.
shame; I'll go to Him be-cause His name A–bove all names, is Je – sus.

I'D RATHER HAVE JESUS

Mrs. Rhea F. Miller, 1894-1966

For to me, to live is Christ and to die is gain. (Philippians 1:21)

The inspiring and challenging words of this hymn, written by Mrs. Rhea Miller, so influenced 23-year-old George Beverly Shea that they determined the direction of his entire life. As he began to compose a melody for these moving lines, he decided to devote his singing talent to God's glory alone.

Growing up with devoted Christian parents, Bev was encouraged to use his fine singing voice often in the services of the Wesleyan Methodist churches of which his father was a minister. Financial needs of the family made it necessary for him to leave college and work in an insurance office. However, he continued singing in churches and for Christian radio programs. Unexpectedly he was offered an audition for a secular singing position in New York City and passed the test. The opportunity for a substantial salary and wide recognition made Bev's decision very difficult.

One Sunday as Bev went to the family piano to prepare a song for the morning service, he found there the poem "I'd Rather Have Jesus." His mother, who collected beautiful quotations and literary selections, had begun to leave some of them around the house for her son to read, hoping to guide him spiritually. Bev was deeply moved with the challenging message of this text. Immediately he began to compose the music for the lines and used the song that same day in his father's church service.

Bev Shea comments: "Over the years, I've not sung any song more than 'I'd Rather Have Jesus,' but I never tire of Mrs. Miller's heartfelt words." As a young man of 23, Bev allowed the message of this text to guide him wisely to a wonderfully productive and worthwhile life of service to Christ as he shared his musical "theme song" with audiences around the world—

I'd rather have Jesus than silver or gold; I'd rather be His than have riches untold; I'd rather have Jesus than houses or land; I'd rather be led by His nail-pierced hand:

I'd rather have Jesus than men's applause; I'd rather be faithful to His dear cause; I'd rather have Jesus than world-wide fame; I'd rather be true to His holy name:

He's fairer than lilies of rarest bloom; He's sweeter than honey from out the comb; He's all that my hungering spirit needs—I'd rather have Jesus and let Him lead:

Refrain: Than to be the king of a vast domain or be held in sin's dread sway! I'd rather have Jesus than anything this world affords today.

❦ *For Today:* Joshua 24:15; Matthew 16:24-26; Romans 1:16; Philippians 3:8

What would be your honest response to this question: "What are you living for and what would you be willing to die for?" Sing this testimony—

George Beverly Shea, 1909-

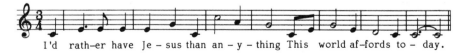

I'd rath-er have Je – sus than an – y – thing This world af–fords to – day.

SATISFIED

Clara Tear Williams, 1858-1937

For He satisfies the thirsty and fills the hungry with good things. (Psalm 107:9)

The lie of the secularist is the notion that contentment in life is dependent upon material possessions. The going expression is "if I only had just a little more." One of the important lessons that we should learn early in life is this: "If I am not satisfied with what I have, I will never be satisfied with what I want." But contentment is an attitude that must be learned and developed. It is foreign to our human behavior. The apostle Paul was shut up in Nero's dungeon in Rome when he penned these words: "I have *learned* the secret of being content in any and every situation . . ." (Philippians 4:12). Paul's contentment was a personal relationship with his Lord. Money can buy many wonderful things, but it never provides this kind of permanent satisfaction. Only an intimate daily relationship with our Creator can truly satisfy the human heart.

In his book *Songs That Lift the Heart* George Beverly Shea tells of his first meeting with the author of this hymn text, Mrs. Clara Tear Williams. It occurred while he was walking one day with his dad:

> "That," said Dad, "was Mrs. Clara Tear Williams. She writes hymns." There was a near reverence in his voice, and though I was only eight years old, I was duly impressed. When Dad and I got home that afternoon, I told Mother about meeting Mrs. Williams, the hymn writer. She smiled knowingly and nodded her head. Then she went to the piano bench and found a hymnal that contained one of Clara Tear Williams' compositions. She explained that Mrs. Williams—a Wesleyan Methodist like us—had written the words, but that the music had been written by Ralph E. Hudson, an Ohio publisher who also was an evangelistic singer. A few years later, when I was in my teens and began to sing solos, I memorized the hymn that Mother played that day and sang it. It was entitled, "Satisfied."

* * * *

All my life long I had panted for a draught, from some clear spring, that I hoped would quench the burning of the thirst I felt within.

Feeding on the husks around me, till my strength was almost gone, longed my soul for something better, only still to hunger on.

Poor I was, and sought for riches, something that would satisfy, but the dust I gathered round me only mocked my soul's sad cry.

Well of water, ever springing, bread of life so rich and free, untold wealth that never faileth, my Redeemer is to me.

Chorus: Hallelujah! I have found Him whom my soul so long has craved! Jesus satisfies my longings—Thru His blood I now am saved.

❧ *For Today:* Psalm 42:1; 81:16; 103:5; Proverbs 13:4; Philippians 4:11, 12

Reflect on this question—"What is the true source of my daily satisfaction?" Then sing this musical testimony as you go—

Ralph E. Hudson, 1843-1901

Hal – le – lu – jah! I have found Him Whom my soul so long has craved!

Je – sus sat – is – fies my long–ings–– Thru His blood I now am saved.

O HAPPY DAY

Philip Doddridge, 1702-1751

I delight greatly in the Lord; my soul rejoices in my God. For He has clothed me with garments of salvation and arrayed me in a robe of righteousness. (Isaiah 61:10)

It is always encouraging to share in a testimonial service by recalling with other believers the time we responded to God's loving invitation for personal salvation. To remember what we were, how we were going, and where we could be today had not God encountered us is truly an important spiritual activity. But we must also be quick to note that the "happy day" of our new birth was never intended to be the final goal for our lives. Rather it was the starting point for developing a Christ-like life and an endless fellowship with our Lord.

Along with Isaac Watts and Charles Wesley, Philip Doddridge is generally ranked as one of England's finest 18th century hymn writers. "O Happy Day," a text which expresses so aptly the sense of joy in a personal relationship with God, is Doddridge's best-known hymn today. The hymn first appeared without the refrain in the 1775 collection of Doddridge's writings, published posthumously, as were all of his 400 hymn texts. The music did not appear for nearly 100 years after the text. It was likely adapted from one of the popular secular tunes of that time.

O happy day that fixed my choice on Thee, my Savior and my God! Well may this glowing heart rejoice and tell its raptures all abroad.

O happy bond that seals my vows to Him who merits all my love! Let cheerful anthems fill His house, while to that sacred shrine I move.

High Heav'n that heard the solemn vow, that vow renewed shall daily hear; till in life's latest hour I bow, and bless in death a bond so dear.

'Tis done, the great transaction's done—I am my Lord's and He is mine; He drew me, and I followed on, charmed to confess the voice divine.

Now rest, my long-divided heart, fixed on this blissful center, rest; nor ever from my Lord depart, with Him of ev'ry good possessed.

Chorus: Happy day, happy day, when Jesus washed my sins away! He taught me how to watch and pray and live rejoicing ev'ry day; happy day, happy day, when Jesus washed my sins away!

❦ ***For Today:*** Psalm 32:11; 70:4; Habakkuk 3:18; Philippians 4:4; 1 John 1:8, 9

Share with someone your conversion experience—the events that prompted the decision when you first fully realized that you were truly God's child. Carry this musical testimony with you—

Edward F. Rimbault, 1816-1876

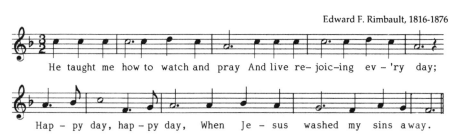

He taught me how to watch and pray And live re-joic-ing ev – 'ry day;

Hap – py day, hap – py day, When Je – sus washed my sins away.

NO ONE EVER CARED FOR ME LIKE JESUS

Words and Music by Charles F. Weigle, 1871-1966

... Where is God my Maker, who gives songs in the night? (Job 35:10)

It is not difficult to sing when all is going well. But often God gives a special song to one of his hurting children during the night times of their life. Believers find new joys in their nights of sorrow and despair, and they discover a greater closeness with their Lord during times of deep need. The apostle John wrote the book of Revelation while on the barren island of Patmos; John Bunyan completed the classic *Pilgrim's Progress* while in the Bedford jail; Beethoven composed his immortal 9th Symphony while totally deaf; and Fanny Crosby once remarked, "If I had not lost my sight, I could never have written all the hymns God gave me."

Charles Weigle's song, "No One Ever Cared For Me Like Jesus," was the product of one of the darkest periods of his life. Weigle spent most of his life as an itinerant evangelist and gospel songwriter. One day after returning home from an evangelistic crusade, he found a note left by his wife of many years. The note said she had had enough of an evangelist's life. She was leaving him. Weigle later said that he became so despondent during the next several years that there were even times when he contemplated suicide. There was the terrible despair that no one really cared for him anymore. Gradually his spiritual faith was restored, and he once again became active in the Christian ministry. Soon he felt compelled to write a song that would be a summary of his past tragic experience. From a heart that had been broken came these choice words that God gave to Charles Weigle:

> I would love to tell you what I think of Jesus since I found in Him a friend so strong and true; I would tell you how He chang'd my life completely—He did something that no other friend could do.
>
> All my life was full of sin when Jesus found me; all my heart was full of misery and woe; Jesus placed His strong and loving arms around me, and He led me in the way I ought to go.
>
> Ev'ry day He comes to me with new assurance, more and more I understand His words of love; but I'll never know just why He came to save me, till some day I see His blessed face above.
>
> **Chorus:** No one ever cared for me like Jesus; there's no other friend so kind as He; no one else could take the sin and darkness from me—O how much He cared for me!

❦ ***For Today:*** Psalm 144:3, 4; Jeremiah 31:2, 3; Ephesians 3:18, 19; 1 John 3:1

With God's help, determine to rise above the problems and hurts that you may be experiencing and turn them into a blessing. Reaffirm your confidence in God's love and care for you by singing this musical truth as you go—

MY SINS ARE BLOTTED OUT, I KNOW!

Words and Music by Merrill Dunlop, 1905-

I, even I, am He who blots out your transgressions, for My own sake, and remembers your sins no more. (Isaiah 43:25)

Forgiveness—when God buries our sins and does not mark the grave.
—*Louis Paul Lehman*

Many Christians have suffered great emotional, mental, and even physical disorders throughout life because they could never accept the fact that God has totally forgiven them. How important it is to realize that when God offers us His forgiveness, it is never a partial but always a total forgiveness—the slate is forever clean. In God's family there are only forgiven children. Then, if we are forgiven by God, we are to accept with gratitude His cleansing provision and, by His help, blot out from our memories all hurting reminders of the past. We should also become a more forgiving person with others, free of the resentments and prejudices that will shackle our spiritual lives. Someone has made this humorous but wise observation: "Christians should keep a cemetery in which to bury the faults and failures of their fellow believers."

The author and composer of this popular gospel hymn, Merrill Dunlop, gives this account of its origin:

It was written in a very few minutes, although only after much deliberation, while I was crossing the Atlantic in 1927 on a liner, *The Leviathan,* and meditating upon the verses in Micah 7:18, 19 and upon the great dimensions of the sea—the breadth and depth and what the Bible says about our sins—buried in those depths—removed—blotted out! Then, making it personal, I said: "My sins are blotted out, I know!" The melody came almost simultaneously with the words. I jotted the chorus down aboard the ship, as I walked the deck. Later, in Ireland, I added the words and music to the stanzas. It took hold immediately and quickly spread across America and across the seas.

* * * *

What a wondrous message in God's Word! My sins are blotted out, I know! If I trust in His redeeming blood, my sins are blotted out, I know!

Once my heart was black, but now what joy; my sins are blotted out, I know! I have peace that nothing can destroy; my sins are blotted out, I know!

I shall stand some day before my King; my sins are blotted out, I know! With the ransomed host I then shall sing: "My sins are blotted out, I know!"

Chorus: My sins are blotted out, I know! My sins are blotted out, I know! They are buried in the depths of the deepest sea: My sins are blotted out, I know!

❦ *For Today:* Psalm 103:1, 3, 11, 12; Isaiah 1:18; 43:25; Micah 7:18, 19

Live in the assurance of God's complete forgiveness. Then determine to forgive and forget the wrongs that others may have done to you. Let your heart be glad as you rejoice in this musical truth—

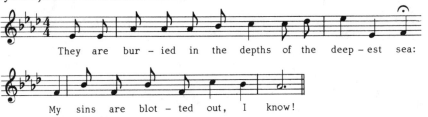

THE HAVEN OF REST

Henry L. Glimour, 1836-1920

We have this hope as an anchor for the soul, firm and secure. It enters the inner sanctuary behind the curtain, where Jesus, who went before us, has entered on our behalf. (Hebrews 6:19)

What stabilizers are to a ship in stormy water, the conscious presence of Christ is to a Christian during the storms and stresses of daily living. Christians have never been promised an exemption from any of life's storms. The Scriptures teach that "man is born to trouble as surely as sparks fly upward" (Job 5:7). It is our reaction to life's storms that reveals the level of our spiritual maturity. We can either become bitter and belligerent, or we can use the experience to develop greater spiritual strength as we learn to rely more fully on our Lord.

Not only do we have the indwelling presence of Christ, but we also have the assurance that Jesus Christ is in heaven today interceding for us. Just as an Old Testament priest stood behind the veil in the tabernacle or the temple to represent the Israelites before God, so Jesus pleads our case in the heavenly realm on the basis of His death and resurrection. What security this gives us!

The author of this text, Henry Gilmour, came to the United States from Ireland as a teenager. He practiced dentistry for a number of years and then spent the last 25 years of his life as a gospel musician. He was a gifted soloist and was greatly respected as a choir director. "The Haven of Rest" first appeared in *Sunlight Songs,* published in 1890.

> My soul in sad exile was out on life's sea, so burdened with sin, and distrest, till I heard a sweet voice saying, "Make me your choice!" And I entered the Haven of Rest.

> I yielded myself to His tender embrace, and faith taking hold of the Word, my fetters fell off, and I anchored my soul—The "Haven of Rest" is my Lord.

> The song of my soul, since the Lord made me whole, has been the old story so blest of Jesus, who'll save whosoever will have a home in the Haven of Rest!

> O come to the Savior—He patiently waits to save by His power divine; Come, anchor your soul in the Haven of Rest, and say, "My Beloved is mine."

> **Chorus:** I've anchored my soul in the Haven of Rest; I'll sail the wide seas no more; the tempest may sweep o'er the wild, stormy deep—In Jesus I'm safe ever more.

❦ *For Today:* Exodus 33:22; Psalm 34:19; 61:2; Isaiah 66:12; Philippians 4:7; Hebrews 4:3; 6:13-20

Regardless of your circumstances, determine to rely more fully on the indwelling Christ and the awareness of your heavenly advocate. Carry this musical testimony with you—

George D. Moore, 19th century

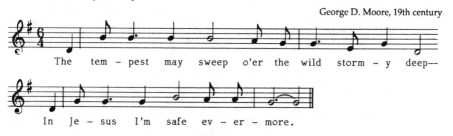

The tem - pest may sweep o'er the wild storm - y deep--

In Je - sus I'm safe ev - er - more.

CHRIST LIVETH IN ME

Daniel W. Whittle, 1840-1901

I have been crucified with Christ and I no longer live, but Christ liveth in me.
(Galatians 2:20)

"Don't you know that you yourselves are God's temple and that God's Spirit lives in you?" (1 Corinthians 3:16). One can almost hear the apostle Paul exhorting the carnal Christians at Corinth with these strong words. How important it is that believers realize with conviction that their earthly bodies are the residence of the living God! Such an awareness should cause us to have an earnest concern for the proper care of our bodies. It is also the motivation we need for Christ-like living—to allow His perfection to be demonstrated in our mortal flesh.

> Oh, to be saved from myself, dear Lord, Oh, to be lost in Thee;
> Oh, that it may be no more I, but Christ that lives in me.   —*C. H. Forrest*

The evidence of true conversion is the growing awareness of Christ within us as the Holy Spirit confirms this fact with our human spirit (Romans 8:16). As we mature in the Christian faith, we appreciate increasingly the biblical truth of the glorious identification and security that are ours: God is in Christ, Christ is in us, and we are in Christ. Nothing can ever defeat or destroy such a divine union.

The author, Daniel W. Whittle, was a most interesting individual. He joined the Illinois Infantry during the Civil War and rose to the rank of major. For the remainder of his life he was known by this title. Following the war he returned to Chicago and became treasurer of the Elgin Watch Company. In 1873, however, he resigned this high position and under D. L. Moody's influence entered the evangelistic ministry. He was unusually successful as an evangelist as well as the author of a number of favorite gospel hymns, most of which he wrote with the pseudonym "El Nathan." "Christ Liveth in Me" first appeared in *Gospel Hymns #6*, which was published in 1891.

> Once far from God and dead in sin, no light my heart could see; but in God's Word the light I found. Now Christ liveth in me.

> As lives the flower within the seed, as in the cone the tree; so, praise the God of truth and grace; His Spirit dwelleth in me.

> With longing all my heart is filled, that like Him I may be, as on the wond'rous thought I dwell that Christ dwelleth in me.

> **Refrain:** Christ liveth in me. O what a salvation this, that Christ liveth in me!

❦ *For Today:* John 17:22, 23; 2 Corinthians 6:16; Galatians 2:19-21; Ephesians 3:16, 17; Colossians 1:27

Live with the confidence of an indwelling Christ who promises to help you do all things through His strength (Philippians 4:13). Sing this musical truth—

James McGranahan, 1840-1907

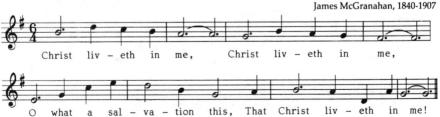

Christ liv - eth in me, Christ liv - eth in me,

O what a sal - va - tion this, That Christ liv - eth in me!

WHY DO I SING ABOUT JESUS?

Words and Music by Albert A. Ketchum, 1894-?

Shout with joy to God, all the earth! Sing to the glory of His name; offer Him glory and praise! (Psalm 66:1, 2)

> Fill me with gladness from above,
> Hold me by strength divine;
> Lord, let the glow of your great love
> Through my whole being shine.   —*Unknown*

The Christian life was meant to be a joyous experience. One of the most effective ways to demonstrate our inner joy is to carry a song upon our lips throughout our daily activities. It was my father who first taught me this truth. As a painter-decorator, Dad became known to his many customers as the "singing painter." Singing his favorite hymns while he worked became his natural way of life. At his funeral, many of his customers, both believers and nonbelievers, told me of the impact my father had upon them as they observed his cheerful attitude while he worked.

It is important that we carry a song of the Lord with us. The world needs to see and hear the story of Jesus and His love. And the song that we carry on the inside will be reflected on our countenance. An inner song and a cheerful countenance are always the result of a life that is enjoying an intimate daily fellowship with our Lord and Savior—the One who sets us free!

Albert Ketchum, the author and composer of "Why Do I Sing About Jesus?", wrote this song while a student at the Moody Bible Institute during the early 1920's. The song first appeared in *Gospel Truth in Song,* published in 1922. It provides believers a fine vehicle for a musical testimony about their Lord:

> Deep in my heart there's a gladness—Jesus has saved me from sin! Praise to His name, what a Savior! Cleansing without and within!

> Only a glimpse of His goodness; that was sufficient for me; only one look at the Savior, then was my spirit set free.

> He is the fairest of fair ones. He is the lily, the rose; rivers of mercy surround Him; grace, love, and pity He shows.

> **Chorus:** Why do I sing about Jesus? Why is He precious to me? He is my Lord and my Savior: Dying, He set me free!

❦ *For Today:* Psalm 32:7; 40:3; 66:16; Proverbs 15:13; Philippians 2:5-11; 1 Peter 2:7

Determine to allow the warmth of God's love to be reflected in all of your activities. Carry this musical testimony with you as you seek to be a witness for Christ even in your working attitudes—

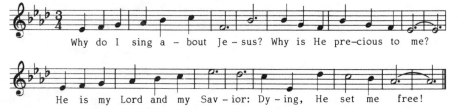

Why do I sing a - bout Je - sus? Why is He pre-cious to me?

He is my Lord and my Sav - ior: Dy - ing, He set me free!

July

• Results of the Gospel • Joy • Peace • Contentment
• Comfort • Security • Heaven
• National Holiday/Independence Day

HE KEEPS ME SINGING

Words and Music by Luther B. Bridgers, 1884-1948

If you obey My commands, you will remain in My love, just as I have obeyed My Father's commands and remain in His love. I have told you this so that My joy may be in you and that your joy may be complete. (John 15:10-11)

Joy is the flag which is flown from the castle of the heart when the King is in residence there. —*Unknown*

Joy should be one of the chief characteristics of our Christian faith. In the New Testament the word *chara* is used 53 times to mean "joy." Only a joyful exuberant Christian is a worthy representative of the transforming power of Christ's gospel. But what is spiritual joy? It is much more than mere laughter or even happiness. It is a life that is at rest in the Lord, regardless of life's circumstances. Such a life cannot help but have a strong impact on nonbelievers. If there were more singing Christians, there would be more Christians.

Often our finest and most effective songs are sung during the midnight experiences of life. It is easy to sing when all is well. But to sing when all is dark requires the indwelling presence of Christ. Luther Bridgers, a Methodist pastor and evangelist from Georgia, is believed to have written both words and music for this joyful hymn in 1910, following the death of his wife and three sons in a fire at the home of his wife's parents while he was away conducting revival meetings in Kentucky.

There's within my heart a melody—Jesus whispers sweet and low, "Fear not, I am with thee—peace, be still," in all of life's ebb and flow.

All my life was wrecked by sin and strife. Discord filled my heart with pain; Jesus swept across the broken strings, stirred the slumb'ring chords again.

Feasting on the riches of His grace, resting 'neath His shelt'ring wing, always looking on His smiling face—That is why I shout and sing.

Tho sometimes He leads thru waters deep, trials fall across the way, tho sometimes the path seem rough and steep, see His feet-prints all the way.

Soon He's coming back to welcome me far beyond the starry sky; I shall wing my flight to worlds unknown; I shall reign with Him on high.

Chorus: Jesus, Jesus, Jesus—Sweetest name I know, fills my ev'ry longing, keeps me singing as I go.

❦ *For Today:* Psalm 40:3; Proverbs 29:6; Isaiah 12:3, 5; 52:9; Acts 16:25; Ephesians 5:19

Determine to live with a singing spirit; be a truly "praising Christian." Carry this musical testimony with you as a help, knowing that—

Je - sus, Je - sus, Je - sus,— Sweet - est name I know;

Fills my ev - 'ry long - ing, Keeps me sing - ing as I go.

IN MY HEART THERE RINGS A MELODY

Words and Music by Elton M. Roth, 1891-1951

Sing to the Lord a new song, for He has done marvelous things; His right hand and His holy arm have worked salvation for Him. Shout for joy to the Lord, all the earth, burst into jubilant song with music. (Psalm 98:1, 4)

King Solomon, one of the wisest men who ever lived, once made this observation: "A happy heart makes the face cheerful, but heartache crushes the spirit" (Proverbs 15:13). The medical profession has also long realized that happy people are the healthiest people. But how does one achieve that happiness—that joy? The child of God knows that it comes from living close to the Savior. And beyond that—joy experienced should also be joy expressed.

This ought to be true in our individual lives as well as when we gather in our church services. True worship must have the ingredient of festal joy. The Psalms insist that we "burst into jubilant song with music" and that we praise our God with "trumpet, lute, harp, timbrel, and loud crashing cymbals." Too often believers give the impression that the Christian experience is a cheerless journey of harsh self-discipline that must be painfully endured until the heavenly rewards are finally realized. Little joy or praise is evident in such a testimony.

The author and composer of this hymn, Elton Roth, was a well-known musician of his day. It was while assisting with evangelistic meetings in Texas on a hot summer day in 1923 that the words and music for this hymn suddenly came to him. Mr. Roth recalls, "That evening I introduced the song by having more than 200 boys and girls sing it at the open air meeting, after which the audience joined in the singing. I was thrilled as it seemed my whole being was transformed into song."

When our worship and personal experience are full of joy and song, it will be easier for our lives to encourage others to know this same happiness also.

> I have a song that Jesus gave me; it was sent from heav'n above; there never was a sweeter melody; 'tis a melody of love.
>
> I love the Christ who died on Calv'ry, for He washed my sins away; He put within my heart a melody, and I know it's there to stay.
>
> 'Twill be my endless theme in glory; with the angels I will sing; 'twill be a song with glorious harmony, when the courts of heaven ring.
>
> **Chorus:** In my heart there rings a melody, there rings a melody with heaven's harmony; in my heart there rings a melody, there rings a melody of love.

❦ ***For Today:*** 1 Chronicles 16:8-10; Nehemiah 8:10; Colossians 3:16

Consider thoughtfully—Am I truly a happy Christian? Does my life express the joy of the Lord? Does my church worship produce joy in my life? Ask God to change whatever may be lacking. Then sing joyfully as you go—

In my heart there rings a mel – o – dy; There rings a mel – o – dy of love.

IT IS WELL WITH MY SOUL

Horatio G. Spafford, 1828-1888

God is our refuge and strength, an ever present help in trouble. (Psalm 46:1)

Inner peace through an implicit trust in the love of God is the real evidence of a mature Christian faith. Only with this kind of confidence in his heavenly Father could Horatio Spafford experience such heart-rending tragedies as he did and yet be able to say, "It is well with my soul."

Spafford had known peaceful and happy days as a successful attorney in Chicago. He was the father of five children, an active member of a Presbyterian church, and a loyal friend and supporter of D. L. Moody and other evangelical leaders of his day. Without warning, however, a series of unexpected events occurred. First, there was the sudden death of the Spaffords' only son. Then a short time after, the great Chicago fire of 1871 wiped out the family's extensive real estate investments. When Mr. Moody and his music associate Ira Sankey left for Great Britain for an evangelistic campaign, Spafford decided to take his family to Europe to lift their spirits and also to assist in the meetings.

In November, 1873, Spafford was detained by urgent business, but he sent his wife and four daughters as scheduled on the *S.S. Ville du Harve*, planning to join them soon. Halfway across the Atlantic, the ship was struck by an English vessel and sank in 12 minutes. All four of the Spafford daughters—Tanetta, Maggie, Annie and Bessie—were among the 226 who drowned. Mrs. Spafford was among the few who were miraculously saved.

Horatio Spafford stood hour after hour on the deck of the ship carrying him to rejoin his sorrowing wife in Cardiff, Wales. When the ship passed the approximate place where his precious daughters had drowned, Spafford received sustaining comfort from God that enabled him to write, "When sorrows like sea billows roll . . . It is well with my soul." What a picture of our hope!

> When peace, like a river, attendeth my way, when sorrows like sea billows roll—Whatever my lot, Thou hast taught me to say, It is well with my soul.

> Tho Satan should buffet, tho trials should come, let this blest assurance control, that Christ hath regarded my helpless estate and shed His own blood for my soul.

> And, Lord, haste the day when my faith shall be sight, the clouds be rolled back as a scroll: The trump shall resound and the Lord shall descend, "Even so"— it is well with my soul.

> **Chorus:** It is well with my soul, it is well, it is well with my soul.

❦ *For Today:* Psalm 31:14; 142:3; Galatians 2:20; 1 Peter 4:19

Ask yourself if you can truthfully say, "It is well with my soul," no matter what the circumstances may be that surround you.

Philip P. Bliss, 1838-1876

It is well..... with my soul..... It is well, it is well with my soul.

THE STAR-SPANGLED BANNER
Francis Scott Key, 1779-1843

Submit yourselves to every ordinance of man for the Lord's sake: Whether it be to the king, as supreme, or to governors, as unto them that are sent by him for the punishment of evildoers, and for the praise of them that do well. (1 Peter 2:13, 14 KJV)

During the War of 1812, while on the deck of a truce ship, Francis Key paced nervously as a fierce battle raged nearby during the British attack on the harbor of Baltimore. As District Attorney of Georgetown and a spiritual lay leader of his church, Key had been sent by President James Madison to negotiate with the British for a physician who had been taken prisoner. All night Key and his party were detained as the heavy bombardment continued. When the firing suddenly stopped just before morning, Key was fearful of the outcome; but as he looked hesitantly across the water, he saw the American flag still triumphantly flying with the assurance of our nation's freedom!

With joyful relief, Key wrote his poem hastily on the back of an envelope and put finishing touches on it after being released later that evening. One month later the song was published, accompanied by an old hunting tune, "Anacron in Heaven," attributed to John Stafford Smith of England. Although enthusiastically received by the people, the song was not officially adopted by Congress as our national anthem until March 3, 1931.

> O say, can you see, by the dawn's early light, what so proudly we hailed at the twilight's last gleaming, whose broad stripes and bright stars, thru the perilous fight, o'er the ramparts we watched, were so gallantly streaming? And the rockets' red glare, the bombs bursting in air, gave proof thru the night that our flag was still there. O say, does that star-spangled banner yet wave o'er the land of the free and the home of the brave?

> O thus be it ever, when free men shall stand between their loved homes and the war's desolation! Blest with vict'ry and peace, may the heav'n-rescued land praise the Pow'r that hath made and preserved us a nation! Then conquer we must, when our cause it is just; and this be our motto: "In God is our trust!" And the star-spangled banner in triumph shall wave o'er the land of the free and the home of the brave!

❦ *For Today:* Proverbs 14:34; Matthew 22:21; Romans 13:1-7; 1 Timothy 2:1, 2; 1 Peter 2:13-21

Write a letter of commendation to a public official for some worthy contribution he has made to the moral and spiritual betterment of our country. May this musical question from our national anthem be a continuing challenge and concern.

Attributed to John Stafford Smith, 1750-1836

O say, does that star-span-gled ban-ner yet wave

O'er the land of the free and the home of the brave?

PEACE, PERFECT PEACE

Edward H. Bickersteth, 1825-1906

I have told you these things, so that in Me you may have peace. In this world you will have trouble. But take heart! I have overcome the world. (John 16:33)

The quest for inner calm and peace has been a universal struggle for mankind throughout the ages. Even for those of us who profess to be followers of Christ, it is difficult to realize with consistency that "God's ways are higher than our ways and His thoughts than our thoughts." It often becomes normal for us to make our own plans without consulting Him for His perfect will.

This comforting hymn, which reminds us that God's perfect peace is found only in Christ Jesus, was written by an English minister of the Anglican church. Edward Bickersteth, Jr. served as the Bishop of Exeter, England, and became well-known for his many books of sermons, poetry, and hymns.

While vacationing in August, 1875, Bickersteth heard a sermon on Isaiah 26:3 and was deeply moved by the way this verse reads in Hebrew: "Thou wilt keep him in *peace, peace* whose mind is stayed on Thee . . ." The repetition of the word conveyed the idea of absolute perfection. That afternoon while visiting a dying aged relative, Bickersteth read this verse from Isaiah to comfort the man. Then at the bedside he quickly composed the lines of this hymn text just as it reads today.

From the Hebrew expression of "peace peace" came the beginning phrase of each stanza, "Peace, perfect peace." Then questions were posed. For each of these five questions Edward Bickersteth supplied a positive spiritual answer.

As these completed lines were read to the dying relative, they were no doubt a source of great comfort—as they have continued to be for troubled hearts throughout the years.

> Peace, perfect peace—in this dark world of sin? The blood of Jesus whispers peace within.
>
> Peace, perfect peace—by thronging duties pressed? To do the will of Jesus, this is rest.
>
> Peace, perfect peace—with sorrows surging round? On Jesus' bosom naught but calm is found.
>
> Peace, perfect peace—with loved ones far away? In Jesus' keeping we are safe, and they.
>
> Peace, perfect peace—our future all unknown? Jesus we know, and He is on the throne.

❦ ***For Today:*** Isaiah 26:3; 32:17; John 14:27; Ephesians 1:14; Philippians 4:7

Experience the perfect peace of God in your life by realizing anew that it is only obtained through the presence of Christ in our lives—He is our peace (Ephesians 1:14). Carry this musical message as you go—

Pax Tecum tune ————————————————————————— George T. Caldbeck, 1852-1918

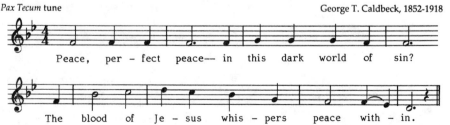

Peace, per - fect peace-- in this dark world of sin?

The blood of Je - sus whis - pers peace with - in.

LIKE A RIVER GLORIOUS

Frances R. Havergal, 1836-1879

If only you had paid attention to my commands, your peace would have been like a river, your righteousness like the waves of the sea. (Isaiah 48:18)

Our gift of salvation includes more than pardon from sin, deliverance from hell, and a guarantee to heaven. It includes everything we need to live victorious lives of "perfect peace and rest" here and now. An untroubled mind is one of life's greatest goals. Many seek it by pursuing money, success, drugs, or alcohol, but all such roads end in failure and frustration. Contentment has been described as that inner satisfaction that enables us to live in quietness, peace, and acceptance. The secret of contentment does not depend on our material possessions; rather, it depends on our spiritual awareness and the appropriation of what we possess by being members of the heavenly family.

This hymn text by Frances Havergal, often called "England's Consecration Poet," reflects so well her personal lifestyle. Her brief life of 43 years was said to be completely dedicated to God and His service. The music was composed for this text by James Mountain, an English Baptist pastor, evangelist and musician. The hymn first appeared in its present form in the *Hymns of Consecration and Faith*, published in 1876. The song was titled "Perfect Peace."

These choice words have made this a favorite hymn of many of God's people through the years, especially when called upon to face difficult problems:

> Like a river glorious is God's perfect peace, over all victorious in its bright increase; perfect, yet it floweth fuller ev'ry day; perfect, yet it groweth deeper all the way.

> Hidden in the hollow of His blessed hand, never foe can follow, never traitor stand; not a surge of worry, not a shade of care, not a blast of hurry touch the spirit there.

> Ev'ry joy or trial falleth from above, traced upon our dial by the Sun of Love; we may trust Him fully all for us to do—They who trust Him wholly find Him wholly true.

> **Refrain:** Stayed upon Jehovah, hearts are fully blest—finding, as He promised, perfect peace and rest.

❦ *For Today:* Psalm 29:11; Isaiah 26:3; John 14:27; Philippians 4:11; Colossians 3:15; James 3:17

Reflect on this statement—"A mind stayed on God produces a sound mind for daily living." Carry this musical truth with you as a reminder—

Wye Valley tune   James Mountain, 1844-1933

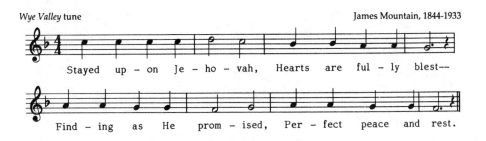

Stayed up - on Je - ho - vah, Hearts are ful - ly blest--

Find - ing as He prom - ised, Per - fect peace and rest.

SWEET PEACE, THE GIFT OF GOD'S LOVE

Words and Music by Peter P. Bilhorn, 1865-1936

Great peace have they who love Your law, and nothing can make them stumble.
(Psalm 119:165)

The blessing of peace is the one prize that often eludes those who seem to have attained everything else in life. Yet peace is one of the choice gifts left to us by our departing Lord. Jesus' mission was to bring God's peace to man by bridging the way for us to enjoy eternal fellowship with our Creator.

Peter Bilhorn, author and composer of this hymn, began writing gospel songs shortly after his conversion at the age of 20. In all he wrote more than 2,000 songs while serving as the song leader for Billy Sunday and other leading evangelists.

One night he sang one of his most popular songs, "I Will Sing the Wondrous Story," at a camp meeting. A friend jokingly remarked, "I wish you would write a song to suit my voice as well as that song suits yours." Bilhorn responded, "What shall it be?" "Oh, any sweet piece." That evening Bilhorn composed the music for the new hymn.

The following winter while travelling on a train, Bilhorn observed a tragic train accident. He saw one poor individual left lying in a pool of blood. That event reminded him of Christ's blood atoning for our sins, which prompted him to write these words there on the train. He completed a hymn that has since moved many to a deeper realization and appreciation of God's "wonderful gift from above."

There comes to my heart one sweet strain, a glad and a joyous refrain; I sing it again and again—sweet peace, the gift of God's love.

Thru Christ on the cross peace was made. My debt by His death was all paid; no other foundation is laid for peace, the gift of God's love.

When Jesus as Lord I had crowned, my heart with this peace did abound; in Him the rich blessing I found—sweet peace, the gift of God's love.

In Jesus for peace I abide, and as I keep close to His side, there's nothing but peace doth betide—sweet peace, the gift of God's love.

Chorus: Peace, peace, sweet peace! Wonderful gift from above! O wonderful, wonderful peace! Sweet peace, the gift of God's love.

❦ *For Today:* Isaiah 57:21; Galatians 5:22; Philippians 4:6, 7; Colossians 3:15

Thank God for the gift of peace that He has provided. A life of peace should lead us to a life of praise—and a life of praise in turn leads to a life of peace. Carry this musical reminder with you—

Peace, peace, sweet peace! Won – der – ful gift from a – bove!

O won–der–ful, won–der–ful peace! Sweet peace, the gift of God's love!

COME, YE DISCONSOLATE

Thomas Moore, 1779-1852, (verses 1 and 2 with alterations)
Thomas Hastings, 1784-1872, (verse 3)

You will seek Me and find Me when you seek Me with all your heart. (Jeremiah 29:13)

God's delight is to administer comfort to wounded spirits.   —*Unknown*

Repeating the plea to "come" and the plaintive promise that "earth has no sorrow that heav'n cannot heal," this hymn of a soulful Irish poet has brought divine peace and consolation to countless troubled individuals. The text assures the anguished, the desolate, the straying one, and the penitent that responding to God's gracious invitation and sharing our burdens with Him will bring us joy, light, hope, and tender comfort.

Thomas Moore was well-known in Ireland for his poems and ballads such as "The Last Rose of Summer" and "Believe Me, If All Those Endearing Young Charms." He became known as the "Voice of Ireland." Moore's prose and poetry were said to be influential in the political emancipation of Ireland. The English seemed to sense in his writings the true spirit of the Irish people, and they were moved to be more sympathetic toward their gaining independence from England.

After Thomas Moore included this hymn in his 1824 collection, *Sacred Songs—Duets and Trios,* a number of revisions were made in the lines by Thomas Hastings, an American hymnist. The third stanza was almost completely rewritten by Hastings. It is generally agreed that these changes made Moore's poem easier to sing and more suitable for evangelical church use. How important to be reminded that "Earth has no sorrow that heaven cannot heal."

Come, ye disconsolate, where'er ye languish—Come to the mercy seat, fervently kneel; Here bring your wounded hearts; here tell your anguish: Earth has no sorrow that heav'n cannot heal.

Joy of the desolate, Light of the straying, Hope of the penitent, fadeless and pure! Here speaks the Comforter, tenderly saying, "Earth has no sorrow that heav'n cannot cure!"

Here see the Bread of Life, see the waters flowing forth from the throne of God, pure from above; come to the feast of love—come ever knowing earth has no sorrow but heav'n can remove.

❦ *For Today:* Matthew 11:28, 29; John 14:1; 2 Corinthians 1:3-7; Hebrews 4:15, 16; 1 Peter 5:7

Bring to the mercy seat whatever is clouding your life, and you will find the consolation and peace that God has promised and that only He can give. Then remember that the world is full of people with heavy hearts. Share this word of encouragement with someone. Carry this musical reminder with you—

Consolator tune   Samuel Webbe, 1740-1816

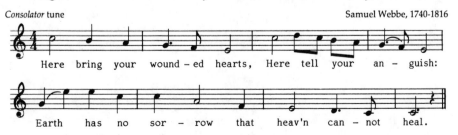

Here bring your wound-ed hearts, Here tell your an-guish: Earth has no sor-row that heav'n can-not heal.

DOES JESUS CARE?

Frank E. Graeff, 1860-1919

And surely I will be with you always, to the very end of the age. (Matthew 28:20)

God whispers in our pleasures but shouts in our pain. ━C. S. *Lewis*

Frank E. Graeff, author of this hymn text, knew what it was to wonder, as most of God's children do at times, if the Lord is really concerned during our times of hurt, when the burdens and cares weigh heavily, when the way seems dark, when temptation seems difficult to resist, or when we must part with our dearest loved one. Yet the answer comes back triumphantly: "I know my Savior cares!"

Known as the "sunshine minister" of the Methodist denomination in the churches of the Philadelphia conference, Frank Graeff was widely liked for his cheerful and winsome personality. C. Austin Miles, writer of the hymn "In the Garden," said of him:

> He is a spiritual optimist, a great friend of children; his bright sun-shining disposition attracts not only children but all with whom he comes in contact. He has a holy magnetism and a child-like faith.

Unknown to others, however, were the many severe testing experiences in Mr. Graeff's life. It was during a time of severe physical agony, doubt, and despondency that he turned to the Scriptures for comfort and strength. First Peter 5:7, which says, "Casting all your care upon Him; for He careth for you," became especially meaningful to him in this time of need. He wrote the lines of "Does Jesus Care?" to express the feelings of assurance that came to him. Mr. Graeff wrote more than 200 hymns in his lifetime, but none has been more consoling to God's people than this text:

> Does Jesus care when my heart is pained too deeply for mirth and song, as the burdens press, and the cares distress, and the way grows weary and long?
>
> Does Jesus care when my way is dark with a nameless dread and fear? As the daylight fades into deep night shades, does He care enough to be near?
>
> Does Jesus care when I've tried and failed to resist some temptation strong, when for my deep grief I find no relief, tho my tears flow all the night long?
>
> Does Jesus care when I've said good bye to the dearest on earth to me, and my sad heart aches till it nearly breaks—Is it aught to Him? Does He see?
>
> **Chorus:** O yes, He cares—I know He care! His heart is touched with my grief; when the days are weary, the long nights dreary, I know my Savior cares.

❦ *For Today:* Psalm 28:7; 42:8; Isaiah 26:4; Mark 5:36; 1 Peter 5:7

In your times of darkness or sorrow, rest in the security of the truth that Jesus truly cares deeply and will ultimately meet your need. Then try to comfort someone else with this musical truth—

J. Lincoln Hall, 1866-1930

O yes, He cares—I know He cares! His heart is touched with my grief;

When the days are wea-ry the long nights drear-y, I know my Sav – ior cares.

NO ONE UNDERSTANDS LIKE JESUS

Words and Music by John W. Peterson, 1921-

For we do not have a high priest who is unable to sympathize with our weaknesses, but we have one who has been tempted in every way, just as we are—yet was without sin. Let us then approach the throne of grace with confidence, so that we may receive mercy and find grace to help in our time of need. (Hebrews 4:15, 16)

Since World War II, the name John W. Peterson has become synonymous with fine gospel music. Over 1,000 gospel songs and hymns, as well as many other musical works such as cantatas, anthems, choral arrangements, and gospel film musicales, have been written by this gifted and dedicated composer. Mr. Peterson gave this account of "No One Understands Like Jesus," written during the early years of his ministry:

> At one time I had a fairly responsible position with a well-known gospel ministry. One day a supervisory position opened up in my department. I was led to believe that I was to be promoted to this position. I was thrilled and challenged by the prospect of a new job. But I was by-passed, and a man from the outside was brought in to fill the position. There followed days of agonizing heart searching. It was all I could do to keep from becoming bitter. One night I had occasion to spend an evening with the man who was brought in for "my" position. For some reason or other, though otherwise a very pleasant fellow, that night he became quite caustic in some of his remarks to me, and I was deeply hurt. Later that evening, after returning home, I was sitting in our living room thinking about the events of the past days and about the bitter experiences of that evening. I began to feel very alone and forsaken. Suddenly, I sensed the presence of the Lord in an unusual way and my mind was diverted from my difficulties to His faithfulness and sufficiency. Soon the thought occurred to me that He fully understood and sympathized with my situation—in fact, no one could ever completely understand or care as did He. Before long, the idea for the song came and I began to write—

* * * *

No one understands like Jesus. He's a friend beyond compare; meet Him at the throne of mercy; He is waiting for you there.

No one understands like Jesus; ev'ry woe He sees and feels; tenderly He whispers comfort, and the broken heart He heals.

No one understands like Jesus when the foes of life assail; you should never be discouraged; Jesus cares and will not fail.

No one understands like Jesus when you falter on the way; tho you fail Him, sadly fail Him, He will pardon you today.

Refrain: No one understands like Jesus when the days are dark and grim; no one is so near, so dear as Jesus—Cast your ev'ry care on Him.

❦ *For Today:* Job 23:10; Psalm 112:7; 131:2; 139:2; Proverbs 14:26

Learn to handle human disappointments and rejection even as Joseph did by realizing this truth—"they meant it for harm, the Lord meant it for good" (Genesis 50:19, 20). Be thankful for Jesus who understands and will never disappoint. Sing as you go realizing that—

No one un-der-stands like Je-sus When the days are dark and grim;

No one is so near, so dear as Je-sus--Cast your ev-'ry care on Him.

GOD WILL TAKE CARE OF YOU

Civilla D. Martin, 1869-1948

Cast your cares on the Lord and He will sustain you; He will never let the righteous fall. (Psalm 55:22)

Do we as Christians trust God for salvation and eternal life yet at times doubt that He will tenderly care for us in our daily life? We all seem to need reassurance of God's concern for us in troublesome times. That's why this hymn has brought comfort and encouragement to so many Christians—it reminds us that the Lord cares deeply for His children. We need not worry no matter how great the task, how difficult the test, how fierce the danger, or how great the need. We can just "lean upon His breast" and be covered by "His wings of love."

Civilla Martin wrote this hymn when she herself needed to learn the lesson of resting in God's care. Her husband, the Reverend W. Stillman Martin, was a well-known Baptist evangelist. One Sunday in 1904, Mrs. Martin became ill suddenly and was unable to accompany her husband to his preaching assignment some distance away. As Mr. Martin considered cancelling his trip, their young son exclaimed, "Father, don't you think that if God wants you to preach today, He will take care of Mother while you're away?" Returning that evening after seeing several people profess Christ as Savior, Mr. Martin found his wife greatly improved and busily writing this text, which had been suggested by her son's words. That same evening, Stillman Martin composed the music, providing God's people with another endearing hymn that has ministered to hurting hearts.

Be not dismayed whate'er betide, God will take care of you; beneath His wings of love abide; God will take care of you.

Thru days of toil when heart doth fail, God will take care of you; when dangers fierce your path assail, God will take care of you.

All you may need He will provide; God will take care of you; nothing you ask will be denied; God will take care of you.

No matter what may be the test, God will take care of you; lean, weary one, upon His breast; God will take care of you.

Chorus: God will take care of you, thru ev'ry day, o'er all the way; He will take care of you; God will take care of you.

🐦 *For Today:* Job 23:10; Psalm 57:1; Isaiah 41:10; 1 Corinthians 10:13; Philippians 4:19; 1 Peter 5:7

Share God's love and concern with someone who is hurting. Encourage the troubled believer with this musical truth—

W. Stillman Martin, 1862-1935

God will take care of you, Thru ev – 'ry day, O'er all the way;

He will take care of you, God will take care of you.

HIDING IN THEE

William O. Cushing, 1823-1902

But the Lord has become my fortress, and my God the rock in whom I take refuge.
(Psalm 94:22)

In childhood when we were frightened we wanted to run and hide in our mother's or father's arms until we felt the danger had passed. In the same way when trouble and sorrow disturb our adult lives, we look for a place of consolation or escape. But we can only find the deep satisfying peace of God in the midst of our storms when we are relying on the God of all peace.

William O. Cushing said that, when he wrote this hymn text in 1876, "it was the outgrowth of many tears, many heart conflicts and yearnings of which the world could know nothing." After the death of his wife in middle age, Cushing was forced to retire from an active ministry because of poor health. He had been a successful pastor in the eastern areas of the United States. He began to be intensely interested in writing hymns, collaborating with many of the leading gospel musicians of that time. One day when Ira Sankey made a special request for a song in his gospel work, Cushing felt it was a direct call from God. He explained:

> I prayed, "Lord, give me something that may glorify Thee." It was while thus waiting that "Hiding in Thee" pressed to make itself known. Mr. Sankey called forth the tune and by his genius gave the hymn wings, making it useful in the Master's work.

William Cushing knew personally the sorrows and turmoil of life, but he also knew where he could find safety and rest—in the "blest Rock of Ages." When this hymn was first published, the author prefaced it with Psalm 31:2—"Be my rock of refuge, a strong fortress to save me."

> O safe to the Rock that is higher than I my soul in its conflicts and sorrows would fly. So sinful, so weary—Thine, Thine would I be: Thou blest "Rock of Ages," I'm hiding in Thee.

> In the calm of the noon-tide, in sorrow's lone hour, in times when temptation casts o'er me its pow'r, in the tempests of life, on its wide, heaving sea, Thou blest "Rock of Ages," I'm hiding in Thee.

> How oft in the conflict, when pressed by the foe, I have fled to my Refuge and breathed out my woe. How often, when trials like sea billows roll, have I hidden in Thee, O Thou Rock of my soul.

> **Chorus:** Hiding in Thee, Thou blest "Rock of Ages," I'm hiding in Thee.

❦ *For Today:* Psalm 4:8; Psalm 31:2; Isaiah 26:3, 4; 2 Corinthians 1:9, 10

Whenever tempests arise in your sea of life, do not hesitate to fly for refuge to the safety of your "Rock of Ages," and rest peacefully there. Sing this musical truth as you go—

Ira D. Sankey, 1840-1908

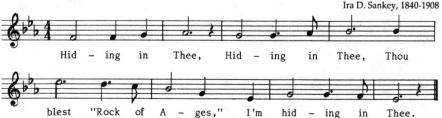

Hid – ing in Thee, Hid – ing in Thee, Thou
blest "Rock of A – ges," I'm hid – ing in Thee.

A SHELTER IN THE TIME OF STORM

Vernon J. Charlesworth, 1838-? with alteration

You are my hiding place; you will protect me from trouble and surround me with songs of deliverance. (Psalm 32:7)

Storms often hit the northern coast of England bringing distress to the many small fishing vessels that ply the coastal waters. It is reported that "A Shelter in the Time of Storm" has long been a favorite song of many of the fishemen in this area, and they are often heard singing it as they approach their harbors during a storm.

The vivid wording of this hymn assures us that we too are safer during life's storms with Christ in control than in the calm times without Him. We as Christians must rest assured that "no fears alarm, no foes affright" in the shelter of His safe retreat. Just as a young bird would never fly if not pushed out of its nest, we would never develop spiritual strength if we did not learn to handle—with absolute confidence in God—the storms He allows to come our way.

The text for this hymn was written by Vernon J. Charlesworth, an English pastor who also served as headmaster of Charles Spurgeon's Stockwell Orphanage. Ira Sankey, American gospel musician and publisher, discovered the song in a small London paper and gave it a singable new melody, adding a refrain that could be easily sung.

The Lord's our Rock, in Him we hide—a shelter in the time of storm, secure whatever ill betide—a shelter in the time of storm.

A shade by day, defense by night—a shelter in the time of storm; no fears alarm, no foes affright—a shelter in the time of storm.

The raging storms may round us beat—a shelter in the time of storm; we'll never leave our safe retreat—a shelter in the time of storm.

O Rock divine, O Refuge dear—a shelter in the time of storm; be Thou our helper ever near—a shelter in the time of storm.

Chorus: O Jesus is a Rock in a weary land, a weary land, a weary land; O Jesus is a Rock in a weary land—a shelter in the time of storm.

❦ *For Today:* Psalm 94:22; Proverbs 14:26; Isaiah 12:2; 26:4; Nahum 1:7; Hebrews 10:22

Thank God for the storms in life that have helped you develop spiritual strength. Seek to encourage someone who may be floundering in a difficult situation. Carry this musical truth with you realizing—

Ira D. Sankey, 1840-1908

O Je - sus is a Rock in a wea - ry land— A

shel - ter in the time of storm.

FROM EVERY STORMY WIND THAT BLOWS

Hugh Stowell, 1799-1865

When you pass through the waters, I will be with you . . . (Isaiah 43:2)

God sometimes shuts the door and shuts us in,
That He may speak, perchance through grief or pain;
And softly, heart to heart, above the din
May teach some precious truth to us again.   *—Unknown*

In Old Testament worship, the mercy seat was the cover of the Ark of the Covenant, which housed the Mosaic tables of stone, a pot of manna, and Aaron's rod that budded. The mercy seat was a most sacred, holy place. It symbolized the place of God's eternal presence with His people.

When the storms of life blow our way, we can either cringe in despair or flee to the heavenly Mercy Seat—the God of all comfort (2 Corinthians 1:3, 4).There we can find the help and strength to be overcomers. Trials can sometimes embitter and harden our spirits. However, if we use the trial to lean more fully on Christ and to learn the lesson He desires to teach us, we become stronger in our faith.

Hugh Stowell, the author, was a minister in the Anglican church and was known as one of the truly evangelical leaders in the church during his time. His ministry was also characterized by a love for children and an active Sunday school in his church. This hymn text was originally titled "Peace at the Mercy Seat" and was first published in 1828 in a collection of poems by the author.

How different life would be "had suff'ring saints no mercy seat." How important it is for God's people to avail themselves of this "calm, sure retreat" by using prayer to commune with Him there on a consistent basis.

From ev'ry stormy wind that blows, from ev'ry swelling tide of woes, there is a calm, a sure retreat—'Tis found beneath the mercy seat.

There is a place where Jesus sheds the oil of gladness on our heads, a place than all besides more sweet—It is the blood-bought mercy seat.

There is a scene where spirits blend, where friend holds fellowship with friend; tho sundered far, by faith they meet around one common mercy seat.

Ah! Whither could we flee for aid when tempted, desolate, dismayed, or how the hosts of hell defeat, had suff'ring saints no mercy seat?

Ah! there on eagle wings we soar, and sin and sense molest no more; and heav'n comes down our souls to greet, while glory crowns the mercy seat.

❧ *For Today:* Psalm 61:2; Isaiah 25:4; Matthew 11:28; 1 Corinthians 1:3-5; Hebrews 4:16

Always remember—for the child of God, life's storms are opportunities to learn more about Him. Thank God even now for His Heavenly Mercy Seat. Reflect on these words as you go—

Retreat tune   Thomas Hastings, 1784-1872

There is a calm, a sure re - treat-- 'Tis found be - neath the mer - cy seat.

HE HIDETH MY SOUL

Fanny J. Crosby, 1820-1915

I will put you in a cleft in the rock and cover you with my hand. (Exodus 33:22)

The beloved blind American poet Fanny Jane Crosby did not begin writing gospel texts until her mid-forties. But from then on, inspiring words seemed to flow constantly from her heart, and she became "the happiest creature in all the land." Friends stopped in frequently to see her with requests for new texts for special occasions.

One day Fanny was visited by William Kirkpatrick, a talented gospel musician who had just composed a new melody that he felt needed suitable words to become a singable hymn. As William sat at the piano and played the tune for Fanny, her face lit up. She knelt in prayer, as was always her custom, and soon the lines to this lovely hymn began to flow freely from her heart:

> A wonderful Savior is Jesus my Lord, a wonderful Savior to me; He hideth my soul in the cleft of the rock, where rivers of pleasure I see.

> A wonderful Savior is Jesus my Lord—He taketh my burden away; He holdeth me up and I shall not be moved; He giveth me strength as my day.

> With numberless blessings each moment He crowns, and, filled with His fullness divine, I sing in my rapture, "O Glory to God for such a Redeemer as mine!"

> When clothed in His brightness transported I rise to meet Him in clouds of the sky; His perfect salvation, His wonderful love, I'll shout with the millions on high.

> **Chorus:** He hideth my soul in the cleft of the rock that shadows a dry, thirsty land; He hideth my life in the depths of His love, and covers me there with His hand, and covers me there with His hand.

The life of Fanny Crosby can be as uplifting to us as her wonderful hymns. When she wrote "rivers of pleasure I see," "with numberless blessings each moment He crowns," and "I sing in my rapture," she revealed the triumph God gave her over a life of blindness. At least 8,000 gospel texts were written by this godly woman. She lived to be 95 years of age and traveled extensively in her later years as a speaker throughout the country. She said it was her continual prayer that God would allow her to lead to Christ every person she contacted. Only eternity will reveal the host of lives that have been directed to God through the life and hymns of Fanny Crosby.

❦ *For Today:* Psalm 27:5; 49:15; Isaiah 51:16; 1 Corinthians 15:57

Do not look at your own strengths and faith but trust the One on whom your faith depends to keep you and make you useful in His service. Sing with confidence as you go—

William J. Kirkpatrick, 1838-1921

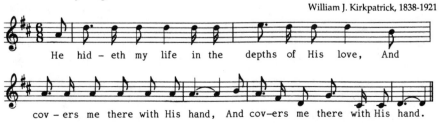

He hid - eth my life in the depths of His love, And cov - ers me there with His hand, And cov-ers me there with His hand.

JESUS NEVER FAILS

Words and Music by Arthur A. Luther, 1891-1960

Heaven and earth will pass away, but my words will never pass away. (Matthew 25:35)

Just when my hopes have vanished, just when my friends forsake,
Just when the fight is thickest, just when with fear I shake,
Then comes a still small whisper, "Fear not my child, I'm near!"
Jesus beings peace and comfort; I love His voice to hear.   —*J. Bruce Evans*

The Bible teaches that some of life's richest lessons are learned only in the valley of tears. The psalmist declared: "It was good for me to be afflicted so that I might learn Your decrees" (Psalm 119:71). Difficult times should be the steppingstones in our spiritual growth and usefulness. This was the case with the author and composer of "Jesus Never Fails." Arthur Luther, pastor and musician, relates the following story regarding the writing of his hymn:

As a school boy Christian I had a burning desire to be a foreign missionary. That was not to be. Later I had an urgent desire to write a song that everyone would sing. I tried a popular song but it was a dismal failure; yet, God, in His own time and way, granted my wish and "Jesus Never Fails" has reached to the uttermost of mission fields and the multitudes have sung it. The song was written at Somerset, Kentucky, while I was there with the Dr. O. E. Williams Evangelistic Party. I received some very disturbing news from my family some 600 miles away. Worried and homesick, I sat down at the old square piano in the "Old Kentucky Home" where we were staying and as my fingers wandered idly, a simple melody developed beneath them which seemed to sing, "Jesus Never Fails." Then and there the words and music of the chorus were born. I accepted this as the answer to my heart's prayer and I thank Him that it proved true. Reassuring news came from home. He did not fail me . . . Scores of testimonies have since come from missionaries, evangelists, and others of the blessing that this simple three-word message has been to them. It has been translated into ten European languages and into Chinese . . . "Jesus Never Fails" has become a sort of musical slogan of Bible-believing Christians everywhere. Men sang it at the battlefront as they girded themselves for the fray. On the homefront, saints sing it as they do battle with the forces of sin, in true confidence that the Captain of their salvation fails not. I surely have every reason to praise God for this song that He gave me in the hour of my need and which has gone on to bless the entire world with its message of triumph. . . .

* * * *

Earthly friends may prove untrue, doubts and fears assail; One still loves and cares for you, one who will not fail.

Tho the sky be dark and drear, fierce and strong the gale, just remember He is near, and He will not fail.

In life's dark and bitter hour love will still prevail. Trust His everlasting pow'r—Jesus will not fail.

Chorus: Jesus never fails; heav'n and earth may pass away, but Jesus never fails.

❦ *For Today:* Matthew 28:20; Acts 18:9; Romans 8:18; 2 Timothy 4:17

Face life confidently with the awareness that the victorious Lord is at your side. He will never fail! Carry this musical truth with you—

Je - sus nev - er fails, Je - sus nev - er fails; Heav'n and

earth may pass a - way, But Je - sus nev - er fails.

UNDER HIS WINGS
William O. Cushing, 1823-1902

He will cover you with His feathers, and under His wings you will find refuge.
(Psalm 91:4)

Daily living is often filled with unexpected dangers. We never know what lies ahead as we begin each new day. How does a person cope with uncertainty and have the stability to live victoriously? For the Christian, daily security is having an unwavering confidence that God is in absolute control and personally involved in every detail of life. The only condition is that we must be willing to accept His help and remain close to Him wherever He leads. Jesus taught this truth to the people of His day; He longed to gather them to Himself even as a mother hen gathers her chicks under her wings when there is an impending storm. The human tragedy then and still today is that people are generally unwilling to accept His gracious offer (Luke 13:34).

The author of this hymn text, William Cushing, wrote these words as an expression of Psalm 17:8—"Hide me under the shadow of Thy wings." After pastoring several large churches, Cushing suddenly was told that he could no longer preach. He had lost the power of speech. Broken in spirit, he cried out to God with the words of the psalmist. God answered by giving him the gift of writing. In all, William Cushing wrote more than 300 gospel hymns, which have had an even wider spiritual influence than his years of successful pastoring. "Under His Wings" first appeared in Ira Sankey's *Sacred Songs No. 1,* published in 1896. It has continued to be a favorite hymn of comfort among God's people.

Under His wings I am safely abiding; tho the night deepens and tempests are wild, still I can trust Him; I know He will keep me; He has redeemed me, and I am His child.

Under His wings, what a refuge in sorrow! How the heart yearningly turns to His rest! Often when earth has no balm for my healing, there I find comfort and there I am blest.

Under His wings, O what precious enjoyment! There will I hide till life's trials are o'er; sheltered, protected, no evil can harm me; resting in Jesus I'm safe evermore.

Refrain: Under His wings, under His wings, who from His love can sever? Under His wings my soul shall abide, safely abide forever.

🐦 *For Today:* Deuteronomy 33:27; 2 Samuel 22:31; Psalm 17:8; 36:7; 57:1; Isaiah 12:2; Matthew 23:37

Realize anew that God Himself desires to protect you and provide for your best welfare. Thank Him for this blessing. Go forth with this musical truth—

Ira D. Sankey, 1840-1908

ALL YOUR ANXIETY

Words and Music by Edward Henry Joy, 1871-1941

Cast all your anxiety on Him because He cares for you. (1 Peter 5:14)

> Upon the Lord your burden cast,
> To Him bring all your care;
> He will sustain and hold you fast,
> And give thee strength to bear.
>
>   *—Unknown*

Worry, anxiety, and depression have been the subjects of many discourses. The reason, of course, is that these conditions are so common to everyone. Many descriptions of these times have been given:

> Worry is nothing more than borrowed trouble.   *—Unknown*

> Worry is unbelief in disguise.   *—Unknown*

> Worry does not relieve tomorrow of its stress—it merely empties today of its strength.
>   *—Unknown*

> The beginning of anxiety is the end of faith, and the beginning of true faith is the end of anxiety.   *—George Mueller*

> Depression is the Devil's tool in thwarting the joy of believers and in immobilizing them in the Lord's service.   *—Unknown*

You cannot read the book of Psalms without sensing the deep cloud of emotional gloom experienced at times even by King David, this man after God's own heart. "Why are you downcast, O my soul? Why so disturbed within me?" (Psalm 43:5). But David also knew the right answer for these dark times. First, he honestly admitted his feelings to God. Second, he re-established his confidence in God. Third, he determined to praise Him—"I will yet praise Him, my Savior and my God." This three-stage antidote for despair is still the cure for our emotional anxieties today.

> Is there a heart o'er-bound by sorrow? Is there a life weighed down by care? Come to the cross—each burden bearing, all your anxiety—leave it there.

> No other friend so keen to help you, no other friend so quick to hear; no other place to leave your burden, no other one to hear your prayer.

> Come then at once—delay no longer! Heed His entreaty kind and sweet; you need not fear a disappointment—You shall find peace at the mercy seat.

> **Chorus:** All your anxiety, all your care, bring to the mercy seat—leave it there; never a burden He cannot bear, never a friend like Jesus!

❦ *For Today:* Psalm 27:5; 37:5; 55:22; 91:1; 138:7; Luke 21:34; 2 Corinthians 1:9, 10; Philippians 4:6

When anxious moments come your way, remember to do what King David did. When we thank and praise God in everything, anxieties must cease.

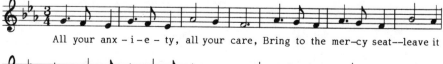

LEAVE IT THERE

Words and Music by Charles A. Tindley, 1851-1933

Why are you downcast, O my soul? Why so disturbed within me? Put your hope in God, for I will yet praise Him, my Savior and my God. (Psalm 42:5)

"Put all your troubles in a sack, take 'em to the Lord, and leave 'em there." These good words of advice were given by Charles Tindley, the distinguished black Methodist pastor from Philadelphia, to one of his worried parishioners. It was the spark that prompted the pastor to develop this thought and pen the words and music of this familiar gospel hymn in 1916.

Charles H. Spurgeon, the noted English Baptist pastor, once gave this similar advice: "If you tell your troubles to God, you put them into the grave. If you roll your burden anywhere else, it will roll back again."

We will never be able to escape the troubles that life brings, but we can always turn to the Lord for strength and deliverance and then . . . "leave it there." When we cannot calmly leave our burdens and affairs in God's hands, we are often tempted to use wrong means to solve our problems, such as relying upon our human wisdom rather than God's guidance. We need to seek relief for our problems by giving them to God.

If the world from you withhold of its silver and its gold, and you have to get along with meager fare, just remember, in His word, how He feeds the little bird—Take your burden to the Lord and leave it there.

If your body suffers pain and your health you can't regain, and your soul is almost sinking in despair; Jesus knows the pain you feel; He can save and He can heal—Take your burden to the Lord and leave it there.

When your enemies assail and your heart begins to fail, don't forget that God in heaven answers prayer; He will make a way for you and will lead you safely thru—Take your burden to the Lord and leave it there.

When your youthful days are gone and old age is stealing on, and your body bends beneath the weight of care, He will never leave you then; He 'Il go with you to the end—Take your burden to the Lord and leave it there.

Chorus: Leave it there, leave it there; take your burden to the Lord and leave it there. If you trust and never doubt, He will surely bring you out—Take your burden to the Lord and leave it there.

❦ *For Today:* Job 13:15; Psalm 55:22; 62:8; Isaiah 26:3, 4; Philippians 4:6; 1 Peter 5:7

Make a mental list of the problems and anxieties that are troubling you. Ask God to show you how to discard these from your mind's preoccupation and simply to leave them with Him. Use this musical message to help—

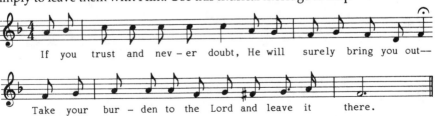

SWEETLY RESTING

Mary D. James, 1810-1883

For in the day of trouble He will keep me safe in His dwelling; He will hide me in the shelter of His tabernacle and set me high upon a rock. (Psalm 27:5)

> Once my hands were always trying,
> Trying hard to do my best;
> Now my heart is sweetly trusting,
> And my soul is all at rest.   *—A. B. Simpson*

Evangelist D. L. Moody once observed that there are three kinds of faith a Christian can have: *a struggling faith, a clinging faith,* or *a resting faith.* A resting faith is not some mystical feeling that we might experience at times in a church service or during a spiritually high moment. It is simply the daily repose of a life that has learned to relax and be comfortable in God's providential care. Such an attitude is the result of ceasing to live for self and starting to live solely for God's glory.

Medical people have long realized the relationship that exists between a happy, calm spirit and a healthy body. Doctors have often stated that many of our physical problems are caused by undue stress. How important it is, then, even for our own well-being, to relax and rest in God, to trust Him implicitly regardless of the circumstances. Since we were created in His image, we are able to find fulfillment and true contentment only as we learn to enjoy His daily fellowship. That's the "resting faith" Moody was talking about.

> In the rifted Rock I'm resting, safely sheltered I abide, all secure in this blest refuge, heeding not the fiercest blast.

> Long pursued by sin and Satan—weary, sad, I longed for rest; then I found the heavenly shelter opened in my Savior's breast.

> Peace which passeth understanding, joy the world can never give, now in Jesus I am finding; in His smiles of love I live.

> In the rifted Rock I'll hide me 'till the storms of life are past, all secure in this blest refuge, heeding not the fiercest blast.

> **Chorus:** Now I'm resting, sweetly resting in the cleft once made for me; Jesus, blessed Rock of Ages, I will hide myself in Thee.

❦ *For Today:* Deuteronomy 33:27; Joshua 1:9; Psalm 38:4; 46:1; 57:1; 62:7; Proverbs 17:22; Hebrews 4:11

If your faith in God is something other than a "resting faith," ask Him to help you move up into this higher spiritual realm. Thank Him for His willingness to help. Carry this musical statement as you go—

W. Warren Bently, (unknown)

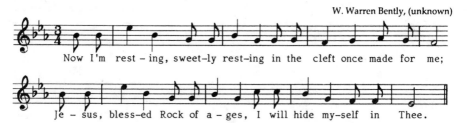

Now I'm rest-ing, sweet-ly rest-ing in the cleft once made for me;

Je - sus, bless-ed Rock of a - ges, I will hide my-self in Thee.

'TIS SO SWEET TO TRUST IN JESUS

Louisa M. R. Stead, c. 1850-1917

That we should be to the praise of His glory, who first trusted in Christ. (Ephesians 1:12 KJV)

Out of one of the darkest hours of her life—the tragic drowning of her husband— a young mother proclaimed through her tears, "'Tis so sweet to trust in Jesus . . . and I know that thou art with me, wilt be with me to the end." As Louisa Stead, her husband and their little daughter were enjoying an ocean side picnic one day, a drowning boy cried for help. Mr. Stead rushed to save him but was pulled under by the terrified boy. Both drowned as Louisa and her daughter watched helplessly. During the sorrowful days that followed, the words of this hymn came from the grief stricken wife's heart.

Soon after this Mrs. Stead and her daughter left for missionary work in South Africa. After more than 25 years of fruitful service, Louisa was forced to retire because of ill health. She died a few years later in Southern Rhodesia. Her fellow missionaries had always loved "'Tis So Sweet to Trust in Jesus" and wrote this tribute after her death:

> We miss her very much, but her influence goes on as our five thousand native Christians continually sing this hymn in their native language.

Out of a deep human tragedy early in her life, Louisa Stead learned simply to trust in her Lord. She was used to "the praise of His glory" for the remainder of her life. Still today, her ministry continues each time we sing and apply the truth of these words:

> 'Tis so sweet to trust in Jesus, just to take Him at His word, just to rest upon His promise, just to know, "Thus saith the Lord."

> O how sweet to trust in Jesus, just to trust His cleansing blood, just in simple faith to plunge me 'neath the healing, cleansing flood!

> Yes, 'tis sweet to trust in Jesus, just from sin and self to cease, just from Jesus simply taking life and rest and joy and peace.

> I'm so glad I learned to trust Thee, Precious Jesus, Savior, Friend; and I know that Thou art with me, wilt be with me to the end.

> **Chorus:** Jesus, Jesus, how I trust Him! How I've proved Him o'er and o'er! Jesus, Jesus, precious Jesus! O for grace to trust Him more!

❦ *For Today:* Psalm 91:4; Isaiah 26:3, 4; Acts 10:43; Romans 1:16, 17; 5:1, 2; Ephesians 1:3-14

Express thanks to God for the lessons of trust He has taught you. Sing with this hymn writer—"O for grace to trust Him more!" Carry this musical reminder with you because—

William J. Kirkpatrick, 1838-1921

Je – sus, Je – sus, how I trust Him! How I've proved Him o'er and o'er!

Je – sus, Je – sus, pre – cious Je – sus! O for grace to trust Him more!

A CHILD OF THE KING

Harriett E. Buell, 1834-1910

We are God's children. Now if we are children, then we are heirs—heirs of God and co-heirs with Christ, if indeed we share in His sufferings in order that we may also share in His glory. (Romans 8:16, 17)

As children of the heavenly kingdom, we should learn to enjoy and possess the rich spiritual blessings that belong to us as heirs of God's riches.

- We have been justified and made acceptable to God—Romans 5:1
- We have been adopted into God's royal family—Romans 8:16, 17
- We have heen given a citizenship in heaven—Philippians 3:20
- We possess the indwelling Holy Spirit—1 Corinthians 6:19
- We have been placed into the kingdom of the Son of God's love—Colossians 1:13
- We have the promise that the best is yet to come—a heavenly home—1 Corinthians 2:9

Whether you are great or small in God's kingdom, you are still God's child. An infant is as truly a child of its parents as is a full-grown person. You are as dear to your heavenly Father as the most prominent member in His family.

Harriett Buell wrote the words for "A Child of the King" one Sunday morning while walking home from her Methodist church service. She sent her text to the *Northern Christian Advocate,* and it was printed in the February 1, 1877 issue of the magazine. John Sumner, a singing school music teacher, saw the words and composed the music without Harriett Buell's knowledge. The hymn has been widely used since then to remind believers who they really are—bearers of God's image (Genesis 1:26) and children of the King of kings.

> My Father is rich in houses and lands; He holdeth the wealth of the world in His hands! Of rubies and diamonds, of silver and gold, His coffers are full—He has riches untold.
>
> My Father's own Son, the Savior of men, once wandered o'er earth as the poorest of them; but now He is reigning forever on high, and will give me a home in heav'n by and by.
>
> I once was an outcast stranger on earth, a sinner by choice and an alien by birth; but I've been adopted; my name's written down—an heir to a mansion, a robe, and a crown.
>
> A tent or a cottage, why should I care? They're building a palace for me over there! Tho exiled from home, yet still I may sing: All glory to God, I'm a child of the King.
>
> **Chorus:** I'm a child of the King! With Jesus, my Savior, I'm a child of the King!

❦ ***For Today:*** Romans 8:14-17; Galatians 4:1-7; Ephesians 1:5; James 2:5

As an heir of God and a citizen of heaven, strive to make your walk and actions consistent with this high calling. Sing as you go—

John B. Sumner, 1838-1918

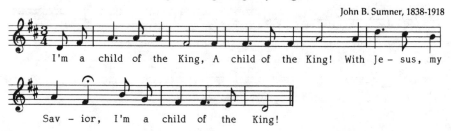

I'm a child of the King, A child of the King! With Je - sus, my

Sav - ior, I'm a child of the King!

O THAT WILL BE GLORY

Words and Music by Charles H. Gabriel, 1856-1932

God will wipe every tear from their eyes. There will be no more death or mourning or crying or pain, for the old order of things has passed away. (Revelation 21:4)

Think of stepping on shore, and finding it heaven!
Of taking hold of a hand, and finding it God's hand,
Of breathing new air, and finding it celestial air;
Of feeling invigorated, and finding it immortality,
Of passing from storm and tempest to an unbroken calm,
Of waking up, and finding it Home!   —*Unknown*

The text for "O That Will Be Glory" was inspired for author and composer Charles Gabriel by his good friend Ed Card, superintendent of the Sunshine Rescue Mission of St. Louis, Missouri. Ed was a radiant believer who always seemed to be bubbling over with the joy of the Lord. During a sermon or prayer, he would often explode with the expression, "Glory!" (Incidentally, there is a biblical precedent for this practice. See Psalm 29:9.) Ed Card's smiling face earned him the nickname "Old Glory Face." It was his custom to close his own praying with a reference to heaven, ending with the phrase "and that will be glory for me!" It is said that Mr. Card had the joy of singing this hymn just before his home going—with the pleasure of knowing that his Christian life had been its inspiration.

Charles H. Gabriel was one of the best-known and most prolific gospel songwriters of the early 20th century era. For most of his hymns, Gabriel wrote and composed both the words and music. His gospel songs were especially used during the large Billy Sunday evangelistic campaigns of the 1910-1920 decade. "O That Will Be Glory" has been translated into many languages and dialects.

When all my labors and trials are o'er and I am safe on that beautiful shore, just to be near the dear Lord I adore will thru the ages be glory for me.

When, by the gift of His infinite grace, I am accorded in heaven a place, just to be there and to look on His face will thru the ages be glory for me.

Friends will be there I have loved long ago; joy like a river around me will flow; yet, just a smile from my Savior, I know, will thru the ages be glory for me.

Chorus: O that will be glory for me, glory for me, glory for me; when by His grace I shall look on His face, that will be glory, be glory for me!

❦ *For Today:* 1 Corinthians 13:12; 2 Corinthians 3:18; Revelation 14:13

Reflect on this truth—One moment of heavenly glory will outweigh a lifetime of suffering. Live with the assurance that God's tomorrow will make today's struggles worth it all. Anticipate this joy by singing as you go—

When by His grace I shall look on His face,

That will be glo - ry, be glo - ry for me!

MY SAVIOR FIRST OF ALL

Fanny J. Crosby, 1820-1915

You have made known to me the path of life; You will fill me with joy in Your presence, with eternal pleasures at Your right hand. (Psalm 16:11)

The strong, triumphant spirit of American hymnwriter Fanny Crosby was an inspiration to everyone who knew her. Even though she was blind from six weeks of age because of improper medical treatment, she never revealed bitterness or depression. At one time a well-intentioned minister remarked to her:

"I think it is a great pity that the Master, when He showered so many gifts upon you, did not give you sight."

"Do you know," replied Fanny, "if at birth I had been able to make one petition to my Creator, it would have been that I should be born blind."

"Why?" asked the surprised clergyman.

"Because when I get to heaven, the first sight that shall ever gladden my eyes will be that of my Savior!"

For Fanny, the anticipation of heaven was the joy of seeing her Lord "face to face." Although she wrote 8,000 or more gospel song texts on many different subjects, the themes of heaven and the Lord's return seem to have been her favorites. In no other hymn does she picture more vividly her hope of seeing the beauty of Christ's welcome, standing by His side, and witnessing firsthand His scars of redemption. What moving scenes Fanny Crosby has created for us to ponder in these vividly worded lines!

When my lifework is ended and I cross the swelling tide, when the bright and glorious morning I shall see, I shall know my Redeemer when I reach the other side, and His smile will be the first to welcome me.

O the soul-thrilling rapture when I view His blessed face and the luster of His kindly beaming eye; how my full heart will praise Him for the mercy, love and grace that prepare for me a mansion in the sky.

O the dear ones in glory, how they beckon me to come, and our parting at the river I recall; to the sweet vales of Eden they will sing my welcome home—but I long to meet my Savior first of all.

Thru the gates to the city, in a robe of spotless white, He will lead me where no tears will ever fall; in the glad song of ages I shall mingle with delight—but I long to meet my Savior first of all.

Chorus: I shall know Him, I shall know Him, and redeemed by His side I shall stand; I shall know Him, I shall know Him by the print of the nails in His hand.

❦ *For Today:* Philippians 3:20, 21; 2 Peter 1:4, 11; Revelation 21:10-21; 22:1-5

Contemplate once more some of the joys of Heaven promised in the Bible. Share your enthusiasm with a Christian who needs this encouragement.

John R. Sweney, 1837-1899

I shall know Him, I shall know Him, By the

print of the nails in His hand.

ON JORDAN'S STORMY BANKS

Samuel Stennett, 1727-1795

If only for this life we have hope in Christ, we are to be pitied more than all men. (1 Corinthians 15:19)

In this day of the "throwaway" and the temporary, Christians must live according to their belief in eternity. The apostle Paul reminded the believers at Corinth that if their hope in Christ were related only to this life, they would be the most miserable men of all (1 Corinthians 15:17-19). The anticipation of God's tomorrow makes it possible for Christians to live joyfully today—regardless of life's circumstances.

> He liveth long who liveth well! All other life is short and vain;
> He liveth longest who can tell of living most for heavenly gain. —*Horatius Bonar*

What Canaan was to God's chosen people of the Old Testament, the "heavenly places" are to New Testament believers. God has raised us up with Christ so that even now we can sit with Him in heavenly places (Ephesians 2:6). Living in Canaan, our spiritual heavenlies, should be the Christian's daily experience as well as a foretaste of our eternal glory. We, like the Israelites, must faithfully follow our Leader and foresee and enjoy our possessions now.

Samuel Stennett was one of the most respected and influential preachers among the dissenting or non-conformist groups of his times. He pastored a Baptist church on Little Wild Street in London, England, for an entire lifetime. The tune, "Promised Land," is one of the many traditional melodies used in the United States during the early part of the 19th century. The hymn was first published in its present form in 1895.

On Jordan's stormy banks I stand and cast a wishful eye to Canaan's fair and happy land, where my possessions lie.

All o'er those wide extended plains shines one eternal day; where God the Son forever reigns and scatters night away.

No chilling winds nor pois'nous breath can reach that healthful shore; sickness and sorrow, pain and death are felt and feared no more.

When shall I reach that happy place and be forever blest? When shall I see my Father's face and in His bosom rest?

Chorus: I am bound for the promised land, I am bound for the promised land; O who will come and go with me? I am bound for the promised land.

❦ *For Today:* Numbers 14 :7-9; Isaiah 35:10; Revelation 21:1-4

Determine to set your sights and values more strongly on eternity and heavenly gain. Go forth with a buoyancy to your step and this song upon your lips—

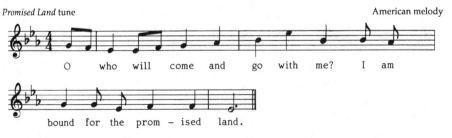

Promised Land tune — American melody

O who will come and go with me? I am bound for the prom - ised land.

HE THE PEARLY GATES WILL OPEN

Fredrick A. Blom, 1867-1927
Translated by Nathaniel Carlson, 1879-1957

But as it is written, eye hath not seen, nor ear heard, neither have entered the heart of man, the things which God hath prepared for them that love Him. (1 Corinthians 2:9 KJV)

Out of the repentant heart of a back-slidden Swedish pastor came this deeply emotional and vividly worded hymn, which expresses his renewed faith in God. After serving as the minister of several churches, Fredrick Arvid Blom somehow fell into deep sin and even was in prison for a time. "I drifted from God," he explained, "and became embittered with myself, the world, and not the least with ministers who looked on me with suspicion because I was a member of the Socialist Party." Then like a "dove when hunted" or "a wounded fawn," Blom cried in anguish to his heavenly Father, who in "love divine" forgave him and healed his broken heart and life. From this restoration came this lovely text, which has since comforted many sorrowful hearts with the assurance of a never-ending divine love and a promise of an eternal heavenly home. God's people need not fear death. Instead we ought to view it as the beginning of a new form of life—the entering into an eternal abode with our loving Savior, who will Himself open heaven's gate to welcome us home.

> Love divine, so great and wondrous, deep and mighty, pure, sublime! Coming from the heart of Jesus—just the same thru tests of time.

> Like a dove when hunted, frightened, as a wounded fawn was I; brokenhearted, yet He healed me—He will heed the sinner's cry.

> Love divine, so great and wondrous! All my sins He then forgave! I will sing His praise forever, for His blood, His pow'r to save.

> In life's even-tide, at twilight, at His door I'll knock and wait; by the precious love of Jesus I shall enter heaven's gate.

> **Chorus:** He the pearly gates will open, so that I may enter in; for He purchased my redemption and forgave me all my sin.

❧ *For Today:* John 14:2, 3; 2 Corinthians 5:1, 6, 8; Revelation 7:9, 16, 17

Try to comfort someone who is ill or fearful of death with the strong promises of Scripture that remind us of the welcome in heaven awaiting each true believer in Christ. Or, if you have opportunity, try to reassure someone who has been away from God that there is forgiveness and divine love for all who will truly repent and turn again to seek renewed fellowship with God. Sing this musical testimony as you go—

Elsie Ahlwen, 1905-

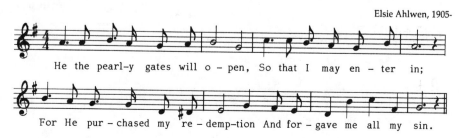

He the pearl-y gates will o - pen, So that I may en - ter in;

For He pur - chased my re - demp-tion And for - gave me all my sin.

FACE TO FACE

Carrie E. Breck, 1855-1934

Dear friends, now we are children of God, and what we will be has not yet been made known. But we know that when He appears we shall be like Him, for we shall see Him as He is. Everyone who has this hope in Him purifies himself, just as He is pure. (1 John 3:2, 3)

For some the concept of heaven is a place of peaceful resting. Others envision it as filled with golden streets and sounds of beautiful music. For most of us the thought of reuniting with loved ones is comforting. However, the most thrilling anticipation for every believer when he reflects about heaven is surely the moment of seeing our Savior "face to face."

The thoughts so well expressed in "Face to Face" were written by a busy wife and mother who by her own admission could not carry a tune. She had only a sense of rhythm. She said, "I penciled verses under all conditions; over a mending basket, with a baby on my arm, and sometimes even when sweeping or washing dishes, my mind moved in poetic meter." Living with her husband and five daughters in Portland, Oregon, Carrie Breck was a deeply committed Christian and life-long member of the Presbyterian church.

Mrs. Breck occasionally sent some of her poems to a composer of gospel hymns, Grant Colfax Tullar, with the hope that he would set them to suitable music. Amazingly, when the verses of "Face to Face" arrived in the mail one day, Mr. Tullar had just completed the music for a song with words that did not fully please him. The lines of Mrs. Breck's text, however, were a perfect fit for the music he had composed.

Face to face with Christ, my Savior, face to face—what will it be? When with rapture I behold Him, Jesus Christ who died for me!

Only faintly now I see Him, with the darkling veil between; but a blessed day is coming, when His glory shall be seen.

What rejoicing in His presence, when are banished grief and pain, when the crooked ways are straightened and the dark things shall be plain.

Face to face—O blissful moment! Face to face—to see and know; face to face with my Redeemer, Jesus Christ who loves me so.

Chorus: Face to face I shall behold Him, far beyond the starry sky; face to face, in all His glory, I shall see Him by and by!

❦ *For Today:* Romans 15:4; 1 Corinthians 13:12; 1 Thessalonians 4:13-17

Anticipate the joy it will be to greet our Savior and to fully "see and know"—when the "crooked ways are straightened" and the "dark things shall be plain." Share this hope with someone. Rejoice with this musical truth as you go—

Grant C. Tullar, 1869-1950

Face to face I shall be - hold Him, Far be - yond the star - ry sky;

Face to face in all His glo - ry, I shall see Him by and by!

AFTER

Words and Music by N. B. Vandall, 1896-1970

. . . weeping may remain for a night, but rejoicing comes in the morning. (Psalm 30:5)

How much more content we are if we know that *after* some trying or painful experience, there will be pleasure and a reward. Such thoughts help to spur on the athlete in competition, a mother during the birth of a child, or a weary workman on his way home to a warm fire and loved ones. It was in the midst of a tragic personal experience that the author and composer of the hymn was moved to express this consoling thought.

N. B. Vandall, a singer and a well-known gospel evangelist, was rushed to the hospital to discover that his son Paul had just been struck by a car and was critically injured. The doctor held out very little hope for recovery. Mr. Vandall recalled:

> For one hour and fifteen minutes, I held on in prayer while they cleaned and sewed up the head wounds and set the broken bones. Wearily I made my way back to my humble home. I tried to comfort my wife, when, in my own heart, I had no assurance. I fell on my knees and tried to pray, saying only, "O God!"
>
> Hardly had those words been uttered when God came. It seemed to me that Jesus knelt by my side and I could feel His arms around me as He said, "Never mind, my child. Your home will be visited with tribulation and sorrow, but in the afterwards to come, these things shall not be. Your home is in heaven, where all tears shall be wiped away!"
>
> Brushing aside my tears, I made my way to the piano and wrote the song "After." Paul did recover from the accident. He is still very nervous and his eyesight is impaired, but I thank God for His goodness in giving him back to us. God in His wisdom, through heartache, gave a song that has since been a comfort to a vast number of His people.

* * * *

After the toil and the heat of the day, after my troubles are past, after the sorrows are taken away, I shall see Jesus at last.

After the heartaches and sighing shall cease, after the cold winter's blast, after the conflict comes glorious peace—I shall see Jesus at last.

After the shadows of evening shall fall, after my anchor is cast, after I list to my Savior's last call, I shall see Jesus at last.

Refrain: He will be waiting for me—Jesus, so kind and true; on His beautiful throne, He will welcome me home—after the day is through.

❧ *For Today:* John 14:2, 3; 1 Corinthians 2:9; 2 Corinthians 5:1, 6, 8; 2 Peter 1:3, 4

Perhaps some sorrowful or stormy time has served to make God's presence more real in your life. Thank Him for this, and for His promise of seeing Jesus "after the day is through." Carry this promise with you as you go—

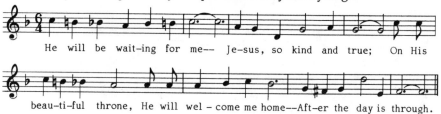

He will be wait-ing for me-- Je-sus, so kind and true; On His beau-ti-ful throne, He will wel - come me home--Aft-er the day is through.

BEYOND THE SUNSET

Virgil P. Brock, 1887-1978

Now we see but a poor reflection as in a mirror; then we shall see face to face. Now I know in part; then I shall know fully, even as I am fully known. (1 Corinthians 13:12)

The ability to see "beyond the sunset"—to anticipate the glories of God's tomorrow—enables a Christian to live joyfully and victoriously in any of life's circumstances. It is difficult for us to imagine heavenly scenes or to describe them with earthly symbols. The Bible does promise us, however, that there will be "eternal joy" in the "glorious presence" of our Savior "on that fair shore."

Virgil P. Brock told how he wrote this favorite hymn about heaven:

> This song was born during a conversation at the dinner table, one evening in 1936, after watching a very unusual sunset at Winona Lake, Indiana, with a blind guest, my cousin Horace Burr, and his wife, Grace. A large area of the water appeared ablaze with the glory of God, yet there were threatening storm clouds gathering overhead. Our blind guest excitedly remarked that he had never seen a more beautiful sunset.
>
> "People are always amazed when you talk about seeing," I told him, "I can see," Horace replied. "I see through other people's eyes, and I think I often see more; I see beyond the sunset."
>
> The phrase "beyond the sunset" and the striking inflection of his voice struck me so forcibly, I began singing the first few measures. "That's beautiful!" his wife interrupted. "Please go to the piano and sing it."
>
> We went to the piano nearby and completed the first verse. Before the evening meal was finished, all four stanzas had been written and we sang the entire song together.

Virgil P. Brock's cheerful and lively manner continued to inspire others as he wrote more than 500 gospel songs and led congregations in vibrant singing until the end of his 91 years. His fruitful life reflected a constant, keen awareness of that land "beyond the sunset."

> Beyond the sunset, O blissful morning, when with our Savior heav'n is begun. Earth's toiling ended, O glorious dawning—beyond the sunset when day is done.
>
> Beyond the sunset no clouds will gather; no storms will threaten, no fears annoy; O day of gladness, O day unending—beyond the sunset, eternal joy!
>
> Beyond the sunset a hand will guide me to God the Father, whom I adore; His glorious presence, His words of welcome, will be my portion on that fair shore.
>
> Beyond the sunset, O glad reunion with our dear loved ones who've gone before. In that fair homeland we'll know no parting—beyond the sunset forevermore!

❦ *For Today:* John 14:2, 3; Philippians 3:20, 21; Revelation 21:4

Practice frequent thoughts about the promises and glories of heaven when you feel yourself giving an undue amount of importance to the trivial events of daily living. Now sing—

Blanche Kerr Brock,1888-1958

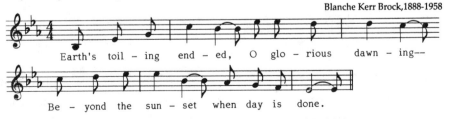

I KNOW I'LL SEE JESUS SOME DAY

Avis B. Christiansen, 1895-1985

When Christ, who is your life, appears, then you also will appear with Him in glory. (Colossians 3:4)

> Lord, we wait for Thine appearing;
> "Even so," Thy people say;
> Bright the prospect is, and cheering,
> Of beholding Thee that day.   —*Thomas Kelly*

Heaven is not an invention of the human imagination. It is as sure as the promise of Christ in the Scriptures: "I am going to prepare a place for you. And if I go and prepare a place for you, I will come back and take you to be with Me that you also may be where I am" (John 14:2, 3). The Bible, however, does not tell us a great deal about the specifics of heaven, simply because our mortal minds are unable to comprehend its riches. The main concern of the Scriptures is to acquaint us with the One who has made our entry into heaven possible. Because of His redemptive work in our behalf, seeing Him personally becomes the real glory of heaven for every believer.

We have all heard the expression that "we can become so heavenly minded that we are of no earthly good." It is possible that we can think and dream about our eternal future to the point that we forget to live effectively for God now. But the greater concern for most of us is that we become so consumed with the enjoyments of this present life that we lose sight of the glories that await us and the anticipation of seeing our Savior. Our hope in Christ for the future should be the real source of joy and strength for our daily lives. It should also be our motive for holy living—"to live self-controlled, upright and godly lives in this present age, while we wait for the blessed hope—the glorious appearing of our great God and Savior, Jesus Christ" (Titus 2:12, 13).

Sweet is the hope that is thrilling my soul—I know I'll see Jesus some day! Then what if the dark clouds of sin o'er me roll? I know I'll see Jesus some day!

Though I must travel by faith, not by sight, I know I'll see Jesus some day! No evil can harm me, no foe can affright—I know I'll see Jesus some day!

Darkness is gath'ring, but hope shines within. I know I'll see Jesus some day! What joy when He comes to wipe out ev'ry sin; I know I'll see Jesus some day!

Chrous: I know I'll see Jesus some day! I know I'll see Jesus some day! What a joy it will be when His face I shall see; I know I'll see Jesus some day!

❦ *For Today:* 2 Corinthians 5:1, 6, 8; Philippians 3:20, 21; Revelation 22:1-5

Let your soul come alive with the thrill of expectation—the glories of heaven and the prospect of personally seeing Jesus. Carry this joy with you as you sing with certainty—

Scott Lawrence, (unknown)

What a joy it will be when His face I shall see,
I know I'll see Je – sus some day!

I'VE GOT PEACE LIKE A RIVER
Spiritual

The Lord gives strength to His people; the Lord blesses His people with peace.
(Psalm 29:11)

> Not merely in the words you say,
> Not merely in your deeds confessed,
> But in the most unconscious way
> Is Christ expressed.
>
> And from your eyes He beckons me,
> And from your heart His love is shed,
> Till I lose sight of you . . .
> And see Christ the Lord instead. —*Unknown*

For the past month we have been considering the benefits and blessings of being a Christian—joy, peace, contentment . . . with rivers of living waters flowing out of such a life (John 7:38). Knowing Christ as personal Savior, experiencing the guiding presence of the Holy Spirit, and living with a glorious hope for eternity should produce a dramatic difference in the personality and lifestyle of every true believer. Christ's redemptive work provides not only for our eternal glory, but also for a full and abundant life now (John 10:10). A professing Christian who is perceived by his family, friends, and colleagues to be continually sour, contentious, and discontent is a disgrace to the gospel and a hindrance in the work of evangelism.

May the words of this little spiritual increasingly become our genuine testimony as we earnestly seek to direct others to Christ the Lord:

> I've got peace like a river in my soul.
>
> I've got joy like a fountain in my soul.
>
> I've got faith like a mountain in my soul.
>
> I've got love like an ocean in my soul.
>
> I've got Christ as my Savior in my soul.

❦ *For Today:* Psalm 107:9; 119:165; Isaiah 26:3; John 14:27; 16:33; Philippians 4:6, 7, 11; 1 Timothy 6:6

Ask God to make your life truly reflect the peace, joy, faith and love of His indwelling presence as you seek to be an effective representative for Him. Allow the Holy Spirit to produce the "rivers of living water" in your daily living. Carry this musical message with you—

Source unknown

August

• Consecration • Commitment • Dedication of Life

I AM THINE, O LORD

Fanny J. Crosby, 1820-1915

Let us draw near to God with a sincere heart in full assurance of faith. (Hebrews 10:22)

Each new day requires a fresh renewal of our dedication to the Lord. The strongest of Christians can be drawn away by the pressures of daily living. And we are vulnerable to the lusts of the flesh and the eyes as well as the subtle temptations that constitute the "pride of life" (1 John 2:16). The warning of Scripture is clear: "Let him that thinketh he standeth take heed lest he fall" (1 Corinthians 10:12). God must always have His rightful place on the throne of the heart. Nothing in life—not job, not recreation, not even family—should have the top priority of our daily concerns. Anything that replaces the Lordship of Christ can become idolatrous and cause us to be susceptible to a spiritual disaster. We must each day say, "I am Thine, O Lord."

Fanny Crosby wrote this consecration hymn while visiting in the home of the composer of the music, William H. Doane, in Cincinnati. The family's conversation that night centered around the blessedness of enjoying the nearness of God. Suddenly in a moment of inspiration, Fanny started giving the words of the hymn—line by line, verse by verse, and then the chorus. Soon after Doane supplied the music, and another of the more than 8,000 Fanny Crosby hymns was born. Since that day in 1875, these moving lines have ministered to and challenged countless numbers of God's people to keep their lives dedicated to their Lord:

I am Thine, O Lord—I have heard Thy voice, and it told Thy love to me; but I long to rise in the arms of faith and be closer drawn to Thee.

Consecrate me now to Thy service, Lord, by the pow'r of grace divine; let my soul look up with a steadfast hope and my will be lost in Thine.

O the pure delight of a single hour that before Thy throne I spend, when I kneel in pray'r and with Thee, my God, I commune as friend with friend.

There are depths of love that I cannot know till I cross the narrow sea; there are heights of joy that I may not reach till I rest in peace with Thee.

Chorus: Draw me nearer, nearer, blessed Lord, to the cross where Thou hast died; draw me nearer, nearer, nearer, blessed Lord, to Thy precious, bleeding side.

❦ *For Today:* Psalm 16:11; 73:28; Romans 12:1, 2; 1 Corinthians 7:22-24; Hebrews 12:28

Begin this new day, with all of its unknown pressures and temptations, with this musical prayer upon your lips—

William H. Doane, 1832-1915

Draw me near – er, near – er, near – er bless – ed Lord,

To Thy pre – cious, bleed–ing side.

NOTHING BETWEEN

Words and music by Charles A. Tindley, 1851-1933

If our hearts do not condemn us, we have confidence before God and receive from Him anything we ask, because we obey His commands and do what pleases Him. (1 John 3:21, 22)

Born to slave parents and separated from them when only five years of age, Charles Tindley was a most remarkable individual. He learned to read and write on his own at the age of 17, attended night school, completed seminary training through correspondence, and was ordained to the Methodist ministry. While attending evening school, young Tindley supported himself as the janitor of the Calvary Methodist Episcopal Church in Philadelphia. In 1902, Charles Tindley was called to pastor this prestigious church where he had once been the janitor. The Calvary Methodist Church prospered greatly under his leadership. Eventually several larger sanctuaries had to be built to accommodate the crowds of all races that came to hear this humble preacher. In 1924, in spite of Tindley's protests, the new church building was renamed the Tindley Temple Methodist Church.

Charles Tindley expresses a concern in this hymn for many of the practices and attitudes that must be rejected if Christians are to be pleasing to their Lord. The hymn reminds us that we must watch out for those allurements and temptations that can easily disrupt our spiritual courses: "Delusive dreams, sinful-worldly pleasures, habits, pride, self or friends." The Bible teaches that we are not to be conformed to this world but should know the transforming power of a spiritually renewed mind (Romans 12:1, 2).

Nothing between my soul and the Savior, naught of this world's delusive dream: I have renounced all sinful pleasure—Jesus is mine! There's nothing between.

Nothing between, like worldly pleasure! Habits of life, tho harmless they seem, must not my heart from Him ever sever—He is my all! There's nothing between.

Nothing between, like pride or station: Self or friends shall not intervene; tho it may cost me much tribulation, I am resolved! There's nothing between.

Nothing between, e'en many hard trials, tho the whole world against me convene; watching with prayer and much self denial—Triumph at last, with nothing between!

Chorus: Nothing between my soul and the Savior, so that His blessed face may be seen. Nothing preventing the least of His favor: Keep the way clear! Let nothing between.

❦ *For Today:* Psalm 51:10; 2 Timothy 2:15; Hebrews 13:6; 1 John 3:18-24

Reflect on this truth: "The price of spiritual power is a purity of heart." Ask God to reveal anything that might hinder His flow of power in your life.

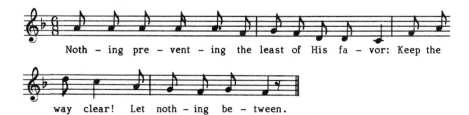

Noth - ing pre - vent - ing the least of His fa - vor: Keep the

way clear! Let noth - ing be - tween.

MY JESUS, AS THOU WILT!

Benjamin Schmolck, 1672-1737
Translated by Jane L. Borthwick, 1813-1897

I desire to do Your will, O my God; Your law is within my heart. (Psalm 40:8)

> My will is not my own till Thou has made it Thine; if it would reach the monarch's throne it must its crown resign. It only stands unbent amid the clashing strife, till on Thy bosom it has leant and found in Thee its life. —*George Matheson*

Following the decision to accept God's provision for salvation, our next most important decision is to do God's will, regardless of what the future may bring. Often, however, we have difficulty in discerning God's will. George Mueller, one of the great men of prayer, has given these insights from his own life regarding this matter:

- Seek to get your heart in such a condition that it has no will of its own in regard to a given matter. Do not depend upon feelings or impressions.
- Seek the will of the Spirit of God through, or in connection with, the Word of God.
- Take into account providential circumstances.
- Ask God in prayer to reveal His will clearly.

> Thus, through prayer to God, the study of His Word, and reflection, I come to a deliberate judgment, and if my mind is thus at peace, and continues so after two or three more petitions, I proceed accordingly. I have found this method always effective.

"My Jesus, As Thou Wilt!" first appeared in a German hymnal in 1704. Later it was translated into English by Jane Borthwick and appeared in the collection *Hymns from the Land of Luther*, published in 1820. These words have since reminded believers that it is only as we yield our wills to God that He can empower us for living victoriously for Him:

> My Jesus, as Thou wilt! O may Thy will be mine! Into Thy hand of love I would my all resign. Through sorrow or through joy, conduct me as Thine own; and help me still to say, "My Lord, Thy will be done."

> My Jesus, as Thou wilt! Though seen through many a tear, let not my star of hope grow dim or disappear. Since Thou on earth hast wept, and sorrowed oft alone, if I must weep with Thee, My Lord, Thy will be done.

> My Jesus, as Thou wilt! All shall be well for me; each changing future scene I gladly trust with Thee. Straight to my home above I travel calmly on, and sing, in life or death, "My Lord, Thy will be done."

❦ *For Today:* Matthew 6:10; Ephesians 5:17; Colossians 1:9; Hebrews 13:21; 1 John 2:17

How do you try to discern God's will for your life? Are you willing to accept and do whatever He may reveal to you? Use this hymn to help in your reflection—

Jewett tune   Carl Maria von Weber, 1786-1826

Through sor - row or through joy, Con - duct me as Thine own;
And help me still to say, "My Lord, Thy will be done."

BREAK THOU THE BREAD OF LIFE

Mary Ann Lathbury, 1841-1913

I am the bread of life. He who comes to Me will never go hungry, and he who believes in Me will never be thirsty. (John 6:35)

As Christians, our supreme occupation must always be with Christ Himself—not merely our church, denomination or religious system. Reading the Bible and spending time in prayer are vital to our spiritual well-being. But even these activities are a means to an end, the end purpose being that they bring us into a closer relationship with God Himself. Notice the words of this hymn:

> Beyond the sacred page I seek Thee, Lord . . . .
> And in Thy book revealed I see the Lord.

Although it is often used as a communion service hymn, this hymn's real teaching is that God's Word—"the Bread of Life" should nourish our spiritual lives and bring us into an ever closer relationship with our Lord.

The hymn's author, Mary Lathbury, was a longtime associate with the Chautauqua Assembly, a Methodist camp meeting located on beautiful Lake Chautauqua in New York. In 1877 at the request of the camp director, Miss Lathbury wrote these words to be used as a theme song for the Bible study sessions. The music was composed by the gifted music director of Chautauqua, William F. Sherwin. The hymn has since been widely used at the camp grounds, as it has been by Christians everywhere for times of quiet reflection upon the things of God.

> Break Thou the bread of life, Dear Lord, to me, as Thou didst break the loaves beside the sea: Beyond the sacred page I seek Thee, Lord; my spirit pants for Thee, O living Word.
>
> Bless thou the truth, dear Lord, to me—to me, as Thou didst bless the bread by Galilee: Then shall all bondage cease, all fetters fall, and I shall find my peace, my All in all.
>
> Thou art the bread of life, O Lord, to me; Thy holy Word the truth that saveth me: Give me to eat and live with Thee above; teach me to love Thy truth, for Thou art love.
>
> O send Thy Spirit, Lord, now unto me, that He may touch my eyes and make me see: Show me the truth concealed within Thy Word, and in Thy book revealed I see the Lord.

❦ *For Today:* Psalm 63:1; 119:45; Jeremiah 15:16; Matthew 14:13-21

Determine that your life will reflect complete peace and contentment as you allow Christ to nourish and fill you with Himself. Use this hymn to help in this spiritual quest.

Bread of Life tune   William F. Sherwin, 1826-1888

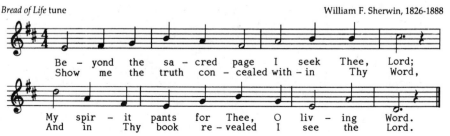

Be - yond the sa - cred page I seek Thee, Lord;
Show me the truth con - cealed with - in Thy Word,

My spir - it pants for Thee, O liv - ing Word.
And in Thy book re - vealed I see the Lord.

OPEN MY EYES, THAT I MAY SEE

Words and Music by Clara H. Scott, 1841-1897

Open my eyes that I may see wonderful things in Your law. (Psalm 119:18)

The Scriptures teach that our faith in Christ employs all of our God-given senses:

> SIGHT—"Look unto me, and be saved, all the ends of the earth" (Isaiah 45:22).
> HEARING—"Hear, and your soul shall live" (Isaiah 55:3).
> SMELL—"Thy name is like ointment poured forth" (Song of Solomon 1:3).
> TOUCH—"If I may but touch His garment, I shall be well" (Matthew 9:21).
> TASTE—"O taste and see that the Lord is good" (Psalm 34:8).

In order to receive God's truth properly, then, we must have our entire being alive and alert to His every prompting. In general, most Christians do not deliberately and dramatically disobey God. Instead we simply do not heed Him by being sensitive to His leading in the small details of our lives. How important that we learn the lesson taught by this hymn text that we should have seeing eyes, hearing ears, a verbal communication of the truth, and a loving heart for sharing God's love. All of this is possible as we are illuminated by the Holy Spirit during times of quiet waiting.

Clara Scott, author and composer of this hymn, taught music in the Ladies' Seminary at Lyons, Iowa. Mrs. Scott was a prolific composer of vocal and instrumental music, including a book of anthems, *The Royal Anthem Book,* published in 1882. These words have since been widely used to help believers have a greater awareness of God's will for their lives and a readiness to obey (James 1:22).

> Open my eyes, that I may see glimpses of truth Thou hast for me; place in my hands the wonderful key that shall unclasp and set me free. Silently now I wait for Thee, ready, my God, Thy will to see; open my eyes—illumine me, Spirit divine!

> Open my ears, that I may hear voices of truth Thou sendest clear; and while the wave-notes fall on my ear, ev'rything false will disappear. Silently now I wait for Thee, ready, my God, Thy will to see; open my ears—illumine me, Spirit divine!

> Open my mouth, and let me bear gladly the warm truth ev'rywhere. Open my heart and let me prepare love with Thy children thus to share. Silently now I wait for Thee, ready, my God, Thy will to see; open my heart—illumine me, Spirit divine!

❦ ***For Today:*** Psalm 40:8; Proverbs 16:9; Matthew 13:6; Luke 8:18; John 7:17

Ask God to activate your senses for receiving His truth and to make you more sensitive to the needs of those who need to hear "the warm truth" and to experience His love. Breathe this musical prayer as you prepare to go forth—

Si - lent - ly now I wait for Thee, Read - y, my God, Thy will to

see; O - pen my eyes— il - lu - mine me, Spir - it di - vine!

I WOULD BE LIKE JESUS

James Rowe, 1865-1933

For those God foreknew He also predestined to be conformed to the likeness of His Son, that He might be the firstborn among many brothers. (Romans 8:29)

I may not understand, Lord, but one day I shall see
Thy loving hand was taking pains to fashion me like Thee.   —*Unknown*

There is much about the word *predestined* that is difficult to understand. One very obvious lesson that can be learned, however, is that God planned ahead of time for His children to be like His Son. The Scriptures teach that Christ has left us an example, and that we should seek to imitate Him and follow in His steps (Galatians 5:1; 1 Peter 2:21). Like our Lord, we have been called to have the spirit of a servant, spending and being spent, meeting the needs of others. But we cannot develop a Christ-like life merely on the basis of religious activity or even an accumulation of biblical knowledge, as important as knowledge and sound doctrine are to Christian living. Rather, spiritual maturity—Christ-like living—is the result of an implicit obedience to God's will for our lives, even as our Lord was always obedient to the will of His Father. This awareness of God's purposes is made possible as the Holy Spirit reveals the truth to us through the Scriptures.

Nothing demonstrates the truthfulness of our verbal witness for Christ more than a life in which the very character of Jesus is clearly evident. This hymn has been used to help Christian people in this spiritual desire and development since it was first written by an American gospel musician, James Rowe, and published in the *Make Christ King Hymnal* in 1912.

Earthly pleasures vainly call me—I would be like Jesus; nothing worldly shall enthrall me—I would be like Jesus:

He has broken ev'ry fetter—I would be like Jesus; that my soul may serve Him better—I would be like Jesus:

All the way from earth to glory—I would be like Jesus; telling o'er and o'er the story—I would be like Jesus:

That in heaven He may meet me, I would be like Jesus; that His words "Well done" may greet me, I would be like Jesus:

Refrain: Be like Jesus—this my song—in the home and in the throng, be like Jesus all day long! I would be like Jesus.

❦ *For Today:* 2 Corinthians 3:8; Galatians 4:19; Ephesians 2:10; Philippians 2:1-11; 1 Peter 2:21

"Great oaks from little acorns grow—and character from deeds you sow." Earnestly seek to bring Christ-like attitudes and actions into every area of life. Sing as you go—

B. D. Ackley, 1872-1958

I WANT A PRINCIPLE WITHIN

Charles Wesley, 1707-1788

So I strive always to keep my conscience clear before God and man. (Acts 24:16)

> Order my footsteps by Thy Word,
> And make my heart sincere;
> Let sin have no dominion, Lord,
> But keep my conscience clear.   —*Unknown*

The Bible has much to say about the importance of a Christian having a strong "inner man" (Ephesians 3:16). For instance the word *conscience* appears more than 30 times throughout the New Testament. The conscience has been described as the "rudder of the soul" or the believer's "principle within." One of the prime responsibilities of Christian living is to keep the conscience clear as to the things of God so that we might live worthy lives before our fellowmen. But the conscience must be continually enlightened and developed by an exposure to God's Word if it is to serve as a reliable guide for our lives. A conscience that is allowed to become hardened and insensitive to sin will ultimately lead to spiritual and moral disaster. We must allow God to develop our consciences and then our consciences are able to develop us.

Charles Wesley was very strong in his teaching about the necessity of an enlightened conscience for believers. Part of the Wesleyan concept for the doctrine of holiness was that God's people should be so sensitive to sin that eventually they would be able to live without known sin in their lives.

This song text first appeared in the 1749 edition of Wesley's *Hymns and Sacred Poems*, with the title "For a Tender Conscience." These words are still a worthy goal for our daily living:

> I want a principle within of watchful, Godly fear, a sensibility of sin, a pain to feel it near. Help me the first approach to feel of pride or wrong desire, to catch the wand'ring of my will and quench the Spirit's fire.

> From Thee that I no more may stray, no more Thy goodness grieve, grant me the filial awe, I pray, the tender conscience give. Quick as the apple of an eye, O God, my conscience make! Awake my soul when sin is nigh and keep it still awake.

> Almighty God of truth and love, to me Thy pow'r impart; the burden from my soul remove, the hardness from my heart. O may the least omission pain my reawakened soul, and drive me to that grace again which makes the wounded whole.

❦ *For Today:* Acts 23:1; Romans 2:15; Ephesians 1:4; 2 Timothy 1:8, 9

Ask God to give you a greater sensitivity to those attitudes and actions that could harden the response of your conscience. Carry this musical prayer with you—

Gerald tune   Louis Spohr, 1784-1859

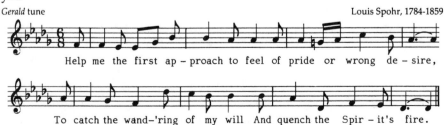

Help me the first ap – proach to feel of pride or wrong de – sire,

To catch the wand-'ring of my will And quench the Spir – it's fire.

TEACH ME THY WAY, O LORD

Words and Music by Mansell Ramsey, 1849-1923

Teach me your way, O Lord; lead me in a straight path. (Psalm 27:11)

> I have held many things in my hands, and I have lost them all; but whatever I have placed in God's hands, that I still possess. —*Martin Luther*

> I thank God for my handicaps, for, through them, I have found myself, my work, and my God. —*Helen Keller*

Whatever absorbs our thinking will ultimately control our actions. It is so important for a Christian, then, to let the ways of the Lord become the controlling force in life. It was C. S. Lewis who reminded us that we are becoming now what we will be in eternity—either something beautiful and full of glory or something hideous and full of darkness.

A spiritual knowledge of Christ is always a personal knowledge. It is not gained through the experiences of others. Knowing the Lord in all of His fullness for every situation we encounter is a lifetime pursuit. Discipleship involves a willingness to be taught and then a desire to follow the ways of the Lord—to go with Him in the same direction He is going. We must be willing to say with David Livingstone, the noted missionary statesman of the past century, "I will place no value on anything I have or may possess except in relation to the kingdom of Christ."

This hymn first appeared in 1920 in England. The author and composer, Benjamin Ramsey, was a well-known local church musician in the Bournemouth area of England. It has since had a wide use by student groups as well as by sincere believers everywhere who genuinely desire to have a greater knowledge of their Lord.

> Teach me Thy Way, O Lord, teach me Thy way! Thy guiding grace afford—teach me Thy way! Help me to walk aright, more by faith, less by sight; lead me with heav'nly light—teach me Thy Way!

> When I am sad at heart, teach me Thy Way! When earthly joys depart, teach me Thy Way! In hours of loneliness, in times of dire distress, in failure or success, teach me Thy Way.

> When doubts and fears arise, teach me Thy Way! When storms o'er spread the skies, teach me Thy Way! Shine thru the cloud and rain, thru sorrow, toil and pain; make Thou my pathway plain—teach me Thy Way!

> Long as my life shall last, teach me Thy Way! Where'er my lot be cast, teach me Thy Way! Until the race is run, until the journey's done, until the crown is won, teach me Thy Way!

❦ *For Today:* Psalm 25:4, 5; 86:11; 90:12; Matthew 11:29; Romans 12:2

Ask God to teach you some fresh insight from the Scriptures about Himself. Use this musical prayer to help—

Camacha tune

Help me to walk a - right, More by faith, less by sight;

Lead me with heav'n - ly light— Teach me Thy Way!

TAKE THE WORLD, BUT GIVE ME JESUS

Fanny J. Crosby, 1820-1915

What good is it for a man to gain the whole world, yet forfeit his soul? Or what can a man give in exchange for his soul? (Mark 8:36, 37)

In every believer there is a constant struggle between the old nature, which is attracted to the world, and the new nature, which responds to God. These two opposing natures will never cease to struggle as long as we are residents of this world. Worldliness can be described as anything that tends to draw us away from God and limits us from being all that He wants us to be. Separation from the world, however, does not mean that we are to live in isolation from individuals within the world, whether they be saint or sinner. We cannot represent our Lord if we remain aloof from the needs of those around us. There must always be that fine balance in our lives between a closeness and total commitment to Christ and an availability and helpful contact with those in our everyday world,.

A Christian's goal in life is to "cease from sin" and thus starve the old nature, which tends to be selfish, hateful, and greedy. Although it is true that we will never achieve a sinless perfection until we reach heaven, this should never keep us from striving and saying with Fanny Crosby, "Take the world, but give me Jesus." Like the blind poetess, the goal of someday having a "clearer, brighter vision" when we see our Lord face to face makes the struggles of this life all worthwhile.

> Take the world, but give me Jesus—All its joys are but a name; but His love abideth ever, thru eternal years the same.

> Take the world, but give me Jesus—Sweetest comfort of my soul; with my Savior watching o'er me, I can sing tho billows roll.

> Take the world, but give me Jesus—Let me view His constant smile; then thruout my pilgrim journey light will cheer me all the while.

> Take the world, but give me Jesus—In His cross my trust shall be; till, with clearer, brighter vision, face to face my Lord I see.

> **Chorus:** O the height and depth of mercy! O the length and breadth of love! O the fullness of redemption—Pledge of endless life above!

❧ *For Today:* Galatians 5:16-18; Ephesians 3:17-19; Philippians 1:20-24; 1 John 2:15

Reflect on your spiritual goals for life. Make a list of the activities and disciplines necessary for their achievement. Invite the Holy Spirit's help. Carry this musical truth as you go—

John R. Sweney, 1837-1899

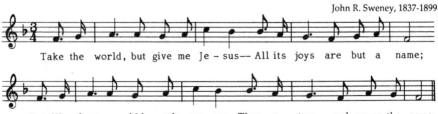

Take the world, but give me Je - sus-- All its joys are but a name;

But His love a - bid - eth ev - er, Thru e - ter - nal years the same.

NEARER, STILL NEARER

Words and Music by Leila N. Morris, 1862-1929

The Lord is near to all who call on Him, to all who call on Him in truth. (Psalm 145:18)

It has often been observed that there were at least four groups of people who had a relationship with Christ while He was here on earth. There was the multitude, those who followed from a distance. They were interested merely in what Jesus could do. They were the spectators of the Savior. There was a second group—the 120 gathered in the upper room at Pentecost. They moved much closer to Christ. They shared in His suffering and crucifixion. There was a still closer group—the 12 (later the 11) disciples who were personally taught by Christ. And even this small band of helpers advanced to a more intimate relationship when Christ announced that they were no longer servants but His friends (John 15:15). But within the family of disciples there was another even closer group—Peter, James, and John. They were the ones who enjoyed the closest fellowship with the Lord and were the ones Jesus counted on the most.

Even today there are various levels of closeness to the Lord. It is possible to be involved in much religious activity that does not really draw us nearer to God. To move into closer relationships with Him, we must employ the spiritual means He has provided: An understanding and application of the Scriptures to our lives and daily communion with our Lord. Our spiritual growth is in direct proportion to this vital truth.

Leila Morris, the author and composer of this hymn, was active in the Methodist Episcopal church and in holiness camp meetings. She wrote more than 1,000 gospel hymns, and she continued writing even after going blind. "Nearer, Still Nearer," was first published in 1898 in the *Pentecostal Praises Hymnal.*

> Nearer, still nearer, close to Thy heart, draw me, my Savior, so precious Thou art; fold me, O fold me close to Thy breast; shelter me safe in that haven of rest.

> Nearer, still nearer, nothing I bring, naught as an offering to Jesus my King: Only my sinful, now contrite heart; grant me the cleansing Thy blood doth impart.

> Nearer, still nearer, Lord, to be Thine. Sin with its follies I gladly resign; all of its pleasures, pomp and its pride, give me but Jesus, my Lord crucified.

> Nearer, still nearer, while life shall last, till safe in glory my anchor is cast; through endless ages, ever to be, nearer, my Savior, still nearer to Thee.

❦ *For Today:* Psalm 119:133; Ephesians 2:13; Philippians 3:10; James 4:8; 2 Peter 3:18

Reflect on those attitudes and actions that would move your life into a higher level of closeness with Christ. Make this your resolve. Carry this musical prayer as you go—

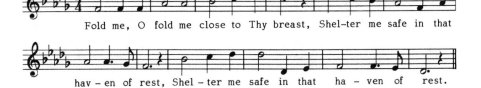

THY WORD HAVE I HID IN MY HEART

Words and Music by Ernest O. Sellers, 1869-1952

The Spirit gives life; the flesh counts for nothing. The words I have spoken to you are spirit and they are life. (John 6:63)

O cleansing Word, O precious Word, Your promises are true;
They keep and purify my heart; Your truths are ever new.   —*Unknown*

God has made provision for each believer to live holy and pure lives—regardless of his or her environment. That provision is the power of His Word. The ability to live above the filth and evil in the daily world around us can be achieved only through listening to and responding to the truth of the Scriptures.

Portions of the wonderful 119th Psalm, with the majority of its 176 verses speaking pointedly regarding the importance of God's Word, were paraphrased by Ernest O. Sellers and set to a melody in 1908 to provide us with a hymn that still has an important place in our hymnals.

The first stanza of this hymn is based on verse 105: "Thy Word is a lamp to my feet, and a light to my path." Stanza two is based on verses 89 and 90: "Forever, O Lord, Thy Word is settled in heaven. Thy faithfulness is unto all generations: Thou hast established the earth, and it abideth." The third stanza is taken from the 44th, the 62nd, and the 164th verses of this psalm: "Seven times a day do I praise Thee, because of Thy righteous judgments. At midnight, I will rise to give thanks unto Thee, because of Thy righteous judgments. So shall I keep Thy law continually forever and ever." The final stanza is based on the 41st verse: "Let Thy mercies come also unto me, O Lord, even Thy salvation according to Thy Word."

For the chorus of his hymn, Mr. Sellers used the words directly from Psalm 119:11. They provide a strong closing summary for the reason we hide God's Word in our hearts: "Thy Word have I hid in my heart—that I might not sin against Thee."

Thy Word is a lamp to my feet, a light to my path alway, to guide and to save me from sin and show me the heav'nly way.

Forever, O Lord, is Thy Word established and fixed on high; Thy faithfulness unto all men abideth forever nigh.

At morning, at noon, and at night I ever will give Thee praise; for Thou art my portion, O Lord, and shall be thru all my days!

Thru Him whom Thy Word hath foretold, the Savior and Morning Star, salvation and peace have been brought to those who have strayed afar.

Chorus: Thy Word have I hid in my heart, that I might not sin against Thee.

❧ *For Today:* Psalm 119:11, 41, 44, 62, 89, 90, 105, 164; 2 Timothy 3:16, 17

Take one of these choice verses from Psalm 119 and let it saturate your life. Carry with you verse 11 in this musical form—

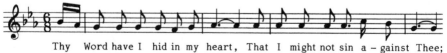

Thy Word have I hid in my heart, That I might not sin a-gainst Thee;
That I might not sin, That I might not sin, Thy Word have I hid in my heart.

DEEPER AND DEEPER

Words and Music by Oswald J. Smith, 1890-1986

I delight to do Thy will, O my God: Yea, Thy law is within my heart. (Psalm 40:8)

These beautifully worded lines with their soulful melody flowed from the heart of Oswald J. Smith after many difficult experiences during the early years of his ministry. He related in his book, *The Story of My Life,* that he was carried through these troublesome times by what he called his "morning watch."

> It was when I walked alone with God that I learned the lessons He would teach. I set aside a time and a place to meet Him, and I have never been disappointed.

Dr. Smith was one of the great evangelical preachers and missionary statesmen of the 20th century. For many years he was the pastor of a church he founded, the People's Church in Toronto, Canada. He described the inspiration that came to him for "Deeper and Deeper:"

> Arriving in Woodstock, Ontario, I was invited to preach one Sunday morning in the largest Methodist Church in that city. As I walked along the street on my way to the church, the melody of this hymn sang itself into my heart and with the words, "Into the heart of Jesus, deeper and deeper I go." I can still recall the joy and buoyancy of youth, the bright sunshine overhead, and the thrill with which I looked forward to my service that Sunday morning, as again and again I hummed over the words. After preaching, I returned to my rented room, and the first thing I did was to write out the melody as God had given it to me. The verses were much more difficult. It was three years later, in the First Presbyterian Church of South Chicago, of which I pastor, that I completed them. The writing of the hymn afforded me much joy. I still love it and always will, for it was the child of my youth. It proves conclusively that God can impart His deepest truths to the hearts of the young, for I doubt if I have ever written anything more profound since.

* * * *

Into the heart of Jesus deeper and deeper I go, seeking to know the reason why He should love me so—Why He should stoop to lift me up from the miry clay, saving my soul, making me whole, tho I had wandered away.

Into the joy of Jesus deeper and deeper I go, rising, with soul enraptured, far from the world below; joy in the place of sorrow, peace in the midst of pain, Jesus will give, Jesus will give—He will uphold and sustain!

Into the love of Jesus deeper and deeper I go, praising the One who brought me out of my sin and woe; and thru eternal ages gratefully I shall sing, "O how He loved! O how He loved! Jesus, my Lord and my King!"

❦ *For Today:* Psalm 42; 16:8, 11; Lamentations 3:26; Isaiah 40:31; 54:2; 1 John 2:17

Determine to know God in a deeper way than ever before. Sing as you go—

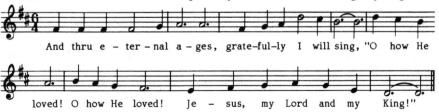

And thru e - ter - nal a - ges, grate-ful-ly I will sing, "O how He loved! O how He loved! Je - sus, my Lord and my King!"

JESUS, I MY CROSS HAVE TAKEN

Henry F. Lyte, 1793-1847

Then Jesus said to His disciples, "If anyone would come after Me, he must deny himself and take up his cross and follow Me." (Matthew 16:24)

Every believer has a cross of some kind that Christ expects him to carry cheerfully each day as a demonstration of his discipleship. Life is a matter of choices. If we have made a decision to follow Christ, there must be purposeful self-denial in our lives or we have not really learned the meaning of true discipleship. Salvation is free, but discipleship is costly. Bearing the cross involves a willingness to look beyond our own affairs and to share the load of others in order that they too may have a personal relationship with the Savior.

Henry Lyte spent the last 23 years of his life ministering to an Anglican parish of humble fishermen in Devonshire, England. In spite of his cross of frail health, Lyte worked tirelessly to build up a Sunday school of more than 800 children, and he contributed to a great spiritual and moral change in the hardened community around him. Also during these years, he had a number of books of poetry published as well as 80 hymn texts.

In everything he attempted amidst numerous difficulties, Henry Lyte demonstrated that he truly denied himself, took up his cross, and faithfully followed and served his Lord.

> Jesus, I my cross have taken, all to leave and follow Thee; destitute, despised, forsaken—Thou from hence my all shalt be. Perish ev'ry fond ambition—all I've sought and hoped and known! Yet how rich is my condition—God and heav'n are still my own!

> Let the world despise and leave me; they have left my Savior too; human hearts and looks deceive me—Thou art not, like man, untrue. And while Thou shalt smile upon me, God of wisdom, love, and might, foes may hate, and friends may shun me—Show Thy face, and all is bright!

> Haste thee, on from grace to glory, armed by faith and winged by prayer; Heav'n's eternal days before thee—God's own hand shall guide thee there. Soon shall close thy earthly mission; swift shall pass thy pilgrim days; hope shall change to glad fruition, faith to sight, and prayer to praise!

❦ ***For Today:*** 2 Kings 18:1-7; Matthew 10:38; Mark 10:21; Luke 9:23, 62; 1 Peter 2:21

Purpose in your heart to deny yourself, cheerfully enduring whatever your cross may be, and then serve God by serving someone else. Begin by reflecting seriously on the words of this hymn—

Ellesdie tune — From Leavitt's *Christian Lyre*, 1831

Je - sus, I my cross have tak - en, All to leave and fol - low Thee;

Yet how rich is my con - di - tion—God and heav'n are still my own!

TAKE TIME TO BE HOLY

William D. Longstaff, 1822 -1894

But just as He who called you is holy, so be holy in all you do; for it is written: "Be holy, because I am holy." (1 Peter 1:15, 16)

The valuable guidelines given in this hymn for living a holy life are just as pertinent for believers today as they were when William Longstaff wrote them more than a century ago. God still requires a holy lifestyle for His people. We sometimes confuse holiness with piety, which can be merely a hypocritical goodness that masks inner deceit or impurity. A truly holy or Christ-like life reveals the virtues mentioned in 2 Peter 1:5, 6: Goodness, knowledge, self-control, perseverance, godliness, brotherly kindness and love. We are surrounded today by so much sham and insincerity that we are often unconsciously affected by such influences. To maintain the quality of life that God demands, we must determine to take time to develop a life that is genuinely and consistently holy in every area.

William Longstaff, though financially independent, (son of a wealthy English ship owner) was a humble and devout Christian layman and a close friend and supporter of the Moody-Sankey evangelistic team that stirred England with great revival campaigns during the late 19th century. After hearing a sermon on 1 Peter 1:16—"Be ye holy, for I am holy"—with reference to the book of Leviticus from which it was originally taken, young William began to make the achievement of holiness his life's goal. Although this was his only hymn, these words have since been an invaluable influence for sincere believers everywhere who truly desire to live a genuine Christian life:

Take time to be holy. Speak oft with thy Lord; abide in Him always and feed on His Word. Make friends of God's children. Help those who are weak, forgetting in nothing His blessing to seek.

Take time to be holy. The world rushes on; spend much time in secret with Jesus alone. By looking to Jesus, like Him thou shalt be; thy friends in thy conduct His likeness shall see.

Take time to be holy. Let Him be thy guide, and run not before Him, whatever betide. In joy or in sorrow still follow thy Lord, and, looking to Jesus, still trust in His Word.

Take time to be holy. Be calm in thy soul—Each thought and each motive beneath His control. Thus led by His Spirit to fountains of love, thou soon shalt be fitted for service above.

❧ *For Today:* Leviticus 20:7, 8; 2 Corinthians 7:1; Ephesians 4:23, 24; 1 Timothy 1:8; Hebrews 12:14

Reflect on all of the various suggestions for holy living listed in this hymn text. Sing these truths as you go realizing you need to—

Holiness tune   George C. Stebbins, 1846-1945

Take time to be ho - ly, Speak oft with thy Lord;

For - get - ting in noth - ing His bless - ing to seek.

HAVE THINE OWN WAY, LORD

Adelaide A. Pollard, 1862-1934

Yet, O Lord, you are our Father, We are the clay, You are the potter; we are all the work of Your hand. (Isaiah 64:8)

An elderly woman at a prayer meeting one night pleaded, "It really doesn't matter what you do with us, Lord, just have your way with our lives." At this meeting was Adelaide Pollard, a rather well-known itinerant Bible teacher who was deeply discouraged because she had been unable to raise the necessary funds for a desired trip to Africa to do missionary service. She was moved by the older woman's sincere and dedicated request of God.

At home that evening Miss Pollard meditated on Jeremiah 18:3, 4:

Then I went down to the potter's house, and behold, he wrought a work on the wheels, and the vessel that he made of clay was marred in the hand of the potter; so he made it again another vessel, as seemed good to the potter to make it.

Before retiring that evening, Adelaide Pollard completed the writing of all four stanzas of this hymn as it is sung today. The hymn first appeared in published form in 1907.

Often into our lives come discouragements and heartaches that we cannot understand. As children of God, however, we must learn never to question the ways of our sovereign God—but simply to say:

Have Thine own way, Lord! Have Thine own way! Thou art the potter, I am the clay. Mold me and make me after Thy will, while I am waiting, yielded and still.

Have Thine own way, Lord! Have Thine own way! Search me and try me, Master, today! Whiter than snow, Lord, wash me just now, as in Thy presence humbly I bow.

Have Thine own way, Lord! Have Thine own way! Wounded and weary, help me, I pray! Power, all power, surely is Thine! Touch me and heal me, Savior divine!

Have Thine own way, Lord! Have Thine own way! Hold o'er my being absolute sway! Fill with Thy Spirit till all shall see Christ only, always, living in me!

❦ *For Today:* Psalm 27:14; Romans 6:13, 14; 9:20, 21; Galatians 2:20

Breathe this ancient prayer: "I am willing, Lord, to receive what Thou givest, to lack what Thou withholdest, to relinquish what Thou takest, to surrender what Thou claimest, to suffer what Thou ordainest, to do what Thou commandest, to wait until Thou sayest 'Go.'" Reflect on these words again as you go—

Adelaide tune   George C. Stebbins, 1846-1945

Mold me and make me af – ter Thy will, While I am
Fill with Thy Spir–it Till all shall see Christ, on–ly,

wait – ing, Yield – ed and still.
al – ways, Liv – ing in me.

NEARER, MY GOD, TO THEE

Sarah R. Adams, 1805-1848

Draw nigh to God, and He will draw nigh to you. (James 4:8 KJV)

This well-loved hymn was written by a talented and charming English woman who lived only 43 years. In spite of her delicate health, Sarah Flower Adams had an active and productive life. After a successful career on the London stage as Sheakespeare's Lady MacBeth, she began to write and became widely known for her literary accomplishments. The cross mentioned in the first stanza of her hymn text may have been the physical handicaps that limited her many ambitions.

Sarah's sister Eliza was gifted musically and often composed melodies for her sister's poems. Together they contributed 13 texts and 62 new tunes for a hymnal that was being compiled by their pastor. One day the Rev. William J. Fox asked for a new hymn to accompany his sermon on the story of Jacob and Esau. Sarah spent much time studying Genesis 28:10-22 and within a short time completed all of the stanzas of "Nearer, My God, to Thee." Since that day in 1840, this hymn has had an unusual history of ministering spiritual comfort to hurting people everywhere.

These lines picturing Jacob sleeping on a stone, dreaming of angels, and naming the place Bethel, meaning "the house of God," seem to reflect the common yearning—especially in times of deep need—to experience God's nearness and presence in a very real way.

> Nearer, my God, to Thee, nearer to Thee! E'en tho it be a cross that raiseth me; still all my song shall be, nearer, my God, to Thee, nearer, my God, to Thee, nearer to Thee!

> Tho like the wanderer, the sun gone down, darkness be over me, my rest a stone, yet in my dreams I'd be nearer, my God, to Thee, nearer, my God, to Thee, nearer to Thee!

> Then with my waking thoughts, bright with Thy praise, out of my stony griefs. Bethel I raise; so by my woes to be nearer, my God, to Thee, nearer my God, to Thee, nearer to Thee!

> Or if on joyful wing, cleaving the sky, sun, moon, and stars forgot, upward I fly, till all my song shall be, nearer, my God, to Thee, nearer, my God, to Thee, nearer to Thee!

❦ *For Today:* Genesis 28:10-22; Psalm 16:7, 8; 73:28; 145:18; Jeremiah 29:13; Acts 17:27

When I seek God, He has promised to draw very close to me. What a joyful experience to know His intimate presence throughout every hour of this day. It causes me to sing—

Bethany tune   Lowell Mason, 1792-1872

Still all my song shall be, Near - er, my God to Thee
Near - er, my God to Thee, Near - er to Thee!

I NEED THEE EVERY HOUR

Annie S. Hawks, 1835-1918
Refrain added by Robert Lowry

In the day of my trouble I will call to You, for You will answer me. (Psalm 86:7)

This deeply personal hymn came from the heart of a busy housewife and mother who had no idea of the spiritual strength that her own hastily written words would bring her later during a sorrowful time in her life.

The author, Annie S. Hawks, has left this account about the writing of her poem in 1872:

> One day as a young wife and mother of 37 years of age, I was busy with my regular household tasks. Suddenly, I became filled with the sense of nearness to the Master, and I began to wonder how anyone could ever live without Him, either in joy or pain. Then the words were ushered into my mind and these thoughts took full possession of me.

Sixteen years later, Mrs. Hawks experienced the death of her husband. Years after, she wrote:

> I did not understand at first why this hymn had touched the great throbbing heart of humanity. It was not until long after, when the shadow fell over my way, the shadow of a great loss, that I understood something of the comforting power in the words which I had been permitted to give out to others in my hour of sweet serenity and peace.

One of the blessings of a victorious Christian life is knowing the closeness of our Lord in every circumstance of life. Like Annie Hawks, it is so important that we develop strong spiritual lives during the peaceful hours in order that we will be able to be victorious when difficulties come, which they surely will to everyone at some time.

I need Thee every hour, most gracious Lord. No tender voice like Thine can peace afford.

I need Thee every hour; stay Thou near by. Temptations lose their pow'r when Thou art nigh.

I need Thee every hour, in joy or pain. Come quickly, and abide, or life is vain.

I need Thee every hour; teach me Thy will, and Thy rich promises in me fulfill.

I need Thee every hour, Most Holy One; O make me Thine indeed, Thou blessed Son.

Refrain: I need Thee, O I need Thee; every hour I need Thee! O bless me now, my Savior—I come to Thee!

🍂 *For Today:* Psalm 4:1; 86; John 15:4, 5; 16:33; 1 Corinthians 10:13; Hebrews 4:16

Consciously practice walking close to the Savior each hour so that whether there are times of joy or grief, He will be there to meet every need. Sing as you go meditating on the fact—

Robert Lowry, 1826-1899

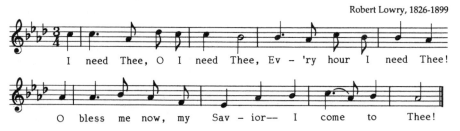

I need Thee, O I need Thee, Ev - 'ry hour I need Thee!

O bless me now, my Sav - ior— I come to Thee!

MAY THE MIND OF CHRIST, MY SAVIOR

Kate B. Wilkinson, 1859-1928

Let this mind be in you, which was also in Christ Jesus. (Philippians 2:5)

In the home Christ-likeness is kindness;
In business it is honesty;
Toward the weak it is burden bearing;
Toward the sinner it is evangelism;
Toward ourselves it is self-control;
Toward God it is reverence, love and worship.   —*Unknown*

Each day our prayer life should include the request that the Holy Spirit reveal the mind of Christ to us. As we mature in the Christian faith, our personalities and characters should take on Christ-like qualities. To have a Christ-like mind, it is vitally important that we nourish our minds daily with quality materials— things "that are true, noble, right, pure, lovely, admirable, and praiseworthy" (Philippians 4:8).

Kate Wilkinson was a member of the Church of England and actively involved in the Keswick Deeper Life Movement. The hymn first appeared in the *Golden Bells Hymnal,* published in 1925.

As a suggestion for your devotional times, take the six prayers of this hymn and use one each day to meditate upon as preparation for your worship on the Lord's Day. What does it mean to have the "mind of Christ," the "Word of God," the "peace of God," the "love of Jesus," the strength of Jesus, and the beauty of Jesus in your life? How would these Christ-like virtues affect your daily living? How would they influence your worship of God?

May the mind of Christ, my Savior, live in me from day to day, by His love and pow'r controlling all I do and say.

May the Lord of God dwell richly in my heart from hour to hour, so that all may see I triumph only thru His pow'r.

May the peace of God, my Father, rule my life in ev'rything that I may be calm to comfort sick and sorrowing.

May the love of Jesus fill me, as the waters fill the sea; Him exalting, self-abasing— this is victory.

May I run the race before me strong and brave to face the foe, looking only unto Jesus as I onward go.

May His beauty rest upon me as I seek the lost to win, and may they forget the channel, seeing only Him.

❧ ***For Today:*** 1 Corinthians 15:49; Ephesians 3:17; Philippians 2:1-16

Try to base every action and decision on the response to this question: What is the Christ-like way for handling this situation? Reflect on this hymn—

St. Leonard's tune   A. Cyril Barnam-Gould, 1891-1953

May the mind of Christ, my Sav-ior live in me from day to day,

By His love and pow'r con - troll - ing All I do and say.

O FOR A CLOSER WALK WITH GOD

William Cowper, 1731-1800

So then, just as you received Christ Jesus as Lord, continue to live in Him, rooted and built up in Him, strengthened in the faith as you were taught, and overflowing with thankfulness. (Colossians 2:6)

The Christian life begins with a step of faith for salvation. Then it continues step by step toward spiritual maturity as we develop a growing closeness to God. If we sincerely desire a more intimate relationship with our Lord, we will need perseverance and often personal denial or sacrifice. This thoughtful hymn text teaches that there may be idols that will hinder a close walk with God. It is only as these are forsaken that our way will be characterized by serenity, love, and purity while we go on with the Lord in a daily walk of faith.

As we endeavor to walk closely with God, unscheduled events will often come into our lives. Yet these unexpected happenings may result in greater blessing than we had ever anticipated. If we learn to be flexible and calmly trust God to lead us in His way, we will not only be drawn closer to Him but will be more aware of "a light to shine upon the road."

The life of William Cowper was filled with troubling events. Early in life he began to be plagued with chronic melancholy and depression that afflicted him at various times until his death. At one time he was in such mental torment that he even attempted to drown himself. Eventually he moved to the little village of Olney, England, where he began a close friendship with John Newton, pastor of the Anglican church there. Each day the two men met in the garden of Cowper's home to write devotional poetry and hymns. In 1779, their combined talents produced the famous *Olney Hymns* hymnal, one of the most important contributions to evangelical hymnody. Cowper wrote 67 of the texts in this book. This hymn text was originally titled "Walking With God," based on Genesis 5:24: "And Enoch walked with God: And he was not; for God took him."

> O for a closer walk with God, a calm and heav'nly frame, a light to shine upon the road that leads me to the Lamb!
>
> The dearest idol I have known, whate' er that idol be, help me to tear it from Thy throne, and worship only Thee.
>
> So shall my walk be close with God, calm and serene my frame, so purer light shall mark the road that leads me to the Lamb.

🐝 *For Today:* Genesis 5:24; Psalm 63:7, 8; 2 Corinthians 5:7; Galatians 5:13-18; Ephesians 5:8-10

Be so sensitive to God's presence and leading that you will be ready to adjust your schedule and represent Him whenever the slightest opportunity comes your way. Allow this hymn to help in this faith adventure—

Beatitudo tune — John B. Dykes, 1823-1876

O for a clos-er walk with God, A calm and heav'n-ly frame,

A light to shine up-on the road that leads me to the Lamb!

CLEANSE ME

J. Edwin Orr, 1912-1988

If we confess our sins, He is faithful and just and will forgive us our sins and purify us from all unrighteousness. (1 John 1:9)

The inspiration of a thrilling revival in New Zealand prompted the late J. Edwin Orr to blend the 23rd and 24th verses of Psalm 139 with a lovely Polynesian melody that has since become one of our most challenging hymns of revival. Dr. Orr's text opens with the prayer that the revival begin in him. Then he reminds us that revival begins only after God's people recognize their sin, receive cleansing from it and surrender their "will, passion, self and pride." The hymn ends appropriately with the assurance of knowing that God will hear and supply our needs.

J. Edwin Orr has been widely known as a challenging evangelist and a noted scholar of historical revival movements. He has written many textbooks and was a professor of world missions. He also lectured and held workshops throughout the world while visiting 150 countries.

"Cleanse Me" was written in 1936 after a stirring Easter convention in Ngaruawahia, New Zealand. Fervent meetings sprang up throughout the city. Inspired by this intense movement of the Holy Spirit, Dr. Orr took time as he left New Zealand to write the verses of "Cleanse Me" on the back of an envelope in the post office. The tune he used was the lovely Maori Song of Farewell, sung to him by four Aborigine girls as he was leaving. In following campaigns in Australia and other parts of the world, Dr. Orr often used this hymn to encourage new spiritual awakenings. His ceaseless prayer was that the people of God would be stirred to pray for yet another world-wide awakening.

> Search me, O God, and know my heart today; try me, O Savior, know my thoughts, I pray. See if there be some wicked way in me; cleanse me from ev'ry sin and set me free.
>
> I praise Thee, Lord, for cleansing me from sin; fulfill Thy Word and make me pure within. Fill me with fire where once I burned with shame; grant my desire to magnify Thy name.
>
> Lord, take my life and make it wholly Thine; fill my poor heart with Thy great love divine. Take all my will, my passion, self and pride; I now surrender, Lord— in me abide.
>
> O Holy Ghost, revival comes from Thee; send a revival—start the work in me. Thy Word declares Thou wilt supply our need; for blessings now, O Lord, I humbly plead.

❦ *For Today:* Leviticus 19:2; Psalm 51:7, 10; 85:6; 139:23, 24; Ephesians 1:4

Ask God to reveal any attitudes or actions that may be displeasing to Him. Confess each specific one, then claim His cleansing forgiveness and go forth with His joy and power. Use the words of this hymn to guide you—

Maori melody

See if there be some wick - ed way in me;

Cleanse me from ev - 'ry sin and set me free.

MORE ABOUT JESUS

Eliza E. Hewitt, 1851-1920

I want to know Christ and the power of His resurrection and the fellowship of sharing in His sufferings, becoming like Him in His death, and so, somehow, to attain to the resurrection from the dead. (Philippians 3:10, 11)

The Christian gospel is thrilling to contemplate. It is so simple that even a small child can understand and respond to its basic message—the necessity of placing one's implicit faith in Christ. But, on the other hand, it is so profound that a lifetime is far too brief to fully comprehend it, since its message is really a person—a growing knowledge and relationship to the eternal Son of God.

The author of this hymn text, Eliza Edmunds Hewitt, was an invalid for an extended period of her life. Out of this experience she developed an intimate relationship with God and the Scriptures and a desire to share her feelings with others through writing. She became a prolific author of children's poetry and Sunday school literature. Various gospel musicians soon became aware of her many fine poems and set them to suitable music. In later years, Eliza's physical condition improved and she was able to be even more active in her Christian ministries. She was a close friend of Fanny Crosby and often met with her for fellowship and discussion of new hymns they had written. "More About Jesus" was first published in 1887. Miss Hewitt's prayer, "Spirit of God, my teacher be, showing the things of Christ to me," was beautifully answered in her many hymns with heart-felt words such as these:

More about Jesus would I know, more of His grace to others show, more of His saving fullness see, more of His love who died for me.

More about Jesus let me learn, more of His holy will discern; Spirit of God my teacher be, showing the things of Christ to me.

More about Jesus—in His Word holding communion with my Lord, hearing His voice in ev'ry line, making each faithful saying mine.

More about Jesus on His throne, riches in glory all His own, more of His kingdom's sure increase, more of His coming——Prince of Peace.

Refrain: More, more about Jesus, more, more about Jesus; more of His saving fullness see, more of His love who died for me.

❦ *For Today:* 2 Corinthians 3:18; Ephesians 3:19; Philippians 3; 1 Peter 2:2; 2 Peter 1:4

A person who has had an intimate relationship with Christ radiates much more gospel truth to our world than volumes of theological arguments do. Strive to experience more of Christ's love so that you may "more of His grace to others show." Sing this prayer as you go—

John R. Sweney, 1837-1899

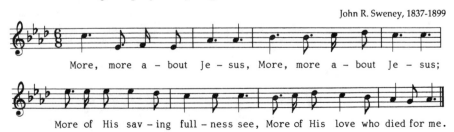

More, more a - bout Je - sus, More, more a - bout Je - sus;

More of His sav - ing full - ness see, More of His love who died for me.

WHITER THAN SNOW

James Nicholson, c. 1828-1876

Cleanse me with hyssop, and I will be clean; wash me, and I will be whiter than snow. (Psalm 51:7)

God's people have been placed in their particular circle of influence so they can demonstrate purity and a concern for righteousness. If we do not fulfill this role, who will? It is easy, however, to become so accustomed and hardened to the lust and sin all about us that we lose that fine edge of our Christian witness. In fact, without God's daily cleansing and renewal, we are easily infiltrated with and influenced by the very lifestyle that we reject in others.

Unconfessed sin becomes a destructive poison in our lives, not only spiritually but also emotionally and physically. Repentance and confession are always the starting points for a restored fellowship with God. Like the psalmist David did in his prayer in Psalm 51, we all need to experience God's cleansing and forgiveness. Only then will we be effective for God in helping others and directing sinners to Him (Psalm 51:13).

This is another fine hymn text written by a Christian layman. James Nicholson spent his entire life as a clerk in the post office in Philadelphia, yet he was always active in the work of the Wharton Street Methodist Episcopal Church. The hymn was first published in a pamphlet titled "Joyful Songs" in 1872. The hymn's popularity greatly increased with its inclusion in the well-known *Gospel Hymns* series published by Sankey and Bliss. It has since provided a musical prayer that needs to be expressed by every Christian on a daily basis:

> Lord Jesus, I long to be perfectly whole; I want thee forever to live in my soul, break down ev'ry idol, cast out ev'ry foe—Now wash me and I shall be whiter than snow.

> Lord Jesus, look down from Thy throne in the skies and help me to make a complete sacrifice. I give up myself and whatever I know—Now wash me and I shall be whiter than snow.

> Lord Jesus, for this I most humbly entreat; I wait, blessed Lord, at Thy crucified feet. By faith, for my cleansing I see Thy blood flow—Now wash me and I shall be whiter than snow.

> Lord Jesus, Thou seest I patiently wait; come now and within me a new heart create. To those who have sought Thee Thou never saidst "No"—Now wash me and I shall be whiter than snow.

> **Refrain:** Whiter than snow, yes, whiter than snow—Now wash me and I shall be whiter than snow.

❦ *For Today:* Psalm 32:3; Isaiah 1:18; Romans 3:24, 25; 1 Corinthians 6:11

Ask the Holy Spirit to reveal any area of sin. Confess it to God and claim His forgiving grace. Pray this prayer with the hymnwriter—

William G. Fischer, 1835-1912

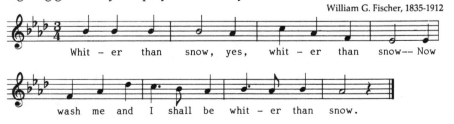

Whit – er than snow, yes, whit – er than snow–– Now wash me and I shall be whit – er than snow.

SITTING AT THE FEET OF JESUS

Source of words and music unknown

Mary has chosen what is better, and it will not be taken away from her. (Luke 10:42)

The story of Martha the worker and Mary the worshiper (Luke 10:38-42) illustrates an important spiritual principle: We please our Lord most when we learn to sit at His feet in adoration and worship before trying to serve Him in our own strength. Sitting implies our humble dependence upon Him and a sense of quietness of soul that indicates our willingness to hear. We can become so busy with life's pursuits, even worthy Christian activities, that we do not hear the still small voice of God. Or sometimes we pursue God in spiritual spectaculars. But like the story of Elijah on Mount Horeb (1 Kings 19:11, 12), the Lord does not always reveal Himself in the wind, fire, or earthquake, but sometimes in the stillness of the small voice.

> Speak, Lord, in the stillness while I wait on Thee;
> Hushed my heart to listen in expectancy.
> Speak, Thy servant heareth! Be not silent, Lord;
> Waits my soul upon Thee for the quick'ning word! —*E. May Grimes*

Learning to listen to God's voice is one of the important factors in our spiritual growth. When we are silent before Him in the enjoyment of His presence and His Word, we gain His wisdom, insights, and the renewal of our strength for daily living. May the people who see and know us say of us even as it was said of the early disciples—"they took note that these men had been with Jesus" (Acts 4:13).

> Sitting at the feet of Jesus, O what words I hear Him say! Happy place—so near, so precious! May it find me there each day! Sitting at the feet of Jesus, I would look upon the past, for His love has been so gracious—It has won my heart at last.
>
> Sitting at the feet of Jesus, where can mortal be more blest? There I lay my sins and sorrows, and, when weary, find sweet rest. Sitting at the feet of Jesus, there I love to weep and pray, while I from His fullness gather grace and comfort ev'ry day.
>
> Bless me, O my Savior, bless me, as I sit low at Thy feet! O look down in love upon me, let me see Thy face so sweet! Give me, Lord, the mind of Jesus; make me holy as He is; may I prove I've been with Jesus, who is all my righteousness.

🐝 *For Today:* 2 Kings 22:19; Psalm 130:5; Isaiah 30:15; 57:15; Matthew 11:29; 2 Corinthians 4:16

Be especially sensitive to God's still small voice in your life. Let this awareness of His presence and concern encourage and empower you. Use this hymn to help—

Constancy tune

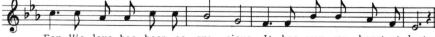

Sit - ting at the feet of Je - sus, I would look up - on the past

For His love has been so gra - cious--It has won my heart at last.

O TO BE LIKE THEE!

Thomas O. Chisholm, 1866-1960

For we are God's workmanship, created in Christ Jesus to do good works, which God prepared in advance for us to do. (Ephesians 2:10)

> Great Master, teach us with Your skillful hand;
> Let not the music that is in us die!
> Great Sculptor, hew and polish us; nor let
> Hidden and lost, Your form within us lie! —*Horatius Bonar*

The Bible teaches that God's goal for His people is that they "become mature, attaining to the whole measure of the fullness of Christ" (Ephesians 4:13). We are to daily "put on Christ"—His love and character—even as we put on our garments (Romans 13:14). Christ-likeness is more than a religious profession or a weekly visit to church. It must become our total way of life. The Scriptures further teach that we are to carry the fragrance of Christ wherever we go—to unbelievers, the smell of death and to fellow believers, the fragrance of life (2 Corinthians 2:14-16).

Our society is in desperate need of more Christ-like believers. The only thing many people will ever know about God is what they see of His radiance reflected in our daily lives. Our ability to represent our Lord worthily is only possible through the enabling power of the Holy Spirit.

This hymn text by Thomas Chisholm is one of his more than 1,200 fine poems, many of which have been set to music and have become enduring hymns of the church. This one, published in 1897, was his first hymn to be widely received.

> O to be like Thee! blessed Redeemer. This is my constant longing and prayer; gladly I'll forfeit all of earth's treasures, Jesus, Thy perfect likeness to wear.

> O to be like Thee! full of compassion, loving, forgiving, tender and kind; helping the helpless, cheering the fainting, seeking the wand'ring sinner to find.

> O to be like Thee lowly in spirit, holy and harmless, patient and brave; meekly enduring cruel reproaches, willing to suffer others to save.

> O to be like Thee! while I am pleading, pour out Thy Spirit, fill with Thy love; make me a temple meet for Thy dwelling; fit me for life and heaven above.

> **Chorus:** O to be like Thee! O to be like Thee, Blessed Redeemer, pure as Thou art! Come in Thy sweetness, come in Thy fullness; stamp Thine own image deep on my heart.

❦ ***For Today:*** Romans 8:29; 1 Corinthians 2:2; 2 Corinthians 3:18; 1 Thessalonians 4:3; Titus 3:3

Reflect on this statement: "He who does not long to know more of Christ really knows nothing of Him yet!" Carry this musical message with you—

William J. Kirkpatrick, 1838-1821

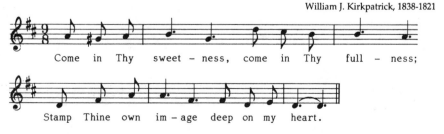

TAKE MY LIFE AND LET IT BE

Frances R. Havergal, 1836-1879

So whether you eat or drink or whatever you do, do it all for the glory of God.
(1 Corinthians 10:31)

In this day of self-centered living and pleasure-oriented lifestyle, the total commitment to God of body, mind, and possessions portrayed in this text is difficult for many Christians to achieve. Even though we realize that we have nothing we have not received and that we are only stewards of the good gifts God has entrusted to us, we often fail to apply this basic truth to our daily lives:

> The gold that came from Thee, Lord, to Thee belongeth still;
> Oh, may I always faithfully my stewardship fulfill.   —*Unknown*

It was said of Frances Ridley Havergal, author of this text, that the beauty of a consecrated life was never more perfectly revealed than in her daily living. She has rightfully been called "The Consecration Poet."

"These little couplets that chimed in my heart one after another" were for Frances Havergal the result of an evening in 1874 passed in pursuing a deeper consecration of herself to God. "Take my voice and let me sing always only for my King" was personally significant for Frances. She was naturally very musical and had been trained as a concert soloist with an unusually pleasant voice. Her musical talents could have brought her much worldly fame. However, she determined that her life's mission was to sing and work only for Jesus. The line "Take my silver and my gold" was also sincerely phrased. At one time Frances gathered together her many fine pieces of jewelry and other family heirlooms and shipped them to the church missionary house to be used for evangelizing the lost. Nearly fifty articles were sent with "extreme delight."

> Take my life and let it be consecrated, Lord, to Thee; take my hands and let them move at the impulse of Thy love;
>
> Take my feet and let them be swift and beautiful for Thee; take my voice and let me sing alway only, for my King.
>
> Take my lips and let them be filled with messages for Thee; take my silver and my gold—not a mite would I withhold.
>
> Take my love—my God, I pour at Thy feet its treasure store; take myself—and I will be ever, only, all for Thee, ever, only, all for thee.

❦ *For Today:* 1 Chronicles 29:5; Matthew 22:37; 1 Corinthians 6:19, 20

Express once more your gratitude for all of God's gifts. Dedicate yourself more completely to His glory and service. Sing these words of consecration as you go—

Hendon tune   H. A. Cesar Malan, 1787-1864

Take my mo - ments and my days— Let them flow in
cease - less praise, Let them flow in cease - less praise.

LIVING FOR JESUS

Thomas O. Chisholm, 1866-1960

Therefore, I urge you, brothers, in view of God's mercy, to offer your bodies as living sacrifices, holy and pleasing to God—which is your spiritual worship. Do not conform any longer to the pattern of this world, but be transformed by the renewing of your mind. (Romans 12:1, 2)

For the Christian, a foremost priority must be to live for Christ and to seek first His kingdom (Matthew 6:33). That does not line up with all the talk we hear today about self-realization. The Christian, however, knows that we were created by God that we might glorify Him. Therefore, we should not live to please ourselves but rather to exalt and serve our Lord. "My dearest treasure the light of His smile"—the ultimate goal of our lives.

"Living for Jesus" was written in 1917 by Thomas Chisholm at the request of the composer, Harold Lowden, who had used his tune two years earlier with another text. Lowden, however, was not satisfied with the union of his tune with the earlier text and wrote Mr. Chisholm, suggesting the title "Living for Jesus" for the new hymn setting. Chisholm felt very inadequate for the task, but within two weeks the words were completed.

Thomas Chisholm had been an editor, a schoolteacher, and a Methodist minister before ill health forced him to begin a less strenuous life as an insurance salesman. His favorite endeavor had always been the writing of poetry, and he continued to do this all through his 94 years. "I have greatly desired," he said, "that each hymn or poem might send some definite message to the hearts for whom it was written." Though humble in spirit and frail in health, Chisholm found that writing encouraging words such as these for God's people to sing was his "pathway of blessing."

Living for Jesus a life that is true, striving to please Him in all that I do, yielding allegiance, glad-hearted and free—this is the pathway of blessing for me.

Living for Jesus who died in my place, bearing on Calv'ry my sin and disgrace—such love constrains me to answer His call, follow His leading and give Him my all.

Living for Jesus thru earth's little while, my dearest treasure the light of His smile, seeking the lost one He died to redeem, bringing the weary to find rest in Him.

Chorus: O Jesus, Lord and Savior, I give myself to Thee, for Thou in Thine atonement didst give Thyself for me. I own no other Master—my heart shall be Thy throne: My life I give, henceforth to live, O Christ, for Thee alone.

❧ ***For Today:*** Mark 12:33; Romans 6:13, 18; 2 Corinthians 4:10, 11

Tomorrow is God's secret, but today is your opportunity to live cooperatively with and for Him. Make it "God's today." Live this day to glorify His Son in every possible way. Sing as you go—

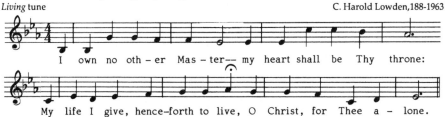

Living tune   C. Harold Lowden,188-1963

I own no oth-er Mas-ter— my heart shall be Thy throne:

My life I give, hence-forth to live, O Christ, for Thee a - lone.

LORD, I WANT TO BE A CHRISTIAN
Spiritual

He has given us His very great and precious promises, so that through them you may participate in the divine nature and escape the corruption in the world caused by evil desire. (2 Peter 1:4)

A CHRISTIAN IS . . .

A mind through which Christ thinks;
A heart through which Christ loves;
A voice through which Christ speaks;
A hand through which Christ helps.   —*Unknown*

"Sir, I want to be a Christian."

The text for this spiritual song is thought to have been an outgrowth of this remark made by a Negro slave to a minister, William Davis, sometime during the mid 18th century.

How would you have replied to this request? Many people today use the term *Christian* simply to mean someone other than a pagan, Buddhist, or Hindu. Or they equate it with a person who is a church member or perhaps someone who has a strong humanitarian concern for others.

The word *Christian* was first used with the people of Antioch because they believed the account of the gospel by personally accepting God's free gift of salvation and making Christ the Savior and Lord of their lives (Acts 11:26). They literally became CHRIST-ians—little Christs. After he has taken the initial step of salvation, a Christian should develop a growing desire to model the virtues of godly living. The Bible teaches that a Christian should make every effort to add to his faith goodness, knowledge, self-control, perseverance, godliness, brotherly kindness, and love (2 Peter 1:5-7). Christians, then, are to be effective representatives for God in a corrupt world and a living demonstration of the transforming power of the gospel.

> Lord, I want to be a Christian in my heart.
>
> Lord, I want to be more loving in my heart.
>
> Lord, I want to be more holy in my heart.
>
> Lord, I want to be like Jesus in my heart.

❦ ***For Today:*** Acts 4:12; 16:30, 31; Romans 10:10; 1 Corinthians 15:49; Colossians 3:9, 10; 2 Peter 1:5-10

Would you be able to explain the term *Christian* if someone should ask? Are you consciously trying to add Christ-like virtues to your faith? Pray that you will be a worthy representative and demonstration of the gospel. Carry this spiritual with you to help—

Traditional Spiritual

Lord, I want to be a Chris – tian in my heart. In my heart,

in my heart, Lord, I want to be a Chris – tian in my heart.

ALL THE WAY MY SAVIOR LEADS ME

Fanny J. Crosby, 1820-1915

For this God is our God forever and ever; He will be our guide even to the end.
(Psalm 48:14)

Often we become discouraged because we cannot see God's long range plan of guidance for our lives. We need to remember that God has promised to guide our steps, not the miles ahead. "The steps of a good man are ordered by the Lord" (Psalm 37:23).

This beloved hymn came from the grateful heart of Fanny Crosby after she had received a direct answer to her prayer. One day when she desperately needed five dollars and had no idea where she could obtain it, Fanny followed her usual custom and began to pray about the matter. A few minutes later a stranger appeared at her door with the exact amount. "I have no way of accounting for this," she said, "except to believe that God put it into the heart of this good man to bring the money. My first thought was that it is so wonderful the way the Lord leads me, I immediately wrote the poem and Dr. Lowry set it to music." The hymn was first published in 1875.

No one knows the importance of guided steps as much as a blind person like Fanny Crosby, who lost her sight at six weeks of age through improper medical treatment. A sightless person is keenly aware that there will be stumbling and uncertainty as he continues on his way. As Fanny wrote, "Cheers each winding path I tread, gives me grace for every trial," she has reminded us that God has never promised to keep us from hard places or obstacles in life. He has assured us, however, that He will go with us, guide each step, and give the necessary grace.

All the way my Savior leads me; what have I to ask beside? Can I doubt His tender mercy, who through life has been my Guide? Heavenly peace, divinest comfort, here by faith in Him to dwell! For I know whate'er befall me, Jesus doeth all things well.

All the way my Savior leads me, cheers each winding path I tread, gives me grace for ev'ry trial, feeds me with the living bread. Though my weary steps may falter, and my soul athirst may be, gushing from the Rock before me, lo! a spring of joy I see.

All the way my Savior leads me; Oh, the fullness of His love! Perfect rest to me is promised in my Father's house above. When my spirit, clothed immortal, wings its flight to realms of day, this my song through endless ages: Jesus led me all the way.

❦ *For Today:* Psalm 32:8; John 10:3-5; Romans 8:28; 1 Corinthians 10:4

Ask God to help you find that "perfect rest" in every stressful situation, confident that He is guiding your every step. Sing this musical truth—

Robert Lowry, 1826-1899

For I know what-e'er be-fall me, Je-sus do-eth all things well.
This my song through end-less a - ges, Je-sus led me all the way.

PRECIOUS LORD, TAKE MY HAND

Thomas A. Dorsey, 1899-1965

*For I am the Lord, your God, who takes hold of your right hand and says to you,
"Do not fear; I will help you."* (Isaiah 41:13)

Out of a broken heart after his wife and newly born son had both died,
Thomas Dorsey cried to his Lord to lead him "through the storm, through the
night." In doing so, he created lines that have since ministered to others in an
unusual way. This tender song, written by a black gospel musician in 1932, has
since been a favorite with Christians everywhere.

Thomas A. Dorsey grew up in Georgia as a "preacher's kid." As he began to
be successful as a composer of jazz and blues songs, however, he drifted away
from God. After it seemed to him that he was miraculously spared in brushes
with death, Dorsey came back to the Lord. As his life dramatically changed he
began to write gospel songs and to sing in church services. It was during a
revival meeting in St. Louis, Missouri, that he received a telegram telling the
tragic news of his wife and infant son. Stunned and grief-stricken, Dorsey cried,
"God, you aren't worth a dime to me right now!"

A few weeks later, however, as Dorsey fingered the keyboard of a piano, he
created the lines of "Precious Lord" to fit a tune that was familiar to him. The
following Sunday the choir of the Ebenezer Baptist Church in South Chicago,
Illnois, sang the new song with Dorsey playing the accompaniment. "It tore up
the church!"

God continued to lead Thomas Dorsey by the hand until he had written more
than 250 gospel songs. He once stated:

> My business is to try to bring people to Christ instead of leaving them where they are. I
> write for all of God's people. All people are my people. What I share with people is love. I try
> to lift their spirits and let them know that God still loves them. He's still saving, and He can
> still give that power."

* * * *

> Precious Lord, take my hand, lead me on, help me stand—I am tired, I am
> weak, I am worn; thro' the storm, thro' the night, lead me on to the light—Take
> my hand, precious Lord, lead me home.

> When my way grows drear, Precious Lord, linger near—when my life is al-
> most gone. Hear my cry, hear my call, hold my hand lest I fall—Take my hand,
> precious Lord, lead me home.

🐦 *For Today:* Psalm 6:11; 27:11; 48:14; John 1:7; 10:3

Enjoy the fellowship of God so strongly that you feel He is holding your hand
and leading you in whatever circumstances you may find yourself. Share this
testimony of Thomas Dorsey as you go—

George N. Allen, 1812-1877
Adapted by Thomas A. Dorsey, 1899-1965

Thro' the storm, thro' the night, Lead me on to the light—

Take my hand, pre - cious Lord, lead me home.

I SURRENDER ALL

Judson W. Van De Venter, 1855-1939

Anyone who does not take his cross and follow Me is not worthy of Me. Whoever finds his life will lose it, and whoever loses his life for my sake will find it. (Matthew 10:38, 39)

The Bible teaches us that brokenness is a prerequisite to blessing and usefulness. No one ever achieves spiritual greatness until he has fully surrendered himself to God. Victorious living comes only as we abandon ourselves to the Lordship of Christ, becoming His loving bond slave. God's best for our lives is not the result of struggle. Rather, it is simply the acceptance of His perfect will and the recognition of His authority in every area of our lives.

> Higher than the highest heaven,
> Deeper than the deepest sea,
> Lord, Thy love at last hath conquered:
> Grant me now my supplication,
> None of self and all of Thee.
>
> —*Unknown*

Judson Van De Venter wrote this text after surrendering his many talents to his all-wise Savior:

> For some time, I had struggled between developing my talents in the field of art and going into full-time evangelistic work. At last the pivotal hour of my life came, and I surrendered all. A new day was ushered into my life, I became an evangelist and discovered down deep in my soul a talent hitherto unknown to me. God had hidden a song in my heart, and touching a tender chord, He caused me to sing.

After making his decision to devote his life to Christian service, Van De Venter ministered with much blessing in extensive evangelistic work both at home and abroad. Billy Graham is one of many who claim that Judson Van De Venter had greatly influenced their lives and ministry.

> All to Jesus I surrender, all to Him I free give; I will ever love and trust Him, in His presence daily live.
>
> All to Jesus I surrender, humbly at His feet I bow; worldly pleasures all forsaken, take me, Jesus, take me now.
>
> All to Jesus I surrender, make me, Savior, wholly Thine; let me feel the Holy Spirit—truly know that Thou art mine.
>
> All to Jesus I surrender, Lord, I give myself to Thee; fill me with Thy love and power; let Thy blessings fall on me.
>
> **Chorus:** I surrender all, I surrender all, all to Thee, my blessed Savior, I surrender all.

❦ ***For Today:*** Romans 6:8-14; 1 Corinthians 6:19, 20; Ephesians 3:16, 17

If you have lost the enthusiasm for Christ that you once had, make a fresh surrender to His will and Lordship. Sing as you go—

Winfield S. Weeden, 1847-1908

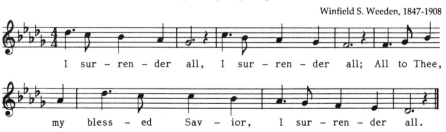

I sur - ren - der all, I sur - ren - der all; All to Thee, my bless - ed Sav - ior, I sur - ren - der all.

ONLY ONE LIFE

Avis B. Christiansen, 1895-1985

And He died for all, that those who live should no longer live for themselves but for Him who died for them and was raised again. (2 Corinthians 5:15)

Find your purpose and fling your life out into it; and the loftier your purpose is, the more sure you will be to make the world richer with every enrichment of yourself!
—*Phillips Brooks*

How tragic it is to see the great number of talented young people who waste their lives on transient things instead of investing them in that which is eternal. Yet this choice must be made by every individual: Will I commit my life to the highest and best—God and His service—or will I settle for that which is self-seeking and cheap? The results of these two styles of living are obvious; merely observe the difference between the quality of life of those who have engaged in self-indulgent, useless living and those who have spent their time faithfully serving God with a concern for the spiritual and physical needs of others. One leads to disillusionment and the other to contentment.

Since it was published in 1937, this thoughtful hymn by Avis B. Christiansen and Merrill Dunlop has been widely used of God to challenge scores of young believers with the importance of committing their lives completely to God's glory and service. Both Mrs. Christiansen and Mr. Dunlop have made other notable contributions to gospel hymnody with their many fine hymns.

These words reinforce and amplify the oft-quoted statement: "Only one life, 'twill soon be past; only what's done for Christ will last."

> Only one life to offer—Jesus, my Lord and King; only one tongue to praise Thee and of Thy mercy sing; only one heart's devotion—Savior, O may it be consecrated alone to Thy matchless glory, yielded fully to Thee.

> Only this hour is mine, Lord—May it be used for Thee; may ev'ry passing moment count for eternity; souls all about are dying, dying in sin and shame; help me bring them the message of Calv'ry's redemption in Thy glorious name.

> Only one life to offer—Take it, dear Lord, I pray; nothing from Thee withholding, Thy will I now obey; thou who hast freely given Thine all in all for me, claim this life for Thine own to be used, my Savior, ev'ry moment for Thee.

❦ *For Today:* Matthew 10:39; Luke 12:15, 34; Romans 12:1, 2; Philippians 1:20, 21; 3:8

Seriously ponder: Do I really have something beyond myself that gives real meaning and purpose to my life? Is that something God and His service? Breathe this musical prayer—

Merrill Dunlop, 1905-

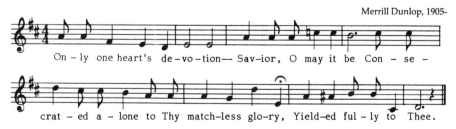

On - ly one heart's de - vo - tion— Sav-ior, O may it be Con - se - crat - ed a - lone to Thy match-less glo-ry, Yield-ed ful - ly to Thee.

September

• The Church • The Worship of God • Adoration of Christ
• The Holy Bible

THE CHURCH'S ONE FOUNDATION

Samuel J. Stone, 1839-1900

. . . Christ is the head of the church, His body, of which He is the Savior. (Ephesians 5:23)

During an especially heated period of theological controversy in Engand in 1866 when liberalism threatened to destroy the great cardinal doctrines of the Anglican church, this hymn was written by Pastor Samuel Stone. He was a strong supporter of the conservative faith and refused to compromise in any way the critical attacks on doctrinal orthodoxy.

It was Stone's desire to write a hymn that would reaffirm the Lordship of Christ as the foundation of the church. To combat the skeptical liberal scholarship, Samuel Stone wrote twelve hymn texts based on the Apostles' Creed. This particular text refers to the ninth article: "The Holy Catholic (Universal) Church, the communion of saints: He is the Head of this body."

Described as the poor man's pastor, Samuel Stone demonstrated his firm belief in the church as the instrument of Christ for meeting the needs of people. He spent much time ministering to the poor and underprivileged people in London's East End. It was said that "he created a beautiful place of worship for the humble folk and made it a center of light in dark places."

This is what the local church was meant to be—a spiritual hospital for hurting humanity, never an exclusive private club for self-righteous Christians. Called out from the world by God for Himself, the church consists of people who meet regularly for worship, inspiration, instruction, and fellowship. After that, Christ our Head sends His own back into the world to represent Him and to model His love for all mankind.

> The Church's one foundation is Jesus Christ her Lord; She is His new creation by water and the Word: from heav'n He came and sought her to be His holy bride; with His own blood He bought her, and for her life He died.

> Elect from ev'ry nation, yet one o'er all the earth, her charter of salvation One Lord, one faith, one birth; one holy name she blesses, partakes one holy food, and to one hope she presses, with ev'ry grace endued.

> Yet she on earth hath union with God the Three in One, and mystic sweet communion with those whose rest is won: O happy ones and holy! Lord, give us grace that we, like them, the meek and lowly, on high may dwell with Thee.

❦ *For Today:* Matthew 16:15-18; 1 Corinthians 3:11; Colossians 1:18

Give thanks to God for your local church as well as for fellow-believers of the church universal everywhere. Affirm your conviction in Christ as the head of the church as you carry this musical truth—

Aurelia tune   Samuel S. Wesley, 1810-1876

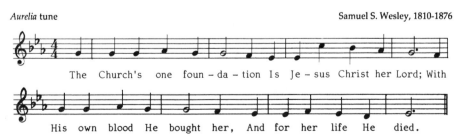

The Church's one foun – da – tion Is Je – sus Christ her Lord; With

His own blood He bought her, And for her life He died.

I LOVE THY KINGDOM, LORD!

Timothy Dwight, 1752-1817

And let us consider how we may spur one another on toward love and good deeds. Let us not give up meeting together, as some are in the habit of doing, but let us encourage one another—and all the more as you see the Day approaching. (Hebrews 10:24, 25)

God honored the tears, prayers, and work of the distinguished president of Yale University, Timothy Dwight, to bring to that campus in 1795 a startling spiritual revival. It soon spread to other nearby universities as well. Prior to his administration, most of the students at Yale and other eastern schools had been infected with the "free thought" of Thomas Paine, Rousseau, and the French Revolution.

Timothy Dwight, grandson of the brilliant and powerful American preacher, Jonathan Edwards, was an unusually successful and distinguished person in many areas. A graduate of Yale University at 17, he was a chaplain in the American Revolution, a Congregational minister, a prosperous farmer, a member of the Connecticut state legislature, a faculty member at Yale and eventually president of the university. Timothy Dwight also wrote a number of scholarly books, authored thirty-three hymn texts, and revised the hymnbook used by New England Congregational and Presbyterian churches for 30 years.

In Dwight's text, the term *kingdom* suggests three different levels of Christ's church:

- **The Church Personal—** "The kingdom of God is within you." (Luke 17:21)
- **The Church Local—** individual congregations (Matthew 11:28, 29)
- **The Church Universal—** believers of every age, race and culture (Revelation 7:9)

The kingdom of God is a living body, not merely an organization. Its purpose is to extend Christ's influence, build up the members of His body, and glorify His name. The promise of Christ is that nothing, not even the gates of hell, will ever triumph over His Church (Matthew 16:18).

I love Thy kingdom, Lord! The house of Thine abode—The Church our blest Redeemer saved with His own precious blood.

I love Thy Church, O God! Her walls before Thee stand, dear as the apple of Thine eye and graven on Thy hand.

Beyond my highest joy I prize her heav'nly ways—Her sweet communion, solemn vows, her hymns of love and praise.

Sure as Thy truth shall last, to Zion shall be giv'n the brightest glories earth can yield, and brighter bliss of heav'n.

❦ *For Today:* Matthew 16:15-18; Ephesians 2:19, 21, 22; 5:23-27

Ask yourself if you are as joyful and enthusiastic about Christ's kingdom and its mission on earth as you should be. Allow this hymn to renew your vision—

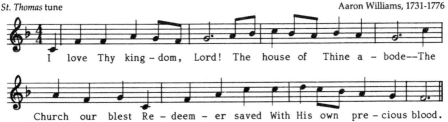

St. Thomas tune   Aaron Williams, 1731-1776

I love Thy king - dom, Lord! The house of Thine a - bode--The Church our blest Re - deem - er saved With His own pre - cious blood.

GLORIOUS THINGS OF THEE ARE SPOKEN

John Newton, 1725-1807

Great is the Lord, and greatly to be praised in the city of our God, in the mountain of His holiness. Beauitiful for situation, the joy of the whole earth is Mount Zion, on the sides of the north, the city of the great King. God is known in her palaces for a refuge. (Psalm 48:1, 2, 3 KJV)

Of the many hymn texts by the noted English clergyman, John Newton, this one is generally considered to be one of his finest and most joyous. In the Old Testament, the city of Zion was the place where God dwelt among His people. It was a haven of refuge, a treasured place. In our New Testament age, Zion refers to the church, a community of God's people, a living and dynamic organism. Newton's hymn refers to God's strong protection of His people, His promise to supply their needs, and His presence to lead His own by the cloud and fire as He did the Israelites of old.

With all its shortcomings and faults, the local church is still God's means of meeting the needs of mankind. As Christians, we are to promote the church, supporting it with enthusiasm and finding our spiritual strength and fellowship in it. Then as members of Christ's universal church, we are commanded to be His worthy representatives to the entire world. We must be actively involved in ministering the "streams of living waters" which "never fail from age to age."

John Newton, the convicted slave trader and sea captain, never stopped praising God for His "sure repose"— "whose Word cannot be broken"—who formed us "for His own abode."

> Glorious things of thee are spoken, Zion, city of our God; He whose word cannot be broken formed thee for His own abode: On the Rock of Ages founded, what can shake thy sure repose? With salvation's walls surrounded, thou mayst smile at all thy foes.
>
> See, the streams of living waters, springing from eternal love, well supply thy sons and daughters and all fear of want remove: Who can faint while such a river ever flows their thirst to assuage? Grace which, like the Lord, the Giver, never fails from age to age.
>
> Round each habitation hov'ring, see the cloud and fire appear for a glory and a cov'ring, showing that the Lord is near! Glorious things of Thee are spoken, Zion, city of our God; He whose word cannot be broken formed thee for His own abode.

🍂 *For Today:* Psalm 87:3; Isaiah 33:20, 21; Matthew 16:18; Romans 12:5

Be thankful for your local church and what it means in your life. Ask for God's special blessing on your pastor, the board members, and your fellow church members. Allow this hymn to help—

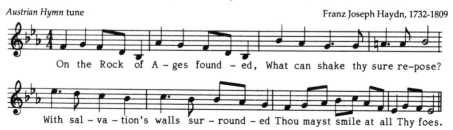

Austrian Hymn tune   Franz Joseph Haydn, 1732-1809

On the Rock of A - ges found - ed, What can shake thy sure re-pose?

With sal - va - tion's walls sur - round - ed Thou mayst smile at all Thy foes.

O BREATH OF LIFE

Bessie P. Head, 1850-1936

I have heard of Your fame; I stand in awe of Your deeds, O Lord. Renew them in our day, in our time make them known. (Habakkuk 3:2)

> Set us afire, Lord, stir us, we pray— while the world perishes, we go our way
> Purposeless, passionless, day after day; set us afire, Lord, stir us, we pray!
>
> —*Unknown*

When the Holy Spirit was poured out at Pentecost for the birth of the church, it was in response to the fervent prayers of God's people. This is still the principle for an effective ministry of any church —determined, persistent prayer for the Holy Spirit's enabling power to accomplish our mission for God.

Vitality is essential to any Christian ministry; complacency is deadly. There must be the fervency of divine life infused into us by God the Holy Spirit. Just as a healthy vine manifests itself in producing foliage and fruit, so it is with a healthy Christian—he will bear evidence of an infectious enthusiasm for the furtherance of the gospel and a life that produces the fruits of the Spirit.

This song of pleading for Holy Spirit power was written by Mrs. Bessie Head, a member of the Church of England. She was the author of numerous hymn texts, several of which appeared in the 1937 *Keswick Hymn Book,* including this hymn.

It would be helpful if each believer, as well as each local church, would use this musical prayer often as a theme song. We need God's continual reviving, renewing, refreshing, comforting, and equipping power if we are to effectively "spread the light" and meet the needs of this hour.

> O Breath of Life, come sweeping through us. Revive Thy Church with life and pow'r; O Breath of life, come, cleanse, renew us, and fit Thy Church to meet this hour.
>
> O Wind of God, come bend us, break us, till humbly we confess our need; then in Thy tenderness remake us, revive, restore, for this we plead.
>
> O Breath of Love, come breathe within us, renewing thought and will and heart; Come, Love of Christ, afresh to win us, revive Thy Church in ev'ry part.
>
> O Heart of Christ, once broken for us, 'tis there we find our strength and rest; our broken contrite hearts now solace, and let Thy waiting Church be blest.
>
> Revive us, Lord! Is zeal abating while harvest fields are vast and white? Revive us, Lord, the world is waiting. Equip Thy Church to spread the light.

❦ *For Today:* Psalm 85:6; Jeremiah 20:9; Luke 11:13; Acts 3:19; Romans 5:5

Why is it that we as individual believers and as a local church easily become complacent about the things of God? What steps can be taken to change this? Carry this musical prayer with you as you reflect on this serious matter—

Det ar ett fast ord tune   Joel Blomquist, 1840-1930

O Breath of Life, come, cleanse, re - new us, And fit Thy
Church to meet this hour.

O DAY OF REST AND GLADNESS

Christopher Wordsworth, 1807-1885

There remains, then, a Sabbath-rest for the people of God; for anyone who enters God's rest also rests from his own work, just as God did from His. Let us, therefore, make every effort to enter that rest. . . . (Hebrews 4:9, 10, 11)

Christopher Wordsworth, a nephew of the renowned English poet, William Wordsworth, reminds us in this hymn that since God rested after His acts of creation, we who are made in His image also need a day of rest and spiritual renewal. We need the encouragement and fellowship of other believers to keep our lives aglow for God. The way we use the Lord's Day reflects our true devotion to God. Very early in the Christian era, the first day of the week replaced the Jewish Sabbath as the day of worship because it was on Sunday that the resurrection took place. Although we do not observe it according to the many set rules such as the Jews had for their Sabbath, Sunday should always be a special day of refreshment and of giving honor and worship to our God.

Christopher Wordsworth was an Anglican bishop, a noted scholar, and a distinguished writer. He composed 127 hymn texts that were intended to teach the truths of Scripture and encourage worship. "O Day of Rest and Gladness," his only hymn widely used today, focuses on the doctrine of the Trinity. In the second stanza, the triune Godhead is compared to three important events or a "triple light" that occurred on the first day of the week: The creation of light (Genesis 1:1), the resurrection of Christ, and the advent of the Holy Spirit. In the final stanza, Wordsworth addresses each member of the Godhead by name, as the church raises its perpetual voice to "Thee, blest Three in One."

O day of rest and gladness, O day of joy and light, O balm of care and sadness, most beautiful, most bright: On thee, the high and lowly, thru ages joined in tune, sing "Holy, Holy, Holy," to the great God Triune.

On thee, at the creation, the light first had its birth; on thee, for our salvation, Christ rose from depths of earth; on thee, our Lord, victorious, the Spirit sent from heav'n; and thus on thee, most glorious, a triple light was giv'n.

New graces ever gaining from this our day of rest, we reach the rest remaining to spirits of the blest. To Holy Ghost be praises, to Father, and to Son; the Church her voice upraises to Thee, blest Three in One.

❦ ***For Today:*** Genesis 1:3-5; Psalm 118:24; Isaiah 58:13, 14; Revelation 22:35

Do you anticipate with joy the Lord's Day, when you can worship God in your local church? How can Sunday become a more meaningful time of renewal and refreshment for you and your family? Reflect on this hymn as you go—

Mendebras tune   German melody arranged by Lowell Mason, 1792-1872

On thee, the high and low – ly, Thru ag – es joined in tune,

Sing "Ho – ly, Ho – ly, Ho – ly," To the great God Tri – une.

BRETHREN, WE HAVE MET TO WORSHIP

George Atkins, 19th century

Ascribe to the Lord the glory due His name. Bring an offering and come before Him; worship the Lord in the splendor of His holiness. (1 Chronicles 16:31)

The apostle Paul's favorite name for fellow believers was "brethren." He used this term at least 60 times throughout his various epistles. Paul's concept of the local church was a worshiping family—the family of God. Of course, we need to worship God daily in our individual devotional lives. But every believer also needs the enriching experience of worshiping and serving God with other family members on a weekly basis. Only a church of faithful worshiping members is adequately prepared to do its work and fulfill its witness in the world.

Our worship of God, both personally and corporately, should share with the young prophet these five elements depicted in Isaiah 6:

- Recognition: "I saw the Lord . . ." (v. 1)
- Praise: "Holy, Holy, Holy . . ." (v. 3)
- Confession: "Woe is me . . ." (v. 5)
- Assurance of Pardon: "This has touched your lips . . . forgiven" (v. 7)
- Dedication: "Here am I . . ." (v. 8)

This interesting hymn has been a favorite, especially in the South, since it first appeared in 1825. Nothing is known of George Atkins, the author of the text.

> Brethren, we have met to worship and adore the Lord our God.
> Will you pray with all your power, while we try to preach the Word?
> All is vain unless the Spirit of the Holy One comes down.
> Brethren, pray, and holy manna will be showered all around.
>
> Brethren, see poor sinners round you slumb'ring on the brink of woe.
> Death is coming, hell is moving—Can you bear to let them go?
> See our fathers and our mothers and our children sinking down.
> Brethren, pray, and holy manna will be showered all around.
>
> Sisters, will you join and help us? Moses' sister aided him.
> Will you help the trembling mourners who are struggling hard with sin?
> Tell them all about the Savior—Tell them that He will be found.
> Sisters, pray, and holy manna will be showered all around.
>
> Let us love our God supremely. Let us love each other too.
> Let us love and pray for sinners till our God makes all things new.
> Then He'll call us home to heaven; at His table we'll sit down;
> Christ will gird Himself and serve us with sweet manna all around.

❦ *For Today:* Isaiah 6:1-9; Psalm 96:4, 9; 107:32; John 4:24; Hebrews 10:25

Make a list of the various activities that you think would improve your church worship service. Share these ideas with your pastor and other concerned leaders. Reflect on the purpose of group worship as you sing this hymn—

Holy Manna tune   Attributed to William Moore, *Columbian Harmony*, 1825

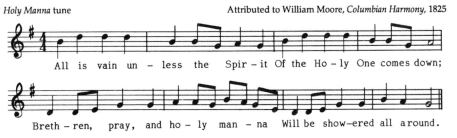

All is vain un-less the Spir-it Of the Ho-ly One comes down;

Breth-ren, pray, and ho-ly man-na Will be show-ered all around.

GREAT GOD OF WONDERS

Samuel Davies, 1723-1761

O Lord my God, You are very great; You are clothed with splendor and majesty.
(Psalm 104:1)

It is possible for Christians to lose a sense of the infinite power and greatness of God and make of Him merely a heavenly friend—a God who is no bigger than our mundane needs. Our personal and intimate relationship with God must always be balanced with the realization that He is still the "Great God of Wonders." This great God is as unbounded in His presence as He is in His glory and power—even the heavens cannot contain Him (1 Kings 8:27). This was the awareness that King Solomon had after building his magnificent temple. He stated in this passage that if God cannot be contained even in the highest heaven, "how much less in this temple I have built." God's great design in all of His works is the manifestation of His own glory. His glory is the result of His very nature and acts. A mark of a mature Christian is the ability to say "not unto us, but unto Thy name be glory" (Psalm 29:2).

The author of this hymn text, Samuel Davies, was an American Presbyterian minister who was appointed president of Princeton University in 1759, succeeding the well-known evangelist, Jonathan Edwards. Dr. Davies was a man of distinguished ability and was highly influential in the fields of religion and education. He wrote a number of fine hymns that had a wide acceptance in the 18th century, especially in England.

Although not a trained musician, composer John Newton could, when necessary, compose the music for texts as well. His musical setting is well-suited to this fine text by Samuel Davies, and it makes a strong vehicle for conveying its majestic quality, especially on the refrain:

> Great God of wonders! all Thy ways are matchless, God-like and divine; but the fair glories of Thy grace more God-like and unrivaled shine, more God-like and unrivaled shine.

> In wonder lost, with trembling joy, we take the pardon of our God: Pardon for crimes of deepest dye, a pardon bought with Jesus' blood, a pardon bought with Jesus' blood.

> O may this strange, this matchless grace, this God-like miracle of love, fill the whole earth with grateful praise, and all th'angelic choirs above, and all th'angelic choirs above.

> **Refrain:** Who is a pard'ning God like Thee? Or who has grace so rich and free? Or who has grace so rich and free?

🐦 *For Today:* 1 Chronicles 29:11; Job 36:5; Psalm 31:19; 145:3; Isaiah 40:26, 28

Reflect again on God's greatness. In what ways do we sometimes try to contain His greatness? Determine to let "God be God" in every situation. Carry this musical question as you go—

John Newton, 1725-1807

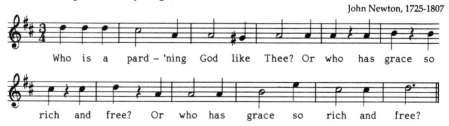

Who is a pard – 'ning God like Thee? Or who has grace so rich and free? Or who has grace so rich and free?

HOLY, HOLY, HOLY

Reginald Heber, 1783-1826

Come, let us bow down in worship, let us kneel before the Lord our Maker; for He is our God and we are the people of His pasture, the flock under His care. (Psalm 95:6, 7)

"O Lord, grant that I may desire Thee, and desiring Thee, seek Thee, and seeking Thee, find Thee, and finding Thee, be satisfied with Thee forever."   —*Augustine*

"Holy, holy, holy is the Lord God Almighty who was, and is, and is to come" (Revelation 4:8). These are the words of worship that believers will proclaim in heaven one day. This majestic text based on these words was written approximtely 150 years ago by an Anglican minister, Reginald Heber, and it is still one of the hymns most frequently used in our corporate worship.

Worship is the cornerstone of a believer's spiritual life. The bedrock of the local church is its worship service, and all aspects of the church's ministry are founded here. It is only as a Christian truly worships that he begins to grow spiritually. Learning to worship and praise God, then, should be a believer's lifetime pursuit. Our worship reflects the depth of our relationship with God. We must learn to worship God not only for what He is doing in our personal lives, but above all for who He is—His being, character, and deeds.

Reginald Heber was a highly respected minister, writer, and church leader, serving for a time as the Bishop of Calcutta. His early death at the age of 43 was widely mourned throughout the Christian world. One year after his death, a collection of 57 of his hymns was published by his widow and many friends as a tribute to his memory and faithful ministry. It is from this collection of 1827 that these words were taken:

Holy, Holy, Holy, Lord God Almighty! Early in the morning our song shall rise to Thee; Holy, Holy, Holy! Merciful and Mighty! God in Three Persons, blessed Trinity!

Holy, Holy, Holy! All the saints adore Thee, casting down their golden crowns around the glassy sea; cherubim and seraphim falling down before Thee, which wert and art and evermore shalt be.

Holy, Holy, Holy! Tho the darkness hide Thee, tho the eye of sinful man Thy glory may not see. Only Thou art holy—there is none beside Thee perfect in pow'r, in love and purity.

Holy, Holy, Holy, Lord God Almighty! All Thy works shall praise Thy name in earth and sky and sea; Holy, Holy, Holy! Merciful and Mighty! God in Three Persons, blessed Trinity!

❧ *For Today:* Psalm 145:8-21; Isaiah 6:3; Revelation 4:5-11; 5:13

What does the term *worship* mean to you? How could your life of worship be improved? Use this hymn to help—

Nicaea tune   John B. Dykes, 1823-1876

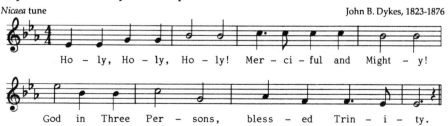

Ho - ly, Ho - ly, Ho - ly! Mer - ci - ful and Might - y!

God in Three Per - sons, bless - ed Trin - i - ty.

IMMORTAL, INVISIBLE

Walter Chalmers Smith, 1824-1908

Now to the King eternal, immortal, invisible, the only God, be honor and glory forever and ever, Amen. (1 Timothy 1:17)

In our enjoyment of a personal relationship with God, we sometimes lose sight of the awe and reverence that should also be part of our worship of Him. Often we tend to forget the supreme holiness and greatness of who God really is. In our hymnody and theology we can carelessly treat our Lord as merely "the friend upstairs."

Consider this ancient advice from a father to his son:

> First of all, my child, think magnificently of God. Magnify His providence; adore His power, pray to Him frequently and incessantly. Bear Him always in your mind. Teach your thoughts to reverence Him in every place for there is no place where He is not. Therefore, my child, fear and worship and love God; first and last, think magnificiently of Him!
>
> Paternus, *Advice to a Son*

The author of the fine worshipful text of "Immortal, Invisible" was Walter Chalmers Smith, a pastor and an important leader of the Free churches of Scotland. He had various volumes of his poetry published, including several hymnals. "Immortal, Invisible" was first published in Smith's 1867 hymnal, *Hymns of Christ and the Christian Life.*

One can reflect at length on the greatness of God as described by these words:

> Immortal, invisible, God only wise, in light inaccessible hid from our eyes, most blessed, most glorious, the Ancient of Days, Almighty, victorious—Thy great name we praise.

> Unresting, unhasting, and silent as light, nor wanting, nor wasting, Thou rulest in might; Thy justice, like mountains, high soaring above Thy clouds, which are fountains of goodness and love.

> To all, life Thou givest—to both great and small; in all life Thou livest—the true life of all; we blossom and flourish as leaves on the tree, and wither and perish—but naught changeth Thee.

> Great Father of glory, pure Father of light, Thine angels adore Thee all veiling their sight; all praise we would render—O help us to see 'tis only the splendor of light hideth Thee!

🍎 *For Today:* Job 37:21-24; Psalm 36:5, 6; 1041-5; Colossians 1:15-17, 19; Revelation 21:23

J. P. Phillips, in his book *Your God Is Too Small,* reminds us that our concept of God is generally too limited. Reflect on this truth as you sing—

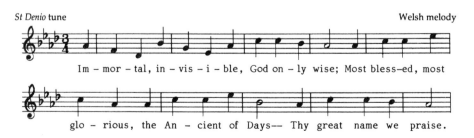

MAJESTY

Words and Music by Jack Hayford, 1934-

O Lord, our Lord, how majestic is Your name in all the earth! (Psalm 8:1)

There are many attributes of the Lord that should prompt our response of adoration and worship: His holiness, His power, His love . . . A very popular contemporary song by the Rev. Jack Hayford, senior pastor of the Church of the Way in Van Nuys, California, also teaches that the very regal majesty of Christ deserves our praise. This text further reminds us that Christ's dominion over principalities, His power, and His absolute majesty in heaven are for the benefit of those who trust and follow Him here and now.

Pastor Hayford relates the following account for the writing of "Majesty:"

> In 1977, my wife Anna and I spent our vacation in Great Britain, traveling throughout the land from the south country and Wales to the northern parts of Scotland. It was the same year as Queen Elizabeth's 25th Anniversay of her coronation, and symbols of royalty were abundantly present beyond the usual.

While viewing many of the ancient castles throughout the land, Pastor Hayford began to reflect on the truth that the provisions of Christ for the believer not only include our forgiveness for sin but provide a restoration to a royal relationship with God as sons and daughters born into the heavenly family through His Majesty.

> As Anna and I drove along together, at once the opening lyrics and melody of "Majesty" simply came to my heart, I seemed to feel something new of what it meant to be His—to be raised to a partnership with Him in His throne. Upon returning to our home in California, I was finally able to complete the song.

Pastor Jack Hayford provides this interpretation for his song:

> "Majesty" describes the kingly, lordly, gloriously regal nature of our Savior—but not simply as an objective statement in worship of which He is fully worthy. "Majesty" is also a statement of the fact that our worship, when begotten in spirit and in truth, can align us with His throne in such a way that His Kingdom authority flows to us—to overflow us, to free us and channel through us. We are rescued from death, restored to the inheritance of sons and daughters, qualified for victory in battle against the adversary, and destined for the Throne forever in His presence.

* * * *

Majesty, worship His majesty—Unto Jesus be all glory, power and praise— Majesty, kingdom authority flow from His throne unto His own, His anthem raise. So exalt, lift up on high the name of Jesus—Magnify, come glorify Christ Jesus, the King. Majesty, worship His majesty—Jesus who died, now glorified, King of all kings.

☙ ***For Today:*** Psalm 29:4; 93:1; Hebrews 1:3; 2:9; Revelation 4:11

Allow your mind to think about the glory and majesty of Christ as the reigning King of Heaven. Worship Him with these words—

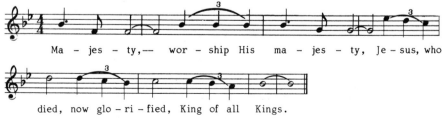

Ma - jes - ty,— wor - ship His ma - jes - ty, Je - sus, who died, now glo - ri - fied, King of all Kings.

O FOR A THOUSAND TONGUES

Charles Wesley, 1707-1788

Let everything that has breath praise the Lord. Praise the Lord. (Psalm 150:6)

Soon after their graduation from Oxford University, John and Charles Wesley decided to sail to America, the new world, to try to minister to the rough colonists under General Oglethorpe in Georgia and to evangelize the Indians. The Wesleys soon became disillusioned with the situation there, however, and after a short time returned to England.

As they crossed the Atlantic, John and Charles were much impressed by a group of devout Moravians, who seemed to have such spiritual depth and vitality as well as genuine missionary zeal. After returning to London, the Wesleys met with a group of Moravians in the Aldersgate Hall. Here in May, 1738, both brothers had a spiritual "heart-warming experience," realizing that even though they had been so zealous in religious activity, neither had ever personally known God's forgiveness or real joy. From that time on their ministry displayed a new dimension of spiritual power.

"O for a Thousand Tongues" was written by Charles in 1749 on the 11th anniversary of his Aldersgate conversion experience. It was inspired by a chance remark of an influential Moravian leader named Peter Bohler, who expressed his spiritual joy in this way: "Oh, Brother Wesley, the Lord has done so much for my life. Had I a thousand tongues, I would praise Christ Jesus with every one of them!"

These words of personal testimony by Charles Wesley have provided a moving vehicle of worship for God's people for more than two centuries:

> O for a thousand tongues to sing my great Redeemer's praise, the glories of my God and King, the triumphs of His grace.
>
> My gracious Master and my God, assist me to proclaim, to spread thru all the earth abroad the honors of Thy name.
>
> Jesus! the name that charms our fears, that bids our sorrows cease, 'tis music in the sinner's ears; 'tis life and health and peace.
>
> He breaks the pow'r of canceled sin; He sets the pris'ner free. His blood can make the foulest clean . . . His blood availed for me.
>
> Hear Him, ye deaf, His praise, ye dumb, your loosened tongues enploy; ye blind, behold your Savior come and leap ye lame, for joy.
>
> Glory to God and praise and love be ever, ever giv'n by saints below and saints above . . . the Church in earth and heav'n.

🎺 **For Today:** Psalm 96:1-4; 103:1-4; 145:2, 3; Romans 14:17

Let this hymn be the desire of your heart as you sing this message—

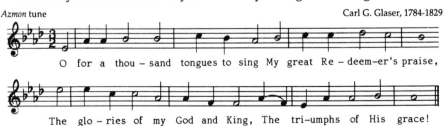

Azmon tune   Carl G. Glaser, 1784-1829

O for a thou - sand tongues to sing My great Re - deem-er's praise,

The glo - ries of my God and King, The tri-umphs of His grace!

O WORSHIP THE KING

Robert Grant, 1779-1838

Sing praises to God, sing praises; sing praises to our King, sing praises. For God is the King of all the earth; sing to Him a psalm of praise. (Psalm 47:6, 7)

The word *worship* is a contraction of an old expression in the English language, *woerth-scipe,* denoting the giving of reverent praise to an object of superlative worth. True worship, then, is an act by a redeemed man, the creature, toward God, his Creator, whereby his will, intellect, and emotions gratefully respond to the revelation of God's person expressed in the redemptive work of Jesus Christ, as the Holy Spirit illuminates the written word to his heart.

The author of this text, Robert Grant, described himself and all of us as "frail children of dust, and feeble as frail," even though he was a member of a distinguished British political family, a member of the Parliament of Scotland, and governor of Bombay, India, for a time. Throughout his entire life, Grant was a devoutly evangelical Christian who strongly supported the missionary outreach of his church and endeared himself to the people of India by establishing a medical college in Bombay.

Although this is the only hymn by Sir Robert Grant in common usage today, it is considered to be a model for worship. Its descriptive names used in exalting the Almighty are significant: Shield, Defender, Ancient of Days, Maker, Defender, Redeemer and Friend. Also the vivid imagery—"pavilioned in splendor," "girded with praise," "whose robe is the light," "whose canopy space," "chariots of wrath," "wings of the storm"—aids us in the worthy praise and adoration of our heavenly King.

O worship the King, all-glorious above, and gratefully sing His pow'r and His love; our Shield and Defender, the Ancient of Days, pavilioned in splendor and girded with praise.

O tell of His might, O sing of His grace, whose robe is the light, whose canopy space; His chariots of wrath the deep thunderclouds form, and dark is His path on the wings of the storm.

Thy bountiful care what tongue can recite? It breathes in the air; it shines in the light. It streams from the hills, it descends to the plain, and sweetly distills in the dew and the rain.

Frail children of dust, and feeble as frail, in thee do we trust, nor find thee to fail; Thy mercies how tender, how firm to the end! Our Maker, Defender, Redeemer and Friend.

❦ **For Today:** Psalm 104; 22 :28-31; 145:1-13; 1 Timothy 6:15, 16

Identify activities in a church service that are often substituted for the worship of God. Reflect again on the message of this hymn—

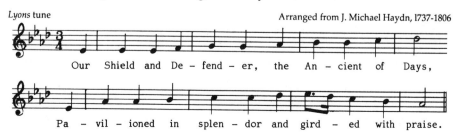

Lyons tune — Arranged from J. Michael Haydn, 1737-1806

Our Shield and De - fend - er, the An - cient of Days,

Pa - vil - ioned in splen - dor and gird - ed with praise.

ALL HAIL THE POWER

Edward Perronet, 1726-1792
Altered by John Rippon, 1751-1836

You are worthy, our Lord and God, to receive glory and honor and power, for You created all things, and by Your will they were created and have their being. (Revelation 4:11)

Sometimes called the "National Anthem of Christendom," this is one of the truly great worship hymns of the church. Written by a young English minister, it was published in 1779 and has been translated into almost every language where Christianity is known. The strong exuberant lines lead us to heartfelt worship of God each time we sing them. But what does it mean to worship?

> It is a quickening of the conscience by the holiness of God; a feeding of the mind with the truth of God; an opening of the heart to the love of God; and a devoting of the will to the purpose of God. —*Unknown*

We can be thankful that God moved an 18th century pastor to write this stirring hymn text that reminds us so forcibly that the angels in heaven and ransomed souls from "every kindred, every tribe" on earth are worshiping with us even now. And we will one day all join together in singing "the everlasting song"—when Christ is crowned "Lord of all."

Edward Perronet came from a family of distinguished French Huguenots who had fled to Switzerland and then England to escape religious persecution. He was ordained to the ministry of the Anglican church but was always more sympathetic to the evangelical movement led by John and Charles Wesley. Soon Edward left the state church to join the Wesleys in their evangelistic endeavors. Although he wrote a number of other hymns, this is the only one for which he will be remembered.

> All hail the pow'r of Jesus' name! Let angels prostrate fall; bring forth the royal diadem, and crown Him Lord of all!
>
> Ye chosen seed of Israel's race, ye ransomed from the fall, hail Him who saves you by His grace, and crown Him Lord of all!
>
> Let ev'ry kindred, ev'ry tribe, on this terrestrial ball, to Him all majesty ascribe, and crown Him Lord of all!
>
> O that with yonder sacred throng ye at His feet may fall! We'll join the everlasting song, and crown Him Lord of all!

🍂 *For Today:* Colossians 1:15-19; Philippians 2:9-11; Hebrews 2:7, 8

Reflect with joyous anticipation upon that time in heaven when our "everlasting song" will be shared throughout eternity with those from "every kindred and every tribe." Prepare even now by singing this hymn—

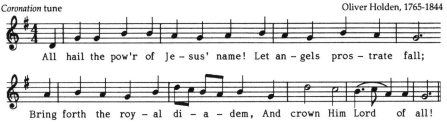

Coronation tune   Oliver Holden, 1765-1844

All hail the pow'r of Je-sus' name! Let an-gels pros-trate fall;

Bring forth the roy-al di-a-dem, And crown Him Lord of all!

OUR GREAT SAVIOR

J. Wilbur Chapman, 1859-1918

Our great God and Savior, Jesus Christ, who gave Himself for us to redeem us from all wickedness and to purify for Himself a people that are His very own, eager to do what is good. (Titus 2:13, 14)

> To the artist, Christ is the one altogether lovely.
> To the builder, He is the sure foundation.
> To the doctor, He is the great physician.
> To the geologist, He is the Rock of Ages.
> To the sinner, He is the Lamb of God who cleanses and forgives sin.
> To the Christian, Jesus Christ is the Son of the Living God, our great Savior.
>
> —*Unknown*

Through the centuries, artists and poets who have been impressed with Christ have tried valiantly to present His portrait both with brush and pen. Yet even the noblest efforts of these dedicated men and women seem feeble and inadequate.

Evangelist J. Wilbur Chapman has provided a worthy text extolling various attributes of Christ as they relate to our personal lives: "Friend of sinners," "Lover of my soul," Strength in weakness," "My victory, help in sorrow, comfort, guide, keeper, pilot." Finally, after reviewing everything that Christ means to a believer, we can do no better than to respond with Chapman's refrain: "Hallelujah! what a Savior! Hallelujah! what a Friend!"

"Our Great Savior" first appeared in its present form in the hymnal *Alexander's Gospel Songs, No. 2*, published in 1910.

> Jesus! what a Friend for sinners! Jesus! Lover of my soul. Friends may fail me, foes assail me; He, my Savior, makes me whole.

> Jesus! what a strength in weakness! Let me hide myself in Him; tempted, tried, and sometimes failing, He, my strength, my vict'ry wins.

> Jesus! what a help in sorrow! While the billows o'er me roll, even when my heart is breaking, He, my comfort, helps my soul.

> Jesus! what a guide and Keeper! While the tempest still is high, storms about me, night o'er-takes me, He, my Pilot, hears my cry.

> Jesus! I do now receive Him; more than all in Him I find; He hath granted me forgiveness; I am His, and He is mine.

> **Chorus:** Hallelujah! what a Savior! Hallelujah! what a Friend! Saving, helping, keeping, loving, He is with me to the end.

❧ *For Today:* Luke 7:34; Romans 3:24, 25; Ephesians 1:7; Colossians 1:18; 1 John 1:7; Revelation 5:9

Give Christ the praise of your heart for all that He really means in life—in your vocation, pursuits, personal relationships . . . Use this musical expression to carry your praise—

Hyfrydol tune

Rowland W. Prichard, 1811-1887

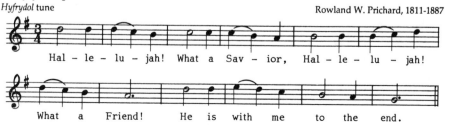

HOW SWEET THE NAME OF JESUS SOUNDS

John Newton, 1725-1807

Unto you therefore which believe He is precious. (1 Peter 2:7 KJV)

One of the important activities we need for our spiritual growth and maturity is to spend time daily in quiet meditation and communion with our Lord. Although Bible reading and prayer are absolutely necessary, it is still possible to engage in these pursuits without ever experiencing real communion with Christ Himself. We must learn to say—

> Once His gifts I wanted, now the Giver own;
> Once I sought for blessing, now Himself alone!   —*A. B. Simpson*

John Newton has given believers an excellent text for extolling and meditating upon Christ. This worship of our Lord reaches its crescendo in the fourth stanza when Newton lists ten consecutive titles for Jesus: Shepherd, Brother, Friend, Prophet, Priest, King, Lord, Life, Way. In the fifth and sixth stanzas, Newton realizes that a Christian's praise of Christ's names will always be inadequate until He is finally viewed in heaven. But we must never cease trying.

The story is told of this converted slave ship captain preaching one of his final sermons before his home-going at the age of 82. His eyesight was nearly gone and his memory had become faulty. It was necessary for an assistant to stand in the pulpit to help him with his sermon. One Sunday Newton had twice read the words, "Jesus Christ is precious." "You have already said that twice," whispered his helper; "go on." "I said that twice, and I am going to say it again," replied Newton. Then the rafters rang as the old preacher shouted, "JESUS CHRIST IS PRECIOUS!"'

> How sweet the name of Jesus sounds in a believer's ear! It soothes his sorrows, heals his wounds, and drives away his fear.
>
> It makes the wounded spirit whole and calms the troubled breast; 'tis manna to the hungry soul and to the weary rest.
>
> Dear name! the Rock on which I build, my Shield and Hiding place, my never failing Treasury filled with boundless stores of grace.
>
> Jesus! my Shepherd, Brother, Friend, my Prophet, Priest and King, my Lord, my Life, my Way, my End, accept the praise I bring.
>
> Weak is the effort of my heart, and cold my warmest thought; but when I see Thee as Thou art I'll praise Thee as I ought.
>
> Till then I would Thy love proclaim with ev'ry fleeting breath; and may the music of Thy name refresh my soul in death.

🐦 *For Today:* Psalm 8:9; 104:34; Song of Solomon 1:3; Matthew 11:28

Ask this question: "How often do I spend time in worship and adoration of Christ simply for who He is?" Begin now by singing this musical message—

St. Peter tune   Alexander R. Reinagle, 1799-1877

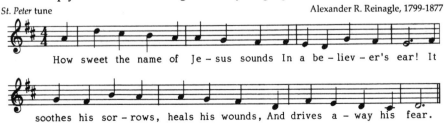

How sweet the name of Je - sus sounds In a be - liev - er's ear! It soothes his sor - rows, heals his wounds, And drives a - way his fear.

HIS MATCHLESS WORTH

Samuel Medley, 1738-1799

Whom have I in heaven but You? And earth has nothing I desire besides You.
(Psalm 73:25)

The distinctiveness of the Christian faith is that it focuses all of its teachings and emphasis on a single person, Jesus Christ—the God-man. All that we really know about our heavenly Father is learned from this One who lived among us for 33 years.

Some people speak eloquently about the Fatherhood of God yet seldom extol the virtues of Christ. But without a biblical knowledge of Christ and a personal relationship with Him, our understanding of God the Father would be incomplete. The Scriptures teach that Christ was the visible representation of the invisible Godhead (John 4:9).

Samuel Medley served in the British Royal Navy until he was wounded in battle at the age of 21. While recuperating from his injury, he was converted to Christ as he was reading a sermon by Isaac Watts. Soon Medley felt the call of God to the ministry and pastored several Baptist churches, including one in Liverpool, where he was especially successful, particularly in work with young sailors.

This hymn text first appeared in Medley's hymnal of 1789. It was originally titled "Praise of Jesus," and it presents a rich picture of our Lord. It extols His matchless worth, unfathomable to the human mind; His redemptive work; His characters and many forms of love; His righteousness; and the fact that He will one day receive us to an eternal heavenly home.

O could I speak the matchless worth, O could I sound the glories forth which in my Savior shine, I'd soar and touch the heav'nly strings, and vie with Gabriel while he sings in notes almost divine, in notes almost divine.

I'd sing the precious blood He spilt, my ransom from the dreadful guilt of sin and wrath divine! I'd sing His glorious righteousness, in which all perfect heav'nly dress my soul shall ever shine, my soul shall ever shine.

I'd sing the characters He bears, and all the forms of love He wears, exalted on His throne: In loftiest songs of sweetest praise, I would to everlasting days make all His glories known, make all His glories known.

Well, the delightful day will come when my dear Lord will bring me home and I shall see His face; then with my Savior, Brother, Friend, a blest eternity I'll spend, triumphant in His grace, triumphant in His grace.

❧ *For Today:* Psalm 73:21-28; Matthew 14:33; 27:54; 28:18; Philippians 2:9-11

Spend a few moments delighting yourself in Christ alone. Then sing as you go—

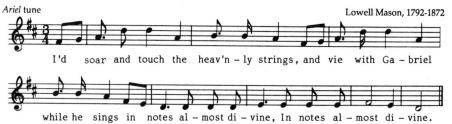

Ariel tune   Lowell Mason, 1792-1872

I'd soar and touch the heav'n-ly strings, and vie with Ga-briel while he sings in notes al-most di-vine, In notes al-most di-vine.

HALLELUJAH, WHAT A SAVIOR!

Words and Music by Philip P. Bliss, 1838-1876

*He was despised and rejected by men, a man of sorrows, and familiar with suffering
. . . He was despised, and we esteemed Him not. (Isaiah 53:3)*

A life of praise is not something that can be worked up. Rather, it is a remembrance and a response to Christ's sacrificial death on our behalf. As we reflect on who Christ is and what He has accomplished for us, what He provides in our daily lives as an advocate before God, and what He has promised for our future, our hearts are melted before Him. We bow at His feet in humble adoration and proclaim with all sincerity, "Hallelujah, What a Savior!"

It is said that the word *Hallelujah* is basically the same in all languages. It seems as though God has given this word as a preparation for the great celebration of heaven, when His children from every tribe, language, people and nation shall have been gathered home to sing their eternal "Hallelujah to the Lamb!"

Philip Bliss, along with Ira Sankey, was one of the truly important leaders and publishers of early gospel music. Before his tragic train accident death at the age of 38, he wrote hundreds of gospel songs, many of which are still widely sung today. "Hallelujah, What a Savior!" is one of the best and most enduring of the songs produced by Bliss. The first four stanzas present Christ's atoning work simply and clearly. The last stanza, "When He comes, our glorious King," is in an entirely different mood, joyful and triumphant in its anticipation of the praise that will continue throughout eternity —"Hallelujah, What a Savior!"

> "Man of Sorrows!" what a name for the Son of God, who came ruined sinners to reclaim! Hallelujah, what a Savior!

> Bearing shame and scoffing rude, in my place condemned He stood—Sealed my pardon with His blood: Hallelujah, what a Savior!

> Guilty, vile and helpless we, spotless Lamb of God was He; full atonement! can it be? Hallelujah, what a Savior!

> Lifted up was He to die, "It is finished," was His cry; now in heav'n exalted high: Hallelujah, what a Savior!

> When He comes, our glorious King, all His ransomed home to bring, then anew this song we'll sing: Hallelujah, what a Savior!

🍂 *For Today:* Isaiah 53:3-6; Philippians 2:7-11; Hebrews 12:2; 1 Peter 2:24

Carry your "Hallelujah, what a Savior!" with you into every situation. Reflect often on Christ's atoning work on your behalf and the glorious promise of His return.

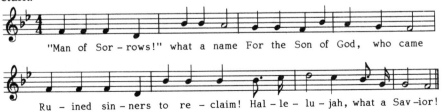

NEAR TO THE HEART OF GOD

Words and Music by Cleland B. McAfee, 1866-1944

When anxiety was great within me, your consolation brought joy. (Psalm 94:19)

O Thou who dry'st the mourner's tears! How dark this world would be,
If, when deceived and wounded here, we could not fly to Thee.   —*Thomas Moore*

Life is often filled with unexpected problems or crises. Unrest and despair will darken the way of even the strongest saint. Yet the Christian—because of the refuge he has in God—should strive to maintain composure and stability in spite of stress and difficulties. We cannot escape the pressures and dark shadows in our lives; but they can be faced with a spiritual strength that our Lord provides. As we are held securely "near to the heart of God," we find the rest, the comfort, the joy and peace that only Jesus our Redeemer can give. Because of this, we can live every day with an inner calm and courage.

This is the message that Cleland McAfee expressed in this consoling hymn at a time when his own life was filled with sadness. While he was serving as pastor of the First Presbyterian Church in Chicago, Dr. McAfee was stunned to hear the shocking news that his two beloved nieces had just died from diptheria. Turning to God and the Scriptures, McAfee soon felt the lines and the tune of this hymn flow from his grieving heart. On the day of the double funeral he stood outside the quarantine home of his brother Howard singing these words as he choked back the tears. The following Sunday the hymn was repeated by the choir of McAfee's church. It soon became widely known and has since ministered comfort and spiritual healing to many of God's people in times of need.

There is a place of quiet rest, near to the heart of God, a place where sin cannot molest, near to the heart of God.

There is a place of comfort sweet, near to the heart of God, a place where we our Savior meet, near to the heart of God.

There is a place of full release, near to the heart of God, a place where all is joy and peace, near to the heart of God.

Chorus: O Jesus, blest Redeemer, sent from the heart of God, hold us who wait before Thee near to the heart of God.

❧ *For Today:* Psalm 34:18; 73:28; Ecclesiastes 5:1; Matthew 11:28-30; Hebrews 4:16

Determine to live courageously regardless of what may come your way—but always with a sensitive awareness of God's nearness. Use this musical prayer to help—

O Je - sus, blest Re - deem - er, Sent from the heart of God,

Hold us who wait be - fore Thee, Near to the heart of God.

ASK YE WHAT GREAT THING I KNOW

Johann C. Schwedler, 1672-1730
Translated by Benjamin H. Kennedy, 1804-1889

For I resolved to know nothing while I was with you except Jesus Christ and Him crucified. (1 Corinthians 2:2)

A question that many struggle with today is "What is the real purpose of living?" Or, "What is the ultimate reality or joy in life?" The testimony of the author of the book of Ecclesiastes would no doubt echo the frustrations of many in contemporary society—"All is vanity, empty and meaningless."

The author of this hymn text, Johann Schwedler, a prominent German minister and hymn writer of his era, discovered quite a different answer for his life—"Jesus Christ, the Crucified"—the consoler, reviver, healer, and final rewarder. For the apostle Paul, all of life also revolved around a personal relationship with Jesus Christ—"For me to live is Christ" (Philippians 1:21).

C. S. Lewis has written: "Either Jesus Christ was what He claimed or He was a liar and we should repudiate Him. Or if He was not what He claimed to be and not a liar, He was a madman, and we should treat Him as such. Or He was what He claimed to be and we should fall at His feet and worship Him."

With doubting Thomas, the apostle Paul, and devout followers of Christ through the centuries, may our purpose in life be expressed in a devoted, daily relationship with our Lord. May we speak out with clarity and conviction: "My Lord and God—my highest joy!"

> Ask ye what great thing I know that delights and stirs me so? What the high reward I win? Whose the name I glory in? Jesus Christ, the Crucified.

> Who defeats my fiercest foes? Who consoles my saddest woes? Who revives my fainting heart, healing all its hidden smart? Jesus Christ, the Crucified.

> Who is life in life to me? Who the death of death will be? Who will place me on His right, with the countless hosts of light? Jesus Christ, the Crucified.

> This is that great thing I know—This delights and stirs me so: Faith in Him who died to save, Him who triumphed o'er the grave, Jesus Christ, the Crucified.

❦ *For Today:* Acts 2:36; Romans 5:1; Galatians 2:20; 6:14; Philippians 3:13, 14; 1 Peter 3:15

Be prepared to speak out if someone should ask about your real purpose in life. Carry this hymn as a help—

Hendon tune   H. A. Cesar Malan, 1787-1864

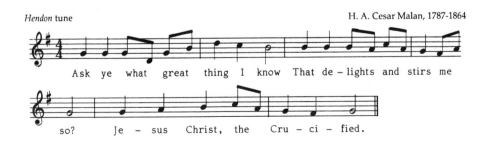

Ask ye what great thing I know That de-lights and stirs me so? Je-sus Christ, the Cru-ci-fied.

JESUS, THE VERY THOUGHT OF THEE

Attributed to Bernard of Clairvaux, 1091-1153
English Translation—Edward Caswall, 1814-1876

As the deer pants for streams of water, so my soul pants for You, O God. My soul thirsts for God, for the living God. (Psalm 42:1, 2)

This hymn text comes from the height of the Middle Ages, a period of history often scornfully called "The Dark Ages." The spiritual and moral darkness of the church had reached a new blackness. The institution founded by Christ some 1,000 years prior was mainly degenerate and corrupt. The moral standards of many of its prominent leaders were characterized by disgrace and shame. Yet within this system of religious confusion, God laid it upon the heart of a dedicated monk to write a devotional poem about his Lord that has since become the text for one of the finest hymns in our hymnals. As was true then and now, God always has a remnant of true believers who maintain His eternal truths.

At an early age Bernard was known for his piety and scholarship. With his natural charms and talents, he had many opportunities open to him for a successful secular life. While still in his early 20's, however, he chose the life of a monk at the monastery of Citeaux, France. Within three years Bernard's forceful personality, talents, and leadership qualities were recognized, and he was asked to form other branches of this order throughout Europe. Within Bernard's lifetime 162 other such orders were founded. One of these new monasteries was at Clairvaux, France, where Bernard was made its abbot or head. Here he remained until his death in 1153.

Jesus, the very thought of Thee with sweetness fills my breast; but sweeter far Thy face to see and in Thy presence rest.

Nor voice can sing, nor heart can frame, nor can the mem'ry find a sweeter sound than Thy blest name, O Savior of mankind.

O hope of ev'ry contrite heart, O joy of all the meek, to those who fall how kind Thou art! how good to those who seek!

But what to those who find? Ah, this nor tongue nor pen can show—the love of Jesus, what it is; none but His loved ones know.

Jesus, our only joy be Thou, as Thou our prize wilt be; Jesus, be Thou our glory now and thru eternity.

❦ *For Today:* Psalm 66:2; 130:7; Jeremiah 17:7; Ephesians 3:19

Earnestly seek to be one of God's faithful remnant—"salt" and "light"—keeping His truths alive for this generation to hear and believe.

St. Agnes tune   John B. Dykes, 1823-1876

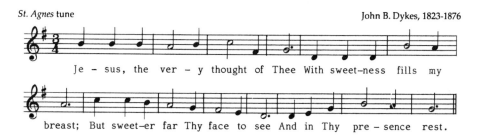

Je - sus, the ver - y thought of Thee With sweet—ness fills my breast; But sweet—er far Thy face to see And in Thy pre - sence rest.

MY FAITH LOOKS UP TO THEE

Ray Palmer, 1808-1887

In whom we have boldness and confidence of access through our faith in Him.
(Ephesians 3:12 RSV)

"My Faith Looks Up to Thee" was written in 1832 by Ray Palmer, a 22-year-old school teacher. Several months after his graduation from Yale University and while still living with the family of the lady who directed the girls' school where he taught, Palmer wrote the text for this hymn. He had experienced a very discouraging year in which he battled illness and loneliness.

> The words for these stanzas were born out of my own soul with very little effort. I recall that I wrote the verses with tender emotion. There was not the slightest thought of writing for another eye, least of all writing a hymn for Christian worship. It is well-remembered that when writing the last line, "Oh, bear me safe above, a ransomed soul!" the thought of the whole work of redemption and salvation was involved in those words, and suggested the theme of eternal praises, and this brought me to a degree of emotion that brought abundant tears.

Two years later, while visiting in Boston, Palmer chanced to meet his friend, Lowell Mason, a well-known name in musical circles during this time. Upon seeing Ray Palmer's text, Mason stated: "Palmer, you may live many years and do many good things, but I think you will be best-known to posterity as the author of 'My Faith Looks Up to Thee'." Lowell Mason composed a melody for this text, a tune which he called "Olivet" in reference to the hymn's message. Soon the hymn appeared in its present form in a hymnal edited by Mason. And from that time on this musical expression has had an important place in nearly every hymnal that has been published:

> My faith looks up to Thee, Thou Lamb of Calvary, Savior divine; now hear me when I pray, take all my sin away; O let me from this day be wholly Thine!

> May Thy rich grace impart strength to my fainting heart, my zeal inspire; as Thou hast died for me, O may my love to Thee pure, warm and changeless be—a living fire!

> While life's dark maze I tread and griefs around me spread, be Thou my guide; bid darkness turn to day, wipe sorrow's tears away, nor let me ever stray from Thee aside.

> When ends life's transient dream, when death's cold sullen stream shall o'er me roll, Blest Savior, then, in love, fear and distrust remove—O bear me safe above, a ransomed soul.

🐚 *For Today:* Psalm 118:8, 9; Romans 1:17; 5:1, 2; 2 Corinthians 12:9

Reflect on this statement—Faith is simply learning to say "Amen" (so be it!) to God. Express your faith by singing—

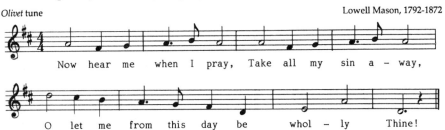

MAJESTIC SWEETNESS SITS ENTHRONED

Samuel Stennett, 1727-1795

But we see Jesus, who was made a little lower than the angels, now crowned with glory and honor because He suffered death, so that by the grace of God He might taste death for everyone. (Hebrews 2:9)

The dominant theme of the beautifully expressed text in this hymn, "Majestic Sweetness Sits Enthroned," is the adoration of Jesus Christ. It is based on the descriptive passage found in the Song of Solomon 5:10-16. Here the awaiting maiden, anticipating the return of her lover, describes him with such terms as: "Chief among ten thousand," "head of pure gold," "body like polished ivory," "altogether lovely. . . ."

The Bible often refers to believers as the bride of Christ. We too are awaiting the return of our lover, the One who is "fairer than all the fair."

This hymn text originally had nine stanzas and was titled "The Chief Among Ten Thousand" or "The Excellencies of Christ." It first appeared in Rippon's famous Baptist collection, *A Selection of Hymns from the Best of Authors,* published in 1787.

The author, Samuel Stennett, was a well-known Baptist pastor in London, England, and was regarded as one of the outstanding evangelical preachers of his day. Dr. Stennett was also an influential writer on numerous theological subjects as well as the author of thirty-nine hymns. Despite his many accomplishments, however, he will always be best remembered for these beautiful words of adoration often used in communion services as well as for spiritual enrichment during times of personal devotions:

Majestic sweetness sits enthroned upon the Savior's brow; His head with radiant glories crowned, His lips with grace o'er flow; His lips with grace o'er flow.

No mortal can with Him compare among the sons of men; fairer is He than all the fair who fill the heav'nly train, who fill the heav'nly train.

He saw me plunged in deep distress and flew to my relief; for me He bore the shameful cross and carried all my grief, and carried all my grief.

To Him I owe my life and breath and all the joys I have; He makes me triumph over death and saves me from the grave, and saves me from the grave.

❦ *For Today:* Song of Solomon 5:10-16; Colossians 1:15-20; Hebrews 1:1-3

Express in your own words your feelings of love and adoration to your heavenly bridegroom for all that He means in your life and the anticipation of someday soon actually seeing Him. Allow these musical truths to help you during this time of personal devotions—

Ortonville tune   Thomas Hastings, 1784-1872

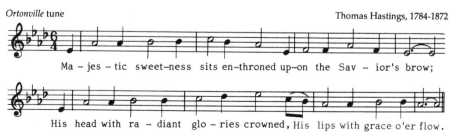

Ma – jes – tic sweet-ness sits en–throned up–on the Sav – ior's brow;

His head with ra – diant glo – ries crowned, His lips with grace o'er flow.

SUN OF MY SOUL

John Keble, 1792-1866

For the Lord God is a sun and shield; the Lord bestows favor and honor; no good thing does He withhold from those whose walk is blameless. O Lord Almighty, blessed is the man who trusts in You. (Psalm 84:11, 12)

Jesus taught that we can learn much from the lilies of the field. How do they grow? By struggling and seeking to display their beauty? No, they simply open themselves to the existing sun, and in their sun-centeredness, they grow and become objects of beauty for all to enjoy. Indeed the sun is one of the most important factors in nature's growth.

We too need sun for our souls—the warmth of God's love and presence in our lives. We were created for this in order to be complete persons. It was St. Augustine who realized this truth centuries ago: "Thou hast made us for Thyself, O God, and our hearts are restless till they find rest in Thee."

John Keble, a professor of poetry at Oxford University for 10 years and later an Anglican minister of the humble parish church in the village of Hursley, wrote this poem in 1820. Seven years later he published a collection of poems titled *The Christian Year* with all of the poems following the church calendar year. "Sun of My Soul" was one of the poems from that collection. The book was extremely successful, going through 109 editions before John Keble's death in 1866.

The poem was originally named "Evening" and was based on the account in Luke 24:29, where Christ went in to dine with the two Emmaus disciples following His resurrection.

This prayer for the constant and unobscured sense of Christ's unwavering presence and blessing, whether in life or death, and finally the full enjoyment of God's love in "heav'n above," is still a worthy goal for each believer.

Sun of my soul, Thou Savior dear, it is not night if Thou be near; O may no earth-born cloud arise to hide Thee from Thy servant's eyes!

When the soft dews of kindly sleep my weary eyelids gently steep, be my last thought; how sweet to rest forever on my Savior's breast!

Abide with me from morn till eve, for without thee I cannot live; abide with me when night is nigh, for without Thee I dare not die.

Be near to bless me when I wake, ere thru the world my way I take; abide with me till in Thy love I lose myself in heav'n above.

❧ *For Today:* Psalm 4:6-8; Luke 1:77-79; 24:29; 2 Corinthians 4:4

Pray with John Keble that "no earth-born cloud" will obscure a sense of Christ's presence and blessing in your life. Carry this musical message to help—

From *Katholisches Gesangbuch*, Vienna, c. 1774

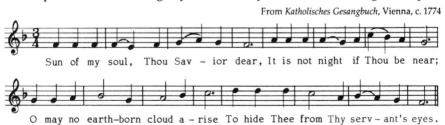

Sun of my soul, Thou Sav - ior dear, It is not night if Thou be near;

O may no earth—born cloud a - rise To hide Thee from Thy serv - ant's eyes.

JESUS, I AM RESTING, RESTING

Jean Sophia Pigott, 1845-1882

In repentance and rest is your salvation, in quietness and trust is your strength.
(Isaiah 30:15)

John Wesley, the flaming evangelist of the 18th century, once stated that Christians must "learn to live with a slack rein." If that were true then, it is even more necessary in the hectic pace lived today. We all need times of relaxation, rest, and renewal. Even Christian workers can experience "burn-out" while engaged in worthwhile activities for God.

Resting in Jesus is an important development in our Christian maturity. It is something we must learn to practice daily regardless of life's pressures and circumstances. It must be in the present tense, not a nostalgic memory from the past. Although this principle is easier stated than practiced, we must consciously learn to relax and enjoy God's presence; to allow God to absorb our inward worries and conflicts; to allow Him to energize us with His love and power.

The author of this thoughtful text, Jean Sophia Pigott, was born and lived in Ireland. She wrote this text in 1876. The composer, James Mountain, was an English Baptist minister, writer, and musician. He is best remembered today for several of his surviving hymn tunes.

The story is told of Hudson Taylor, missionary statesman to China, in the terrible days of the Boxer uprising there. As one report followed another of mission stations being destroyed and missionaries massacred, Taylor remained quietly at his desk, singing softly these words that he loved so dearly:

> Jesus, I am resting, resting in the joy of what Thou art; I am finding out the greatness of Thy loving heart. Thou hast bid me gaze upon Thee, and Thy beauty fills my soul, for by Thy transforming power Thou hast made me whole.

> Simply trusting Thee, Lord Jesus, I behold Thee as Thou art, and Thy love, so pure, so changeless, satisfies my heart—Satisfies its deepest longings, meets, supplies its ev'ry need, compasseth me round with blessings. This is love indeed!

> Ever lift Thy face upon me as I work and wait for Thee. Resting 'neath Thy smile, Lord Jesus, earth's dark shadows flee. Brightness of my Father's glory, sunshine of my Father's face, keep me ever trusting, resting; fill me with Thy grace.

❧ *For Today:* Isaiah 23:3, 4; 32:17; Matthew 11:28; 2 Timothy 2:2; Hebrews 4:9

Determine to spend some time each day in refreshment and renewal of your body, mind and spirit. Sing this musical truth as you go—

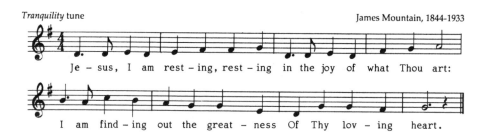

Tranquility tune   James Mountain, 1844-1933

Je - sus, I am rest - ing, rest - ing in the joy of what Thou art:

I am find - ing out the great - ness Of Thy lov - ing heart.

FADE, FADE, EACH EARTHLY JOY

Jane C. Bonar, 1821-1884

Love the Lord, all His saints! The Lord preserves the faithful, but the proud He pays back in full. Be strong and take heart, all you who hope in the Lord. (Psalm 31:23, 24)

Each of us was created for the purpose of enjoying the fellowship of Almighty God. Our souls were made for eternity, not for this brief earthly pilgrimage alone. The Christian life should be lived each day as though we were already enjoying the blessings of heaven. We deprive ourselves of one of life's greatest treasures when we lose this perspective and become bogged down with the trivialities of earthly living.

An intimate fellowship with our Lord should produce at least three basic differences in our living:

- **More humility**—a greater realization of our finiteness and the need for dependence upon God.
- **More happiness**—a realization that this life has purpose and dignity as we represent God. And then a promised eternity in heaven with our Lord.
- **More holiness**—a greater desire to be a worthy representative for God and to live a life of absolute purity.

The author of this lovely devotional hymn text, Jane C. Bonar, was the wife of Dr. Horatius Bonar, generally regarded as the greatest of evangelical Scottish preachers and hymn writers. Jane, too, was a very gifted writer and Christian leader. For more than 40 years the Bonars shared life's sorrows and joys together in a rich ministry for God. These devotional thoughts are still the sentiments of every spiritually mature follower of Christ:

Fade, fade, each earthly joy—Jesus is mine; break, ev'ry tender tie—Jesus is mine. Dark is the wilderness; earth has no resting place; Jesus alone can bless—Jesus is mine.

Tempt not my soul away—Jesus is mine; here would I ever stay—Jesus is mine. Perishing things of clay, born but for one brief day, pass from my heart away—Jesus is mine.

Farewell, ye dreams of night—Jesus is mine; lost in this dawning bright—Jesus is mine. All that my soul has tried left but a dismal void; Jesus has satisfied—Jesus is mine.

Farewell, mortality—Jesus is mine; welcome, eternity—Jesus is mine, welcome, O loved and blest, welcome, sweet scenes of rest; welcome, my Savior's breast—Jesus is mine.

🍂 *For Today:* Psalm 16:8, 11; 37:4, 23; 40:8; Proverbs 11:20; Colossians 3:2

Allow the awareness of God's presence to produce in your life more HUMILITY, HAPPINESS, and HOLINESS as you seek to represent Him.

Lundie tune — Theodore E. Perkins, 1831-1912

Fade, fade, each earth - ly joy— Je - sus is mine;

Break ev - 'ry ten - der tie — Je - sus is mine.

WHEN ALL THY MERCIES, O MY GOD

Joseph Addison, 1672-1719

Oh, give thanks unto the Lord, for He is good; for His mercy endureth forever.
(1 Chronicles 16:11 KJV)

A reflection upon God's blessings will always result in a response of worship and praise; a neglect of gratitude will eventually produce a lifestyle of self-centeredness.

Joseph Addison, the author of this hymn, wrote this introduction for his text:

> If gratitude is due from man to man, how much more from man to his Maker. The Supreme being does not only confer upon us those bounties which proceed immediately from His hand, but even those benefits which are conveyed to us by others. Any blessing which we enjoy, by what means soever derived, is the gift of Him who is the great author of good and the Father of mercies.

Joseph Addison was recognized in his era as one of England's literary greats. He was not only a writer and a moralist, but a man of affairs in his government. He was elected to Parliament and then appointed successively as Under Secretary, Secretary for Ireland, and finally Secretary of State.

These words are thought to have been written by Joseph Addison following his rescue from a shipwreck during a storm off the Coast of Genoa, Italy. The hymn originally had 13 stanzas. It was published on August 9, 1712, in a London daily paper, *The Spectator,* of which Addison served for a time as editor. The surviving four stanzas have since provided God's people with a meaningful aid in expressing grateful worship to God for all of His enduring mercies:

> When all Thy mercies, O my God, my rising soul surveys, transported with the view I'm lost in wonder, love and praise.

> Unnumbered comforts to my soul Thy tender care bestowed before my infant heart conceived from whom those comforts flowed.

> When worn with sickness, oft hast Thou with health renewed my face; and, when in sins and sorrows bowed, revived my soul with grace.

> Thru ev'ry period of my life Thy goodness I'll pursue, and after death, in distant worlds, the glorious theme renew.

❦ ***For Today:*** Psalm 63:1-5; 86:5-17; 89:1; 103:8-14; James 3:17

Reflect with this author upon God's mercy of comfort, His mercy of physical and spiritual healing, His mercy of reviving grace—then, respond to Him with grateful expressions of worship and praise. Allow this hymn to help—

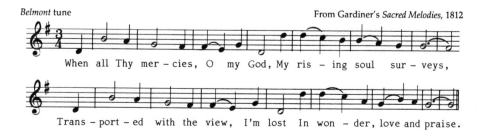

Belmont tune — From Gardiner's *Sacred Melodies,* 1812

When all Thy mer-cies, O my God, My ris-ing soul sur-veys,

Trans-port-ed with the view, I'm lost In won-der, love and praise.

THE SANDS OF TIME ARE SINKING

Anne Ross Cousin, 1824-1906

And I—in righteousness I will see Your face; when I awake, I will be satisfied with seeing Your likeness. (Psalm 17:15)

What beautiful pictures of Christ and our relationship to Him as His bride are portrayed for us in this lovely hymn text which was inspired by the dying words of a 17th century Scottish preacher. The colorful imagery enhances the truths of these very thoughtful lines.

"And glory, glory dwelleth in Immanuel's Land" were the final triumphant words spoken by Samuel Rutherford, a forceful evangelical preacher who suffered much persecution in Scotland for his support of the non-conformist movement. His open opposition to the state church resulted in banishment from his pulpit and home. When his courageous loyalty to Christ continued throughout his life, Rutherford was eventually charged with high treason, which could mean being beheaded. Already on his death bed, however, he sent, back this message: "I behoove to answer my first summons, and ere your day for me arrive, I will be where few kings and great folks come."

Two hundred years after the death of Rutherford in 1661, his victorious life, writings, and final words so impressed Anne Ross Cousin that she was moved to write this remarkable text. Mrs. Cousin describes vividly the glories of heaven. Her wonderful closing proclamation that "the Lamb is all the glory" is a fitting climax to the hymn's vibrant exaltation of Christ and His eternal abode.

> The sands of time are sinking, the dawn of heaven breaks; the summer morn I've sighed for—the fair, sweet morn awakes. Dark, dark hath been the midnight, but day-spring is at hand, and glory, glory dwelleth in Immanuel's land.
>
> O Christ, He is the fountain, the deep, sweet well of love! The streams on earth I've tasted more deep I'll drink above: There to an ocean fulness His mercy doth expand, and glory, glory dwelleth in Immanuel's land.
>
> O I am my Beloved's, and my Beloved's mine! He brings a poor vile sinner into His "house of wine." I stand upon His merit—I know no other stand, not e'en where glory dwelleth in Immanuel's land.
>
> The Bride eyes not her garment but her dear Bridegroom's face; I will not gaze at glory but on my King of grace, not at the crown He giveth but on His pierced hand: The Lamb is all the glory of Immanuel's land.

❧ *For Today:* John 17:3; Romans 13:14; Ephesians 3:14-21; Hebrews 12:2

Learn to say—"My goal is Christ Himself, not joy, nor peace, not even heaven—but Himself, my Lord." Even now, as we anticipate the joy of "Immanuel's land" and the sight of our Savior's face, let us look away from ourselves and the cares of life and focus on the author and finisher of our faith.

Rutherford tune   Chretien Urhan, 1790-1845

And glo — ry, glo — ry dwell — eth In Im — man — uel's land.
The Lamb is all the glo — ry Of Im — man — uel's land.

O WORD OF GOD INCARNATE

William W. How, 1823-1897

All Scripture is God-breathed and is useful for teaching, rebuking, correcting and training in righteousness, so that the man of God may be thoroughly equipped for every good work. (2 Timothy 3:16, 17)

Everyone has a basic premise for his life's convictions. The Christian begins with Jesus Christ, who came to earth to reveal God to man. The Christian also believes in the absolute historicity of Jesus as recorded in the Scriptures, the only authentic record of our Lord's life and works. For God's people, then, the Bible is the most important book in life. Though written by forty different writers from Moses to John over a period of 1600 years, there is a perfect harmony throughout all 66 books. This is proof that the book is truly "God-breathed" and that the real author was the Holy Spirit.

The writer of this hymn text, William W. How, was a bishop of the Anglican church in London, England. He was known as an outstanding hymnist, the composer of sixty excellent hymns of which 25 are still in use.

In the first stanza of this hymn, Bishop How affirms that the Bible is God's Truth revealed and is a light from one age to another. In the second stanza, he states that Christ has entrusted His Holy Word to the Church so that it might be revealed as a light to all the world. Then he describes the Bible in picturesque language in stanza three and closes the hymn with a prayer that the Church may always continue to bear God's revealed truth to all people everywhere.

O Word of God Incarnate, O Wisdom from on high, O Truth unchanged, unchanging, O Light of our dark sky: We praise Thee for the radiance that from the hallowed page, a lantern to our footsteps, shines on from age to age.

The Church from her dear Master, received the gift divine, and still that light she lifteth o'er all the earth to shine. It is the sacred casket, where gems of truth are stored; it is the heav'n-drawn picture of Thee, the living Word.

It floateth like a banner before God's host unfurled; it shineth like a beacon above the dark'ning world. It is the chart and compass that o'er life's surging sea, 'mid mists and rocks and quick sands, still guides, O Christ, to Thee.

O make Thy Church, dear Savior, a lamp of purest gold, to bear before the nations Thy true light as of old. O teach Thy wandering pilgrims by this their path to trace, till, clouds and darkness ended, they see Thee face to face.

❦ *For Today:* Psalm 60:4; 119:105, 130, 160; Mark 13:31; John 1:1, 2

Breathe a prayer of thanks to God for the Bible——our guide for this life and our road map for heaven. Reflect on this musical truth as you go—

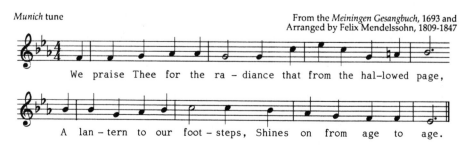

Munich tune

From the *Meiningen Gesangbuch*, 1693 and Arranged by Felix Mendelssohn, 1809-1847

We praise Thee for the ra – diance that from the hal–lowed page,

A lan – tern to our foot – steps, Shines on from age to age.

HOLY BIBLE, BOOK DIVINE

John Burton, Sr., 1773-1822

Oh, how I love Your law! I meditate on it all day long. (Psalm 119:97)

Nobody ever outgrows Scripture; the Book widens and deepens with our years.
—*Charles H. Spurgeon*

The Bible is truly an amazing book. It has rightfully been called "The Book of Books." The first book ever printed was the Bible—the German Gütenberg Bible between the years 1450-1455. Today, it is printed in more than 600 languages, and portions of it are printed in more than 1,000 tongues and dialects. It has long been the world's best seller.

In addition to being God's love letter and self-disclosure of Himself, the Bible clearly spells out His plan for our redemption and restored fellowship. It is also our final authority for all matters of faith, morals, and practice. Through the inspired Word, God the Holy Spirit illuminates and guides believers in their Christian walk and also prepares them for their future heavenly destination.

Our finite minds will never be able to comprehend all of the teaching of Scripture, but the essential truths related to our redemption and Christ-like living cannot be misunderstood. It was Abraham Lincoln who once observed: "Read the Bible for whatever reason you can accept and take the rest on faith, and you will live and die a better man."

John Burton, author of "Holy Bible, Book Divine," was an English Sunday school teacher with a concern for teaching spiritual truths to children. This text appeared in 1806 in Burton's Sunday school hymnal, which was titled *Incentives for Early Piety.* These words have since been spiritually profitable for both young and old:

> Holy Bible, Book divine, precious treasure, thou art mine; mine to tell me whence I came, mine to teach me what I am;
>
> Mine to chide me when I rove, mine to show a Savior's love; mine thou art to guide and guard, mine to punish or reward;
>
> Mine to comfort in distress—Suff 'ring in this wilderness; mine to show, by living faith, man can triumph over death;
>
> Mine to tell of joys to come and the rebel sinner's doom: O thou holy Book divine, precious treasure, thou art mine.

❧ *For Today:* Matthew 24:35; John 15:7; 2 Timothy 3:15-17; Hebrews 4:12

It was George Mueller who said: "The vigor of our spiritual life will be in exact proportion to the place held by the Word in our life and thoughts." Determine to give the Bible a greater place in your life. Sing this child-like hymn as you go—

Aletta tune   William B. Bradbury, 1816-1868

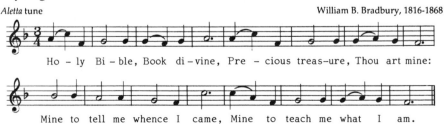

Ho - ly Bi - ble, Book di -vine, Pre - cious treas–ure, Thou art mine:

Mine to tell me whence I came, Mine to teach me what I am.

THE SPIRIT BREATHES UPON THE WORD

William Cowper, 1731-1800

Your Word is a lamp to my feet and a light for my path. (Psalm 119:105)

The Bible is the only book whose Author is always present when one reads it.
—Unknown

We can never really be exposed to the truths of God's Word without our lives being affected. Either we become more desirous of becoming like the author of the Book, or we become increasingly hardened to its truths. It has been said that we must know the Word of God in order to know the God of the Word. However, a study of God's Word must never stop at merely gaining biblical knowledge. It must always lead us to a more intimate relationship with God Himself.

Although William Cowper, the author of this hymn text, was regarded as one of the leading English poets of his day, he suffered periods of severe depression throughout his lifetime. Yet during times of normalcy he wrote great literary works and worked with John Newton to produce the important *Olney Hymns* hymnal of 1779, to which Cowper contributed 67 texts. "The Spirit Breathes Upon the Word" was from this collection.

This hymn teaches an important truth: The same Spirit of God who authored the Bible is the One who enlightens it for our understanding and guidance— "The hand that gave it still supplies the gracious light and heat." May we increasingly use this enlightened Word as we pursue the steps of Christ till they lead us to "brighter worlds above."

> The Spirit breathes upon the Word, and brings the truth to sight; precepts and promises afford a sanctifying light.

> A glory gilds the sacred page, majestic like the sun: It gives a light to ev'ry age; it gives but borrows none.

> The Hand that gave it still supplies the gracious light and heat; His truths upon the nations rise; they rise but never set.

> Let everlasting thanks be Thine for such a bright display as makes a world of darkness shine with beams of heav'nly day.

> My soul rejoices to pursue the steps of Him I love, till glory breaks upon my view in brighter worlds above.

❦ **For Today:** Deuteronomy 4:2; Matthew 4:4; 24:35; 1 Timothy 3:14, 15; 2 Timothy 3:15-17; 1 Peter 2:2

Determine to enter into a fresh study of God's Word with the desire that the Holy Spirit will bring some new truth and insight into your daily life. Carry this musical truth with you—

Ortonville tune   Thomas Hastings, 1784-1872

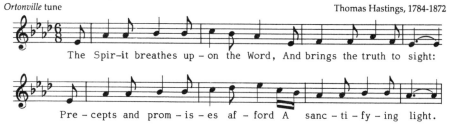

The Spir-it breathes up-on the Word, And brings the truth to sight:

Pre-cepts and prom-is-es af-ford A sanc-ti-fy-ing light.

October

• *Christian Witness* • *Christian Warfare* • *Social Concerns*
• *Reformation Day*

LORD, SPEAK TO ME

Frances R. Havergal, 1836-1879

We are therefore Christ's ambassadors, as though God were making his appeal through us. We implore you on Christ's behalf: Be reconciled to God. (2 Corinthians 5:20)

As Christ's personal ambassadors, we should be people of double resolve: To hear what God has to say to us and then to share that message with others.

> Use me, God, in Thy great harvest field,
> Which stretcheth far and wide like a wide sea;
> The gatherers are so few; I fear the precious yield
> Will suffer loss. Oh, find a place for me!   —*Christina G. Rossetti*

Effective service must always begin with prayer—asking God to use us to accomplish His eternal purposes in the lives of others. But we must not dictate to our Lord as to how and when we should be used. We are simply to be available whenever He directs in a particular situation. Then our representation for Him is simply to speak His truth boldly but always in love. Imploring lost people to be reconciled to God is far different from merely engaging them in theological arguments. We must always remember that the real need of people is to hear about the historical Christ as a personal Savior and Lord and to be guided to a living and vital relationship with Him.

Frances Ridley Havergal, the author of this text, has often been called the "consecration poet" because of her deep commitment to Christ. This text first appeared in 1872 in leaflet form with the title "A Worker's Prayer," accompanied by the scripture verse: "For none of us lives to himself and none dies to himself" (Romans 14:17). These words have since been widely used in leading others to a deeper consecration of their lives to God:

> Lord, speak to me that I may speak in living echoes of Thy tone; as Thou hast sought, so let me seek Thy erring children lost and lone.
>
> O lead me, Lord, that I may lead the wand'ring and the wav'ring feet; O feed me, Lord, that I may feed the hung' ring ones with manna sweet.
>
> O teach me, Lord, that I may teach the precious things Thou dost impart; and wing my words that they may reach the hidden depths of many a heart.
>
> O fill me with Thy fullness, Lord, until my very heart o'er-flow in kindling tho't and glowing word, Thy love to tell, Thy praise to show.
>
> O use me, Lord, use even me, just as Thou wilt, and when, and where, until Thy blessed face I see —Thy rest, Thy joy, Thy glory share.

❦ *For Today:* Psalm 119:9-16; Luke 17:21; John 13:15; Acts 1:8; John 2:17

Ask God to engineer the circumstances that will allow you to represent Him effectively to some needy person. Use this musical prayer—

Canonbury tune   Robert Schumann, 1810-1856

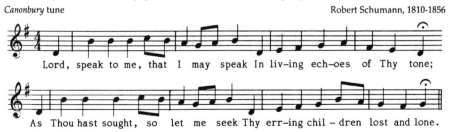

Lord, speak to me, that I may speak In liv-ing ech—oes of Thy tone;

As Thou hast sought, so let me seek Thy err—ing chil – dren lost and lone.

RESCUE THE PERISHING

Fanny J. Crosby, 1820-1915

The Spirit of the Lord God is upon me; because the Lord hath anointed me to preach good tidings unto the meek; He hath sent me to bind up the brokenhearted, to proclaim liberty to the captives . . . . (Isaiah 61:1 KJV)

One of the most tragic words in our vocabulary is the word *perishing*. Yet it was a word that Jesus Himself often used (Matthew 18:14; Luke 13:3, 5) to describe people who are spiritually alienated from God.

Fanny Crosby, often called the "queen of gospel music," recalled how she wrote this challenging hymn:

> I remember writing that hymn in the year 1869. Like many of my hymns, it was written following a personal experience at the New York City Bowery Mission. I usually tried to get to the mission at least one night a week to talk to "my boys." I was addressing a large company of working men one hot summer evening, when the thought kept forcing itself on my mind that some mother's boy must be rescued that night or he might be eternally lost. So I made a pressing plea that if there was a boy present who had wandered from his mother's home and teaching, he should come to me at the end of the service. A young man of 18 came forward—
>
> "Did you mean me, Miss Crosby? I promised my mother to meet her in heaven, but as I am now living, that will be impossible."
>
> We prayed for him and suddenly he arose with a new light in his eyes— "Now I am ready to meet my mother in heaven, for I have found God."

A few days before, William Doane, composer of the music, had sent Fanny Crosby a tune for a new song to be titled "Rescue the Perishing." It was to be based on the text "Go out into the highways and hedges, and compel them to come in, that my house may be filled" (Luke 14:23).

> Rescue the perishing, care for the dying, snatch them in pity from sin and the grave; weep o'er the erring one, lift up the fallen, tell them of Jesus, the mighty to save.
>
> Down in the human heart, crushed by the tempter, feelings lie buried that grace can restore; touched by a loving heart, wakened by kindness, chords that are broken will vibrate once more.
>
> Rescue the perishing, duty demands it; strength for thy labor the Lord will provide; back to the narrow way patiently win them; tell the poor wand'rer a Savior has died.
>
> **Refrain:** Rescue the perishing, care for the dying; Jesus is merciful, Jesus will save.

❦ ***For Today:*** Ezekiel 18:32; Luke 14:23; Romans 9:2, 3; 2 Peter 3:9

Reflect seriously that it is the divine image in every person (Genesis 1:26, 27) that gives life an intrinsic dignity and worth—regardless of race, color, sex, age, or social standing. That's what makes each person worthy of being rescued from eternal damnation. Sing this musical challenge as you go—

William H. Doane, 1832-1915

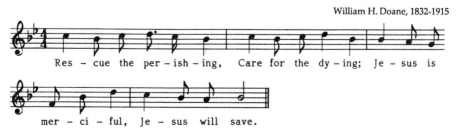

Res - cue the per - ish - ing, Care for the dy - ing; Je - sus is mer - ci - ful, Je - sus will save.

YE SERVANTS OF GOD, YOUR MASTER PROCLAIM

Charles Wesley, 1707-1788

. . . salvation belongs to our God, who sits on the throne, and to the Lamb. (Revelation 7:10)

The proclamation of the gospel requires a devoted, zealous spirit. The real purpose of this proclamation is to affect a personal conversion in the hearer, and this experience implies a radical change of lifestyle. The Bible speaks of this change as becoming a "new creation" (2 Corinthians 5:17). It involves the convert in at least three new and conscious relationships: To Christ, to the church, and to the world. Conversion means nothing if it does not result in a change from self-centered living to devotion to God and a life of sacrificial service for Him.

Charles Wesley wrote this text in 1744, a year of unusually severe persecution for the Wesleys and their followers. During this trying year the Wesleys wrote several hymn pamphlets titled *Hymns for Times of Trouble and Persecution.* One of these booklets included "Ye Servants of God, Your Master Proclaim." The text was based on Psalm 93:1-4 and Revelation 7:9-12. The purpose of this text was to encourage their persecuted followers to concentrate on the One "whose kingdom is glorious—who rules over all." As is generally true, Christians flourish best for God during times of persecution. This was certainly true of the Wesleys and the early Methodists. "God is on the throne; therefore let us cry aloud, and honor His Son and our Savior" became the battlecry. And the more severe the opposition, the stronger became their proclamation of the gospel.

May our proclamation, too, always focus on Jesus Christ as the Savior, Lord, and Master of life and eternity. May we not become side-tracked with our own ideas, pet themes, or personal experiences.

> Ye servants of God, your Master proclaim, and publish abroad His wonderful name; the name all victorious of Jesus extol: His kingdom is glorious; He rules over all.

> "Salvation to God who sits on the throne," let all cry aloud and honor the Son; the praises of Jesus the angels proclaim, fall down on their faces and worship the Lamb.

> Then let us adore and give Him His right—all glory and pow'r, and wisdom and might, all honor and blessing, with angels above, and thanks never ceasing, and infinite love.

🕭 *For Today:* Psalm 93:1-4; 96:1-10; Mark 10:43, 45; Revelation 7:9-12

Ask God to keep your spirit consistently zealous for Him. Carry this musical reminder with you—

Hanover tune   William Croft, 1678-1727

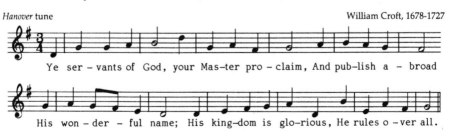

Ye ser - vants of God, your Mas-ter pro - claim, And pub-lish a - broad

His won - der - ful name; His king-dom is glo-rious, He rules o -ver all.

I LOVE TO TELL THE STORY

A. Catherine Hankey, 1834-1911

The fruit of the righteous is a tree of life, and he who wins souls is wise. (Proverbs 11:30)

Soul-winning should be the normal product of our commitment to discipleship and a daily intimate relationship with the Lord. Soul-winning is not salesmanship, in which we try to manipulate or subdue lost individuals to a decision. It is simply taking a message, the objective historical truths of the gospel, and then speaking with the authority of Jesus Christ in the power and love of the Holy Spirit.

Sharing our personal faith should be a joyful and satisfying experience, just as it was with Kate Hankey, author of this hymn's text. Although she was born into the home of a wealthy English banker and a member of the Anglican church, Kate early in life developed a fervent evangelical concern. She began organizing Sunday school classes for rich and poor throughout London. These classes had a strong influence in the city, with a large number of the young students in turn becoming zealous Christian workers.

When Kate was only 30 years old, however, she experienced a serious illness. During a long period of recovery, she wrote a lengthy poem on the life of Christ. The poem consisted of two main sections, each containing 50 verses. The first section of the poem was titled "The Story Wanted," later adapted for another of Catherine Hankey's familiar hymn texts, "Tell Me the Old, Old Story," still widely sung today. Later that same year while recovering from her illness, Kate completed the second part of her poem, titled "The Story Told," which became the basic part of "I Love to Tell the Story."

I love to tell the story of unseen things above, of Jesus and His glory, of Jesus and His love. I love to tell the story because I know 'tis true. It satisfies my longings as nothing else can do.

I love to tell the story, more wonderful it seems than all the golden fancies of all our golden dreams. I love to tell the story—It did so much for me, and that is just the reason I tell it now to thee.

I love to tell the story, for those who know it best seem hungering and thirsting to hear it like the rest. And when in scenes of glory I sing the new, new song, 'twill be the old, old story that I have loved so long.

Refrain: I love to tell the story! 'Twill be my theme in glory to tell the old, old story of Jesus and His love.

❦ *For Today:* Daniel 12:3; Matthew 4:19; Acts 4:12; 1 Peter 3:15; 1 John 4:9, 10

Reflect seriously on this often quoted description of soul-winning—"It is proclaiming the good news just as one contented beggar tells a starving beggar friend where there is food." Sing this musical testimony—

William G. Fischer, 1835-1912

CHANNELS ONLY

Mary E. Maxwell, 20th century

If a man cleanses himself from the latter, he will be an instrument for noble purposes, made holy, useful to the Master and prepared to do any good work. (2 Timothy 2:21)

A vessel He will make of you, if small or great, 'twill surely do—
Great joy and peace will always fill the one who's yielded to His will.   —*Unknown*

To be a channel of the purposes of God is the highest calling in life. Every believer has been given at least one spiritual gift for this work (1 Peter 4:10). When we use that gift, our own lives are blessed and enriched by God as we bless others. For instance, after a visit to a nursing home or an invalid person, we often come away spiritually rejuvenated. Ministering to the needs of others is one of the best remedies for self-centeredness and joyless living.

Our ministry to others, however, is always based on what we have first received and experienced from God. We can never give out spiritual nourishment until we have first taken it in ourselves. Our experiences of suffering can be used to equip us to help others who suffer as we do. Difficulties can either make us bitter or they can fill us with a compassion and sensitivity for the hurts of others. People who are hurting can sense when we really understand and care for them in Christian love.

Our Lord is seeking representatives who realize their insufficiencies but are willing to be a channel filled with His power and love. That's the vessel He can use.

How I praise Thee, precious Savior, that Thy love laid hold of me;
Thou hast saved and cleansed and filled me that I might Thy channel be.

Emptied that thou shouldest fill me, a clean vessel in Thy hand,
with no pow'r but as Thou givest graciously with each command.

Witnessing Thy pow'r to save me, setting free from self and sin,
Thou who boughtest to possess me, in Thy fullness, Lord, come in.

Jesus, fill now with Thy Spirit hearts that full surrender know,
that the streams of living water from our inner man may flow.

Chorus: Channels only, blessed Master—but with all Thy wondrous pow'r flowing thru us, thou canst use us ev'ry day and ev'ry hour.

❦ *For Today:* Romans 6:19; 2 Corinthians 4:1-7; Galatians 5:13; 2 Timothy 2:14-26; James 1:22

Ask the Holy Spirit to show you your particular gift in channeling God's love to others. Share an encouraging, comforting word with someone you know is hurting. Use this musical message to help—

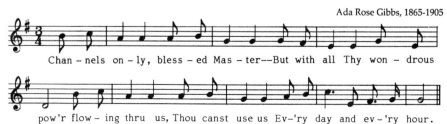

Ada Rose Gibbs, 1865-1905

Chan – nels on – ly, bless – ed Mas – ter—But with all Thy won – drous pow'r flow – ing thru us, Thou canst use us Ev-'ry day and ev-'ry hour.

MAKE ME A BLESSING

Ira B. Wilson, 1880-1950

Through the blessing of the upright a city is exalted, but by the mouth of the wicked it is destroyed. (Proverbs 11:11)

> Nothing is lost that is done for the Lord,
> Let it be ever so small;
> The smile of the Savior approves of the deed
> As though it were greatest of all.
>
> *—Unknown*

We are of little value to our Lord if we do not produce fruit for Him. In fact, the command of Scripture is to bear "much fruit." Regardless of the task to which God calls us, whether it be great or small, it will receive His promised blessing when we do it faithfully and with sincere motives. The Scriptures also teach that our deeds of compassion and mercy must be done with cheerfulness, never simply out of duty (Romans 12:8). St. Francis of Assisi said, "It is not fitting when one is in God's service to have a gloomy face or a chilling look." Representing Christ and serving others must become a normal, happy lifestyle as we "carry the sunshine where darkness is rife."

The text of this hymn was written in 1909 by Ira Wilson, a musician associated for many years with the Lorenz Publishing Company, serving as editor of the popular periodicals for church choirs, *The Choir Leader* and *The Choir Herald*. The music for the hymn was added 15 years later by George Schuler, who served for more than 40 years in the music department of the Moody Bible Institute. Throughout his lifetime Mr. Schuler contributed much fine music for both vocal and keyboard use. "Make Me a Blessing" was first introduced in 1924 at a Sunday school convention in Cleveland, Ohio, where Schuler had 1,000 copies of the song printed for the occasion. It was received with much enthusiasm, and these words have since been widely used to challenge believers to make their lives useful to God.

> Out in the highways and byways of life many are weary and sad; carry the sunshine where darkness is rife, making the sorrowing glad.
>
> Tell the sweet story of Christ and His love. Tell of His pow'r to forgive; others will trust Him if only you prove true every moment you live.
>
> Give as 'twas given to you in your need. Love as the Master loved you; be to the helpless a helper indeed; unto your mission be true.
>
> **Chorus:** Make me a blessing, make me a blessing! Out of my life may Jesus shine. Make me a blessing, O Savior, I pray. Make me a blessing to someone today.

🐝 *For Today:* Isaiah 6:8; Matthew 5:13-16; Acts 20:24; 2 Corinthians 1:4; 2 Timothy 2:21

Simply breathe this musical prayer as you go forth to represent Christ.

George S. Schuler, 1882-1973

Make me a bless - ing, O Sav - ior I pray, Make me a bless - ing to some - one to - day.

STAND UP AND BLESS THE LORD

James Montgomery, 1771-1854

Stand up and praise the Lord your God, who is from everlasting to everlasting.
(Nehemiah 9:5)

Many excellent opportunities to witness for the Lord are lost each day simply because of our timidity. Or perhaps we are with a group of colleagues when the Lord's name is blasphemed, the gospel derided, the church's hypocrites ridiculed . . . and we remain silent. How tragic that our noble words of praise on Sunday often leave us during the week when they are needed most.

> Ye call Me Master and obey not, Ye call Me Light and see Me not, Ye call Me Way and walk not, Ye call Me Life and desire Me not, Ye call Me Wise and follow Me not, Ye call Me Fair and love Me not, Ye call Me rich and ask Me not, Ye call Me Eternal and see Me not, Ye call Me Noble and serve Me not, Ye call Me Mighty and honor Me not, Ye call Me just and fear Me not. —*Found on an old slab in the Cathedral of Lubeck, Germany*

"Stand Up and Bless the Lord" was written by James Montgomery in 1824 especially for a Sunday school anniversary in Sheffield, England. It was based on Nehemiah 9:5. Montgomery was the editor of a newspaper in Sheffield and was known as an outspoken advocate for many humanitarian causes, especially abolition of slavery. His ideas for social reform were considered so radical that he was imprisoned two times. Other causes he championed included hymn singing in the Anglican church services, foreign missions, and the British Bible Society. James Montgomery wrote more than 400 hymns, earning him a lasting place as one of England's finest hymn writers. May this challenge help you today.

> Stand up and bless the Lord, ye people of His choice; stand up and bless the Lord your God with heart and soul and voice.
>
> Though high above all praise, above all blessing high, who would not fear His holy name and laud and magnify?
>
> O for the living flame, from His own altar brought, to touch our lips, our minds inspire, and wing to heav'n our thought!
>
> God is our strength and song, and His salvation ours; then be His love in Christ proclaimed with all our ransomed pow'rs.
>
> Stand up and bless the Lord— the Lord your God adore; stand up and bless His glorious name henceforth forevermore.

🍒 *For Today:* 1 Chronicles 23:30; Psalm 51:15; 1 Corinthians 15:58; Hebrews 12:28

Refuse to be intimidated by those who seem hostile or indifferent to our Lord. Speak His praise graciously but boldly. Use this musical truth to help—

Altus tune   John Willared, 1921-

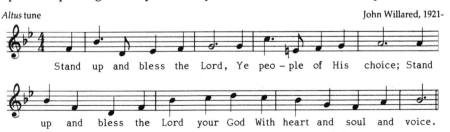

Stand up and bless the Lord, Ye peo-ple of His choice; Stand up and bless the Lord your God With heart and soul and voice.

"ARE YE ABLE?" SAID THE MASTER

Earl Marlatt, 1892-1976

Can you drink the cup I am going to drink? (Matthew 20:22)

> A Christian is a person who, when getting to the end of his/her rope, ties a knot and determines to hang on, realizing that human extremity now becomes God's opportunity.
> —*Unknown*

The mission for each Christian is to proclaim and live the good news of the gospel and to urge individuals everywhere to be converted—to experience a personal reconcilation and relationship with God. This persuasion must always be done with openness and honesty. In our desire to have people make a decision for Christ, we must always be forthright with them. We cannot conceal the cost of discipleship involved in receiving God's provision of salvation. And we must tell them of the importance of giving Jesus Christ His rightful place in every area of life and of becoming an active member of the believing community.

Earl Marlatt, a professor of religion at Boston University and later at Southern Methodist University, wrote this text in 1925 for a consecration service at the Boston University School of Religious Education. It was based on Christ's pointed question to His disciples in Matthew 20:22: "Can you drink the cup I am going to drink?" "We can," they answered. The hymn was originally titled "Challenge." And still today, as in generations past, "heroic spirits answer, 'Lord, we are able.'"

"Are ye able," said the Master, "to be crucified with Me?" "Yea," the sturdy dreamers answered, "To the death we follow Thee:"

"Are ye able" to remember, when a thief lifts up his eyes, that his pardoned soul is worthy of a place in paradise?

"Are ye able?" still the Master whispers down eternity, and heroic spirits answer now as then in Galilee:

Chorus: "Lord, we are able"— our spirits are Thine; remold them — make us like Thee, divine: Thy guiding radiance above us shall be a beacon to God, to love and loyalty.

❦ *For Today:* Ecclesiastes 12:7; Mark 10:35-40; Luke 14:27; 23:39-43; John 12:2

Are we sometimes at fault for giving the illusion to non-Christians that becoming a follower of Christ is the end of all of life's difficulties? Should we not tell them about the cost of life-long discipleship? Seek to engage someone in conversation about the characteristics of true Christianity. Sing this truth as you go—

Beacon Hill tune

Harry S. Mason, 1881-1964

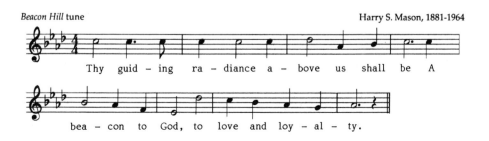

Thy guid - ing ra - diance a - bove us shall be A bea - con to God, to love and loy - al - ty.

YE CHRISTIAN HERALDS

Bourne H. Draper, 1775-1843

How beautiful on the mountains are the feet of those who bring good news, who proclaim peace, who bring good tidings, who proclaim salvation, who say to Zion, "your God reigns!" (Isaiah 52:7)

Many of us are often guilty of taking our pastors, missionaries, and Christian leaders for granted. Seldom do we take time to really know them as persons or to let them know how much we appreciate their ministries.

Where would our world be today had there never been any missionaries and ministers of the gospel? Wherever the gospel has been preached, churches, schools, hospitals, social improvements, and advances in civilization have followed. Even in our own local communities it is often the rescue missions and other Christian organizations that are doing the most effective work in meeting the total needs of people. How important it is, then, that we as God's children support these leaders and organizations with our prayers and financial gifts.

"Ye Christian Heralds" is taken from a seven-verse poem titled "Farewell to Missionaries," which first appeared in an English newspaper in about 1803. Two years later it was reprinted in a hymnal with the title "On the Departure of the Missionaries." One of the poem's omitted verses not found in our hymnals is of interest:

> Set up thy throne where Satan reigns, on Afric shores, on India's plains;
> On wilds and continents unknown, and be the universe thine own.

The author of this text, Bourne Draper, was a Baptist minister who served most of his life in the Baptist church in Southampton, England. Although he authored a number of other works, Draper is best known today for this one hymn written as a young man while he was preparing for the Christian ministry.

> Ye Christian heralds, go proclaim salvation through Emmanuel's name;
> to distant climes the tidings bear, and plant the Rose of Sharon there.

> God shield you with a wall of fire; with holy zeal your hearts inspire;
> bid raging winds their fury cease, and calm the tempests into peace.

> And when our labors all are o'er, then we shall meet to part no more;
> meet with the ransomed throng to fall, and crown our Savior Lord of all!

❦ *For Today:* Psalm 96; Isaiah 6:8; Mark 16:15; Acts 1:8; Romans 10:13-15; 1 Corinthians 3:9

Determine to read in the near future a biography of some great missionary statesman. Also write a personal letter to one of your church missionaries. Then let your pastor know how much you appreciate his ministry. Reflect again on this hymn—

Missionary Chant tune   Heinrich C. Zeuner, 1795-1857

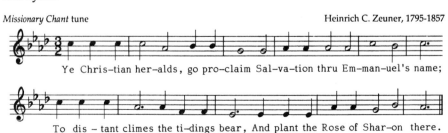

Ye Chris-tian her-alds, go pro-claim Sal-va-tion thru Em-man-uel's name;

To dis - tant climes the ti-dings bear, And plant the Rose of Shar-on there.

WORK, FOR THE NIGHT IS COMING

Annie L. Coghill, 1836-1907

As long as it is day, we must do the work of Him who sent Me. Night is coming when no one can work. (John 9:4)

> Do not pray for easy lives; pray to be stronger men! Do not pray for tasks equal to your powers. Pray for powers equal to your tasks. Then the doing of your work shall be no miracle, but you shall be a miracle. —*Phillips Brooks*

Diligence is a law of life. We are to put forth our very best effort into whatever work God gives us to do. For the Christian, every occupation is sacred when it is done for God's glory. What counts in God's sight is not only the actual work we do, but the attitude with which we do it. The story is told of three men who worked on a large church building, all doing similar tasks. When asked what they were doing, one replied, "I'm making mortar." Another, "I'm helping put up this great stone wall." The third, "I'm building a cathedral for God's glory." The right attitude makes all the difference.

This hymn, which emphasizes the joy and dignity of work, especially Christian service, was written in 1854 by an 18 year-old Canadian girl, known then as Annie Louise Walker. (Annie married a wealthy merchant, Harry Coghill, in 1883.) Her poem was first published in a Canadian newspaper and later in her own book, *Leaves From the Back Woods.* Mrs. Coghill eventually attained prominence as a poet and author, producing several volumes which enjoyed wide circulation.

Philosophers and writers have made many profound statements about the intrinsic value of labor; but none has been able to state more simply and meaningfully the joy of being co-workers with God in worthy labor than has Annie Louise Coghill in this hymn text:

> Work, for the night is coming. Work thru the morning hours; work while the dew is sparkling; work 'mid springing flow'rs. Work when the day grows brighter. Work in the glowing sun; work for the night is coming, when man's work is done.

> Work, for the night is coming. Work thru the sunny noon; fill brightest hours with labor—rest comes sure and soon. Give ev'ry flying minute something to keep in store; work for the night is coming when man works no more.

> Work, for the night is coming under the sunset skies: While their bright tints are glowing, work, for daylight flies. Work till the last beam fadeth, fadeth to shine no more; work, while the night is dark'ning, when man's work is o'er.

❦ ***For Today:*** Psalm 128:1, 2; Proverbs 6:6; 10:4; Isaiah 21:11; 61:1-3; Romans 10:14,15; Galatians 6:9

John Wesley once said: "Never be unemployed and never be triflingly employed." See your work as a sacred trust from God. Use this musical reminder—

Lowell Mason, 1792-1872

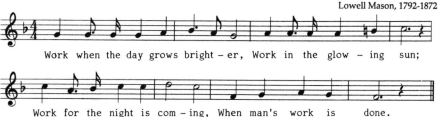

Work when the day grows bright - er, Work in the glow - ing sun;

Work for the night is com - ing, When man's work is done.

REVIVE US AGAIN

William P. Mackay, 1839-1885

Will You not revive us again, that Your people may rejoice in You? (Psalm 85:6)

The most desperate need of our day is a spiritual and moral renewal. This revival must begin with God's people, you and me—the Church. It must be more than a mere increase in church membership and attendance. There must be an individual resurgence of God consciousness, moral righteousness, and Christ-like living. It must include the elements of humbling ourselves and turning from our wicked ways (2 Chronicles 7:14). Although spiritual renewal cannot be "worked up" by human effort, we can prayerfully desire and seek it. We can ask God sincerely for a fresh touch of His love and the desire to represent and serve Him more effectively.

> Let none hear you idly saying, "There is nothing I can do,"
> While the souls of men are dying, and the Master calls for you.
> Take the task He gives you gladly. Let His work your pleasure be;
> Answer quickly when He calleth, "Here am I, send me, send me!"   *—Unknown*

The author of this text, William Paton Mackay, was a Scottish Presbyterian minister. After his education at the University of Edinburgh, he practiced medicine for a number of years before being called to the Christian ministry in 1868. Written in 1863 but revised four years later, this hymn text was based on Habakkuk 3:2: "Lord, I have heard of Your fame; I stand in awe of Your deeds, O Lord. Renew them in our day, in our time make them known; in wrath remember mercy." The hymn was included in Ira Sankey's *Gospel Hymns and Sacred Songs* of 1875, under the title "O Lord, Revive Thy Work."

> We praise Thee, O God, for the Son of Thy love, for Jesus who died and is now gone above.
>
> We praise Thee, O God, for Thy Spirit of light, who has shown us our Savior and scattered our night.
>
> All glory and praise to the Lamb that was slain, who has borne all our sins and has cleansed every stain.
>
> Revive us again; fill each heart with Thy love; may each soul be rekindled with fire from above.
>
> **Chorus:** Hallelujah, Thine the glory! Hallelujah, amen! Hallelujah, Thine the glory! Revive us again.

🎄 *For Today:* 2 Chronicles 7:14; Psalm 85:6; 2 Corinthians 4:16-18; Titus 3:4-8

Ask God to show you the areas in life that need a spiritual renewal. Pray for a genuine revival in your local church. Be willing to pray, however, "Lord, let it begin in me." Carry this musical prayer with you as you go—

John J. Husband, 1760-1825

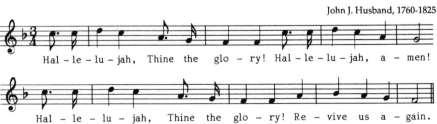

Hal – le – lu – jah, Thine the glo – ry! Hal – le – lu – jah, a – men!

Hal – le – lu – jah, Thine the glo – ry! Re – vive us a – gain.

LEAD ON, O KING ETERNAL

Ernest W. Shurtleff, 1862-1917

I have fought the good fight, I have finished the race, I have kept the faith. Now there is in store for me the crown of righteousness, which the Lord, the righteous Judge, will award to me on that day—and not only to me, but also to all who have longed for His appearing. (2 Timothy 4:7, 8)

One of the thrilling experiences in life is to watch a loved one or friend walk across a stage in cap and gown and receive that long awaited diploma. Today's hymn was written for just such an event.

Ernest Shurtleff, author of this text, was about to graduate from Andover Seminary in 1887. His classmates at the seminary, recognizing the poetic ability of their colleague, shortly before graduation one day approached Shurtleff with this request:

> "Ernest, why don't you write our class poem. After all, you have already published two volumes of poetry—What's the use of having a distinguished author in the class if he cannot rise to the occasion and do his class the honor of writing a good poem just for them?"
>
> "Let's make it a hymn that we can all sing," replied Shurtleff, "We've been spending days of preparation here at seminary. Now the day of march has come and we must go out to follow the leadership of the King of kings, to conquer the world under His banner."

Although the metaphors and expressions in this hymn were intended to challenge the graduating class of 1887 at Andover Seminary, the truths of this text can be applied to our lives today. This is not the time for any of us to slacken our efforts in the service of our Lord. The crown awaits the conquest— "Lead on, O God of Might!"

> Lead on, O King Eternal, the day of march has come! Henceforth in fields of conquest Thy tents shall be our home. Thru days of preparation Thy grace has made us strong, and now, O King Eternal, we lift our battle song.

> Lead on, O King Eternal, till sin's fierce war shall cease; and holiness shall whisper the sweet Amen of peace; for not with swords loud clashing nor roll of stirring drums, with deeds of love and mercy the heav'nly kingdom comes.

> Lead on, O King Eternal, we follow, not with fears; for gladness breaks like morning where'er Thy face appears. Thy cross is lifted o'er us; we journey in its light: The crown awaits the conquest—lead on, O God of might.

❦ **For Today:** Psalm 25:4, 9, 10; Isaiah 48:17; 1 Corinthians 16:13; Philippians 1:27-30

Ask God to lead you to greater spiritual conquests than you have yet known and to enable you to win the victory "with deeds of love and mercy." Carry these musical truths with you—

Lancashire tune   Henry Smart, 1813-1879

Thru days of prep – a – ra – tion Thy grace has made us strong,

And now, O King E – ter – nal, We lift our bat – tle song.

ONWARD, CHRISTIAN SOLDIERS

Sabine Baring-Gould, 1834-1924

Thou therefore endure hardness, as a good soldier of Jesus Christ. (2 Timothy 2:3 KJV)

The Christian life is often compared in Scripture to a warfare—the struggle of sin against righteousness and of the flesh versus the spirit. Each follower of Christ is called to be a "good" soldier. This involves motivation, training, discipline, good equipment, and endurance.

This hymn text reminds us that the church universal, the "called out" body of believers from every age, race, and culture, is to be an aggressive, unified body. It must always be moving forward in its mission. We cannot allow ourselves to become stagnant and contented with the status quo.

The author of this text, Sabine Baring-Gould, a Church of England minister, has left this account regarding the writing of this hymn:

> It was written in a very simple fashion, without thought of publication. Whitmonday is a great day for school festivals in Yorkshire, and one Whitmonday it was arranged that our school should join forces with that of a neighboring village. I wanted the children to sing while marching from one village to the other, but couldn't think of anything quite suitable, so I sat up at night resolved to write something myself. "Onward, Christian Soldiers" was the result. It was written in great haste, likely in less than 15 minutes.

Yet these words that were written hurriedly for marching children became the text for a hymn that God ordained to inspire lives around the world, challenging Christians with their responsibility to be aggressive in advancing His cause both individually and with other members of the "Church of God."

> Onward, Christian soldiers marching as to war, with the cross of Jesus going on before! Christ, the royal Master, leads against the foe; forward into battle see His banner go!

> Like a mighty army moves the Church of God; brothers, we are treading where the saints have trod. We are not divided, all one body we—One in hope and doctrine, one in charity.

> Onward, then, ye people, join our happy throng; blend with ours your voices in the triumph song. Glory, laud and honor unto Christ the King—This thru countless ages men and angels sing.

> **Refrain:** Onward, Christian soldiers, marching as to war, with the cross of Jesus going on before!

❦ *For Today:* 1 Corinthians 16:13; Ephesians 6:10-18; 1 Timothy 6:11, 12

Consider how the outreach ministry of your local church could be advanced more effectively in the community. Sing this musical truth to help as you reflect on this concern—

St. Gertrude tune   Arthur S. Sullivan, 1842-1900

On - ward, Chris - tian sol - diers, March - ing as to war,

With the cross of Je - sus, Go - ing on be - fore!

A CHARGE TO KEEP I HAVE

Charles Wesley, 1707-1788

As a prisoner for the Lord, then, I urge you to live a life worthy of the calling you have received. (Ephesians 4:1)

All of us as Christians have been given a general charge— a God to glorify. We have also been given a particular charge or calling that is unique. Our response to these charges is what gives life purpose and meaning. Fulfillment and contentment in life are not measured alone by our accomplishments. We must have the satisfaction that we are in the place and doing the task that God has destined for us—whether it be great or small.

Charles Wesley is said to have been inspired to write the text for this hymn while reading Matthew Henry's commentary on the book of Leviticus. In his thoughts on Leviticus 8:35, Henry wrote, "We shall everyone of us have a charge to keep, an eternal God to glorify, an immortal soul to provide for, one generation to serve." This hymn text first appeared in Wesley's *Short Hymns on Select Passages of Holy Scriptures*, published in 1762. It was printed under the title "Keep the Charge of the Lord, That Ye Die Not."

This hymn text reflects the strength and zeal of the early Methodists. John Wesley once remarked upon hearing of his followers' persecution: "Our people die well." On another occasion a physician said to Charles Wesley, "Most people die for fear of dying; but I never met with such people as yours. They are none of them afraid of death, but calm and patient and resigned to the last."

Being a Christian who worthily represents the Lord has never been and will never be a life of ease. It requires our very best, the total commitment of our lives.

> A charge to keep I have—a God to glorify, who gave His Son my soul to save and fit it for the sky.

> To serve the present age, my calling to fulfill—O may it all my pow'rs engage to do my Master's will!

> Arm me with jealous care, as in Thy sight to live; and O Thy servant, Lord, prepare a strict account to give!

> Help me to watch and pray, and on Thyself rely; and let me ne'er my trust betray, but press to realms on high.

❦ ***For Today:*** Leviticus 8:35; Joshua 24:15; Galatians 1:15-24; 1 Peter 4:10, 11

Ask God to redefine your sense of divine calling in life and to help make you more contented right where He has placed you. Carry this musical challenge with you—

Boylston tune   Lowell Mason, 1792-1872

A charge to keep I have-- A God to glo - ri - fy, Who gave His Son my soul to save And fit it for the sky.

STAND UP FOR JESUS

George Duffield, 1818-1888

Finally, be strong in the Lord and in His mighty power. (Ephesians 6:10)

A great city-wide revival swept across Philadelphia in 1858. It was called "the work of God in Philadelphia." Of the participating ministers none was more powerful that the 29-year-old Episcopalian, Dudley Tyng, who was known as a bold and uncompromising preacher.

In addition to pastoring his own church, Dudley Tyng began holding noonday services at the downtown YMCA. Great crowds came to hear this dynamic young preacher. On Tuesday, March 30, 1858, over 5,000 men gathered for a noon mass meeting to hear Tyng preach from the text "Ye that are men, go and serve the Lord" (Exodus 10:11). Over 1,000 of these men committed their lives to Christ. At one point, the young preacher exclaimed:

> I must tell my Master's errand, and I would rather that this right arm were amputated at the trunk than that I should come short of my duty to you in delivering God's message.

The very next week, while visiting in the country and watching the operation of a corn threshing machine in a barn, young Tyng accidentally caught his loose sleeve between the cogs; the arm was lacerated severely with the main artery severed and the median nerve injured. As a result of shock and a great loss of blood, the Rev. Dudley Tyng died.

On his death bed when asked by a group of sorrowing friends and ministers for a final statement, he feebly whispered, "Let us all stand up for Jesus."

The next Sunday, Tyng's close friend and fellow worker, the Rev. George Duffield, pastor of the Temple Presbyterian Church in Philadelphia, preached his morning sermon as a tribute to his departed friend. He closed his sermon by reading a poem that he had just finished writing, inspired, as he told his people, by the dying words of his esteemed friend.

> Stand up, stand up for Jesus; ye soldiers of the cross; lift high His royal banner—it must not suffer loss. From vict'ry unto vict'ry His army shall He lead, 'till ev'ry foe is vanquished and Christ is Lord indeed.

> Stand up, stand up for Jesus; the trumpet call obey; forth to the mighty conflict in this His glorious day. Ye that are men now serve Him against unnumbered foes; let courage rise with danger and strength to strength oppose.

> Stand up, stand up for Jesus; the strife will not be long; this day the noise of battle—the next, the victor's song. To Him that overcometh a crown of life shall be; He with the King of Glory shall reign eternally.

❦ **For Today:** 2 Corinthians 1:20-22; Ephesians 6:10-18; James 1:12

Determine to live boldly and unashamedly for God in the strength and wisdom that He will provide. Sing as you go—

Webb tune   George J. Webb, 1803-1887

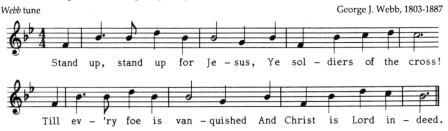

MUST JESUS BEAR THE CROSS ALONE?

Thomas Shepherd, 1665-1739

Then He called the crowd to Him along with His disciples and said: "If anyone would come after Me, he must deny himself and take up his cross and follow Me." (Mark 8:34)

The scriptural qualifications for discipleship are very clear: Self-denial and a resolve to bear a cross of consecration for the sake of the gospel. Each true follower of Christ will have a cross to bear at various times throughout life. The cross is the badge that identifies us as a worthy representative and servant of our Master. For some, the cross might be a physical weakness; for others it could be an unachieved goal, a discouraging situation, or a concern for a loved one. Whatever it may be, the way we bear our individual cross can in itself be a testimony to the power of the gospel as well as a source of encouragement to weaker Christians.

The text for this hymn was the work of several different authors through the centuries. Thomas Shepherd, a 17th century English dissenter preacher, published a volume of poems in 1693 titled *Penitential Cries.* At least the first stanza with some possible alterations is believed to have come from that volume. One of the original stanzas from this work reads as follows:

> Shall Simon bear the Cross alone, and other Saints be free?
> Each Saint of Thine shall find his own— And there is one for me.

George Nelson Allen, music teacher at Oberlin College, collected the verses and composed the music for the text in 1844 for inclusion in his collection, *Oberlin Social and Sabbath School Hymn Book.* "Must Jesus Bear the Cross Alone?" has since challenged Christians in their commitment to Christ and His service with the realization that an earthly cross always precedes the heavenly crown.

> Must Jesus bear the cross alone and all the world go free? No, there's a cross for ev'ry one, and there's a cross for me.

> The consecrated cross I'll bear till death shall set me free, and then go home my crown to wear, for there's a crown for me.

> How happy are the saints above, who once went sorrowing here! But now they taste unmingled love, and joy without a tear.

> O precious cross! O glorious crown! O resurrection day! Ye angels, from the stars come down and bear my soul away.

❧ *For Today:* Matthew 16:24-27; Philippians 3:10; 1 Peter 2:21-24

Reflect on the example of our Lord, "who for the joy set before Him endured the cross, scorning its shame . . ." (Hebrews 12:2). Relate this to the cross you may be bearing. Carry this musical truth with you—

Maitland tune

George N. Allen, 1812-1877

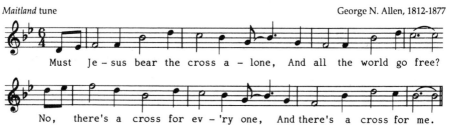

Must Je – sus bear the cross a – lone, And all the world go free?

No, there's a cross for ev – 'ry one, And there's a cross for me.

MY SOUL, BE ON THY GUARD

George Heath, 1750-1822

Therefore I do not run like a man running aimlessly; I do not fight like a man beating the air. I beat my body and make it my slave so that after I have preached to others, I myself will not be disqualified for the prize. (1 Corinthians 9:26, 27)

There is nothing more tragic than to see a Christian negate a lifetime of worthy living and service for God through some spiritual defeat and dishonor to the gospel. Imagine the shame of Job when Eliphaz the Temanite rebuked him with these cutting words:

Think how you have instructed many, how you have strengthened feeble hands. Your words have supported those who stumbled; you have strengthened faltering knees, but now trouble comes to you, and you are discouraged; it strikes you, and you are dismayed. Should not your piety be your confidence and your blameless ways your hope? (Job 4:3-6)

The apostle Paul's fervent concern for his life, that after he had preached to others he himself might be disqualified by God through careless living, seems to apply to the writer of this hymn text. George Heath was an English independent minister, who in 1770 became pastor of a Presbyterian church at Honiton, Devonshire. Later, proving himself unworthy of this office, he was deprived of his parish "for cause." Eventually, it seems, he became a Unitarian minister. It is difficult to understand how a person could write such a stirring challenge on the subject of spiritual steadfastness and then change so drastically in later years. Yet the Scriptures are clear that the Christian life is a lifetime of perseverance, and whoever puts his hand to the plow and looks back is unfit for service in God's kingdom (Luke 9:62). We must have the enabling power of the Holy Spirit each day if we intend to be on guard.

My soul, be on thy guard—ten thousand foes arise. The hosts of sin are pressing hard to draw thee from the skies.

O watch and fight and pray; the battle ne'er give o'er; renew it boldly ev'ry day, and help divine implore.

Ne'er think the vict'ry won, nor lay thine armor down; the work of faith will not be done till thou obtain thy crown.

Fight on, my soul, till death shall bring thee to thy God; He'll take thee, at thy parting breath, to His divine abode.

❦ **For Today:** Matthew 26:41; 1 Corinthians 15:58; 16:13; Hebrews 10:23

Be alert to the many distractions that can easily undermine your spiritual life. Resolve to keep short accounts with God. Depend on the Holy Spirit for your inner strength. Reflect on this musical message as you go—

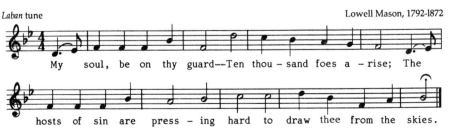

WHO IS ON THE LORD'S SIDE?

Frances R. Havergal, 1836-1879

. . . offer yourselves to God, as those who have been brought from death to life; and offer the parts of your body to Him as instruments of righteousness. (Romans 6:13)

As Christians, we are to take our places in God's army and not be ashamed to be counted as one of His. Believers are too often content to sit on the sidelines and merely observe the spectacle. The work of the gospel, inviting individuals to be personally reconciled with God, is an urgent task, not a spectator sport. It demands our whole-hearted, zealous involvement.

This militant hymn text by Frances Havergal was originally titled "Home Missions," and was written in October, 1877. It was based on the Scripture setting in 1 Chronicles 12:1-18, where a very select group of soldiers was preparing to join King David in warfare against the enemy. The poem later appeared in *Loyal Responses,* published by the author in 1878. "Who Is on the Lord's Side?" has been used for more than a century to challenge Christians to make a definite commitment to follow Christ in spiritual warfare.

Who is on the Lord's side? Who will serve the King? Who will be His helpers, other lives to bring? Who will leave the world's side? Who will face the foe? Who is on the Lord's side? Who for Him will go?

Not for weight of glory, not for crown and palm, enter we the army, raise the warrior psalm; but for Love that claimeth lives for whom He died: He whom Jesus nameth must be on His side.

Jesus, Thou hast bought us, not with gold or gem, but with Thine own life-blood, for Thy diadem. With Thy blessing filling each who comes to Thee. Thou has made us willing; Thou hast made us free.

Fierce may be the conflict, strong may be the foe, but the King's own army none can overthrow. Round His standard ranging, vict'ry is secure, for His truth unchanging makes the triumph sure.

Refrain: 1. By Thy call of mercy, by Thy grace divine,

2. By Thy love constraining, by Thy grace divine,

3. By Thy grand redemption, by Thy grace divine,

4. Joyfully enlisting, by Thy grace divine,

WE ARE ON THE LORD'S SIDE—SAVIOR, WE ARE THINE!

❦ *For Today:* Joshua 24:15; 1 Chronicles 12:1-18; Mark 8:24-38; 2 Corinthians 5:11; 1 Timothy 6:12

Determine to do or say something to a non-Christian that publicly identifies you as a follower/soldier of Christ. Carry this musical truth as a help—

Armageddon tune

C. Luise Reichardt, c. 1780-1826
Arranged by John Goss, 1800-1880

We are on the Lord's side-- Sav - ior, we are Thine!

AM I A SOLDIER OF THE CROSS?

Isaac Watts, 1674-1748

Endure hardship with us like a good solder of Christ Jesus. No one serving as a soldier gets involved in civilian affairs——he wants to please his commanding officer. (2 Timothy 2:3, 4)

The Church founded by Christ has been built on the blood of martyrs. It has been estimated that at least 50 million persons have had a martyr's death since the crucifixion of our Lord. Even today, in our 20th century civilized culture, large numbers of believers live under conditions of harassment and persecution.

All of Christ's apostles were persecuted by the enemies of their Master. According to historical tradition, the following was their fate:

Matthew—suffered martyrdom by being slain in the city of Ethiopia.
Mark—died at Alexandria, after being dragged through the streets of that city.
Luke—hanged on an olive tree in the classic land of Greece.
John—put in boiling oil. Afterward branded at Patmos.
Peter—crucified at Rome with his head downward.
James the Lesser—thrown from a pinnacle of the temple, then beaten to death.
Bartholomew—flayed alive.
Andrew—bound to a cross, where he preached to his persecutors until he died.
Jude—shot to death with arrows.
Matthias—first stoned and then beheaded.
Barnabas of the Gentiles—stoned to death at Salonica.
Paul—after various tortures and persecutions, beheaded at Rome by Emperor Nero.

In Isaac Watts' time, much persecution was inflicted upon the English Dissenters—those who had split from the official, state Anglican church. Stalwarts such as Isaac Watts became resolute and fearless in their proclamation and defense of the gospel. "Am I a Soldier of the Cross?" was written in 1724, following a sermon by Watts titled "Holy Fortitude or Remedies Against Fears." These words are still a challenge for us today:

Am I a soldier of the cross? A foll'wer of the Lamb? And shall I fear to own His cause or blush to speak His name?

Must I be carried to the skies on flow'ry beds cf ease, while others fought to win the prize and sailed thru bloody seas?

Are there no foes for me to face? Must I not stem the flood? Is this vile world a friend to grace, to help me on to God?

Sure I must fight if I would reign—Increase my courage, Lord! I'll bear the toil, endure the pain, supported by Thy Word.

🍂 *For Today:* 1 Corinthians 16:13; Ephesians 6:10-20; 1 Timothy 6:12; Jude 3

Even now, pray for those who are suffering for Christ and the work of the gospel in difficult areas around the world. Reflect on these musical questions—

Arlington tune   Thomas A. Arne, 1710-1778

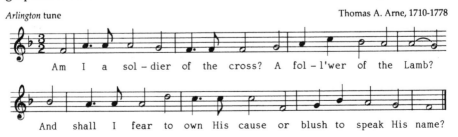

Am I a sol – dier of the cross? A fol – l'wer of the Lamb?

And shall I fear to own His cause or blush to speak His name?

THE SON OF GOD GOES FORTH TO WAR

Reginald Heber, 1783-1826

Be on your guard; stand firm in the faith; be men of courage; be strong.
(1 Corinthians 16:13)

This text was written in 1812 by Reginald Heber, an important 19th century Anglican church hymn writer. Heber wrote it especially for use on St. Stephen's Day, which occurs the first day after Christmas. On this day the liturgical churches honor the memory of Stephen, the first Christian martyr.

The hymn's first stanza portrays Christ as the leader of a great army going forth to win His kingly crown. The challenge is given: "Who follows in His train?" The response: Those who demonstrate that they can bear the cross patiently here below.

The second stanza reminds us of Stephen's martyrdom. The scriptural account tells us that Stephen saw Jesus "standing at God's right hand," with Stephen praying for his murderers, "Lord, do not hold this sin against them" (Acts 7:54-60).

The third stanza refers to the day of Pentecost when the Holy Spirit was given to "the chosen few." The verse then reminds us of the twelve apostles and their martyrdom for the sake of the gospel. The final stanza is a picture in heaven of the noble martyrs throughout the ages before God's throne—men, boys, matrons, maids—dressed in robes of white.

> The Son of God goes forth to war, a kingly crown to gain: His blood-red banner streams afar: Who follows in His train? Who best can drink His cup of woe, (Christ's suffering on the cross) triumphant over pain? Who patient bears His cross below, he follows in His train.

> The martyr first, whose eagle eye could pierce beyond the grave, who saw His Master in the sky and called on Him to save—Like Him, with pardon on his tongue in midst of mortal pain, he prayed for them that did the wrong: Who follows in his train?

> A glorious band, the chosen few on whom the Spirit came, twelve valiant saints, their hope they knew, and mocked the cross and flame—They met the tyrant's brandished steel, the lion's gory mane. They bowed their necks the death to feel: Who follows in their train?

> A noble army, men and boys, the matron and the maid, around the Savior's throne rejoice, in robes of light arrayed—They climbed the steep ascent of heav'n thru peril, toil and pain: O GOD, TO US MAY GRACE BE GIVEN TO FOLLOW IN THEIR TRAIN!

❦ *For Today:* Ephesians 6:10-20; 1 Timothy 6:12; 2 Timothy 2:3, 4

Let this musical statement be your response of faith—

All Saints New tune   Henry S. Cutler, 1824-1902

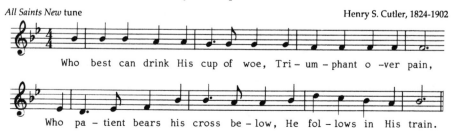

Who best can drink His cup of woe, Tri- um - phant o -ver pain,

Who pa - tient bears his cross be - low, He fol - lows in His train.

FIGHT THE GOOD FIGHT
WITH ALL THY MIGHT

John S. B. Monsell, 1811-1875

Fight the good fight of the faith. Take hold of the eternal life to which you were called when you made your good confession in the presence of many witnesses. (1 Timothy 6:12)

As Christians, one of our chief characteristics should be courage, especially when it involves our spiritual defense of the gospel. How easily, however, our noble intentions for this kind of fortitude are changed into attitudes of despair and defeat because of annoying circumstances, the secular media, or disappointment in others. To avoid these courage-defeating forces, we must have our "inner man" renewed daily with spiritual nourishment. We cannot be truly strong if we do not gain the inner strength that comes from God.

When John Monsell wrote this hymn text, he provided ten strong imperatives for a triumphant Christian life: 1) Fight the good fight; 2) Lay hold of life; 3) Run the straight race; 4) Lift up thine eyes; 5) Seek His face; 6) Cast care aside; 7) Lean on thy Guide; 8) Trust and prove; 9) Faint not nor fear; and 10) Only believe. Each of these is worthy of further pondering.

John Monsell was an Anglican clergyman who published a hymnal in 1863 titled *Love and Praise for the Church Year.* In that song book this hymn first appeared under the title "The Fight for Faith." This respected man of the pulpit was also known as a strong advocate of vigorous congregational singing, constantly persuading his people that congregational singing should be fervent and joyous. "We are too distant and reserved in our praises," he would say. "We sing, but not as we should sing to Him who is the chief among ten thousand, the altogether lovely." Perhaps there is a stronger relationship between our times of joyous praise and our ability to "fight the good fight" than we generally realize.

> Fight the good fight with all thy might! Christ is thy strength, and Christ thy right; lay hold on life, and it shall be thy joy and crown eternally.

> Run the straight race through God's good grace. Lift up thine eyes and seek His face; life with its way before us lies; Christ is the path and Christ the prize.

> Cast care aside, lean on thy Guide; His boundless mercy will provide; trust and thy trusting soul shall prove Christ is its life and Christ its love.

> Faint not nor fear; His arms are near; He changeth not, and thou art dear; only believe, and thou shalt see that Christ is all in all to thee.

🍂 ***For Today:*** Deuteronomy 31:6; Romans 8:36-39; 1 Corinthians 16:13

Allow God to renew your inner man through quiet meditation with His Word and a time of communion with Him. Reflect on these musical truths—

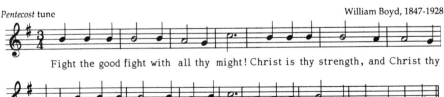

Pentecost tune   William Boyd, 1847-1928

Fight the good fight with all thy might! Christ is thy strength, and Christ thy

right; Lay hold on life, and it shall be Thy joy and crown e-ter-nal - ly.

SOLDIERS OF CHRIST, ARISE

Charles Wesley, 1707-1788

Finally, be strong in the Lord and in His mighty power. Put on the full armor of God so that you can take your stand against the devil's schemes. (Ephesians 6:10, 11)

Followers of Christ are also His soldiers—called to do battle with the forces of Satan and evil. Victories are never won while resting in the barracks. God's soldiers must always be alert and dressed in full armor. That armor includes six important pieces: (Ephesians 6:10-20)

- The belt of truth (warriors with absolute integrity).
- The breastplate of righteousness (people must see our good works).
- Sandals of peace (though soldiers, we are called to be peacemakers).
- Shield of faith (for extinguishing all of Satan's doubts and fears).
- Helmet of salvation (one of Satan's chief attacks is the mind).
- Sword of the Spirit—the Word of God (our only offensive weapon).

In addition to wearing armor, the Christian soldier is to face every occasion with prayer and to remember the fellow saints in prayer (v. 18). Ultimately, however, the battle is not ours but God's (2 Chronicles 20:15). He knows the battle plan. Our responsibility is only to be active and obedient in the small duty wherever He has placed us on the battlefield.

Charles Wesley knew much about the Christian life as warfare. Many times both John and Charles were physically abused for their evangelical ministries. This text was first published in 1749 and was titled "The Whole Armor of God—Ephesians VI." The hymn has often been referred to as "the Christian's bugle blast" for its strong call to arms.

Soldiers of Christ, arise and put your armor on, strong in the strength which God supplies thru His eternal Son; strong in the Lord of hosts and in His mighty pow'r: Who in the strength of Jesus trusts is more than conqueror.

Stand then in His great might, with all His strength endued, and take, to arm you for the fight, the panoply of God; that having all things done, and all your conflicts past, ye may o'ercome thru Christ alone and stand entire at last.

Leave no unguarded place, no weakness of the soul; take ev'ry virtue, ev'ry grace, and fortify the whole. From strength to strength go on; Wrestle and fight and pray; tread all the pow'rs of darkness down and win the well-fought day.

❦ *For Today:* 1 Corinthians 15:57, 58; Ephesians 6:10-20; Philippians 1:27-30; 1 Timothy 6:12

Reflect on the words of Maltbie D. Babcock— "We are not here to play, to dream, to drift; we have hard work to do, and loads to lift. Shun not the struggle; face it—'tis God's gift." Go forth in your full armor and in the power of His might. Carry this musical encouragement with you—

Diademata tune   George J. Elvey, 1816-1893

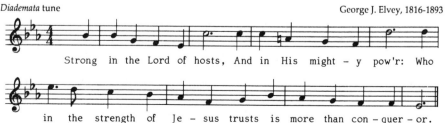

Strong in the Lord of hosts, And in His might - y pow'r: Who in the strength of Je - sus trusts is more than con - quer - or.

GOD OF OUR FATHERS

Daniel C. Roberts, 1841-1907

If my people, who are called by My name, will humble themselves and pray and seek My face and turn from their wicked ways, then will I hear from heaven and will forgive their sin and will heal their land. (2 Chronicles 7:14)

> After what I owe to God, nothing should be more dear or more sacred to me than the love and respect I owe my country. —*Jacques Auguste de Thou*

We need to be reminded that a nation can receive God's blessing only when He is recognized as ruler and Lord. Christian people in every land have an awesome responsibility—to be models of God's righteousness— "salt" and "light" for a sinful and hurting society. The moral strength of a nation rests upon the knees of God's people.

"God of Our Fathers" also reminds us that concerned citizens of the heavenly kingdom should also be involved citizens of their earthly kingdom. The hymn text was written in 1876, the year that America was preparing to celebrate its 100th anniversary of the signing of the Declaration of Independence. Daniel Crane Roberts, a 35-year-old rector of a small Episcopal church in Brandon, Vermont, felt that the country should have a new national hymn for the occasion. His new song was sung for the first time by the parishioners of the Brandon village church for their worship service on July 4th, 1876.

Later, at the time of the actual National Centennial Observance commemorating the adoption of the Constitution, Roberts' hymn text was chosen as the official hymn for that event. These words remind us well that the God who has so richly blessed our land in the past is the One still needed to be "our ruler, guardian, guide, and stay."

> God of our fathers, whose almighty hand leads forth in beauty all the starry band; of shining worlds in splendor thru the skies, our grateful songs before Thy throne arise.

> Thy love divine hath led us in the past, in this free land by Thee our lot is cast; be thou our ruler, guardian, guide and stay, Thy word our law, Thy paths our chosen way.

> From war's alarms, from deadly pestilence, be Thy strong arm our ever sure defense; Thy true religion in our hearts increase; Thy bounteous goodness nourish us in peace.

> Refresh Thy people on their toilsome way. Lead us from night to never ending day; fill all our lives with love and grace divine, and glory, laud, and praise be ever Thine.

❦ ***For Today:*** Exodus 3:15; Psalm 33:12; Proverbs 14:34

Breathe a prayer of thanks for the heritage of Christianity and for God's continued guidance of our land.

National Hymn tune   George W. Warren, 1828-1902

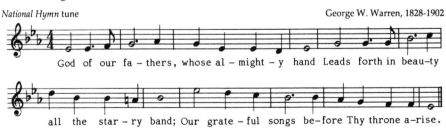

God of our fa – thers, whose al – might – y hand Leads forth in beau–ty all the star – ry band; Our grate – ful songs be–fore Thy throne a–rise.

FAITH OF OUR FATHERS

Frederick W. Faber, 1814-1863

Contend for the faith that was once for all entrusted to the saints. (Jude 3)

If you don't have a cause that is worth dying for, you very likely don't have anything worth living for. —*Unknown*

Often we fail to realize the great price many of our forefathers paid to establish and preserve the Christian faith. It is good for us to be reminded often that the history of the Christian faith is a rich heritage of countless people whose faith in God was considered more dear than life itself. Much could said about the first century Christians and their persecution by the Roman Empire, or even the religious persecutions of our American forefathers in their quest for a new land where they could enjoy religious freedom.

The "faith of our fathers" referred to in this hymn, however, is the faith of the martyred leaders of the Roman Catholic church during the 16th century. Although he was raised as a Calvinist and later was a minister in the Anglican church, Frederick Faber left the state church and joined the Roman Catholic fold. He became known as Father Wilfrid. Faber began to make it his life's mission to write hymns that promoted the history and teachings of the Catholic church. Frederick Faber wrote 150 such hymns before his early death at the age of 49. His "Faith of Our Fathers" text first appeared in 1849 in the author's collection, *Jesus and Mary; or Catholic Hymns for Singing and Reading.* It was always Faber's hope that someday England would be brought back to the Papal fold.

The three stanzas found in our hymnals, however, are very usable for evangelical worship and can be reinterpreted to challenge our commitment and loyalty to the gospel that our spiritual fathers often died to defend:

Faith of our fathers, living still in spite of dungeon, fire and sword—O how our hearts beat high with joy whene'er we hear that glorious word!

Our fathers, chained in prisons dark, were still in heart and conscience free; how sweet would be their children's fate if they, like them, could die for thee!

Faith of our fathers, we will love both friend and foe in all our strife; and preach thee too, as love knows how, by kindly words and virtuous life.

Refrain: Faith of our fathers, holy faith, we will be true to thee till death.

❦ *For Today:* Psalm 22:4, 5; 1 Timothy 6:13, 14; 2 Timothy 4:7; Hebrews 11

Reflect on the great gallery of Old Testament saints listed in Hebrews 11. Ask God to make your Christian faith something that future generations will want to emulate. Carry this tune with you—

St. Catherine tune

Henri F. Hemy, 1818-1888
Adapted by James G. Walton, 1821-1905

Faith of our fa – thers, ho – ly faith, We will be true to thee till death.

FAITH IS THE VICTORY

John H. Yates, 1837-1900

. . . this is the victory that has overcome the world, even our faith. (1 John 5:4)

Saving faith must always be reflected in a working faith. Our response of faith to the redemptive work of Christ transforms us; but then we need a daily motivating faith if we want to live overcoming lives. To live by faith is to believe with conviction that God's purposes for us will ultimately prevail. In fact, prevailing faith anticipates victory and celebrates in advance. For example, read the Old Testament account of how singers preceded the warriors into battle and the defeat of the enemy was accomplished (2 Chronicles 20:20-22).

Our faith does not develop merely through intellectual assent to biblical dogma or through wishful thinking. Rather, it is a lifetime commitment to the person of Christ with a response of obedience to His Word (Romans 10:17).

This hymn of faith and victory was first published in 1891 in the *Christian Endeavor Hymnal*. The author, John Henry Yates, was a licensed Methodist preacher who was later ordained by the Baptists. Ira Sankey, the composer, is often called the "father of the gospel song."

> Encamped along the hills of light, ye Christian soldiers rise, and press the battle ere the night shall veil the glowing skies. Against the foe in vales below let all our strength be hurled; faith is the victory, we know, that overcomes the world.

> His banner over us is love, our sword the Word of God; we tread the road the saints above with shouts of triumph trod. By faith they like a whirl-wind's breath swept on o'er ev'ry field; the faith by which they conquered death is still our shining shield.

> On ev'ry hand the foe we find drawn up in dread array; let tents of ease be left behind, and onward to the fray! Salvation's helmet on each head, with truth all girt about: The earth shall tremble 'neath our tread and echo with our shout.

> To him that overcomes the foe white raiment shall be giv'n; before the angels he shall know his name confessed in heav'n. Then onward from the hills of light, our hearts with love aflame; we'll vanquish all the hosts of night in Jesus' conq'ring name.

> **Chorus:** Faith is the victory! Faith is the victory! O glorious victory that overcomes the world.

🍂 *For Today:* Galatians 2:20; James 2:18; 1 John 5:1-12; Jude 3

Ask God to make you a vivid demonstration to your associates and friends of a triumphant faith in Christ—an exclamation of faith, not a question mark. Sing this musical truth as you go—

Ira D. Sankey, 1840-1908

Faith is the vic – to – ry! Faith is the vic – to – ry! O glo – ri – ous vic – to – ry That o – ver – comes the world.

O FOR A FAITH THAT WILL NOT SHRINK

William H. Bathurst, 1796-1877

The apostles said to the Lord, "Increase our faith!" He replied, "If you have faith as small as a mustard seed, you can say to this mulberry tree, 'Be uprooted and planted in the sea,' and it will obey you." (Luke 17:5, 6)

> When the world seems at its worst, Christians must be at their best. —*Unknown*

> Faith is to believe what we do not see, and the reward of faith is to see what we believe. —*St. Augustine*

Discouragement can easily cause our faith to shrink, and we may even at times consider quitting our service for God. Perhaps we have all experienced these sentiments:

> I've taught a class for many years; borne many burdens, toiled through tears—
> But folks don't notice me a bit, I'm so discouraged, I'll just quit. —*Unknown*

One of the chief characteristics of spiritual maturity is the ability to persevere—even in the face of adversity. God often permits difficulties to come into our lives simply to allow our faith in Him to become stronger. A faith that is never tested and strengthened soon becomes a shrinking one. But if our faith is real, it will stand every test and prove to be an overcoming faith.

This hymn text, which is an exposition of Luke 17:5, is from William Bathurst's *Psalms and Hymns for Public and Private Use.* The song was originally titled "The Power of Faith." The first three stanzas describe a victorious faith amidst some of the most difficult circumstances in life. The final stanza affirms the believer's desire to have such trust that even now life becomes a foretaste of heaven it self.

William Hiley Bathurst was an Anglican minister who wrote more than 200 hymn texts. The composer of the music, William H. Havergal, the father of Frances Ridley Havergal, was also prominent in the Church of England, as a minister and writer of many hymns.

> O for a faith that will not shrink tho pressed by many a foe, that will not tremble on the brink of any earthly woe.

> That will not murmur nor complain beneath the chast'ning rod, but in the hour of grief or pain will lean upon its God.

> A faith that shines more bright and clear when tempests rage without, that, when in danger, knows no fear, in darkness feels no doubt.

> Lord, give me such a faith as this, and then, whate'er may come, I'll taste e'en now the hallowed bliss of an eternal home.

❦ *For Today:* Romans 1:17; Galatians 6:9; Ephesians 6:16; 2 Timothy 1:7

Ponder this question—Could I stand to lose everything and still have an implicit faith in God and know with certainty that He is in absolute control? Carry this musical resolve—

Evan tune

William H. Havergal, 1793-1870

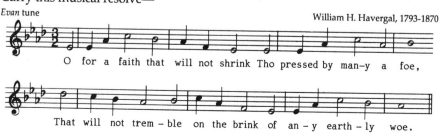

O for a faith that will not shrink Tho pressed by man-y a foe,

That will not trem-ble on the brink of an-y earth-ly woe.

RISE UP, O MEN OF GOD!

William P. Merrill, 1867-1954

. . . that you stand firm in one spirit, contending as one man for the faith of the gospel without being frightened in any way by those who oppose you. (Philippians 1:27, 28)

Our world is filled with much physical and social suffering. Often we prefer to close our eyes to these painful situations that are all around us. It is much more comfortable to associate only with those who live as we do. This kind of attitude within the church will turn any body of believers into nothing more than a religious club.

If we want to represent our Lord with integrity, we must not compartmentalize the church's mission. Soul winning and social responsibility are woven intrinsically together and constitute an inherent part of the ministry. A starving person needs both his stomach as well as his soul cared for. Christ's earthly ministry is a prime model of an ideal balance of caring for body as well as the soul of needy individuals.

The author of this call-to-action text, William Pierson Merrill, was a Presbyterian minister. He served churches in Philadelphia and Chicago, and he pastored the Brick Presbyterian Church in New York until his retirement in 1938. Merrill wrote "Rise Up, O Men of God!" especially for the brotherhood movement within the Presbyterian churches in 1911. Merrill was also a prolific writer of hymn texts and theological books.

An important secret of individual happiness is to be employed continually in doing something of value, to be "done with lesser things," to be totally involved in serving "the King of kings." And even the cup of water given in Christ's name will not go unrewarded (Matthew 10:42).

Rise up, O men of God! Have done with lesser things; give heart and mind and soul and strength to serve the King of kings.

Rise up, O men of God! His kingdom tarries long. Bring in the day of brotherhood and end the night of wrong.

Rise up, O men of God! The Church for you doth wait, her strength unequal to her task; rise up, and make her great!

Lift high the cross of Christ! Tread where His feet have trod. As brothers of the Son of man, rise up, O men of God!

🍎 *For Today:* Deuteronomy 11:13-32; John 12:26; Acts 20:28; 1 Corinthians 16:13; Ephesians 6:7

Determine by word and example to be a challenge to the members of your church by being more aggressively involved in an outreach ministry to your community. Reflect again on this musical truth—

St. Thomas tune

From "Williams' Psalmody," 1770

Rise up, O men of God! Have done with less-er things, Give
heart and mind and soul and strength to serve the King of Kings.

O MASTER, LET ME WALK WITH THEE

Washington Gladden, 1836-1918

He has showed you, O man, what is good. And what does the Lord require of you?
To act justly and to love mercy and to walk humbly with your God. (Micah 6:8)

Go labor on: Spend and be spent, my joy to do the Father's will;
It is the way the Master went, should not the servant tread it still?   —*H. Bonar*

As God's representatives, we must make it our life's mission to make the invisible Christ visible to lost and needy people through both word and deed. We can do this most effectively by dealing justly with others and by showing compassion and understanding to those who are less privileged than we are.

This hymn, published in 1879, comes from a period of religious history in America when there was much emphasis given to the social implications of the gospel. The Civil War had ended and the country was in the midst of a great industrial revolution. As is often true in such times, the individual is exploited in the name of economic progress.

Many of our country's more liberal clergymen became enthusiastic champions for the cause of social justice. One of the recognized leaders of the social gospel movement was Washington Gladden, known not only for his influential pulpiteering and writing but also for his negotiations in various national labor disputes and strikes. It was always his conviction that it was the duty of the Christian Church to "elevate the masses not only spiritually and morally, but to be concerned about their social and economic welfare as well." Although Gladden was widely known in his day for his persuasive preaching and writing, he is remembered particularly today for this one hymn text, which teaches us so well that our service for God must always be based on an intimate fellowship with Him.

O Master, let me walk with Thee in lowly paths of service free; tell me Thy secret—help me bear the strain of toil, the fret of care.

Help me the slow of heart to move by some clear, winning word of love; teach me the wayward feet to stay and guide them in the homeward way.

Teach me Thy patience! still with Thee in closer, dearer company, in work that keeps faith sweet and strong, in trust that triumphs over wrong.

In hope that sends a shining ray far down the future's broad'ning way, in peace that only Thou canst give, with Thee, O Master, let me live.

❦ *For Today:* Amos 3:3; Matthew 25:31-46; Ephesians 4:1 Philippians 2:5-7; Titus 3: 8

Actively seek to do for someone at least one good deed that you might otherwise be hesitant to attempt. Allow this musical message to help—

Maryton tune   H. Percy Smith, 1825-1898

O Mas - ter, let me walk with Thee In low-ly paths of Serv - ice free;

Tell me Thy se - cret--help me bear The strain of toil, the fret of care.

WHERE CROSS THE CROWDED WAYS OF LIFE

Franklin Mason North, 1850-1935

Defend the cause of the weak and fatherless; maintain the rights of the poor and oppressed. Rescue the weak and needy; deliver them from the hand of the wicked. (Psalm 82:3, 4)

Henry David Thoreau, noted American writer, philosopher, and naturalist of the past 19th century, once described the large city as "a place where people are lonely together." This loneliness is not the result of an absence of people; rather, it is due to a lack of genuine caring relationships.

If Thoreau's observation was true in the past, it has become increasingly true in the present, and the prediction is that it will become alarmingly more so in the near future. In 1950 there were only seven cities in the world with more than five million people. Only two of these were in the Third World. Today there are 34 cities with more than five million people, 22 of which are in the Third World. And by the middle of the 21st century, there will be nearly 100 cities with at least five million people, with 80 of these in Africa, Asia, and Latin America. Twenty percent of the world's population will be living in the slums and squatter settlements of Third World countries.

The author of this text, Franklin North, was a Methodist minister in New York City. He wrote this hymn in response to a request from the Methodist hymnal committee for a hymn about big city life, which Pastor North knew well and to which he was most sympathetic. The hymn first appeared in 1903 in the publication *The Christian City*, of which North was the editor. God help us to be people with sensitivity and compassion.

> Where cross the crowded ways of life, where sound the cries of race and clan, above the noise of selfish strife, we hear Thy voice, O Son of man!

> The cup of water giv'n for Thee still holds the freshness of Thy grace; yet long these multitudes to see the sweet compassion of Thy face.

> O Master, from the mountain side, make haste to heal these hearts of pain; among these restless throngs abide; O tread the city streets again:

> Till sons of men shall learn Thy love and follow where Thy feet have trod; till glorious, from Thy heav'n above, shall come the city of our God.

❦ *For Today:* Zechariah 7:8; Matthew 10:42; 22:9; Luke 4:18; 1 Peter 2:21

Determine to become better acquainted with a person from another culture or race. Perhaps invite him or her to your home for dinner. Ask God to help you think globally, to understand and accept a multicultural world. Reflect on these musical thoughts as you go—

Germany tune

Gardiner's *Sacred Melodies*,1815

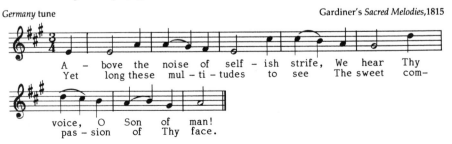

HOLD THE FORT

Words and Music by Philip P. Bliss, 1838-1876

Only hold on to what you have until I come. (Revelation 2:25)

God's call to each believer is to be obedient and faithful—not to seek a life of earthly success. Difficulties and defeats are a normal part of every Christian's life. Our response to negative situations can either shatter us or they can intensify our perseverance and confidence in a sovereign God. It has been said that a mark of a champion athlete is not how he/she responds to a victory, but how a difficult loss on a previous day has been met.

As was true of so many of Philip P. Bliss's gospel songs, this stirring hymn was inspired by an illustration used by Major Whittle, an officer in the American Civil War, while addressing a YMCA meeting on the text from Revelation 2:25. Major Whittle's illustration was about a small Northern force of soldiers in charge of guarding a great quantity of supplies. They were being hard pressed by greatly superior Confederate forces. Finally, the Confederate general, General French, commanded the Federal troops to surrender. At that moment the troops saw a signal from their leader, General Sherman, on a hill some miles away, which said, "Hold the fort, I am coming. Sherman." The story so captivated Bliss's interest that he could not retire that evening until he had completed both the text and the music for this rousing gospel song. It later became a great favorite in the Moody-Sankey campaigns both in Great Britain and in the United States.

We too have a commander now in heaven who has promised to return for us. Victory is certain! Our responsibility is to faithfully "hold the fort" and to "occupy till He comes" (Luke 19:13 KJV).

> Ho, my comrades, see the signal waving in the sky! Reinforcements now appearing, victory is nigh.
>
> See the mighty host advancing, Satan leading on; Mighty men around us falling, courage almost gone!
>
> See the glorious banner waving! Hear the trumpet blow! In our Leader's name we triumph over ev'ry foe.
>
> Fierce and long the battle rages, but our help is near; Onward comes our great Commander—cheer, my comrades, cheer!
>
> **Chorus:** "Hold the fort, for I am coming," Jesus signals still; wave the answer back to heaven, "By Thy grace we will."

❧ *For Today:* Matthew 10:22; Romans 5:3; 2 Timothy 2:10; Hebrews 12:2, 6, 7; James 1:12

Reflect seriously on these lines: "Christ's cause is hindered everywhere, and people are dying in despair. The reason why? Just think a bit—The church is full of those who quit." Carry this musical truth with you—

A MIGHTY FORTRESS

Words and Music by Martin Luther, 1483-1546
English Translation by Frederick H. Hedge, 1805-1890

God is our refuge and strength, an ever present help in trouble. Therefore we will not fear, though the earth give way and the mountains fall into the heart of the sea. (Psalm 46:1, 2)

October 31, 1517, is perhaps the most important day in Protestant history. This was the day when Martin Luther, an Augustinian monk and a professor of theology, posted on the doors of the Cathedral of Wittenberg, Germany, his 95 theses (complaints) against the teachings and practices of the medieval Roman Church. With this event, the 16th century Protestant Reformation was formally born.

The Protestant Reformation movement was built on three main tenets:

- The re-establishment of the Scriptures.
- Clarifying the means of salvation.
- The restoration of congregational singing.

"A Mighty Fortress" was written and composed by Martin Luther. The date of the hymn cannot be fixed with any exact certainty. It is generally believed, however, to have been written for the Diet of Spires in 1529 when the term "protestant" was first used. The hymn became the great rallying cry of the Reformation.

A mighty fortress is our God, a bulwark never failing; our helper He amid the flood of mortal ills prevailing. For still our ancient foe doth seek to work us woe— His craft and pow'r are great, and, armed with cruel hate, on earth is not his equal.

Did we in our own strength confide our striving would be losing, were not the right Man on our side, the Man of God's own choosing. Dost ask who that may be? Christ Jesus, it is He—Lord Sabaoth His name, from age to age the same—and He must win the battle.

And tho this world, with devils filled, should threaten to undo us, we will not fear, for God hath willed His truth to triumph thru us. The prince of darkness grim—we tremble not for Him; His rage we can endure; for lo! his doom is sure— One little word shall fell him.

That word above all earthly pow'rs—no thanks to them—abideth; the Spirit and the gifts are ours thru Him who with us sideth. Let goods and kindred go, this mortal life also; the body they may kill; God's truth abideth still—His kingdom is forever.

🐝 ***For Today:*** Deuteronomy 33:27; 2 Samuel 22:2; Psalm 46; Isaiah 26:4

Breathe a prayer of thanks to God for reformers such as Martin Luther, who laid the foundations for our evangelical faith. Praise Him on this Reformation Day for this truth—

Ein' Feste Burg tune

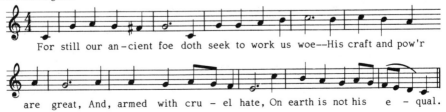

For still our an–cient foe doth seek to work us woe––His craft and pow'r are great, And, armed with cru – el hate, On earth is not his e – qual.

November

• Praise • Thanksgiving • All Saints Day

COME, CHRISTIANS, JOIN TO SING

Christian Henry Bateman, 1813-1889

Come, let us sing for joy to the Lord; let us shout aloud to the Rock of our salvation. Let us come before Him with thanksgiving and extol Him with music and song. (Psalm 95:1)

A New Testament church should always be a singing church, for sacred song is the natural outpouring of joyous Christian hearts. Of all the world's religions, only Christianity is a singing faith. But singing should not be limited to the church services; rather, it should become the Christian's normal daily lifestyle.

Singing God's praises provides many important benefits to believers. There is the awareness that God is pleased when the voice is lifted in praise: "He who offers praise honors me" (Psalm 50:23). Then we learn many important spiritual truths and concepts when we sing. For many of us, our first awareness that God loves us and that He loves all the children of the world was gained through a song sung at our mother's knee or in the Sunday school nursery. Singing will also provide encouragement and comfort in times of need. Often when we are experiencing periods of discouragement and despondency, a simple hymn will come to mind and will be used of God to mend our fragile emotions. Also, singing is one of our best preparations for heaven. The Bible teaches that we will enjoy giving praise and singing throughout eternity.

This hymn was originally titled "Come, Children, Join to Sing." It first appeared in 1843 in a collection *Sacred Melodies for Sabbath Schools and Families,* edited by the author of this text, Christian H. Bateman. Bateman served three Congregational churches in Scotland and England and then was ordained in the Anglican church.

Come, Christians, join to sing—Alleluia! Amen! Loud praise to Christ our King—Alleluia! Amen! Let all, with heart and voice, before His throne rejoice; praise is His gracious choice: Alleluia! Amen!

Come, lift your hearts on high—Alleluia! Amen! Let praises fill the sky—Alleluia! Amen! He is our Guide and Friend; to us He'll condescend; His love shall never end: Alleluia! Amen!

Praise yet our Christ again—Alleluia! Amen! Life shall not end the strain—Alleluia! Amen! On heaven's blissful shore His goodness we'll adore, singing forevermore, "Alleluia! Amen!"

❦ ***For Today:*** Psalm 95; 150; Ephesians 5:19; Colossians 3:16; 1 Peter 2:9

When tempted to complain or feel despondent, determine to sing a song of praise. It is one of the best ways to experience calm and contentment when life becomes bleak. Try this musical message as you go—

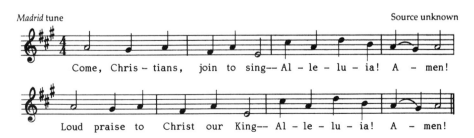

Madrid tune · Source unknown

Come, Chris-tians, join to sing-- Al – le – lu – ia! A – men!

Loud praise to Christ our King-- Al – le – lu – ia! A – men!

HOLY GOD, WE PRAISE THY NAME

From the *Te Deum*, c. 4th century, Attributed to Ignace Franz, 1719-1790
English Translation by Clarence Walworth, 1820-1900

In God we make our boast all day long, and we will praise Your name forever.
(Psalm 44:8)

Much of the origin of this noble expression of praise and worship is lost in obscurity. Through the centuries the "Te Deum" has been one of the supreme triumphal expressions of praise used by the Christian Church.

The original setting of "Te Deum Laudamus" was likely composed by Bishop Ambrose, Bishop of Milan, Italy, in A.D. 387, and an important leader in the development of early church music. Paraphrases of this fourth century "Te Deum" have been written in many languages, including this text in German, from which it was later translated into English by an American Catholic priest, Clarence A. Walworth. The hymn is still an important part of the morning service liturgy in Anglican churches and it is sung frequently in all Protestant churches.

The fourth stanza is one of the strongest hymn affirmations of the doctrine of the Triune Godhead. The Trinity was an important controversy in the early church. Arius, c. A.D. 250-336, was a proponent of the doctrine of Arianism, which maintained that "if the Father was God, then the Son was a creature of the Father"—a middle Being between God and the world—a divine Being but not to be worshiped as God. At the Council of Alexandria (A.D. 321) and later at the Council of Nicaea (A.D. 325), this teaching was thoroughly branded as heresy. However, this controversy on the person and deity of Christ has continued even to the present time in the teachings of various cults.

> Holy God, we praise Thy name—Lord of all, we bow before Thee! All on earth Thy scepter claim; all in heav'n above adore Thee: Infinite Thy vast domain, everlasting is Thy reign.
>
> Hark, the loud celestial hymn angel choirs above are raising; cherubim and seraphim, in unceasing chorus praising, fill the heav'ns with sweet accord—Holy, holy, holy Lord!
>
> Lo, the apostolic train joins Thy sacred name to hallow; prophets swell the glad refrain and the white-robed martyrs follow; and, from morn to set of sun, thru the Church the song goes on.
>
> Holy Father, Holy Son, Holy Spirit, three we name Thee; while in essence only one, undivided God we claim Thee, and adoring bend the knee, while we sing our praise to Thee.

❦ *For Today:* Numbers 14:21; 1 Chronicles 29:11; Psalm 107:8; Isaiah 6:3; Revelation 15:3

Take time to worship and praise the triune Godhead. Use these words to help—

Grosser Gott tune   From *Katholisches Gesangbuch*, Vienna, c. 1774

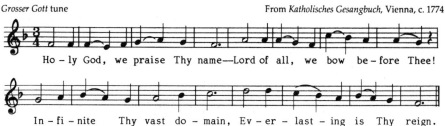

Ho - ly God, we praise Thy name—Lord of all, we bow be - fore Thee!

In - fi - nite Thy vast do - main, Ev - er - last - ing is Thy reign.

THE GOD OF ABRAHAM PRAISE

Thomas Olivers, 1725-1799
Based on the revised *Yigdal* of Daniel ben Judah, 14th century

You who fear the Lord, praise Him! All you descendants of Jacob, honor Him!
(Psalm 22:23)

The story of God's dealing with Israel is an incredible one: the sovereign God preserving and directing throughout history the affairs of His chosen people. Beginning with Abraham, "the father of many nations," the Jewish people have been persecuted frequently, yet never destroyed. From the Jews we have received the Ten Commandments and eventually our Messiah-Redeemer. "Salvation is from the Jews" (John 4:22).

Thomas Olivers, author of "The God of Abraham Praise," was one of John Wesley's 18th century evangelists. He traveled extensively throughout England and Ireland, fearlessly preaching the gospel but often encountering violent opposition. Olivers states that he wrote this hymn after listening to the preaching of a Jewish rabbi at the Duke's Place Synagogue, Oldgate, London. There he also heard Meyer Lyon (Leoni), a well-known Jewish cantor, sing the Doxology of *Yigdal* from the Hebrew liturgy. Composed around 1400, the *Yigdal* was based upon the 13 articles of Jewish faith. Olivers was so impressed by the service and especially the music that he began writing this text to fit the meter of the tune he had heard. The name of the melody used, "Leoni," was in honor of Cantor Meyer Lyon.

The God of Abraham is still our God today and is worthy of our praises to Father, Son, and Holy Ghost—both now and through eternity.

> The God of Abraham praise, who reigns enthroned above, ancient of everlasting days, and God of love. Jehovah, great I AM, by earth and heav'n confessed, I bow and bless the sacred Name forever blest.
>
> The God of Abraham praise, at whose supreme command from earth I rise and seek the joys at His right hand. I all on earth forsake, its wisdom, fame and pow'r, and Him my only portion make, my shield and tow'r.
>
> He by Himself hath sworn—I on His oath depend; I shall, on eagles' wings upborne, to heav'n ascend. I shall behold His face, I shall His pow'r adore, and sing the wonders of His grace forevermore.
>
> The whole triumphant host give thanks to God on high; "Hail, Father, Son and Holy Ghost!" they ever cry. Hail, Abraham's God and mine! I join the heav'nly lays; all might and majesty are Thine and endless praise.

❧ *For Today:* Exodus 3:14; 15:1-19; Lamentations 5:19; Hebrews 13:8

Ask God to give you opportunity to witness to a Jewish person and graciously tell him that Jesus Christ, his long-awaited Messiah, has come and desires to be his personal Redeemer-Lord. Praise the God of Abraham as you go—

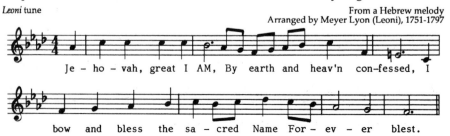

Leoni tune

From a Hebrew melody
Arranged by Meyer Lyon (Leoni), 1751-1797

Je - ho - vah, great I AM, By earth and heav'n con—fessed, I
bow and bless the sa - cred Name For - ev - er blest.

PRAISE TO THE LORD, THE ALMIGHTY

Joachim Neander, 1650-1680
Translated by Catherine Winkworth, 1829-1878

Let the people praise Thee, O God; let all the people praise Thee. (Psalm 67:3)

Great expressions of praise to God have come from many different traditions and backgrounds. Throughout the centuries God has used the talents of people from various cultures to provide His church with hymns of praise so His people might be known as people of praise and thanksgiving.

The author of this inspiring hymn text, Joachim Neander, has often been called the greatest of all German-Calvinist Reformed hymn writers. He wrote approximately 60 hymns and composed many tunes. Nearly all of his hymns are triumphant expressions of praise.

This hymn is a free paraphrase of Psalm 103:1-6, which begins, "Bless [praise] the Lord, O my soul: And all that is within me, bless His holy name." The translator of this text, Catherine Winkworth, is regarded as one of the finest translators of the German language. Her translations helped to make German hymns popular in England and America during the 19th century. The tune, "Lobe Den Herren" ("Praise to the Lord"), first appeared in a German hymnal in 1665. It is said that Neander personally chose this tune for his text, and the words have never been used with any other melody.

> Praise to the Lord, the Almighty, the King of creation! O my soul, praise Him, for He is thy health and salvation! All ye who hear, now to His temple draw near; join me in glad adoration.

> Praise to the Lord, who o'er all things so wondrously reigneth, shelters thee under His wings, yea, so gently sustaineth! Hast thou not seen how thy desires e'er have been granted in what He ordaineth?

> Praise to the Lord, who with marvelous wisdom hath made thee, decked thee with health, and with loving hand guided and stayed thee; How oft in grief hath not He brought thee relief, spreading His wings for to shade thee!

> Praise to the Lord! O let all that is in me adore Him! All that hath life and breath, come now with praises before Him! Let the Amen sound from His people again: Gladly for aye we adore Him!

❦ ***For Today:*** Psalm 100; 103:1-6; 104; 150; Colossians 1:15-20

It has been said that "he who sincerely praises God will soon discover within his soul an inclination to praise goodness in his fellow men." Make this your day's goal. Sing as you go—

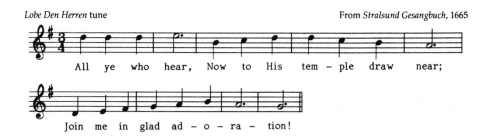

Lobe Den Herren tune   From *Stralsund Gesangbuch*, 1665

All ye who hear, Now to His tem - ple draw near;

Join me in glad ad - o - ra - tion!

PRAISE, MY SOUL, THE KING OF HEAVEN

Henry F. Lyte, 1793-1847

Praise the Lord, all His works everywhere in His dominion. Praise the Lord, O my soul. (Psalm 103:22)

> The Christian life that is joyless is a discredit to God and a disgrace to itself.
> —*Maltbie D. Babcock*

A life of praise and an inner joy and contentment are interwoven—they are complements of each other. Such a life is the result of being absorbed with God. For such an individual the pursuit of God's glory, the Lordship of Christ, and the worship and praise of our Creator-redeemer become a natural way of living. To this person the blessings of God never become commonplace.

> *Forgives all our iniquities; heals our diseases, redeems our life from destruction; crowns us with loving kindness and mercy; satisfies us with good things; renews our youth, works righteousness and judgment for the oppressed; gives guidance to His people; is merciful; is gracious and slow to anger while plenteous in mercy: knows all about us; will never forsake. (Psalm 103:3-10)*

Although Henry Lyte, the author of this hymn text, experienced many difficulties in life, including a frail body, this hymn helps us realize that we as believers can rise above our problems and lift voices of praise in spite of any circumstances. The text is a summary of the psalmist's admonition in Psalm 103 to praise and to remember all of the good things about God. It first appeared in Lyte's collection of new paraphrases of the Psalms, published in 1834. Interestingly, the hymn has the distinction of being the requested processional for the wedding of Queen Elizabeth II at Westminister Abbey on November 20, 1947, exactly 100 years after author Henry Lyte's death.

> Praise, my soul, the King of heaven; to His feet thy tribute bring; ransomed, healed, restored, forgiven, evermore His praises sing: Alleluia! Praise the Everlasting king!

> Father-like, He tends and spares us, well our feeble frame He knows; in His hands He gently bears us, rescues us from all our foes: Alleluia! Widely yet His mercy flows!

> Angels in the height, adore Him; ye behold Him face to face; Sun and moon, bow down before Him, dwellers all in time and space: Alleluia! Praise with us the God of grace!

🐝 *For Today:* 1 Chronicles 29:10-13; Psalm 47:6, 7; 103; 1 Timothy 1:17

Remember—A cheerful word of praise and encouragement will mean more to those with whom we live than acres of flowers we may give when they are gone. Carry this song of triumph with you—

Zion tune   Thomas Hastings, 1784-1872

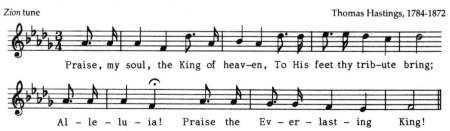

Praise, my soul, the King of heav-en, To His feet thy trib-ute bring;

Al – le – lu – ia! Praise the Ev – er – last – ing King!

I SING THE MIGHTY POWER OF GOD

Isaac Watts, 1674-1748, with alterations by others

He shall have dominion also from sea to sea, and from the rivers unto the ends of the earth. (Psalm 72:8 KJV)

Isaac Watts, the father of English hymnody, had a fervent concern about the dismal state of congregational singing that had developed in the English-speaking churches during the late 17th and early 18th centuries. He wrote many new paraphrased versions of the Psalms to replace the ponderous literal settings that had long been used. Watts also believed that writers should be free to express praise and devotion to God in their own words. These texts became known as "hymns of human composure." For having such convictions, Isaac Watts was often known as a revolutionary churchman of his day. Yet his ambition, according to his own words, was as follows: "My design was not to exalt myself to the rank and glory of poets, but I was ambitious to be a servant to the churches, and a helper to the joy of the meanest Christian."

Although he never married, Isaac Watts always loved children and wrote much for them. In 1715 he wrote a book of songs especially for young people titled *Divine Songs for Children*. This hymnal, the first ever written exclusively for children, includes the text for "I Sing Mighty Power of God."

How important it is, whether child or adult, that we recognize and praise the mighty power of our Creator God. This hymn also teaches that we should sing of His goodness and wisdom as well as His omnipresence. God's people have much to sing about!

I sing the mighty pow'r of God that made the mountains rise, that spread the flowing seas abroad and built the lofty skies. I sing the wisdom that ordained the sun to rule the day; the moon shines full at His command, and all the stars obey.

I sing the goodness of the Lord that filled the earth with food; He formed the creatures with His word and then pronounced them good. Lord, how Thy wonders are displayed where'er I turn my eye: If I survey the ground I tread or gaze upon the sky!

There's not a plant or flow'r below but makes Thy glories known; and clouds arise and tempests blow by order from Thy throne. While all that borrows life from Thee is ever in Thy care, and ev'rywhere that man can be, Thou, God, art present there.

❧ *For Today:* 1 Chronicles 29:11-13; Psalm 95:3-5; 107:8; Isaiah 40:26, 28; Revelation 4:11

Try to catch a new awareness of God's great power, goodness, and wisdom. Thank Him for His promise to be at your side. Praise Him as you go—

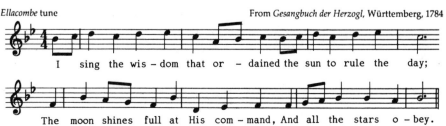

FOR ALL THE SAINTS

William How, 1823-1897

Therefore, since we are surrounded by such a great cloud of witnesses, let us throw off everything that hinders and the sin that so easily entangles, and let us run with perseverance the race that is marked out for us. (Hebrews 12:1)

Someone has described a "saint" as any Christian who makes it easier for others to believe in God. One of the neglected liturgical days in many Protestant churches is All Saints Day, which occurs on the first Sunday in November. This neglect is understandable because the tradition of the day is rooted in medieval Catholicism. Homage is given on this day to the departed canonized saints of the church.

There is, however, an underlying meaning to this day that evangelical Christians should use and recognize. Here, for example, are some lessons it can teach us:

- Every believer whom God has called by His grace and sanctified by His Spirit has been called to sainthood.

- A thankful spirit for the memories of those believers from our local church who were called to their heavenly home during the past year.

- Then, for many of us, there has often been one particular individual who has especially influenced our lives—directing us to God, tutoring us in truth, and modeling the virtues of the Christian life.

Bishop William W. How wrote the text of "For All the Saints" in 1864, for use in the Anglican church liturgy commemorating All Saints Day. It was originally titled "Saints Day Hymn—Cloud of Witnesses—Hebrews 12:1."

How do we best honor the memory of loved ones and friends who have contributed to our lives? By rededicating our own life to God, obeying Him implicitly, and reaching out to the needs of others.

> For all the saints who from their labors rest, who Thee by faith before the world confessed, Thy name, O Jesus, be forever blest: Alleluia! Alleluia!

> Thou wast their Rock, their Fortress and their Might; Thou, Lord, their captain in the well-fought fight; and Thou, in darkness drear, their one true light: Alleluia!Alleluia!

> From earth's wide bounds, from ocean's farthest coast, thru gates of pearl streams in the countless host, singing to Father, Son, and Holy Ghost: Alleluia! Alleluia!

🍂 *For Today:* Psalm 22:4, 5; 1 Thessalonians 4:13-17; Revelation 6:11; 7:9

Recall the various individuals who have especially influenced your life for God. Breathe a prayer of thanks for their memory.

Sine Nomine tune   Ralph Vaughan Williams, 1872-1958

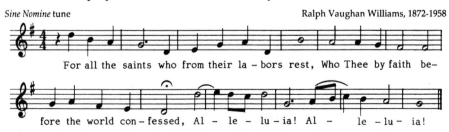

For all the saints who from their la - bors rest, Who Thee by faith be- fore the world con - fessed, Al - le - lu - ia! Al - le - lu - ia!

Music: *Sine Nomine*. Copyright © Oxford University Press. All rights reserved. Used by Permission.

MAY JESUS CHRIST BE PRAISED

German hymn, c. 1800
Translated by Edward Caswall, 1814-1878

I will extol the Lord at all times: His praise will always be on my lips. (Psalm 34:1)

Forms of worship services vary according to the cultural backgrounds, personalities, and traditions of the believers. Some Christians feel that true worship is best achieved when it is conducted in a structured, liturgical, and meditative setting. Other believers prefer a more free, spontaneous, informal praise and testimony type of service. Forms of worship are not important in themselves. In fact, a variety of worship forms is healthy within the evangelical community. However, we must never get so caught up in the forms and means of worship that we fail to focus on the object of all worship—the praise of Jesus Christ!

One of the important sources of English hymnody is the wealth of worthy hymns translated from earlier Greek, Latin, and German sources during the mid 19th century. Many English writers' interest in the hymns from these other cultures was largely a part of a movement within the Anglican church known as the Oxford Movement. The rediscovery of earlier and ancient hymns became especially important during this time. One of the leaders of this movement was Edward Caswall, a well-known scholar, minister, and translator. Caswall is also the translator of another important hymn about our Lord, "Jesus, the Very Thought of Thee." Throughout his life Caswall kept adding new verses to "May Jesus Christ Be Praised" until eventually this hymn included 28 stanzas.

These words still have an important place in our church services as they direct our attention to the basic purpose of all worship:

When morning gilds the skies, my heart awaking cries: May Jesus Christ be praised! Alike at work and prayer to Jesus I repair: May Jesus Christ be praised!

Does sadness fill my mind? A solace here I find: May Jesus Christ be praised! Or fades my earthly bliss? My comfort still is this: May Jesus Christ be praised!

In heav'n's eternal bliss the loveliest strain is this: May Jesus Christ be praised! The pow'rs of darkness fear when this sweet chant they hear: May Jesus Christ be praised!

Be this, while life is mine, my canticle divine: May Jesus Christ be praised! Be this th' eternal song thru all the ages long: May Jesus Christ be praised!

❦ *For Today:* Psalm 5:3; 57:7; 69:34; John 14:6, 9; 20:31; Revelation 11:15; 17:14

What does the term *worship* mean to you? Is your understanding founded on the praise of Christ? Identify activities in a church service as well as in our own devotional lives that are often substituted for the true worship of God. Determine to praise Christ throughout the day with this hymn—

Laudes Domini tune

Joseph Barnby, 1838-1896

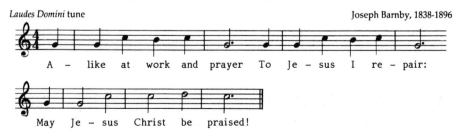

A - like at work and prayer To Je - sus I re - pair:

May Je - sus Christ be praised!

PRAISE THE SAVIOR

Thomas Kelly, 1796-1854

In Him we were also chosen, having been predestined according to the plan of Him who works out everything in conformity with the purpose of His will, in order that we, who were the first to hope in Christ, might be for the praise of His glory. (Ephesians 1:11, 12)

God's people have always been and will always be a "praising people." God created and chose us in order that we "might be for the praise of His glory," the sum of all that God is and does. The song of praise began at creation when "the morning stars sang together and all the angels shouted for joy" (Job 38:7). It was furthered during the Old Testament period by the Israelites, who were widely known for their "singing faith." The song of praise was echoed by the angelic chorus announcing Christ's birth. It has been proclaimed and published by pastors, hymn writers, and singers throughout the centuries. And it is rehearsed each week by worshiping believers everywhere as they prepare for the new song of praise and worship that will continue throughout eternity.

Thomas Kelly is considered to be one of the most distinguished spiritual poets of the 19th century. After his dismissal from the Anglican church for his zealous evangelical preaching, especially on the subject of "justification by faith"— a doctrinal taboo by the High Church, he associated himself with the dissenting Congregationalists, becoming known as a magnetic preacher throughout his ministry.

These inspiring two-line verses by Thomas Kelly, based on Psalm 88:1, were published in 1809. The melody of this hymn is of unknown German origin.

> Praise the Savior, ye who know Him! Who can tell how much we owe Him? Gladly let us render to Him all we are and have.

> Jesus is the name that charms us; He for conflict fits and arms us. Nothing moves and nothing harms us while we trust in Him.

> Trust in Him, ye saints, forever—He is faithful, changing never. Neither force nor guile can sever those He loves from Him.

> Keep us, Lord, O keep us cleaving to Thyself, and still believing, till the hour of our receiving promised joys with Thee.

> Then we shall be where we would be; then we shall be what we should be. Things that are not now, nor could be, soon shall be our own.

🐝 *For Today:* Psalm 66:2; 88:1; 96:7, 8; 100:4; Hebrews 13:15; Revelation 4:11

The psalmist declared that he praised God seven times a day for His righteous laws (Psalm 119:164). Determine to spend some time throughout this day in offering your voice of praise to the Lord. Use this hymn to help—

Acclaim tune   German melody

Praise the Sav - ior, ye who know Him! Who can tell how

much we owe Him? Glad-ly let us ren - der to Him All we are and have.

PRAISE HIM! PRAISE HIM!

Fanny J. Crosby, 1820-1915

I will praise the Lord all my life; I will sing praise to my God as long as I live.
(Psalm 146:2)

Christianity is not a theory or speculation, but a life; not a philosophy of life, but a living presence. This realization can turn any gloom into a song.   —*S. T. Coleridge*

Praise is our Lord's most righteous due. It is not an option whether we will offer praise—it is one of God's commands. Scriptures clearly teach that we are to offer a sacrifice of praise to God continually (Hebrews 13:15, 16). Our daily sacrifice of praise should include joyful songs for who Christ is—"our blessed redeemer." Then we need to praise God for all of His daily blessings, which are beyond number. We should offer praise even for the trials of life for they are often blessings in disguise. Finally, our sacrifice should include praise for His leading in ways yet to be experienced.

This is another of the many favorite gospel hymns written by Fanny Crosby, blind American poetess. In all she wrote between 8,000 and 9,000 gospel hymn texts and supplied our hymnals with more beloved hymns that are still sung today than any other writer.

"Praise Him! Praise Him!" first appeared in a Sunday school hymnal, *Bright Jewels*, which was published in 1869. The song was originally titled "Praise, Give Thanks." And still today, these words evoke praise from each believing heart—

Praise Him! praise Him! Jesus, our blessed Redeeemer! Sing, O earth, His wonderful love proclaim! Hail Him! hail Him! highest archangels in glory; strength and honor give to His holy name! Like a shepherd Jesus will guard His children. In His arms He carries them all day long:

Praise Him! praise Him! Jesus, our blessed Redeemer! For our sins He suffered, and bled and died; He, our Rock, our hope of eternal salvation, Hail Him! hail Him! Jesus the Crucified. Sound His praises! Jesus who bore our sorrows; love unbounded, wonderful, deep and strong:

Praise Him! praise Him! Jesus, our blessed Redeemer! Heavenly portals loud with hosannas ring. Jesus, Savior, reigneth forever and ever; Crown Him! crown Him! Prophet and Priest and King! Christ is coming! over the world victorious, pow'r and glory unto the Lord belong:

Refrain: Praise Him! praise Him! tell of His excellent greatness; praise Him! praise Him! ever in joyful song!

❦ *For Today:* Psalm 71:23; Hebrews 1:3-8; 13:8; Revelation 1:5, 6; 5:11-14

Go forth with a renewed awareness of Christ's presence in your life. Offer Him this sacrifice of praise—

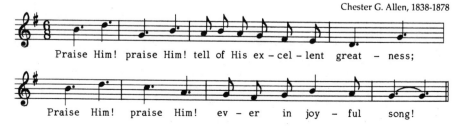

Chester G. Allen, 1838-1878

Praise Him! praise Him! tell of His ex – cel – lent great – ness;

Praise Him! praise Him! ev – er in joy – ful song!

SING PRAISE TO GOD WHO REIGNS ABOVE

Johann J. Schutz, 1640-1690
Translated by Frances E. Cox, 1812-1897

The Lord reigns, let the earth be glad; let the distant shores rejoice. (Psalm 97:1)

Following the Protestant Reformation, which was climaxed by Martin Luther's posting of the 95 theses at the Cathedral of Wittenberg in 1517, Lutheranism became the dominant religious force in Germany and throughout much of Europe. In the 17th century, there was an important renewal movement within the Lutheran Church known as Pietism. The leader of this spiritual movement was a Lutheran pastor in Frankfort, Germany, Philip J. Spener (1635-1705). Mainly through small cell prayer and Bible study groups, he sought to influence nominal church people who had become accustomed to the dead orthodoxy that had overtaken the church. Spener taught them the meaning of inner personal faith in Christ and the demands that such faith makes upon the believer for holy Christian living.

One of the important characteristics of the 17th century Pietistic Movement was the involvement of laymen in the church. Many of the hymn writers and important voices in the church at this time were the lay people from all walks of life. Such was the case with Johann J. Schutz, an authority in civil and canon law, living in Frankfort, Germany. He was closely allied with Philip Spener and the practice of the Pietists in establishing small cell groups within the church. Schutz wrote a number of religious publications as well as five hymns. This is his only hymn still in use.

As is true with any spiritual renewal, the Pietist Movement give birth to a great revival of hymnody throughout Germany.

> Sing praise to God who reigns above, the God of all creation, the God of pow'r, the God of love, the God of our salvation; with healing balm my soul He fills, and ev'ry faithless murmur stills: To God all praise and glory!

> The Lord is never far away, but, thru all grief distressing, an ever present help and stay, our peace and joy and blessing; as with a mother's tender hand He leads His own, His chosen band: To God all praise and glory!

> Thus all my toilsome way along I sing aloud Thy praises, that men may hear the grateful song my voice unwearied raises; be joyful in the Lord, my heart! Both soul and body bear your part: To God all praise and glory!

❦ *For Today:* 1 Chronicles 16:25-36; Psalm 97:1, 6; 139:7; Isaiah 12:2-5; Hebrews 13:15

Raise your voice in praise to the omnipotent God of all creation; yet He is the One who has promised never to be far away and to be your "ever present help and stay." Allow this musical expression to help—

Mit Freuden Zart tune

From the Bohemian Brethren's Hymnal *Kirchengesänge* of 1566

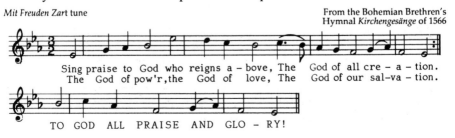

Sing praise to God who reigns a - bove, The God of all cre - a - tion.
The God of pow'r, the God of love, The God of our sal - va - tion.

TO GOD ALL PRAISE AND GLO - RY!

I WILL PRAISE HIM!

Margaret J. Harris, 19th century

To Him who loves us and has freed us from our sins by His blood, and has made us to be a kingdom and priests to serve His God and Father—to Him be glory and power for ever and ever! Amen. (Revelation 1:6)

An attitude of happiness in life is a matter of our will. Abraham Lincoln once stated that "most people are as happy as they make up their minds to be." Closely related to a Christian's happiness is the determination to live a life of praise to God. The goal of every believer should be the overflowing of praise, regardless of the circumstances. Knowing God in Christ is the most compelling reason to have such a life. Each day is a new opportunity for offering a praise sacrifice to God. Instead of dwelling on the negatives of our lives, we should seek fresh reasons daily for praising our Lord.

Praise is our highest spiritual exercise. There is more said in the Scriptures about our praise life than even our times of prayer. In prayer it is possible to approach God out of selfish motives; in praise, we worship Him for what He is Himself. Praise is also an encouragement to our fellowmen—"the afflicted hear and rejoice" (Psalm 34:2). Weak hearts will be strengthened and trembling saints revived when they hear our testimonies of praise.

One of the most important times to sing praise to God is when we feel imprisoned by the circumstances of life. Like the experience of Paul and Silas in the Roman prison (Acts 16: 24, 25), it is often uncanny how prayer and praise open the doors of our lives to new dimensions of opportunity and spiritual power.

When I saw the cleansing fountain, open wide for all my sin, I obeyed the Spirit's wooing when He said, "Wilt thou be clean?"

Tho the way seems straight and narrow, all I claimed was swept away; my ambitions, plans and wishes at my feet in ashes lay.

Then God's fire upon the altar of my heart was set aflame: I shall never cease to praise Him—Glory, glory to His name!

Blessed be the name of Jesus! I'm so glad He took me in: He's forgiven my transgressions; He has cleansed my heart from sin.

Glory, glory to the Father! Glory, glory to the Son! Glory, glory to the Spirit! Glory to the Three in One!

Chorus: I will praise Him! I will praise Him! Praise the Lamb for sinners slain; give Him glory, all ye people, for His blood can wash away each stain.

❦ *For Today:* Psalm 34:1; 86:12; 145:2; Romans 11:36; 1 Timothy 1:17

Begin searching your life for fresh reasons to rejoice and sing praise to God. Allow this musical truth to be your theme—

Margaret J. Harris, 19th century

I will praise Him! I will praise Him! Praise the Lamb for sin-ners slain;

Give Him glo-ry, all ye peo-ple, For His blood can wash a – way each stain.

BLESSED ASSURANCE

Fanny J. Crosby, 1820-1915

Let us draw near to God with a sincere heart in full assurance of faith, having our hearts sprinkled to cleanse us from a guilty conscience and having our bodies washed with pure water. Let us hold unswervingly to the hope we profess, for He who promised is faithful. (Hebrews 10:22, 23)

Beware of despairing about yourself. You are commanded to put your trust in God, and not in yourself.   —*St. Augustine*

Some people claim to have accepted Christ as Savior, yet they live in the tragic uncertainty of doubting their personal relationship with God. The Scriptures teach, however, that we can know with absolute confidence that we have the life of God within us (1 John 5:13). This confidence is not based on inner feelings or outer signs. Rather, this assurance is founded upon the promises of a faithful God and His inspired Word. It depends not on the amount of our faith but on the object of our faith—Christ Himself.

Though blinded at six weeks of age through improper medical treatment, Fanny Crosby wrote more than 8,000 gospel songs texts in her lifetime of 95 years. Her many favorites such as "Blessed Assurance" have been an important part of evangelical worship for the past century. Only eternity will disclose the host of individuals whose lives have been spiritually enriched through the texts of Fanny Crosby's many hymns. Engraved on Fanny J. Crosby's tombstone at Bridgeport, Connecticut, are these significant words taken from our Lord's remarks to Mary, the sister of Lazarus, after she had anointed Him with costly perfume—"She hath done what she could" (Mark 14:8).

Blessed assurance, Jesus is mine! O what a foretaste of glory divine! Heir of salvation, purchase of God, born of His Spirit, washed in His blood.

Perfect submission, perfect delight! Visions of rapture now burst on my sight; angels descending bring from above echoes of mercy, whispers of love.

Perfect submission—all is at rest; I in my Savior am happy and blest; watching and waiting, looking above, filled with His goodness, lost in His love.

Chorus: This is my story, this is my song, praising my Savior all the day long; this is my story, this is my song, praising my Savior all the day long.

❦ *For Today:* Isaiah 12:2; Romans 8:16, 17; 15:13; Titus 2:13, 14; 1 John 5:13; Revelation 1:5, 6

If you have accepted Christ as personal Savior, live with the absolute conviction and triumphant faith that the apostle Paul had when he exclaimed—"I know whom (not merely what) I have believed . . . (2 Timothy 1:12). Carry Fanny Crosby's musical praise with you—

Phoebe P. Knapp, 1839-1908

REJOICE, YE PURE IN HEART

Edward H. Plumptre, 1821-1891

Sing joyfully to the Lord, you righteous; it is fitting for the upright to praise Him.
(Psalm 33:1)

The hallmark of the Christian life is a joyous spirit. The Bible teaches that "a cheerful heart is good medicine, but a crushed spirit dries up the bones" (Proverbs 17:22). And singing has an important part in the life of joy. It can be the mind's greatest solace and can express its noblest inspiration. For the person who learns to enjoy it, singing has therapeutic value.

A joyous, singing spirit should not be limited to a Sunday worship experience. Every day is the time to rejoice. Let us never forget that "to glorify God and to enjoy Him forever" should be the ultimate goal of all human existence.

Edward H. Plumptre, the author of this hymn, was a graduate of Oxford University and a minister in the Anglican state church. He was recognized as a brilliant scholar and was appointed to be a member of the Old Testament Committee for the revision of the Authorized Version of the Bible. He authored a number of scholarly works, translated numerous Latin hymns, and had several volumes of his own poetry published.

This hymn was written for the annual choir festival at Peterborough Cathedral, England, May, 1865. It was used as a processional when the choirs from a number of different communities entered and sang in the great cathadral. The hymn first appeared in the 1868 appendix to *Hymns Ancient and Modern*, the well-known Anglican hymnal of the past century. These words still inspire believers to "rejoice, give thanks, and sing!"

> Rejoice, ye pure in heart; rejoice, give thanks, and sing; your festal banner wave on high, the cross of Christ your King.

> With all the angel choirs, with all the saints on earth, pour out the strains of joy and bliss, true rapture, noblest mirth!

> Still lift your standard high, still march in firm array; as warriors through the darkness toil till dawns the golden day.

> Yes, on through life's long path, still chanting as you go; from youth to age, by night and day, in gladness and in woe.

> Then on, ye pure in heart, rejoice, give thanks, and sing; your festal banner wave on high, the cross of Christ your King

> **Refrain:** Rejoice, rejoice, rejoice give thanks, and sing!

❦ *For Today:* Psalm 24:3, 4; 32:11; 33:1; 51:10-13

Say with the psalmist David: "This is the day which the Lord hath made; I will rejoice and be glad in it" (Psalm 118: 24). Sing this musical reminder—

Marion tune   Arthur H. Messiter, 1834-1916

Re - joice, re - joice, Re - joice give thanks, and sing!

DOXOLOGY
Thomas Ken, 1637-1711

I will praise You, O Lord my God, with all my heart; I will glorify Your name forever. (Psalm 86:12)

The lines of the "Doxology" have been the most frequently sung words of any known song for more than 300 years. Even today nearly every English-speaking Protestant congregation unites at least once each Sunday in this noble overture of praise. It has been said that the "Doxology" has done more to teach the doctrine of the Trinity than all the theology books ever wiritten.

Instead of being merely a perfunctory hymn that is sung each week, the "Doxology" should be regarded by Christians as an offering or sacrifice of praise to God for all of His blessings in the past week (Hebrews 13-15). True worship always involves an offering. In the Old Testament period, Levitical priests offered blood sacrifices to God on behalf of their people. In this New Testament era, God wants our sacrifice of praise. Other sacrifices desired by God of New Testament believer-priests include: Our bodies (Roman 12:1); the service of our faith (Philippians 2:17); our material gifts (Philippians 4:18); our good works and communication (Hebrews 13:16).

The author of this text was a bold, outspoken 17th century Anglican bishop named Thomas Ken. Ken's illustrious career in the ministry was stormy and colorful. He served for a time as the English chaplain at the royal court in the Hague, Holland. He was so outspoken, however, in denouncing the corrupt lives of those in authority at the Dutch capital that he was compelled to leave after a short stay.

Upon his return to England, he was appointed by King Charles II to be one of his chaplains. Ken continued to reveal the same spirit of boldness in rebuking the moral sins of his dissolute English monarch. Despite this, Charles always admired his courageous chaplain, calling him "the good little man." The king rewarded Thomas Ken by appointing him to the bishopric of the Bath and Wales area. The historian Macaulay gave this tribute to Bishop Ken: "He came as near to the ideal of Christian perfection as human weakness permits."

Praise God, from whom all blessings flow; praise Him, all creatures here below: praise Him above, ye heav'nly host; praise Father, Son and Holy Ghost. Amen.

❦ *For Today:* Psalm 97:1; 100; 150:6

It has been said that a Christian's theology must become his doxology. As a believer-priest, are you offering to God the sacrifices that He desires? Give Him your praise even now as you sing the "Doxology"—

Old Hundredth tune   Louis Bourgeois, c. 1510-c. 1561

Praise God from whom all bless - ings flow; Praise
Fa - ther, Son, and Ho - ly Ghost. A - men.

COME, THOU FOUNT OF EVERY BLESSING

Robert Robinson, 1735-1790

O Lord, You are my God: I will exalt You and praise Your name, for in perfect faithfulness You have done marvelous things, things planned long ago. (Isaiah 25:1)

It would be enlightening if the people in the pew could stand on the platform and observe the congregational singing during an average church service. One would soon concur that there are many who appear to have attended church without the express purpose of having a personal encounter with God. Comparatively few people reveal evidence of losing themselves in worship and praise or of appropriating the great truths about which they sing.

How different would be our times of corporate praise if each of us would heed the apostle Paul's teaching of "singing with the Spirit and with the understanding also" (1 Corinthians 14:15). Not all of us are able to sing tunefully, but everyone in whom the Spirit of God dwells can and should respond with joyful praise when the opportunity is presented.

During his early teen years, Robert Robinson lived in London, where he mixed with a notorious gang of hoodlums and led a life of debauchery. At the age of 17 he attended a meeting where the noted evangelist George Whitefield was preaching. Robinson went for the purpose of "scoffing at those poor, deluded Methodists" and ended up professing faith in Christ as his Savior. Soon he felt called to preach the gospel and subsequently became the pastor of a rather large Baptist church in Cambridge, England. Despite his young age, Robinson became known as an able minister and scholar, writing various theological books as well as several hymns, including these words written when he was just 23 years of age:

> Come, Thou Fount of ev'ry blessing, tune my heart to sing Thy grace; streams of mercy, never ceasing, call for songs of loudest praise. Teach me some melodious sonnet sung by flaming tongues above; praise the mount—I'm fixed upon it—mount of Thy redeeming love.

> Here I raise mine Ebenezer—hither by Thy help I'm come; and I hope by Thy good pleasure safely to arrive at home. Jesus sought me when a stranger wand'ring from the fold of God; He to rescue me from danger interposed His precious blood.

> O to grace how great a debtor daily I'm constrained to be! Let Thy goodness like a fetter bind my wand'ring heart to Thee: Prone to wander—Lord, I feel it—prone to leave the God I love; here's my heart—O take and seal it; Seal it for Thy courts above.

🐝 ***For Today:*** 1 Samuel 7:10-12; Psalm 68:19; Zechariah 13:1; Romans 5:2

Why not raise your "Ebenezer" (a memorial to God's faithfulness) with these words—

Nettleton tune   John Wyeth, 1770-1858

FOR THE BEAUTY OF THE EARTH

Folliott S. Pierpoint, 1835-1917

Whatever is right, whatever is pure, whatever is lovely, whatever is admirable—if anything is excellent or praiseworthy—think about such things. (Philippians 4:8)

One of the delights that we as adults have in being around children is to hear their squeals of pleasure as they observe and discover some ordinary object about them. No doubt our heavenly Father is also pleased when His children take time to observe and appreciate His creation and then to simply express joyous gratitude to Him for His countless blessings. Today's hymn reminds us of the common blessings of life that many of us often take for granted—the beauties of nature, our parents, family, friends, church. The lyrics then direct our "grateful praise" to God Himself, the giver of every good and perfect gift.

Not much is known about Folliott Sandford Pierpoint, author of this lovely text. He was born in the intriguing old town of Bath, England. Even today Bath is most interesting and lovely, nestled in the hills surrounding this ancient city. Here one can still view the large pools of natural mineral baths for which the town was named. The inspiration for this hymn text is said to have come to this young author as he was strolling about his native town one day in the late spring, entranced by the beautiful countryside with the winding Avon River in the distance. His heart no doubt swelled up within him as he enjoyed the beauties of God's creation—the sun, the flowers, the shining stars. Pierpoint also recalled his social blessings—friends and home—those relationships that bring such enriching dimensions to our lives. Above all, however, were the spiritual blessings as represented by the Church—God's chosen agency for accomplishing His divine purposes in the world. Each of these blessings is then directed to God with a "hymn of grateful praise."

> For the beauty of the earth, for the glory of the skies, for the love which from our birth over and around us lies: CHRIST OUR GOD, TO THEE WE RAISE THIS OUR HYMN OF GRATEFUL PRAISE!

> For the joy of human love, brother, sister, parent, child, friends on earth and friends above, for all gentle thoughts and mild: CHRIST OUR GOD, TO THEE WE RAISE THIS OUR HYMN OF GRATEFUL PRAISE!

> For Thy Church that evermore lifteth holy hands above, off'ring up on ev'ry shore her pure sacrifice of love: CHRIST OUR GOD, TO THEE WE RAISE THIS OUR HYMN OF GRATEFUL PRAISE!

❦ *For Today:* Psalm 9:1, 2; 69:30, 31; 107:21, 22; John 1:3; James 1:17

Determine to fill your mind with things that are pure . . . . Sing this musical prayer to the One who has made it all possible—

Dix tune   Conrad Kocher, 1786-1872

Christ our God, to Thee we raise, This our hymn of grate-ful praise.

WE PLOW THE FIELDS, AND SCATTER

Matthias Claudius, 1740-1815
Translated by Jane M. Campbell, 1817-1878

Yet He has not left Himself without testimony: He has shown kindness by giving you rain from heaven and crops in their seasons; He provides you with plenty of food and fills your hearts with joy. (Acts 14:17)

The Scriptures have many important lessons to teach us about harvests. One of these lessons is that there is always a waiting time between the planting of the seed and the gathering of the fruit or grain. This is true in spiritual matters as well. God often has to give us a waiting period for the full bloom of the Spirit's fruit to be produced in our lives. The lesson of patience must be learned when sharing God's love with others.

We can also learn from the harvest that a planted seed must first die before it can spring forth in new life. The way to personal spiritual fruitfulness is first death to self-centeredness (Matthew 10:30). Another truth is that a bountiful harvest is directly proportionate to the amount of sowing that has been done. "Whoever sows sparingly will also reap sparingly, and whoever sows generously will also reap generously" (2 Corinthians 9:6). And finally, harvesting is a cooperative affair. We may spread the seeds of the gospel and cultivate and water the spiritual soil in an individual's life, but ultimately it is God who gives the harvest (1 Corinthians 3:6, 9).

"We Plow the Fields, and Scatter" first appeared in Germany in 1782 and was known as "The Peasants' Song." It was part of a dramatic sketch portraying a harvest festival in a farm home in northern Germany. It first appeared in England in 1861.

> We plow the fields, and scatter the good seed on the land, but it is fed and watered by God's almighty hand; He sends the snow in winter, the warmth to swell the grain, the breezes and the sunshine, and soft refreshing rain.

> We thank Thee, then, O Father, for all things bright and good, the seed-time and the harvest, our life, our health, our food; no gifts have we to offer, for all Thy love imparts, but that which Thou desirest, our humble, thankful hearts.

> **Chorus:** All good gifts around us are sent from heaven above; then thank the Lord, O thank the Lord for all His love.

❦ ***For Today:*** Genesis 1:11-18; 2:4, 5; Psalm 55:9-11; Isaiah 55:10, 11; Hebrews 11:3; James 1:17

"But that which Thou desirest, our humble, thankful hearts." Is there a spiritual harvest in my life? Am I contributing to a harvest time in the lives of others? Reflect on this musical truth as you go—

Wir Pflügen tune   Johann A. P. Schulz, 1747-1800

All good gifts a - round us are sent from heav'n a - bove;

Then thank the Lord, O thank the Lord for all His love.

HIS LOVING KINDNESS

Samuel Medley, 1738-1799

How priceless is Your unfailing love! Both high and low among men find refuge in the shadow of Your wings. (Psalm 36:7)

A Christian should never lose his reason for singing about the Lord and His constant loving kindness. "His praise should continually be in our mouths (Psalm 34:1). Loving kindness has been described as "love in action." God's loving kindness was the act of sending Christ to be our Redeemer "while we were still sinners" (Romans 5:8).

Samuel Medley, a Baptist minister, lived a dissipated life in the British Navy until he was severely wounded in a sea fight between the French and English in 1759, off Cape Lagos, Portugal. While convalescing, he read a sermon by Isaac Watts on Isaiah 42:6, 7. These verses ultimately led to Medley's conversion and later to his becoming a minister of the gospel. "His Loving Kindness" was written as a personal testimony of thanksgiving to God. The text first appeared in published form in 1782. For 27 years Samuel Medley pastored the Baptist church in Liverpool with much success, especially as a preacher to the sailors. Medley wrote a large number of hymns but always stated in the preface of his books that his only purpose for writing was to "comfort Christians and to glorify Christ." It has been said that the underlying purpose of Samuel Medley's ministry, both in preaching and in hymn writing, was to "humble the pride of man, exalt the grace of God in his own salvation, and promote real holiness in the hearts and lives of believers."

The spritely music for this text is an American camp meeting melody in popular use throughout the South before its publication in the 19th century.

God's loving kindness . . . "how free," "how great," "how good,"—a comfort in death and a source of eternal joy.

> Awake, my soul, to joyful lays, and sing thy great Redeemer's praise; He justly claims a song from thee, His loving kindness, oh, how free!

> He saw me ruined by the fall, yet loved me not withstanding all; He saved me from my lost estate, His loving kindness, oh, how great!

> When trouble, like a gloomy cloud, has gathered thick and thundered loud, He near my soul has always stood, His loving kindness, oh, how good!

> Soon shall we mount and soar away to the bright realms of endless day, and sing, with rapture and surprise, His loving kindness, in the skies.

> **Refrain:** Loving kindness, loving kindness, His loving kindness, oh how free!

❦ *For Today:* 2 Samuel 22:3, 4; Nehemiah 9:17; Psalm 31:21; 36:5-10; 59:10; Isaiah 54:8, 10; Ephesians 2:4-7

Recount your salvation experience; reflect on God's leading; anticipate the eternal joys of heaven—then sing as you go—

Loving Kindness tune   William Caldwell, 19th century

MY REDEEMER

Philip P. Bliss, 1838-1876

In Him we have redemption through His blood, the forgiveness of sins, in accordance with the riches of God's grace that He lavished on us with all wisdom and understanding. (Ephesians 1:7, 8)

The text for "My Redeemer," though a joyful note of praise, was found in the wreckage of a train accident which had just claimed the life of its author, Philip P. Bliss.

Philip Bliss was influential in promoting the growth of early gospel hymnody in this country. In addition to being known as a man with a commanding stature and impressive personality for leading congregational singing, Philip Bliss was highly regarded by his fellow colleagues. George Stebbins, also a noted gospel song writer of this time, once paid Bliss this tribute: "There has been no writer of verse since his time who has shown such a grasp of the fundamental truths of the gospel, or such a gift for putting them into poetic and singable form."

Yet, at the age of 38, at the very height of his fruitful music ministry, Bliss' life was suddenly ended in a tragic train accident. He had visited his mother at his childhood home in Rome, Pennsylvania, during the Christmas season of 1876 and was returning by train to Chicago on December 29 with his wife Lucy when a railroad bridge near Ashtabula, Ohio, collapsed. Their train plunged into a ravine 60 feet below and caught fire. One hundred passengers perished miserably. Bliss survived the fall and escaped through a window but frantically returned to the wreckage in an attempt to rescue his wife. As a result, he perished with her in the fire. Neither body was ever recovered.

Quite miraculously, however, among Bliss' belongings in the train wreckage was found a manuscript on which Bliss had been working. It contained these significant words:

I will sing of my Redeemer and His wondrous love to me; on the cruel cross He suffered, from the curse to set me free.

I will tell the wondrous story, how, my lost estate to save, in His boundless love and mercy, He the ransom freely gave.

I will praise my dear Redeemer, His triumphant pow'r I'll tell, how the victory He giveth over sin and death and hell.

I will sing of my Redeemer and His heav'nly love to me; He from death to life hath bro't me, Son of God with Him to be.

Chorus: Sing, O sing of my Redeemer; with His blood He purchased me; on the cross He sealed my pardon, paid the debt and made me free.

❦ *For Today:* Isaiah 53:4-12; 2 Corinthians 2:14, 15; Galatians 2:20

Make this musical truth your desire as you go—

James McGranahan, 1840-1907

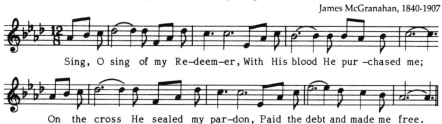

Sing, O sing of my Re–deem–er, With His blood He pur –chased me;

On the cross He sealed my par–don, Paid the debt and made me free.

GREAT IS THY FAITHFULNESS

Thomas O. Chisholm, 1866-1960

Because of the Lord's great love we are not consumed, for His compassions never fail. They are new every morning; great is Your Faithfulness. (Lamentations 3:22, 23)

One of the important lessons the Children of Israel had to learn during their wilderness journey was that God's provision of manna for them was on a morning by morning basis. They could not survive on old manna nor could it be stored for future use (Exodus 16:19-21).

While many enduring hymns are born out of a particular dramatic experience, this was simply the result of the author's "morning by morning" realization of God's personal faithfulness in his daily life. Shortly before his death in 1960, Thomas Chisholm wrote:

> My income has never been large at any time due to impaired health in the earlier years which has followed me on until now. But I must not fail to record here the unfailing faithfulness of a covenant keeping God and that He has given me many wonderful displays of His providing care which have filled me with astonishing gratefulness.

Thomas Obediah Chisholm was born in a crude log cabin in Franklin, Kentucky. From this humble beginning and without the benefit of high school or advanced education, he somehow began his career as a school teacher at the age of 16 in the same country school where he had received his elementary training. After accepting Christ as Savior, he became editor of *The Pentecostal Herald* and later was ordained as a Methodist minister. Throughout his long lifetime, Mr. Chisholm wrote more than 1,200 sacred poems, many of which have since become prominent hymn texts.

> Great is Thy faithfulness, O God my Father! There is no shadow of turning with Thee; Thou changest not; Thy compassions, they fail not: As thou hast been Thou forever wilt be.

> Summer and winter, and springtime and harvest, sun, moon and stars in their courses above, join with all nature in manifold witness to Thy great faithfulness, mercy and love.

> Pardon for sin and a peace that endureth, thine own dear presence to cheer and to guide, strength for today and bright hope for tomorrow—blessings all mine, with ten thousand beside.

> **Chorus:** Great is Thy faithfulness! Great is Thy faithfulness! Morning by morning new mercies I see; all I have needed Thy hand hath provided—Great is Thy faithfulness, Lord, unto me.

🐝 *For Today:* Psalm 9:10; 36:5-7; 102:11, 12; James 1:17

Live with this spirit of grateful praise—

William M. Runyan, 1870-1957

All I have need-ed Thy hand hath pro-vi-ded— Great is Thy faith-ful-ness, Lord, un-to me!

COME, YE THANKFUL PEOPLE, COME

Henry Alford, 1810-1871

It is a good thing to give thanks unto the Lord, and to sing praises unto Thy name,
O most high. (Psalm 92:1 KJV)

Our early American leaders wisely realized the importance of having a special day each year in which people could recount their blessings and express gratitude to God for all of His goodness.

The first thanksgiving was decreed by Governor Bradford in 1621 to commemorate the Pilgrims' harvest. Later George Washington proclaimed November 26, 1789, as a national day of thanksgiving, but the holiday was not repeated on a national basis until Abraham Lincoln named it a national Harvest Festival on November 26, 1861. After that time, the holiday was proclaimed annually by the President and the governors of each state. Finally in 1941, Congress passed a bill naming the fourth Thursday of each November as Thanksgiving Day.

The first stanza of this harvest hymn is an invitation and an exhortation to give thanks to God in His earthly temple—our local church—for the heavenly care and provision of our earthly need. The following two stanzas are an interesting commentary on the Parable of the Wheat and the Tares as recorded in Matthew 13:24-30, 36-43. The final stanza is a prayer for the Lord's return—"the final harvest home."

> Come, ye thankful people, come—raise the song of harvest home; all is safely gathered in ere the winter storms begin. God, our Maker, doth provide for our wants to be supplied: Come to God's own temple, come—raise the song of harvest home.

> All the world is God's own field, fruit unto His praise to yield: Wheat and tares together sown, unto joy or sorrow grown. First the blade and then the ear, then the full corn shall appear: Lord of harvest, grant that we wholesome grain and pure may be.

> For the Lord our God shall come and shall take His harvest home: From His field shall in that day all offenses purge away—give His angels charge at last in the fire the tares to cast, but the fruitful ears to store in His garner evermore.

> Even so, Lord, quickly come to Thy final harvest-home: gather Thou Thy people in, free from sorrow, free from sin; there, forever purified, in Thy presence to abide: come, with all Thine angels, come—raise the glorious harvest-home.

❦ *For Today:* 1 Chronicles 16:8, 9; Psalm 68:19; Matthew 13:24-30; 36-43; Hebrews 13:15

The worship most acceptable to God comes from a thankful heart. Carry this musical truth with you—

St. George's Windsor tune   George J. Elvey, 1816-1893

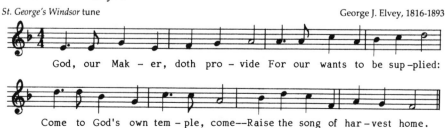

God, our Mak - er, doth pro - vide For our wants to be sup -plied:

Come to God's own tem - ple, come--Raise the song of har - vest home.

COUNT YOUR BLESSINGS

Johnson Oatman, Jr., 1856-1922

Praise be to the God and Father of our Lord Jesus Christ, who has blessed us in the heavenly realms with every spiritual blessing in Christ. (Ephesians 1:3)

For the Christian, gratitude should be a life attitude.

"Count Your Blessings" was written by one of the prolific gospel song writers of the past century, a Methodist lay preacher named Johnson Oatman. In addition to his preaching and the writing of more than 5,000 hymn texts, Oatman was also a successful business man, engaged in a shipping business and in his later years as an administrator for a large insurance company in New Jersey.

It is good for each of us periodically to take time to rediscover the simple but profound truths expressed by Mr. Oatman in the four stanzas of this hymn. In the first two verses he develops the thought that counting our blessings serves as an antidote for life's discouragements and in turn makes for victorious Christian living. The third stanza of this hymn teaches us that counting our blessings can be a means of placing material possessions in proper perspective when compared to the eternal inheritance awaiting believers. Then as we review our individual blessings, we certainly would have to agree with Mr. Oatman's fourth verse: The provision of God's help and comfort to the end of our earthly pilgrimage is one of our choicest blessings.

Each of us could spare ourselves much despair and inner tension if we would only learn to apply the practical teaching of this hymn to our daily living.

> When upon life's billows you are tempest tossed, when you are discouraged, thinking all is lost, count your many blessings—name them one by one, and it will surprise you what the Lord hath done.
>
> Are you ever burdened with a load of care? Does the cross seem heavy you are called to bear? Count your many blessings—ev'ry doubt will fly, and you will be singing as the days go by.
>
> When you look at others with their lands and gold, think that Christ has promised you His wealth untold; count your many blessings—money cannot buy your reward in heaven nor your home on high.
>
> So amid the conflict, whether great or small, do not be discouraged. God is over all; count your many blessings—angels will attend, help and comfort give you to your journey's end.
>
> **Chorus:** Count your blessings—name them one by one; count your blessings—see what God hath done.

�された *For Today:* Psalm 28:7; 68:19; 69:30, 31; James 1:17

Make a list of God's blessings. Share this list with your friends and family.

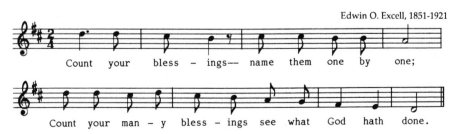

Edwin O. Excell, 1851-1921

Count your bless – ings—— name them one by one;

Count your man – y bless – ings see what God hath done.

NOW THANK WE ALL OUR GOD

Martin Rinkart, 1586-1649
English Translation—Catherine Winkworth, 1827-1878

Who shall separate us from the love of Christ? Shall trouble or hardship or persecution or famine or nakedness or danger or sword? No, in all these things we are more than conquerors through Him who loved us. (Romans 8:35, 37)

From some of the severest human sufferings imaginable during the 30 Years' War of 1618-48—a war that has been described as the most devasting in all history—this great hymn of the church was born.

Martin Rinkart was called at the age of 31 to pastor the state Lutheran church in his native city of Eilenberg, Germany. He arrived there just as the dreadful bloodshed of the 30 Years' War began, and there Rinkart spent the remaining 32 years of his life faithfully ministering to these needy people.

Germany, the battleground of this conflict between warring Catholic and Protestant forces from various countries throughout Europe, was reduced to a state of misery that baffles description. The German population dwindled from 16 million to 6 million. Because Eilenberg was a walled city, it became a frightfully over-crowded refuge for political and military fugitives from far and near. Throughout these war years several waves of deadly diseases and famines swept the city, as the various armies marched through the town, leaving death and destruction in their wake. The plague of 1637 was particularly severe. At its height Rinkart was the only minister remaining to care for the sick and dying.

Martin Rinkart's triumphant, personal expressions of gratitude and confidence in God confirm for each of us this truth taught in Scripture, that as God's children, we too can be "more than conquerors through Him who loved us."

Now thank we all our God with hearts and hands and voices, who wondrous things hath done, in whom His world rejoices; who from our mothers' arms hath blessed us on our way with countless gifts of love, and still is ours today.

O may this bounteous God thru all our life be near us, with ever joyful hearts and blessed peace to cheer us; and keep us in His grace, and guide us when perplexed, and free us from all ills in this world and the next.

All praise and thanks to God the father now be given, the Son and Him who reigns with Them in highest heaven—The one eternal God whom earth and heav'n adore—for thus it was, is now, and shall be evermore.

❦ *For Today:* 1 Chronicles 16:36; Psalm 147; 1 Corinthians 15:57, 58

God wants us to be victors and not the victims of life. With His presence we can overcome and not be overwhelmed. Carry this musical truth with you—

Nun Danket tune   Johann Crüger, 1598-1662

Now thank we all our God with hearts and hands and voic – es; Who from our

moth–ers' arms hath blessed us on our way—And still is ours to – day.

WE GATHER TOGETHER

Source Unknown
Translation by Edward Kremser, 1838-1914

Devote yourselves to prayer, being watchful and thankful. (Colossians 4:2)

Thanksgiving is not merely a day to be observed once each year; for the Christian it must be a way of daily living.

No Thanksgiving Day gathering would be complete without the singing of this traditional Dutch hymn. Today we sing this hymn as an expression of thanks to God as our defender and guide throughout the past year. The text was originally written by an anonymous author at the end of the 17th century to celebrate the Dutch freedom from the Spanish overlords, who had been driven from their land. Freedom was now theirs, both politically from Spain and religiously from the Catholic church.

"We Gather Together" must be understood and appreciated in its historical setting. For many years, Holland had been under the scourge of Spain, and in 1576, Antwerp was captured and sacked by the Spanish armies. Again, in 1585, it was captured by the Spanish and all of the Protestant citizens were exiled. Many other Dutch cities suffered similar fates. During the 17th century, however, there developed in Holland a time of great prosperity and rich post-reformation culture. Commerce was expanded around the world, and this was the period of great Dutch art, with such well-known painters as Rembrandt and Vermeer. In 1648 the Spanish endeavors to control Holland were finally destroyed beyond recovery.

One can readily see the references to these historical events throughout the hymn's text: "The wicked oppressing now cease from distressing," as well as the concern in the final stanza that God will continue to defend—"and pray that Thou still our defender will be."

> We gather together to ask the Lord's blessing; He chastens and hastens His will to make known. The wicked oppressing now cease from distressing: Sing praises to His name—He forgets not His own.

> Beside us to aide us, our God with us joining, ordaining, maintaining His kingdom divine. So from the beginning the fight we were winning: Thou, Lord, wast at our side—all glory be Thine!

> We all do extol Thee, Thou Leader triumphant, and pray that Thou still our defender wilt be; let Thy congregation escape tribulation: Thy name be ever praised! O Lord, make us free!

🍎 **For Today:** Psalm 4:11, 12; John 16:33; Romans 8:31; Hebrews 12:5-7

Share with others, perhaps your family members, how God has guided and protected your lives throughout this past year. Sing this hymn together before enjoying the Thanksgiving meal—

Kremser tune

Netherlands melody
Arranged by Edward Kremser 1838-1914

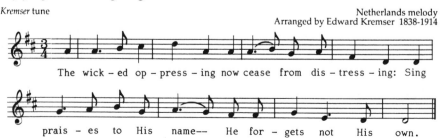

THANK YOU, LORD

Words and Music by Seth Sykes, 1892-1950 and Bessie Sykes, 1905-

Thanks be to God for His indescribable gift! (2 Corinthians 9:15)

The gift of salvation—a personal relationship with almighty God—what an indescribable gift! Yet how often do we sincerely thank our Lord for all that He has done in making this possible? Our lack of praise and thanksgiving for His gift of salvation can be likened to the response of the ten lepers after being miraculously healed by Christ (Luke 17:11-19). Only one returned to express gratitude. The interest of the other nine was centered more in what had happened to them personally than in remembering the One who had performed the miracle in their lives. Are we ever guilty of this same carelessness?

It is interesting to imagine the life-long remorse that characterized these nine ungrateful lives:

> I meant to go back, but you may guess I was filled with amazement, I cannot express
> To think that after those horrible years, that passion of loathing and passion of fears,
> Of sores unendurable—eaten, defiled—my flesh was as smooth as the flesh of a child.
> I was drunken with joy; I was crazy with glee; I scarcely could walk and I scarcely could see,
> For the dazzle of sunshine where all had been black; but I meant to go back, Oh, I meant to go back!
> I had thought to return, when people came out; there were tears of rejoicing and laughter and shout;
> My cup was so full I seemed nothing to lack! But I meant to go back, Oh, I meant to go back!   —*Unknown*

The words of this hymn have been greatly used of God since they were written in 1940 to allow believers to offer praise for the gift of their salvation—

> Some thank the Lord for friends and home, for mercies sure and sweet; but I would praise Him for His grace—in prayer I would repeat:

> Some thank Him for the flow'rs that grow, some for the stars that shine. My heart is filled with joy and praise because I know He's mine.

> I trust in Him from day to day; I prove His saving grace; I'll sing this song of praise to Him until I see His face.

> **Chorus:** Thank you, Lord, for saving my soul; thank you, Lord, for making me whole. Thank you, Lord, for giving to me Thy great salvation so rich and free.

❧ *For Today:* Psalm 100:4; 116:12, 14; 147:7; Philippians 4:6, 7; Colossians 2:7; 1 Thessalonians 5:18

Pause even now and praise God for Himself and His gift of personal salvation on your behalf. Carry this musical prayer with you—

Thank you, Lord, for sav-ing my soul, Thank you, Lord for mak-ing me whole; Thank you, Lord, for giv-ing to me Thy great sal-vation so rich and free.

THANKS TO GOD!

August Ludvig Storm, 1862-1914
Translated by Carl E. Backstrom, 1901-

Always giving thanks to God the Father for everything, in the name of our Lord Jesus Christ. (Ephesians 5:20)

A thankful spirit, both for the good and the difficult, is one of the important indicators of a believer's spiritual condition. To be able to say—

> I thank Thee, God, that all our joy is touched with pain, that shadows fall on brightest hours, that thorns remain;
> So that earth's bliss may be our guide, and not our chain. I thank Thee, Lord, that Thou has kept the best in store;
> We have enough, but not too much to long for more—a yearning for a deeper peace, not known before. —*Adelaide A. Procter*

A prayer like this requires a life that knows and practices the intimate presence of Christ in daily living.

August Storm, the author of "Thanks to God!", lived most of his life in Stockholm, Sweden. As a young man he was converted to Christ in a Salvation Army meeting. Soon he joined the Salvation Army Corps and in time became one of its leading officers. He wrote this hymn's text for the Army's publication, *Stridsropet (The War Cry)*, on December 5, 1891. The original Swedish version had four stanzas, with each verse beginning with the word *tack* "thanks," having a total of 32 "thanks" in all. The gratitude expressed to God ranges from the "dark and dreary fall" to the "pleasant, balmy springtime," "pain as well as pleasure," "thorns as well as roses."

These words have come from the heart of one who lived and practiced what his lips and pen proclaimed:

> Thanks, O God, for boundless mercy from Thy gracious throne above; thanks for ev'ry need provided from the fullness of Thy love! Thanks for daily toil and labor and for rest when shadows fall; thanks for love of friend and neighbor and Thy goodness unto all!

> Thanks for thorns as well as roses; thanks for weakness and for health; thanks for clouds as well as sunshine; thanks for poverty and wealth! Thanks for pain as well as pleasure—all thou sendest day by day; and Thy Word, our dearest treasure, shedding light upon our way.

> Thanks, O God, for home and fireside, here we share our daily bread; thanks for hours of sweet communion, when by Thee our souls are fed! Thanks for grace in time of sorrow and for joy and peace in Thee; thanks for hope today, tomorrow, and for all eternity!

❦ ***For Today:*** Psalm 68:19; 103:1-10; 116:12; Revelation 7:12

"A grateful person is a happy one." Become even more aware of God's daily blessings in life. Carry this portion of today's hymn with you—

Tack, O Gud tune

John Alfred Hultman, 1861-1942

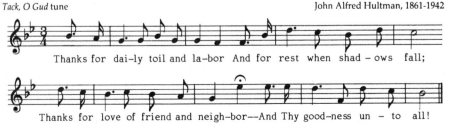

Thanks for dai-ly toil and la-bor And for rest when shad – ows fall;

Thanks for love of friend and neigh-bor––And Thy good-ness un – to all!

LET US WITH A GLADSOME MIND

John Milton, 1608-1674

Give thanks to the Lord, for He is good. His love [mercy] endures forever. (Psalm 136:1)

A thankful heart is not only the greatest virtue, but the parent of all other virtues.
—Cicero

A gladsome, joyous mind is the product of a grateful, praising heart. Gratefulness is the opposite of selfishness. The selfish person is boastful of his accomplishments. The grateful Christian, however, realizes that all achievements and blessings come only from God's bountiful hand. This realization results in a life of praise.

Far too often our prayer life consists only of a series of personal requests. God wants our requests, but He also desires to hear our praise for His eternal kindness and love in response to our daily needs.

This hymn text of praise was written by John Milton in 1621 when he was only 15 years of age. It was based on verses 1, 2, 7, and 23 of Psalm 136, a psalm that refrains each of its 26 verses with the reminder that God's love/mercy/kindness endure forever. This hymn is one of 19 poetic versions of various psalms written by Milton. Today, however, John Milton is best remembered as the brilliant, blind English poet who wrote the classic masterpieces, *Paradise Lost* and *Paradise Regained.* He is also credited with having much influence on the later hymn writings of Isaac Watts ("the father of English hynnody") and Charles Wesley (author of 6,500 hymn texts).

Let us with a gladsome mind praise the Lord, for He is kind:
For His mercies shall endure, ever faithful, ever sure.

Let us blaze His name abroad; for of gods He is the God:
For His mercies shall endure, ever faithful, ever sure.

He with all-commanding might filled the new-made world with light:
For His mercies shall endure, ever faithful, ever sure.

All things living He doth feed; His full hand supplies their need:
For His mercies shall endure, ever faithful, ever sure.

Let us then with gladsome mind praise the Lord, for He is kind:
For His mercies shall endure, ever faithful, ever sure.

❧ *For Today:* Psalm 63:1-5; 103:2; 136; 145:9; James 1:17

It is always inspiring to read about the work of God in the life of a Bible character or some great leader in history. But it is even more profitable for us to recount the mercies of God in our own past life and to offer Him praise for His eternal love. Why not do so with this little hymn?

Composer unknown

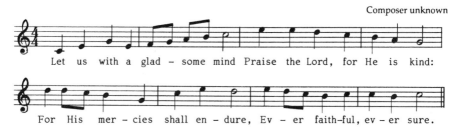

Let us with a glad – some mind Praise the Lord, for He is kind:

For His mer – cies shall en – dure, Ev – er faith–ful, ev – er sure.

JESUS CALLS US

Mrs. Cecil F. Alexander, 1818-1895

Whoever serves Me must follow Me; and where I am, my servant also will be. My Father will honor the one who serves Me. (John 12:26)

God's call for discipleship comes to every believer, not just a special few. Whether or not we hear God's call depends on our spiritual sensitivity.

The last Sunday in November is known as St. Andrew's Day. It has traditionally been an important day in the liturgical worship of the Anglican church. It commemorates the calling of Andrew by Jesus as recorded in Matthew 4:18-20 and Mark 1:16-18. "At once they [Simon and his brother Andrew] left their nets and followed Him." Andrew has become the patron saint of Scotland, and the oblique cross on which tradition says he was crucified is part of the Union Jack of the British flag.

This is another of the quality hymn texts written by Cecil Frances Alexander, recognized as one of England's finest women hymn writers. It is one of the few of Mrs. Alexander's hymns not specifically written for children; nearly all of her more than 400 poems and hymn texts were intended for reaching and teaching children with the gospel.

Following her marriage in 1850 to the distinguished churchman, Dr. William Alexander, who later became archbishop for all of Ireland, Mrs. Alexander devoted her literary talents to helping her husband with his ministry, including writing appropriate poems that he could use with his sermons. One fall day, two years after their marriage, Dr. Alexander asked his wife if she could write a poem for a sermon he was planning to preach the following Sunday for his St. Andrew's Day sermon. The pastor closed his sermon that day with the new poem written by his wife. These words have since been widely used in all churches to challenge God's people to hear Christ's call as Andrew did and then to follow, serve, and love Him "best of all."

Jesus calls us o'er the tumult of our life's wild, restless sea; day by day His sweet voice soundeth, saying, "Christian, follow Me."

Jesus calls us from the worship of the vain world's golden store, from each idol that would keep us, saying, "Christian, love Me more."

In our joys and in our sorrows, days of toil and hours of ease, still He calls, in cares and pleasures, "Christian, love Me more than these."

Jesus calls us: by Thy mercies, Savior, may we hear Thy call, give our hearts to Thy obedience, serve and love Thee best of all.

❧ *For Today:* Isaiah 6:8; Matthew 4:18-20; Mark 1:16-18; Luke 9:23

May we respond as Andrew did and become one of Christ's faithful followers and a "fisher of men." Carry this musical message as you go—

Galilee tune   William H. Jude, 1851-1922

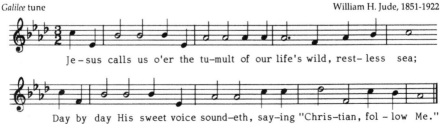

Je-sus calls us o'er the tu-mult of our life's wild, rest-less sea;

Day by day His sweet voice sound-eth, say-ing "Chris-tian, fol-low Me."

TO GOD BE THE GLORY

Fanny J. Crosby, 1820-1915

So that with one heart and mouth you may glorify the God and Father of our Lord Jesus Christ. (Romans 15:6)

The aim and final reason for all music should be nothing else but the glory of God and the refreshment of the spirit. —*J. S. Bach*

To give glory to God should be the greatest desire of every Christian. Not only should this be the supreme goal for our individual lives, but it should also be true whenever we gather in our local churches. "In the presence of the congregation I will sing Your praises" (Hebrews 2:12). We must always be alert in recognizing God's leading in our midst and in acknowledging His hand of blessing upon our corporate endeavors—the "great things He hath taught us and the great things He hath done." Without this sensitive awareness and gratitude, churches, like individuals, can easily lose the focus of their mission and develop a false sense of self-worth and sufficiency.

This fine gospel hymn first appeared in a Sunday school collection, *Brightest and Best,* compiled by William Doane and Robert Lowry in 1875. In 1952 the Billy Graham Crusade Team went to England, where they first made extensive use of the hymn in their meetings. It was an immediate success. Upon their return to the United States, they found the same enthusiastic response by American audiences. It has been a favorite hymn ever since.

"To God Be the Glory" differs from most of the hymns written by Fanny Crosby in that it is a more objective praise of God rather than the typical subjective testimony or Christian experience type of song. It is a fine blend of the characteristics of both the hymn and the gospel song.

To God be the glory—great things He hath done! So loved He the world that He gave us His Son, who yielded His life an atonement for sin and opened the Lifegate that all may go in.

O perfect redemption, the purchase of blood! To ev'ry believer the promise of God; the vilest offender who truly believes, that moment from Jesus a pardon receives.

Great things He hath taught us, great things He hath done, and great our rejoicing thru Jesus the Son; but purer and higher and greater will be our wonder, our transport, when Jesus we see.

Chorus: Praise the lord, Praise the Lord, let the earth hear His voice! Praise the Lord, Praise the Lord, let the people rejoice! O come to the Father thru Jesus the Son, and give Him the glory—great things He hath done.

❦ *For Today:* Psalm 29:2; Romans 11:36; Galatians 1:4, 5; Ephesians 3:21

Reflect seriously on whether God's glory is really the desire of your life. Also, give Him a testimony of praise for His blessings upon your local church.

William H. Doane, 1832-1915

O come to the Fa – ther thru Je – sus the Son, And give Him the glo – ry–– great things He hath done.

December

• The First Advent • Christ's Name • His Birth
• His Second Advent • Eternal Reign

HOW TEDIOUS AND TASTELESS
THE HOURS

John Newton, 1725-1807

Whom have I in heaven but You? And earth has nothing I desire beside You.
(Psalm 73:25)

The gospel of Jesus Christ revolves around the two Advents of the Savior: The first when He came as the humble baby in Bethlehem's manger (Philippians 2:6-8); the second when He returns as King of kings with power and great glory to establish His eternal kingdom (Luke 21:27). Christ's first coming assures us that we now have a God who identified Himself with us in every aspect of life from birth to death. The anticipation of His second coming assures us that we will live and reign with Him forever. Such a hope keeps this life from becoming "tedious and tasteless"—regardless of the seasons or situations.

The ultimate source of inner joy is God Himself, not our circumstances. Without an intimate sense of His daily presence, however, our lives can easily become wintry and frigid.

"BUT WHEN I AM HAPPY WITH HIM, DECEMBER'S AS PLEASANT AS MAY."

"How Tedious and Tasteless the Hours" is another of the fine hymns by John Newton. It first appeared in his 1779 collection titled *The Olney Hymns*. The hymn was originally titled "Fellowship with Christ"—based on Psalm 73:25. These words still speak vividly to us of the importance of maintaining a close personal relationship with our Lord:

> How tedious and tasteless the hours when Jesus no longer I see! Sweet prospects, sweet birds, and sweet flowers have all lost their sweetness to me. The midsummer sun shines but dim; the fields strive in vain to look gay; but when I am happy with Him, December's as pleasant as May.

> Content with beholding His face, my all to His pleasure resigned, no changes of season or place would make any change in my mind: While blest with a sense of His love, a palace a toy would appear; and prisons would palaces prove, if Jesus would dwell with me there.

> Dear Lord, if indeed I am Thine, if Thou art my sun and my song, say, why do I languish and pine, and why are my winters so long? Oh, drive these dark clouds from my sky; Thy soul-cheering presence restore; or take me unto Thee on high, where winter and clouds are no more.

🍂 *For Today:* Nehemiah 8:10; Psalm 9:2; 70:4; Romans 14:17, 18

God has made you a steward of this day, regardless of the weather or circumstances. May it count for Him. Consciously practice His presence. Reflect on this musical truth—

De Fleury tune   American Folk tune

The mid – sum – mer sun shines but dim; The fields strive in vain to look gay; But when I am hap – py with Him, De – cem – ber's as pleas–ant as May.

O COME, O COME, EMMANUEL

Latin hymn from 12th century
English translation by John M. Neale, 1818-1866

He will be great and will be called the Son of the Most High. The Lord God will give Him the throne of His father David, and He will reign over the house of Jacob forever; His kingdom will never end. (Luke 1:32, 33)

The preparation for the celebration of our Lord's birth begins four Sundays before Christmas Day. This begins the period known as the Advent season. Advent centers on the Old Testament prophecies concerning a coming Messiah and His establishment of an earthly kingdom. The Messiah's coming was prophesied 600 years before His birth. At the time the Jewish people were living in captivity in Babylon. For centuries thereafter faithful Jews earnestly anticipated the Deliverer-Messiah with great longing and expectation, echoing the prayer that He would "ransom captive Israel." And finally the long awaited heavenly announcement came— "Unto you is born this day in the city of David a Savior, which is Christ the Lord!" (Luke 2:11).

"O Come, O Come, Emmanuel" was originally used in the medieval church liturgy as a series of antiphons—short musical statements that were sung for the week of vesper services just before Christmas Eve. Each of these antiphons greets the anticipated Messiah with one of the titles ascribed Him throughout the Old Testament: Wisdom, Emmanuel, The Lord of Might, The Rod of Jesse, Day Spring, and The Key of David.

The haunting modal melody for the verses is also of ancient origin. It is based on one of the earliest forms of sacred music known—the Chant or Plain Song.

> O come, O come, Emmanuel, and ransom captive Israel, that mourns in lonely exile here until the Son of God appear.

> O come, O come, Thou Lord of might who to Thy tribes, on Sinai's height, in ancient times didst give the law in cloud and majesty and awe.

> O come, thou Rod of Jesse, free Thine own from Satan's tyranny; from depths of hell Thy people save and give them vict'ry o'er the grave.

> O come, Thou Day-spring, come and cheer our spirits by Thine advent here; O drive away the shades of night and pierce the clouds and bring us light.

> O come, Thou Key of David, come and open wide our heav'nly home where all Thy saints with Thee shall dwell—O come, O come, Emmanuel!

> **Refrain:** Rejoice! rejoice! Emmanuel shall come to thee, O Israel.

❧ ***For Today:*** Isaiah 7:14; 9:6; 11:1; 22:22; Matthew 1:22, 23; Luke 1:78, 79; Galatians 4:45

Christ came not only to be the Emmanuel—"God with us"—but even in a more personal way, *God in us.* Carry this truth throughout the Advent Season.

Veni Emmanuel tune — Plainsong, 13th century

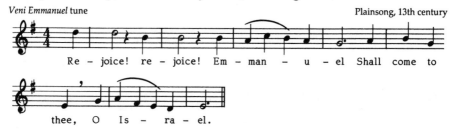

Re - joice! re - joice! Em - man - u - el Shall come to thee, O Is - ra - el.

COME, THOU LONG-EXPECTED JESUS

Charles Wesley, 1707-1788

I will shake all nations, and the desire of all nations shall come. . . . (Haggai 2:7 KJV)

Anticipation is a necessary and important part of every believer's life. In Old Testament times the people anxiously awaited a Messianic Kingdom. Today we should be waiting with the same urgent expectancy as did the Israelites of old. But our anticipation is the Lord's second advent—the piercing of the clouds and the sound of the trumpet—when victory over sin and death will be complete and final.

> Not only looking, but longing the blessed Lord's return to greet;
> Our crowns of glory to gather and cast them with joy at His feet,
> Not only waiting, but watching, wistfully scanning the skies;
> Anticipating that daybreak when the world's true Sun shall arise.   —*Unknown*

The Old Testament prophecies were very specific concerning our Lord's first advent. The prophets gave the exact location of His birth (Micah 5:2) as well as the sign that He would be virgin born (Isaiah 7:14). Likewise the New Testament gives clear instructions regarding the second advent: "There shall be signs in the sun, and in the moon, and in the stars; and upon the earth distress of nations . . . and when these things begin to come to pass, then look up, and lift up your heads; for your redemption draweth near" (Luke 21:25-28 KJV).

"Come, Thou Long-expected Jesus" is another of the more than 6,500 hymns written by Charles Wesley. It was first published in 1744 in a small collection of 18 poems titled *Hymns for the Nativity of Our Lord.* The vibrant "Hyfrydol" tune was composed by a 20-year-old Welshman, Rowland H. Prichard, in about 1830. The tune means "good cheer." It has been used with many of our popular hymns.

Just as Christ's birth 2,000 years ago dramatically changed the course of human history, so will the return of our Lord as the King of kings. With the saints of the ages we pray, "Come, Thou Long-expected Jesus."

> Come, thou long-expected Jesus, born to set Thy people free; from our fears and sins release us: Let us find our rest in Thee; Israel's Strength and Consolation, hope of all the earth thou art; dear Desire of ev'ry nation, joy of ev'ry longing heart.

> Born Thy people to deliver, born a child and yet a King; born to reign in us forever, now Thy gracious Kingdom bring. By Thine own eternal Spirit rule in all our hearts alone; by Thine all sufficient merit, raise us to Thy glorious throne.

❦ *For Today:* Isaiah 9:6, 7; Daniel 7:13, 14; Matthew 1:22, 23; Luke 1:32-35

Rejoice in the truth that God's eternal promises are unchangeable: Christ was born and He will return. Sing this truth as you go—

Hyfrydol tune   Rowland H. Prichard, 1811-1887

Is - rael's Strength and Con-so-la - tion, Hope of all the earth Thou art;

Dear De - sire of ev - 'ry na - tion, Joy of ev - 'ry long-ing heart.

BLESSED BE THE NAME

W. H. Clark, 19th century, Refrain by Ralph E. Hudson, 1843-1901

I will exalt You, my God the King; I will praise Your name for ever and ever. . . . for you have exalted above all things Your name and Your Word. (Psalm 145:1 and Psalm 138:2)

The Bible teaches that there are two things our Lord honors above all else: *His Name* and *His Word*. These two priorities should also be the most sacred trusts in our spiritual lives. A name is an individual's main identification, as well as the carrier of his reputation. In the Bible, God renamed individuals—Jacob to Israel (Genesis 32:22-32) and Saul to Paul (Acts 13:9)—to reflect more accurately their changed lifestyles. It is only normal, then, to defend one's name at all costs.

To many people today, the names "Jesus" and "God" are merely words to use in blasphemy. To those of us who associate these names with divine love, such talk cannot be dismissed lightly. Christ Himself spoke out against becoming sacrilegious in our speaking when He cautioned His disciples never even to swear either by heaven or earth (Matthew 5:34-37). And it should be remembered that one tenth of the moral law deals with profaning God's name, with this serious warning—"The Lord will not hold him guiltless . . . " (Deuteronomy 5:11). Even our approach to the heavenly Father in prayer must always be done with reverence—in the name of Jesus (John 16:23).

Let us determine to use this Christmas season to truly magnify His name and to proclaim His worth together:

> "Jesus"—O how sweet the name, "Jesus" —every day the same;
> "Jesus" —let all saints proclaim its worthy praise forever.   —W. C. Martin

The stanzas of "Blessed Be the Name" first appeared in 1891 in *Hymns of the Christian Life*. The melody was likely one of the early folk hymn tunes used in the 19th century campmeetings.

> All praise to Him who reigns above in majesty supreme, who gave His Son for man to die, that He might man redeem!
>
> His name above all names shall stand, exalted more and more, at God the Father's own right hand, where angel-hosts adore.
>
> Redeemer, Savior, Friend of man, once ruined by the fall, Thou hast devised salvation's plan, for Thou hast died for all.
>
> His name shall be the Counselor, the mighty Prince of Peace, of all earth's kingdoms Conqueror, whose reign shall never cease.
>
> **Refrain:** Blessed be the name, blessed be the name of the Lord.

❦ *For Today:*   Job 1:20, 21; Psalm 8:1; 34:3; Isaiah 42:8; John 10:3

Reflect on this truth: We are bearers of the divine name—CHRISTians. Worship your Lord with this musical expression—

Ralph E. Hudson, 1843-1901
Arranged by Wm. J. Kirkpatrick, 1838-1921

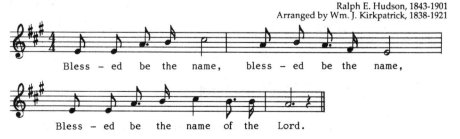

Bless - ed be the name, bless - ed be the name,

Bless - ed be the name of the Lord.

THAT BEAUTIFUL NAME

Jean Perry, 1865-1935

She will give birth to a son, and you are to give Him the name Jesus, because He will save His people from their sins. (Matthew 1:21)

There is no name so sweet on earth, no name so sweet in heaven,
The name, before His wondrous birth, to Christ the Savior given.   —*George W. Bethune*

There are many wonderful names and titles ascribed to Christ throughout the Bible. A study of these titles is not only interesting but also important since each name reveals an insight into our Lord's character. Ivor Powell, in his book *Bible Names of Christ* (Kregel Publications), discusses 80 different titles including:

Counselor— Isaiah 9:6
Emmanuel— Matthew 1:23
Helper— Hebrews 13:6
Messiah— Daniel 9:25
Judge— John 5:22
Rose of Sharon— Song of Solomon 2:1
Sun of Righteousness— Malachi 4:2

But the sweetest name of all to every believer is *Jesus.* When He was eight days old, Mary's infant Son was circumcised and given the Hebrew name *Joshua* (*Jesus* in Greek), which literally means "the Lord saves." And the Scriptures affirm without qualification that "there is no other name given among men, whereby we must be saved" (Acts 4:12).

"That Beautiful Name" first appeared in *The Voice of Thanksgiving, No. 2,* a hymnal published in 1916 especially for use at the Moody Bible Institute. The hymn has since found a place in the affections of Christian people everywhere.

I know of a Name, a beautiful Name, that angels brought down to earth; they whispered it low, one night long ago, to a maiden of lowly birth.

I know of a Name, a beautiful Name, that unto a Babe was giv'n; the stars glittered bright thruout that glad night, and angels praised God in heav'n.

The One of that Name my Savior became, my Savior of Calvary; my sins nailed Him there; my burdens He bare; He suffered all this for me.

I love that blest Name, that wonderful Name, made higher than all in heav'n; 'twas whispered, I know, in my heart long ago—to Jesus my life I've giv'n.

Chorus: That beautiful Name, that beautiful Name from sin has pow'r to free us! That beautiful Name, that wonderful Name, that matchless Name is Jesus

❦ *For Today:* Matthew 10:32; 1 Corinthians 1:2; Philippians 2:9-11; Hebrews 1:4

Raise your voice in praise and worship to the One who was given to save us from our sins. Sing as you go—

Mabel Johnston Camp, 1871-1937

That beau –ti –ful Name, That won – der – ful Name, That

match – less Name is Je – sus!

HIS NAME IS WONDERFUL

Words and Music by Audrey Mieir, 1916-

For unto us a child is born, unto us a son is given, and the government shall be upon His shoulder; and His name shall be called Wonderful, Counselor, the Mighty God, the Everlasting Father, The Prince of Peace. (Isaiah 9:6 KJV)

More than 2,500 years ago, the prophet Isaiah told of One who would be the hope of mankind, the long awaited Messiah who would establish an eternal kingdom based on justice and righteousness. Isaiah's important pronouncement told that this one would be a God-man: a child born—His humanity; a son given—His deity. The quintuplet of names ascribed to this One gives further insight into His character and ministry:

- **Wonderful**— He would be wonderful in what He would accomplish for the fallen human race.
- **Counselor**— He would be our guide through life, and our advocate before the heavenly Father.
- **The Mighty God**— He would be the God before whom every knee shall one day bow.
- **The Everlasting Father**— He would be the God of eternity.
- **The Prince of Peace**— He would be the one who would ultimately bring a true tranquility among all nations.

Audrey Mieir has been widely known for several decades as the composer and author of many fine gospel songs and choruses. "His Name Is Wonderful," written in 1959, is one of her finest. She tells in her biography how the inspiration for this song occurred while she watched the annual Christmas program given at her Bethel Union Church in Duarte, California. After the usual procession of angels, shepherds, Mary and Joseph, the singing of "sleep in heavenly peace," the pastor of the church suddenly exclaimed—"His Name Is Wonderful." Audrey Mieir tells that she quickly grabbed her Bible, searched the concordance for names given to Jesus in the Scriptures, and soon composed this song, which has since been sung around the world:

> His name is Wonderful, His name is Wonderful, His name is Wonderful, Jesus, my Lord; He is the mighty King, Master of ev'rything; His name is Wonderful, Jesus, my Lord; He's the great Shepherd, the Rock of all ages, Almighty God is He; bow down before Him, love and adore Him; His name is Wonderful, Jesus my Lord.

❧ ***For Today:*** Psalm 72:19; Proverbs 18:10; 22:1; John 1:12; Acts 4:12; Philippians 2:9,10

The more intimately we know the "child-Son," the deeper grows our love and devotion for Him. Worship Him even now and throughout the day with the singing of this song—

He is the might - y King, Mas - ter of ev - 'ry - thing,

His name is Won - der - ful, Je - sus, my Lord.

JOIN ALL THE GLORIOUS NAMES

Isaac Watts, 1674-1748

Praise be to His glorious name forever; may the whole earth be filled with His glory. (Psalm 72:19)

"Wisdom," "love," "power," "prophet," "priest," "king," "almighty Lord," "conqueror," "captain"—these are the names and titles used throughout the stanzas of this hymn to describe our Lord. But the conclusion is this: The most glorious names that either men or angels could devise would still be "too poor to speak His worth." Words are limited in their ability to convey the deep feelings of the soul. We can and should extol our Lord with great hymns of praise such as this, especially during this joyful season. But beyond our verbal expressions there must be a life deeply devoted to His person and the extension of His kingdom.

"Join All the Glorious Names" was first published in 1707 in Isaac Watts' *Hymns and Spiritual Songs, Book 1.* This hymn is generally regarded as one of Isaac Watts' finest among his more than 600 hymns and psalm paraphrases. These numerous works have earned him the title of the "father of English hymnody."

A growing love relationship with our Lord and an appreciation of His worth should result in a life of praise and worship. We should also be led to respond in loving obedience with a willingness to say with this hymn writer—"Behold I sit in willing bonds beneath Thy feet."

Join all the glorious names of wisdom, love and pow'r, that ever mortals knew, that angels ever bore: All are too poor to speak His worth, too poor to set my Savior forth.

Great Prophet of my God, my tongue would bless Thy name; by Thee the joyful news of our salvation came: The joyful news of sins forgiv'n, of hell subdued, and peace with heav'n.

My Savior and my Lord, my Conq'ror and my King, Thy scepter and Thy sword, Thy reigning grace I sing: Thine is the pow'r—behold I sit in willing bonds beneath Thy feet.

Now let my soul arise and tread the tempter down; my Captain leads me forth to conquest and a crown: A feeble saint shall win the day, tho death and hell obstruct the way.

❦ *For Today:* Exodus 20:7; Proverbs 18:10; Matthew 12:21; John 1:12; Acts 4:12; 1 Timothy 6:15

Earnestly try to show your love and devotion to Christ in some special way during this Christmas season. Worship Him even now by singing this hymn—

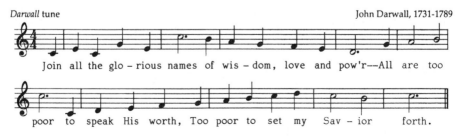

Darwall tune

John Darwall, 1731-1789

Join all the glo - rious names of wis - dom, love and pow'r—All are too poor to speak His worth, Too poor to set my Sav - ior forth.

O COME, ALL YE FAITHFUL

Latin hymn, 18th century
English translation by Frederick Oakeley, 1802-1880

When the angels had left them and gone into heaven, the shepherds said to one another, "Let's go to Bethlehem and see this thing that has happened, which the Lord has told us about!". . . . (Luke 2:15, 20)

The songs of the Christmas season comprise some of the finest music known to man, and this hymn is certainly one of our universal favorites. It was used in Catholic churches before it became known to Protestants. Today it is sung by church groups around the world since it has been translated from its original Latin into more than 100 other languages. The vivid imagery of the carol seems to have meaning and appeal for all ages in every culture.

The original Latin text consisted of four stanzas. The first calls us to visualize anew the infant Jesus in Bethlehem's stable. The second stanza is usually omitted in most hymnals, but it reminds us that the Christ-child is very God Himself:

> God of God and Light of Light begotten, Lo, He abhors not the Virgin's womb; Very God, begotten, not created—O come, let us adore Him.

The next stanza pictures for us the exalted song of the angelic choir heard by the lowly shepherds. Then the final verse offers praise and adoration to the Word, our Lord, who was with the Father from the beginning of time.

For many years this hymn was known as an anonymous Latin hymn. Recent research, however, has revealed manuscripts that indicate that it was written in 1744 by an English layman named John Wade and set to music by him in much the same style as used today. The hymn first appeared in his collection, *Cantus Diversi*, published in England in 1751. One hundred years later the carol was translated into its present English form by an Anglican minister, Frederick Oakeley, who desired to use it for his congregation. The tune name, "Adeste Fideles," is taken from the first words of the original Latin text, and translated literally means "be present or near, ye faithful."

> O come, all ye faithful, joyful and triumphant; come ye, O come ye to Bethlehem; come and behold Him, born the King of angels:

> Sing, choirs of angels, sing in exultation; sing all ye bright hosts of heav'n above; glory to God, all glory in the highest:

> Yea, Lord, we greet Thee, born this happy morning; Jesus, to Thee be all glory giv'n; Word of the Father, now in flesh appearing:

> **Refrain:** O come, let us adore Him, Christ, the Lord.

❦ *For Today:* Matthew 2:1, 2; Luke 2:9-14; John 1:14

Ask God to help you and your family make this Christmas season the most spiritual one you have yet known. Worship Him— Christ, the Lord!

Adeste Fideles tune   From Wade's *Cantus Diversi*, 1751

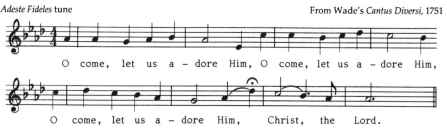

O come, let us a - dore Him, O come, let us a - dore Him,

O come, let us a - dore Him, Christ, the Lord.

JOY TO THE WORLD!

Isaac Watts, 1674-1748

But the angel said to them, "Do not be afraid, I bring you good news of great joy that will be for all the people." (Luke 2:10)

As one of the most joyous of all Christmas hymns, this carol omits references to shepherds, angelic choruses, and wise men. It emphasizes instead the reverent but ecstatic joy that Christ's birth brought to mankind. For centuries hearts had yearned for God to reveal Himself personally. At last it happened as "the Word became flesh and dwelt among us." The entire Advent season should be filled with solemn rejoicing as we contemplate anew God's great gift, providing the means whereby sinful man might live eternally.

"Joy to the World" is a paraphrase of the last part of Psalm 98:

Make a joyful noise unto the Lord, all the earth; make a loud noise and rejoice and sing praise. Let the floods clap their hands; let the hills be joyful together before the Lord; for He cometh to judge the earth; with righteousness shall He judge the world, and the people with equity.

Although it was originally a song of rejoicing for Jehovah's protection of His chosen people and the anticipation of the time when He would be the God of the whole earth, this psalm was intended by Watts to be a New Testament expression of praise. It exalts the salvation that began when God became incarnate as the Babe of Bethlehem who was destined to remove the curse of Adam's fall. The text was originally titled "The Messiah's Coming and Kingdom" when it first appeared in Watts' hymnal of 1719. The music for this popular carol is thought to have been adapted by Lowell Mason, an American church musician, from some of the phrases used in parts of George Frederick Handel's beloved oratorio, *The Messiah*, first performed in 1742.

Through the combined talents of an English literary genius of the 18th century, a German-born musical giant from the same period, and a 19th century American choir director and educator, another great hymn was born.

> Joy to the world! the Lord is come! Let earth receive her King; let ev'ry heart prepare Him room, and heav'n and nature sing.

> Joy to the earth the Savior reigns. Let men their songs employ, while fields and floods, rocks, hills and plains repeat the sounding joy.

> No more let sins and sorrows grow, nor thorns infest the ground; He comes to make His blessings flow far as the curse is found.

> He rules the world with truth and grace, and makes the nations prove the glories of His righteousness and wonders of His love.

❦ *For Today:* Genesis 3:17 18; Psalm 98; Romans 5:20, 21

Express gratitude for our Savior's birth with these words—

Antioch tune

Adapted from G. F. Handel 1685-1759
Arranged by Lowell Mason, 1792-1872

Joy to the world! the Lord is come! Let earth re - ceive her King.

WHAT CHILD IS THIS?

William C. Dix, 1837-1898

When they had seen Him, they spread the word concerning what had been told them about this child . . . (Luke 2:17)

The question asked in this well-loved carol must have been uppermost in the minds of those present at Jesus' birth. We can almost hear the question being asked from one to another as they gazed into the humble manger. How difficult it must have been for them to understand that the babe who lay in "such mean estate" was truly the promised Messiah. And through the centuries men have continued to ponder who Christ really is—how can He be fully God and still fully man? Only through divine faith comes the revealed answer.

> He who is the Bread of Life began His ministry hungering. He who is the Water of Life ended His ministry thirsty. Christ hungered as man, yet fed the multitudes as God. He was weary, yet He is our rest. He prayed, yet He hears prayers. He was sold for 30 pieces of silver, yet He redeems sinners. He was led as a lamb to the slaughter, yet He is the Good Shepherd. He died, and by dying destroyed death. —*Unknown*

How beautifully the triumphant answer to this imposing question bursts forth in the refrain— "This, this is Christ the King."

This thoughtful text was written by William Dix, one of our finest lay hymn writers. While a successful insurance salesman in Glasgow, Scotland, he was stricken with a sudden serious illness at the age of 29. Dix was confined to bed for an extended period and suffered deep depression until he called out to God and "met Him in a new and real way." Out of this spiritual experience came many artistic and distinctive hymns, including this delightful carol. It was taken from a longer Christmas poem, "The Manger Throne," written by William Dix about 1865. The melody "Green Sleeves" is a traditional English folk tune.

> What Child is this, who, laid to rest, on Mary's lap is sleeping? Whom angels greet with anthems sweet, while shepherds watch are keeping?

> Why lies He in such mean estate where ox and ass are feeding? Good Christian, fear—for sinners here the silent Word is pleading.

> So bring Him incense, gold and myrrh—come, rich and poor, to own Him; the King of kings salvation brings—let loving hearts enthrone Him.

> **Refrain:** This, this is Christ the King, whom shepherds guard and angels sing: Haste, haste to bring Him laud—the Babe, the Son of Mary.

❦ *For Today:* Matthew 2:1-12; Luke 1:26-28; 2:6-20

As you read and study the gospel account about Christ, begin a study of both His claims and demonstrations that prove that He was truly God—truly deity, the Messiah sent from heaven. Sing this musical truth as you go—

Green Sleeves melody   English melody before 1642

This, this is Christ the King, whom shep–herds guard and an–gels

sing: Haste, haste to bring Him laud––the Babe, the Son of Ma – ry.

O LITTLE TOWN OF BETHLEHEM

Phillips Brooks, 1835-1893

So Joseph also went up from the town of Nazareth in Galilee to Judea, to Bethlehem the town of David, because he belonged to the house and line of David. (Luke 2:4)

In the same way that God's "wondrous gift" came to Bethlehem, silently, so Christ comes into our lives today and casts out our sins and fears if we are willing to have Him abide in our lives. Then "the dear Christ enters in." How beautifully the glorious message of Christmas is told in this well-phrased hymn by Phillips Brooks, one of America's most outstanding ministers of the past century.

During a trip to the Holy Land in 1865, Brooks went to the Church of the Nativity in Bethlehem on Christmas Eve and worshiped there. He was deeply moved by this experience. Three years later, while pastoring the Holy Trinity Church in Philadelphia, Brooks desired to have a special carol for the children to sing in their Sunday school Christmas program. Recalling the peaceful scene in the little town of Bethlehem, Brooks completed the writing of the text in just one evening. He gave a copy of the words to his organist, Lewis R. Redner, and requested him to compose a melody that would be easy for the children to sing. On the evening just before the program was to be given, Redner awakened suddenly from his sleep with the present melody in his mind—and he quickly wrote it out. "O Little Town of Bethlehem" has been a favorite with children and adults around the world since that time.

O little town of Bethlehem, how still we see thee lie! Above thy deep and dreamless sleep the silent stars go by; yet in thy dark streets shineth the everlasting Light—the hopes and fears of all the years are met in thee tonight.

For Christ is born of Mary—and gathered all above, while mortals sleep, the angels keep their watch of wond'ring love. O morning stars, together proclaim the holy birth, and praises sing to God the King, and peace to men on earth.

How silently, how silently the wondrous gift is giv'n! So God imparts to human hearts the blessings of His heav'n. No ear may hear His coming, but, in this world of sin, where meek souls will receive Him still the dear Christ enters in.

O holy Child of Bethlehem descend to us, we pray; cast out our sin and enter in—be born in us us today. We hear the Christmas angels the great glad tidings tell; O come to us, abide with us, our Lord Emmanuel!

🐦 *For Today:* Micah 5:2; Matthew 2:1-12; Luke 2:1-7

In the midst of all the rush and activity of the Christmas season, take time to rejoice in the joy of Christ's birth and ask Him to abide with you in a special way.

St. Louis tune   Lewis H. Redner, 1831-1908

O come to us, a - bide with us, Our Lord Em - man - u - el.

AWAY IN A MANGER

Source unknown (stanzas 1, 2), John Thomas McFarland, 1851-1913 (stanza 3)

And she gave birth to her firstborn, a son. She wrapped Him in cloths and placed Him in a manger, because there was no room for them in the inn. (Luke 2:7)

The shepherds had an angel	Christ watches me, His little lamb,
The wise men had a star	Cares for me day and night,
But what have I, a little child,	That I may be His own in heaven;
To guide me home from far,	So angels clad in white
Where glad stars sing together	Shall sing their "Glory, glory,"
And singing angels are?	For my sake in the height.

—Christina Rossetti

No Christmas song is more loved than this tender children's carol. With its simply worded expression of love for the Lord Jesus and trust in His faithful care, the hymn appeals to young and old alike. It is usually one of the first Christmas songs learned in early childhood; yet its pleasing melody and gentle message preserve it in our affections all through life.

For some time "Away in the Manger" was titled "Luther's Cradle Hymn." It was thought to have been written by Martin Luther for his own children and then passed on by German mothers. Modern research discounts this claim, however. Stanzas one and two first appeared in the *Little Children's Book,* published in Philadelphia in 1885. The third verse was written by a Methodist minister, Dr. John T. McFarland, in the early 1900's when an additional stanza for this carol was desired for use at a church children's day program.

How important it is that we take time to help our children see beyond the glitter of the Christmas season and teach them the true meaning of Christ's birth. The most thrilling story ever known to man began in Bethlehem at Christmas.

> Away in a manger, no crib for a bed, the little Lord Jesus laid down His sweet head; the stars in the sky looked down where He lay, the little Lord Jesus, asleep an the hay.

> The cattle are lowing; the Baby awakes, but little Lord Jesus, no crying He makes; I love Thee, Lord Jesus! look down from the sky, and stay by my cradle till morning is nigh.

> Be near me, Lord Jesus, I ask Thee to stay close by me forever, and love me, I pray; bless all the dear children in Thy tender care, and fit us for heaven, to live with Thee there.

❦ **For Today:** Matthew 8:20; Mark 10:13-16; Luke 2:12, 16

Use this season to enjoy times of family worship. Include the reading of the Christmas story—Luke 2:1-20 (perhaps from different versions), share personal insights from the story, dramatize the various events, sing and play the carols, pray together, and discuss how the family could share their joy with others.

Mueller tune   James R. Murray, 1841-1905

ANGELS, FROM THE REALMS OF GLORY

James Montgomery, 1771-1854

An angel of the Lord appeared to them, and the glory of the Lord shone around them, and they were terrified. (Luke 2:9)

> All my heart this night rejoices as I hear, far and near,
> Sweetest angel voices. "Christ is born" their choirs are singing,
> Till the air everywhere now with joy is ringing.   —Paul Gerhardt

"Angels, From the Realms of Glory" is considered by many students of hynnody to be one of our finest Christmas hymns. In a unique style it addresses first the angelic chorus in the first stanza, then the shepherds in the second stanza, the wise men in the third, and finally today's believers—calling all to worship Christ our King. Worship is the very essence of the entire Christmas story.

James Montgomery was known as a deeply devoted, noble person who made an important contribution to English hymnody through his many inspiring texts. At the age of 23 he was appointed editor of the weekly *Sheffield Register* in London, maintaining this position for the next 31 years. As editor of this paper Montgomery championed many different causes, such as the abolition of slavery. "Angels, From the Realms of Glory" first appeared as a poem in Montgomery's newspaper on December 24, 1816. Later it was published in a hymnal titled *Montgomery's Original Hymns* and was known as "Good Tidings of Great Joy to All People."

> Angels, from the realms of glory, wing your flight o'er all the earth; ye who sang creation's story, now proclaim Messiah's birth:

> Shepherds, in the fields abiding, watching o'er your flocks by night, God with man is now residing; yonder shines the infant Light:

> Sages, leave your contemplations, brighter visions beam afar; seek the great desire of nations; ye have seen His natal star:

> Saints before the altar bending, watching long in hope and fear, suddenly the Lord, descending, in His temple shall appear:

> **Refrain:** Come and worship, come and worship, worship Christ, the new-born King.

❦ *For Today:* Isaiah 7:14; Haggai 2:7; Matthew 2:1-9, 23; Luke 2:7-20; John 1:14

Just as the angels, shepherds, and wise men all bowed their knee in the worship of Christ, may we pause in our busy lives to do the same. Carry this musical reminder with you—

Regent Square tune   Henry Smart, 1813-1879

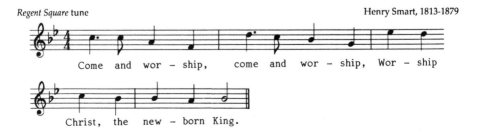

Come and wor - ship,   come and wor - ship,   Wor - ship

Christ,   the   new - born King.

ANGELS WE HAVE HEARD ON HIGH

Traditional French Carol

Glory to God in the highest, and on earth peace to men on whom His favor rests. (Luke 2:14)

As vast numbers of angels swiftly descended toward earth through the star sprinkled sky, the leading angel halted them with a sign. They hovered with folded wings over a silent field near Bethlehem. "There they are," said the leading angel, "the humble shepherds who have been chosen by God to receive our message. It will be the most wonderful news that mortal man has ever received. Are you ready with your great angelic chorus?"

The leading angel drifted slightly downward so that he could be seen by the shepherds below. They were terrified! Each one of them covered his face in the brilliance of the light but earnestly listened with awe as the vision before them began to speak in their own language:

"Do not be afraid. I bring you good news of great joy that will be for all the people. Today in the town of David a Savior has been born to you; He is Christ the Lord."

Instantly surrounding the angel was the brilliant heavenly host, and echoing through the sky was the most beautiful singing that the shepherds had ever heard, exulting and praising God for the long-awaited gift of His Son. They made haste to see the Savior with their own eyes.

The Bible teaches that angels are the ministering servants of God and that they are continually being sent to help and protect us, the heirs of salvation. Certainly their most important task, however, was this momentous occasion announcing Christ's arrival on earth!

Although little is known of its origins, this inspiring 18th century French carol has become a universal favorite.

> Angels we have heard on high, sweetly singing o'er the plains, and the mountains, in reply, echoing their joyous strains.

> Shepherds, why this jubilee? Why your joyous strains prolong? What the gladsome tidings be which inspire your heav'nly song?

> Come to Bethlehem and see Him whose birth the angels sing; come, adore on bended knee Christ the Lord, the new-born King.

> See Him in a manger laid, Jesus, Lord of heav'n and earth; Mary, Joseph, lend your aid, with us sing our Savior's birth.

> **Refrain:** Gloria in excelsis Deo!

❧ *For Today:* Luke 1:46-55; Luke 2:7-20

Rejoice that His angels are concerned about you and are sent to protect you personally. Sing this musical refrain—

Gloria tune   French melody, 18th century

Glo . . . . ri - a—

in ex – cel – sis De – o!

HARK! THE HERALD ANGELS SING

Charles Wesley, 1707-1788

But you, Bethlehem Ephrathah, though you are small among the clans of Judah, out of you will come for Me One who will be ruler over Israel, whose origins are from old, from ancient times. (Micah 5:2)

Christmas carols as we know them now were abolished by the English Puritan parliament in 1627 because they were a part of a "worldly festival," which they considered the celebration of Christmas to be. As a result, there was a scarcity of Christmas hymns and carols in the 17th and early 18th centuries. Charles Wesley's "Hark! The Herald Angels Sing" was one of the few written during this period. Wesley's fine text and the melody by master composer Felix Mendelssohn have given this hymn its great popularity and its standing as a classic among Christmas songs.

Like many of Charles Wesley's more than 6,500 hymns, this text clearly presents biblical doctrine in poetic language. The first stanza describes the song of the angels outside Bethlehem with an invitation to join them in praise of Christ. The following verses present the truths of the virgin birth, Christ's deity, the immortality of the soul, the new birth, and a prayer for the transforming power of Christ in our lives.

For more than 200 years, believers have been enlightened and blessed by the picturesque manner in which Charles Wesley has retold the truths of our Savior's birth.

Hark! the herald angels sing, "Glory to the new-born King; peace on earth, and mercy mild—God and sinners reconciled!" Joyful, all ye nations rise, join the triumph of the skies; with th'angelic hosts proclaim, "Christ is born in Bethlehem!" Hark the herald angels sing, "Glory to the new-born King!"

Christ, by highest heav'n adored, Christ, the everlasting Lord! Late in time behold Him come, offspring of the virgin's womb. Veiled in flesh the God-head see; hail th' incarnate Deity, pleased as man with men to dwell, Jesus, our Emmanuel. Hark! the herald angels sing, "Glory to the new-born King."

Hail the heav'n-born Prince of Peace! Hail the Sun of Righteousness! Light and life to all He brings, ris'n with healing in His wings. Mild He lays His glory by, born that man no more may die, born to raise the sons of earth, born to give them second birth. Hark! the herald angels sing, "Glory to the new-born King."

❦ *For Today:* Matthew 2:1-12; Luke 2:1-7, 14

Be so in tune with the exultant song of the angels during this Christmas time that others may see and hear that Christ dwells with you.

Mendelssohn tune   Felix Mendelssohn, 1809-1847

Hark! the her – ald an – gels sing, "Glo – ry to the new – born King."

THE FIRST NOEL

English carol, before 1823

And there were shepherds living out in the fields nearby, keeping watch over their flocks at night. (Luke 2:8)

Although no Christmas season would be complete without the melodious singing of this tuneful carol, very little is known about its origin. It is believed to have had its rise in France during the 15th century. *Noel* is a French word originating from Latin meaning "birthday." The song is thought to have been brought across the channel to England by the wandering troubadours. The carol under the English form, "Nowell," became a great favorite for Christmas Eve, especially in the west of England. This was when the entire village gathered for singing and celebrating the bringing in of the Yule log. At this time carols were thought of as popular religious songs meant to be sung outside the church rather than within.

"The First Noel" portrays in vivid narrative style the story of the birth of Christ. All six verses are needed to complete the entire event when the hymn is sung. The sixth stanza urges us to join together to sing praises to God for the marvels of His creation and for the salvation provided through Christ's shed blood. The repetition of the joyous "noel" in the refrain is equivalent to our singing out "happy birthday" to someone.

It is interesting to observe that the "King of Israel" was first announced to "certain poor shepherds" only, but in the final stanza the phrases "let us all" and "mankind hath brought" remind us that Christ came to redeem the whole world.

> The first noel the angel did say was to certain poor shepherds in fields as they lay—in fields where they lay keeping their sheep on a cold winter's night that was so deep.
>
> They looked up and saw a star shining in the east, beyond them far; and to the earth it gave great light, and so it continued both day and night.
>
> And by the light of that same star, three wise men came from country far; to seek for a king was their intent, and to follow the star wherever it went.
>
> This star drew nigh to the northwest; o'er Bethlehem it took its rest; and there it did both stop and stay, right over the place where Jesus lay.
>
> Then entered in those wise men three, full rev'rently upon their knee, and offered there, in His presence, their gold and myrrh and frankincense.
>
> Then let us all with one accord sing praises to our heav'nly Lord, that hath made heav'n and earth of naught, and with His blood mankind hath bought.
>
> **Refrain:** Noel, noel! Noel, noel! Born is the King of Israel!

❦ *For Today:* Matthew 2:1-12; Luke 2:8-20

Let's allow the joy of Christ's birth to be reflected on our faces and heard in our glad singing of praises to Him all through this Christmas season.

Sandys' *Christmas Carols*, 1833

No - el, no - el! No - el, no - el! Born is the King
of Is - ra - el!

IT CAME UPON THE MIDNIGHT CLEAR

Edmund H. Sears, 1810-1876

Suddenly a great company of the heavenly host appeared with the angel, praising God and saying, "Glory to God in the highest, and on earth peace to men on whom His favor rests." (Luke 2:13)

The peace of Christmas, proclaimed by the heavenly chorus, is one of God's greatest gifts to mankind. "God was reconciling the world unto Himself" (2 Corinthians 5:19). This message of reconciliation involves us on three different levels: Peace with God, peace with our fellowmen, and peace within ourselves. It is this blessed concept that Edmund Sears wanted to emphasize in his unusual carol.

In the second stanza Sears stressed the social aspects of the angels' message—the hope of Christians spreading peace and good will to others who are burdened and painfully toiling. The hymn was written in 1849, a time preceding the Civil War when there was much tension over the question of slavery, the industrial revolution in the North and the frantic gold rush in California. The final verse looks forward optimistically to a time when all people will enjoy the peace of which the angels sang.

This carol is one of the finest ever written by an American. After graduation from Harvard Divinity School, Edmund Sears spent most of his life in small pastorates in the East.

It came upon the midnight clear, that glorious song of old, from angels bending near the earth to touch their harps of gold: "Peace on the earth, good will to men, from heav'n's all gracious King!" The world in solemn stillness lay to hear the angels sing.

And ye, beneath life's crushing load, whose forms are bending low, who toil along the climbing way with painful steps and slow, look now! for glad and golden hours come swiftly on the wing: O rest beside the weary road and hear the angels sing.

For lo, the days are hast'ning on, by prophet bards foretold, when with the ever circling years comes round the age of gold when peace shall over all the earth its ancient splendors fling, and the whole world give back the song which now the angels sing.

❦ *For Today:* Luke 2:9-14; Ephesians 2:14; Hebrews 1:6

Just as the angelic announcement of peace was given at a time of much turmoil caused by the heavy rule of the Roman Empire, so today does God's message of peace comes despite life's stormy circumstances.

Carol tune   Richard S. Willis, 1819-1900

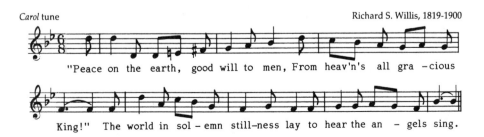

"Peace on the earth, good will to men, From heav'n's all gra –cious King!" The world in sol – emn still–ness lay to hear the an – gels sing.

THERE'S A SONG IN THE AIR!

Josiah G. Holland, 1819-1881

Suddenly a great company of the heavenly host appeared with the angel, praising God. . . . (Luke 2:13)

What a beautiful scene is drawn for us in this joyful Christmas hymn! As we visualize once more the glorious chorus of angels, the brilliant star, and Mary watching over her babe in the lowly manger, we feel like joining the "heavenly throng" in their "tumult of joy" to greet our Savior and King!

Josiah G. Holland created one of the most thoughtful and thrilling of all the carols that we sing during this season. It is no wonder that the angels' song rang out so jubilantly: They knew it was the King of heaven and earth they serenaded. How little did those who followed the brilliant light of the star realize that through the ages the whole earth would be illumined by Christ the Lord (Revelation 22:16). Like those who saw the star, we "rejoice in the light, and we echo the song. . . ."

Born in Belchertown, Massachusetts, Josiah Gilbert Holland began his professional career as a medical doctor. But soon he became involved in writing and editorial work and eventually helped establish *Scribner's Magazine.* "There's a Song in the Air" first appeared in a Sunday school collection in 1874 and five years later in Holland's *Complete Poetical Writings.* The present tune, "Christmas Song," was composed for these words by Karl P. Harrington approximately 25 years later. The composer was a recognized church musician, serving in various Methodist churches as organist and choir director. He was also one of the musical editors for the *Methodist Hymnal* of 1905, when the present version of the carol first appeared.

> There's a song in the air! There's a star in the sky! There's a mother's deep prayer and a baby's low cry! And the star rains its fire while the beautiful sing, for the manger of Bethlehem cradles a King!

> There's a tumult of joy o'er the wonderful birth, for the Virgin's sweet Boy is the Lord of the earth. Ay! the star rains its fire while the beautiful sing, for the manger of Bethlehem cradles a King!

> In the light of that star lie the ages impearled, and that song from afar has swept over the world. Ev'ry hearth is aflame—and the beautiful sing in the homes of the nations that Jesus is King!

> We rejoice in the light, and we echo the song that comes down thru the night from the heavenly throng. Ay! we shout to the lovely evangel they bring, and we greet in His cradle our Savior and King!

❦ **For Today:** Matthew 2:10; Luke 1:3, 68, 69; Luke 2:9-20, 29-32

Sing the words of this hymn with exuberance as though you were actually joining with the angels in their song that continues to ring—

Christmas Song tune   Karl P. Harrington, 1861-1953

And the star rains its fire while the beau-ti-ful sing, For the man-ger of Beth-le-hem cra-dles a King!

WHILE BY OUR SHEEP

German carol, Translated by Theodore Baker, 1851-1934

The shepherds returned, glorifying and praising God for all the things they had heard and seen, which were just as they had been told. (Luke 2:20)

It was a cold, clear night. The stars twinkled above and an air of peaceful serenity settled calmly over the field outside of Bethlehem. The fire was burning low as the shepherds sprawled out to rest among their sheep. "What is the meaning of that star?" asked one of the younger boys. As some turned to look, the star seemed to sparkle with a glorious glow, almost hanging over Bethlehem. Then suddenly they were blinded by a brilliant light! They cried out in fright and hid their faces on the ground. The consoling voice of an angel calmed their spirits as they listened in rapture to the blessed announcement of the long-awaited Messiah. How great was their joy!

Have you ever wondered why these simple, uncouth shepherds without wealth, power, or social position were the first to receive heaven's glorious message? Prophecy foretold that salvation would be offered first to Israel. Thus the Jewish shepherds were allowed to adore the Savior before the arrival of the Gentile wise men. Perhaps the humble shepherds were also chosen to receive the angels' message because God wanted to send His only Son to be associated with the seemingly unimportant of this world rather than among the proud and wealthy. Also God knew that these lowly shepherds would receive His news of salvation with open hearts and would return with great joy to share what they had heard and seen.

Originating as it does from 17th century Germany, this vivid description of the first Christmas night reminds us of the various lands and cultures that have provided our many lovely carols, giving us a rich musical and spiritual heritage.

> While by our sheep we watched at night, glad tidings bro't an angel bright:
>
> There shall be born, so he did say, in Bethlehem a Child today:
>
> There shall the Child lie in a stall, this Child who shall redeem us all:
>
> This gift of God we'll cherish well—Jesus, our Lord Emmanuel:
>
> **Refrain:** How great our joy! (Great our joy!) Joy, joy, joy! (Joy, joy, joy!) Praise we the Lord in heav'n on high! (Praise we the Lord in heav'n on high!)

🍂 *For Today:* Isaiah 40:11; Jeremiah 31:10; Luke 2:8-20

Take your place with the shepherds when the heavenly announcement was given. Move with them to the manger and worship in awe. Return with the song of praise upon your lips (hear the gentle echo in the night's stillness). Share your joy with others.

17th century carol, *Trier Gesangbuch*

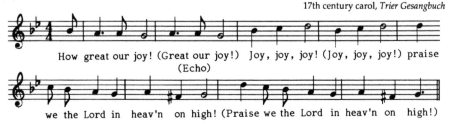

How great our joy! (Great our joy!) Joy, joy, joy! (Joy, joy, joy!) praise (Echo)

we the Lord in heav'n on high! (Praise we the Lord in heav'n on high!)

WHILE SHEPHERDS WATCHED THEIR FLOCKS

Nahum Tate, 1652-1715

Today in the town of David a Savior has been born to you; He is Christ the Lord.
(Luke 2:11)

In the spring of the year, the lambing season, shepherds in ancient times would sit all night beside their flocks, watching for wolves or other dangers and even feeding orphan lambs with milk on a soaked rag. No doubt this is why these shepherds were seated on the ground the night Jesus was born, for biblical scholars believe the event was actually some time in April. It would be natural for these humble men to be fearful, not only for themselves but also for their flock, when the brilliant light and the voices of the angels pierced the silent night. But with what wonder and exultation they must have heard the astounding news! Are we surprised that they forgot their duty to their flocks and hastened joyfully, though perhaps doubtfully, to see the Holy Babe in the manger with their own eyes?

This clearly written, colorful narrative of the angels' announcement to the shepherds was written by Nahum Tate, the son of an Irish clergyman. After education at Trinity College, Dublin, he was appointed Poet Laureate of England during the reign of William and Mary. His life as a drunkard and a spendthrift resulted in degradation, however, and he died at the age of 63 in a debtor's refuge in London, England.

No doubt the popularity of this carol has been enhanced by the tuneful melody, which has been adapted from a work by master composer George Frederick Handel.

> While shepherds watch'ed their flocks by night, all seated on the ground, the angel of the Lord came down, and glory shone around, and glory shone around.

> "Fear not!" said he, for mighty dread had seized their troubled mind; "glad tidings of great joy I bring to you and all mankind."

> "To you in David's town this day is born, of David's line, the Savior who is Christ the Lord, and this shall be the sign;

> "The heav'nly Babe you there shall find to human view displayed, all meanly wrapt in swathing bands and in a manger laid."

> "All glory be to God on high, and to the earth be peace: Good will henceforth from heav'n to men begin and never cease!"

❦ *For Today:* Luke 2:8-14; Romans 1:3

Out of gratefulness to God for the precious gift of His Son, we should be anxious to spread His peace and good will to others whenever we can.

Christmas tune

Arranged from George F. Handel, 1685-1759
in Weyman's *Melodia Sacra*, 1815

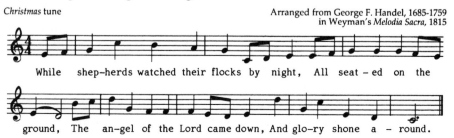

While shep-herds watched their flocks by night, All seat - ed on the
ground, The an-gel of the Lord came down, And glo-ry shone a - round.

WE THREE KINGS OF ORIENT ARE

Words and Music by John H. Hopkins, 1820-1891

And when they were come into the house, they [the wise men] saw the young child with Mary His mother, and fell down, and worshiped Him; and when they had opened their treasures, they presented unto Him gifts: gold, frankincense, and myrrh. (Matthew 2:11)

Each of the participants involved with Christ's birth—Mary and Joseph, the inn keeper, the angels, shepherds, and wise men—has much to teach us.

Although there is no scriptural basis for stating dogmatically that there were three wise men, the fact that three distinct gifts are mentioned has given rise to this traditional idea. Master artists throughout the centuries have depicted three wise men on camels as one of their favorite nativity themes.

The number of wise men is not important, but the fact that they persisted in following the light that was given them until they found the object of their search, that they responded in worship, and that they returned home to share their experience with others—all has much to tell us. Also, the gifts presented to the Christ-child were both significant and appropriate: gold, symbolic of His kingly reign; frankincense, symbolic of His priestly ministry; myrrh, symbolic of our redemption through His death. How important it is that our gifts of love and devotion be offered to Christ after we have first found Him and then have bowed in true adoration before Him.

The author and composer of this well-known Christmas hymn was an Episcopalian minister from Pennsylvania. John Hopkins has been credited with contributing much to the development of music in his denomination during the 19th century, writing a number of fine hymns and hymn tunes. One of his publications, *Carols, Hymns and Songs,* enjoyed four editions.

> We three kings of Orient are, bearing gifts we traverse afar, field and fountain, moor and mountain, following yonder star.

> Born a King on Bethlehem's plain, gold I bring to crown Him again, King forever, ceasing never over us all to reign,.

> Frankincense to offer have I; incense owns a Deity nigh; prayer and praising, all men raising, worship Him, God on high.

> Myrrh is mine; its bitter perfume breathes a life of gathering gloom: Sorr'wing, sighing, bleeding, dying, sealed in the stone-cold tomb.

> Glorious now behold Him arise, King and God and Sacrifice; alleluia, alleluia! Earth to heav'n replies.

❦ *For Today:* Matthew 2:1-11

Follow the light of God's Word and the leading of His Holy Spirit to worship Christ and to share His love. Carry this tuneful message—

Kings of Orient tune   John H. Hopkins, 1820-1891

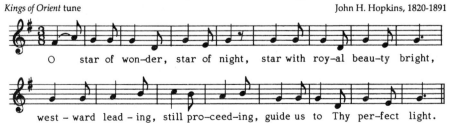

GOOD CHRISTIAN MEN, REJOICE

Latin carol, 14th century
Translation by John M. Neale, 1818-1866

Shout for joy, O heavens; rejoice, O earth; burst into song, O mountains! For the Lord comforts His people and will have compassion on His afflicted ones. (Isaiah 49:13)

As this spritely carol reminds us, Christmas should be the most joyous season of the year for all true Christians. Our lives should be filled with gratitude to God for the immeasurable love shown to us in the gift of His Son. Out of joyous hearts we should be exuberant in "heart and soul and voice!" This ancient hymn uses frequent repetition to impress upon us that the birth of Christ won for us "endless bliss" by opening the way to heaven and conquering our fear of death through His assurance of eternal life.

The festive spirit of Christmas, however, should not fade away as the holiday passes. The joy and peace that Christ brings to our lives should enable us to be continually rejoicing Christians, regardless of the circumstances. The blessings that came to us on Christmas morn have illuminated our lives forever!

"Good Christian Men, Rejoice" is an unusual combination of 14th century Latin phrases and vernacular German expressions. The original Latin text was titled "In Dulci Jubilo," meaning "in sweet shouting." Over the years German people added their own wording, making this a "macaronic carol"—one that combines two or more languages. The carol was later given a free rendering English translation by John M. Neale, the noted 19th century scholar and translator of ancient hymns. It first appeared in *Neale's Carols for Christmastide* in 1853.

Good Christian men, rejoice with heart and soul and voice; give ye heed to what we say: News! news! Jesus Christ is born today! Ox and ass before Him bow, and He is in the manger now: Christ is born today! Christ is born today!

Good Christian men, rejoice with heart and soul and voice; now ye hear of endless bliss: Joy! joy! Jesus Christ was born for this! He has opened heaven's door, and man is blessed evermore: Christ was born for this! Christ was born for this!

Good Christian men, rejoice with heart and soul and voice; now ye need not fear the grave: Peace! peace! Jesus Christ was born to save! Calls you one and calls you all to gain His everlasting hall: Christ was born to save! Christ was born to save!

❦ *For Today:* Isaiah 40:1-11; Luke 1:77-79; Luke 2:10-20; Ephesians 1:3-12

Determine by God's help to maintain the joy of Christmas in your life. Seek to minister an encouraging word to some lonely person. Share this musical message—

Dulci Jubilo tune — German melody, 14th century

Good Chris-tian men, re-joice with heart and soul and voice;

Give ye heed to what we say: News! news! Christ is born to-day!

I HEARD THE BELLS ON CHRISTMAS DAY

Henry W. Longfellow, 1807-1882

And He will be their peace. (Micah 5:5)

The cruel miseries caused by the Civil War greatly distressed the beloved American poet, Henry Wadsworth Longfellow. With heaviness of spirit he put his thoughts into words to create this fine carol. Since he was the most influential American poet of his day, Longfellow brought fresh courage and renewed faith to many of his countrymen who read this poem. Although he was a member of the Unitarian church, he maintained a strong belief in God's goodness and personal concern for His people.

"I Heard the Bells on Christmas Day" was written in 1864 for the Sunday school of the Unitarian Church of the Disciples in Boston, Massachusetts. It originally had seven stanzas and was titled "Christmas Bells." References to the Civil War are prevalent in the omitted verses. The plain, direct wording of the present five stanzas gives this clear message: God is still in command and in His own time will cause the right to triumph and will bring peace and good will once more. The beautiful chiming bells of Christmas reassure us of this important truth.

The personal peace of Longfellow's life was shaken again 18 years after he wrote this poem. His second wife, to whom he was very devoted, was tragically burned in a fire. Her death was a devastating shock to him. In his remaining years he continued to write, however, and some of his greatest works came during this period of his life. After his death, his bust was placed in the Poets' Corner of London's Westminster Abbey as one of the immortal American writers.

I heard the bells on Christmas day their old familiar carols play, and wild and sweet the words repeat of peace on earth, good will to men.

I thought how, as the day had come, the belfries of all Christendom had rolled along th' unbroken song of peace on earth, good will to men.

And in despair I bowed my head: "There is no peace on earth," I said; "hate is strong, and mocks the song of peace on earth, good will to men."

Yet pealed the bells more loud and deep: "God is not dead, nor doth He sleep; the wrong shall fail, the right prevail, with peace on earth, good will to men."

Then ringing, singing on its way, the world revolved from night to day—a voice, a chime, a chant sublime of peace on earth, good will to men!

❦ *For Today:* Luke 2:13, 14; John 14:27; 16:33; Romans 12:10; Ephesians 2:14

"Peace on earth among men of good will!" This is the blessed promise of Christmas. It is the antidote for any fear or hysteria that may enter our lives. Let the glorious sounds of Christmas remind you of this truth—

Waltham tune   J. Baptiste Calkin, 1827-1905

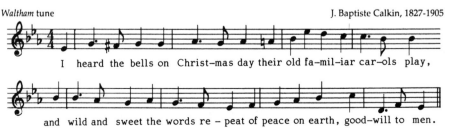

I heard the bells on Christ-mas day their old fa-mil-iar car-ols play,

and wild and sweet the words re - peat of peace on earth, good-will to men.

SILENT NIGHT! HOLY NIGHT!

Joseph Mohr, 1792-1848
English translation by John F. Young, 1820-1885

Today in the town of David a Savior has been born to you: He is Christ the Lord.
(Luke 2:11)

When this beloved hymn was written by two humble church leaders for their own mountain village parishioners, little did they realize how universal its influence would eventually be.

Joseph Mohr, assistant priest in the Church of St. Nicholas in the region of Tyrol, high in the beautiful Alps, and Franz Gruber, the village schoolmaster and church organist, had often talked about the fact that the perfect Christmas hymn had never been written. So Father Mohr had this goal in mind when he received word that the church organ would not function. He decided that he must write his own Christmas hymn immediately in order to have music for the special Christmas Eve mass. He did not want to disappoint his faithful flock. Upon completing the text, he took his words to Franz Gruber, who exclaimed when he saw them, "Friend Mohr, you have found it—the right song—God be praised!"

Soon Gruber completed his task of composing an appropriate tune for the new text. His simple but beautiful music blended perfectly with the spirit of Father Mohr's words. The carol was completed in time for the Christmas Eve mass, and Father Mohr and Franz Gruber sang their new hymn to the accompaniment of Gruber's guitar. The hymn made a deep impact upon the parishioners even as it has on succeeding generations.

When the organ repairman came to the little village church, he was impressed by a copy of the Christmas carol and decided to spread it all around the region of Tyrol. Today it is sung in all major languages of the world and is a favorite wherever songs of the Christmas message are enjoyed.

Silent night! holy night! all is calm, all is bright round yon virgin mother and Child, holy Infant, so tender and mild—sleep in heavenly peace, sleep in heavenly peace.

Silent night holy night! shepherds quake at the sight; glories stream from heaven afar; heav'nly hosts sing alleluia—Christ the Savior is born! Christ the Savior is born!

Silent night! holy night! Son of God, love's pure light radiant beams from Thy holy face with the dawn of redeeming grace—Jesus, Lord at Thy birth, Jesus, Lord at Thy birth.

❦ *For Today:* Matthew 2:9, 10; Luke 1:77-79; Luke 2:7-20

Allow the peaceful strains of this carol to help you worship in awe with the shepherds and sing alleluia with the angels for God's "redeeming grace"—

Stille Nacht tune   Franz Gruber, 1787-1863

THOU DIDST LEAVE THY THRONE

Emily E. S. Elliott, 1836-1897

I have come that they might have life, and have it to the full. (John 10:10)

This spiritually enriching text differs from the usual Christmas songs since it focuses not only on Jesus' birth but also on His life on earth, His suffering and death, and the ultimate triumph of His second advent.

This hymn was written by Emily Elliott to teach children the truths of the advent and nativity seasons. Emily's life was filled with benevolent activities in rescue missions and in the work of the Sunday school movement of that time. Although she wrote this text for the children of her father's church, St. Mark's Anglican Church in Brighton, England, the easily understood wording, the poetic imagery, and the spiritual truths found in these excellent lines soon made the hymn a widespread favorite everywhere.

The clear message of each verse is accentuated by the use of contrasting sentences, each beginning with the word "but." Then in the fifth stanza, the contrast is reversed with the rejoicing at Christ's return and the prospects of being at His side throughout eternity. The refrain after each verse effectively personalizes the truth presented. This fine hymn has proved to be an inspiration not only to children but to adults as well, during the Christmas season and also throughout the entire year.

> Thou didst leave Thy throne and Thy kingly crown when Thou camest to earth for me; but in Bethlehem's home was there found no room for Thy holy nativity.

> Heaven's arches rang when the angels sang, proclaiming Thy royal degree; but of lowly birth didst Thou come to earth, and in great humility.

> The foxes found rest, and the birds their nest in the shade of the forest tree; but Thy couch was the sod, O Thou Son of God, in the deserts of Galilee.

> Thou camest, O Lord, with the living word that should set Thy people free; but with mocking scorn and with crown of thorn they bore Thee to Calvary.

> When the heav'ns shall ring and the angels sing at Thy coming to victory, let Thy voice call me home, saying, "Yet there is room—there is room at My side for thee," My heart shall rejoice, Lord Jesus, when thou comest and callest for me!

> **Refrain (vv. 1-4):** O come to my heart, Lord Jesus— there is room in my heart for Thee!

🍂 *For Today:* Matthew 1:18-25; 2 Corinthians 8:9; Philippians 2:5-11

The Christmas story must become very personal in our individual lives. Carry this musical response with you—

Margaret tune   Timothy R. Matthews, 1826-1910

O come to my heart, Lord Je-sus--There is room in my heart for Thee!

GO TELL IT ON THE MOUNTAIN

Stanzas by John W. Work, 1871-1925

You who bring good tidings to Zion, go up on a high mountain. You who bring good tidings to Jerusalem, lift up your voice with a shout, lift it up, do not be afraid; say to the towns of Judah, "Here is your God!" (Isaiah 40:9)

For many people, another Christmas season is merely a rerun of the trivial and the sentimental. But for the devoted Christian, Christmas is much more than a once a year celebration. It is a fresh awareness that a Deliverer was sent from the ivory palaces of heaven to become personally involved in the redemption and affairs of the human race. The impact of this realization becomes a strong motivation to share the good news with needy and desperate people who need to know that there is an Emmanuel available who can meet their every need. Men everywhere must hear these glad tidings if they are to benefit from them. With absolute clarity they must hear the message, "Here is your God!"

Negro spirituals had their roots in the late 18th and early 19th century camp meetings throughout the South as well as in the active evangelical ministry carried on among the black people during this time. However, few of their traditional songs were collected or published prior to about 1840. The stanzas for "Go Tell It on the Mountain" were written by John W. Work, Jr. He and his brother, Frederick J. Work, were early leaders in arranging and promoting the cause of Negro spirituals. Today's song was first published in *Folk Songs of the American Negro* in 1907. These traditional spirituals have since become an important part of the American folk and sacred music heritage and are greatly appreciated and enjoyed by all of God's people.

> While shepherds kept their watching o'er silent flocks by night, behold, throughout the heavens there shone a holy light.

> The shepherds feared and trembled when lo! above the earth rang out the angel chorus that hailed our Savior's birth.

> Down in a lowly manger the humble Christ was born, and God sent us salvation that blessed Christmas morn.

> **Refrain:** Go tell it on the mountain, over the hills and ev'rywhere—go tell it on the mountain that Jesus Christ is born!

❦ ***For Today:*** Isaiah 42:11, 12; Luke 14:23; Romans 12:11; 1 Corinthians 15:58; Ephesians 2:10

Reflect on this: How have I grown spiritually throughout this Christmas season? What new insights have I gained regarding this message? How can I share my faith in the living Christ more effectively in the days ahead? Use this musical reminder to help—

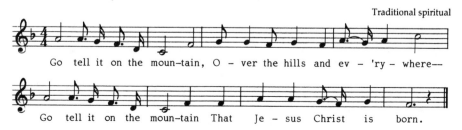

Traditional spiritual

Go tell it on the moun–tain, O – ver the hills and ev – 'ry – where—

Go tell it on the moun–tain That Je – sus Christ is born.

LO! HE COMES, WITH CLOUDS DESCENDING

Charles Wesley, 1707-1788

Look, He is coming with the clouds, and every eye will see Him, even those who pierced Him, and all the peoples of the earth will mourn because of Him. So shall it be! Amen. (Revelation 1:7)

When Jesus made His first entrance to earth, He was seen by only a small group of people—a few lowly shepherds and later by some wandering wise men. Bethlehem's stable birth attracted little attention and had limited immediate effect upon the rest of the world. It was nearly 30 years before Christ's earthly ministry gained much notice.

What a contrast it will be when He returns for His second advent—every eye "shall see the Son of man coming in the clouds of heaven with power and great glory" (Matthew 24:30). Even those who crucified God's Son will see and mourn, as will people from every tribe and nation because of their rejection of Him. But for those who have trusted in His redemptive work, the days of mourning will be over, not just beginning. For the Christian, the anticipation of Christ's return is a joyous prospect—"O come quickly, Alleluia! come, Lord, come!"

In 1758 Charles Wesley published in his *Hymns of Intercession for all Mankind* a four stanza text, "Lo, He Comes with Clouds Descending." Eight years earlier an associate of the Wesleys, John Cennick, had written a hymn with a similar text. This present version first appeared in 1760 and is really a combination of both Cennick's and Wesley's texts.

This is an excellent scriptural hymn and one that should be used much more frequently when believers contemplate and anticipate their Lord's return.

> Lo! He comes, with clouds descending, once for our salvation slain; thousand thousand saints attending, swell the triumph of His train: Alleluia! alleluia! God appears on earth to reign.

> Ev'ry eye shall now behold Him, robed in dreadful majesty; those who set at naught and sold Him, pierced and nailed Him to the tree, deeply wailing, deeply wailing, shall the true Messiah see.

> Yea, Amen! let all adore Thee high on Thine eternal throne; Savior, take the pow'r and glory, claim the kingdom for Thine own. O come quickly, O come quickly, Alleluia! come, Lord come!

🍂 ***For Today:*** Matthew 16:27, 28; Mark 13:26, 27; Luke 21:27, 28; 1 Thessalonians 4:16, 17; 2 Peter 3:13, 14

Although you have enjoyed celebrating our Lord's birth, reflect on what a dramatic event His second advent will be. Rejoice in the truth that you will have an important place in His eternal glory. Raise your alleluias even now—

Sicilian Mariners tune   From Tattersall's *Psalmody*, 1794

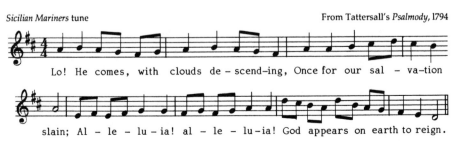

Lo! He comes, with clouds de-scend-ing, Once for our sal-va-tion slain; Al-le-lu-ia! al-le-lu-ia! God appears on earth to reign.

CHRIST RETURNETH!

H. L. Turner, 19th century

I will come again, and receive you unto Myself. (John 14:3 KJV)

The promise of Christ's return has been a source of much comfort to God's people through the centuries. However, it has also caused disagreement and even some divisions within the church. Not all Bible students and groups of Christians are agreed on the outline of future events. Even a casual acquaintance with the study of eschatology (the doctrine of the last things) will soon introduce such conflicting terms and interpretations as postmillennialism, amillennialism, premillennialism, posttribulation, midtribulation, and pretribulation.

Each of these positions has the support of excellent biblical scholarship and many sincere Christian followers. It is easy for believers to get confused with the many aspects of Christ's return.

Although Christians may disagree on some of the specifics related to future prophecy, most will agree on these basics: Christ will return personally—Acts 1:11; His return will be visible—Revelation 1:7; He will come in power and glory—Mark 13:26; and His coming will consumate His salvation and judgment—John 5:21-29; Hebrews 9:27, 28. The anticipation of Christ's coming places a responsibility upon believers both individually and corporately even now: To live lives of purity (1 John 3:3) and to be involved in getting the gospel to every nation before His return (Matthew 24:14; Mark 13:10).

"Christ Returneth" first appeared in Ira D. Sankey's *Gospel Hymns, No. 3* in 1878. It has since been widely used to impress and challenge God's people with the truth of the imminent return of their Lord.

> It may be at morn, when the day is awaking, when sunlight thru darkness and shadow is breaking, that Jesus will come in the fullness of glory to receive from the world His own.
>
> It may be at mid-day; it may be at twilight; it may be, perchance, that the blackness of midnight will burst into light in the blaze of His glory, when Jesus receives His own.
>
> O joy! O delight should we go without dying, no sickness, no sadness, no dread and no crying, caught up thru the clouds with our Lord into glory, when Jesus receives His own.
>
> **Chorus:** O Lord Jesus, how long, how long ere we shout the glad song— Christ returneth! Hallelujah! Hallelujah! Amen, Hallelujah! Amen.

❦ *For Today:* Matthew 24:30, 31; 25:13; Mark 13:32-37; 14:62; Luke 12:35-40; 1 Thessalonians 2:19

Live in the simple enjoyment that Christ will fulfil His promise—He will return—perhaps even this day. Sing this musical prayer—

James McGranahan, 1840-1907

O Lord Je - sus, how long, how long Ere we shout the glad song--Christ re-turn--eth! Hal-le- lu –jah! Hal-le - lu –jah! A - men, Hal-le-lu- jah! A - men.

THERE'LL BE NO DARK VALLEY

William O. Cushing, 1823-1902

He will wipe every tear from their eyes. There will be no more death or mourning or crying or pain, for the old order of things has passed away. (Revelation 21:4)

> There is a land of pure delight, where saints immortal reign;
> Eternal day excludes the night, and pleasures banish pain.   —*Isaac Watts*

In every life there will be some "dark valleys." Difficult days cannot be avoided. In fact, the lives of some believers seem to be filled with affliction and suffering. But for the child of God, there is glorious relief just ahead . . . the return of Christ and the promise of a land of endless delight. The prospect of Gods' tomorrow also means a time of joyous reunion with loved ones who have preceded us. Truly "there'll be songs of greeting when Jesus comes. . . ."

William Orcutt Cushing knew the meaning of "dark valleys" in his life. After more than 20 years of successfully pastoring Disciples of Christ churches in the state of New York, he suddenly lost the ability to speak. Then his wife died at the age of 47. During this "valley period" Cushing became interested in hymn writing and wrote more than 300 hymn texts, including such other favorites as: "Under His Wings," "When He Cometh," and "Hiding in Thee."

Ira David Sankey, the hymn's composer, worked as a soloist and songleader with evangelist D. L. Moody for nearly 30 years in campaigns throughout the United States and the British Isles. "There'll Be No Dark Valley" was widely used by Sankey in many of these meetings. The hymn's simple repetitive message and singable melody still provide encouragement and comfort to God's people.

> There'll be no dark valley when Jesus comes; there'll be no dark valley when Jesus comes; there'll be no dark valley when Jesus comes to gather His loved ones home.
>
> There'll be no more sorrow when Jesus comes; there'll be no more sorrow when Jesus comes; but a glorious morrow when Jesus comes to gather His loved ones home.
>
> There'll be songs of greeting when Jesus comes; there'll be songs of greeting when Jesus comes; and a joyful meeting when Jesus comes to gather His loved ones home.
>
> **Refrain:** To gather His loved ones home, to gather His loved ones home; there'll be no dark valley when Jesus comes to gather His loved ones home.

🍒 *For Today:* 1 Thessalonians 4:16, 17; 2 Peter 3:13, 14; Revelation 22:5, 12.

Hear these words of encouragement "I will come back and take you to be with me . . ." (John 14:1-3). Carry this musical truth with you—

Ira D. Sankey, 1840-1908

JESUS SHALL REIGN

Isaac Watts, 1674-1748

The Mighty One, God, the Lord, speaks and summons the earth from the rising of the sun to the place where it sets. (Psalm 50:1)

The spread of Christianity has been phenomenal. In spite of cruel persecution of Christ's followers in the first three centuries A.D. and from time to time through the years since, His kingdom has continued to spread to "realms and people of every tongue." Periods of attack on believers have served only to increase their fervor and growth. Then in recent years, with the rapid development of technology—radio, television, gospel films, Bible translations and distributions—the preaching of the gospel has been heard by more people than ever before in the history of mankind.

When this stirring hymn was written in 1719, however, the evangelical missionary movement that we know in our time had scarcely begun. In 1779 William Carey was one of the first to try to persuade Christians to carry the gospel message to heathen countries of the world. Isaac Watts was certainly quite prophetic when he paraphrased this text from Psalm 72. It is still considered one of the finest missionary hymns ever written and has been sung in countless native tongues. In the South Sea Islands in 1862, 5,000 primitive people sang this hymn as the king abolished their native laws and established a Christian constitution.

It is thrilling for us to realize that the praise of Jesus, Bethlehem's humble Babe, is continuing to spread and that some day soon His kingdom will "spread from shore to shore" and every tribe, language, people, and nation will bow down and exalt His name together.

> Jesus shall reign where'er the sun does his successive journeys run, His kingdom spread from shore to shore till moons shall wax and wane no more.

> From north to south the princes meet to pay their homage at His feet, while western empires own their Lord and savage tribes attend His word.

> To Him shall endless prayer be made and endless praises crown His head: His name like sweet perfume shall rise with ev'ry morning sacrifice.

> People and realms of ev'ry tongue dwell on His love with sweetest song, and infant voices shall proclaim their early blessings on His name.

❦ *For Today:* Psalm 10:16; 72; Isaiah 33:17; Zechariah 14:9; Revelation 11:15

Rejoice in the many endeavors in our day that work to spread the gospel around the world. Resolve to do more personally to assist through prayer and financial support. Reflect on the truth of this hymn—

Duke Street tune   John Hatton, c. 1710-1793

His king - dom spread from shore to shore— Till

moons shall wax and wane no more.

THE LORD IS KING!

Freely adapted from Josiah Condor, 1789-1855

For the Lord is the great God, the great King above all gods. (Psalm 95:3)

As we reflect on the joys, failures, and blessings of the past year, we can rejoice in the truth that we are personally related to the Lord Jehovah, who is king of heaven and earth and will reign forever. Some day we shall see Him and begin to enjoy His eternal presence.

This vibrant hymn stirs us to praise and gratefulness for all of God's leading in the past year. We will never "murmur at His wise decrees" if we remember His promises and reflect on how good and great He is. We are also reminded by this triumphant text that we must submit ourselves in humility to God's will in our lives, trusting "His tender care" for us. Then we are to sing and shout His praise throughout each day! What a victorious life this suggests for us as believers as we approach another new year.

The text of this fine hymn is an adaptation of one written earlier by Josiah Condor, a respected non-conformist lay preacher in the Congregational church of England. The music for this text was arranged from a tune found in *The Sacred Harp*, a collection of early American sacred music.

> The Lord is King! Lift up, lift up thy voice—sing His praise, sing His praise! All heav'n and earth before Him now rejoice—sing His praise, sing His praise! From world to world the joy shall ring, for He alone is God and King; from sky to sky His banner fling—sing His praise, sing His praise!

> The Lord is King! Let all His worth declare—great is He, great is He! Bow to His will and trust His tender care—great is He, great is He! Nor murmur at His wise decrees, nor doubt His steadfast promises; in humble faith fall on thy knees—great is He!

> The Lord is King! And bow to Him ye must—God is great, God is good! The judge of all to all is ever just—God is great, God is good! Holy and true are all His ways: Let ev'ry creature shout His praise; the Lord of Hosts, Ancient of Days—God is great, God is good!

> The Lord is King! Throughout His vast domain He is all, all in all! The Lord Jehovah evermore shall reign—He is all, all in all! Through earth and heav'n one song shall ring, from grateful hearts this anthem spring: Arise, ye saints, salute thy King—all thy days, sing His praise!

❧ ***For Today:*** Psalm 10:16; 145:11-13; Luke 1:33; 1 Timothy 6:15; Revelation 11:15

Have you truly made God the King in your life? How would you measure your spiritual progress during this past year? Let us earnestly seek to know Him in a deeper way in this coming year.

All Is Well tune   *The Sacred Harp*, 1844

From world to world the joy shall ring, For He a-lone is God and King;

From sky to sky His ban-ners fling—All thy days, sing His praise!

Hymn Index

Scripture Index

Songwriter Index

Additional Hymn Stories
by Kenneth W. Osbeck

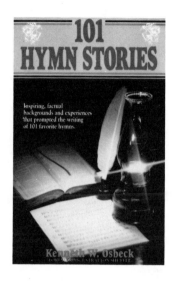

101 Hymn Stories

A thrilling collection of the stories behind your favorite hymns. The exciting events which produced such classic expressions of praise as *A Mighty Fortress, Fairest Lord Jesus, How Great Thou Art, Jesus Loves Me, Holy, Holy, Holy, Rock of Ages,* and *The Old Rugged Cross* are brought to life in vivid, inspiring detail. This book will revitalize your worship and can be used for devotions, sermon illustrations, and bulletin inserts.

ISBN 0-8254-3416-5   288 pp   paperback

101 More Hymn Stories

A companion volume to *101 Hymn Stories* with additional stories behind your favorite hymns. The background stories to such well-known hymns like *Am I a Soldier of the Cross?, Burdens Are Lifted at Calvary, Because He Lives, Joy to the World, Trust and Obey, Turn Your Eyes Upon Jesus,* and *Worthy Is the Lamb* are brought to life in inspiring detail. This book will enhance personal or family devotions and can be used as sermon illustrations, introductions to congregational singing, and as bulletin inserts.

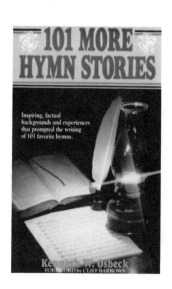

ISBN 0-8254-3420-3   328 pp   paperback